Private Equity and Management Buy-outs

Private Equity and Management Buy-outs

Edited by

Mike Wright

Professor of Financial Studies and Director, Centre for Management Buy-out Research, Nottingham University Business School, UK, Visiting Professor, Rotterdam School of Management, Erasmus University Rotterdam, The Netherlands and Editor, Journal of Management Studies

Hans Bruining

Associate Professor of Strategic Management, Rotterdam School of Management, Erasmus University Rotterdam, The Netherlands

Edward Elgar

Cheltenham, UK • Northampton, MA, USA

Published by
Edward Elgar Publishing Limited
The Lypiatts
15 Lansdown Road
Cheltenham
Glos GL50 2JA
UK

Edward Elgar Publishing, Inc.
William Pratt House
9 Dewey Court
Northampton
Massachusetts 01060
USA

A catalogue record for this book
is available from the British Library

Library of Congress Control Number: 2008927979

ISBN 978 1 84720 725 8

Printed and bound in Great Britain by MPG Books Ltd, Bodmin, Cornwall

Contents

Contributors

Kevin Amess, Nottingham University Business School, UK

Nicolas Bacon, Nottingham University Business School, UK

Rod Ball, Nottingham University Business School, UK

Marcel Bonnet, Erasmus University Rotterdam, The Netherlands

Paul Boselie, Tilburg University, The Netherlands

Hans Bruining, Erasmus University Rotterdam, The Netherlands

Trevor Buck, Loughborough University and Nottingham University Business School, UK

Andrew Burrows, Nottingham University Business School, UK

Lowell W. Busenitz, University of Oklahoma, USA

David Citron, Cass Business School, London, UK

Jay Dial, Case Western Reserve University, USA

Igor Filatotchev, Cass Business School, London, UK

Richard Harris, University of Glasgow, UK

Robert E. Hoskisson, University of Arizona, USA

Ranko Jelic, University of Birmingham, UK

Motoya Kitamura, Mitsubishi Research Institute, Japan

Erkki Nikoskelainen, Swedish School of Economics and Business Administration, Helsinki, Finland

Luc Renneboog, Tilburg University, The Netherlands and ECGI, Belgium

Fred Rippington, Cass Business School, London, UK

Brahim Saadouni, UMIST, Manchester, UK

M. Louise Scholes, Nottingham University Business School, UK

Donald S. Siegel, University at Albany, State University of New York, USA

Tomas Simons, Tilburg University, The Netherlands

Charlie Weir, The Robert Gordon University, Aberdeen, UK

Paul Westhead, Durham Business School, UK

Mike Wright, Nottingham University Business School, UK, Erasmus University Rotterdam, The Netherlands and Editor, *Journal of Management Studies*

Preface

As private equity markets have gained in importance worldwide over the last decade there has been a growing debate about the role of private equity in the firm and society at large. Private equity firms are facing different challenges, notably: increased pressure to be more transparent in their value creation and governance role with regard to shareholders and employees of the buy-out firm; increased pressure to be more transparent about the short- and long-term economic and social effects, for instance their role in the upside potential of buy-outs and impact on human resources management; increased pressure to be transparent about the determinants of exit strategies; increased pressure to test the acceptability of financial leverage in the financial structures of buy-outs; increased importance of their intermediary role as adviser to vendors and buyers in family buy-outs; increased pressure to combine financial expertise with technological and management control expertise in buy-out firms. For the first time the broad issues now facing private equity and buy-outs are brought together through the contributions in this volume.

A major problem with the current debate regarding private equity is that it has been conducted largely in the absence of serious consideration of the scientific evidence. This book aims to be a timely attempt to present a scholarly view on private equity backed buy-outs based on a review of international market trends and the evidence in a collection of articles published between 2000 and 2007 in highly regarded journals. This evidence represents the results of a systematic research programme by the Centre for Management Buy-out Research (CMBOR) and its associates. We hope that the content will be of interest to and stimulate further debate among practitioners, researchers, students and policymakers in the area of financing and strategic management of growing and restructuring firms.

We would like to thank the contributors of the chapters on which this volume is based. We would also like to thank colleagues and associates of CMBOR, especially Kevin Amess, Rod Ball, Andrew Burrows, Douglas Cumming, Miguel Meuleman, Louise Scholes and Donald Siegel. Thanks are also due to Francine O'Sullivan and Ben Booth of Edward Elgar for their encouragement and forbearance.

Acknowledgements

The authors and the publishers wish to thank the following who have kindly given their permission for the use of copyright material.

Academy of Management (NY) for 'Entrepreneurial growth through privatization: the upside of management buyouts', M. Wright, R. Hoskisson, L. Busenitz and J. Dial, *Academy of Management Review*, **25** (3), July 2000, 591–600.

Elsevier Science for 'Why do public firms go private in the UK? The impact of private equity investors, incentive realignment and undervaluation', L. Renneboog, T. Simons and M. Wright, *Journal of Corporate Finance*, **13** (4), September 2007, 591–628; 'Management control systems and strategy change in buyouts', H. Bruining, M. Bonnet and M. Wright, *Management Accounting Research*, **15** (2), June 2004, 155–77; 'Management buyouts and restructuring Japanese corporations', M. Wright, M. Kitamura and R. Hoskisson, *Long Range Planning*, **36** (4), August 2003, 355–73; and 'The impact of corporate governance mechanisms on value increase in leveraged buyouts', E. Nikoskelainen and M. Wright, *Journal of Corporate Finance*, **13** (4), September 2007, 511–37.

MIT Press Journals for 'Assessing the impact of management buyouts on economic efficiency: plant-level evidence from the United Kingdom', R. Harris, D.S. Siegel and M. Wright, *Review of Economics and Statistics*, **87** (1), February 2005, 148–53.

Springer Science and Business Media for 'Information sharing, price negotiation and management buy-outs of private family-owned firms', L. Scholes, M. Wright, P. Westhead, A. Burrows and H. Bruining, *Small Business Economics*, **29** (3), October 2007, 329–49.

Taylor and Francis for 'The wage and employment effects of leveraged buyouts in the UK', K. Amess and M. Wright, *International Journal of Economics and Business*, **14** (2), July 2007, 179–95; 'The impact of business ownership change on employee relations: buy-outs in the UK and The Netherlands', H. Bruining, P. Boselie, M. Wright and N. Bacon, *International Journal of Human Resource Management*, **16** (3), March 2005, 345–65; and 'Entrepreneurial orientation in management buy-outs and the contribution of venture capital', H. Bruining and M. Wright, *Venture Capital*, **4** (2), April 2002, 147–68.

Wiley Blackwell Publishing Ltd for 'Post-privatisation effects of management and employee buy-outs', M. Wright, T. Buck and I. Filatotchev, *Annals of Public and Cooperative Economics*, **73** (3), September 2002, 303–52; 'Performance of private to public MBOS: the role of venture capital', R. Jelic, B. Saadouni and M. Wright, *Journal of Business and Accounting*, **32** (3/4), April/May 2005, 643–81; 'Secured creditor recovery rates from management buy-outs in distress', D. Citron, M. Wright, R. Ball and F. Rippington, *European Financial Management*, **9** (2), June 2003, 141–61; and 'Irrevocable commitments, going private and private equity', M. Wright, C. Weir, and A. Burrows, *European Financial Management*, **13** (4), September 2007, 757–75.

Every effort has been made to trace all the copyright holders but if any have been inadvertently overlooked, the publishers will be pleased to make the necessary arrangements.

PART I

Introduction

1. Private equity and management buy-outs: international trends, evidence and policy implications[1]

Mike Wright and Hans Bruining

1. INTRODUCTION

The international surge of private equity markets during the first decade of this century has been accompanied by concerns about their effects, both positive and negative (see for example Financial Services Authority, 2006; PSE Group in European Parliament, 2007). These concerns emphasize a need to evaluate the impact of these transactions on organizations and on society as a whole.

This chapter reviews the development and effects of private equity and management buy-outs internationally. Section 2 briefly defines private equity and buy-out transactions. Section 3 reviews developments in key private equity and buy-out markets. Section 4 analyses aspects of the operation of private equity firms. In particular, we consider approaches to the negotiation of transactions; competition and collusion issues relating to bidding for deals; deal pricing; the different nature of funds providers; leverage and financial instruments; the extent of deal refinancing; and the role of the taxation regime. Section 5 reviews evidence on the antecedents of public to private buy-outs in particular, that is the factors driving their occurrence. Section 6 reviews the evidence on the financial performance of private equity and buy-outs in terms of returns to shareholders and bondholders at the time of the buy-out transaction; returns to investors; and issues relating to creditors and distress costs. Section 7 examines the real effects of private equity and buy-outs in terms of the impact on productivity; investee firm strategy; employees and HRM; the nature of entrepreneurial buy-outs; and the factors that drive the gains in private equity and buy-out investments. Section 8 discusses realizations and exits in terms of, first, the trends in different OECD countries and, second, the post-exit effects on buy-out firms. Section 9 discusses implications for further research and policy. Finally, Section 10 outlines the chapters of the volume.

2. DEFINITIONS OF PRIVATE EQUITY AND BUY-OUTS

In general, buy-outs involve the creation of a new independent entity in which ownership is concentrated in the hands of management and private equity firms, if present, with substantial funding also provided by banks. Private equity provides equity capital to enterprises not quoted on a stock market. Private equity can be used to develop new products and technologies, to expand working capital, to make acquisitions, or to strengthen a company's balance sheet. It can also resolve ownership and management issues. A succession in family-owned companies, or the buy-out and buy-in of a business by experienced managers may be achieved using private equity funding (EVCA, 2007)

Private equity firms become active investors through taking board seats and specifying contractual restrictions on the behaviour of management which include detailed reporting requirements. Lenders also typically specify and closely monitor detailed loan covenants (Citron et al., 1997).

Buy-outs may take a number of forms. In a leveraged buy-out (LBO), typically a publicly quoted corporation or a large division of a group is acquired by an LBO association. In the USA, the resulting private company is typically controlled by a small board of directors representing the LBO association, with the CEO usually the only insider on the board (Jensen, 1993). As the name suggests, these deals are generally highly leveraged, with the private equity firm acquiring a significant equity stake. The same institutions may be involved as debt and equity subscribers – under a so-called 'strip financing' arrangement – or, alternatively, specialist institutions may be involved with debt instruments ranging from secured loans to junk bonds (Jensen, 1993).

Investor-led buy-outs (IBOs) involve the acquisition of a whole company or a division of a larger group in a transaction led by a private equity firm and are also referred to as bought deals or financial purchases. The private equity firm will typically either retain existing management to run the company or bring in new management to do so, or employ some combination of internal and external management. Incumbent management may or may not receive a direct equity stake or may receive stock options. IBOs developed in the late 1990s when private equity firms were searching for attractive deals in an increasingly competitive market and where corporate vendors or large divisions were seeking to sell them through auctions rather than giving preference to incumbent managers. These deals have similarities with LBOs. The differences can be summarized in terms of the metamorphosis of LBO associations into private equity firms as the industry has developed. As the names suggest, IBOs tend to have lower leverage than

LBOs and may be expected to create value through developing the company, not just through efficiency improvements.

By contrast, a management buy-out (MBO) usually involves the acquisition of a divested division or subsidiary or of a private family-owned firm by a new company in which the existing management takes a substantial proportion of the equity. In place of the LBO association, MBOs usually require the support of a private equity firm. The former parent may retain an equity stake, perhaps to support a continuing trading relationship. In smaller transactions management is likely to obtain a majority of the voting equity (CMBOR, 2005). MBOs typically involve a small group of senior managers as equity-holders but depending on circumstances equity-holding may be extended to other management and employees, creating a management–employee buy-out (MEBO). MEBOs may occur, for example, where it is important to tie in the specific human capital of the employees, where a firm is widely spread geographically making direct management difficult, or on privatization, where there is a need to encourage trade unions to support the transfer of ownership (e.g. in bus services and transportation).

A management buy-in (MBI) (Robbie et al., 1992) is simply an MBO in which the leading members of the management team are outsiders. Although superficially similar to MBOs, MBIs carry greater risks as incoming management does not have the benefits of the insiders' knowledge of the operation of the business. Venture capitalists have sought to address this problem by putting together hybrid buy-in/management buy-outs (so-called BIMBOs) to obtain the benefits of the entrepreneurial expertise of the outside managers and the intimate internal knowledge of the incumbent management.

Leveraged build-ups (LBUs) involve the development of a corporate group based on an initial buy-out or buy-in which serves as a platform investment to which is added a series of acquisitions. LBUs developed as private equity firms sought new means of generating returns from buy-out-type investments. The initial platform deal may need to be of a sufficiently large size to attract the management with the skills and experience to grow a large business through acquisition. LBUs may be attractive in fragmented industries with strong demand prospects, for example the fruit and soft drinks industry in Europe. The potential problems with LBUs relate to the identification, purchase and subsequent integration of suitable acquisition candidates.

3. TRENDS IN BUY-OUTS

Since the development of highly leveraged transactions involving listed companies in the USA in the late 1970s, buy-outs have become an international phenomenon. In Europe, the UK led the way, with activity levels growing rapidly in the early 1980s (Wright et al., 2000). The Continental European buy-out market first saw growth later in the decade (Wright et al., 1992), with France and the Netherlands in particular seeing considerable buy-out activity. Initially activity in Germany was slower to develop but has recently become much more important.

Buy-outs have been an important feature of the privatization of state assets during the transition from communism to a market economy in Central and Eastern Europe since the beginning of the 1990s, including some countries that are now part of the OECD (Wright et al., 2002). The need for major restructuring in Japan and Korea has given an impetus to buy-outs in the Far East, with buy-outs now spreading in significant numbers to Asia.

In the first part of this section we analyse the general trends in private equity and management buy-outs. We then discuss international developments in transactions involving the taking private of listed corporations. This is followed by an analysis of cross-border private equity investments.

3.1 Market Overview

3.1.1 General trends

Whilst it is notoriously difficult to obtain consistent data on the private equity (PE) market, various information sources can be used to provide an overall picture of global trends. Although not distinguishing between investment phases, some of the findings of the PWC Global Private Equity Report are useful in pointing towards buy-out market trends within the wider PE context.

Global fundraising increased from $87 billion in 2003 to $131 billion in 2004, although this is still well short of the peak of $262 billion raised at the height of the dot.com boom in 2000. Two-thirds of venture capital and private equity money is sourced in North America; however, investment opportunities have become increasingly global. Considering cumulative data from 1998 to 2004, 57 per cent was invested in North America, 28 per cent in Europe and 10 per cent in Asia Pacific, with the remainder being spread between the Middle East, Africa and Central and South America.

In terms of fundraising specifically for buy-outs, €183 billion was raised in the USA in 2005 compared to only €42 billion in 2004 (Buyouts, 2006). According to EVCA the expected allocation of funds raised for buy-outs across Europe rose from €17.8 billion in 2004 to €57.7 billion in 2005 (EVCA, 2006).

Recent trends have seen huge growth in European PE market value, with 39 per cent of the 2004 total invested in Europe compared to 41 per cent in the USA, whilst there has also been a move towards the Asia Pacific region in recent years, which received 16 per cent of the total investment in 2004.

Management buy-outs have typically accounted for less than 10 per cent of the total number of investments made by PE firms in Europe (EVCA, 2006). However, generally over half of the total funding raised has been invested into MBO/MBIs. In recent years more funds have been targeted at later-stage deals such that in 2005 approximately one-fifth of all investments made were into buy-outs, accounting for over 70 per cent of the total private equity capital invested in 2005.

The US market started to develop during the mid-1970s but in Western Europe, only the UK and the Netherlands had shown significant activity by the mid-1980s. The US market remained relatively flat during the 1990s following the problems brought about by the recession of the early 1990s. Since 2001 the US buy-out market has seen significant growth in deal activity and value, with a total number of 549 buy-outs/buy-ins valued at €179 billion in 2006 (Table 1.1 and 1.2).

Table 1.1 *Number of buy-outs/buy-ins*

Country	1997	1998	1999	2000	2001	2002	2003	2004	2005	2006
USA	203	178	187	302	175	160	167	306	422	549
Austria	7	5	4	13	7	18	12	14	14	7
Belgium	10	19	16	19	25	24	20	37	28	26
Denmark	16	13	18	18	12	18	12	14	30	20
Finland	32	16	19	15	23	29	28	27	32	15
France	139	150	148	131	126	124	141	159	228	155
Germany	99	79	53	66	91	108	105	111	124	136
Ireland	8	15	9	12	16	20	14	11	7	14
Italy	25	32	43	31	18	38	44	43	45	49
Netherlands	61	75	66	79	60	62	74	73	85	75
Norway	6	4	8	7	9	12	16	13	16	19
Portugal	3	5	6	5	1	6	5	3	5	5
Spain	23	37	30	28	37	42	52	34	50	48
Sweden	20	23	32	25	49	25	24	39	38	35
Switzerland	65	51	56	54	50	36	31	35	30	23
UK	709	690	658	623	643	639	713	706	691	617
Australia	8	10	17	7	25	17	25	18	27	19
Canada	5	8	12	29	22	20	11	21	28	33
Japan		1	10	13	31	24	49	56	43	1
S. Korea					2	2			1	3

Source: CMBOR/Barclays Private Equity/Deloitte/ Thomson Financial/JBORI.

Table 1.2 Value of buy-outs/buy-ins (€ m)

Country	1997	1998	1999	2000	2001	2002	2003	2004	2005	2006
USA	11 510	16 633	20 590	32 308	18 462	31 538	72 308	105 385	152 308	179 231
Austria	128	95	680	734	47	154	303	110	287	41
Belgium	414	820	2 595	342	1 744	517	1 448	2 270	4 257	588
Denmark	263	267	2 520	1 313	500	1 391	848	260	7 089	13 369
Finland	440	560	1 085	675	1 047	480	1 039	977	2 163	881
France	5 281	6 153	8 387	6 502	6 387	15 568	8 767	11 520	21 623	23 282
Germany	3 538	5 230	4 642	14 879	7 229	8 252	11 974	17 915	12 928	20 622
Ireland	69	243	1 475	259	5 021	4 930	747	977	773	1 004
Italy	3 121	670	2 997	2 560	1 107	3 428	7 773	2 940	17 527	6 392
Netherlands	1 059	3 397	2 906	1 856	4 433	1 899	4 958	7 614	10 338	25 782
Norway	180	22	225	1 004	1 370	142	308	431	470	1 581
Portugal	64	84	206	83	2	26	54	8	76	94
Spain	374	854	1 715	941	1 532	2 069	934	2 279	9 391	4 100
Sweden	1 375	928	2 686	3 169	3 005	1 116	2 226	1 701	4 702	5 435
Switzerland	2 426	1 347	1 013	1 772	715	2 766	865	1 584	1 081	924
UK	17 114	23 270	26 869	38 419	31 346	24 851	23 574	30 155	35 411	38 261
Australia	78	1 293	3 433	168	1 315	553	478	752	1 147	3 911
Canada	10	598	30	2 365	228	1 979	916	2 279	1 704	2 404
Japan		24	956	1 074	1 473	711	5 121	4 745	2 734	24
S. Korea					769	491			673	1 093

Source: CMBOR/Barclays Private Equity/Deloitte/Thomson Financial.

Private equity markets in many Western European countries are now well established. Deal value across Western Europe was negligible in the mid-1980s but two decades later has become substantial. The UK has historically been the biggest buy-out market in Europe and generally contributed half of the total value. However, since 2001 the UK share has fallen to just over a quarter of the total value as other countries' markets have begun to mature (Tables 1.1 and 1.2).

Markets in most countries in Europe initially developed with the advent of relatively small buy-outs initiated by the management team. Deals have since grown in size, with the average value across Europe in 2006 being €114 million, up from €21 million in 1996. In addition, management buy-ins (MBIs), including institutional buy-outs (IBOs), have become much more influential since the mid-1990s and now account for nearly 90 per cent of the total European market value and 50 per cent of the volume of all transactions. The number of employees working for firms that have undergone a management buy-out is a significant part of the overall workforce. Estimates are that this has increased across the whole of Europe, from 450 000 in new deals completed in 2003 to 850 000 for new deals done in 2005 (CMBOR data), the latter figure including the buy-out of the cleaning and building maintenance firm ISS in Denmark with 273 000 employees. However, the vast majority of buy-outs are SMEs (Figure 1.1).

The UK is clearly the most mature of the European regions and has been the largest buy-out market in Europe, both by volume and value, for many

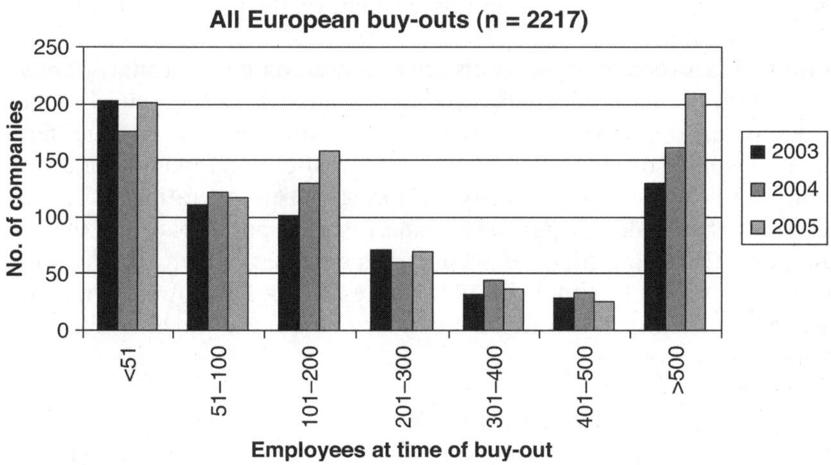

Source: CMBOR.

Figure 1.1 Employee distribution of buy-outs

years. France and Germany have been the second and third most active markets in Europe for many years (Table 1.1). Well-established if relatively small markets are observed in Australia and Canada (Tables 1.1 and 1.2) and buy-out markets are also beginning to develop in Japan and Korea.

3.1.2 Vendor source of deals

The largest share of European buy-outs now comes from family/private firms, often resulting from a situation where there is no obvious family successor, with the company subsequently sold to the incumbent management team (Figure 1.2). Family/private deals were the most common source of buy-outs in seven of the 12 majority European countries in 2005. During the 1980s and the 1990s the local parent firm was the most important source due to the high level of restructuring of firms across industries. As Figure 1.2 shows, it still is the second most important buy-out source.

Secondary buy-outs, involving private equity firms buying and selling companies between themselves, have become increasingly important lately both as an exit mechanism and source of deals. Secondary buy-outs accounted for 15 per cent of all activity in 2005.

Public-to-private (PTP) buy-outs, whereby a company is de-listed from the stock exchange, has become another important feature of the buy-out market in some countries in recent years. Although the number of this type of buy-out is relatively small, the total value can be significant. The size of PTP deal has increased with, for example, the total value of PTP deals in the UK in 2005, equating to 30 per cent of the total value from just 3 per cent of all activity. We focus on this segment of the private equity market in more detail below.

In the USA secondary buy-outs are also becoming increasingly popular and now equate to 5 per cent by value and volume of all buy-outs. In Japan buy-outs arising from Japanese company divestments are the most common source of buy-out, with very few arising from foreign firm divestments (indicative of the paucity of foreign firms operating in Japan). Secondary buy-outs in Japan are also increasing in popularity, as is the case in other OECD countries. No secondaries were recorded by the Japanese Buy-out Research Institute (JBORI) before 2001 but eight were completed in 2006. We comment further on secondary buy-outs as an alternative exit route in Section 8.1.

3.1.3 Relative size of individual markets

In order to give an indication of the relative importance of the buy-out market to the economy in each country, figures for gross domestic product (GDP) have been used to compare total buy-out value (i.e enterprise value: debt plus equity) as a proportion of GDP.

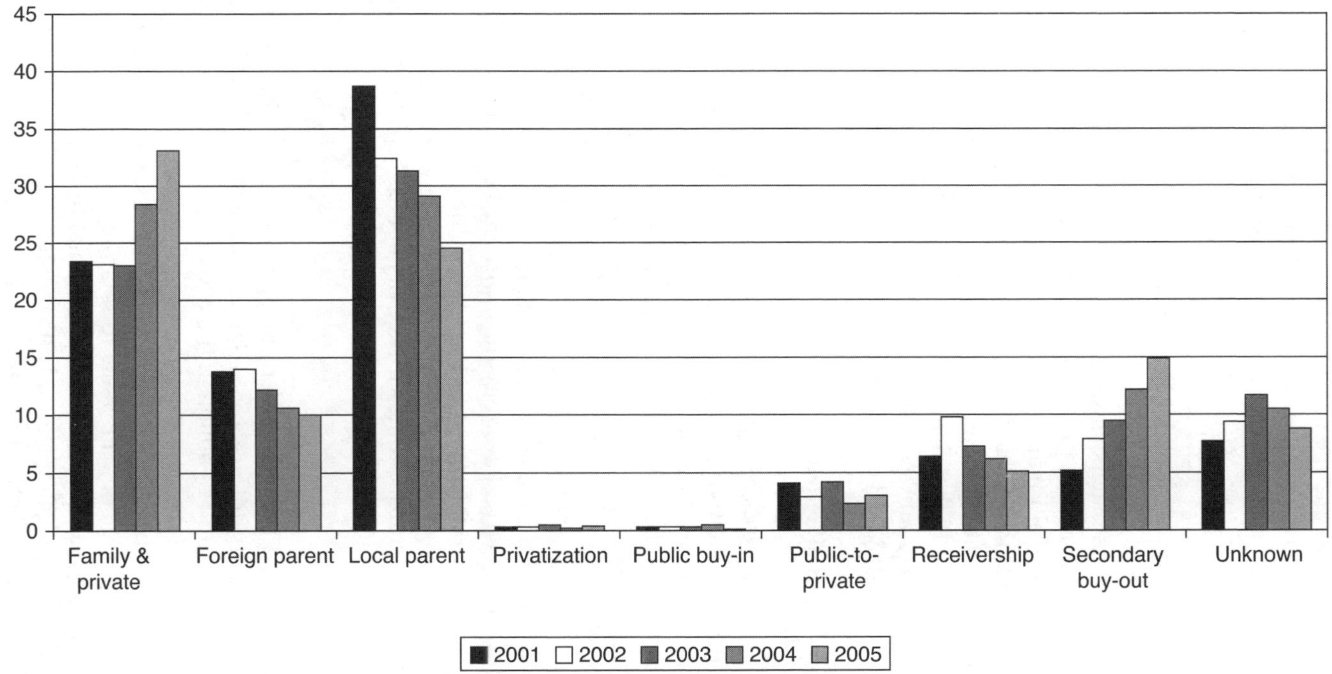

Source: CMBOR/Barclays Private Equity/Deloitte.

Figure 1.2 Buy-outs/buy-ins by source in Europe – percentage of total number

On this basis, the USA and the UK have the world's most developed LBO markets and had a record buy-out value during 2005 which equated to 1.6 per cent of these countries' gross domestic product. UK buy-out value reached its second highest level in 2005, with the proportion of buy-out value to GDP at 1.9 per cent (Figure 1.3). When the figures for the two most mature markets are compared with some of the major European economies it can be seen that countries such as France, Germany and Italy still trail not just in absolute but also in relative terms and that increased activity in these markets could therefore be possible. The small countries such as Denmark and the Netherlands owe their high rankings in Figure 1.3 to a few large deals that took place in 2005 and 2006, for example cleaning and maintenance company ISS (€2.9 billion), telecommunications company TDC A/S (€13 billion), publisher VNU (€8.7 billion) and Philips Semiconductors NXP (€7.4 billion).

In Australia, Canada and South Korea, total buy-out value was only around 0.2 per cent of GDP in 2005 and less than 0.1 per cent in Japan.

3.2 Public-to-Private Buy-outs (PTPs)

Recent years have seen the public-to-private (PTP) sector as a growing influence on the buy-out markets of both the USA and Europe, with PTPs also evident in Japan and Australia. Both the USA and the UK saw a surge in large deal activity in the going-private sector at the end of the 1980s, with food giant RJR Nabisco still one of the highest-profile LBOs of all time with a value of $30.2 billion in 1989. The record for the world's largest LBO remained intact up until 2006, when HCA, a US healthcare group, finally surpassed Nabisco with a value of $32.1 billion. The late 1980s also provided one of the UK's largest ever buy-outs, with the £2.2 billion Gateway transaction. Following this surge in PTP activity in the late 1980s, and some subsequent poor returns from these transactions, there was a slowdown in both US and UK PTP transactions, with activity not really picking up until a decade later.

3.2.1 USA

The increased size of PE funds under management has resulted in these funds having the ability to target ever larger transactions. PTP buy-out value surged to a record $120 billion in the USA in 2006 from around $75 billion in 2005 (Figure 1.4).

In the USA the high value of some PTP transactions has led to an increase in the percentage of PTP value to total buy-out market value. In 2002 this stood at just 16 per cent, but provisional figures for 2006 show PTP value at over 60 per cent of total LBO market value. This is a considerable way above the corresponding share for Europe; see below.

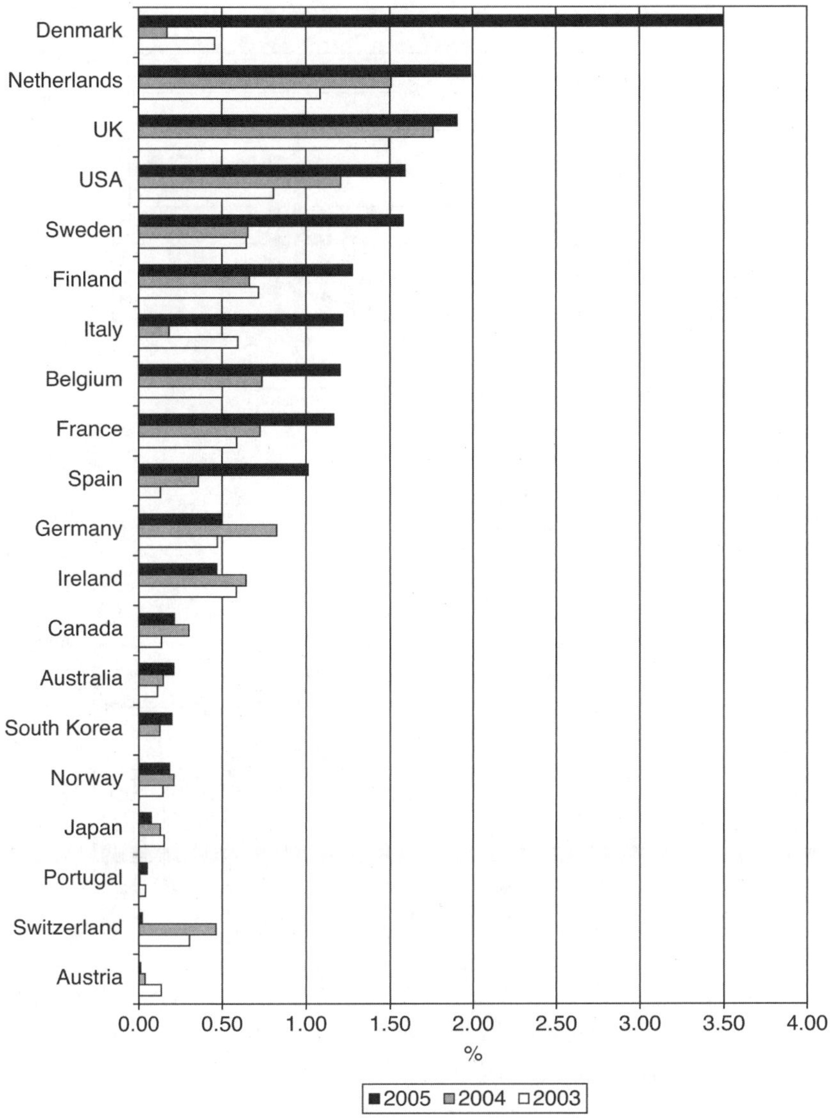

Source: CMBOR/Barclays Private Equity/Deloitte/OECD/Thomson Financial.

Figure 1.3 Buy-outs as a percentage of GDP

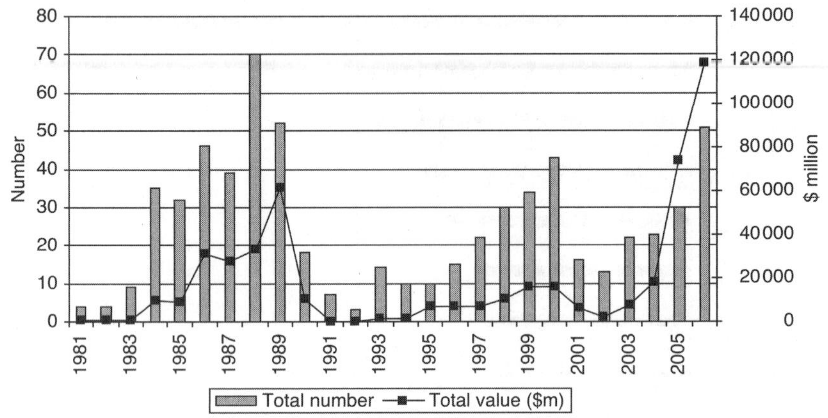

Source: Thomson Financial.

Figure 1.4 PTP buy-outs in the USA

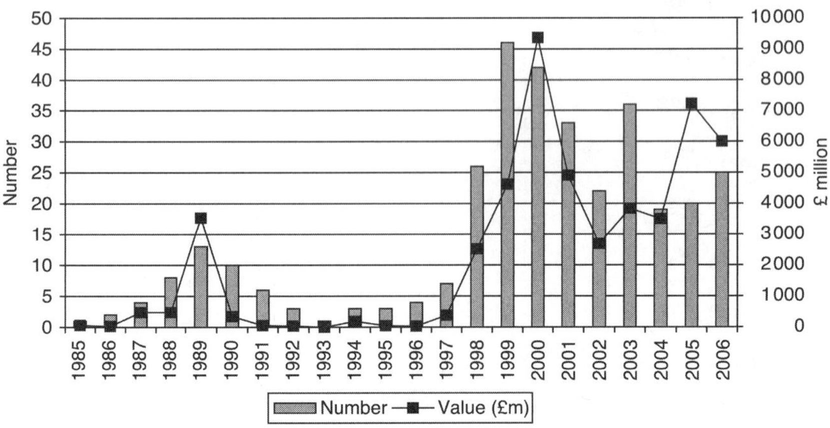

Source: CMBOR/Barclays Private Equity/Deloitte.

Figure 1.5 PTP buy-outs in the UK

3.2.2 Europe

The UK PTP market reached an initial high in 1989 with 13 transactions in that year having a combined value of over £3.5 billion (Figure 1.5), although the majority of that was accounted for by the buy-out of supermarket chain Somerfield/Gateway at almost £2.2 billion. This was by far the largest UK buy-out of any kind up to that date and remained so until

2000 when business property company MEPC was taken private for £3.5 billion.

The UK PTP market fell to relatively low levels in the early 1990s, with very little activity taking place until 1998 when 26 deals completed for £2.5 billion. From then, both the number and value of PTP buy-outs rose rapidly, with a record 46 in 1999 (£4.6 billion invested) followed by 42 in 2000 and a record value that year of £9.4 billion. This peak in investment value came during a period of record stock market valuations and a boom in technology stocks, with subsequent events showing that many quoted companies had been highly overvalued. Following the high levels of investment in 2000, the market then fell to £2.7 billion in 2002, with only 22 transactions. Going privates have since built up momentum once more, with 2005 having a value of £7.2 billion, although this fell in 2006 to £5.8 billion. PTP deal flow has remained relatively low in recent years, with just 20 in 2005 and 24 in 2006.

Although the PTP sector has become a large source of buy-out market value, the number of transactions remains relatively low when compared to the wider buy-out sector. Recent figures in the UK show that PTPs account for only between 2.5 and 5 per cent of total buy-out volume but between 20 and 30 per cent of total buy-out market value, having risen as high as two-fifths of market value in 2000. However, the first half of 2007 saw the buy-out of the first FTSE 100 company when the healthcare and beauty retail firm Boots was acquired in a deal led by Kohlberg Kravis Roberts (KKR).

The PTP market in Continental Europe also saw a surge in activity in the late 1980s, with 15 deals in 1989 having a combined value of €2.4 billion. This was followed by 13 in 1989 at €1.9 billion. Mirroring the UK market, Europe then saw little activity in the 1990s until 1998, when there was another surge in activity to €5.2 billion from 31 transactions (Figure 1.6).

From 2004 the Continental European PTP market has also shown marked growth. In 2006, €25.7 billion was invested in 16 transactions, although almost €22 billion of this total (85 per cent) is accounted for by two huge transactions – the €13 billion Danish telecommunications company (TDC) buy-out and publisher VNU at €8.7 billion. In Continental Europe PTPs have made up only between 2 and 4 per cent of the total buy-out market by volume since 2000 but have contributed between a tenth and a quarter of total market value during the same period.

The two largest PTP transactions of all time in Europe both took place in 2006 with Danish telecommunications company TDC having a value of €13 billion. This was a syndicated transaction with Blackstone, KKR and Providence Equity Partners of the USA teaming with Permira and Apax Partners of the UK to provide the equity funding for the deal. VNU, headquartered in the Netherlands, had a value of €8.7 billion and was also a

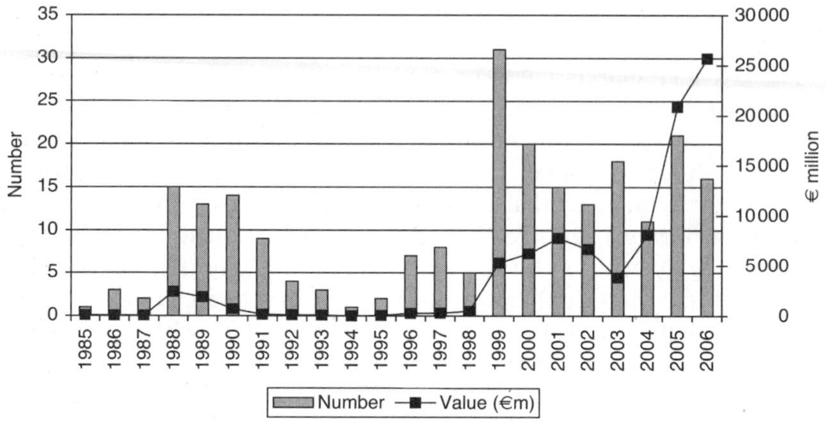

Source: CMBOR/Barclays Private Equity/Deloitte.

Figure 1.6 PTP buy-outs in Continental Europe

syndicated buy-out involving Blackstone, Carlyle Group, KKR, Thomas H. Lee Partners, Hellman & Friedman and Alpinvest. Both these transactions had employment levels in the tens of thousands.

The relatively small size of other international LBO markets means that PTP activities have been quite low but there have been some noteworthy transactions, especially in Japan and Australia. In Japan from 2000 to 2003 there were only 12 PTP transactions with a combined value of ¥115 billion (Figure 1.7).

The largest of these, Toshiba Tungaloy, a manufacturer of machinery, was a ¥35.7 billion buy-out led by Nomura in December 2003. Since then the Japanese market has seen 12 further PTP transactions by the end of 2006 and the value has rocketed to over ¥1000 billion (€7 billion). Evidence of the growing interest in the Japanese PTP market was demonstrated in 2006 when restaurant and retail chain Skylark became the largest Japanese PTP: the deal was led by Nomura and CVC Capital Partners and had a value of ¥257 billion (€1.8 billion). In Australia the PTP market has also remained relatively small although there were four transactions as long ago as 1990 for a total value of €272 million. Activity then stalled until 2001, with six PTPs completing to the end of 2006.

3.3 Cross-border Private Equity Investments

The past several years have seen a boom in international private equity activity. According to the European Venture Capital and Private Equity

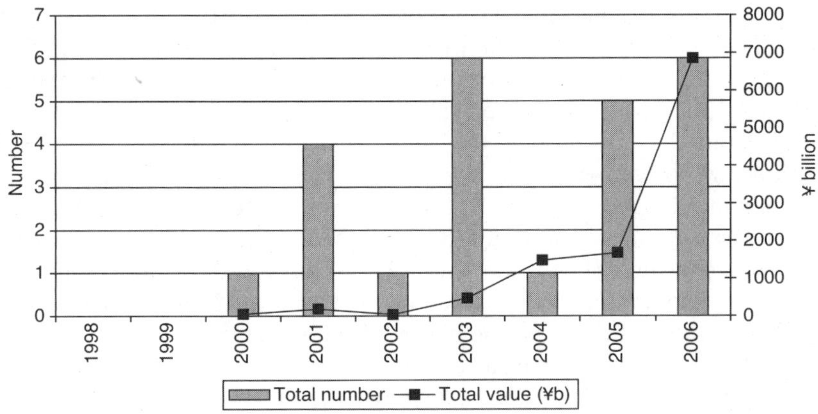

Source: Japan Buy-out Research Institute.

Figure 1.7 PTP buy-outs in Japan

Association (EVCA) cross-border investments represent almost 38 per cent of the total amount of early-stage and later-stage private equity investments in 2005. This is a significant increase compared to 2000, when the total amount of cross-border investment equalled 27 per cent.

Several factors have contributed to the internationalization of the industry: internationalization of capital sources, increased competitiveness of the domestic market, need for risk diversification, more and more firms pursuing global strategies, growth of developing economies, and increasing opportunities for exiting investments due to further development of IPO markets. A critical factor in the growth of international private equity investing has been the perception of the increasing difficulty of finding enough attractive private equity investments in the home market. Further, in many markets, foreign PE inflows fill untapped market demand. Also, even though domestic players have better knowledge with respect to local market conditions, in Europe UK PE investors often have more experience and can easily use their industrial expertise from around the globe with respect to private equity investing and, therefore, are able to add significant value to cross-border investments.

Cross-border activity of some of the major US private equity firms has been a critical factor behind the growth of European buy-out value in recent years. Buy-outs led by US private equity firms reached another record value in Europe in 2005 at €26 billion, with both the UK and Continental Europe seeing very large-scale completions. The largest US-backed buy-out in 2005 was in France, where distributor of electrical equipment and supplies Rexel was bought by a consortium led by Clayton Dubilier & Rice for €3.7 billion. In Table 1.3, we report the number of buy-out investments by UK private equity investors in Continental Europe for a 15-year time period. We include all the investments by PE firms that originated from the UK even if they invested through a local branch. For example, an investment made by Barclays Private Equity France will be included in the figures reported. It is clear from the total number of investments abroad that the international focus of UK private equity firms increased considerably during the 1990s. The upward trend in foreign investment activity reached a maximum in 1999 with 132 investments, after which a significant drop can be observed. However, the absolute amount invested overseas has grown steadily.

Syndication with domestic partners is often used as an internationalization strategy in order to obtain access to local market information and to facilitate monitoring. Further, by syndicating, the increased risk associated with international investments can be reduced. From a domestic provider perspective, syndication with foreign investors can build networks that provide access to foreign stock markets and overseas customers that might otherwise be difficult to achieve. Over the period 1991–2006, almost 50 per cent of the international investments by UK PE investors were syndicated. There is also a general downward trend in the percentage of investments that are syndicated by UK firms entering European markets. One reason for this is that more and more UK private equity investors have local offices in Continental European countries with local partners, which reduces the need to rely on domestic PE players through syndication; moreover in the early 1990s there was relatively little local private equity capacity.

The percentage of deals syndicated by UK PE investors varies across European countries (Table 1.4). In Germany, Portugal and Switzerland less than 40 per cent of the investments made by UK PE investors are syndicated, which represents the lowest level of syndication activity by UK PE investors for continental European investments. At the top end of the distribution we find Austria and the Netherlands, in which more than 60 per cent of the deals are syndicated. As syndication might be used to reduce the extent of uncertainty when entering a country, one would expect less syndication activity the more experience UK PE investors gain with a certain country. This does not appear to be the case. For example, the extent of syndication in the French market is still relatively high. One reason for this might be that France is still considered a challenging destination from a legal and cultural perspective.

Table 1.3 Distribution of foreign investments by UK investors (by number)

Country	1991	1992	1993	1994	1995	1996	1997	1998	1999	2000	2001	2002	2003	2004	2005
Austria	0	4	2	0	0	0	0	0	3	2	0	0	1	1	0
Belgium	0	0	1	0	0	1	2	6	6	2	1	1	4	7	3
Denmark	0	0	1	0	0	0	1	0	2	2	2	0	2	0	2
Finland	0	0	0	0	2	2	1	1	0	1	1	5	3	3	2
France	10	22	13	25	25	33	43	29	52	37	32	29	18	15	25
Germany	2	10	9	19	20	24	22	24	20	26	10	11	13	15	14
Ireland	0	3	0	6	3	1	5	5	3	4	4	4	1	0	0
Italy	6	5	8	13	3	8	10	9	13	10	1	7	5	4	3
Netherlands	2	1	3	11	9	4	5	6	5	6	4	4	8	8	3
Norway	0	0	0	0	0	1	0	0	1	0	0	0	0	0	0
Portugal	0	0	0	0	1	0	0	0	1	1	0	1	0	0	1
Spain	2	0	5	11	9	9	11	15	14	11	13	5	3	8	8
Sweden	1	0	2	1	5	5	2	1	7	2	4	3	2	7	5
Switzerland	0	0	1	0	2	2	6	4	5	6	1	8	1	4	1
Eastern Europe	0	0	0	0	0	0	0	0	0	1	0	0	4	1	4
Other	0	0	0	0	0	1	2	2	0	1	0	1	0	0	1
Total	23	45	45	86	79	91	110	102	132	112	73	78	65	73	72

Source: CMBOR/Barclays Private Equity/Deloitte.

Table 1.4 Syndication by UK PE firms in different European countries (1991–2006)

Country	Sole investment	Syndication	Total
Austria	5	8	13
	38.46%	61.54%	100
Belgium	18	17	35
	51.43%	48.57%	100
Denmark	8	6	14
	57.14%	42.86%	100
Finland	9	12	21
	42.86%	57.14%	100
France	199	220	419
	47.49%	52.51%	100
Germany	162	86	248
	65.32%	34.68%	100
Ireland	22	18	40
	55%	45%	100
Italy	59	50	109
	54.13%	45.87%	100
Netherlands	31	52	83
	37.35%	62.65%	100
Norway	3	0	3
	100%	0%	100
Portugal	3	2	5
	60%	40%	100
Spain	69	61	130
	53.08%	46.92%	100
Sweden	25	24	49
	51.02%	48.98%	100
Switzerland	26	16	42
	61.9%	38.1%	100
Eastern Europe	7	4	11
	63.64%	36.36%	100

Source: CMBOR/Barclays Private Equity/Deloitte.

4. MARKET OPERATION

In this section we analyse aspects of the operation of private equity firms. In particular, we reflect on approaches to the negotiation of transactions; competition and collusion issues relating to bidding for deals; deal pricing; the different nature of funds providers; leverage and financial instruments; the extent of deal refinancing; and the role of the taxation regime.

4.1 Negotiations

Private equity firms can improve the chances of success in negotiating a buy-out of a listed corporation by seeking irrevocable commitments from significant shareholders to accept the bidder's bid before the offer is made public. Gaining these commitments means that the bidder is sending a signal to other non-committed shareholders that the deal is a good one. The announcement of substantial irrevocable commitments may also make other potential bidders less likely to enter the contest with an alternative bid. The initial commitment ensures that, without any higher alternative bid, the agreement to sell the share becomes binding. Private equity bidders for listed companies may use irrevocable commitments in an attempt to ensure the success of a PTP proposal and reduce the costs associated with failure, as well as avoiding a bidding contest that would potentially reduce their returns from the investment. Weir et al. (2007) find that those proposing a management buy-out (MBO) are more likely to gain the backing of other shareholders the greater the bid premium and the more likely the private equity backer is to be reputable.

Informational asymmetries between vendors and purchasers may affect buy-outs involving private family firm succession. Flows of information may affect both succession planning and the buy-out negotiation process. A number of negotiation issues are raised, which centre around information asymmetries between founders and managers, as well as the extent to which negotiations are dominated by one or the other party or whether they are collaborative (Howorth et al., 2004). Scholes et al. (Chapter 5 in this volume) find lower information asymmetry problems if family firm vendors and the existing management team are equally involved in succession planning. However, they find that negotiations were less likely to involve a mutually agreed price where the succession process was driven by the vendor.

4.2 Competition and Collusion

Increasing attention is being directed to some of the regulatory issues surrounding private equity transactions. There may be the possibility of collusion in club deals if rival firms have been encouraged not to bid for a particular deal during an auction process so that the bid price remains low, with the non-bidding firms then being offered a stake in the target after terms have been agreed.

Private equity firms have denied any form of collusion and have argued that with ever-increasing deal values, clubs must be formed. Clearly, although buy-out funds have seen a dramatic increase in size over recent years, no one particular fund will want to over-allocate a large amount of capital to one transaction. Some of the largest US private equity firms now seem to be countering the possibility of increased government scrutiny with the recent formation of their own trade association. The Private Equity Council (PEC) has been formed in Washington DC by such private equity heavyweights as KKR, the Blackstone Group, the Carlyle Group and Bain Capital as an advocate of the PE industry, the aim being to bring increased recognition to the industry's role in the wider economy.

The behaviour of PE firms needs to be considered in the wider context of the market for corporate control and corporate governance. The ability of syndicates of PE firms to bid for larger listed corporations may add to the market for corporate control where other more traditional corporate bidders may be absent or find it difficult to acquire control. UK evidence indicates that PTPs have higher incidence of the two posts of CEO and board chair being held by the same person than traditional acquisitions of corporations and are associated with lower valuations and greater board ownership (Weir and Wright, 2006). The potential downsides from possible collusion by syndicates may therefore need to be weighed against the performance benefits to be derived from the improved corporate governance and incentives mechanisms they introduce, like the management equity share and debt ratio.

4.3 Pricing

An indication that private equity firms are prepared to pay more for buy-out targets can be seen in the relationship between profit before interest and tax (PBIT) and total transaction value (P/E ratio). This has risen consistently over the LBO market's development (see e.g. Figure 1.8).

In Continental Europe, where buy-outs with an enterprise transaction value of over $150 million have grown significantly from just 30 in 1998 to a record 109 in 2005, there has been a marked increase in P/E ratios from around 11 in 2000 to almost 19 in 2006. In the USA purchase price multiples for buy-outs have also shown a generally rising trend in recent years. Using data from Standard & Poor that track transaction value as a multiple of earnings before interest, taxes, depreciation and amortization (EBITDA), US buy-outs over $250 million have seen a rise in the average P/E ratio from under 6 in 1995 to over 7.5 by the end of 2005. For buy-outs between $250 million and $499 million, S&P data show multiples having risen to a peak in 1998 at around 8.7 and then falling back to 6.5 in 2001

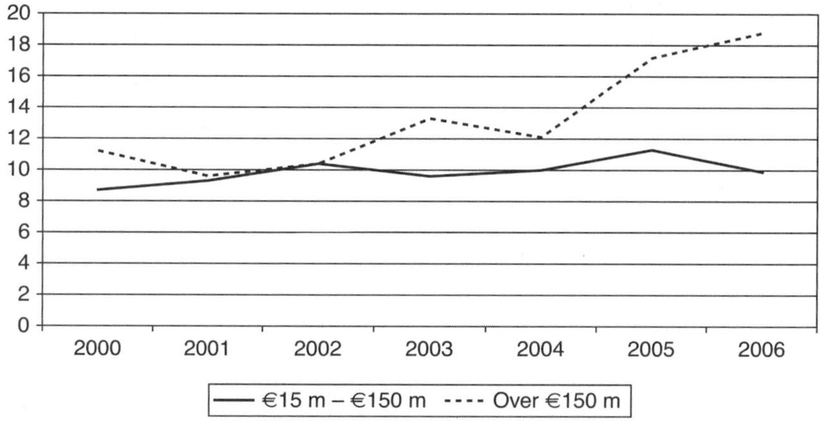

Source: CMBOR/Barclays Private Equity/Deloitte.

Figure 1.8 Continental Europe buy-out PBIT ratios

before rising to end 2005 at around 8.5. LBOs above $500 million followed a similar pattern and peaked in 1998 at just under 9 before falling to 6.7 in 2001 and rising again to end 2005 at 8.8.

Meuleman and Wright (2007) examine the relationship between private equity industry concentration and the extent of interfirm networking through syndication on the prices that private equity firms pay to acquire investment targets using data from the population of 988 UK buy-out targets in the period 1993 to 2002. Their results indicate that higher levels of market concentration are associated with lower prices when using total transaction value and transaction-value-to-EBIT (earnings before interest and taxes) as dependent variables.

The development of networks of private equity firms may reduce competitive rivalry, increase tacit collusion and hence lower prices. However, Meuleman and Wright (2007) find some evidence that the density of networks of individual private equity firms is associated with higher transaction values and insignificantly associated with transaction-value-to-EBIT multiples paid. Private equity firms with a higher market share were willing to pay a higher price to acquire investment targets, perhaps reflecting their greater efficiency and ability to create more value.

They also find that private equity firms are willing to pay higher prices the larger the amount invested by the management of the buy-out firm, and if the vendor retains a financial stake in the buy-out target, private equity investors are willing to pay a premium, indicating that these send a positive signal of the value of the underlying buy-out target. More successful private equity firms were willing to pay a higher price and the inflow of funds in the industry has a positive impact on the prices investors pay to acquire targets. They also find that the higher the number of investors active in a given year, the lower the prices associated with buy-out firms; this finding may be associated with lower prices attracting more private equity investors.

4.4 Funds Providers

In the USA, private equity investors in buy-outs tend to be limited partners, while in Europe, private equity firms that are divisions of banks and insurance companies play a more important role. These different firms may have varying investment time horizons and differences in their balance of general monitoring and specific sector skills. Hedge funds have also emerged recently as players in the buy-out market. These funds have traditionally been less actively involved in their investments than private equity investors. They also require greater liquidity and have had shorter time horizons than private equity firms.

Hedge funds may trigger restructuring and focus on cost reduction over the relatively shorter term. If this is the case, it raises doubts regarding the ability of hedge funds to generate long-run value in the buy-out firms that they invest in. Another concern is whether hedge funds will seek to exit quickly when one of their buy-out investments becomes financially distressed or whether they will become actively involved in restructuring. Different types of hedge funds may emerge with different mandates and a focus on different types of buy-out. Such funds may begin to recruit executives with private equity expertise. Further research, then, is needed to analyse the different buy-out market segments occupied by private equity firms and hedge funds, the different involvement of these types of investors in their deals and the performance impacts.

The resurgence of club deals has enabled syndicates of private equity firms, albeit smaller than in the 1980s, to bid for very large buy-outs that would otherwise be too risky to fund on their own.[2] In addition to this risk-spreading rationale, they may bring together the diverse specialist skills required to restructure and regenerate a particular deal (Wright and Lockett, 2003). Despite the presence of 'drag along' and similar provisions, coordination may be problematic when restructuring of distressed buy-outs is required (Citron et al., 2006).

4.5 Leverage and Financial Instruments

A buy-out is called an LBO (leveraged buy-out) when the new company's capital structure incorporates a particularly high level of debt, much of which is normally secured against the company's assets or cash flows. The objective of the PE firm is to achieve higher returns than would be possible through a stock market investment. Their instruments are financial leverage, dividend payments and control of managing the companies in the investment portfolio.

The first wave of LBOs in the USA was associated with concerns about excessive leverage (Kaplan and Stein, 1993). Similarly, while the percentage of debt in buy-out deals peaked in the late 1980s in the UK and sharply declined in the early 1990s, this has recently increased. In the average deal transacted in 2005, senior secured debt represented 51 per cent of the purchase price, with subordinated (mezzanine) debt accounting for around 5 per cent of the deal price (CMBOR, 2006). The average share of debt in financing structures varies markedly across deal sizes, with larger deals having the larger shares of senior and mezzanine debt (Table 1.5). Among the very largest deals, the average combined share of financing structures accounted for by senior and mezzanine debt has increased from 55 per cent in 2000 to 67.3 per cent in 2006, with the major part of this increase accounted for by senior debt. These increases have prompted regulatory concerns about conflicts of interest between different classes of finance providers as well as the likelihood of collapse of large private equity deals and the impact on lenders, purchasers of the debt and orderly markets (FSA, 2006).

4.5.1 Equity

The equity in buy-out transactions is provided by both private equity firms and management. On average, in UK transactions with a deal value of at least £10 million, management share ownership equity stake has generally been around 33 per cent, although in 2006 the figure was 42 per cent. The equity finance provided by private equity firms is obtained principally from pension funds in independent private equity firms and from their parent organization in captive private equity firms.

In the UK, the level of equity deployed in buy-outs has generally been on average between 35 per cent and 45 per cent of the total transaction value of the buy-out throughout the history of the market. Although CMBOR data on Continental European buy-outs have been recorded over a shorter timeframe than for the UK market, it is evident that on average European deals have also been purchased using a similar proportion of equity. This average has also ranged roughly between 35 per cent and 45 per cent since data collection started in 1999.

Pension funds are now the largest single contributor of capital raised for the European private equity market, accounting for 25 per cent of total European funds raised in 2005 according to EVCA figures. This amounted

Table 1.5 Average financing structures by deal size for all European MBOs/MBIs

Panel A: Deal size below €50 million

Type of finance (average %)	2000	2001	2002	2003	2004	2005	2006
Equity	51.6	43.2	37.0	43.0	43.3	38.9	36.7
Mezzanine	4.8	3.5	3.0	0.9	2.9	2.4	4.6
Debt	38.3	44.8	46.6	48.8	45.2	47.3	48.9
Loan note	2.3	2.5	6.9	3.5	4.9	3.6	3.8
Other finance	3.3	5.9	6.5	3.8	3.7	7.9	6.0
Total financing (€ m)	4635	3971	2429	2224	2274	2623	1743

Panel B: Deal size €50–€250 million

Type of finance (average %)	2000	2001	2002	2003	2004	2005	2006
Equity	38.7	31.6	31.6	39.1	35.6	33.2	35.0
Mezzanine	6.1	11.7	6.2	6.5	8.1	9.3	9.9
Debt	50.8	47.8	53.7	51.3	53.4	53.9	50.7
Loan note	0.9	4.4	4.3	0.4	0.5	1.8	2.7
Other finance	3.5	4.4	4.2	2.6	2.3	1.7	1.7
Total financing (€ m)	9807	7298	7416	8464	8795	9752	6274

Panel C: Deal size above €250 million

Type of finance (average %)	2000	2001	2002	2003	2004	2005	2006
Equity	27.8	29.3	29.1	30.5	29.4	29.3	33.0
Mezzanine	10.8	7.1	10.2	9.7	9.7	10.5	9.0
Debt	52.1	49.7	51.3	56.6	58.6	58.2	57.0
Loan note	0.1	2.2	2.1	0.0	1.2	0.0	0.2
Other finance	9.2	11.8	7.3	3.2	1.1	2.0	0.8
Total financing (€ m)	23 882	22 332	36 886	34 305	37 938	56 795	47 730

Panel D: Deal size above €500 million

Type of finance (average %)	2000	2001	2002	2003	2004	2005	2006
Equity	28.0	24.8	26.1	31.4	28.9	29.8	32.2
Mezzanine	8.0	8.2	8.8	9.6	9.5	11.6	8.3
Debt	47.0	48.8	49.4	54.1	59.6	57.0	59.0
Loan note	0.1	3.5	2.1	0.0	0.6	0.0	0.3
Other finance	16.9	14.7	13.7	4.9	1.4	1.6	0.2
Total financing (€ m)	17 384	15 858	30 214	29 339	32 874	49 716	40 279

Source: CMBOR/Barclays Private Equity/Deloitte.

to €16.8 billion, although clearly, private equity remains a relatively small part of total pension fund allocation, with about 1 or 2 per cent invested in the asset class on average. It is not yet fully clear what effect the Basel II Accord, which includes new norms of credit management for PE firms to control the financial risks of their portfolio investments, will have on the private equity market when it comes into force in 2008. However, it is believed that in countries such as Germany, where banks have held a great many underperforming long-term loans in small and medium-sized companies, there may have to be a rebalancing of capital, with long-term loans being replaced by equity. It is thought that this could help boost private equity investment in the country.

4.5.2 Debt

The debt in buy-out structures may be provided in a number of forms, depending on the ability of the buy-out firm to provide the lender with collateral and/or evidence of a stable cash flow to enable repayment of the interest and capital and/or the ability of the firm to sell off surplus assets to pay down some of the debt.

Senior debt, that is debt secured on the assets of the business, can take different forms with different interest and repayment conditions attached. The most typical layer is a straightforward repayment loan (so-called 'A' tranche). Other layers (so-called 'B' and 'C' tranches) may have longer maturities and repayment conditions that involve the roll-up of interest at a higher rate than the 'A' tranche and capital repayment delayed until the buy-out exits.

Senior debt has begun to take a higher proportion of total structuring in buy-outs over recent years. In addition to record levels of buy-out funds in the USA in recent years, new issuance of leveraged loans continues to climb. Value reached $246 million in the USA in 2005 compared to $195 million in 2004. The first quarter of 2006 alone saw $90 billion (Standard & Poor's).

Debt levels in Europe have indeed risen over recent years, with the total proportion of senior debt used in buy-outs in the UK in 2005 at over 50 per cent for the first time in the history of the market. This proportion has risen from just 36 per cent in 1992. This was, however, in the early days of the market when buy-outs were generally quite small and bank base rates were between 7 and 10 per cent rather than around the 5 per cent level seen in the UK in 2006. Debt in Europe has also reached high levels in the last few years, rising to a peak of over 55 per cent in 2003 and staying high in 2005 at over 53 per cent and around 54 per cent in 2006.

In large buy-outs the debt is underwritten by an investment bank or a large commercial bank and then syndicated. Recently this debt has been increasingly purchased by hedge funds and collateralized debt obligations (CDOs) or collateralized loan obligations (CLOs) funds. A CDO fund is a pooled investment vehicle which invests in a diversified group of debt assets. To finance its investments the pool vehicle issues bonds/notes to investors. The servicing and repayment of these notes is linked directly to the performance of the underlying assets. The majority of CDO funds invest in one or a combination of the following: senior secured loans; mezzanine loans; high-yield bonds; investment grade loans (these are loans that are rated BBB– or Baa3 and above); and SME (small and medium-sized enterprise)/emerging markets/mortgage-backed loans. Depending on the underlying asset combination, certain acronyms are used: CDOs imply a combination of loans and high yield instruments, whereas CLOs imply a loan-only fund. The packaging of debt into financial instruments such as CDOs and CLOs is causing concerns as to whether it is known who actually owns the large amount of leveraged loans now being issued. In the USA as in Europe there is a degree of caution surrounding hedge fund activity as it is often seen as a risky choice to provide leverage.

Second-lien debt has come into the buy-out market in recent years as an alternative to mezzanine financing. It is effectively a tranche of senior debt with some contractual subordination and because of this offers a higher yield. Where a C tranche of senior debt has typically been priced at around 3.25 per cent over Euribor (euro interbank offered rate) for large deals in recent years, second lien has been priced at around 5.50 per cent over Euribor.

Lenders typically specify and closely monitor detailed loan covenants to help ensure that the buy-out maintains its ability to service the debt. MBO lending agreements typically contain on average both more and a greater variety of accounting-based and non-accounting covenants than do general bank lending agreements. Various covenants may be used, but the most important are minimum cash-flow-based interest coverage ratio covenants, net worth covenants and dividend covenants (Citron et al., 1997). Breaching of covenants provides an early warning signal of liquidity problems. If covenants are breached, the lender has the power to take corrective action before the point is reached where the firm is unable to pay the interest.

Banks may have been encouraged to loosen lending criteria because they are now more able to pass on risk to hedge funds and other investors. Figures from Merrill Lynch covering the US market indicate that there has been a weakening of loan covenants on leveraged loans, with the average number falling to 2.8 in the second quarter of 2006 from 4.7 covenants per loan in 1997.

The share of debt in the financial structure reveals only one aspect of leverage. It is also important to consider the ability of a target firm to support a larger share of debt in the financing structure either in terms of the stability of its earnings, expected growth in earnings or through asset disposals. Hence a critical figure is the income gearing in a particular deal, i.e. the number of times interest payments are covered by cash flows. The debt/EBIT ratio provides an approximation of this figure: the higher the ratio, the riskier is the gearing. CMBOR data covering the European market also show a steep rise in the average debt/EBIT ratio over recent years, with a figure of over 9 recorded in 2006 from just 4.2 in 1999 for buy-outs valued at over €100 million. It is believed that the benign economic environment seen over recent years, of low inflation, low interest rates and robust economic growth, has produced a virtuous circle for buy-outs. If this were to change, the wholesale disposal of some of the more esoteric debt products could follow, with implications for the wider financial system that are difficult to predict. As buy-outs become bigger and account for a significant and growing share of employment, there is growing policy awareness of the potential implications of a sudden rise in interest rates or slowdown in economic growth for the buy-out sector. In the UK the Financial Services Authority (FSA) has recently begun investigating the possible effects of the growing influence of private equity and the implications of excessive leverage on the wider economy. However, despite these concerns many investors continue to be attracted to the European senior debt and mezzanine market by low default rates, opportunities for diversification from the USA and the prospects of high yields.

Average debt multiples to EBITDA in the USA fell at the top end of the market in 2005 to 5.7 from 5.9 in 2004 for buy-outs valued at over $1 billion (Standard & Poor's data). Buy-outs from $500 million to $1 billion also fell to 5 from 5.9 in 2004. Buy-outs below $500 million had an average debt to EBITDA multiple of 4.7 in 2005 from around 4.5 in 2004.

4.5.3 Mezzanine

In some cases, notably where a significant premium is paid on asset value, the buy-out firm may have insufficient assets to provide collateral to enable senior debt to be obtained, but it may have a strong stable cash flow. In these cases, mezzanine or subordinated debt may be obtained. For the lender, this is riskier than senior debt as there is less security; a higher rate of interest and possibly an equity option may be paid to the lender to compensate.

Mezzanine finance was until recently usually provided by dedicated mezzanine companies, but is now offered by many of the major banking sector debt providers. In continental Europe mezzanine has recently made up around 7 to 8 per cent of total deal structuring but in 2005 reached a new high of 10 per cent of average buy-out financing. In the UK, mezzanine does not appear to be so widely used and only amounts to around

4 per cent of deal structuring on average. However, mezzanine tranches have grown in size in the past few years, with the gambling and leisure group Gala Clubs in the UK using a record €683 million in 2005 for the acquisition of Coral Group. This was soon eclipsed in 2006 by the €1 billion used in the €2.1 billion secondary LBO of internet and telecom provider Casema (NL). Mezzanine providers report that much of the recent increased issuance of mezzanine has been taken up by hedge funds and CLO/CDO funds which are relatively new entrants to the LBO market.

4.6 Refinancing Buy-outs

In addition to the concern about the higher leverage being deployed in the private equity market, questions have also been raised relating to the refinancing of some recent deals and whether equity is being replaced by debt so that straight cash payments or dividends can be paid to investors. The result could be even higher leverage levels in the buy-out market than the entry buy-out structuring data would suggest.

Data for the European market show a rapid rise in company restructurings in the last four years. After falling to just €7 billion in 2002, refinancings rose rapidly to €45 billion by the end of 2005. This has fallen back in 2006 but provisional data still show over €36 billion raised to refinance European buy-outs (Table 1.7).

Examining the data for acquisitions by European companies which were formerly a buy-out (leveraged build-ups), it is clear that a large part of the

Table 1.6 Number and value of European restructurings by buy-outs

Refinancing year	No.	Value (€ m)
1995	33	201
1996	32	986
1997	111	1 641
1998	110	4 395
1999	97	3 115
2000	124	8 807
2001	110	17 632
2002	116	7 303
2003	92	11 837
2004	139	33 077
2005	135	45 200
2006	102	36 179

Source: CMBOR/Barclays Private Equity/Deloitte.

Table 1.7 Number and value of European acquisitions by buy-outs

Acquisition year	No.	Value (€ m)
1995	2	0
1996	8	488
1997	22	824
1998	50	162
1999	69	4267
2000	189	17248
2001	167	6810
2002	129	6057
2003	126	1724
2004	144	6143
2005	203	17838
2006	163	4515

Source: CMBOR/Barclays Private Equity/Deloitte.

refinancing total can be accounted for by the acquisitions of other companies (Table 1.7). In 2003 the total value of acquisitions by private equity backed companies was only €1.7 billion in Europe, but this figure rose sharply to €17.8 billion by the end of 2005. A sizeable proportion of this total is accounted for by the purchase of Coral Group by Gala Clubs for €3.2 billion, with a €4.1 billion debt and mezzanine package being used to help finance this acquisition. The refinancing of buy-outs has several other possibilities in addition to dividend recaps, i.e. for the acquisition of another company, for expansion of operations, or to obtain a new debt package on more favourable terms. However, the sharp increase in refinancing totals in recent years does add weight to the premise that an increasing number of large LBOs are now returning to the debt market in order to release capital to investors.

4.7 Taxation Regime

Tax relief on interest payments is a significant part of virtually all corporation taxes around the world and a company can reduce its after-tax cost of capital by increasing debt relative to equity. Legislation covering the taxation of private equity companies differs from one country to another and can encourage or discourage private equity investment activity; the impact on borrowing behaviour may differ as the resulting interest deductions may be different. Anti-avoidance provisions are in place in the UK, Spain, France, Germany, the Netherlands, the USA and Japan to determine the validity of tax deductions, for example the maximum rate of interest for which a tax deduction is available (Devereux et al., 2006).

In the UK the Finance Bill of 2005 extended the existing transfer pricing rules to private equity transactions, thus disallowing some tax deductions and also delayed tax relief payments related to interest on debt. Both of these changes were seen as negative by the private equity industry.

According to EVCA, Germany ranks only eighteenth in its private equity framework provisions out of the 21 major European countries. The tax situation has been unfavourable in Germany for some time, with, for example, a penal tax regime for those investing in certain types of foreign investment funds. In addition, by the year 2000 private equity managers had moved their funds out of Germany and had set up funds in Jersey, Luxembourg and Switzerland where tax treatments were well established and understood. The new German coalition government is in the process of reforming the legislation, in the shape of the Private Equity Act, which may encourage the setting up of German-based funds and may attract foreign investors. Indeed, the forthcoming German 2008 tax reform will bring Germany somewhat into line with the USA with regard to these anti-avoidance regulations.

Canada introduced a new Tax Fairness Plan in October 2006 which removed the tax advantages of publicly traded income trusts and partnerships compared to conventional Canadian public corporations, a move that may affect the private equity community in the USA and Canada as many firms divested their portfolio companies into the Canadian income trust public market. This may force private equity firms to look at alternative exit strategies.

5. ANTECEDENTS

A major theoretical argument for the taking private of listed corporations and divisions of such corporations through a buy-out concerns the existence of agency costs arising from under-incentivized and weakly monitored management in firms funded largely through equity where the pressure to service funding was low. It was argued that these buy-outs were more likely to be in mature sectors with high levels of free cash flow.

Much of the early evidence relating to the antecedents to the taking private of listed firms relates to 1980s buy-outs in the USA. US studies of the role of free cash flow in the decision to go private have produced mixed results. Lehn and Poulsen (1989) and Singh (1990) report that firms going private have greater free cash flow than firms remaining public but lower sales growth. However, Kieschnick (1998) reworked Lehn and Poulsen's sample using a weighted logistic regression and found free cash flow and sales growth to be insignificant. In addition, Opler and Titman (1993) find that leveraged buy-outs are more likely to exhibit only the *combined* characteristics of low Tobin's Q (market value/asset value) and high cash flow than firms remaining public. Further, Halpern et al. (1999) also find no evidence to support the free cash flow hypothesis. This US evidence, therefore, suggests that going private is not being driven by the need to return free cash to the shareholders.

A second argument concerns the opportunity to reap benefits from tax reductions associated with changing the funding of corporations from equity to debt where interest on debt is treated more favourably than dividends on shares for tax purposes. Kaplan (1989b) estimates the tax benefits of US PTPs to be between 21 per cent and 72 per cent of the premium paid to shareholders to take the company private for the first half of the 1980s.

Singh (1990) reports that US MBOs were significantly more under takeover pressure prior to the MBO than a sample of matched firms. DeAngelo (1986) finds no evidence of systematic manipulation of pre-buy-out accounting data by incumbent management. Wu (1997) does show evidence consistent with the view that managers manipulate earnings downwards prior to the MBO proposal. Asquith and Wizman (1990), Cook et al. (1992) and Warga and Welch (1993) show that bondholders with covenants offering low protection against corporate restructuring lose some percentage of their investment.

More recently, the development of corporate governance codes (Keasey et al., 1997) may lead to at least a *prima facie* convergence of internal governance mechanisms across firms. Improved internal governance may reduce the need for external governance in the form of hostile takeovers or for PTPs. As internal governance improves, agency problems may be reduced and it becomes more difficult for managers to protect their own interests by rejecting an outside bid. Weir et al. (2005a) show for the UK that, before they go private, PTPs tend to separate the functions of CEO and chair of the board less often than those firms remaining public (in contrast to suggestions by the Combined Corporate Governance Code) but do not have fewer outside directors. The authors also show that companies going private have higher CEO and outside blockholders than firms remaining public.

Weir and Wright (2006) report that UK PTPs have higher duality of CEO and board chair than traditional acquisitions of corporations. The authors also report that PTP buy-outs had lower valuations than traditional acquisition of listed corporations by other corporations, indicating managerial private information, and greater board ownership, suggesting that outside bidders have been deterred from bidding for the firms because of the potential difficulties involved in dealing with significant board ownership.

Australian PTP evidence indicates that insider ownership is not significantly higher in PTPs than for traditional acquisitions of listed corporations (Evans et al., 2005).

Opler and Titman (1993) consider financial distress cost, measured by R&D intensity, as a factor deterring a PTP buy-out and lowering the shareholder value gains. Weir et al. (2008) extend Opler and Titman's US work by testing the financial distress costs hypothesis in the context of the UK, a contract-based distress resolution system, and by considering the role of private equity firms. Using a dataset covering 115 PTP buy-outs completed in the period 1998 to 2001 and 115 randomly selected firms that remained public, they find contrasting evidence to that for US PTPs. Consistent with the financial distress costs model, firms going private are more likely to have better asset collateralization, have less debt and be more diversified. However, in contrast to the USA, UK PTPs did not have lower R&D. This may reflect the third antecedent of greater involvement of private equity firms in buy-outs in the UK than in the USA and the relatively high level of innovative activity post buy-out.

R&D intensity, however, is not an accurate measure of bankruptcy risk or distress costs. Sudarsanam et al. (2007) employ a direct measure of bankruptcy risk and financial distress estimated from stock market data and using the option pricing model. These are the default probability and proximity to default. They find that 20 out of their sample of 199 UK PTPs completed in the period 1997 to 2005 were in the high risk of default category using Moody's KMV model. Controlling for other factors reported in earlier studies as contributing to the PTP decision, and comparing their PTP sample with a control sample of similar firms not going private, Sudarsanam et al. (2007) find that going private companies have significantly higher default probability. They report a cumulative abnormal return (CAR) of 15 per cent for a seven-day announcement period for firms subject to going private, but that returns are higher for target firms faced with higher bankruptcy risk, suggesting a strong turnaround motivation for the PTP deal. Hence, in contrast to US evidence, the UK evidence shows that financial distress does not deter a PTP buy-out.

6. FINANCIAL PERFORMANCE OF BUY-OUTS AND PRIVATE EQUITY

6.1 Returns to Shareholders

For listed corporations, the value vendors place on a business is reflected in the share price response to the announcement of an attempt to take a firm private. A series of US studies in the 1980s (DeAngelo et al., 1984; Kaplan, 1989a; Lehn and Poulsen, 1989; Marais et al. 1989) finds a large abnormal gain for the target's shareholders when a going private LBO deal is announced. Kaplan (1989a) reports a median abnormal gain of 42 per cent for 76 US buy-outs in the period 1980–86. Similar stock market studies of voluntary divestments as LBOs by diversified companies (e.g. Hite and Vetsuypens, 1989; Markides, 1992) reveal small but significant positive announcement effects.

There is the possibility of systematically lower premia where insiders involved in the buy-out take action to reduce the apparent valuation in order to buy out at a price that is advantageous to themselves. This could be passive, where managers simply exploit asset prices which appear (to them) to be too low or it could be the result of some deliberate misrepresentation or concealment by them. Evidence on the former has been obtained from abnormal stock market returns for announced and then withdrawn LBOs (DeAngelo et al., 1984; Marais et al., 1989). Smith (1990) argues that abandoned, hidden-information buy-outs should show the same subsequent performance gains as completed ones and hence the same market response, assuming the buy-out is solely motivated by insider information. She finds no such evidence and hence concludes against the hidden-information view. However, the stock market response appears to depend substantially on whether or not a subsequent bid occurs (Lee, 1992), whilst existing owners returns are greater when competitive bids are received (Easterwood et al., (1994).

Insiders may manage earnings prior to a management bid in order to reduce the profits base for valuing the business. The evidence is somewhat contradictory: DeAngelo (1986) reports none, whilst Perry and Williams (1994) find evidence of consistent falls in the last complete financial year prior to an announcement. Kaplan and Stein (1993) analyse the structure of MBO pricing across the whole 1980s. They suggest that deal prices rose with the level of leverage, leading to overheating and a sharp rise in the failure rate at the end of the decade. Thus, if there were initial transfers from the pre-MBO owners, this trend was reversed across the period.

Renneboog et al. (2007) find that, in UK PTPs from 1997 to 2003, on average, pre-transaction shareholders reap a premium of approximately 40 per cent when the transaction is consummated and a 30 per cent abnormal return. They find that the principal sources of shareholder wealth gains are undervaluation of the pre-transaction target firm, increased interest tax shields and incentive realignment. Weir et al. (2005b) also identify undervaluation as a major rationale for going private in the UK during this period. An expected reduction of free cash flows does not determine the premiums, nor are PTPs a defensive reaction against a takeover. This evidence is only partly consistent with the early US evidence cited above, the undervaluation argument being more important in the UK, perhaps reflecting the significant numbers of PTPs completed where the founder had retained a significant equity stake.

The wealth of existing bondholders will be adversely affected if new debt, issued at the time of the restructuring, impacts adversely on the perceived riskiness of the original debt. Marais et al. (1989) fail to detect any such wealth transfer but Asquith and Wizman (1990) report a small average loss of market value, but those original bonds with protective covenants showed a positive effect. As buy-outs typically substitute debt for equity they tend to reduce corporate tax liabilities, but this tax saving generally accounts for only a small fraction of the value gain in buy-outs (Kaplan, 1989b; Schipper and Smith, 1988).

6.2 Returns to Investors

The substitution of leverage for equity in private equity deals enables investors in the remaining equity to increase their returns. Senior and subordinate debt providers have greater security for the finance they provide than equity holders and so seek a lower return. Funds providers to private equity firms (limited partners, LPs) receive the capital gain when the investments in the shares of the private equity deals are liquidated through trade sale, IPO or a secondary buy-out (see below). Private equity firms typically receive a management fee on the funds they raise from LPs of the order of 1.5–2 per cent and a share of the capital gain (known as carried interest, or 'the carry') above some predetermined hurdle rate and generally of the order of 20 per cent (Gompers and Lerner, 1999).

Fund-level data published by national venture capital associations and EVCA consistently show that the internal rates of return (IRRs) on buy-out funds outperform any other form of private equity/venture capital investment (Table 1.8).

Groh and Gottschalg (2006) provide evidence of a positive and significant effect of buy-outs from a sample of 199 US buy-out fund investments from 1984 to 2004. The authors show that buy-out investors select transactions in industries with low operating risk while successfully leveraging their investments and transferring transaction risks to lenders.

Previous research has also demonstrated that buy-out specialists play an important role in structuring the debt used to finance the LBO and in monitoring management in the post-LBO firm (Cotter and Peck, 2001). Buy-out specialists that control a majority of the post-LBO equity tend to have less debt and, thus, are less likely to experience financial distress. Buy-out specialists that closely monitor managers through stronger representation

Table 1.8 Pan-European returns (IRR) achieved on private equity

	1999	2000	2001	2002	2003	2004	2005
Early	21.6	21.9	15.7	8.0	5.4	4.2	2.3
Development	13.7	13.8	13.4	10.0	8.5	7.4	9.0
Balanced	19.0	16.8	20.5	12.8	11.2	10.7	8.5
All venture capital	17.6	16.8	15.8	9.5	7.4	6.7	6.2
Buy-out	23.9	21.0	19.8	17.8	17.0	16.5	17.8
Generalist	14.3	13.9	11.1	6.7	6.9	6.4	8.8
All private equity	19.4	18.3	17.2	12.2	10.9	10.6	10.6

Note: Pooled IRR is obtained by taking cash flows from inception together with the residual value for each fund and aggregating them into a pool as if it were a single fund.

Source: EVCA/Thomson Venture Economics.

on the board also tend to use less debt. Active monitoring by a buy-out specialist substitutes for tighter debt terms in monitoring and motivating managers of LBOs.

Nikoskelainen and Wright (2007) find an average (median) return of 22.2 per cent (−5.3 per cent), net of market index returns, and that IPO exits outperform trade sales and secondary buy-outs. Their analysis indicates that a balance of interrelated firm-level corporate governance mechanisms is critical for value increase in buy-outs, and the importance of these mechanisms for enhancing returns is context dependent in relation to the size of the transaction, among other things. Return characteristics and the probability of a positive return are mainly related to size of the buy-out target, acquisitions carried out during the holding period and differences between insider-driven buy-outs and outsider-driven buy-ins.

Cumming and Walz (2004) compare buy-out returns to the returns to other stages of venture capital and private equity investment using a large international sample in 39 countries. They show returns are greater in countries with stronger legal conditions, which demonstrates the importance of the legal environment for facilitating external corporate governance mechanisms.[3] The structure of the investment enhances returns: returns are high for syndicated investments but lower for co-investments, which suggests that the capital from a follow-on fund is used to bail out the bad investments from earlier funds. Cumming and Walz (2004) also show that convertible securities enhance returns.

Fund characteristics are equally important for returns. For instance, more established funds achieve higher returns (see also Kaplan and Schoar, 2005). Funds that invest in fewer projects per fund manager achieve higher returns, suggesting that smaller portfolio sizes per manager provide improved screening and greater value-added (Kanniainen and Keuschnigg, 2003, 2004; Schmidt, 2006; Cumming, 2006).

6.3 Creditors and Distress Costs

A further class of investors that need to be considered is creditors, ranging from senior secured to junior subordinated. Returns to these investors may involve either interest only or a combination of interest and the return on equity warrants (options) which are converted on exit or some other crystallization point. The returns to these investors also warrant attention when LBOs and private equity deals become distressed. Andrade and Kaplan (1998) find that for US buy-outs that defaulted, the leveraged buy-out companies retained approximately the same value that they had obtained before the buy-out. In UK buy-outs that defaulted, secured creditors recovered on average 62 per cent of their investment, and many of these companies were eventually restructured and sold as going concerns (Citron et al., 2003). Evidence on the returns to subordinated creditors in such cases is generally lacking.

Distress regimes vary across institutional environments (Armour and Cumming, 2006). As private equity firms internationalize, different distress regimes may affect both where they undertake deals but also the returns they and the debt providers who invest alongside them earn. Andrade and Kaplan's (1998) study showed that the distress costs of highly leveraged LBOs in the USA were low; the costs of financial distress in these firms amounted to 10–23 per cent of firm value. Betker (1997) finds that the ratio of direct costs of bankruptcy to assets for traditional Chapter 11 cases is lower if the firm is a highly leveraged transaction (HLT) than for distressed firms in general and suggests that this is because HLTs reduce creditor coordination problems.

Citron et al. (2006) analyse the determinants of bankruptcy costs under the UK's receivership regime. They find that the direct costs of receivership consume a significant percentage of the receivership proceeds, with both mean and median receivership costs equal to about 20 per cent of total receivership proceeds, while continuing trading costs consume a further 29 per cent of total receivership proceeds. In comparison with Franks and Sussman's (2005) more general population of small firms, where the direct costs of bankruptcy appear to be relatively high, with a mean ranging between 24.3 per cent and 42.4 per cent (median 18.5 per cent to 26.8 per cent) of total bankruptcy proceeds, these MBOs experienced fewer going-concern realizations in receivership (30 per cent), made a lower average repayment to secured creditors and made fewer 100 per cent repayments to these creditors. These results contrast with expectations about buy-outs following Jensen (1989). That these MBOs entered formal insolvency procedures despite the presence of specialized lender monitoring suggests that these cases will have been the ones considered most difficult to reorganize.

Citron et al.'s (2006) findings do not support the argument that multiple lenders create inefficiencies resulting in significantly lower secured creditor recovery rates. However, when there are multiple secured lenders, the senior secured lender gains at the expense of other secured creditors as the lender first registering the charge over assets obtains priority. They also find that receivership costs are positively related to the proportion of secured debt repaid and that, consistent with the presence of a scale effect, the relative significance of receivership costs declines as firm size grows.

Kaplan and Stein (1993) in a study of larger US buy-outs and Wright et al. (1996a) for the UK provide strong evidence that higher amounts of debt were associated with an increased probability of failure or need to be restructured. Wright et al. (1996a) also find that the higher turnover per employee and the reduction of employment on buy-out is negatively-associated with failure; this suggests the importance of measures taken to restructure an underperforming company early in the buy-out life cycle.

More recently, our examination of the 451 UK private-equity-backed deals completed from 1996 with a transaction value of at least £10 million that had exited up to the end of November 2006 provides some systematic evidence relating to the issue of whether high leverage is associated with buy-out failure (Table 1.9). Among all these exited buy-outs, those that entered bankruptcy had slightly higher proportions of senior secured debt in their initial financing structures. A more fine-grained breakdown shows that those buy-outs in the deal size range of £10–49.9 million that entered receivership had starting financial structures with larger proportions of senior debt than those that exited through other routes. The small number of deals in the £100 million deal range that entered receivership had the highest average proportion of senior debt and this was also substantially above that for other exits in the size range. However, these differences are not statistically significant. Looking at all forms of debt in these exited buy-outs, that is senior secured debt, mezzanine debt, high-yield debt and vendor loans, a similar pattern of differences emerges, except that for some deal size categories non-receivership exits had slightly higher percentages of debt than receivership exits. Overall, the differences in the proportion of funding structures accounted for by all forms of debt were not statistically significantly different between buy-outs that entered receivership and those that exited by flotation, trade sale or secondary buy-out.

Table 1.9 Leverage and bankruptcy in private equity backed exited UK buy-outs

Deal size range	No.	Senior debt as % of total financing	Total debt as[2] % of total financing
1. At least £10 m			
All exited deals	451	51.4	61.9
Receiverships	73	53.7	61.1
Other exits[1]	378	51.0	62.1
2. £10–£49.9 m			
All exited deals	273	50.8	59.3
Receiverships	59	53.6	61.1
Other exits	214	50.0	58.7
3. £10m–£99.9 m			
All exited deals	356	51.4	60.8
Receiverships	69	53.4	60.7
Other exits	287	51.0	60.9
4. At least £100 m			
All exited deals	95	51.3	66.1
Receiverships	4	58.0	67.9
Other exits	91	51.0	66.0

Notes:
[1] Includes flotations, trade sale, secondary buy-out.
[2] Includes senior secured debt, mezzanine debt, high-yield debt and vendor loans.

Source: CMBOR/Barclays Private Equity/Deloitte.

Sudarsanam et al. (2007) extend their finding that PTPs have a higher default probability before buy-outs than non-PTPs by examining whether PTPs that eventually exit through bankruptcy had higher initial default probability and distance to default than PTPs that exited through IPO, trade sale, secondary buy-out or no exit. They find that PTPs that end up in bankruptcy as an exit mode have the highest default probability, amounting to 376 basis points and 2.76 standard deviations to the default threshold.

6.4 Accounting Performance

Research on US LBOs during the 1980s indicates substantial mean improvements in profitability and cash flow measures over the interval between one year before the transaction and two or three years after to it (Kaplan, 1989a; Kaplan and Stein, 1993; Smith, 1990; Muscarella and Vetsuypens, 1990;

Opler, 1992; Smart and Waldfogel, 1994). Similarly, UK evidence indicates that the vast majority of buy-outs show clear improvements in profitability and working capital management (Wright et al., 1992). Financial ratio analysis of 73 medium-sized MBOs in the Netherlands related to cash flow, sales and return on investment showed that they had significantly better than average financial ratios of the industries in which they were involved (Bruining, 1992). Wright et al. (1996b) concluded using a sample of UK firms experiencing an MBO in the mid-1980s that they generated significantly higher increases in return on assets than comparable firms that did not experience an MBO over a period from two to five years after buy-out.

Desbrières and Schatt (2002) find that MBO firms in France outperform comparable firms in the same industry both before and after the buy-out. However, the performance of French MBO firms declines after the transaction is consummated. This downturn in performance is reported to be especially notable in former family businesses.

A representative survey of private-equity-backed buy-outs completed in the EU between 1992 and 1997 showed that the average EBIT as a percentage of turnover initially jumped from 4.2 per cent in the first year after buy-out and rose to approximately 7 per cent by year 3. Almost two-thirds of respondents (65 per cent) to this survey reported that their turnover had improved in comparison with competitors since the buy-out. About the same proportion of managers (67.3 per cent) also reported their belief that EBIT had grown more than their competitors' profits since the buy-out had taken place (CMBOR/EVCA, 2002).

Of course, financial statements may be subject to manipulation around the time of the buy-out. On the one hand, DeAngelo (1986), Kaplan (1989a) and Lee (1992) cast doubt on the manipulation and insider trading arguments. In contrast, Wu (1997) shows earnings manipulation in 87 management buy-outs during 1980–87, consistent with the notion that managers manipulate earnings downwards before the MBO proposal. Chou et al. (2006) find positive and significant discretionary current accruals coincident with offerings of reverse LBOs, and this earnings manipulation has a significant effect on the post-issue performance. Earnings manipulation may also affect the market's ability to assess the quality of buy-outs (Gilson, 2000).

Overall, recent evidence on buy-out performance reviewed here and also in Cumming et al. (2007) is consistent with superior risk-adjusted performance relative to industry benchmarks. Buy-out returns are significantly enhanced by corporate governance mechanisms, that is equity incentives for managers, board representation by private equity firms and the need to meet debt servicing commitments.

6.5 Debt, Monitoring and Incentives

Some indications of the effects of monitoring mechanisms introduced in buy-outs are given by comparing alternative organizational forms. For example, leveraged recapitalizations, which simply substitute debt for equity in quoted companies, have been shown to raise shareholder value (Denis and Denis, 1993) but they do not appear to have the same performance impact as LBOs, which also involve managerial ownership and institutional involvement (Denis, 1994). Similarly, defensive employee stock ownership plans (ESOPs), in which leveraged employee share purchases are used to forestall takeovers, do not appear to perform as well as LBOs. (Chen and Kensinger, 1988). Thompson et al. (1992) found that the management team shareholding size had by far the larger impact on relative performance in UK MBOs. Similarly, Phan and Hill (1995) found that managerial equity stakes had a much stronger effect on performance than debt levels for periods of three and five years following the buy-out.

A CMBOR survey of 300 management buy-outs across Europe questioned management teams about the nature of the contribution of their private equity provider (CMBOR/EVCA, 2001). Other than the provision of funding, the single most important contributions of the private equity firm were, in order of declining importance, financial advice and financial contacts, acting as a sounding board for management ideas, and providing strategic advice. Some 84 per cent of respondents claimed that without private equity support the firm would no longer have existed.

A recent study by Gottschalg and Wright (2008) shows that some private equity firms are repeatedly able to create real and lasting value through their investments. Indeed, their buy-outs enhance the competitive position and long-term prospects of the acquired companies. What makes a difference is their capacity to work actively with the management of their portfolio companies to improve strategy and operational effectiveness.

This study finds that private equity firms help build better businesses as their deep experience in making buy-out deals helps them take the right decisions during the deal and after the acquisition. Second, a clear strategic focus on specific target industries enables these private equity firms to build up and leverage expertise. Third, early and honest communication of what the buy-out means for the company and its employees, including targets, risks and rewards, is important in creating the motivation necessary to meet ambitious business plans. Fourth, a strong and trust-based relationship between company management and private equity investors is the basis for value-added involvement in strategic and operational decisions. Finally, keeping a balance between the growth in capital under management and available managerial resources is required for a private equity firm's continuing success.

7. REAL EFFECTS OF BUY-OUTS

7.1 Productivity

Amess (2002, 2003) presents UK evidence on the effects of full-firm MBOs on productivity, based on company-level data. Using plant-level data, Lichtenberg and Siegel (1990) find that US MBO plants had higher total factor productivity (TFP) than representative establishments in the same industry before they changed owners. However, they also reported that MBO plants experienced significant improvements in TFP after the MBO. More importantly, the authors also found that this enhancement in economic performance could not be attributed to reductions in R&D, wages, capital investment, or layoffs of blue-collar personnel.

Harris et al. (2005), analysing longitudinal data for approximately 36 000 UK manufacturing establishments, extended the Lichtenberg and Siegel (1990) study. The authors found that UK MBO establishments were less productive than comparable plants before the transfer of ownership. They also reported that MBO plants experienced a substantial increase in productivity after a buy-out and that these post-buy-out productivity gains are pervasive across industries. The results imply that the improvement in economic performance may be due to measures undertaken by new owners or managers to reduce the labour intensity of production, through the outsourcing of intermediate goods and materials. This evidence suggests that MBOs may be a useful mechanism for reducing agency costs between new owner-managers and new shareholders, and enhancing economic efficiency.

7.2 Strategy

Buy-outs are a means for refocusing the strategic activities of the firm (Seth and Easterwood, 1993; Phan and Hill, 1995). Both Wright et al. (1992) and Zahra (1995) find that buy-outs are followed by significant increases in new product development and other aspects of corporate entrepreneurship such as engaging in entrepreneurial ventures, technological alliances, R&D staff size and capabilities. Bruining (1992) provides case study evidence that MBOs improve their economic performance by making explicit strategic choices for growing internally and externally.

US evidence strongly supports the view that capital investment falls immediately following the LBO as a result of the increased leverage

(Kaplan, 1989a; Smith, 1990). The evidence on UK MBOs is rather different. Wright et al. (1992) report that asset sales are offset by new capital investment, particularly in plant and equipment. The effect of buy-outs on R&D is less clear, although on balance there seems to be a reduction (Long and Ravenscraft, 1993; Lichtenberg and Siegel, 1990; Smith, 1990). However, as many LBOs are in low R&D industries, the overall effect may be insubstantial. There is some evidence that in buy-outs that do have R&D needs this expenditure is used more effectively (Zahra, 1995).

7.3 Employees and Human Resource Management

The effects of private equity transactions on employment and wages in particular have been at the centre of considerable heated recent policy debate. Evidence on the effects of buy-outs on employment is mixed. Opler (1992), Kaplan (1989a) and Smith (1990) – but not Muscarella and Vetsuypens (1990) – report small increases in total firm employment following LBOs. Kaplan (1989a) and Smith (1990), however, report that buy-outs do not expand their employment in line with industry averages. Lichtenberg and Siegel (1990) report an 8.5 per cent fall in non-production workers, over a three-year period, with production employment unchanged. Early UK evidence suggested that job losses occur most substantially at the time of the change in ownership (Wright et al., 1992).

Bruining et al. (2005) report that MBOs in the UK and The Netherlands result in an improvement in human resource management (HRM) practices. Specifically, they found that there were higher levels of employment, employee empowerment and wages. These effects were found to be stronger in the UK than in the Netherlands, and emphasize the importance of understanding different institutional contexts even within Europe.

Amess et al. (2007) report that employees in UK MBO firms have more discretion over their work practices than comparable workers at non-MBO firms. Skilled employees, in particular, were found to have very low levels of supervision at MBO firms. Amess and Wright (2007) show in a panel of 1350 UK LBOs observed over the period 1999–2004 that when LBOs are disaggregated, employment growth is 0.51 of a percentage point higher for MBOs after the change in ownership and 0.81 of a percentage point lower for MBIs. More detailed data indicate that employment in the MBOs dips initially after the buy-out but then continues to rise, on average. In contrast, for MBIs, the employment level remains below the pre-buy-out level (Table 1.10). These findings are consistent with the notion that MBOs lead to the exploitation of growth opportunities, resulting in higher employment growth. The same patterns do not emerge from MBIs, typically because the latter transactions involve enterprises that require considerable

Table 1.10 The post-MBO and post-MBI changes in employment and remuneration per employee

Variables	Years relative to year of deal					
	t+1	*t*+2	*t*+3	*t*+4	*t*+5	*t*+6
MBO						
Employment (%)	−2.28	2.96	7.46	21.43	26.02	36.19
	(−0.63)	(0.63)	(1.28)	(3.31)***	(3.15)***	(2.44) **
% deals with positive change	60.19	65.12	66.08	64.32	61.70	61.42
% deals with negative change	35.73	33.22	32.16	34.02	36.17	36.22
% deals with no change	4.08	1.66	1.77	1.66	2.13	2.36
Remuneration per	6.30	11.22	15.05	19.89	26.91	28.27
employee (%)	(3.80)***	(6.07)***	(6.62)***	(6.86)***	(5.05)***	(6.47)***
% deals with positive change	71.47	75.67	77.30	81.67	83.96	86.61
% deals with negative change	28.53	24.33	22.70	18.33	16.04	13.39
% deals with no change	0	0	0	0	0	0
Number of deals	319	301	283	241	188	127
MBI						
Employment (%)	−10.22	−9.70	−11.10	−3.35	−5.02	−18.26
	(−1.46)	(−1.24)	(1.24)	(−0.31)	(−0.37)	(−0.55)
% deals with positive change	57.5	59.82	58.65	56.32	55.93	64.86
% deals with negative change	36.66	36.61	38.46	39.08	42.37	35.10
% deals with no change	5.83	3.57	2.88	4.60	1.69	0
Remuneration per	5.49	10.04	15.47	17.59	25.03	38.84
employee (%)	(1.57)	(2.56)**	(3.46)***	(3.03)***	(3.33)***	(4.74)***

Table 1.10 (continued)

Variables	Years relative to year of deal					
	$t+1$	$t+2$	$t+3$	$t+4$	$t+5$	$t+6$
% deals with positive change	63.87	72.07	81.55	79.07	86.21	94.49
% deals with negative change	35.13	27.93	18.45	20.93	13.79	5.41
% deals with no change	0	0	0	0	0	0
Number of deals	120	112	104	87	59	37

Notes: (1) column $t+s$ ($s=1, 2, \ldots, 6$) shows the percentage change in the relevant variable s years after the deal compared to the year before the deal ($t-1$) on a deal-by-deal pairing. Thus the employment change of 21.43 per cent four years after the deal indicates that employment grew by 21.43/5 = 4.29 per cent per annum; (2) paired t-statistics of equality between $t-1$ and $t+s$ years after the deal are in parentheses; (3) ***, ** and * indicate significance at the 1, 5 and 10 per cent levels, respectively.

Source: The employment and remuneration data are obtained from FAME and matched with the CMBOR database that provides information on the date of deals and exits. Due to exits, the number of deals in the analysis declines over time. This means that caution must be taken when comparing changes in different buy-out periods. The advantage of this approach, however, is that we use all available deals and do not introduce bias by discarding deals in order to keep the sample size the same in each post-buy-out period.

restructuring. In the context of the findings of Harris et al. (2005) noted above that total factor productivity in buy-outs is on average lower than comparable non-buy-out counterparts before the change in ownership, it is perhaps not surprising that some labour shedding occurs. In the light of evidence from Wright et al. (1996a), such action appears to reduce the likelihood that the firm will subsequently fail, with the likely even higher loss of employment.

Amess and Wright (2007) find that on average wages in both MBOs and MBIs are lower than their non-buy-out industry counterparts. Amess and Wright do not examine the trend pre-buy-out, so it is not possible to tell whether buy-outs had a higher or lower wages trend than non-LBOs and hence whether the position is worse, better or the same after buy-out. Moreover, it needs to be asked why the position is different as between MBOs and MBIs. It is not possible from Amess and Wright to tell what the position was before the LBO, but evidence from elsewhere is clear that MBIs typically were underperforming, problem cases (e.g. Robbie and Wright, 1996). This evidence also shows that post-MBI restructuring is greater than for MBOs and that MBI performance is below that for MBOs. Evidence from CMBOR also shows a higher failure rate of MBIs compared to MBOs (CMBOR, 2006). All this evidence points to MBIs being more problematic. It is, therefore, too simplistic to take a wholly negative view of MBIs since the *status quo ante* may not have been sustainable. Further analysis is needed to link these factors to wages and employment.

7.4 Entrepreneurial Buy-outs

Auctions and a stronger emphasis on shareholder value by corporations in recent years, as corporate governance has become more active, affect private equity returns. It may be more difficult to generate target financial returns simply through financial engineering; rather private equity firms may need to deliver changes in strategy and product development (Kester and Luehrman, 1995). While some private equity funds are persistently good performers, not all are, as evidenced by the differences in the median returns for different performance quartiles. Buy-outs may thus be attractive that involve businesses where managers identify entrepreneurial opportunities for new products and markets but become frustrated with a bureaucratic corporate structure that rejects their proposals for investment (Wright et al., 2000a; Robbie et al., 1999).

'Busted tech' or turnaround buy-outs, where owner-managers may already have the skill set and the incentives to pursue strategic innovations and/or where there may have been little monitoring over management, also offer opportunities for strategic shifts that were not feasible before the change in ownership (Wright et al., 2001). The opportunity for a buy-out may arise when the firm encounters difficulties, either through liquidity problems or poor execution of the business plan due to a lack of technological expertise. In this case, a buy-out may constitute a mechanism for providing superior governance expertise relating to an innovative opportunity.

In the USA, UK and The Netherlands, respectively, Zahra (1995), Wright et al. (1992) and Bruining and Wright (2002) find that buy-outs are followed by significant increases in new product development and other aspects of corporate entrepreneurship. CMBOR/EVCA (2001) found that 69.6 per cent of private-equity-backed buy-outs increased their product range, 62.5 per cent expanded into new markets, 53.7 per cent invested in new sites or locations and 52 per cent developed existing sites. Bruining and Wright (2002) observe important roles for the private equity funders in keeping added-value strategies on track, assisting in new ventures and broadening market focus, and in having the knowledge to be able to assess invest in product development. Bruining et al. (2004) provide detailed case analysis of how private equity firms can contribute to the development of management control systems that facilitate strategic change in different types of buy-out. Analysis of buy-outs in Japan suggests that there is scope to restructure both keiretsus and listed corporations through private-equity-financed buy-outs (Wright et al., 2003). Wright et al. (2003) suggest that in some contrast to the West, buy-outs in Japan are likely to be of particular relevance in the spinning off of underperforming divisions where management's opportunities for growth are frustrated by bureaucratic internal control systems, creating scope for revitalization, that is involving catch-up investment, and entrepreneurial buy-outs.

8. REALIZATION AND EXITS

Private equity (PE) firms are under significant pressure to achieve their target returns and hence work towards a timely exit.

8.1 Exit Trends

The common forms of exit are trade sales, flotations, secondary buy-outs and bankruptcy (receivership). The popularity of the different types of exit depends on the prevailing economic conditions and has thus varied over time. Trade sales have been the most common form of exit in the UK, except in the early 1990s when the recession led to receiverships. Flotations or initial public offerings (IPOs) were often chosen in the late 1980s, when the stock markets were relatively healthy, but have been less popular since then.

Secondary buy-outs have gained importance since the mid-1990s and now account for almost a third of all exits in the UK. A number of factors have driven the need for financial investors to sell off their portfolio firms to other PE firms. These reasons include the difficulties in exiting buy-outs via IPOs, the reduced acquisition appetite by corporations seeking to refocus (especially for smaller deals), and the need for private equity firms to exit from deals when PE funds come to the end of their life.

In a secondary buy-out, an initial buy-out deal is refinanced with a new ownership structure including, typically, a new set of private equity financiers while the original financiers and possibly some of the management exit. Such deals account for a large proportion of the value of the UK market. Moreover, as buy-out markets mature, we also observe tertiary and fourth-time-around deals (CMBOR, 2006). At the end of 2006, a total of 16 companies in the UK (20 across the rest of Europe) had gone through at least three buy-outs. These tend to be mid-range deals that are cash generative in mature sectors, such as the retail sector, which can be easily re-leveraged.

There is considerable debate about the longevity of buy-out structures. Evidence from the 1980s in both the USA (Kaplan, 1991) and UK (Wright et al., 1995) shows that buy-outs have a heterogeneous life cycle; that is, some are exited in a relatively short period of time, while others remain with the buy-out structure for periods in excess of five years. On average larger deals exit significantly sooner than small deals. That there have been some recent very short periods to exit of private equity deals is not new and should not be surprising. Some deals fail quickly while others may receive unsolicited bids by trade buyers within a short time after buy-out. However, it is important to consider the time of exit of a particular cohort, i.e. deals completed in a particular year, as a whole (Table 1.11). The average period to exit for recent years is quite low, reflecting the small number of buy-outs that exit in a short period of time. The very long average exit periods for deals completed in the first half of the 1980s reflects the lower emphasis on exit at that time.[4] These extremities apart, the most common timing of exit for those deals that had exited to mid-2007 is in the range of four to five years.

Financial distress and receivership represent the negative aspect of exits. Since the mid-1980s there have been 12 923 UK buy-outs, of which 1480 have so far entered receivership. The receivership rate varies according to vintage year, peaking at 21 per cent for buy-outs completed in the boom years of 1988–90 which subsequently encountered problems in the recession of the early 1990s. The failure rate of buy-outs completed during the

Table 1.11 Average time to exit to end mid-2007 for UK buy-outs/buy-ins by vintage year

Year of deal	Number of deal	Number of exits to date	Average time to exit (months)
1981	152	66	103.3
1982	247	105	99.3
1983	252	110	79.2
1984	251	117	78.8
1985	294	141	68.0
1986	370	175	68.2
1987	436	236	64.3
1988	501	260	66.0
1989	529	281	59.7
1990	606	276	63.2
1991	581	251	53.8
1992	597	225	58.5
1993	493	201	56.0
1994	565	243	56.1
1995	599	268	54.9
1996	647	280	52.3
1997	709	280	49.1
1998	690	293	49.3
1999	659	246	47.4
2000	623	212	46.1
2001	644	194	40.4
2002	639	165	47.4
2003	714	155	27.6
2004	706	118	22.1
2005	692	65	16.3
2006	682	7	6.9

Source: CMBOR/Barclays Private Equity/Deloitte.

first half of the 1990s was approximately 12 per cent by September 2005. In addition, the large majority of receiverships occur in smaller firms. CMBOR data indicate that 94 per cent of the receiverships were from buy-outs with initial deal values of less than £20 million.

As traditional forms of exit have become more difficult, refinancings and partial sales have become more frequent as they are a mechanism for PE firms to cash out part of their investments while at the same time keeping control of their portfolio companies. Exiting through refinancing may involve either the PE firm having the business borrow more and then paying

Table 1.12 Number and value of UK and Continental Europe partial sales by year

Partial sale year	UK		Continental Europe	
	No.	Value (€ m)	No.	Value (€ m)
2000	77	4237.3	34	420.0
2001	92	8855.0	29	50.7
2002	70	4466.0	30	2643.7
2003	77	2056.7	34	921.9
2004	70	2982.2	45	2938.0
2005	98	9047.0	50	2235.8
2006	59	5744.5	34	2856.7

Source: CMBOR/Barclays Private Equity/Deloitte.

themselves special dividends from the borrowings, or engaging in a sale and leaseback of property assets to a third party and transferring the proceeds from the sale to the PE firm in the form of a dividend. An example of refinancing is the 2004 Dutch buy-out of publisher PCM bought out by Apax Partners of the UK, and of partial sales the fashion retailer KBB bought out by K Capital Partners of the USA. With respect to exit through refinancing, in the UK, for example, in 2005 total refinancings accounted for over a third of the total value realized, compared to a little over a tenth in 1997 (CMBOR, 2006). Between 55 and 90 recapitalizations have been recorded each year in the UK. The total value returned through recapitalization in 2005 was €19 billion, significantly adding to the €33 billion realized through full exit.

A partial sale of the portfolio company provides another means of realizing part of the initial investment without losing control. The sale of a subsidiary business is another means by which the private equity house may seek to return some or all of the original capital investment. Partial sales made up just over a third of the total value realized in the UK in 2001, when the value of the FTSE 100 fell sharply, but have since become less frequent and accounted for just under a quarter of the total in 2005. The number of partial sales recorded is generally between 70 and 100 per annum, with a further €9 billion value realized through partial sales in the UK in 2005 (Table 1.12).

Across Continental Europe secondary buy-outs have dominated over the last few years, pushing trade sale exits into second place, IPOs being once again the least favoured exit option. Exit values were at record levels in 2006, driven largely by these major exits through secondaries. The total

Table 1.13 Exit numbers and exit values for European buy-outs/buy-ins

	UK		Continental Europe	
	Number of exits	Total exit value (€ m)	Number of exits	Total exit value (€ m)
1999	250	9 752.6	127	9 059.5
2000	289	14 786.0	141	11 965.9
2001	258	12 676.2	109	7 352.3
2002	279	16 266.5	98	5 799.9
2003	249	13 281.2	126	10 545.3
2004	330	27 339.6	150	20 789.2
2005	343	32 805.6	221	43 342.3
2006	318	39 149.3	229	55 807.2

Source: CMBOR/Barclays Private Equity/Deloitte.

value of exits reached a record of €39 billion in the UK compared to €56 billion in Continental Europe (Table 1.13). In Continental Europe, refinancing also accounted for just over a third of total exit value in 2005. Partial sales now account for less than 5 per cent of the total in 2005. The effect of these forms of exit on returns to private equity investments has yet to be analysed.

In the USA, figures for secondary buy-outs suggest a similar trend to that observed in Europe, with the contribution from secondary buy-outs equating to about 5 per cent by value and volume of all buy-outs since 2003 compared to between 1 per cent and 2 per cent in the period before then (Thomson Venture Economics, 2006).

According to the Japanese Buy-out Research Institute (JBORI), there were between 25 and 27 exits over the last three years and the majority of these were trades sales, accounting for about half of all exits by number. As expected, in line with other OECD countries, secondary buy-outs are becoming more popular and have accounted for about a fifth of exits over the same period.

8.2 Post-exit Effects

An important issue is whether the claimed benefits of private equity deals are sustained once the private buy-out structure ends. Holthausen and Larcker (1996) find that while leverage and management equity falls when US buy-outs return to market (reverse buy-outs), they remain high relative to comparable listed corporations that have not undergone a buy-out.

Pre-IPO, buy-outs' accounting performance is significantly higher than the median for the buy-outs' sector. Following the IPO, accounting performance remains significantly above the firms' sector for four years but declines during this period. Consistent with other studies, Holthausen and Larcker find that the change is positively related to changes in insider ownership but not to leverage. Bruton et al. (2002) also find that agency cost problems did not reappear immediately following a reverse buy-out but took several years to re-emerge.

Private-equity-backed MBOs in the UK tend to make IPOs earlier than their non-private-equity-backed counterparts (Jelic et al., 2005). There is some evidence that they are more underpriced than MBOs without private equity backing but not that they perform better than their non-private-equity-backed counterparts in the long run. In contrast to the grandstanding hypothesis relating to early-stage venture capital firms (Gompers, 1996), PTP MBOs backed by more reputable private equity firms in the UK tend to exit earlier, and these MBOs performed better than those backed by less prestigious private equity firms.

9. RESEARCH AND POLICY

In this section we develop an agenda for further research and then consider policy implications concerning private equity and buy-outs.

9.1 Agenda for Future Research

There remain a number of areas for further investigation. This section elaborates some particularly important areas.

9.1.1 Vendor sources

Two of the major changes in vendor sources of deals that have become prevalent are PTP transactions and secondary buy-outs. A third area of international importance concerns the role of private equity transactions in the succession of family firms.

There is a need for further research to examine how PTP buy-outs differ in the 1990s/2000s from those of the 1980s. What factors are influential in determining private equity deals now compared to the 1980s? Comparative analysis of the 1980s with the current period might usefully examine differences in vendor and sector deal source and consider to what extent these are associated with changes in the generation of deal opportunities, changes in regulatory conditions, developments in financing techniques and entry of new types of financiers, exit strategies, etc.

A further issue, to which we return below, concerns the effects of PTP transactions on the financial and economic performance of firms. This analysis needs to compare PTP cases with other listed corporations that do not go private. In particular, while it is often claimed by managers and investors that taking a corporation private was the only way to effect changes, this view has been challenged by those who suggest that the incentive and governance arrangements available to listed corporations should enable changes to take place without the need for delisting. This is a long-established debate going back at least to the exchange between Jensen (1989) and Rappaport (1990) almost two decades ago. However, since the 1980s, considerable developments have taken place in corporate governance and executive remuneration, as well as in the perspectives of institutional investors and the nature of the market for corporate control. There is, therefore, a need to examine these issues in the environment of the 2000s.

PTP LBOs have also taken place in recent years in countries where they were previously absent. These developments add to the growing interest in the influence of contextual factors in finance and governance. How do the determinants of private equity deals in different countries differ from those relating to the USA?

Further examination is required relating to the attractiveness to private equity firms of secondary buy-outs. How do management in private-equity-backed secondary buy-outs differ from those in first-time buy-outs in terms of their motivations and strategies to create value?

Internationally, transactions involving family firms facing succession problems account for significant shares of buy-out markets, yet relatively little work has been focused on this aspect. Increasing recognition of agency issues in family firms (Schulze et al., 2003) draws attention to the information asymmetry problems that may occur in negotiating buy-outs on succession. What are the implications of pre-buy-out governance and ownership structure in family firms for the scope for a management buy-out in addressing succession issues? How do venture-backed and non-venture-backed buy-outs of family firms compare in terms of negotiating a deal that is satisfactory to both the family owners and the non-family owners buying out? A further issue in family firm succession concerns the changes to the interlinked systems of family, ownership and management, especially with respect to whether buy-out leads to a replacement of 'familiness' by 'professionalization' and the impact upon performance. To what extent is this the case in buy-outs of family firms or to what extent is there an emergence of a new form of family ownership in the hands of the new owner-managers?

9.1.2 Private equity organizational forms and alternatives

Limited attention has been paid to the nature and effects of the organizational form of the private equity firms involved. Private equity firms can take several organizational forms, including: independent limited partnerships established and managed by professional private equity firms or leveraged buy-out associations that act as general partners in managing the fund on behalf of the limited partners, captive funds that obtain their funding from a parent financial institution, semi-captive firms that obtain their finance partly from their parent and partly by raising closed-end funds, and public sector funds. How do different organizational forms affect private equity firms' investment behaviour, including the types of deals sought, screening of investments and the sources of deal value that are sought, the degree of their involvement in monitoring and value-adding activities, and their investment time horizon? Relatedly, to what extent are these different dimensions associated with the use of different forms of financial instruments and incentives for management?

New types of entrants to the private equity market are also emerging that, on the one hand, provide competition for traditional private equity firms, and, on the other, seek to extend the private equity model into new areas. For example, hedge funds have become attracted to making private equity investments, yet systematic research is needed to compare their role with that of traditional private equity firms. What are the impacts on deal sourcing, pricing, structuring and monitoring and on post-deal strategic changes? How are distressed private equity deals restructured depending on whether they are funded by hedge funds or traditional private equity firms?

9.1.3 The effects of financial leverage

Further research is also required that examines the relationship between financial leverage and the financial performance and stability of private equity deals. Earlier research has suggested that higher leverage is associated with greater likelihood of financial distress, for example by weaker balance sheets, but this evidence relates principally to the 1980s and early 1990s (Wright et al., 1996a; Kaplan and Stein, 1993). It is therefore important to examine whether private equity firms are now seeking more actively to realize the growth potential of leveraged buy-outs as a source of value creation than in the early days of the market.

A further aspect of leverage concerns the impact on taxation revenue. Further analysis is needed that compares the loss to taxation revenue from the leverage effect with any offsetting benefits to taxation revenue from the greater performance that successful private equity deals may generate.

9.1.4 Adding value in MBOs

Extensive media and union criticism of private equity deals has focused on their alleged use of labour shedding as a principal means of generating returns. While the systematic evidence indicates that this view is too sweeping, if not misplaced (Amess and Wright, chapter 12, this volume), further analysis is required of how private equity firms add value.

The heterogeneity of private equity deals raises important questions regarding approaches to adding value. Evidence indicates different employment and wage effects in MBOs and MBIs. To what extent are these associated with the exploitation of opportunities that could not be pursued before the transaction took place or to problems of underperformance being addressed that were present before the buy-out? In essence, this distinction highlights the entrepreneurship versus efficiency perspectives regarding private equity transactions (Wright et al., 2000b, 2001). Further systematic analysis is required to test these arguments and to identify the effects of different approaches. In what circumstances is each type of approach to adding value adopted and appropriate? To what extent is there a need for both types of approach to adding value? To what extent do cost reductions in private equity transactions constrain the ability of firms to adapt to changed market conditions?

Relatedly, private equity firms are also heterogeneous in their objectives, business models, experience and expertise. Private equity firms that are focused in a particular sector may have the expertise to create higher value. On the other hand, private equity firms may possess specialist expertise in sharpening up the strategy and control of firms that can be transferred to other sectors. Research is needed to identify the relative importance of these two aspects of private equity firm expertise. A further issue concerns the extent to which more active involvement by private equity firms leads to greater added value and where the limits of their involvement lies. The experience of private equity funds that have established themselves in the market may mean that they have learnt how to add value. Further research might compare the performance of experienced and inexperienced private equity firms and also compare the behaviour of private equity firms between their first and subsequent funds.

9.1.5 Effects on employment and HRM

Our review has provided some indications of the effects of private equity transactions on employment and HRM. Further, more fine-grained analysis is needed of the nature of employment changes following buy-out. To what extent do changes affect non-managerial employees more or less than managerial employees? To what extent do part-time jobs replace full-time jobs? There is a need for longitudinal studies that chart the development of

HRM mechanisms. Previous research has either examined the managerial or the employee or the union perspective. Future research needs to involve multiple perspectives that include management, employees, unions and investors in order to identify and attempt to reconcile potential differences.

A further issue concerns the extent and drivers of union derecognition. Evidence from the 1980s suggests that union derecognition is relatively rare following a buy-out but may be influenced by employee frustrations with the behaviour of union representatives (Wright and Coyne, 1985). Research is needed to examine these aspects in the environment of the 2000s. To what extent is derecognition driven by management or employees? What mechanisms, if any, replace the role of unions?

9.1.6 Exiting MBOs

Private equity firms have had to develop new forms of exit, such as the widespread growth in secondary buy-outs, but these raise questions concerning the returns that can be generated and the willingness of limited partners to invest in the same deal a second time through a follow-on fund. What is the role of secondary LBOs and releveraging in enhancing the longevity of private equity deals? What are the implications of secondary LBOs for returns to private equity funds and limited partners? It is also necessary to examine the effect of secondary LBOs on the motivation and involvement of the participating management of the buy-out firm.

9.2 Policy Implications

The evidence presented in this volume seeks to contribute to 'the private equity debate' by providing a balanced assessment of the effects of private equity and leveraged buy-outs for the respective stakeholders. In this section we discuss key policy issues.

There have been extensive pressures from trade unions in Germany, the UK and elsewhere, Socialist MEPs and others for tighter regulation of the private equity industry. These pressures have arisen from allegations that private equity firms strip the assets of their portfolio firms to the detriment of employees and their longer-term performance, and 'flip' them as IPOs or trade sales in short periods of time (e.g. PSE Group in European Parliament, 2007). These pressures have resulted, *inter alia*, in demands for restrictions on employment shedding following buy-out, increased transparency, and an end to the favourable tax treatment of interest on debt and on carried interest.

With regard to the issue of governance in LBOs, it is essential to combine the study of the wealth effects of going private for shareholders with the evidence on the impact of buy-outs on human resource management, wage and employment effects. In our view, it is a myth that the governance in LBOs focuses merely on shareholders' interests and that the new investors and new managers/owners neglect human resource issues and the pursuit of longer-term entrepreneurial goals. As the systematic evidence presented in this chapter shows, efficiency of the business post-MBO is often improved by saving on labour costs by cutting jobs around the time of the change in ownership. Indeed, on average MBO/I plants had lower total factor productivity before the buy-out than their non-buy-out counterparts, suggesting a degree of overmanning (Harris et al., 2005); it is perhaps not surprising that some labour shedding occurs.

The evidence shows subsequent recovery in employment, notably in MBOs. While this is not the case on average for MBIs, it needs to be recognized that MBIs are typically more likely to be firms that have been underperforming and require restructuring to restore viability; as such, pre-buy-out employment levels may not have been sustainable for the business to survive (Robbie and Wright, 1996). The majority of both MBOs and MBIs, however, display increases in employment. Indeed, the origins of buy-outs in the UK and The Netherlands at least were very much focused on saving jobs through restructuring troubled businesses (Wright and Coyne, 1985; Bruining, 1992). Where there is little alternative except closure, a private equity deal even with a reduced workforce may have its attractions. In the light of evidence from Wright et al. (1996a), actions to restructure the business on buy-out, including labour shedding, appear to reduce the likelihood that the firm will subsequently fail, with the likely even higher loss of employment. The recent private equity acquisition of Chrysler from Daimler illustrates this point (Healy et al., 2007). Similarly, in the UK, there were reported plans for significant labour shedding in the buy-outs of AA and Birds Eye before buy-out (Work Foundation, 2007). One important policy issue in such deals concerns dealing with pension fund commitments.

Relatedly, findings regarding the lower average wage levels in MBOs and MBIs relative to non-buy-outs need to be considered with care, since pre-buy-out remuneration may not have been sustainable if firms had been underperforming. However, the current debate has also raised important issues concerning the distribution of gains between private equity executives, senior executives of the investee firms and the wider body of employees of the investee firms. One approach to addressing the policy concerns regarding the distribution of the gains from private equity transactions may be to extend the use of employee stock ownership plans (ESOPs), which allow for direct participation by the wider body of employees in the upside benefits. Such schemes may not be appropriate to motivate and remunerate employees in all cases. Rather, ESOP mechanisms may be more appropriate in cases where employees have specific human capital, where there are problems in direct monitoring or where there are strong unions. These schemes have tended to be more widely used in privatization cases but may have an important role to play in firms where employees are widely distributed geographically. These mechanisms may also not motivate employees as owners where they are not accompanied by the involvement of employees in the direction of the firm (Pendleton et al., 1998). If policies are introduced to stimulate ESOPs, therefore, there is a need to be clear about their purpose.

Private equity firms using debt to fund buy-outs typically make use of tax relief benefits that are also available to other firms using debt finance. However, an area of concern is that high levels of debt in the PE system currently could pose potential dangers, although as yet there have been very few large-scale defaults. Interest rate rises could still play a big part in the LBO market's fortunes. Evidence from the peak period of buy-outs in the 1980s shows that high leverage and low firm liquidity are associated with buy-out failure (Wright et al., 1996a). It is important to distinguish income and capital gearing. While much attention has focused on capital gearing, income gearing is arguably more important since cash flow coverage of interest payments is a stronger indicator of ability to service debt. Private equity deals can sustain high capital gearing if they have high and stable interest coverage. A problem with deals completed in the late 1980s with high leverage was that insufficient attention was paid to the stability of cash flows in recessionary conditions. High levels of consumer debt especially in the USA and UK could be vulnerable to any unforeseen economic shock. A subsequent slowdown in GDP could threaten the buy-out market and make it more difficult to service large amounts of debt. There is a need for close monitoring of developments.

Our review has shown that the buy-out market has always been marked by innovation in financial instruments and funding structures. The emergence of second-lien bonds and loans, typically with fewer covenants than first-lien debt but sharing collateral with senior debt providers, introduces the possibility of longer maturities and more attractive interest rates. Such debt instruments may limit future finance options by creating conflicts of interest between first- and second-lien providers. Vertical strip financing, where finance providers invest both in equity and debt-like instruments, is one mechanism to help resolve some of these conflicts.

Potential dangers in changing the tax rate payable on private equity gains are the likely negative impacts in terms of encouraging private equity firms to shift their investments abroad, whether it drives a relatively small number of UK-domiciled executives to relocate abroad for tax purposes and whether other forms of risky investment are discouraged, with adverse implications for the benefits of start-up entrepreneurship. This debate needs to examine the net effects on total tax revenue as a result of private equity deals, also incorporating the tax implications of the treatment of interest and possible increased taxes arising from the enhanced revenue and profits generated as a result of the buy-out.

There are also concerns that the returns to private equity and buy-outs are sucking talented executives from listed corporations to private equity firms or their investee firms, to the detriment of listed corporations. This is an unduly pessimistic view of the managerial labour market as a zero-sum game. The increase in competition in the managerial labour market represented by private equity transactions suggests that listed corporations need to react to remunerate their executives in a more appropriate performance-related way. Regulation of listed corporations that focuses too much on the accountability aspect of corporate governance at the expense of the enterprise aspect, such as Sarbanes–Oxley in the USA, may also be contributing to any shift of talented executives out of listed corporations.

The evidence presented in this chapter shows that few private equity deals can be described as involving the flipping of transactions within a short period of time following the buy-out. As we have shown, secondary buy-outs are becoming increasingly popular as exit routes for private equity internationally. The growing number of large secondary buy-outs provides useful liquidity for the buy-out market at a time when alternative exit routes have become difficult. These deals may lead to the prolongation of disintermediation from public markets but may maintain the positive benefits of private equity governance and incentives as a longer-term organizational form. However, these transactions raise important and challenging unresolved issues relating to performance evaluation. In particular, if the original private equity financiers were effective, how likely is it that further performance gains can be achieved?

For the incoming investors in secondary buy-outs, an important issue is: will managers be buyers or sellers in the deal, and what will be the impact on performance? Furthermore, when management increases its equity stake, there may be a corresponding reduction in control by the private equity firm. This may result in management embarking on risky growth strategies with little monitoring. There are anecdotal examples of the effects of secondary buy-outs (Robbie and Wright, 1990) and Nikoskelainen and Wright (2007) provide initial evidence that returns to exiting through secondary buy-out are lower than for IPOs and sales to corporate buyers. An unresolved issue about secondary buy-outs concerns the possibility that limited partners will be asked by private equity firms to invest again in the same deal through a subsequent fund, and presumably at a higher price than the first time around. While exit from the first buy-out allows the realization of capital gains, limited partners may take some convincing that further significant capital gains will be forthcoming.

A further area of concern for limited partners in private equity investments concerns the extent of fund management, deal completion fees and post-deal advisory fees. Downward pressure on fund management fees may be expected if the costs of managing mega-funds are proportionately less than for smaller funds. Deal completion fees may be especially problematic if they incentivize private equity executives to complete a deal to the detriment of post-deal performance. There may be some concern that post-deal advisory fees should revert to the limited partners rather than going in full to the general partners; but assessment of this issue needs to take account of the possible trade-offs in increased value when an investee is exited. Similarly, there may be concerns over whether a fair price is being paid if sell-offs of parts of buy-outs are made to other firms within a private equity firm's portfolio. However, from a portfolio perspective the effect may be at worst neutral if it adds at least an equivalent value to the purchasing firm in the portfolio.

Finally, it needs to be borne in mind that a major problem in implementing regulatory changes aimed at the private equity market is that some of the alleged benefits they receive are not exclusive to private equity firms. Designing policy to focus specifically on private equity firms may thus be problematic. A further issue is that much of the criticism of private equity firms has ignored their positive benefits. The potential danger is that in seeking to restrict alleged abuses, the benefits of rethinking the strategy and effectiveness of the buy-out firm's operations by using ownership change may be lost.

When new organizational forms such as private equity backed buy-outs emerge, it is difficult for the outsider to form a well-balanced judgement regarding the net effects of these forms. There is, therefore, a need for a cost–benefit assessment of private equity and buy-outs. The systematic evidence that we present in this volume and the wider literature that we have reviewed in this chapter indicate that private equity and buy-outs bring particularly important economic and social benefits.

10. OVERVIEW OF THE BOOK

10.1 Theoretical Perspectives (Part II)

The book begins with an outline of the theoretical perspectives that explain how buy-outs emerged in the business economy. Agency theory, with an emphasis on managerial incentives to improve firm efficiency, is combined with an entrepreneurial cognition perspective that stimulates catching up and exploiting innovation. These theoretical perspectives help the reader to make vital judgements in a given industry regarding the future development of the buy-out and the appropriate role of management and private equity. The two interrelated theories offer a typology that covers the wide variety of organizational forms that buy-outs take. It classifies buy-out performance research, making visible which buy-out attributes and strategic decision-making modes fit with individual cognition and managerial incentives. In this way the typology offers a plan to create arrangements, combining ownership with entrepreneurial and/or managerial orientation, and professional management that fit with the financing and governance structures of buy-outs.

Entrepreneurial growth through privatization: the upside of management buyouts (Chapter 2)

The typology presented in Chapter 2 incorporates different buy-out rationales of cost reduction and strategic orientation in mature sectors to creating value in technology sectors through product development and innovation. Wright, Hoskisson, Busenitz and Dial illustrate the resulting buy-out types with examples from buy-out privatization, and place them in a matrix of buy-out attributes that extends agency theory and widens the conceptual basis to include the entrepreneurial cognition view. The efficiency-oriented buy-out combines ownership and management to align incentives with productivity gains to stimulate efficiency, and leaves the management with limited discretion. The revitalization buy-out shows a combination of efficiency buy-out complemented by process and imitation innovations, providing the management with some discretion to pursue revitalization. The entrepreneurial buy-out represents a form where the entrepreneurial cognition of managers and the incentives to foster strategic innovation may establish a basis for competitive advantage, thus expanding managerial discretion. The failure buy-out is a mismatch between managers with an entrepreneurial cognition having innovative skills and financial incentives rewarding efficiency gains. These forms make us conscious that judgements of management and private equity investors about the future of the firm in a given industry are crucial.

10.2 Sources of Buy-out (Part III)

Buy-outs represent a heterogeneous collection of firms that emerge from various sources: MBO, MBI, IBO, going private and family firms. Therefore it is necessary to develop a heterogeneity view on these kinds of firms that undergo a change of ownership. In an MBO the incumbent management seeks support of the private equity firm to purchase a major stake in the firm and to fund the transaction in taking the firm private; IBOs are deals that consist solely of institutional investors and private equity firms, if managers stay they receive a modest share or an equity ratchet; and in an MBI a team of outside managers or entrepreneurs purchases most of the equity. If the buy-out leads to a delisting, then the transaction is named a 'going private' and if the transaction takes place in a privately held family firm then it is labelled as a family buy-out.

The chapters in this part cover a wide range of buy-out sources and how these buy-outs come into being. However, they take a shared point of analysis: the negotiation processes to transfer ownership. First we present research on the expected gains of going private that tests if wealth is created for shareholders according to the motives that govern the negotiation process. Then we examine at the start of the negotiation process what role irrevocable commitments of the vendor can play in preventing failure in the bidding process. The last chapter enquires how information asymmetry behaviour can be dealt with in negotiations designed for management buy-outs of family-owned firms.

Why do public firms go private in the UK? The impact of private equity investors, incentive realignment and undervaluation (Chapter 3)

Chapter 3 is one of the first finance articles on the anticipated value effects of delisting by means of a buy-out in the UK. In a sample of 177 PTP transactions from 1997 to 2003 in the UK we make acquaintance with important sources of buy-outs that can take a firm private: management buy-outs (MBOs), management buy-ins (MBIs) and institutional buy-outs (IBOs).

The shareholders of the firm that is taken private are usually earning a premium that amounts to 40 per cent or a cumulative abnormal return of 30 per cent. These premiums are even higher for firms with lower levels of managerial ownership. The chapter examines the empirical basis for the expected shareholder wealth gains from PTPs by analysing premiums and events. Renneboog, Simons and Wright find that higher premiums are paid for firms with low leverage, providing some support for the tax benefits after the PPT transaction resulting from an additional tax shield. However, the gain in shareholder wealth is more strongly determined by undervaluation of the target firm for which the new shareholders are willing to pay a premium. They see potential additional value to be generated once the firm reaches its private position, thereby realizing increased incentive realignment with the new managers/owners in the private firm. Lower premiums and cumulative abnormal returns are paid for firms with strong outside blockholders such as, for example, corporations as shareholders. In those cases there is less scope of improvements in the post-PTP period. The study did not find evidence that PTPs are arranged to reduce high free cash flows.

Irrevocable commitments, going private and private equity (Chapter 4)

The market for corporate control shows increased interest in PTPs. As of the early 2000s, these transactions represent 30 per cent of all acquisitions in the UK, with only 4 per cent during the early 1990s. Irrevocable commitments are undertakings given by existing shareholders to agree to sell their shares to the bidder before the bid is announced. According to Wright, Weir and Burrows, they play a central role in the sale process of PTPs that is characterized by a very low level of public bidding. A bid failure may mean that the bidder is left as a minority holder, facing the difficulties of unloading shares to repay debt in what may be an illiquid market. Private equity firms play an important role in negotiating and financing PTPs. The costs of undertaking a PTP that fails to complete can amount to 10 per cent of the transaction value. Irrevocable commitment may be regarded as a means of avoiding these costs. Therefore it is relevant to analyse the involvement in gaining irrevocable commitments. In the UK corporate law and takeover codes these commitments are explicitly recognized and can alleviate some of the uncertainties associated with the bid process. The level of these commitments is studied in the UK during the period 1998–2003 in 155 PTP transactions. The chapter identifies four factors that affect the extent of irrevocable commitments negotiated by potential buyers before the public announcement of the bid, e.g. the value of the bid, the premium offered to other shareholders, the extent of takeover speculation and the reputation of the private equity provider and board ownership. The results seem to suggest that irrevocable commitments are also used to prevent alternative bidders from entering the bidding process.

Information sharing, price negotiation and management buy-outs of private family-owned firms (Chapter 5)

Perspectives relating to agency theory, information asymmetries and game theory are utilized to explore two outcomes associated with the management buy-out (MBO) or management buy-in (MBI) of former private firms: whether information is shared equally between vendors (i.e. family firm owners) and purchasers (i.e. MBO/I management teams) and whether a price is mutually agreed. Scholes, Wright, Westhead, Burrows and Bruining present survey evidence with regard to ownership, governance structure and company objectives gathered from the managers of 114 former private family firms located across Europe that recently reported an MBO/I. Multiple logistic regression analysis shows that respondents in founded (first-generation) family firms and those reporting a strong focus on the strategic importance of the market value increment are more likely to report that 'information is shared equally between vendors and purchasers'. Respondents backed by venture capitalists involved in succession planning that have not identified a suitable successor, but with a strong focus on the strategic importance of the market value increment, are more likely to report that 'a mutually agreed sale price has been negotiated'.

The findings suggest that incumbent managers should make themselves more aware whether the family owners are seeking continued involvement in the business after the transaction or are looking for maximum value from the sale. The founder may seek, as a potential vendor, to develop cooperative relationships with management well in advance of the ownership transfer event. For a mutual beneficial price solution, both the vendor and the purchaser need to consider a venture capitalist firm that can develop adviser or intermediary relationships with more family firm owners that face succession issues.

10.3 Entrepreneurship and Value Creation (Part IV)

Simplifying strategies (heuristics) to make strategic decisions allow one to make inferences and set a future course of action based on experience and a deep understanding of the market that has yet to be systematically spelled out. Entrepreneurs use a heuristic-based approach to decision-making more extensively, which enables them more quickly to make sense of uncertain and complex situations, with limited information, allowing them more readily to navigate through a wide array of problems and irregularities inherent in the development of new opportunities. To pursue comprehensive and quantifiable information before making strategic decisions, as people do with a managerial mindset, will typically mean that a decision will never get made or the window of opportunity will pass before full information is obtained. This perspective can be used to understand different types of buy-out, particularly where innovation is involved, and provides a complementary approach to the traditional agency theory lens.

All the chapters in this part examine buy-out firms that revitalize with catching-up innovations in addition to improving efficiency and buy-outs that undertake innovative projects leading sooner or later to an IPO. The case studies from the first chapter illustrate that top management implementing changes in strategy after an MBO needs newer control systems that stimulate opportunity-seeking and learning that were previously lacking. The second chapter shows us firms that act more entrepreneurially after the MBO and highlights the role of the venture capitalist in enhancing the entrepreneurial orientation of the firm in order to achieve upside potential. Finally, the last chapter focuses on restructuring and buy-outs in Japan. It examines the effectiveness of buy-outs as a tool for reorganizing corporations in Japan. Three main buy-out types are discussed from

Japanese parent groups: efficiency buy-outs, revitalization buy-outs and entrepreneurial buy-outs.

Management control systems and strategy change in buy-outs (Chapter 6)
A significant share of MBOs divested from parent companies face changes to a more growth-oriented strategy and the process of strategy formulation. This chapter analyses why and how management control systems are used in buy-outs to implement strategy change.

Evidence from two cases provides an explanation of how the MBO fits into a classification of levers of control, and why and how certain buy-out characteristics will affect strategy and control. Bruining, Bonnet and Wright develop four arguments as to why the management approaches pre- and post-MBO fundamentally differ, to explore management control in these newer forms of MBO. The first is the renewed strategic orientation post-MBO enabling participants throughout the firm to respond to perceived opportunities and threats, thus allowing *interactive* control systems that stimulate search and learning, and allow new strategies to emerge. The second characteristic is the higher level of commitment to the implementation of a growth strategy, stimulating *beliefs* as a tool for the buy-out management to provide inspiration and organizational direction for purposive entrepreneurial activity by its employees. As a third characteristic they propose that buy-out managers experience more autonomy and flexible decision-making, which will require of them to formulate and communicate specific *boundaries* for employees post-MBO, for example return on investment, selection of product markets and business conduct rules.

The fourth characteristic is the discipline to allocate resources to operations with the strongest cash flow and eliminate unprofitable operations, triggered by the debt and fixed dividend commitments. *Diagnostic* controls will therefore play an important role after the buy-out to achieve the financial targets agreed upon between management and investors.

In buy-outs that need at least some innovation, opportunity search is stimulated by the lever of belief, and learning is fostered by the interactive control lever and plays an important role in controlling the incremental changes in strategy. The levers of control found post-MBO offer an additional explanation for performance improvement following buy-out that goes beyond agency cost arguments involving efficiency improvements to protect the firm against downside risks.

Entrepreneurial orientation in management buy-outs and the contribution of venture capital (Chapter 7)
Bruining and Wright show that MBOs backed by venture capital can lead to significant changes in a firm's ownership composition, and can affect its

subsequent rate of growth, size, strategy, organizational structure and last but not least its entrepreneurial practices. In contrast to studies that highlight the role of the venture capitalist (VC) in start-up firms, research into how the role of the VC fits into this newer growth orientation in management buy-outs is lacking. Traditional LBO associations have been joining forces with VCs for this reason. Many VCs label themselves today as long-term committed and active shareholders that have a 'buy-and-build' strategy.

This chapter analyses the entrepreneur–venture capitalist relationship in two mature buy-out firms in order to obtain insights into where and how the VC's commitment contributes to the entrepreneurial practices in the MBO firm. It focuses on the development of entrepreneurial orientation (EO) after a management buy-out and on the role played by venture capital firms in enhancing EO. The authors present the results of two case studies of divisional buy-outs with regard to their EO and the areas where the VC has been of greatest help. They discuss their contribution to proactiveness, innovativeness, risk-taking, marketing aggressiveness and autonomy elements of the EO of the buy-out firm in contrast to the situation before the MBO. Pre-MBO the firms face investment restrictions, because the firms are peripheral to the product line of the parent company. This diminishes the possibilities of responding entrepreneurially to market development. After the MBO this situation is reversed. Instead of obeying orders from headquarters that block innovation and investment in order to optimize goals, the buy-out managers have discretionary power to decide what is best for the business and how the business plan can be carried out most profitably for them as a firm.

Management buyouts and restructuring Japanese corporations (Chapter 8)

The inability of complex organizational structures of keiretsu groups to adapt swiftly to changes in the marketplace became evident largely when the Japanese economy experienced a long period of economic downturn in the 1980s and 1990s. Following corporations in the USA and Europe, keiretsu-affiliated companies and other Japanese corporations are actively involved in implementing strategies to refocus on their core business by divesting unprofitable and non-core business. Wright, Kitamura and Hoskisson explain that this has led to rationales for divestment by buy-outs and the need to facilitate and support them by institutional changes, e.g. promoting entrepreneurship among managers, governmental support scheme and the presence of private equity. This chapter presents the first examination of management and leveraged buy-outs as a tool for restructuring Japanese corporations. Using archival research, a survey of private equity firms and management buy-outs, and case study evidence, it examines the issues concerning the pressures for change. It studies what factors are facilitating the use of buy-outs in the Japanese economy and how buy-outs might contribute to the restructuring process. It argues that pressures in Japan are more likely to give rise to revitalizing buy-outs than buy-outs focusing solely on efficiency improvements.

10.4 Impact of Buy-outs (Part V)

Most recently, there has been much discussion of the investor's role and the strategic view of private equity companies. Some consider that they aim at short-term profits and thus neglect the long-term goals of the companies they buy. Others consider them as useful guardians of company strategies, because it may be that a company is underperforming but that the management is not aware of the other possibilities there may be, or is not willing to change its direction into a more successful one that a private equity firm forecasts. Nevertheless, there is a growing need for information that reviews and synthesizes studies of the effects of buy-outs backed by private equity.

Empirical evidence in this part of the book is presented in terms of the impact on economic efficiency, employment, employee relations and wages, thus not only on financial parameters that measure the success of investment in buy-outs but also on social parameters that capture their contribution to human resource practices post-MBO.

Instead of focusing exclusively on the effect of MBOs on financial stakeholders, the first chapter examines the impact of buy-outs on economic efficiency at the plant level in more detail by using large data samples from US and UK buy-outs. The second chapter introduces a source of buy-outs we have not yet mentioned, namely the management and employee buy-out (MEBO) that is generally used in privatizations of state-owned companies. Empirical studies from *developed* and *transition* economies are used to compare the effect of these buy-outs for this literature review. The third chapter sheds light on the development of human resource policies and employee relations post-MBO, and compares two different institutional contexts, the UK and the Netherlands. The last chapter in Part V takes a closer look at the impact of management buy-outs and management buy-ins on wage and employment effects of leveraged buy-outs in the UK.

Assessing the impact of management buyouts on economic efficiency: plant-level evidence from the United Kingdom (Chapter 9)

In this chapter by Harris, Siegel and Wright, the total factor productivity for 35 752 manufacturing plants across the industries during 1994–98 is compared before and after the MBO. The chapter shows that MBO plants appear to be less productive than comparable plants before the buy-out. After the MBO these firms show a strong increase in efficiency, substantially more than comparable plants, indicating that new ownership shift resources to more efficient use by strongly downsizing their workforce. Post-MBO productivity increases substantially and, given a reduction of the capital/labour ratio, this could be caused by the measures undertaken by the new owners to reduce labour intensity of production through outsourcing of intermediate goods and materials.

Post-privatization effects of management and employee buy-outs (Chapter 10)

After explaining the governance shortcomings of the state as an enterprise as the basis for privatization, Wright, Buck and Filatotchev discuss the pros and cons of several privatization methods. It reviews evidence of MEBOs for developed and transition economies regarding the impact of privatization buy-outs on human resources management, productivity, restructuring and employment changes. In most privatization MEBOs where top management dominates as shareholder, employees have little participation in decision-making. High levels of employee ownership in privatization MEBOs are more compassionate, with a greater degree of employee-oriented HRM strategies, including bonus systems. Institutional arrangements are discussed to facilitate this involvement. Post-privatization MEBO employment is reduced, with subsequent recovery in developed countries in contrast to the transition economies. Restructuring may be greater where insiders have purchased the shares rather than having acquired them for free by vouchers. Special attention is paid to the longevity of privatization buy-outs, which in the Western economies is more dependent on industrial dynamics. In transition economies the privatization buy-out has facilitated the separation of the state from the industry, thereby enabling quick reforms.

The impact of business ownership change on employee relations: buy-outs in the UK and the Netherlands (Chapter 11)

Little is known about the impact of buy-outs on employee relations. This chapter aims to address this gap. The authors, Bruining, Boselie, Wright and Bacon, focus on two main questions. First, what are the effects of a buy-out on employee relations in an organization? Second, does the national institutional context affect the impact of buy-outs on employee relations? The chapter reports employee relations' changes in buy-outs in the contrasting institutional environments of the UK and the Netherlands. The chapter links theoretical insights from the fields of finance, corporate governance, strategy and HRM to study the effect of ownership change on HRM policies and practices within buy-out companies. Overall, the authors find that buy-outs positively affect HR practices, with increases in training, employee involvement, the number of employees and pay. The positive effects appear to be significantly stronger in a less institutionalized environment such as the UK than the more institutionalized environment of the Netherlands.

The wage and employment effects of leveraged buyouts in the UK (Chapter 12)

This study by Amess and Wright determines and quantifies the effects of leveraged buy-outs (LBOs) from the period 1999–2004 on wages and employment in 1350 LBOs and finds that all LBOs taken together have an insignificant effect on employment growth but have significantly lower wage growth than non-LBOs. Both MBOs and MBIs are found to have a negative impact on wage growth. With regard to employment, MBOs have higher employment growth and MBIs have lower employment growth than cohorts in the same industry. The results indicate that MBOs and MBIs have a differing impact on firms' wage and employment behaviour, and should not be treated as homogeneous. The results are consistent with: (1) MBOs exploiting growth opportunities that lead to greater employment growth; and (2) MBIs not creating new employment opportunities.

10.5 Investment Realization: Success and Failure (Part VI)

As buy-out markets have developed in Europe and the USA, key attention has focused on the longevity of such structures and the means and timing of harvesting private equity investment. Buy-outs involve a fusion of different objectives of managers, financiers and the companies themselves. A major aspect concerns the long-term plans of managers and financiers for the company, and how both parties can realize their investment in a manner that is optimum for each of them, which in turn may have implications for the optimum life cycle of the company itself. Although these issues may well have been addressed at the time of the buy-out, significant actual and potential conflicts of interest may remain and be increased by financial and acquisition market conditions that are considerably different from those foreseen at the time of the buy-out. These different conditions affect the ability of the parties concerned to harvest the investment at the time and by the means initially envisaged. Therefore, it is important to look at the empirical facts of investment realization.

The chapters in Part VI examine how new shareholders have realized the capital gain from their investment through an initial public offering (IPO) or a so-called 'going public'. They pay attention to the relative influence of governance mechanisms such as the manager's share in the equity and the firm's debt coverage ratio on the firm's exit value increase, and to the credit recovery of lenders in case buy-outs become financially distressed.

The impact of corporate governance mechanisms on value increase in leveraged buyouts (Chapter 13)

In this chapter, Nikoskelainen and Wright present evidence on internal rates of return of enterprise value and of invested equity from different sources of exit: 52 IPOs, 92 trade sales, 57 secondary buy-outs and 121 receiverships. The investor returns are calculated as the value increase between the time of the LBO transaction and the time of exit, and are linked with buy-out governance structure that affects the value increment. As governance factors are taken measures of the management's share of equity and the debt coverage ratio. The actions of the buy-out companies are controlled for with acquisitions and divestments, in order to be sure whether a change in operating performance is caused by external or organic growth, or by measures to streamline the buy-out firm. Effects relating to the governance structure of buy-outs are isolated from effects of market movement by adjusting the exit time value for index movement during the holding period. The authors find that the governance mechanisms in LBOs are not the main drivers of value increase: the returns are driven by size of the buy-out company and acquisitions during the holding time. This provides support for the importance of incentives for entrepreneurial management to realize growth opportunities rather than focus on downsizing, and contrasts strongly with the buy-in returns that are driven by streamlining the target company operations.

Performance of private to public MBOs: the role of venture capital (Chapter 14)

Jelic, Saadouni and Wright study the financial performance and venture capital involvement in 167 MBOs exiting through IPOs on the London Stock Exchange during 1964–97. The sample represents about 65 per cent of all buy-outs that exited through IPO during that period and use as a benchmark non-VC-backed MBOs. The results show for both groups significant positive initial premiums. An interesting result of the comparison is the relative lack of long-term underperformance of VC-backed MBOs, which is in contrast to the findings of other UK IPO studies. Venture-backed MBOs tend to be larger and exit earlier than their non-venture-backed counterparts. On average the time to exit for VC-backed MBOs is 45 months, whereas it is 57 months for the non-VC-backed MBOs. They are also more underpriced than MBOs without venture capital backing. Last but not least, no evidence was found that VC-backed MBOs show better market-adjusted returns for the longer term than their non-VC-backed counterparts; however, MBOs backed by more prestigious VCs perform better than MBOs backed by less prestigious VCs.

Secured creditor recovery rates from management buy-outs in distress (Chapter 15)

Buy-outs can go bankrupt due to trading problems, too high financial leverage or managerial shortcomings, but if the going-concern value of the firm is still high, the secured creditors can recover part of their money. Of this, in general least preferred exit route, Citron, Wright, Ball and Rippington document results of a study into the determinants of the amount of repayment to secured creditor in case of buy-outs in financial distress. The chapter identifies three main determinants of repayment: the characteristic causes of the MBO failure; the nature of the MBO monitoring process; and the effectiveness of the receivership process. The findings show some evidence of an increase in recovery rate if the buy-out failure is caused by managerial factors. The rate decreases the larger the size of the buy-out, and if the audit report identifies going concern uncertainties. The number of secured creditors has no adverse effects. The percentage of secured credit recovered goes up when the distressed buy-out is sold as a going concern.

NOTES

1. This chapter has benefited from the contributions of Mike Wright, Hans Bruining, Kevin Amess, Rod Ball, Andrew Burrows, Douglas Cumming, Miguel Meuleman, Louise Scholes and Donald Siegel. An earlier version of part of this chapter was commissioned by the OECD.
2. For example, in the years 1985–89, when the UK market was immature, the top ten buy-outs were funded by, on average, ten equity providers, 11 debt providers and two mezzanine providers. However, in the ten largest buy-outs over the period 2001–2005, there were, on average, three equity providers, four debt providers and one mezzanine provider.
3. The legality index is a weighted average of legal index variables relating to civil versus common law, efficiency of the judicial system, rule of law, corruption, risk of expropriation, risk of contract repudiation, and shareholder rights (La Porta et al., 1998). The higher index in the USA than in the UK is principally attributable to the higher scoring of the USA in terms of the rule of law as identified in the International Country Risk Guide. Note that there is some debate about the appropriateness of these measures in the VC sector (Armour and Cumming, 2006; Wright et al., 2005).
4. This probably also reflects the dominance of 3i in the 1980s, which at that time placed less emphasis on exiting its straight ordinary shares.

REFERENCES

Amess, K. (2002), 'Management buy-outs and firm-level productivity: evidence from a panel of UK manufacturing firms', *Scottish Journal of Political Economy*, **49**, 304–17.

Amess, K. (2003), 'The effects of management buy-outs and on firm-level technical efficiency: evidence from a panel of U.K. machinery and equipment manufacturers', *Journal of Industrial Economics*, **51**, 35–44.
Amess, K. and Wright, M. (2007), 'The wage and employment effects of leveraged buyouts in the U.K.', *International Journal of the Economics of Business*, **14** (2), 179–95.
Amess, K., Brown, S. and Thompson, S. (2007), 'Management buyouts, supervision and employee discretion', *Scottish Journal of Political Economy*, **54** (4), 447–74.
Andrade, G. and Kaplan, S. (1998), 'How costly is financial (not economic distress)? Evidence from Highly Leveraged Transactions that became distressed', *Journal of Finance*, **53**, 1443–94.
Arena, M. and Ferris, S. (2007), 'When managers bypass shareholder approval of board appointments: evidence from the private security market', *Journal of Corporate Finance*, **13** (4), 485–510.
Armour, J. and Cumming, D. (2006), 'The legislative road to replicating Silicon Valley', *Oxford Economic Papers*, **58**, 596–635.
Asquith, P. and Wizman, T. (1990), 'Event risk, covenants, and bondholder returns in leveraged buyouts', *Journal of Financial Economics*, **27**, 195–213.
Betker, B. (1997), 'The administrative costs of debt restructurings: some recent evidence', *Financial Management*, **26** (4), 56–68.
Bruining, H. (1992), 'Performance improvement post-management buy-out', unpublished dissertation, Erasmus University Rotterdam, Haveka.
Bruining, H. and Wright, M. (2002), 'Entrepreneurial orientation in management buyouts and the contribution of venture capital', *Venture Capital: An International Journal of Entrepreneurial Finance*, **4**, 147–68.
Bruining, H., Bonnet, M. and Wright, M. (2004), 'Management control systems and strategy change in buy-outs', *Management Accounting Research*, **15**, 155–77.
Bruining, H., Boselie, P., Wright, M. and Bacon, N. (2005), 'The impact of business ownership change on employee relations: buyouts in the U.K. and the Netherlands', *International Journal of Human Resource Management*, **16**, 345–65.
Bruton, G.D., Keels, J.K. and Scifres, E.L. (2002), 'Corporate restructuring: an agency perspective on the complete buyout cycle', *Journal of Business Research*, **55** (9), 709–24.
Buyouts (2006), Thomson Financial Publication, issue 24, 4 December.
Chen, A.H. and Kensinger, J.W. (1988), 'Puttable stock: a new innovation in equity financing', *Financial Management*, **17** (1), 27–37.
Chou, D.W., Gombola, M. and Liu, F.Y. (2006), 'Earnings management and stock performance of reverse leveraged buyouts', *Journal of Financial and Quantitative Analysis*, **41**, 407–28.
Citron, D., Robbie, K. and Wright, M. (1997), 'Loan covenants and relationship banking in MBOs', *Accounting and Business Research*, **27**, 277–96.
Citron, D., Wright, M., Rippington, F. and Ball, R. (2003), 'Secured creditor recovery rates from management buy-outs in distress', *European Financial Management*, **9**, 141–62.
Citron, D., Wright, M., Rippington, F. and Ball, R. (2006), 'Bankruptcy costs, leverage & multiple secured creditors: the case of MBOs', paper presented at Multinational Finance Conference, Edinburgh, 26 June.
CMBOR (2005), 'Trends in UK buyouts', *Management Buyouts: Quarterly Review*, Nottingham: CMBOR, Spring, 1–14.

CMBOR (2006), *European Management Buy-Out Review*, Nottingham: CMBOR, Jan.–Dec.
CMBOR/EVCA (2001), *Survey of the Economic and Social Impact of Management Buy-outs and Buy-ins in Europe*, EVCA publication.
CMBOR/EVCA (2002), *Survey of the Economic and Social Impact of Venture Capital in Europe*, EVCA publication.
Cook, D.O., Easterwood, J. and Martin, J.D. (1992), 'Bond holder wealth effects of management buyouts', *Financial Management*, **21**, 102–13.
Cotter, J.F. and Peck, S.W. (2001), 'The structure of debt and active equity investors: the case of the buy-out specialist', *Journal of Financial Economics*, **59**, 101–47.
Cumming, D. (2006), 'The determinants of venture capital portfolio size: empirical evidence', *Journal of Business*, **79**, 1083–26.
Cumming, D. and Walz, U. (2004), 'Private equity returns and disclosure around the world', mimeo, available at SSRN: http://ssrn.com/abstract=514105.
Cumming, D., Siegel, D.S. and Wright, M. (2007), 'Private equity, leveraged buy-outs and governance', *Journal of Corporate Finance*, **13** (4), 439–60.
DeAngelo, H., DeAngelo, L., and Rice, J.L. (1984), 'Going private: the effects of a change in corporate ownership structure', *Midland Corporate Finance Journal*, **2**, 35–43.
DeAngelo, L. (1986), 'Accounting numbers as market valuation substitutes: a study of management buyouts of public stockholders', *Accounting Review*, **61**, 400–20.
Denis, D.J. (1994), 'Investment opportunities and the market reaction to equity offerings', *The Journal of Financial and Quantitative Analysis*, **29** (2), 159–77.
Denis, D.J. and Denis, K. (1993), 'Managerial discretion, organizational structure and corporate performance: a study of leveraged recapitalizations', *Journal of Accounting and Economics*, **16**, 209–36.
Desbrières, P. and Schatt, A. (2002), 'The impacts of LBOs on the performance of acquired firms: the French case', *Journal of Business Finance and Accounting*, **29**, 695–729.
Devereux, M.P., Mokkas, S., Pennock, J. and Wharrad, P. (2006), 'Interest deductability for UK corporation tax', Oxford University Centre for Business Taxation, Working Paper.
Easterwood, J.C., Singer, R., Seth, A. and Lang, D. (1994), 'Controlling the conflict of interest in management buyouts', *Review of Economics and Statistics*, **76**, 512–22.
EVCA (2006), *EVCA Yearbook 2006*, Zaventem: European Venture Capital Association.
EVCA (2007), *EVCA Yearbook 2007*, Zaventem: European Venture Capital Association.
Evans, J., Poa, M. and Rath, S. (2005), 'The financial and governance characteristics of Australian companies going private', *International Journal of Business Studies*, **13**, 1–24.
Financial Services Authority (2006), 'Private equity: a discussion of risk and regulatory engagement', Discussion Paper DP06/6. London: Financial Services Authority.
Franks, J.R. and Sussman, O. (2005), 'Financial distress and bank restructuring of small-to-medium size UK companies', *Review of Finance*, **9**, 65–96.
Gilson, S.C. (2000), 'Analysts and information gaps: lessons from the UAL buy-out', *Financial Analysts Journal*, **56**, 82–110.

Gompers, P.A. (1996), 'Grandstanding in the venture capital industry', *Journal of Financial Economics*, **42** (1), 133–56.

Gompers, P.A. and Lerner, J. (1999), *The Venture Capital Cycle*, Cambridge: MIT Press.

Gottschalg, O. and Wright, M. (2008), 'Understanding the buyers' role in private equity returns: the influence of skills, strategy and experience', CMBOR Occasional Paper, University of Nottingham.

Groh, A. and Gottschalg, O. (2006), 'The risk-adjusted performance of US buyouts', Working Paper. HEC: Paris.

Halpern, P., Kieschnick, R. and Rotenberg, W. (1999), 'On the heterogeneity of leveraged going private transactions', *Review of Financial Studies*, **12**, 281–309.

Harris, R., Siegel, D.S. and Wright, M. (2005), 'Assessing the impact of management buyouts on economic efficiency: plant-level evidence from the United Kingdom', *The Review of Economics and Statistics*, **87**, 148–53.

Healy, J., Carty, S., Woodyard, C. and Krantz, M. (2007), 'Unprecedented auto deal: Daimler essentially pays to part ways with Chrysler', *USA Today Money*, 15 May, 1B–2B.

Hite, G. and Vetsuypens, M. (1989), 'Management buyouts of divisions and shareholder wealth', *Journal of Finance*, **44**, 953–70.

Holthausen, D. and Larcker, D. (1996), 'The financial performance of reverse leverage buyouts', *Journal of Financial Economics*, **42**, 293–332.

Howorth, C., Westhead, P. and Wright, M. (2004), 'Buyouts, informational asymmetry and the family–management dyad', *Journal of Business Venturing*, **19**, 509–34.

Jelic, R., Saadouni, B. and Wright, M. (2005), 'Performance of private to public MBOs: the role of venture capital', *Journal of Business Finance and Accounting*, **32**, 643–82.

Jensen, M.C. (1989), 'Eclipse of the public corporation', *Harvard Business Review*, Sept.–Oct., 61–74.

Jensen, M.C. (1993), 'The modern industrial revolution: exit and the failure of internal control systems', *Journal of Finance*, **48**, 831–80.

Kanniainen, V. and Keuschnigg, C. (2003), 'The optimal portfolio of start-up firms in venture capital finance', *Journal of Corporate Finance*, **9**, 521–34.

Kanniainen, V. and Keuschnigg, C. (2004), 'Start-up investment with scarce venture capital support', *Journal of Banking and Finance*, **28**, 1935–59.

Kaplan, S. (1989a), 'The effects of management buy-outs on operating performance and value', *Journal of Financial Economics*, **24**, 217–54.

Kaplan, S. (1989b), 'Management buyouts: evidence on taxes as a source of value', *Journal of Finance*, **3**, 611–32.

Kaplan, S. (1991), 'The staying power of leveraged buyouts', *Journal of Financial Economics*, **29**, 287–313.

Kaplan, S.N. and Schoar, A. (2005), 'Private equity returns: persistence and capital flows', *Journal of Finance*, **60**, 1791–823.

Kaplan, S.N. and Stein, J.C. (1993), 'The evolution of buyout pricing in the 1980s', *Quarterly Journal of Economics*, **108**, 313–57.

Keasey, K., Thompson, S. and Wright, M. (1997), *Corporate Governance: Economic and Financial Issues*, New York: Oxford University Press.

Kester, W.C. and Luehrman, T.A. (1995), 'Rehabilitating the leveraged buyout: a look at Clayton, Dubilier and Rice', *Harvard Business Review*, **73**, 119–30.

Kieschnick, R. (1998), 'Free cash flow and stockholder gains in going private transactions revisited', *Journal of Business Finance and Accounting*, **25** (1–2), 187–202.

La Porta, R., López de Silanes, F., Shleifer, A. and Vishny, R. (1998), 'Law and finance', *Journal of Political Economy*, **106**, 1113–55.
Lee, S. (1992), 'Management buyout proposals and inside information', *Journal of Finance*, **47**, 1061–80.
Lehn, K. and Poulsen, A. (1989), 'Free cash flow and stockholder gains in going private transactions', *Journal of Finance*, **44**, 771–88.
Lichtenberg, F.R. and Siegel, D.S. (1990), 'The effect of leveraged buy-outs on productivity and related aspects of firm behavior', *Journal of Financial Economics*, **27**, 165–94.
Long, W.F. and Ravenscraft, D.J. (1993), 'LBOs, debt and R&D intensity', *Strategic Management Journal*, **14**, 119–35
Marais, L., Schipper, K. and Smith, A. (1989), 'Wealth effects of going private on senior securities', *Journal of Financial Economics*, **23**, 155–91.
Markides, C.C. (1992), 'Consequences of corporate refocusing: ex ante evidence', *Academy of Management*, Journal **35** (2), 398–412.
Meuleman, M. and Wright, M. (2007), 'Industry concentration, syndication networks and competition in the UK private equity market', CMBOR Occasional Paper.
Muscarella, C.J. and Vetsuypens, M.R. (1990), 'Efficiency and organisational structure: a study of reverse LBOs', *The Journal of Finance*, **13** (5), 1389–413.
Nikoskelainen, E. and Wright, M. (2007), 'The impact of corporate governance mechanisms on value increase in leveraged buyouts', *Journal of Corporate Finance*, **13** (4), 629–46.
Opler, T. (1992), 'The performance of leveraged buyout firms: evidence from 1986–1989', *Financial Management*, **21**, 27–34.
Opler, T. and Titman, S. (1993), 'The determination of leveraged buyout activity: free cash flow vs. financial distress costs', *The Journal of Finance*, **48** (5), 1985–99.
Pendleton, A., Wilson, N. and Wright, M. (1998), 'Employees attitudes in buy-outs of privatised bus companies', *British Journal of Industrial Relations*, March, 99–124.
Perry, S.E. and Williams, T. (1994), 'Earnings management preceding management buyout offers', *Journal of Accounting and Economics*, **18**, 152–79.
Phan, P.H. and Hill, C.W.L. (1995), 'Organizational restructuring and economic performance in leveraged buyouts: an ex post study', *Academy of Management Journal*, **38** (3), 704–39
PSE Group in European Parliament (2007), 'Hedge funds and private equity: a critical analysis', Report of the PSE Group in European Parliament.
Rappaport, A. (1990), 'The staying power of the public corporation', *Harvard Business Review*, **68**, 96–104.
Renneboog, L.D.R., Simons, T. and Wright, M. (2007), 'Why do public firms go private in the UK?', *Journal of Corporate Finance*, **13** (4), 591–628.
Robbie, K. and Wright, M. (1990), 'The case of Maccess', in S. Taylor and S. Turley (eds), *Cases in Financial Reporting*, Oxford: Philip Allan.
Robbie, K., Wright, M. and Thompson, S. (1992), 'Management buy-ins in the UK', *Omega*, **20**, 445–56.
Robbie, K. and Wright, M. (1996), *Management Buy-ins: Entrepreneurship, active investors and corporate restructuring*, Manchester: Manchester University Press.
Robbie, K., Wright, M. and Albrighton, M. (1999), 'High-tech management buyouts', *Venture Capital: An International Journal of Entrepreneurial Finance*, **1**, 219–40.

Schipper, K. and Smith, A. (1988), 'Corporate income tax of management buyouts', mimeo, University of Chicago.
Schmidt, D. (2006), 'Private equity versus stocks: do the alternative asset's risk and return characteristics add value to the portfolio?', *Journal of Alternative Investments*, Summer.
Schulze, W.S., Lubatkin, M.H. and Dino, R.N. (2003), 'Toward a theory of agency and altruism in family firms', *Journal of Business Venturing*, **18**, 473–90.
Seth, A. and Easterwood, J. (1993), 'Strategic redirection in large management buyouts: the evidence from post-buyout restructuring activity', *Strategic Management Journal*, **14** (4), 251–73.
Singh, H. (1990), 'Management buy-outs: distinguishing characteristics and operating changes prior to public offering', *Strategic Management Journal*, **11**, 111–29.
Smart, S.B. and Waldfogel, F. (1994), 'Measuring the effect of restructuring on corporate performance: the case of management buyouts', *The Review of Economics and Statistics*, **76** (3), 503–11.
Smith, A. (1990), 'Corporate ownership structure and performance: the case of management buyouts', *Journal of Financial Economics*, **13**, 143–65.
Sudarsanam, S., Wright, M. and Huang, J. (2007), 'Going private buyouts and shareholder wealth gains: impact of bankruptcy risk' CMBOR Occasional Paper, January.
Thompson Venture Economics (2006), Database, Thomson Venture Economics.
Thomson, S., Wright, M. and Robbie, K. (1992), 'Management equity ownership, debt and performance: some evidence from UK management buy-outs', *Scottish Journal of Political Economy*, **39**, 413–30.
Warga, A. and Welch, I. (1993), 'Bondholder losses in leveraged buyouts', *Review of Financial Studies*, **6**, 959–82.
Weir, C., Laing, D. and Wright, M. (2005a), 'Incentive effects, monitoring mechanisms and the threat from the market for corporate control: an analysis of the factors affecting public to private transactions in the UK', *Journal of Business Finance and Accounting*, **32**, 909–44.
Weir, C., Laing, D. and Wright, M. (2005b), 'Undervaluation, private information, agency costs and the decision to go private', *Applied Financial Economics*, **15**, 947–61.
Weir, C., Wright, M. and Scholes, L. (2008), 'Public-to-private buy-outs, distress costs and private equity', *Applied Financial Economics*, forthcoming.
Weir, C. and Wright, M. (2006), 'Governance and takeovers: are public to private transactions different from traditional acquisitions of listed corporations?', *Accounting and Business Research*, **36** (4), 289–308.
Work Foundation (2007), 'Inside the dark box: shedding light on private equity', London: Work Foundation.
Wright, M. and Coyne, J. (1985), *Management Buy-outs*, Beckenham: Croom Helm.
Wright, M. and Lockett, A. (2003), 'The structure and management of alliances: syndication in venture capital investments', *Journal of Management Studies*, **40**, 2073–104.
Wright, M., Thompson, S. and Robbie, K. (1992), 'Venture capital and management-led leveraged buyouts: a European perspective', *Journal of Business Venturing*, **7**, 47–71.
Wright, M., Thompson, S., Robbie, K. and Wong, P. (1995), 'Management buy-outs in the short and long term', *Journal of Business Finance and Accounting*, **22**, 461–82.

Wright, M., Wilson, N., Robbie, K. and Ennew, C. (1996a), 'An analysis of failure in UK buy-outs and buy-ins', *Managerial and Decision Economics*, **17**, 57–70.
Wright, M., Wilson, N. and Robbie, K. (1996b), 'The longer term effects of management-led buyouts', *Journal of Entrepreneurial and Small Business Finance*, **5**, 213–34.
Wright, M., Chiplin, B., Robbie, K. and Albrighton, M. (2000a), 'The development of an organisational innovation: management buy-outs in the UK 1980–1997', *Business History*, **42**, 137–84.
Wright, M., Hoskisson, R., Busenitz, L. and Dial, J. (2000b), 'Entrepreneurial growth through privatization: the upside of management buyouts', *Academy of Management Review*, **25**, 591–601.
Wright, M., Hoskisson, R. and Busenitz, L. (2001), 'Firm rebirth: buyouts as facilitators of strategic growth and entrepreneurship', *Academy of Management Executive*, **15**, 111–25.
Wright, M., Buck, T. and Filatotchev, I. (2002), 'Post-privatization effects of management and employee buy-outs', *Annals of Public and Cooperative Economics*, **73**, 303–52.
Wright, M., Kitamura, M. and Hoskisson, R. (2003), 'Management buy-outs and restructuring Japanese corporations', *Long Range Planning*, **36**, 355–74.
Wright, M., Pruthi, S. and Lockett, A. (2005), 'International venture capital research: from cross-country comparisons to crossing borders', *International Journal of Management Reviews*, **7**, 135–66.
Wu, T.W. (1997), 'Management buyouts and earnings management', *Journal of Accounting Auditing and Finance*, **12**, 373–89.
Zahra, S.A. (1995), 'Corporate entrepreneurship and financial performance: the case of management leveraged buyouts', *Journal of Business Venturing*, **10**, 225–47.

PART II

Theoretical Perspectives

2. Entrepreneurial growth through privatization: the upside of management buyouts

Mike Wright, Robert E. Hoskisson, Lowell W. Busenitz and Jay Dial

In most academic treatments of buyouts, researchers have focused on agency-based explanations that limit managerial discretion to create gains through a focus on efficiency (Jensen, 1989). Although applications of managerial and behavioral perspectives have been limited (see Fox and Marcus, 1992, for an exception), we use an entrepreneurial cognition perspective in this chapter to explain how managerial discretion can lead to upside growth in buyouts.

Buyouts cover a variety of closely related organizational forms, in which a group of individuals or investors (as opposed to publicly owned entities) attains significant equity ownership in an enterprise. The sale of state and local government-owned enterprises, ultimately based on disappointment with their performance (Megginson, Nash and van Randenborgh, 1994), is representative of a growing trend toward privatization buyouts and also represents an increasingly common conduit for change and entrepreneurial pursuits (Filatotchev, Wright, Buck and Zhukov, 1999). We argue that buyout enterprises, restricted by political and other organizational constraints, may generate performance improvements in three main ways: by enhancing efficiency, by catching up with industry-wide innovations, and by exploiting new and radical innovations. These three rationales are inherent in the model that we develop in Table 2.1 and in the arguments that follow.

MODEL DEVELOPMENT

The interrelated theories of agency and property rights have application for both the private (Demsetz, 1967; Jensen and Meckling, 1976) and public sectors (Andrews and Dowling, 1998; Uhlenbruck and De Castro, 1998).[1] They emphasize the importance of incentives for efficiency (Kaplan, 1989;

Table 2.1 Incentives and cognition in buyouts

Managerial incentives	Individual cognition	
	Managerial cognition	Entrepreneurial cognition
Managerial incentives directed toward efficiency gains	**Quadrant 1: Efficiency-oriented buyout** *Buyout attributes:* Combine ownership and management to align incentives with productiveness gains in buyouts in need of efficiency gains. *Decision mode:* Limit managerial discretion. Monetary incentives.	**Quadrant 4: Buyout failure** *Buyout attributes:* Financial incentives reward efficiency gains, but managers with entrepreneurial cognition have innovative skills. Buyout failure is the likely result. *Decision mode:* Expand managerial discretion. Heuristic-based decisions – representativeness.
Managerial incentives to foster strategic innovation	**Quadrant 2: Revitalization buyout** *Buyout attributes:* Process and imitation innovations complement an efficiency focus. After a season of neglect, newly privatized firms adapt various incremental innovations in pursuit of revitalization. *Decision mode:* With management and ownership aligned, long-term incentives encourage innovation and some managerial discretion.	**Quadrant 3: Entrepreneurial buyout** *Buyout attributes:* Strategic innovation emerges because high-powered incentives and discretion are given to owner/managers. Managers with heuristic-based logic pursue radical strategic innovation. *Decision mode:* Expand managerial discretion. Heuristic-based decisions – representativeness. Long-term monetary incentives.

Phan and Hill, 1995), and even catch-up innovation or revitalization (Holmstrom, 1989), but that such incentives are also limited. Furthermore, many buyouts across the global landscape have gone beyond efficiency incentives to become a vehicle for entrepreneurial initiatives and the expansion of managerial discretion (Zahra, 1995). Accordingly, we propose that significant strategic innovations often emerge in buyouts with a change in managerial mindset.

If there are fundamental differences in the way buyout managers think and make decisions, these differences might represent sources of advantage. For example, because it may be difficult to shift from a managerial to an entrepreneurial cognitive mindset, the cognitive approach may represent a source of sustained competitive advantage (Barney, 1991).[2] Alternatively, if the wrong cognitive approach is in place, 'core rigidity' or sustained competitive disadvantage may occur (Leonard-Barton, 1992). By recognizing that strategic decisions can effectively involve heuristics, we point to a possible connection between cognitive theories of decision making, strategic management, and buyout performance.

The term *heuristics* refers to simplifying strategies that individuals (entrepreneurial managers in this case) use to make strategic decisions, especially in complex situations where less complete or uncertain information is available. *Entrepreneurial cognition* refers to the more extensive use of heuristics and individual beliefs that impact decision making. *Managerial cognition* refers to more systematic decision making, in which management uses accountability and compensation schemes, the structural coordination of business activities across various units, and quantifiable budgets to justify future developments.

We build a new model to explain incentive differences from agency theory (short term versus long term) and describe how fundamental differences in individual cognitive orientation (managerial versus entrepreneurial) can be combined to explain different strategic buyout attributes. Rooted in cognitive psychology, entrepreneurial cognition (Baron, 1998; Busenitz and Lau, 1996) indicates that strategic decisions are significantly influenced by individual heuristics and that an understanding of strategic decision making is significantly limited without attention to these cognitive processes (Hitt and Tyler, 1991). This has particular implications for entrepreneurs, because they regularly find themselves in situations that tend to maximize the potential impact of various heuristics (Baron, 1998).

When probing these cognitive processes, it is important first to understand the utility of such decision making. Entrepreneurs typically operate under the conditions of decision uncertainty and decision complexity. Given the level of uncertainty they face, entrepreneurs frequently use heuristics to piece together limited information to make decisions in the face of much turbulence. Without heuristic-based logic, the pursuit of new opportunities becomes too overwhelming and costly for those decision makers who seek a more factual base. The decision-making contexts entrepreneurs face also tend to be more complex. Without the elaborate policies, procedural routines, and structural mechanisms common to established organizations, heuristics may be quite useful in enabling entrepreneurs to make decisions that exploit brief windows of opportunity (Hambrick and Crozier, 1985; Tversky and Kahneman, 1974).

There also may be an important link between the use of decision heuristics and learning in the entrepreneurship context. Central to most models of learning is the issue of achieving new understandings, interpretations, and insights (Daft and Weick, 1984). Sources of competitive advantage are also thought to evolve around knowledge creation and decision-making capabilities (Barney, 1991). Lower-level learning tends to follow the more rational model, with a focus on repetitious observations and routinized learning. Such learning tends to be short term and temporary (Fiol and Lyles, 1985). There are few changes in underlying policies or values (Argyris, 1983), which is consistent with the notion of single-loop learning. These learning modes tend to be slower and more imitable (Lei, Hitt, and Bettis, 1996), in part because decision makers usually wait on results from repeated outcomes of success or failure to reach their decisions.

Higher-level learning involves the formation and use of heuristics to generate new insights into unsolved problems and opportunities (Lei et al., 1996). Although heuristic-based logic may use less information and be less accurate, use of individual-specific clusters of knowledge facilitates quick adjustments to emerging trends (Krabuanrat and Phelps, 1998). For example, decision makers can integrate new information with their heuristic-based logic to make inferences and adjust evolving innovations (Daft and Weick, 1984; Lei et al., 1996). We suggest that faster learning is enhanced by the more extensive use of heuristic-based decision making. Such higher-level learning also tends to produce specialization (Levitt and March, 1988) and sometimes a unique understanding of an entrepreneurial situation, which may be a source of competitive advantage, because high specialization is more likely to result in successful outcomes in rapidly changing environments (Lei et al., 1996).

In sum, we contend that entrepreneurs use a heuristic-based approach to decision making more extensively, and this enables them to make sense out of uncertain and complex situations more quickly, often leading to faster learning and unorthodox interpretations (innovations). The more extensive use of heuristics by entrepreneurs allows them to navigate more readily through a wide array of problems and irregularities inherent in the development of new opportunities.

The different assumptions of our entrepreneurial cognition approach, including individual behavior, role of managerial ownership, managerial decision situation, view of risk, information, and innovation are shown in Table 2.2. We also compare and contrast these assumptions with those of agency theory. The agency cost and the entrepreneurial cognition per-

Table 2.2 Entrepreneurial cognition and agency theory comparisons

Attributes	Entrepreneurial cognition	Agency theory[a]
View of individual behavior	Individual behavior is heuristic based.	Managers respond only to monetary incentives.
Role of managerial ownership	Firm ownership facilitates exploitation of entrepreneurial skills.	Ownership and management are combined to align incentives.
Managerial decision situation	Heuristics are used to quickly interpret the complex and changing business environment to detect emerging trends.	With efficiency as the effectiveness criterion, decisions are based largely on quantifiable information and corporate procedures.
View of risk	Risk concerns are overruled by opportunity recognition.	Individuals are risk averse.
Information	Strategic information, unavailable in the marketplace, emerges from experience and heuristic-based logic.	Information is a purchasable commodity.
Innovation	Heuristic-based reasoning complements entrepreneurial learning, which leads to evolution of radical innovations.	With some long-term incentives, implemented innovations tend to be incremental and imitated from competitors.

Source: [a] Adapted from Eisenhardt (1989, p. 59, Table 1).

spectives developed here each offer important insights for understanding why different types of buyouts have emerged in many international locations.

Accordingly, we now develop each quadrant of the model in Table 2.1, using both agency theory and entrepreneurial cognition in a complementary manner to specify different buyout attributes and the associated managerial decision modes and incentives that fit the strategic buyout purpose. This creates a framework for understanding why different buyout attributes have emerged globally and how to better manage them.

Efficiency-Oriented Buyouts (Quadrant 1)

Buyout attributes

Proponents of the agency cost approach as applied to buyouts hitherto have largely focused upon reducing the problems of overdiversification, overinvestment, and insufficient accountability that result from the misalignment of management incentives and weak monitoring in mature industries with substantial free cash flows (Jensen, 1989). More concentrated ownership, stricter governance, and a more efficient incentive scheme can effectively mitigate the *downside* problems that plague mature firms when costs become inflated. However, firms that are focused on efficiency moves are very likely to further decrease their R&D intensity from what is already a low base (Long and Ravenscraft, 1993). In these buyouts the shareholder value creation might more appropriately be termed the prevention of value destruction from overinvestment in mature or declining industries. Here, the expectation is that financial leverage will be quite high, acting as a limit on managerial discretion.

In centrally planned economies, such as that of the former Soviet system, strategic decisions generally were made at the center, by the ministries, with management carrying out only routine, planned operations (Pelikan, 1987). Many of the so-called Red Directors of the former Soviet system tended to be all powerful within their enterprises (Puffer, 1994), but the perverse nature of incentives and the inflexibility of central planning procedures typically led to valuable inputs being converted into finished goods of low value (Filatotchev et al., 1999).

However, a privatization buyout, either through a purchase with debt finance, as in Hungary (Karsai and Wright, 1994), or through vouchers, as in Russia (Filatotchev, Hoskisson, Buck and Wright, 1996), has facilitated the implementation of incentive and control mechanisms, which has increased the probability of a more viable organizational existence. For example, the foreign trade company Transelektro Kereskedelmi (specializing in the management of foreign construction consortia) was bought out from the Hungarian government in 1992 for HUF 800 million. Fourteen managers obtained 72 per cent of the equity, and 144 of the 400 employees obtained 18 per cent, with the remaining ownership retained by the government. Some 75 per cent of the purchase price was financed by debt from two Hungarian banks over a ten-year period, with interest payable from the start but debt repayment beginning only two years after buyout. The balance was paid in cash. The firm's assets were used as collateral, and the banks obtained informational and control rights over the financial management of the company. Since the buyout, the company has improved efficiency by closing down loss-making businesses in Germany and Dubai, and has focused primarily on its core work in infrastructure projects, such as Ganz-Roeck Boiler and Power Equipment.

Decision mode

In this quadrant business leaders with a managerial (versus entrepreneurial) cognition are likely to respond favorably to the enhanced monetary incentives introduced in a buyout (Jensen and Meckling, 1976). Empirical studies indicate that efficiency-oriented buyouts do increase operating performance and cash flow (Kaplan, 1989). Although management discretion in the pursuit of strategic innovations is unlikely in this quadrant, these buyouts generally occur in mature and stable industries where a lack of innovation is less prone to engender competitive disadvantage. Here, the expectation is that financial leverage will remain fairly high.

Evidence from Hungarian privatization buyouts indicates that although management obtained significant equity holdings, high levels of debt provided relatively little discretion to make investment decisions (Karsai and Wright, 1994).

Revitalization Buyouts (Quadrant 2)

Buyout attributes

Business entities often need to pursue at least some level of innovation and change for survival, but innovative activity usually is characterized by long time horizons, high risk, unpredictability, labor intensity, and numerous idiosyncratic factors (Holmstrom, 1989). Holmstrom and Milgrom (1990) have shown how limitations on discretion and incentive alignment can be used as substitutes, depending on whether the loss of efficiency from restricted managerial discretion is larger or smaller than the cost of providing the right incentives. Francis and Smith (1995), however, have provided evidence that innovation is difficult to accomplish through agency incentives and monitoring and often too costly for diffuse ownership structures. This is particularly problematic in large, integrated organizations, which often lack reliable performance measures because of increased costs of obtaining information. This, in turn, leads to bureaucratic measures to ensure performance. However, these contractual and bureaucratic arrangements tend to be unfriendly toward major innovative efforts, since they restrict experimentation (Francis and Smith, 1995; Holmstrom, 1989).

Similarly, Williamson (1985) tackled the issue of integrated versus nonintegrated firms and concluded that high-powered incentives and hybrid organizations are required for innovation. Substituting debt for equity in a moderately leveraged capital structure can help to concentrate ownership, thus creating potentially higher-powered incentives with longer time horizons.

These arguments suggest that independence might be an important antecedent for innovation, and we propose revitalization buyouts as one organizational hybrid capable of innovation. These buyouts are often directed at firms with few recent improvements or upgrades, operating at relatively inefficient levels. As shown in Table 2.1, this situation provides a good match for the 'managerial cognition' archetype that typically characterizes the leadership in these types of buyouts, since bureaucratic measures of performance are likely to screen out innovative personalities (Holmstrom, 1989, p. 306). Relative to Quadrant 1, longer-term incentives are emphasized, enabling these individuals to accommodate incremental, revitalizing innovation with long-term payoffs, as well as to meet current cash flow demands (Sahlman, 1990).

Privatization by buyout of state-owned enterprises might provide the opportunity to introduce improved incentives and control systems. It also may break the link with ministries, avoiding political interference in management's non-routine decision making (Boycko, Shleifer and Vishny, 1993), and provide the opportunity to address a need for revitalization. Consistent with the overall decline in R&D intensity that tends to occur in leveraged buyout (LBO) firms (Long and Ravenscraft, 1993), we predict that firms in this quadrant will be frugal with R&D expenditure but that the limited expenditures will be very effective (Zahra, 1995).

Prior to the management–employee buyout in 1987, Unipart was the spare parts subsidiary of the then UK state-owned Austin Rover. The majority of Unipart's sales were to the parent, and growth and product development were held back because of restrictions on investment by the loss-making parent. Shortly after its buyout, Unipart signed new long-term contracts with the former parent, undertook investment in a new parts delivery system, and developed a service culture among equity-holding employees. In the medium term, catch-up innovation involved adoption of Japanese production methods and the development of a worldwide customer base that included Toyota and General Motors (GM). The company remains an independent private company with a well-articulated focus on the longer term.

Decision mode

This quadrant extends previous applications of agency theory to buyouts to include cases where some degree of innovation is required. Revitalizing innovation based on a managerial cognition orientation is most appropriate for firms in this quadrant, where managers need to evaluate and implement innovative approaches to determine whether to implement them. Such managers tend to be good at systematically evaluating and overseeing specific innovations for their financial value to the entire business.

In going beyond pure efficiency buyouts, the challenge of this quadrant is to have individuals with a managerial cognition orientation as buyout owner/managers and then to implement rewards for effective short-term cash flows and long-term monetary incentives that foster prudent investments in innovation. Usually, these buyouts have somewhat less leverage and more equity than those in Quadrant 1 providing more flexibility.

Entrepreneurial Buyouts (Quadrant 3)

Buyout attributes

Buyouts generally have been associated with efficiency gains and decreases in R&D intensity, but there is evidence that strategic innovation and R&D intensity are central to many privatized firms (Wright, Hoskisson, Filatotchev and Buck, 1998; Zahra, 1995). Long and Ravenscraft (1993) found that R&D-intensive LBOs outperformed both their non-LBO industry peers and other LBOs without R&D expenditures. Given all the agency costs associated with innovation, high concentrations of management ownership become an important way of encouraging and governing R&D activity (Francis and Smith, 1995). Where major innovation opportunities exist, however, performance gains are more likely to result from management with superior and idiosyncratic skills (Castanias and Helfat, 1991). Consequently, managers with more traditional managerial cognition orientations might be unable to take advantage, even with enhanced incentives.

In the LBO literature one finds remarkably little attention given to the entrepreneurial side of buyouts, in part because of the central emphasis of agency theory on managerial incentives. However, we argue that there is also a need to consider the cognitive skills of the individual managers. The heuristic-based logic employed by entrepreneurial managers facilitates fresh learning perspectives and decision-making ability under great uncertainty and ambiguity. The success of entrepreneurial buyouts at facilitating entrepreneurial decision modes (relative to larger organizations attempting to promote corporate entrepreneurship) results from high-powered ownership incentives that encourage risk taking and long-term rewards in combination with heuristic-based logic, which nurtures the innovation process.

Management buyouts of divisions of both private and public sector corporations often take place because the infrastructure and information-processing capabilities of a diversified firm are too limiting to allow recognition and exploitation of most entrepreneurial opportunities that emerge (Hill and Pickering, 1986). Evidence from over two hundred private and public sector divestments of high-technology divisions indicates that (1) buyout companies were often non-core businesses, (2) the parent did not understand the technology, (3) managers sought autonomy in order to develop their own strategy, and (4) managers sought to earn greater remuneration away from the parents' constrained system (Robbie, Wright and Albrighton, 1999).

Istel's public sector privatization from the highly cash-constrained automobile producer Austin Rover is instructive (Wright, Thompson and Robbie, 1993). Prior to buyout, Istel was regarded as peripheral to the main automobile-producing activities of the parent, and prebuyout sales were focused primarily on a narrow range of computer services, with cash constraints on the loss-making parent restricting the ability of the management of Istel to exploit growth opportunities. The buyout enabled the management to become a global competitor in advanced telecommunication services, electronic document interchange, and factory automation, based on the company's data communications network. Infotrac. The radically different market conditions in which the Istel buyout operated strongly suggest that it was not possible to quantify all the relevant information before making the decision to develop these new products. This, in turn, suggests that an entrepreneurial cognition approach was operating in the Istel situation.

As in Quadrant 2, substituting debt for equity helps facilitate incentives by concentrating ownership. However, leverage likely will be lower here than in either Quadrant 1 or 2 so that debt does not crowd out entrepreneurial or innovative opportunities or unduly constrain R&D investments.

Decision mode

In corporate settings managers with an entrepreneurship orientation are likely to become frustrated with a bureaucratic corporate structure and its stifling attitude toward innovations and renewal (Busenitz and Barney, 1997). When proposals for new ventures are presented, corporate managers regularly reject them because of the lack of quantifiable information and because the information available does not fit into formal corporate decision-making procedures.

One heuristic that might be both particularly salient and prevalent among entrepreneurs is representativeness (Busenitz and Barney, 1997). Representativeness occurs when decision makers are willing to make judgments about a given phenomenon based on an available cluster of information or based on a small, nonrandom sample (Tversky and Kahneman, 1974). This type of reasoning typically results in a satisficing rather than optimal solution that emerges from rational reasoning and the gathering of large amounts of relevant data over time (Krabuanrat and Phelps, 1998). Decision makers using heuristic-based logic will tend to link relevant experiences and personal decision rules quickly to reach a specific decision regarding the new problem or opportunities. If the initial decision solution is rejected, other alternatives will be developed, facilitating a rapid learning process.

Evidence indicates that severing ties with the corporate infrastructure through an entrepreneurial buyout usually increases buyout managers' flexibility to initiate innovations and growth opportunities more freely, with potential long-term rewards (Burgelman, 1995; Wright, Thompson, Chiplin and Robbie, 1991). Risk concerns about new ideas and innovations tend to be overruled because of the opportunity managers' recognized initially. In essence, entrepreneurial buyout managers have expanded discretion to fund those creative ideas they perceive have the greatest long-term payoff, well before solid quantitative data is available to support the project. Such decision making also might facilitate speed that is often crucial to success in entrepreneurial situations.

Buyout Failures (Quadrant 4)

Quadrant 4 represents a mismatch that, if implemented, likely would lead to buyout failure. Entrepreneurial managers want to undertake a buyout and have the skill set to pursue strategic innovations; the incentive system imposed by a system directed at efficiency, however, severely restricts most creative pursuits of the entrepreneurial managers (Ghoshal and Moran, 1996). Accordingly, the misalignment of an entrepreneurial cognition orientation and agency incentives creates a high probability of failure. Managers might be entrepreneurial in applying efficiency, but these issues are fully covered in Quadrants 1 and 2.

DISCUSSION

In this chapter we have attempted to explain more fully the strategic rationales associated with buyout privatizations by using a matrix of buyout attributes that both extends previous application of agency theory to buyouts (Quadrant 2) and widens the conceptual bases beyond agency cost explanations to include an entrepreneurial cognition view (Quadrant 3). The outcomes of heuristic-based logic in entrepreneurial buyouts may have both upside and downside implications for policy makers and managers.

Heuristic-based logic in decision making is very economical and usually provides valuable estimations of the entrepreneurial decisions (Tversky and Kahneman, 1974), especially because of the scarcity of quantifiable information available for a more rational decision. It is virtually impossible to undertake an entrepreneurial endeavor without some confidence in heuristic-based logic. From an agency point of view, the data are too costly (see Table 2.2). The use of heuristics also can provide the impetus for the venture to press forward after the 'go' decision has been made. Failing to gather comprehensive information can lead to errors, but acting on available information and heuristic-based inferences allows decision makers to learn and move ahead with perceived opportunities quickly.

Of course, in the face of uncertainty and ambiguity, a heuristic-based logic may lead to bad decisions in privatizations as well. Entrepreneurial managers might make incorrect judgments about where the future of their firm and a given industry lies. Sometimes, heuristics lead to severe errors (Tversky and Kahneman, 1974), and errors in the case of privatization could likely lead to firm failure (see the case of Coated Electrodes in Wright et al., 1991). Policy makers and managers need to consider when heuristic-based decision making leads to competitive advantage and disadvantage. In addition, they may need to identify particular types of incentives with particular buyout attributes and decision modes associated with each quadrant. For instance, we might expect to see monetary incentives based on cash-flow targets characterize Quadrant 1, whereas Quadrants 2 and 3 might include a mixture of equity ownership to enhance a long-term perspective and monetary incentives based on sales growth, reflecting the upside opportunities. Quadrant 2 reflects shorter-term, incremental revitalization efforts, whereas Quadrant 3's equity incentives would be more consistent with the riskier, longer-term payoffs characteristic of entrepreneurial ventures.

In order to aid policy makers and managers, further examination is needed in which researchers compare the performance of buyouts in the different quadrants and also link this to a buyout manager's cognitive orientation. We also need additional research regarding how specialized incentives might be different among the various quadrants in order to facilitate the accomplishment of a buyout's strategic intent.

There are also implications for policy makers and managers with respect to the conditions under which a move from one quadrant to another may be more appropriate and how such a move may be effected. First, consider privatization buyouts in Central and Eastern Europe. Individuals with more managerial cognition skills might be expected to focus their attention on ensuring the economic viability of the enterprise through cost control measures and more routine catching up (Quadrant 1). This 'shallow restructuring' may be appropriate in the short term, but more radical innovation ('deep restructuring'; European Bank for Reconstruction and Development [EBRD], 1997, 76) might be necessary in the long term, requiring either long-term incentives for revitalizing innovation (a move to Quadrant 2) or heuristic-based logic (a move to Quadrant 3). Without active investor outside blockholders or an urgent need to receive outside financing (both of which may arise in Central and Eastern Europe), however, managers (and employees) with significant organizational property rights might engage in entrenchment behavior at the expense of efficiency improvements. This problem may be exacerbated by weak bankruptcy legislation that enables unviable enterprises to remain in business (EBRD, 1997).

Second, the possibility of buyout failure represented by Quadrant 4 also raises important implications. In principle, no buyout type should fit this quadrant. In the typical buyout environment of asymmetric information, however, and where managers have not been running the business as owner/managers, mismatches may arise and buyouts may be completed. LBO associations and private equity investors might attempt to undertake appropriate screening of potential investees and their management, but in such circumstances this might be imperfect (Robbie and Wright, 1995). In order to avoid failure, investors either may attempt to tightly monitor management with entrepreneurial cognition attributes or replace them with individuals who have the managerial cognition attributes. In this way effort is expended to shift the situation to Quadrant 1. Alternatively, where there is a need to undertake strategic innovation (a shift to Quadrant 3), management may exert pressure to refinance the buyout to allow this to happen, or it may be necessary to introduce new management with an entrepreneurial cognition perspective.

Third, in public sector cases, incumbent managers may not be able to exploit entrepreneurial opportunities. In many privatizations it may be best to change senior management by creating a management buy-in or investor-led buyout. These arrangements, combining ownership, an entrepreneurial orientation, and more professional management, can lead to more constructive outcomes, helping to take the firm to more advanced stages of growth. This suggests a change from Quadrant 1 to Quadrant 2, if managers with a traditional cognitive orientation are brought in from the outside. More radical change to Quadrant 3 may be possible if managers with an entrepreneurial orientation are employed. A move to Quadrants 2 and 3 may be more difficult, however, because outside managers do not have the strategic understanding of incumbent managers (Baysinger and Hoskisson, 1990). For researchers, there is a need to examine when a combination of incumbent and outside managers creates an appropriate mindset that might prove fruitful for understanding success of public sector buyouts.

Finally, an important empirical issue is whether there are significant differences in the financing and governance structures of the buyouts in the four quadrants. As we have suggested, buyouts focusing on efficiency (Quadrants 1 and 2) may tend to have higher levels of debt, whereas we expect higher equity levels in buyouts emphasizing long-term strategic thinking and innovation (Quadrant 3). Although this inverse relationship has not been directly tested, Long and Ravenscraft (1993) found a decline in R&D following an LBO, but LBOs with high levels of R&D may actually experience an increase in R&D following an LBO. Robbie et al. (1999) have found that high-tech buyouts make slightly less use of senior debt and correspondingly more use of subordinated debt than non-high-tech buyouts. In future research scholars should systematically examine this issue.

CONCLUSIONS

With our model we seek to provide a more parsimonious explanation for both publicly traded and public sector buyout privatizations oriented toward a variety of strategic purposes. In prior conceptualizations of buyouts, researchers have focused primarily on limiting managerial discretion, whereas in our approach we include rationales for buyouts that expand managerial discretion to foster entrepreneurial opportunity. To accomplish this, we develop agency explanations along with those of the cognitive approach. In so doing, we argue that significant entrepreneurial progress is made not through managerial incentives alone but through a cognitive shift from a managerial to an entrepreneurial mindset. In addition, we suggest that our model makes a contribution to strategic management by illustrating how cognitive skills, which are hard to change, may lead to competitive advantage or disadvantage.

ACKNOWLEDGMENTS

We thank Hicheon Kim, Bill Wan, three anonymous reviewers, and Isabel Gutierrez for their comments on an earlier draft of this chapter.

NOTES

1. Andrews and Dowling (1998) argue that the public at large can be seen as the principal and managers as the agents in state-owned enterprises and that, since the public has little motivation or power to influence the way a state-owned enterprise is managed, management may be relatively unconstrained in pursuing its own interests.
2. Our assumption here is that individual differences do exist and that these differences generally make it difficult for decision makers to alter their decision mode (systematic versus the heuristic mode in this chapter). Although opinions differ on this issue, in recent empirical work Hitt and Tyler (1991) and Wally and Baum (1994) found that individual differences among decision makers affect strategic decision-making activities.

REFERENCES

Andrews, W. and Dowling, M. (1998), 'Explaining performance changes in newly privatized firms', *Journal of Management Studies*, **35**, 601–18.

Argyris, C. (1983), 'Action science and intervention', *Journal of Applied Behavioral Science*, **19**, 115–40.

Barney, J.B. (1991), 'Firm resources and sustained competitive advantage', *Journal of Management*, **17**, 99–120.

Baron, R. (1998), 'Cognitive mechanisms in entrepreneurship: why and when entrepreneurs think differently than other people', *Journal of Business Venturing*, **13**, 275–94.

Baysinger, B. and Hoskisson, R.E. (1990), 'The composition of boards of directors and strategic control: Effects on corporate strategy', *Academy of Management Review*, **15**, 72–87.

Boycko, M., Shleifer, A. and Vishny, R. (1993), 'Privatizing Russia', *Brookings Papers on Economic Activity*, **2**, 139–92.

Burgelman, R. (1995), *Strategic Management of Technology and Innovation*, Boston: Irwin.

Busenitz, L.W. and Barney, J.B. (1997), 'Differences between entrepreneurs and managers in large organizations: biases and heuristics in strategic decision-making', *Journal of Business Venturing*, **12**, 9–30.

Busenitz, L.W. and Lau, C. (1996), 'A cross-cultural cognitive model of new venture creation', *Entrepreneurship Theory and Practice*, **20**(4), 25–39.

Castanias, R. and Helfat, C. (1991), 'Managerial resources and rents', *Journal of Management*, **17**, 155–72.

Daft, R. and Weick, K. (1984), 'Toward a model of organizations as interpretation systems', *Academy of Management Review*, **9**, 284–95.

Demsetz, H. (1967), 'Toward a theory of property rights', *American Economic Review*, **57**, 347–59.

Eisenhardt, K. (1989), 'Agency theory: an assessment and review', *Academy of Management Review*, **14**, 57–74.

European Bank for Reconstruction and Development (EBRD) (1997), *Transition Report 1997*, London: EBRD.

Filatotchev, I., Hoskisson, R.E., Buck, T. and Wright, M. (1996), 'Corporate restructuring in Russian privatizations: implications for U.S. investors', *California Management Review*, **38**(2), 87–105.

Filatotchev, I., Wright, M., Buck, T. and Zhukov, V. (1999), 'Corporate entrepreneurs and privatized firms in Russia, Ukraine and Belarus', *Journal of Business Venturing*, **14**, 475–92.

Fiol, C.M. and Lyles, M.A. (1985), 'Organizational learning', *Academy of Management Review*, **10**, 803–13.

Fox, I. and Marcus, A. (1992), 'The causes and consequences of leveraged management buyouts', *Academy of Management Review*, **17**, 62–85.

Francis, J. and Smith, A. (1995), 'Agency costs and innovation: some empirical evidence', *Journal of Accounting and Economics*, **19**, 383–409.

Ghoshal, S. and Moran, P. (1996), 'Bad for practice: a critique of the transaction cost theory', *Academy of Management Review*, **21**, 13–47.

Hambrick, D. and Crozier, L. (1985), 'Stumblers and stars in the management of rapid growth', *Journal of Business Venturing*, **1**, 31–45.

Hill, C.W.L. and Pickering, J. (1986), 'Divisionalization, decentralization and performance of large UK companies', *Journal of Management Studies*, **23**, 26–50.

Hitt, M.A. and Tyler, B.B. (1991), 'Strategic decision models: integrating different perspectives', *Strategic Management Journal*, **12**, 327–51.

Holmstrom, B. (1989), 'Agency costs and innovation', *Journal of Economic Behavior and Organization*, **12**, 305–27.

Holmstrom, B. and Milgrom, P. (1990), 'Regulating trade among agents', *Journal of Institutional and Theoretical Economics*, **146**, 85–105.

Jensen, M. (1989), 'Eclipse of the public corporation', *Harvard Business Review*, **67**(5), 61–74.

Jensen, M. and Meckling, W. (1976), 'Theory of the firm: managerial behavior, agency costs and ownership structure, *Journal of Financial Economics*, **3**, 305–60.

Kaplan, S. (1989), 'The effects of management buyouts on operating performance and value', *Journal of Financial Economics*, **24**, 217–54.

Karsai, J. and Wright, M. (1994), 'Governance, finance and accountability in Hungarian buyouts', *Europe–Asia Studies* (formerly *Soviet Studies*), **46**, 997–1016.

Krabuanrat, K. and Phelps, R. (1998), 'Heuristic and rationality in strategic decision making: an exploratory study', *Journal of Business Research*, **41**, 83–93.

Lei, D., Hitt, M.A. and Bettis, R. (1996), 'Dynamic core competences through meta-learning and strategic context, *Journal of Management*, **22**, 549–69.

Leonard-Barton, D. (1992), 'Core capabilities and core rigidities: a paradox in managing new product development', *Strategic Management Journal*, **13**, Summer Special Issue, 363–80.

Levitt, B. and March, J.G. (1988), 'Organizational learning', *Annual Review of Sociology*,**14**, 319–340.

Long, W.F. and Ravenscraft, D.J. (1993), 'LBOs, debt and R&D intensity', *Strategic Management Journal*, **14**, Summer Special Issue, 119–35.

Megginson, W., Nash, R. and van Randenborgh, M. (1994), 'The financial and operating performance of newly-privatized firms: an international empirical analysis', *Journal of Finance*, **49**, 403–52.

Pelikan, P. (1987), 'The formation of incentive mechanisms', in S. Hedlund, (ed.), *Incentives and Economic Systems*, Beckenham, UK: Croom Helm, pp. 27–56.

Phan, P. and Hill, C. (1995), 'Organizational restructuring and economic performance in leveraged buyouts: an ex post study', *Academy of Management Journal*, **38**, 704–39.

Puffer, S. (1994), 'Understanding the bear: a portrait of Russian business leaders', *Academy of Management Executive*, **8**(1), 41–54.

Robbie, K. and Wright, M. (1995), 'Managerial and ownership succession and corporate restructuring: the case of management buy-ins', *Journal of Management Studies*, **32**, 527–50.

Robbie, K., Wright, M. and Albrighton, M. (1999), 'High technology buy-outs', *Venture Capital – An International Journal of Entrepreneurial Finance*, **1**, 219–40.

Sahlman, W. (1990), 'The structure and governance of venture-capital organizations', *Journal of Financial Economics*, **27**, 473–521.

Tversky, A. and Kahneman, D. (1974), 'Judgment under uncertainty: Heuristics and biases', *Science*, **185**, 1124–31.

Uhlenbruck, N. and De Castro, J. (1998), 'Privatization from the acquirer's perspective: a mergers and acquisitions based framework', *Journal of Management Studies*, **35**, 619–40.

Wally, S. and Baum, J.R. (1994), 'Personal and structural determinants of the pace of strategic decision making', *Academy of Management Journal*, **37**, 932–56.

Williamson, O.E. (1985), *The Economic Institutions of Capitalism*, New York: Free Press.

Wright, M., Hoskisson, R.E., Filatotchev, I. and Buck, T. (1998), 'Revitalizing privatized Russian enterprises', *Academy of Management Executive*, **12**(2), 74–85.

Wright, M., Thompson, S., Chiplin, B. and Robbie, K. (1991), *Buy-ins and Buyouts: New strategies in corporate management*, London: Graham & Trotman.

Wright, M., Thompson, S. and Robbie, K. (1993), 'Finance, accountability and control in privatization by management buy-out', *Financial Accountability and Management*, **9**(2), 75–99.

Zahra, S. (1995), 'Corporate entrepreneurship and financial performance: the case of management leveraged buyouts', *Journal of Business Venturing*, **10**, 225–47.

PART III

Sources of Buy-out

3. Why do public firms go private in the UK? The impact of private equity investors, incentive realignment and undervaluation

Luc Renneboog, Tomas Simons and Mike Wright

1. INTRODUCTION

In the Anglo-American corporate landscape, the public corporation is believed to have numerous advantages over its private counterpart. A stock exchange listing combined with the separation of ownership and control allows access to capital markets, specialization in managerial skills, investors' wealth diversification with liquid portfolios, a higher degree of media exposure, risk diversification by founders and entrepreneurs, the use of stock-price-based remuneration packages, and so on. However, this concept of the corporation has a major drawback: an unaccountable management could create substantial agency costs leading to corporate value destruction. The size of the inefficiencies induced by agency conflicts led Jensen (1989) to predict that the eclipse of the public corporation was near. This provocative claim was an exaggeration but, in the 1980s, a first important wave of leveraged public to private transactions (PTPs)[1] with a value of approximately US$250 billion occurred in the US (Opler and Titman, 1993). The phenomenon traversed the Atlantic, with the first UK PTP leveraged buyout (LBO) seeing daylight in 1985 (Wright et al., 2000a, b). Although much smaller in scale, activity in the UK market for PTPs kept pace with the US, reaching a peak in 1989.

Most that is currently known about PTPs results from US research analysing US samples covering the 1980s (see Jensen, 1993, and Renneboog and Simons, 2005, for reviews). However, while a vibrant, and economically important, PTP market has developed in the UK from the late 1990s onwards, there has to date been virtually no systematic research on the sources of shareholder wealth gains of UK going-private transactions. It is questionable whether this US evidence on the sources of wealth gains from leveraged PTPs is generalizable to the UK for the following reasons. First, the nature and extent of debt financing in US PTPs differs substantially from UK deals. Whereas US LBOs are (and were especially in the 1980s) partially financed with junk bonds, privately placed mezzanine was and still is the standard in the UK (Toms and Wright, 2005). Since these two sources of funds have different characteristics (in terms of flexibility, interest rates, maturity, covenants and gearing levels), it is not unlikely that the choice of financing between the two will influence all phases of a PTP. Also, the debt levels associated with UK transactions (across the 1980s and 1990s) are generally lower than the gearing ratio in US deals. Second, while tax motives have been shown to be a very important source of wealth gains in the US, it is unclear whether this result can be extrapolated to the UK given that the tax laws differ. Third, the US market for corporate control counts relatively more hostile takeovers than the UK market. Hence, the takeover defence hypothesis as a reason for PTPs is less likely to hold in the UK. Fourth, Toms and Wright (2005) argue that UK venture capital and buyout markets have traditionally been more closely linked than in the US. Consequently, public to private activity in the UK has focused more on growth opportunities, whereas US LBOs have occurred more frequently in mature, cash-rich industries. Last but not least, whereas US state regulation has been able to stringently regulate unsolicited takeover activity, the UK system has preferred self-regulation (the City Code on Takeovers and Mergers), thus favouring the unrestricted functioning of market forces (Miller, 2000). For all these reasons, a study on the second PTP wave in the UK is compelling and provides an important contribution to the PTP and LBO/MBO literature.

Our sample includes all 177 of the UK PTPs from 1997 (the start of the second wave) until 2003. These leveraged deals can be subdivided into management buyouts (MBOs), management buyins (MBIs) and institutional buyouts (IBOs).[2] In a typical UK MBO, the incumbent management seeks institutional support from private equity firms to purchase a major stake in the firm and to fund the transaction which aims at taking the firm private (Wright et al., 1991). IBOs (also called bought deals or finance purchases) are deals where the bidding group consists solely of institutional investors and private equity houses. When the management stays on, its performance is rewarded with a modest equity stake and/or an equity ratchet.[3] In terms of equity ownership, what separates MBOs from IBOs is whether the management team gained its equity stakes through being part of the bidding group (MBO), or as a component of a remuneration package (IBO). In an MBI, a team of outside managers or entrepreneurs purchases (most of) the equity. The premium for the average UK

PTP amounts to about 40%. In addition, the market reaction to the announcement of a PTP as measured by the cumulative abnormal returns (CAARs) over an 11-day event window centred around the announcement day, are also high at about 30%. These premiums and wealth effects are not dissimilar to the US findings.

We obtain the following results: an important source of expected shareholder wealth gains (as captured by the premiums and CAARs) is the undervaluation of the target firms' share prices over a one-year period prior to the first PTP announcement. The higher premiums offered for such a firm reflect the potential additional value that will be generated once the firm reaches its private status. This effect is stronger for MBOs and IBOs than for MBIs, which may arise due to differences in asymmetric information. In contrast to US research, there is no relation between a target firm's tax burden prior to the PTP and the expected wealth gains. However, the fact that higher premiums are paid for firms with low leverage does provide some support for the tax benefits hypothesis. The unused debt capacity is likely to create a large additional tax shield.

The potential for increased incentive realignment in the private firm is also an important determinant of the shareholder wealth gains as both the premiums and CAARs are higher for firms with lower levels of managerial ownership. We also report evidence supporting the control hypothesis: in firms with stronger outside blockholders, the premiums and CAARs are lower. This negative relation is especially strong in firms with monitoring by corporations as pre-PTP shareholders. This supports the fact that in firms monitored by this type of outside shareholders, there is less scope of operating performance improvements in the post-PTP period.

The free cash flow hypothesis is not sustained as firms are not taken private to reduce high free cash flows, which is consistent with most US studies. Prior takeover interest in the firm does not lead managers to pay more to take their firms private in order to pre-empt potential raiders. Not surprisingly, when at the announcement of a takeover, multiple bidders emerge, the shareholder wealth gains are higher.

The chapter is organized as follows. Section 2 provides an overview of the worldwide evolution of PTPs while Section 3 embeds the hypotheses in the literature. Section 4 discusses the sample selection, lists the data sources and presents the descriptive statistics. Section 5 explains the methodology. Section 6 shows the premiums and CAARS and discusses the results from the cross-sectional regression models and the robustness checks. Section 7 concludes and provides suggestions for future research.

2. WAVES OF PUBLIC TO PRIVATE TRANSACTIONS

One of the more remarkable features of the way business was conducted in the 1960s and 1970s was the lack of focus on shareholder value. For instance, corporate diversification was still considered as a valid business model and growth was believed to generate value increases almost automatically. The deficiencies in corporate governance regulation and the lack of managerial incentives to focus on corporate value were addressed in the 1980s by a wave of corporate restructurings (Wright et al., 2006, Martynova and Renneboog, 2005 and 2006). Not only did the number of (hostile) corporate takeovers surge,[4] but also LBOs and MBOs arose as a powerful catalyst to reduce the excess capacity in what Jensen (1991) calls 'complacent corporate America'. In less than a decade, the US going-private buyout market developed from less than $1 billion (in 1979) to a peak of more than $60 billion (in 1988). However, the culmination of this LBO wave was associated with many bankruptcies and fierce public and political resistance (anti-takeover legislation) such that activity slowed down abruptly, to less than $4 billion in 1990 (Kaplan and Stein, 1993). In the ten years' timeframe of the 'deal decade', $1.3 trillion in total asset value had changed hands (Shleifer and Vishny, 1991). Holmstrom and Kaplan (2001) argue that the 1980-style deals are not necessary anymore, because the focus on shareholder value has since been institutionalized by corporations. Nevertheless, from 1997 onwards, a modest rise in US PTPs can be observed (see Figure 3.1A). Since 2000, PTPs have been motivated by the decline of the stock markets which seems to make the sale of public equity too costly as a source of funds.[5]

Although smaller in scale, the activity in the UK public to private market kept pace with the US and the first wave culminated in 1989 (Figure 3.1B). Public controversy over increased hostility in transactions that year induced the Panel on Takeovers andMergers to adopt new rules regarding the procedures in PTPs (Wright et al., 1991). As in the US, the sudden drop in deals after 1989 made it seem as if the public to private transaction had already outlived its short life. Nevertheless, a new wave of public to private transactions started in 1997. Explanations for the second PTP wave generally emphasize the increased presence of private equity and debt financiers, target shareholder support (e.g. through irrevocable undertakings), the increased use of inducement fees and 'hard' exclusivity agreements, and the expectation that 100% of the shares can be acquired (e.g. through squeeze-out provisions) (Ashurst et al., 2002; Davis and Day, 1998; CMBOR, 2002).However, a much more important reason seems to be the disregard for small companies by institutional investors. For example, upon going private, Mr Ainscough, CEO of Wainhomes Plc, said: 'We feel unloved and

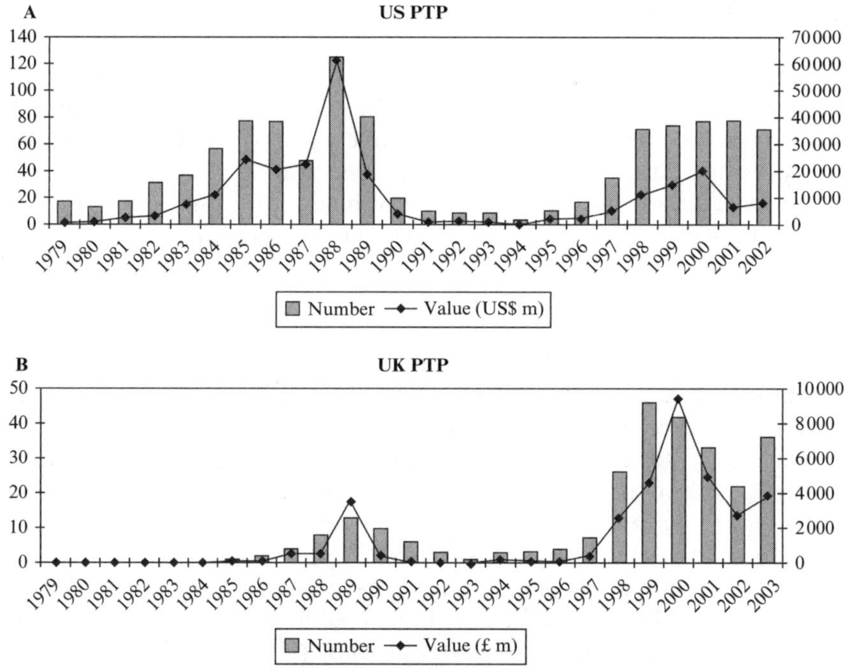

Note to Panel A: This figure shows the number of PTPs (left-hand scale) and the value in US$ m (right-hand scale).

Note to Panel B: This figure shows the number of PTPs (left-hand scale) and the value in £m (right-hand scale).

Source for both panels: Centre for Management Buy-out Research/Barclays Private Equity/Deloitte and Touche.

Figure 3.1 Public to private activity: US (Panel A) and UK (Panel B)

unwanted. There has been a lack of investor appetite for small company shares over the last two or three years. This made it difficult to fund expansions and acquisitions through the issue of new shares, which is one of the main reasons for going public in the first place' (*FT*, 4 March 1999). The lack of liquidity and the need for expansion capital as a consequence of the cut-off of institutional equity finance drove small companies into the arms of private equity firms.[6] The present PTP wave culminated in 1999–2000 in terms of deal numbers, but the value of PTPs remains high, reaching a peak of £7.9 billion in 2004. As increasingly larger corporations were being targeted, the mean deal value rose from £169 million in 1999 to £793 million in 2004 (CMBOR, 2005).

3. HYPOTHESES

Essentially, several sources of wealth gains[7] may motivate the going-private decision. These are: tax savings, reduction of agency costs (due to incentive realignment, control concentration or free cash flow reduction), wealth transfers from stakeholders to shareholders, transaction costs reduction, takeover defenses, and corporate undervaluation. In this section, we formulate these hypotheses and embed them in the literature.

3.1 The Tax Benefit Hypothesis

As the vast majority of PTP transactions take place with a substantial increase in leverage, the increase in interest deductions constitutes an important source of expected wealth gains. Interest tax deductibility on the new loans constitutes a major tax shield increasing the pre-recapitalization value.[8] Clearly, the extent to which tax benefits play a role depends on the fiscal regime and the marginal tax rates a company is subject to. Kaplan (1989b) estimates the tax benefits of US PTPs to be between 21% and 72% of the premium paid to shareholders to take the company private for the first half of the 1980s. Still, he adds that 'a public company arguably could obtain many of the tax benefits without going private'. Lowenstein (1985, p. 759) is critical and calls for a restriction of the tax benefits ('truffles from the tax man') in LBOs, judging that tax-related benefits 'are so large as to dispense the need to create the other, real gains', a claim supported by Frankfurter and Gunay (1992).

Under the tax hypothesis, firms with high tax bills benefit from going private, mainly because the large amount of debt used to finance the transaction creates a considerable additional tax shield which augments the value of the pre-recapitalization firm. Hence:

> *Hypothesis 1: The expected shareholder wealth gains from a PTP are positively related to high tax levels and low leverage ratios of the pre-transaction target firms.*

Testing this hypothesis is not straightforward because a high level of taxes not only represents potential savings in cash outflows (by creating leverage-induced tax shields) but may also reflect past accounting profitability. We therefore also include in the regressions discussed in Section 6.2 both the tax variable and an interaction term of taxes and high performance (a dummy that equals 1 if the return on assets is above the median). A positive relation between the wealth gains and the tax–performance interaction term reflects that the bidders are willing to pay more for firms with good past earnings profitability as it is believed that the tax shields resulting from the leveraged buyout will be sustainable due to high earnings profitability. It should also be noted that in a competitive market for corporate control, the tax benefits are predictable and hence may be appropriated by pre-buyout investors (and are hence fully reflected in the anticipated wealth effects).[9]

3.2 The Agency Costs-related Hypotheses

From the basics of agency theory, three important hypotheses underlie the motives of public to private transactions: incentive realignment, control and free cash flow.

3.2.1 The incentive realignment hypothesis

The insights of Adam Smith (1776) on the divergence of interests between managers and stockholders in a joint stock company are formalized by Jensen and Meckling (1976). When manager/entrepreneurs are also the sole residual claimants, they extract pecuniary rents and non-pecuniary[10] benefits. The optimal mix follows from a deliberation of the marginal costs and utilities associated with the type of benefit. When managers sell a portion of the residual claims to outsiders, the marginal costs of the non-pecuniary benefits decrease as they will bear only a fraction of those costs. Consequently, managers may increase their private benefits, which decreases the firm's value. The need to realign the incentives of managers with those of shareholders is frequently mentioned as an important factor in PTPs (Kaplan, 1989a). Under the incentive realignment hypothesis, the reunification of ownership and control will improve the incentive structure and is expected to increase managerial effort to maximize firm value. Hence:

> *Hypothesis 2: The expected shareholder wealth gains in MBOs and IBOs are negatively related to managerial equity ownership in the pre-transaction firm.*

The effects of the incentive realignment hypothesis at higher levels of managerial ownership are contested because entrenchment effects may render management – even in the wake of poor performance – immune to board restructuring and may delay corporate restructuring (Franks et al., 2001).

3.2.2 The control hypothesis

Grossman and Hart (1980) describe the free-rider problem associated with monitoring managerial actions in public corporations with a dispersed shareholder structure. As the investment in monitoring by an individual shareholder becomes a public good for all shareholders, individual shareholders owning small equity stakes may underinvest in monitoring activities. The presence of strong ownership concentration involving closer monitoring by outside shareholders prior to the PTP implies that fewer wealth gains from going private are expected as the pre-transaction firm is less likely to suffer from high agency costs. Hence:

Hypothesis 3: The expected shareholder wealth gains from PTPs are negatively related to the degree of concentration of equity claims in the hands of monitoring outside shareholders.

As different classes of ownership have different monitoring abilities, we expect a strongly negative relation between wealth gains and the presence of corporations, and individuals or families controlling large share stakes. In the UK, there has traditionally been little evidence of institutional investor activism although there are currently signs of the opposite (Crespi and Renneboog, 2002). Furthermore, the PIRC surveys since 1999 on institutional voting trends conclude that overall proxy voting levels have increased to over 50%.

3.2.3 The free cash flow hypothesis

Free cash flow (FCF) is usually defined as the cash flow in excess of that required to fund all projects that have a positive net present value (NPV) when discounted at a relevant cost of capital. Using empirical results on executive remuneration and corporate performance, Murphy (1985) argues that managers have incentives to retain resources and grow the firm beyond its optimal size – so-called 'empire building' – which is in direct conflict with shareholders' interests. This problem is most severe in cash-rich industries with low growth prospects. By exchanging debt for equity, managers credibly precommit to pay out future cash flows rather than retaining them to invest in negative NPV projects. The increased risk of default resulting from the recapitalization of the LBOs constitutes a motivating factor to make the firm more efficient (Jensen, 1986). In the carrot and stick theory of Lowenstein (1985), the carrot represents the increased managerial share ownership that allows managers to reap more of the benefits from their efforts. The stick appears when firms borrow heavily in order to effect this incentive alignment, which forces the managers to efficiently run the company to avoid default (Cotter and Peck, 2001). In a study of MBOs in the 1980s, Singh (1990) demonstrates that MBOs have substantially higher levels of cash flows than matched firms.

Under the free cash flow hypothesis, high leverage associated with PTPs will reduce wasting FCF by bonding managers to pay out more cash flows to service the debt. This will be especially beneficial to firms that generate large amounts of FCF, on which there are little 'hard' claims by outside investors. Hence:

Hypothesis 4: The expected shareholder wealth gains from PTPs are positively related to levels of free cash flows in the pre-transaction firm.

However, relying on debt to motivate managers may induce the agency costs of debt as debt gives managers the incentive to substitute low-risk assets for high-risk assets (an asset-substitution problem).

3.3 The Transaction Costs Hypothesis

DeAngelo et al. (1984) note that the costs of maintaining a stock exchange listing are very high. For UK companies with a market capitalization of £100 million, the admission fee to the London Stock Exchange (LSE) amounted to £43 700 in 2003 with an annual listing fee of £6280. These costs vary with the size of the corporation and the type of market on which it is listed. For example, for large firms, the direct costs of a listing on the Alternative Investment Market (AIM) are only half those of the official market.[11] In addition, the indirect costs of a listing on the AIM are likely to be much lower than those of a listing on the official market because the listing and disclosure requirements are lower on the AIM.[12] Depending on the size of the company, Benoit (1999) reports that for UK quoted firms, the fees paid to stockbrokers, registrars, lawyers, merchant bankers and financial PR companies, as well as the exchange fee and the auditing, printing and distribution of accounts, can even amount to £250 000.[13]

In short, the transaction costs hypothesis suggests that the wealth gains from going private are largely the result of the elimination of the direct and indirect costs associated with maintaining a stock exchange listing. Hence:

Hypothesis 5: The expected shareholder wealth gains from PTPs are positively related to the cost savings from eliminating the stock market listing.

3.4 The Takeover Defence Hypothesis

Lowenstein (1985) reports that some corporations have gone private via an MBO 'as a final defensive measure against a hostile shareholder or tender offer'. Afraid of losing their jobs when the hostile suitor takes control, management may take the company private. Singh (1990) reports that US MBOs were significantly more under takeover pressure prior to the MBO than a sample of matched firms. Stulz (1988) constructs a model in which pressures from the market for corporate control interact with managerial ownership and finds a curvilinear relationship with firm value. The high levels of equity ownership of firms where management is entrenched make it unlikely that these firms are taken over by outside parties (Jensen and Ruback, 1983). However, maintaining control over the company can put management in the predicament of having too much of their personal wealth invested in the firm (Halpern et al., 1999; Hubbard and Palia, 1995). In short, the takeover defence hypothesis suggests that the premiums in PTPs reflect the fact that the management team may intend to buy out the other shareholders in order to insulate itself against an unsolicited takeover. Hence:

Hypothesis 6: The expected shareholder wealth gains from PTPs are positively related to takeover pressure from the market for corporate control.

3.5 The Undervaluation Hypothesis

As a firm is a portfolio of projects, there may be asymmetric information between management and outsiders about the maximum value that can be realized with the assets in place. It is possible that management, which has superior private information, perceives that the share price is undervalued in relation to the true potential of the firm. This problem may be exacerbated where listed corporations, especially smaller ones, find it troublesome to use the equity market to fund expansion, as it may be difficult to attract the interest of institutional shareholders and fund managers. The lack of interest in such shares creates illiquidity and implies that they are likely to remain lowly valued, which provides an impetus to go private. Furthermore, if institutions attempt to sell shares in firms that experience thin trading, it is likely to have a noticeable effect on the share price, which will reduce the value of any remaining holdings.

There is some anecdotal and empirical evidence from the UK for this perceived undervaluation by management.[14] Lowenstein (1985) argues that, when management is the acquiring party, it may employ specific accounting techniques to depress the pre-announcement share price (see also Schadler and Karns, 1990). By manipulating dividends, refusing to meet with security analysts or even deliberately depressing earnings, managers can use the information asymmetry to their advantage prior to an MBO or IBO. Still, DeAngelo (1986) finds no evidence of systematic manipulation of pre-buyout accounting data by incumbent management.[15] The undervaluation hypothesis states that when the pre-transaction firm's stock is underperforming the management or an LBO specialist are able to pay higher premiums in a PTP transaction as they are expected to create additional shareholder value once the firm is private. Hence:

Hypothesis 7: The expected shareholder wealth gains from PTPs are positively related to the degree of ex ante share price undervaluation.

3.6 The Wealth Transfer Hypothesis

There are three main mechanisms through which a firm can transfer wealth from bondholders to stockholders: (i) by an unexpected increase in the risk of investment projects, or (ii) by (large increases in) dividend payments, or (iii) by an unexpected issue of debt of higher or equal seniority. In PTPs, the third mechanism in particular can lead to substantial bondholder wealth expropriation. Cook et al. (1992) and Warga and Welch (1993) show that bondholders with covenants offering low protection against corporate restructuring lose some percentage of their investment. Still, Amihud (1989) explains that the wealth transfer does not represent a loss for bondholders, but is rather a recuperation of the protection which was greater than was originally contracted for.

Hypothesis 8: The expected shareholder wealth gains from PTPs are positively related to the degree of bondholder protection in debt covenants.

The degree of bondholder protection can be examined by verifying whether or not debt covenants include provisions curbing dividend payouts or limiting the issue of new debt senior to the debt outstanding.[16]

The empirical literature has paid much less attention to wealth transfers other than those related to bondholders. Shleifer and Summers (1988) suggest that new investors in takeovers can break the implicit contracts between the firm and stakeholders, like employees by reducing employment and wages. Nevertheless, Weston et al. (1998) note that such hostility against employees is not observed in PTPs, although there is some evidence of large falls in employment after adjustment for industry effects in both the US and UK (Kaplan, 1989a; Smith, 1990; Harris et al., 2005).

4. DATA SOURCES, DESCRIPTIVE STATISTICS AND METHODOLOGY

4.1 Sample Selection and Data Sources

We retrieved all 181 UK public to private transactions completed between January 1997 and February 2003 from the database of the Centre for

Management Buy-out Research (CMBOR), which comprises the European population of leveraged buyouts and buy-ins and does not have a lower size threshold for inclusion. We excluded four firms due to data availability[17] and hence retain a sample of 177 firms. In addition to the firm name, the year of deal completion and the acquirer, the CMBOR database on these transactions contains data on deal value, firm activities, the financial structure underlying the transaction and certain post-transaction variables. We supplemented these data by collecting accounting information, bid details, the ownership structure and share price data from the following sources. Accounting data were gathered in the first instance from Extel cards (Thomson Research) and subsequently from the Worldscope database (LexisNexis). Where these two databases contained incomplete information, we consulted the annual reports. The details of the PTP bids were collected from Mergerstat reports which comprise the contextual anecdote on each buyout, a description of the business operations of the target and a financial summary on both firm and deal. These reports were complemented with information from the offer documents collected from Thomson Mergers, information from Securities Data Company (SDC), and press articles in the *Financial Times* over a period up to five years prior to each PTP transaction. We verified the data and eliminated inconsistencies by consulting the Regulatory News Service (RNS) announcements provided by UK-Wire Ltd. Access to the databases was granted by Deloitte Corporate Finance (Amsterdam).

Data on beneficial equity ownership stakes held by the management and by outside shareholders were collected from the last annual reports prior to the PTP.[18] All press articles on the 177 sample firms in the *Financial Times* for the five years leading up to the buyout transaction were collected to find data on flotations, restructurings, earnings warnings and CEO turnover. We complemented these data using the Chairman's Statements in annual reports and the offer documents. If no information was found in the *Financial Times* or in the annual reports, we assumed that a flotation, restructuring, earnings warning, or CEO removal did not take place.

Share prices adjusted for dividends and stock splits as well as the market capitalization by firm were collected from DataStream. From this database, we also downloaded the three-month Treasury Bill rate and the FTSE All Share Index. Our final sample of 177 PTPs is larger than most US studies (with exception of the studies by Goh et al., 2002 and Lehn and Poulsen, 1989). Also, while some authors restrict their sample only to the larger transactions (e.g. Kaplan, 1989a; Amihud, 1989), our study does not have a size bias.

4.2 Descriptive Statistics

4.2.1 Accounting and share-price-based measures

The summary statistics on accounting-based measures and share price performance are displayed in Table 3.1 for every type of transaction. The size of the average firm measured by total assets amounts to £200.7 million. While average size is similar to that of US LBOs in the Kaplan (1989a) sample, our median size is substantial lower. The largest firm in our sample is MEPC Plc, with an asset size of roughly £4 billion. In order to successfully complete the larger deals, sophisticated financial engineering techniques are imperative.[19] Consequently, large firms are more likely to be targeted by institutional buyers with specialized financial engineering capabilities, rather than by management teams, which Table 3.1 confirms. The average debt–equity ratio amounts to 34.5%. Firms retain 11% of their assets in cash or cash equivalents.

Our sample firms have a return on assets (ROA) of 3.7% but there are significant differences by type of deal (Table 3.1). Firms with negative accounting returns, indicating an underperforming management, are more likely to be subject to an MBI. IBOs focus on better performing firms which have on average an ROA of 5.7%. Panel A of Table 3.2 shows that the share price returns of UK PTP candidates have substantially underperformed the market, especially in the peak years of the equity boom (1998–99). This suggests that MBOs, MBIs and IBOs have a disciplinary nature.[20] However, an alternative interpretation is that these corporate control transactions are merely a reaction to the undervaluation of the target firms' shares. This is especially likely for small cap firms, which, on average, underperformed the market in the 1990s by 6% per year,[21] only to revive in 1999. One of the reasons for this phenomenon was the decreasing institutional interest in small caps due to consolidation in the fund management industry (CMBOR, 2002). Barred from equity funding, small, listed companies experienced considerable problems to gain access to growth capital to fund acquisitions or organic expansion. Private equity firms have taken advantage of this need for funds by taking undervalued firms private. The returns made by shareholders in the process reattracted institutional interest towards the end of 1999.

Panel B of Table 3.2 compares the market capitalization of the 44 sample firms floated since 1993 at the flotation date, and the market capitalization based on the offer price at the PTP announcement. On average, these firms lost £382.2 million or 12.8% of their value at flotation. Some subsamples managed to generate a positive share price return (4.8% in 1999, 8.8% in 2000, 3.7% in 2001), but even here the annualized returns are small.

Table 3.1 Descriptive statistics on accounting, cash flow and share-price-based measures

		Mean	Median	Std dev.	Min.	Max.
All sample firms (n=177)						
Firm size	Total sales (£ million)	158.6	56.3	347.8	0.8	2574.2
	Total assets (£ million)	200.7	62	453.9	0.9	4065.7
	Total market value (£ m)	87	33.9	161.7	0.6	1370.7
Performance	Return on assets (%)	3.7	5.6	19.2	−190	36
Leverage and taxes	Debt to equity (%)	34.5	12.1	53	0	284.5
	Taxes (% of sales)	2.5	1.8	2.8	−2.4	18.7
Cash flow and retention	Cash to assets (%)	11	4.9	16.1	0	95.9
	Free cash flow (% of assets)	5	5.9	16.6	−100	48.1
MBO (137 firms)						
Firm size	Total sales (£ million)	103.5	52.1	186.6	1.5	1815.8
	Total assets (£ million)	153.2	58.6	337.7	0.9	3296
	Total market value (£ m)	62.5	30.9	91.1	0.6	655.5
Performance	Return on assets (%)	3.9	6.1	21.1	−190	36
Leverage and taxes	Debt to equity (%)	32.4	9	53	0	284.5
	Taxes (% of sales)	2.7	2	2.8	−0.6	18.7
Cash flow and retention	Cash to assets (%)	11.9	6.6	16.9	0	95.9
	Free cash flow (% of assets)	5.4	5.9	17.3	−100	48.1
MBI (18 firms)						
Firm size	Total sales (£ million)	299.2	67.1	580.4	8.4	1889.8
	Total assets (£ million)	232.9	65.6	408.5	12.7	1608.4
	Total market value (£ m)	112.3	23.6	202.9	6.9	738.7
Performance	Return on assets (%)	−1.0	1.8	12.7	−47.7	9
Leverage and taxes	Debt to equity (%)	48.1	28	66.2	0	257
	Taxes (% of sales)	1.1	0.3	1.6	−0.3	5.2
Cash flow and retention	Cash to assets (%)	10.5	2	16.5	0	50
	Free cash flow (% of assets)	0.7	1.9	15.9	−48.5	30.9
IBO (22 firms)						
Firm size	Total sales (£ million)	387.1	121.7	651.2	0.8	2574.2
	Total assets (£ million)	469.6	164.5	872.8	10.1	4065.7
	Total market value (£ m)	218.8	110.3	330.8	8.1	1370.7
Performance	Return on Assets (%)	5.7	6	8.3	−18.7	24.9
Leverage and taxes	Debt to equity (%)	37	20.4	39.8	0	136.6
	Taxes (% of sales)	2.3	1.5	3.2	−2.4	12.3
Cash flow and retention	Cash to assets (%)	5.9	2.6	7.9	0	28.3
	Free cash flow (% of assets)	6.1	6.5	11.6	−23.3	28

Note: This table summarizes the descriptive statistics on accounting data and share-price-based measures.

Sources: Extel Cards, *Financial Times*, annual reports and own calculations.

Table 3.2 Average share price performance in the year prior to PTP and performance since flotation

Panel A: average market-adjusted share return by year

Year	Firms	Share return – FT All Shares return (%)	*t*-value	FT All Share return (%)	*t*-value
1997	7	−11.9	−1.796	15.1	6.360***
1998	27	−36.4	−5.863***	22.9	18.423***
1999	46	−31.8	−7.549***	5.6	5.864***
2000	42	−6.8	−2.644**	11.1	12.557***
2001	32	−1.2	−1.169	−2.0	−1.920*
2002	20	4.6	−0.981	−16.3	−13.085***
2003	3	−7.8	−0.592	−19.3	−7.838***

Panel B: market cap (in £ millions) of sample firms floated since 1993, measured at the flotation and at the first announcement date of the PTP

Year of PTP	Firms	Market cap at flotation date	Market cap at offer price of PTP	Difference	Return (%)
1997	2	84.6	86.0	1.4	1.7
1998	10	543.9	483.2	−60.7	−11.7
1999	14	508.0	532.4	24.4	4.8
2000	7	744.0	809.5	65.5	8.8
2001	5	332.3	344.7	12.4	3.7
2002	6	771.7	346.4	−425.3	−55.1
Total	44	2984.5	2602.3	−382.2	−12.8

Notes: Panel A shows the share price performance in the year prior to the PTP. The share price performance is measured from –300 to –41 days before the first announcement of takeover interest that eventually led to the PTP. The performance of the FTSE All Shares Index was calculated in the same way for each individual firm. Panel B shows the market capitalization for those sample firms that were floated after 1993, at the floatation date and at the first announcement data of the PTP transaction. ***, **, and * stand for statistical significance at the 1, 5 and 10% levels.

Source: Own calculations.

4.2.2 Industry composition

Our sample contains companies from the wider business spectrum. Practically half of the deals in 1998 took place in the business services sector, representing about 25% of PTP value that year. In 1999, the business services sector again broke records in terms of number of deals, although the average value remained modest. Roughly 40% of the MBO transactions took place in two sectors: manufacturing and business services. In 1999, manufacturing accounted for the largest share of total deal value, followed by retail distribution. MBIs account for more than one-third of all deals done in retail distribution, a sector characterized by high cash generation and stable competition. In 2000, the property sector experienced the largest deal observed so far with the £3.5 billion IBO of MEPC Plc. In value terms, the sector represents nearly a third of total transactions, but in terms of number of deals only accounts for 20% of the total PTP activity. The takeover battle for Hillsdown Plc was the second largest deal in 2000 and emphasizes the importance of the manufacturing sector among PTPs. After 2000, the total value of the deals decreased in this sector, but it still remained in second place. Few PTP deals have been completed in the financial sector, but Willis Corroon's Plc management buyout of £851 million was a substantial transaction. Few high-tech firms went private after economic conditions changed radically when the bubble burst in 2000. Contrary to our expectations, more deals were completed in this sector before the bubble rather than after. It is remarkable that IBOs, representing merely 12.5% of the full sample, account for one-third of all transactions in the high-tech sector.[22]

4.2.3 Deal characteristics

Table 3.3 summarizes the characteristics of our PTPs, as well as presenting data on the company histories for the five years preceding the event. Following previous studies (e.g. Goergen and Renneboog, 2004), a transaction is classified as hostile when the board of the target rejects the first offer. Panel A reveals that 7.3% of the PTPs were hostile, which is largely due to the fact that about a third of MBIs were opposed by the target board.[23] Private equity firms try to avoid hostile transactions as they frequently result in the loss of company specific information and skills if the incumbent management departs.[24] In certain IBOs, the continuing involvement of the executive directors is sometimes an explicit condition in the offer.[25]

Bidder competition involves a long-standing debate regarding PTPs. In order to protect minority shareholders, Lowenstein (1985) argued for its institutionalization, while Amihud (1989) concluded that this would deter possible buyers from making a bid in the first place. Paul Myners,[26] former head of fund manager Gartmore, recently argued for a prohibition on management increasing their initial offer in the event of a higher bid, as a method to 'reduce the scope for executives to take shareholders for too much of a ride'. Our sample contains only eleven transactions with more than one bidder in the PTP process, evenly distributed over deal types.[27] In these cases, the management initiated an MBO immediately after having been approached by an outside bidder.[28] White knight

Table 3.3 Descriptive statistics on deal characteristics and company history

	All sample firms (177 firms)		137 MBOs		18 MBIs		22 IBOs	
	Number	%	Number	%	Number	%	Number	%
Panel A: deal characteristics								
Hostile bid	13	7.3	6	4.4	5	27.8	2	9.1
Bidder competition	11	6.2	8	5.8	1	5.6	2	9.1
Defensive action	4	2.3	4	2.9	0	0.0	0	0.0
Financial distress	5	2.8	3	2.2	1	5.6	1	4.5
Deal equity value> £100 m	52	29.4	36	26.3	4	22.2	12	54.5
Deal equity value between £50 m and 100 m	37	20.9	32	23.4	2	11.1	2	9.1
Panel B: company history								
Prior acquisition interest	34	19.2	26	19.0	6	33.3	2	9.1
LBO	12	6.8	10	7.3	0	0.0	2	9.1
AIM	11	6.2	9	6.6	2	11.1	0	0.0
IPO 3	17	9.6	11	8.0	3	16.7	3	13.6
IPO 5	32	18.1	26	19.0	3	16.7	3	13.6
Restructuring 3	28	15.8	17	12.4	4	22.2	7	31.8
Restructuring 5	48	27.1	35	25.5	4	22.2	9	40.9
Profit warning 3	67	37.9	50	36.5	9	50.0	8	36.4
Profit warning 5	81	45.8	59	43.1	12	66.7	10	45.5
CEO 3	44	24.9	35	25.5	4	22.2	5	22.7
CEO 5	61	34.5	47	34.3	6	33.3	8	36.4

Notes: This table shows descriptive statistics on deal characteristics and company history by PTP type. Hostile is a dummy variable that equals 1 if the first bid was rejected. Bidder competition equals 1 if there was more than 1 bidder. Defensive transaction equals 1 if the PTP was enacted to protect against unwanted possible takeover. Financial distress equals 1 if the firm depends on the benevolence of banks to survive. LBO equals 1 if the firm was subject to an LBO before. AIM equals 1 if the firm is listed on the Alternative Investment Market. IPO 3 (5) equals 1 if firm was floated 3 (5) years before the PTP. Restructuring 3 (5) equals 1 if the firm's assets were restructured 3 (5) years before the PTP. Profit warning 3 (5) equals 1 if the firm issued a profit warning 3 (5) years before PTP. CEO 3 (5) equals 1 if CEO was replaced 3 (5) years before PTP.

Source: Annual reports, *Financial Times*, Regulatory News Service and own calculations.

transactions were not found to be present among MBIs and IBOs. Five firms were in financial distress before the transaction and dependent on the benevolence of banks for the continuation of their operations. In three of these five cases, the banks had actually announced that they were terminating their investments, such that these firms had to seek a new life-line.

As expected from the numbers presented in Table 3.1, most of the larger deals involving an equity investment of more than £100 million are IBOs.

4.2.4 Company history

Panel B of Table 3.3 presents summary statistics for the recent company history leading up to the public to private transaction. On average, 19% of the sample firms experience some type of takeover pressure (e.g. published rumors, takeover negotiations, or an offer for the shares) in the year prior to going private. For 12 firms, the PTP was not the first encounter with leveraged buyouts: they had undergone an LBO, an MBO, or in most cases, a divisional buyout in the past. The time between the first and the second transaction was sufficiently large not to distinguish these firms from the others in the sample. Eleven firms were listed on the AIM when going private. Lower entry criteria, a less stringent regulatory regime and certain tax benefits for investing in AIM firms[29] seriously reduce the burden of a listing on the AIM.

Almost 20% of our firms were floated less than five years before returning to private ownership. Lowenstein (1985) describes how a decline in stock markets following a hot issue market can be misused by founder/managers with large shareholdings. In the presence of a collective action problem amongst dispersed shareholders, they can take the company private at a depressed share price. The controversy stems from the impression that these types of transactions, in the short period that they reside on the public equity markets, transfer a disproportionally large share of the firm's risk onto the claims of the outside shareholders for which they are not compensated by sharing in potential future improvements.

Forty-eight firms engaged in asset restructurings in the five years leading up to the transaction, with 28 restructurings concentrated in the last three years. Firms that go private through an MBO restructure significantly less frequently over the three years prior to the buyout. This is not surprising given that management can time the MBO.[30] If management undertakes major asset restructuring before the PTP, less additional value can be created after the PTP. Firms that restructured are more likely to go private through an IBO. Almost half the firms have given a profit warning at least once during the five years prior to their PTP. This provides some support for the fact that PTPs are important mechanisms to restructure poorly performing companies. Table 3.3 also gives some data on board restructuring: in a quarter of the sample, the CEO had to depart in the three-year period leading up to the PTP. A new CEO could, for instance, initiate a new strategy, with going private as a key element in a successful restructuring.[31]

4.2.5 Ownership

All large shareholders (owning share stakes of at least 3%) were categorized into one of nine categories: banks, investment and pension funds, insurance companies, industrial and commercial companies, individuals or families, the government, real estate companies, directors and venture capitalists. As documented above, good monitors reduce agency and information asymmetry problems. More specifically, Franks and Nyborg (1996) show that outside blockholders increase the probability of corporate restructuring.[32] The Herfindahl index in Table 3.4 shows that there is large dispersion of share stakes in the sample firms. On average, the dominant shareholder owns 23.5% of the shares.

The nature of ownership is also an important dimension of the ownership structure (Holderness and Sheehan, 1988). For example, Franks et al. (2001) find that institutional investors do not perform a monitoring role in the UK. These institutional investors have a stake larger than 3% in almost 90% of the sample firms, and are the largest shareholder in 45% of the sample firms. The average holding of a substantial director/shareholder is higher, at 12.5%. Prior to the PTP, venture capitalists were the largest shareholder in only three sample firms. Table 3.4 also presents the ownership data by deal type. Not surprisingly, in the firms that go private through an MBO, directors have larger ownership stakes (which is significantly different from the other types at the 1% level). The fact that directors of firms that go private through MBIs own 9.2% of the equity explains the high level of hostility in this type of transaction. Firms that go private through an IBO have lower equity stakes in the hands of directors (significantly lower at the 1% level), while the average stake controlled by an institution is considerably higher (at the 5% level of significance).

4.2.6 Summary

The descriptive statistics have shown that the sample firms are not drawn from a homogeneous population. MBOs typically are smaller firms, in which the directors possess a larger share of the firm's equity. Their deal characteristics are generally characterized by a low hostility rate, and are occasionally driven by defensive measures. MBIs seem to be the exact counterpart. They are typically larger than MBOs, and seem to occur in mature industries with high levels of free cash flow. On average they suffer

Table 3.4 Descriptive statistics on substantial shareholdings

	Mean (%)	Median (%)	Std dev. (%)	Presence (%)	Dominance (%)
All firms					
Banks	3.4	0.0	5.5	40.1	7.9
Investment and pension funds	10.5	8.9	8.9	89.8	34.5
Insurance companies	2.2	0.0	3.5	37.3	3.4
Industrial and commercial co's	2.2	0.0	7.4	14.1	6.2
Individual or family	3.7	0.0	10.1	31.6	6.2
Real estate funds	1.6	0.0	6.0	8.5	5.6
Directors	12.5	4.2	17.6	58.2	32.2
Venture capital and private equity	1.6	0.0	4.9	14.1	4.0
Herfindahl index	11.0	6.6	12.1	na	na
Dominant shareholder	23.5	18.7	16.0	na	100.0
MBO					
Banks	3.3	0.0	5.3	38.7	8.0
Investment and pension funds	9.8	8.6	7.6	89.8	32.1
Insurance companies	2.2	0.0	3.4	37.2	2.9
Industrial and commercial co's	1.8	0.0	5.9	12.4	5.8
Individual or family	3.5	0.0	9.2	34.3	5.1
Real estate funds	1.6	0.0	6.1	8.0	5.1
Directors	14.1	7.6	18.4	63.5	37.2
Venture capital and private equity	1.3	0.0	4.3	12.4	3.6
Herfindahl index	11.0	6.6	12.1	na	na
Dominant shareholder	23.4	18.6	15.9	na	100.0
MBI					
Banks	4.1	0.0	7.6	38.9	11.1
Investment and pension funds	8.6	7.0	6.3	88.9	16.7
Insurance companies	1.9	0.0	3.5	27.8	0.0
Industrial and commercial co's	7.5	0.0	15.9	27.8	16.7
Individual or family	6.8	0.0	18.2	27.8	16.7
Real estate funds	3.1	0.0	8.0	16.7	11.1
Directors	9.2	1.6	15.9	50.0	22.2
Venture capital and private equity	2.4	0.0	6.5	16.7	5.6
Herfindahl index	14.1	9.3	14.2	na	na
Dominant shareholder	28.1	23.5	18.8	na	100.0
IBO					
Banks	3.8	1.7	4.5	50.0	4.5
Investment and pension funds	16.0	13.5	14.7	90.9	63.6
Insurance companies	2.8	0.0	4.2	45.5	9.1

Table 3.4 (continued)

	Mean (%)	Median (%)	Std dev. (%)	Presence (%)	Dominance (%)
Industrial and commercial co's	0.6	0.0	1.8	13.6	0.0
Individual or family	2.0	0.0	5.1	18.2	4.5
Real estate funds	0.6	0.0	2.8	4.5	4.5
Directors	5.3	0.0	10.2	31.8	9.1
Venture capital and private equity	2.8	0.0	6.8	22.7	4.5
Herfindahl index	8.6	5.8	10.2	na	na
Dominant shareholder	20.8	16.0	13.9	na	100.0

Note: This table shows the substantial shareholdings (>5%) by category of owner. It should be noted that the means, medians and standard deviations are calculated conditional on the presence of a stake of that specific shareholder type. The Herfindahl index captures the concentration of the shareholdings. Dominance shows in which percentage of the firms the shareholder of a particular type is the largest shareholder. Dominant shareholder shows the average percentage of ownership of the largest shareholder regardless of his category.

from negative accounting performance, although this does not result in lower share price performance than for the other deal types. A relatively large proportion of MBIs involve hostile bids. IBOs are typically larger in size and seem to have better prospects than the other deal types. Their ownership structure is characterized as one where directors typically own a small proportion of the shares and institutional investors are the dominant shareholders. The low cash-to-assets ratio seems to confirm that these firms are growth firms that may provide good platforms for buy-and-build strategies of private equity firms.

5. METHODOLOGY

The shareholder wealth effects in buyout research are generally analysed through two different methodologies: a premiums analysis or an event study. Each method has its own advantages but they can jointly increase the power of econometric tests in PTP research.

5.1 Event Study Methodology

When the marketplace is rational, the informational content of an event should be immediately reflected in asset prices (Campbell et al., 1997). The problem with LBO research is that the abnormal returns (ARs) may be cross-sectionally incomparable, due to the non-uniformity of the information releases. Two subsamples can be distinguished. For the first subsample, the initial announcement is e.g. a recommended offer, a (hostile) tender offer, a firm intention, a mandatory offer triggered by the activation of rule nine of the City Code,[33] or simply a notification of negotiations with a disclosed party. Consequently, investors know what type of deal has emerged (i.e. a leveraged PTP of the type MBO, MBI or IBO). For the second subsample, the information reaches the market in two stages: there is an initial notification of an imminent deal[34] (event 1), but the announcement disclosing the deal type only follows later (event 2). Some earlier research has taken the second date as the event date. It is clear that such results are biased due to the fact that the initial announcement (event 1) has a large effect on the share price and that event 2 could be regarded as a correction to event 1. Hence, a correct analysis of the shareholder wealth effects of the announcement of an MBO, MBI or IBO requires the definition of two events:

Event 1: The very first announcement of takeover interest in the target firm that eventually leads to the PTP.
Event 2: The very first announcement that identifies a going-private proposal.

For 64% of our sample, events 1 and 2 coincide, but in 36%, the first announcement that starts the takeover process does not reveal the identity of the bidding party. For these firms, there are on average 51 working days between the two events and this period does not vary substantially between MBOs, MBIs and IBOs. Therefore, we add the cumulative average abnormal returns (CAARs) for events 1 and 2 (while excluding overlap in event windows). Thus, the resulting CAARs of the two subsamples may be more comparable.

5.1.1 Abnormal return estimation

ARs are calculated as the difference between the daily logarithmic returns corrected for dividends and stock splits, and the expected returns as predicted by the CAPM. The risk-free rate is proxied by the three-month treasury bill rate. The systematic risk is estimated over a period of 235 until 41 trading days prior to event 1 (day 0) using the FTSE All Shares Index. We correct the betas for non-synchronous trading (Dimson, 1979), apply a correction for regression to the mean and winsorize the betas at the 5% and 95% level.

To test the null hypothesis that ARs are equal to zero, the parametric significance tests based on the variance of ARs in the estimation window are employed as in Kothari and Warner (1997). We also compute a nonparametric generalized sign test (see Cowan, 1992) to verify the robustness of the results (see Appendix 3A).

5.2 Analysis of Premiums

As an alternative to abnormal returns, many papers (e.g. Kaplan, 1989a,b; Lehn and Poulsen, 1989; Halpern et al., 1999) confine the measurement of wealth effects to the premium offered to the shareholders. The premium is the logarithm of the final price offered by the acquiring party divided by the share price before the first announcement (events 1+2 for the firms with information releases in stages): premium=ln(final price offered/pre-takeover share price). Under this specification, the measured premium impounds the informational value of any announcement made during the going-private process, such as (amended) bid prices, bidder competition, and the identification of the acquiring party. Thus, the premium is calculated over a period comprising event windows 1 and 2 and the period in between.

There are several variations on the definitions of the 'final price offered' and the 'pre-takeover share price'. As the final price, we take the final offer price of the winning bid (as do e.g. Harlow and Howe, 1993). Alternatively, Halpern et al. (1999) and Lehn and Poulsen (1989) use the final traded price of the shares in the market before the delisting. They believe that the final traded price best reflects the market value of a bid comprising securities. However, as a PTP bid frequently contains payment in loan notes,[35] the market value of such an offer cannot be inferred from the last traded share price. The reason is that the shares which are tendered are not sold to the bidder via the market. Instead, in the UK, shareholders can accept or reject a tender offer for their shares by completing and returning the form of acceptances.[36] This means that the price movements observed in the market are speculative only. The last, true assessment of the final bid is not observable from stock market data.

The difficulty with the benchmark 'pre-takeover share price' is the choice of the date. To allow for the share price run-up in the period preceding the first announcement of takeover interest, a period of 20 or 40 days prior to the event date is chosen. We call this the 'anticipation window'. Kaplan's (1989a) LBO study on the US and Goergen and Renneboog's (2004) study on European M&As both mention that the anticipation window spans approximately two months before the initial announcement. We also opt for 40 working days.[37] The test statistics are given in Appendix 3A.

6. RESULTS

6.1 Wealth Effects of Leveraged PTPs: Abnormal Returns and Premiums

Panel A of Table 3.5 shows the premiums offered in all UK PTPs, 1997–2003: a shareholder selling his shares to the final bidder will earn a premium of approximately 41%. This is in line with the US evidence from the 1980s where the premium ranges from 33% to 56% (Table 3.6). The most recent UK study by Weir et al. (2005a) shows a premium of 45% (Table 3.6). The premiums by transaction type are presented in panel B of Table 3.5. IBOs, MBOs and MBIs generate premiums of 43%, 42% and 41%, respectively. The difference (across anticipation windows of various lengths) is not statistically significant. Out of the 177 UK PTPs, five are in financial distress and have an important negative impact on the average premium. Excluding the five distressed firms increases the premium by 3.5% in Table 3.5. At the other extreme, the highest premium offered for a company was almost 180%.[38]

Table 3.5 Premiums by type of leveraged PTP and by anticipation window

Panel A: premiums by anticipation window, 1997–2003 (sample = 177 firms)

Anticipation window	Obs.	Mean	*t*-value	Min.	25% quartile	Median	75% quartile	Max.
1 day	177	37.0	9.247***	−96.3	20.8	35.5	55.6	175
10 days	177	41.1	9.889***	−96.3	22.5	38.7	60.2	179.7
20 days	177	41.0	9.993***	−96.1	25.0	39.5	58.7	171.1
40 days	177	40.1	8.786***	−96.9	25.7	38.5	56.9	171.1

Panel B: premiums by type of PTP

Deal type	Anticipation window	Obs.	Mean (%)	*t*-value
MBO	20 days	137	40.6	8.314***
	40 days		39.1	7.579***
MBI	20 days	18	42.0	4.382***
	40 days		38.8	2.957**
IBO	20 days	22	42.6	3.970**
	40 days		47.4	2.957**

Notes: The premiums (%) are calculated as follows: the anticipation window is the number of days prior to the announcement date of the leveraged PTP. Obs. stands for the number of observations (firms). ***, ** and * stand for statistical significance at the 1%, 5% and 10% levels, respectively.

Source: Own calculations.

Table 3.6 International evidence on premiums paid in PTPs

Study	Sample period/country	Type of deal	Anticipation window	*N*	Mean premium offered (%)
DeAngelo, DeAngelo and Rice (1984)	1973–1980 US	ALL	40 days	72	56.3
Lowenstein (1985)	1979–1984 US	MBO	30 days	28	56.0
Lehn and Poulsen (1989)	1980–1987 US	ALL	20 days	257	36.1
Amihud (1989)	1983–1986 US	MBO	20 days	15	42.9
Kaplan (1989a,b)	1980–1985 US	MBO	2 months	76	42.3
Asquith and Wizman (1990)	1980–1988 US	ALL	1 day	47	37.9
Harlow and Howe (1993)	1980–1989 US	ALL	20 days	121	44.9
Travlos and Cornett (1993)	1975–1983 US	ALL	1 month	56	41.9
Easterwood et al. (1994)	1978–1988 US	MBO	20 days	184	32.9
Weir et al. (2005a)	1998–2000 UK	ALL	1 month	95	44.9

Notes: This table shows the studies that estimate the shareholder wealth effects using a premiums analysis. ALL = all going private deals. MBO = MBO deals only. *N* is the number of sample firms.

The wealth effects corrected for market reactions as captured by the CAARs are given in Table 3.7. The left-hand side of the table presents the abnormal returns over different event windows for the first announcement of the PTP. Over the event window [–5, 5], the CAARs amount to 26%, while over longer windows, the CAARs modestly increase to 29% (panel A of Table 3.7). Panel B shows that the wealth effects of the different types of PTP transactions are very similar. In contrast to M&A research, we find that there is little evidence of a price run-up due to leakage of information or trading on rumours (not reported in the tables). Although the CAARs are negative in the [–40, –6] event window, this is entirely caused by the financially distressed firms. The distressed firms reduce the wealth effects of the PTP announcements. Excluding these firms from our sample increases the CAARs by about 4%.

As pointed out in the methodology section, for some firms the first announcement of a PTP only relates to a takeover (event 1) and does not reveal the bidding party nor the type of PTP. The deal type follows in a subsequent press release (event 2). Figure 3.2 shows that it is important to

Table 3.7 CAARs for leveraged PTPs

Panel A: CAARs by event window (observations =177)

Window	Event 1				Events 1+2			
	CAAR (%)	Simple *t*-stat.	K and W *t*-stat.	Gen. sign test	CAAR (%)	Simple *t*-stat.	K and W *t*-stat.	Gen. sign test.
[–1, 0]	22.68	13.889***	66.111***	13.522***	25.17	11.229***	72.245***	13.824***
[–5, 5]	25.53	11.573***	30.908***	13.673***	28.17	10.034***	33.710***	13.673***
[–40, 40]	29.28	10.439***	12.335***	13.673***	30.79	8.042***	12.590***	13.673***

Panel B: CAARS by deal type

Deal type	Event 1				Events 1+2			
	Window	Mean (%)	*t*-value	Median	Deal type	Mean (%)	*t*-value	Median
MBO	[–1, 0]	22.7	14.444***	18.3	MBO	24.3	10.724***	21.5
(Obs. = 137)	[–5, 5]	25.7	11.414***	24.8		28.2	9.030***	27.9
	[–40, 40]	30.8	12.252***	29.7		33.4	8.575***	31.3
MBI	[–1, 0]	22.6	5.536***	18.3	MBI	27.7	6.194***	26.3
(Obs. = 18)	[–5, 5]	24.4	6.345***	19.8		27.5	5.104***	22.3
	[–40, 40]	36.1	5.676***	31.5		37.7	4.636***	43.5
IBO	[–1, 0]	23.73	2.597**	21.64	IBO	30.21	2.622**	23.62

(Obs. = 22)	[–5, 5]	26.24	2.303*	24.39		29.88	2.672**	32.53
	[–40, 40]	27.39	2.263*	29.11		32.00	2.785**	33.54

Notes: This table shows the CAARs of firms going private in the UK over the period 1997–2003 for different event windows. Event 1 is the first date of any takeover interest that eventually leads to the PTP. For 36% of the sample, the information on the PTP arrives in stages: a first announcement of takeover interest (event1) and a second one in which the bidding party is revealed and it becomes clear that the bid is a leveraged buyout (event 2). Events 1 + 2 combines the CAARS of both events provided there is no overlap in event windows. Expected returns were calculated with the CAPM corrected for thin trading and mean reversion. The betas were trimmed at the 5% and the 95% level of the distribution. The estimation window spans transaction days –235 to –41 whereby 0 stands for the first announcement date. The FTSE All Share Index is the market index. The details on the calculationof the test statistics are given in Appendix A. Obs. stands for the number of observations (firms).***, ** and * stand for statistical significance at the 1%, 5% and 10% levels, respectively.

Source: Own calculations.

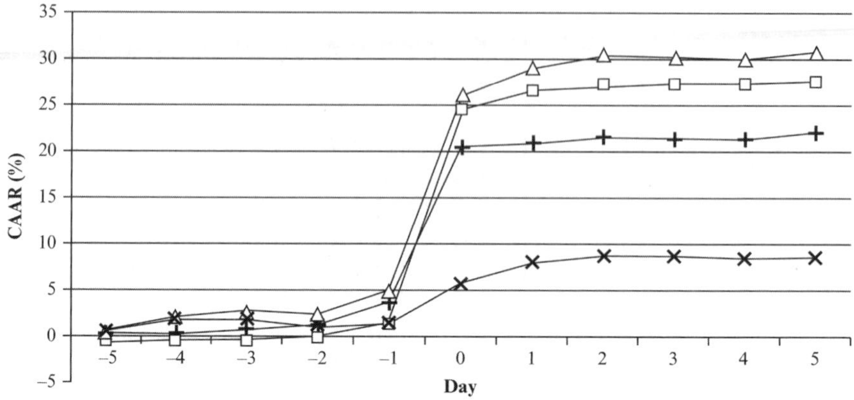

Legend: All information released at once: □=CAAR of 'all-in-one' PTP announcement (event 1) (1).
Information is released in stages:
+ =CAAR of takeover announcement (event 1) but the identity of acquirer and type of deal is not yet announced (2).
×=CAAR of announcement of the identity of the acquirer and the type of deal for firms about which only partial information had been released earlier (event 2) (3).
Δ combines + and ×: CAAR of events 1 and 2 combined for firms with information releases in stages (4).

Notes: This figure shows the cumulative average abnormal returns of firms going private in the UK from 1997 to 2003. The figure distinguishes 4 lines: (1) shows the 'all-in-one' CAAR, for those announcements by which the bidder or the type of deal is identified, (2) shows the CAAR for those announcements in which the bidder is not revealed, (3) shows the average CAAR for those PTP announcements for which an earlier announcement was made that a takeover was imminent without specifying the details of the type of deal (events 1 and 2 do not coincide), (4) shows an artificial CAAR constructed by summing the CAARs of event 1 (line 2) and event 2 (line 3). The CAARs are summed, provided that the announcement date of event 2 does not fall within the event window of event 1. The sample contains 177 observations. Expected returns were calculated with the CAPM, and the CAPM parameters were calculated from a market model regression, corrected for thin trading and mean reversion of the systematic risk. The beta parameters were trimmed at the 5% and the 95% distribution range. The estimation window was run from –235 to –41 days before the first announcement of takeover, and the FTSE All Share Index was used as the market index.

Figure 3.2 Shareholder wealth effects by type of announcement

consider both events 1 and 2 for firms in which the PTP announcement comes in stages. When only considering event 1 or event 2 – as traditional PTP research frequently has – the wealth effects are downward biased. The right-hand side of Table 3.7 shows the combined effects of events 1 and 2. Table 3.8 enables us to compare our findings with those from the US and to conclude that UK PTPs generate market reactions that are largely similar to those in the US.

Table 3.8 Previous evidence of CAARs in PTPs

Study	Sample period/country	Type of deal	Event window	*N*	CAAR (%)
DeAngelo, DeAngelo and Rice (1984)	1973–1980 US	ALL	[–1, 0] days	72	22.27
			[–10, 10] days	72	28.05
Torabzadeh and Bertin (1987)	1982–1985 US	ALL	[–1, 0] months	48	18.64
			[–1, 1] months	48	20.57
Lehn and Poulsen (1989)	1980–1987 US	ALL	[–1, 1] days	244	16.30
			[–10, 10] days	244	19.90
Amihud (1989)	1983–1986 US	MBO	[–20, 0] days	15	19.60
Kaplan (1989a,b)	1980–1985 US	MBO	[–40, 60] days	76	26.00
Marais et al. (1989)	1974–1985 US	ALL	[0, 1] days	80	13.00
			[–69, 1] days	80	22.00
Slovin et al. (1991)	1980–1988 US	ALL	[–1, 0] days	128	17.35
			[–15, 15] days	128	24.86
Lee (1992)	1973–1989 US	MBO	[–1, 0] days	114	14.90
			[–69, 0] days	114	22.40
Frankfurter and Gunay (1992)	1979–1984 US	MBO	[–50, 50] days	110	27.32
			[–1, 0] days	110	17.24
Travlos and Cornett (1993)	1975–1983 US	ALL	[–1, 0] days	56	16.20
			[–10, 10] days	56	19.24
Lee et al. (1992)	1983–1989 US	MBO	[–1, 0] days	50	17.84
			[–5, 0] days	50	20.96
Van de Gucht and Moore (1998)	1980–1992 US	ALL	[–1, 1] days	187	15.60
			[–10, 10] days	187	20.20
Goh et al. (2002)	1980–1996 US	ALL	[–20, 1] days	323	21.31
			[0, 1] days	323	12.68

Notes: This table shows papers that estimate shareholder wealth effects via event studies. ALL = all going private deals. MBO = MBO deals only. All CAARs are statistically significant at the 1% level.

6.2 The Determinants of Shareholder Wealth Gains from Going Private

We test the hypotheses of Section 3 by estimating cross-sectional regressions using both the premium (with an anticipation window of 20 and 40 days) and the CAARs (with event windows [–2, 2] and [–10, 10]) as dependent variables. As explained above, we add the CAARs of event 2 to those of event 1 in case of information releases in stages. Although the full sample of PTPs consists of 177 observations, we exclude the five financially distressed firms as most of the hypotheses are not applicable to these companies. We briefly discuss the motives for distressed PTPs below. All models are tested for the presence of heteroscedasticity by means of a White test (White, 1980) and the results are not biased by multicollinearity.[39]

The tax benefit hypothesis predicts that firms with higher pre-transaction tax bills will benefit more from the interest deductibility associated with increased leverage. Hence, as in previous research (e.g. Lehn and Poulsen, 1989; Kieschnick, 1998; Halpern et al., 1999), we include taxes-to-sales and expect a positive relation between this variable and the wealth effects (see Table 3.9). As discussed in Section 3, a significantly positive relation between the wealth gains and the interaction term of taxes and performance may imply that bidders are willing to pay more for a firm with high past earnings profitability. This may indicate that the tax shields

Table 3.9 Summary of hypotheses and findings

Hypothesis	Abbreviation	Expected sign	Result
H1: Tax benefit	Taxes (as % of sales)	+	Not significant
	Taxes* performance (1 if ROA > median)	+	Not significant
	Debt/equity ratio	–	Negative
H2: Incentive realignment	Managerial ownership	–	Strongly negative
H3: Control	Institutional blockholder	–	Negative
	Corporation blockholder	–	Strongly negative
	Family blockholder	–	Not significant
H4: Free cash flow	Free cash flow	+	Not significant
H5: Transaction costs	AIM listing (1=yes)	–	Negative
H6: Takeover defence	Prior takeover interest (1=yes)	+	Not significant
H7: Undervaluation	Share performance* MBO	–	Strongly negative
	Share performance* MBI	–	Not significant
	Share performance* IBO	–	Strongly negative
Control variables	Hostile bid (1=yes)	–	Not significant
	CEO was removed past 2 years (1=yes)	–	Strongly negative
	Corporate restructuring in past 5 years (1=yes)	–	Not significant
	Pre-2000	+	Not significant
	Bidder competition (1=yes)	+	Strongly positive

induced by the increased leverage are high and will be sustainable in the future.

Table 3.10 reveals that the tax coefficients are not significant but that bidders are willing to pay higher premiums for firms with lower debt–equity ratios. The fact that the tax variables are not significant stands in contrast with the findings for US PTPs (e.g. Kieschnick, 1998; Kaplan, 1989b). Both Dicker (1990) and Weir et al. (2005a) point out that the tax advantages of financing firms with debt are smaller in the UK than in the US. Still, we conclude that higher premiums are paid for firms with low leverage, which proxies both for the tax advantage of additional interest deductibility and for the ease of financing the takeover operation.

We hypothesize that the gains from going private arise from a stronger alignment of incentives in the post-transaction private firm. Firms where managers own only small equity stakes are expected to benefit most from going private, as the buyout is expected to reduce potential agency problems. As mentioned above, the validity of this relation is contested for higher levels of managerial ownership when agency problems induced by managerial entrenchment may dominate. Therefore, we include a dummy variable for those firms where management controls more than 25% of the firm's equity, which corresponds to the highest quartile of managerial ownership of the sample. This threshold is also equal to the entrenchment level documented by Morck et al. (1988). Table 3.10 supports the incentive realignment hypothesis: higher premiums are paid and higher CAARs are realized for firms with low managerial stakes. The additional negative impact of very high managerial equity ownership (>25%) is also consistent with the fact that this share block discourages other bidders (not belonging to the management) to make a counter bid (Stulz, 1988).

Under the control hypothesis, we expect that strong outside shareholders monitor the firm such that there is less scope for performance improvement once the firm is private. This is reflected in a lower premium and a lower CAAR. A strong outsider shareholder is defined as a shareholder controlling an equity stake of 3% of more in the pre-buyout firm and is an institutional investor (bank, pension fund, investment fund or trust, or insurance company), an individual or family, or a corporation.

We find support for the control hypothesis, especially for corporations as good monitors. The strongly negative relation for the outside control dummy variable of corporations shows that lower levels of control by corporations in the pre-transaction firm are associated with larger expected wealth gains upon going private. This finding is consistent with the fact that corporations owning large equity stakes perform a monitoring task. In contrast, the presence of family blockholders is not correlated with wealth

Table 3.10 Cross-sectional regressions for premiums/CAARs in PTP transactions

Variable	Model 1		Model 2		Model 3		Model 4	
	Dep. var. = premium 20 days		Dep. var. = premium 40 days		Dep. var. = CAR [–2, 2]		Dep. var. = CAR [–10, 10]	
	Coef.	*t*-value	Coef.	*t*-value	Coef.	*t*-value	Coef.	*t*-value
Constant	0.5806	7.119***	0.4925	6.446***	0.4363	5.169***	0.5092	5.109***
IBO (1=yes)	−0.0066	−0.128	0.0025	0.315	−0.0396	−0.739	−0.1013	−0.936
MBI (1=yes)	0.0073	0.148	0.0065	0.222	0.0254	0.494	0.3056	0.557
Taxes								
Taxes (as % of sales)	−0.1713	−0.239	−0.2068	−0.331	−1.133	−1.526	−1.052	−1.205
Taxes * performance (1 if ROA > median)	−0.6935	−0.932	−0.4836	−0.560	0.0127	0.016	0.0208	0.317
Debt/equity ratio	−0.0708	−2.305**	−0.0773	−2.259**	−0.0295	−0.927	−0.0300	−0.783
Incentive realignment								
Managerial ownership	−0.0016	−2.143**	−0.0028	−2.072**	−0.0027	−3.378***	−0.0026	2.894***
Managerial stake >25% (1=yes)	−0.0482	−1.666*	−0.0417	−1.640*	−0.0460	−1.538	−0.0541	−1.492
Ownership and control								
Institutional blockholder >5% (yes=1)	−0.0794	−2.290**	−0.0836	−2.401***	−0.0648	−1.804*	−0.0561	−1.649*
Corporation blockholder >5% (yes=1)	−0.0807	−2.808***	−0.0699	−1.994**	−0.0920	−3.094***	−0.0866	−2.755***
Family blockholder >5% (yes=1)	−0.0121	−0.389	−0.0343	−1.047	0.0365	1.136	0.0404	1.221
Free cash flow								
Free cash flow	0.0130	0.133	0.0227	0.488	0.0463	0.458	0.0446	0.502
Transaction costs								
AIM listing (1=yes)	−0.0383	−1.922*	−0.0427	−1.573*	0.0026	0.127	0.0300	0.355

Takeover defence								
Prior takeover interest (1=yes)	0.0549	1.620	0.0637	1.599	0.0106	0.301	0.0092	0.249
Undervaluation								
Share performance*MBO	−0.1327	−3.679***	−0.2003	−0.344***	−0.1039	−2.782***	−0.1150	−2.936***
Share performance*MBI	−1.1500	−1.251	0.1424	−1.114	0.0272	0.219	0.0463	0.994
Share performance*IBO	−0.2702	−1.954*	−0.2080	−1.567	−0.5615	−3.924***	−0.4630	−1.899*
Return on assets	−0.0006	−0.440	−0.0011	−0.698	0.0011	0.800	0.0016	0.552
Control variables								
Hostile bid (1=yes)	−0.0118	−0.240	−0.0116	−0.200	−0.0762	−1.495	−0.0893	−1.604
Bidder competition (1=yes)	0.1308	2.562**	0.2471	2.669***	−0.1026	−1.041	−0.1054	−1.285
CEO was removed past 2 years (1=yes)	−1.1025	−3.282***	−0.0997	−2.463***	−0.1301	−4.025***	−0.1463	−3.155***
Corporate restructuring in past 5 years (1=yes)	−0.0053	−0.165	−0.0182	−0.633	0.0481	1.441	0.0533	1.428
Size (ln of total assets)	0.0041	0.307	0.0056	0.463	0.0014	0.101	0.0009	0.266
PTP occurred pre-2000 (1=yes)	−0.0321	−1.037	−0.0392	−1.410	−0.0080	−0.249	−0.0080	−0.364
Industry dummies	Yes	Yes	Yes	Yes	Yes	Yes	Yes	Yes
F-value	3.390***		4.002***		2.854***			2.631***
R-squared	0.419		0.382		0.378			0.352
Adjusted *R*-squared	0.295		0.271		0.245			0.234

Notes: This table shows the cross-sectional regressions estimating the determinants of the premiums/CAARs in PTP transactions. The anticipation windows for the premiums are 20 and 40 days. The CARs are calculated for event 3 (see Methodology section) and are over a 5-day window centred around the event day. The number of observations is 172. ***, ** and * stand for statistical significance at the 1%, 5% and 10% levels, respectively.

Source: Own calculations.

gains in PTP transactions. We also find that the presence of significant share stakes held by institutional investors is negatively related to shareholder wealth gains (Table 3.10). This negative relation may be the result of institutional shareholder activism which implies that lower performance improvements will be generated (as reflected in the premium and the CAARs) once the firm reaches its private status. However, interviews with institutional investors give more credibility to an alternative explanation: the low premiums in firms with institutional investors as the dominant shareholders reflect the fact that these institutional investors are locked in to poorly performing firms with little prospect of improvement. Hence, institutional investors contribute little monitoring value and are relieved to sell out (see also Franks et al., 2001).

According to the free cash flow (FCF) hypothesis, firms that generate large free cash flows may waste resources. Exchanging equity for debt in a PTP will reduce the amount of resources under managerial discretion and will bond management. This is expected to make the firm's capital budgeting decisions more efficient. Thus, we include the FCF-to-sales ratio as we expect that the higher the FCF, the more wealth gains can be created through a PTP. Our findings in Table 3.10 show that going private is not driven by the need to return FCF to the shareholders.

Under the transaction costs hypothesis, the gains from going private are primarily caused by the elimination of the costs related to a stock exchange listing. We are only able to estimate the impact of the direct costs of maintaining a listing. As mentioned above, the listing costs for AIM-listed firms are lower than for firms listed on the official market of the LSE such that we expect that an AIM listing is related to lower expected wealth effects. A listing on the AIM may also proxy for the lower indirect costs of a listing resulting from more flexible listing requirements. As predicted, the expected sign is negative for the premium regression.

The takeover defence hypothesis predicts that firms go private as a defensive strategy. Thus, pressure from the market for corporate control is expected to force up the premiums paid in PTPs. In MBOs, the management will have to come with a high bid to pre-empt bidding by other contestants. As a proxy for takeover pressure, we take a dummy variable which equals 1 if there has been any takeover interest in the year leading up to the PTP announcement. We expect a positive sign. Table 3.10 reveals that the relation is indeed positive but falls short of being statistically significant (11–12% in models 1 and 2). We therefore reject the takeover defence hypothesis as an explanation for the premium (as do Weir et al., 2005a in their model explaining the decision to go private).

The wealth gains from going private may also be caused by undervaluation. The higher the discrepancy between the market value of a firm and the potential value under private ownership, the larger will be the wealth gains in a PTP. For each type of PTP transaction, past performance is captured by share price returns over a one-year period prior to the PTP ending one month before the first announcement. The expected sign is negative for all deal types, although the magnitude of the effect is expected to be different per type. Due to information asymmetry, managers are best placed to identify undervaluation such that we expect that the impact of past share price performance on the premium and wealth effects is larger for MBOs and IBOs (which frequently retain the incumbent management) than for MBIs. Table 3.10 confirms the undervaluation hypothesis: lower share price performance in case of MBOs and IBOs leads to higher premiums and CAARs. The past share price performance for firms going private through an MBI is not significant.

We also include several control variables. When takeovers are contested, the expected premium and CAARs are higher than in friendly acquisitions. Obviously, hostility is more likely to occur in IBOs or MBIs. Maybe due to the small number of hostile bids in our sample (13 out of 172), Table 3.10 shows that hostility does not seem to influence the wealth effects. Bidder competition is also likely to push up the premium and CAARs, which is confirmed in models 1 and 2 of Table 3.10.

We also control for past corporate or board restructuring. The reason is that the outcome of such restructuring is already reflected in the share prices such that less additional shareholder value may be created through operating performance improvements. We include dummy variables which are equal to one if (i) a major asset restructuring has taken place within the five years prior to the announcement of the PTP and (ii) the CEO was removed within a two-year period prior to the PTP. While the former variable is not significant, the second is strongly negative.

We also include a dummy variable indicating whether the transaction took place prior or subsequent to 2000 in order to control for the equity market decline which started in March 2000. While our univariate statistics indicate that the premium is substantially higher (by more than 10%) in the pre-2000 period, this result is not upheld in all the models.

We conclude that this study weakly supports the tax benefits hypothesis in PTP transactions as a higher premium is paid for firms with low debt–equity ratios. Incentive realignment is also a source of value. We also report some evidence for the control hypothesis, but the most convincing results relate to the undervaluation hypothesis for MBOs and IBOs. Another reason to go private also seems to be the avoidance of the direct costs of maintaining a stock exchange listing. In contrast, going-private transactions are not initiated to curb free cash flows or to avoid unsolicited takeovers. The reported adjusted R-squared shows that the models explain about 23–30% of the sample variation in the dependent variable. Compared to previous research on PTPs' wealth effects, the models fit the data reasonably well.

From the cross-sectional analysis, we have excluded the five financially distressed firms as most of the hypotheses described above are not applicable to these firms. In this small number of firms, the PTPs are used to avoid bankruptcy or could even be regarded as a pre-packaged sale of bankrupt firms.

6.3 Robustness Checks

For reasons of conciseness, we only report the regressions with a premium over 20 and 40 days and the CAARs over a five-day and a 21-day window centred around the event day. We have run specifications using premiums (in logs and percentages) measured over these windows: 1, 5, 10, 20, 40 and 60 (working) days. The CAARs are calculated for the following windows [–1, 0], [–2, 2], [–5, 5], [–10, 10], [–40, 40], [–40, 6], [6, 40], [–10, 5]. The reason for considering these windows is to verify whether the anticipated wealth gains are concentrated closely around the event date or whether the gains of the transaction (and the transaction itself) has triggered share price corrections prior to the first public announcement. As long as the event day [–1, 0] is included in the window, we obtain results similar to the ones reported in Table 3.10.

As free cash flow may be to a large extent industry-driven, we replaced our free cash flow measure in Table 3.10 by industry-adjusted free cash flow to sales. We still fail to find support for the free cash flow hypothesis. We also investigate whether the growth prospects of the firm (measured by Tobin's Q) are also related to the expected value gains in public to private transactions. We find that this is not the case (Tobin's *Q* was not included into the specifications of Table 3.10 in order to avoid multicollinearity). Substituting our size variable by total sales, market capitalization, and return on assets by return on equity does not change any of the reported results. We have also replaced the cut-off measure used to capture strong ownership concentration held by management (a dummy variable equalling 1 when the aggregate managerial ownership is at least 25%) by lower cut-offs. The results remain valid with cut-offs between 20% and 25% but not for lower cut-off levels (10% and 15%). Whereas ownership concentration by category of owner influences the anticipated wealth effect (Table 3.10), total ownership concentration across all categories of owner (as measured by the Herfindahl index) does not. Financial distress (measured by low interest coverage) does not influence the results reported in Table 3.10.

7. CONCLUSIONS AND SUGGESTIONS FOR FUTURE RESEARCH

In the 1990s a vibrant and economically important public to private (PTP) market developed in the UK. Nevertheless, to date there has been virtually no systematic research into the sources of wealth gains in UK going-private transactions. On this topic, most insights relate to the first wave of leveraged buyouts in the US during the 'deal decade' (the 1980s). This chapter analyses a large sample comprising the population of UK PTP transactions in the second going-private wave that started in the latter half of the 1990s. We employ two methods to capture the expected wealth effects of leveraged buyouts: a premium analysis and an event study. We find that on average, PTPs generate premiums of more than 40% and the wealth effects corrected for expected returns amount to almost 30%.

In contrast to US research, the taxes paid by the target firm prior to the PTP transaction are not related to the wealth effects the deal is expected to generate. However, the fact that higher premiums are paid for firms with low leverage provides weak support for the tax benefits hypothesis. The unused debt capacity is likely to create a large additional tax shield.

Our strongest result relates to the undervaluation hypotheses. Consistent with most US studies, this chapter identifies a positive relation between pre-transaction undervaluation and the expected shareholder gains at the PTP transaction. This effect is found to be stronger for MBOs and IBOs (which mostly retain part of the incumbent management) than in MBIs, as the former are better placed to exploit undervaluation issues due to informational asymmetries.

The potential for increased incentive realignment in the private firm also seems an important determinant of the shareholder wealth effects in PTP transactions as both the premium and CAARs are higher for firms with lower levels of managerial ownership. We also report evidence supporting the control hypothesis: in firms with stronger outside blockholders, the premiums and CAARs are lower. This negative relation is especially strong in firms with strong corporations as shareholders. This supports the fact that in firms monitored by this type of outside shareholders, there is less scope for operating performance improvements in the post-transaction period.

We do not find any evidence sustaining the free cash flow hypothesis: firms are not taken private to reduce high free cash flows as Jensen (1989) predicts. This is consistent with most US studies and with the recent UK study by Weir et al. (2005a). While we are not able to test the total cost savings a firm can realize by abandoning a stock exchange listing, we test the relative effect of maintaining a listing on the AIM compared to the official market of the LSE. The negative relation between an AIM listing and the wealth effects does not contradict the hypothesis that less value is created by abandoning the AIM listing and its less expensive listing requirements.

Prior takeover interest in the firm does not lead managers to pay more to take their firms private in order to pre-empt potential raiders. Not surprisingly, when at the announcement of a takeover multiple bidders emerge, the shareholder wealth gains are higher. In contrast, hostile bids do not trigger higher CAARs or premiums.

The realization of these expected wealth gains for our sample firms is difficult to measure currently due to limited data availability; only 20% of the 177 companies in this study underwent an exit up till now. Three were floated again through a secondary IPO (within five years since their delisting). Sixteen firms were sold by their management or the LBO specialist via a trade sale and 17 had a secondary buyout. Exit values are provided for only some of these transactions.

As this chapter is one of the first finance contributions on the anticipated value effects of delistings in the UK, there is scope for further research. Particularly interesting is whether and by which channels the anticipated value is realized after the firm has gone private. Furthermore, a follow-up study on the decision process and the determinants of going-private transactions is interesting. Hardly anything is known about the LBO market in Continental Europe. One reason is that few Continental LBOs were listed in the past, but this situation is changing rapidly especially in France and Scandinavian countries where an increasing number of LBOs of listed firms have recently taken place (CMBOR, 2006). As the equity markets in Continental Europe are less developed, the exit decision by LBO sponsors and specialists probably differs from that in the US or the UK. Another interesting research route is the study of the direct and indirect costs across countries of maintaining a listing as well as of the impact of the differences in corporate governance and listing regulations on corporate value. Further research analysing the differences between Continental Europe and Anglo-American LBOs seems called for.

APPENDIX 3A CALCULATION OF TEST STATISTICS

To test for the significance of average abnormal returns (AAR) and CAARs, Kothari and Warner (1997) describe the followings test statistics.

The one-day test statistic:

$$t_{\mathrm{AR}_t} = \frac{\mathrm{AAR}_t}{\sigma_{\mathrm{AR}}}, \text{ where}$$

$$\sigma_{AR} = \sqrt{\frac{1}{T-1}\sum_{t=-E_1}^{t=E_2} (AAR_t = A\bar{A}R)^2} \tag{3A.1}$$

$$\mathrm{AAR}_t = \frac{1}{N}\sum_{j=1}^{N} \mathrm{AR}_{jt}, \quad \text{for } j = 1, \ldots, N \tag{3A.2}$$

and

$$A\bar{A}R = \frac{1}{T}\sum_{t=E_1}^{E_2} \mathrm{AAR}_t \tag{3A.3}$$

E_1 and E_2 refer to beginning and the end of the estimation window. T is the number of working days in the estimation window, namely 195. This one-day statistic follows a t-distribution. The CAR for security j is computed as follows, for $j = 1, \ldots, N$:

$$\mathrm{CAR}_{j,t1,t2} = \sum_{t=t_2}^{t_1} \mathrm{AR}_{jt}, \tag{3A.4}$$

where t_1 and t_2 are the first and last day of the event window. The CAR over events 1 and 2, CAR^{1+2}, is computed as follows, for $j = 1, \ldots, N$:

$$\mathrm{CAR}^{1+2}_{j,w} = \begin{cases} \mathrm{CAR}^{1}_{j,w,t^1_1,t^1_2} + \mathrm{CAR}^{2}_{j,w,t^2_1,t^2_2} \text{if } t^2_1 > t^1_2 \\ \end{cases} \tag{3A.5}$$

$\mathrm{CAR}^{1}_{j,W,t^1_1 t^1_2}$ and $\mathrm{CAR}^{2}_{j,W,t^2_1 t^2_2}$ are the CARs for event 1 and event 2, respectively, with equal event windows W. t^1_1, t^1_2 and t^2_1, t^2_2 are the beginning and end dates of each event's window W. The cross-sectional average of the individual CARs (whether based on events 1, 2 or 1+2), is computed as follows for $j = 1, \ldots, N$:

$$\mathrm{CAAR}_{t_1,t_2} = \frac{1}{N}\sum_{j=1}^{N}\mathrm{CAR}_{j,t_1,t_2}$$

The test statistic for CAAR is:

$$t_{\mathrm{CAAR}} = \frac{\mathrm{CAAR}_{t_1,t_2}}{\sigma_{\mathrm{AR}}\sqrt{T_2}}, \quad \text{where} \tag{3A.6}$$

where σ_{AR} is given by Eq. (3A.1) and T_2 is the amount of days in the event window.

The second parametric test is a simple t-test for the significance of the sample means.[40] While the test statistics in Kothari and Warner (1997) compute the ARs' variance from the estimation window, this simple t-test uses the variance of event-induced abnormal returns, calculated for each day in the event window individually:

$$t^{s}_{\mathrm{AR}_t} = \frac{\mathrm{AAR}_t}{\sigma^{s}_{\mathrm{AR}_t}/\sqrt{N}}, \tag{3A.7}$$

$$\sigma^{s}_{\mathrm{AR}_t} = \sqrt{\frac{1}{N-1}\sum_{j=1}^{N}(\mathrm{AR}_{jt} - \mathrm{AAR}_t)^2} \quad \text{for } j = 1,\ldots N. \tag{3A.8}$$

where AAR_t is defined as in Eq. (3A.3).

The test statistic for CAAR is then computed as follows:

$$t^{s}_{\mathrm{CAAR}} = \frac{\mathrm{CAAR}_{t_1,t_2}}{\sigma^{s}_{\mathrm{CAAR}}/\sqrt{N}}, \text{ where} \tag{3A.9}$$

$$\sigma^{s}_{\mathrm{CAAR}}\sqrt{\frac{1}{N-1}\sum_{j=1}^{N}(\mathrm{CAR}_{j,t_1,t_2} - \mathrm{CAAR}_{t_1,t_2})^2} \quad \text{for } j = 1,\ldots,N, \tag{3A.10}$$

where $\mathrm{CAAR}t_1t_2$ is defined as in Eq. (3A.6), $\mathrm{CAR}jt_1t_2$ is defined as in Eq. (3A.4) for events 1 and 2, and as in Eq. (3A.5) for events 1 + 2.

We also estimate a non-parametric test: the generalized sign test which compares the proportion of positive abnormal returns around an event to the proportion from a period unaffected by the event (Cowan, 1992).

Cowan (1992) shows that in ideal econometric conditions, Corrado's (1989) rank test is more powerful than the generalized sign test. However, Cowan also demonstrates that the rank test is misspecified under thin trading, while the generalized sign test remains correctly specified. As the securities in our sample are likely to suffer from thin trading, we opt for the generalized sign test:

$$\hat{p} = \frac{1}{N}\sum_{j=1}^{N}\frac{1}{T}\sum_{t=E_1}^{E_2} S_{jt} \quad \text{for } j = 1, \ldots, N, \tag{3A.11}$$

where

$$S_{jt} = \begin{cases} 1 \text{ if } AR_{jt} > 0 \\ 0 \text{ otherwise} \end{cases} \tag{3A.12}$$

E_1, E_2 and T are defined as in Eq. (3A.2). The test statistic uses the normal approximation to the binomial distribution of parameter $\hat{p}$. If we define w as the number of positive CAAR_{j,t_1,t_2} in the event window, the test statistic then becomes:

$$Z_G = \frac{w - N\hat{p}}{[N\hat{p}(1-\hat{p})]^{\frac{1}{2}}} \tag{3A.13}$$

We test the null hypothesis that premiums are equal to zero as follows, where $P_{j,\text{AW}}$ is the premium, calculated with anticipation AW for firm j:

$$t^{P}_{AW} = \frac{\bar{P}_{AW}}{\sigma_{AW}/\sqrt{N}}, \quad \text{where}$$

$$\bar{P}_{\text{AW}} = \frac{1}{N}\sum_{j=1}^{N} P_{j,\text{AW}} \quad \text{for } j = 1, \ldots, N,$$

$$\text{and } \sigma_{\text{AW}} = \sqrt{\frac{1}{N-1}\sum_{j=1}^{N}(P_{j,\text{AW}} - \bar{P}_{\text{AW}})^2}$$

APPENDIX 3B CORRELATION TABLE

N=177	AIM	HOSTILE	PRIOR	BIDCOMP	MANEQ	ManEq>25	MBO	MBI	IBO	RESTR	CEO
AIM	1	0.01	−0.07	−0.07	0.24***	0.17*	0.04	0.06	−0.1	−0.06	−0.05
HOSTILE	0.01	1	0.08	0.11	−0.09	0.02	−0.21***	0.26***	0.03	0.12	−0.01
PRIOR	−0.07	0.08	1	0.05	−0.25***	−0.42***	−0.01	0.12	−0.1	0.02	0 22***
BIDCOMP	−0.07	0.11	0.05	1	−0.13*	−0.27**	−0.03	−0.01	0.04	0.14**	0.01
MANEQ	0.24***	−0.09	−0.25***	−0.13*	1	0.33**	0.24***	−0.1	−0.22***	−0.06	−0.15**
ManEq >25	0.17*	0.02	−0.42***	−0.27**	0.33**	1	0.39***	−0.40***	−0.37**	−0.10	−0.08
MBO	0.04	−0.21***	−0.01	−0.03	0.24***	0.39***	1	−0.62***	−0.7***	−0.17**	0.03
MBI	0.06	0.26***	0.12	−0.01	−0.1	−0.40***	−0.62***	1	−0.13*	0.06	−0.02
IBO	−0.1	0.03	−0.1	0.04	−0.22***	−0.37**	−0.7***	−0.13*	1	0.17**	−0.02
RESTR5	−0.06	0.12	0.02	0.14**	−0.06	−0.10	−0.17**	0.06	0.17**	1	0.36***
CEO5	−0.05	−0.01	0.22***	0.01	−0.15**	−0.08	0.03	−0.02	−0.02	0.36***	1
SHAREPERF	−0.02	0.04	0.06	−0.03	0.02	0.15	0.01	0.04	−0.05	−0.06	−0.06
FCF	−0.14*	0.13*	0.09	0.06	−0.05	−0.24	0.04	−0.09	0.03	−0.08	−0.06
TAX	−0.07	0.08	−0.05	−0.07	0	−0.11	0.12	−0.16**	−0.01	−0.09	−0.03
Tax * Perf.	0.01	0.14	−0.10	0.06	0.09	−0.04	0.16	−0.18*	−0.11	0.03	0.05
LNASS	−0.32***	0.16**	0.2**	0.09	−0.36***	−0.50***	−0.19***	0.04	0.2***	0.22***	0.24***
DEBT/EQ	−0.05	0.02	0.11	−0.07	−0.15**	−0.22*	−0.08	0.09	0.02	−0.12	−0.1
ROA	−0.2**	0.03	−0.02	0.05	0.04	0.01	0.03	−0.08	0.04	−0.02	−0.06
INSTIT	−0.13	0.17	−0.15	−0.11	−0.25	−0.20**	0.14	0.31***	0.26**	0.02	0.04
CORP	−0.03	−0.08	−0.14	−0.09	−0.20**	−0.24***	0.16	0.22**	0.16	0.01	−0.1
FAMILY	−0.04	−0.19*	−0.09	−0.15	−0.17**	−0.16	−0.08	0.15	0.06	0.01	0.04

N=177	SH.PERF	FCF	TAX	Tax * Perf	LNASS	DEBT/EQ	ROA	INSTIT	CORP	FAMIL
AIM	−0.02	−0.14*	−0.07	0.01	−0.32***	−0.05	−0.2***	−0.13	−0.03	−0.04
HOSTILE	0.04	0.13*	0.08	0.14	0.16**	0.02	0.03	0.17	−0.08	−0.19*

PRIOR	0.06	0.09	−0.05	−0.10	0 2***	0.11	−0.02	−0.15	−0.14	−0.09
BIDCOMP	−0.03	0.06	−0.07	0.06	0.09	−0.07	0.05	−0.11	−0.09	−0.15
MANEQ	0.02	−0.05	0	0.09	−0.36***	−0.15**	0.04	−0.25	−0.20**	−0.17**
ManEq >25	0.15	−0.24	−0.11	−0.04	−0.50***	−0.22*	0.01	−0.20**	−0.24***	−0.16
MBO	0.01	0.04	0.12	0.16	−0.19***	−0.08	0.03	0.14	0.16	−0.08
MBI	0.04	−0.09	−0.16**	−0.18*	0.04	0.09	−0.08	0.31***	0.22**	0.15
IBO	−0.05	0.03	−0.01	−0.11	0 2***	0.02	0.04	0.26**	0.16	0.06
RESTR5	−0.06	−0.08	−0.09	0.03	0.22***	−0.12	−0.02	0.02	0.01	0.01
CEO5	−0.06	−0.06	−0.03	0.05	0.24***	−0.1	−0.06	0.04	−0.1	0.04
SHAREPERF	1	0.31***	0.23***	0.48***	0.06	0.18**	0.27***	0.14*	0.26**	−0.14
FCF	0.31***	1	0.27***	0.34***	0.29***	0.16**	0.54***	0.18*	0.21**	−0.18
TAX	0.23***	0.27***	1	0 46***	0.26***	0.11	0.16**	0.13*	−0.05	−0.1
T\ax * Perf.	0.48***	0.34***	0.46***	1	0.21**	0.13	0.35***	0.14	0.07	−0.14
LNASS	0.06	0.29***	0.26***	0.21**	1	0.32***	0.22***	0.30**	−0.11	−0.27***
DEBT/EQ	0.18**	0.16**	0.11	0.13	0.32***	1	0.02	0.22**	0.06	−0.21**
ROA	0.27***	0.54***	0.16**	0.35***	0.22***	0.02	1	0.17	0.14	0.22*
INSTIT	0.14*	0.18*	0.13*	0.14	0.30**	0.22**	0.17	1	−0.19**	−0.27***
CORP	0.26**	0.21**	−0.05	0.07	−0.11	0.06	0.14	−0.19**	1	−0.05
FAMILY	−0.14	−0.18	−0.1	−0.14	−0.27***	−0.21**	0.22*	−0.27***	−0.05	1

Notes: MBO equals 1 if transaction is a management buyout. MBI is 1 if the transaction is a management buy-in. IBO is 1 if the transaction is an institutional buyout. HOSTILE is 1 when first bid is rejected. PRIOR is 1 if there was takeover interest in year before going private. BIDCOMP is 1 if more than 1 bidder is involved. FCF (free cash flow) is operating income before depreciation + taxes (corrected for deferred charges + gross interest expense + dividends paid on common stock) / Total sales. FCF is averaged over last 2 years before going private and is trimmed at –100%. ROA (return on assets) is net income plus interest expenses (net of tax) over average total assets. LNASS (log of total assets) is total assets at end of last fiscal year before going private (GBP m). DEBT/EQ is long-term debt over market value of common stock, 4 months before first takeover announcement. SHAREPERF is the log of share price performance from days –300 to –41 before announcement minus log-return of FTSE All Share Index. TAX (corrected for deferred charges) to sales at the end of last fiscal year before going private. AIM is 1 if firm is listed on Alternative Investment Market. MANEQ is percentage of shares owned by executive directors. ManEq >25 equals 1 if the combined managerial stake is 25% or more. INSTIT is 1 if institutional investors hold a stake of 5% or more. CORP is 1 if corporations hold a stake of 5% or more. FAMILY is 1 if families or individuals hold a stake of 5% or more. CEO5 equals 1 if CEO was replaced 5 years before going private. RESTR5 equals 1 if firm restructured 5 years before going private. ***, **, and * indicate whether or not the correlation is statistically significant from 0 at the 1, 5 or 10% level.

ACKNOWLEDGEMENTS

We gratefully acknowledge suggestions by the referee, the guest editors, Marco Becht, Rafel Crespi, Douglas Cumming, Marc Goergen, Jacob de Kerle, Marina Martynova, Joe McCahery, Arnin Schwienbacher, Peter Szilagyi, Tomas de Victoria, Charlie Weir, Chendi Zhang, and the participants and discussant Jarrett Kotrozo at the *Journal of Corporate Finance* conference at the Rensselaer Polytechnic Institute, NY. We are grateful to Rolf Visser (Deloitte Corporate Finance), who allowed us to use his firm's databases. Luc Renneboog is grateful to the Netherlands Organization for Scientific Research for a replacement subsidy of the programme 'Shifts in Governance' and to the European Commission via the 'New Modes of Governance' project (NEWGOV) led by the European University Institute in Florence; contract nr. CIT1-CT-2004-506392. The opinions in the chapter are those of the authors and not necessarily those of their employers. Mike Wright thanks Deloitte and Barclays Private Equity for financial support for CMBOR.

NOTES

1. We use the terms going-private transaction and public to private transaction as synonyms.
2. In the US literature, IBOs and MBIs are usually called leveraged buyouts (LBOs).
3. Performance contingent contract operating as an incentive device enabling management to increase its equity holdings in a post-buyout firm upon meeting ex ante specified performance targets (Kaplan and Strömberg, 2001).
4. Mitchell and Mulherin (1996) state that 57% of US quoted firms were then takeover targets or were restructured.
5. Small companies in particular experienced strong adverse effects from low trading volumes (Kuhn Capital, 2003). More importantly, though, the implementation of the Sarbanes–Oxley Act is said to increase the costs of a listing substantially.
6. *Financial Times*, 11 June 1999.
7. The anticipated wealth gains are proxied by the short term wealth effects (the realized return around the event date over and a benchmark return) and the premium (see Sections 5.1 and 5.2 for details on the calculations).
8. For the US LBOs in the 1980s, Kaplan (1989b) mentions asset step-ups as another source of tax-related benefits. In this procedure, the tax basis of the pre-transaction assets is inflated to the 'appraised fair market value'. The premium is attributed to goodwill on the seller's books, which leads to tax deductions via goodwill amortization.
9. The fact that tax shields are predictable and are hence reflected in the takeover premium leaves no tax-related incentives for the post-buyout investors to take a company private.
10. These non-pecuniary (also called non-marketable perquisites or private benefits) are not transferable and are investor specific. Possible benefits could be the reputation or 'psychic' value of beingin control (Aghion and Bolton, 1992), salary, and the value expropriated from shareholders (Dyck and Zingales, 2004).
11. The Alternative Investment Market was started 19 June 1995, to facilitate the trading in the securities of smaller, growing companies, which are unable to meet the full criteria for the admission to the official list of the UK Listing Authority or for whom a less rigid

regulatory environment is considered more appropriate. In July 2003, 706 companies were trading on AIM, with a total market capitalization of £12 699 million.

12. An elaborate enumeration of these differences can be obtained from the London Stock Exchange, or found on www.Londonstockexchange.com.
13. Some UK CEOs estimate that these costs may even be higher: Roy Hill, the CEO of Liberfabrica, estimated, just after his company was acquired in 1999, these costs at £400 000. Likewise, Jurek Piasecki, CEO of Goldsmiths, put City-associated costs at £500 000, three months after his firm went private in 1999. An even higher estimate comes from the executive chairman of Wainhomes, who, upon the announcement of taking the company private, estimated the costs of maintaining a listing at £1 million (*Financial Times*, 31 August 1999).
14. For example, the chief executive of Allied Textiles stated that the market was not reflecting the intrinsic value of the company, and the chairman of the building firm Ward claimed that the housing boom had not been reflected in the company's share price (*Financial Times*, 2000). Weir et al. (2005b) use data on perceived and actual undervaluation prior to going to private, controlling for other factors, to identify the importance of undervaluation in the PTP decision. They also find that undervalued firms had relatively high institutional shareholdings, suggesting that the buyout provides institutions with a means of exiting firms with poor market valuation, particularly during a time of limited pressure from the takeover market.
15. Both Harlow and Howe (1993) and Kaestner and Liu (1996) report that MBOs are preceded by significant abnormal share purchases by insiders, whereas outsider-induced buyouts are not. They suggest that pre-buyout insider trading is associated with private managerial information. Occasionally, specialized outsiders (like institutions or private equity investors) realize that a firm has substantial unrealized locked-up value which incentivizes them to buy a toehold stake followed by a management or institutional buyin.
16. We are not able to test this hypothesis due to the fact that hardly any LBO firms in Europe have traded bonds outstanding. In order to calculate abnormal bond returns, we would need a sufficiently large, liquid and standardized European bond market enabling us to construct robust, closely fitted pricing benchmarks. Hence, such a study is necessarily limited to the Eurobond market (which exists for relatively safe, investment-grade firms). Renneboog and Szilagyi (2006) are only able use a sample of 75 target firms in all European takeovers over the period 1997–2004.
17. Doncasters Plc is based in England but its shares were traded on foreign exchanges (not on the London Stock Exchange); Charnos Plc only delisted its preference shares; Crown Sports Plc did not go private after the hostile buyin attempt, but made a settlement with the suitor; Locker Group Plc delisted from the Official List 6 months before its MBO announcement, and therefore no updated share prices were available.
18. In accordance with section 325 of the Companies Act 1985, directors are required to notify the Register of Director's Interests of their holdings and publish all their interests and those held by their immediate families (including other affiliated persons within the meaning of section 346 of the Companies Act 1985) in the annual report. Under sections 198 to 208 of the Companies Act 1985, firms are also required to publish the identity and holdings of all substantial shareholders with an equity stake over 3%.
19. *Financial Times*, 28 September 2000.
20. The executive board of Sears Plc for example, was said to have a 'shocking disregard for shareholder value' (see *FT*, 21 January 1999) and many firms were taken private with the motivation to be restructured away from the public arena.
21. *Financial Times*, 5 June 1999.
22. This may be related to the notion of 'busted-techs' where listed technology corporations encounter control problems with existing management and need to undergo a buyout to enable greater control to be exercised (Wright et al., 2000a,b).
23. Goldstein (2000) applies a stricter classification that excludes seemingly hostile behaviour that could be a simple price bargaining. He accepts 'true' hostility, e.g., in case of litigation or the search for a white knight. We also use a stricter definition, namely a bid is hostile when the independent directors do not recommend the bid until at least a majority of the

shares is in the hands of the hostile suitor. The main motivation of those directors to oppose is the fact that the individual holdout in the cases with high levels of bid acceptances could result in a highly illiquid claim for the shareholder, once the firm is delisted. Under this second definition, only five cases in our sample are truly hostile. Three of the truly hostile transactions were observed for MBIs, while MBOs and IBOs both experienced one such deal. In the rest of the chapter, our first definition of hostility will be used.

24. The IBO of Esporta Plc is a well-documented example of a hostile public to private transaction.
25. In the IBO of the Finelist Group Plc, the continued involvement of the management was claimed to be crucial to the success of the buyout, although the company failed shortly afterwards amidst fraud allegations.
26. *Financial Times*, 15 May 2003.
27. This provides some support for the hypothesis that PTPs generally involve listed corporations where shareholders have few alternatives but to accept a buyout offer.
28. In the case of Hogg Robinson Plc, the prior bid was never officially tabled, but the resistance to the unofficial bid was so explicitly reported in the *FT* that we categorized it as a defensive MBO.
29. Inland Revenue considers companies traded on AIM as non-quoted for tax purposes. As a result of this, the taper relief, which reduces the taxable capital gains made on the sale of shares, is higher for AIM-quoted firms than for firms traded on the main market.
30. Management may undertake restructuring and then make a buyout offer before the benefits appear in the operating income. There is mixed evidence relating to the ability of management to manipulate earnings (DeAngelo, 1986; Perry and Williams, 1994).
31. An example from the sample is Mid Kent Holdings Plc, which went private as part of the restructuring programme started by its new CEO. He intended to reduce the cost of capital and attract new capital to face the ever stronger competition in the water industry.
32. Phillips and Drew Fund Management, the UK's third largest pension fund manager, takes an active stand towards the large blocks of shares it invests in. On several occasions, this has led to a large restructuring, takeover, or even a PTP, as in the case of Sears Plc (*Financial Times*, 24 December 1998).
33. Rule nine of the UK's City Code on Takeovers and Mergers requires that any person acquiring 30% or more of the voting rights is required to make a bid for the whole firm at the highest price paid by him for such shares in the previous 12 months (see Paul, 1994 for a good review of the City Code).
34. The City Code requires firms to disclose takeover negotiations when there are rumours, speculation, or an untoward price movement in the shares, if it can reasonably be determined to be caused by the bidders' actions (Paul, 1994). Typically, this type of announcements does not embody more than the notification of a negotiation that 'may or may not lead to an offer for the shares of the company'.
35. In UK buyouts, it is common for the bidder to offer the vendor the option to receive part of the payment in the form of loan notes (CMBOR, 2005). These notes are issued by the bidder and usually guaranteed by the sponsor of the buyout/buy-in. The issuance of loan notes has advantages for both buyer and seller. Subject to Internal Revenue clearance, loan notes allow the seller to defer the tax charge arising from the sale. Due to the low rate of interest on loan notes in public offers, the buyer enjoys a lower cost of financing the acquisition.
36. The form of acceptance is a document attached to the offer document, which shareholders have to complete and return to the receiving agent who is contracted by the bidder. In case of acceptance of the bid, the share certificates need to be enclosed.
37. Some studies (e.g. Kaplan, 1989b; Asquith and Wizman, 1990; and Easterwood et al., 1994) use hybrid methodologies which correct the premium for a benchmark return (e.g. the S&P500). However, these approaches boil down to an event study with a flexible event window.
38. In this specific case, Firth Rixson Plc, the buyer was an institutional investor who wanted to take the company private under a buy-and-build strategy, for which this company was meant to be the platform.

39. The correlation matrix is given in Appendix 3B and shows that multicollinearity is not an issue. The variance inflation factors of the regression confirm this. We also looked at one set of explanatory variables at a time and compared it with the significance when all sets of explanatory variables are included in the model. For space reasons, these results are not reported here but are both statistically and economically similar to the full models, providing additional evidence that our findings are not driven by multicollinearity.
40. See for a discussion of its statistical properties Strong (1992, p. 545).

REFERENCES

Aghion, P. and Bolton, P. (1992), 'An incomplete contract approach to financial contracting', *Review of Economic Studies*, **59**, 473–94.

Amihud, Y. (1989), *Leveraged Management Buy-Outs*, New York: Dow-Jones Irwin.

Ashurst, Morris, Crisp (2002), 'Public-to-private takeovers in Germany', Ashurst, Morris, Crisp Investment Banking Briefing.

Asquith, P. and Wizman, T. (1990), 'Event risk, covenants, and bondholder returns in leveraged buyouts', *Journal of Financial Economics*, **27**, 195–213.

Benoit, B. (1999), 'Companies and finance: UK: professional expenses prove a deterrent to maintaining stock market exposure: but costs of public-to-private deals can also be considerable', Bertrand Benoit reports. The *Financial Times* of August 31, p. 18.

Campbell, J., Lo, A. and MacKinlay, A.C. (1997), 'Event-study analysis', in *The Econometrics of Financial Markets*, Princeton, NJ: Princeton University Press, ch. 4.

CMBOR (2002), 'Public-to-private buy-outs', in the UK and Continental Europe', Section 3 in *UK Quarterly Review*, Centre for Management Buy-out Research, University of Nottingham, Summer.

CMBOR (2005), 'Public-to-private buy-outs in the UK and Continental Europe', Section 3 in *UK Quarterly Review*, Centre for Management Buy-out Research, University of Nottingham, Winter.

CMBOR (2006), 'European management buy-outs', Centre for Management Buy-out Research, University of Nottingham.

Cook, D.O., Easterwood, J.C. and Martin, J.D. (1992), 'Bondholder wealth effects of management buyouts', *Financial Management*, **21**, 102–13.

Corrado, C.J. (1989), 'A nonparametric test for abnormal security-price performance in event studies', *Journal of Financial Economics*, **23**, 385–95.

Cotter, J. and Peck, S. (2001), 'The structure of debt and active equity investors: the case of the buyout specialist', *Journal of Financial Economics*, **59**, 101–47.

Cowan, A.R. (1992), 'Nonparametric event study tests', *Review of Quantitative Finance and Accounting*, **2**, 343–58.

Crespi, R. and Renneboog, L. (2002), 'Coalition formation and shareholder monitoring in the UK', Working Paper CentER, Tilburg University.

Davis, S. and Day, R. (1998), 'Public-to-private deals: reducing the risk and removing the uncertainty', *UK Venture Capital Journal*, **5**, 1–6.

DeAngelo, L. (1986), 'Accounting numbers as market valuation substitutes: a study of management buyouts of public stockholders', *The Accounting Review*, **61**, 400–420.

DeAngelo, H., DeAngelo, L. and Rice, E.M. (1984), 'Going private: minority freezeouts and stockholder wealth', *Journal of Law and Economics*, **27**, 367–401.

Dicker, A. (1990), 'Tax issues', in B. De Caires (ed.), *Corporate Restructuring*, Euromoney Publications, London.

Dimson, E. (1979), 'Risk measurement when shares are subject to infrequent trading', *Journal of Financial Economics*, **7**, 197–226.
Dyck, A. and Zingales, L. (2004), 'The private benefits of control: an international comparison', *Journal of Finance*, **59**, 537–600.
Easterwood, J., Singer, R., Seth, A. and Lang, D. (1994), 'Controlling the conflict of interest in management buyouts', *Review of Economics and Statistics*, **76**, 512–22.
Frankfurter, G.M. and Gunay, E. (1992), 'Management buy-outs: the sources and sharing of wealth between insiders and outside shareholders', *Quarterly Review of Economics and Finance*, **32**, 82–95.
Franks, J. and Nyborg, K. (1996), 'Control rights, debt structure and the loss of private benefits: the case of the U.K. insolvency code', *Review of Financial Studies*, **9**, 1165–210.
Franks, J., Mayer, C. and Renneboog, L. (2001), 'Who disciplines management of poorly performing companies?', *Journal of Financial Intermediation*, **10**, 209–48.
Goergen, M. and Renneboog, L. (2004), 'Shareholder wealth effects of European domestic and cross-border takeover bids', *European Financial Management Journal*, **10**, 9–45.
Goh, J., Gombola, M., Liu, F.Y. and Chou, D.W. (2002), 'Going-private restructuring and earnings expectations: a test of the release of favorable information for target firms and industry rivals', Working Paper.
Goldstein, D. (2000), 'Hostile takeovers as corporate governance? Evidence from the 1980s', *Review of Political Economy*, **12**, 381–400.
Grossman, S.J. and Hart, O.D. (1980), 'Take-over bids, the free-rider problem and the theory of the corporation', *Bell Journal of Economics*, **11**, 42–64.
Halpern, P., Kieschnick, R. and Rotenberg, W. (1999), 'On the heterogeneity of leveraged going private transactions', *Review of Financial Studies*, **12**, 281–309.
Harlow, W.V. and Howe, J.S. (1993), 'Leveraged buyouts and insider nontrading', *Financial Management*, **22**, 109–18.
Harris, R., Siegel, D. and Wright, M. (2005), 'Assessing the impact of management buyouts on economic efficiency: plant-level evidence from the United Kingdom', *Review of Economics and Statistics*, **87**, 148–53.
Holderness, C.G. and Sheehan, D. (1988), 'The role of majority shareholders in publicly held corporations', *Journal of Financial Economics*, **20**, 317–46.
Holmstrom, B. and Kaplan, S.N. (2001), 'Corporate governance and merger activity in the U.S.: making sense of the '80s and '90s', *Journal of Economic Perspectives*, **15**, 121–44.
Hubbard, G. and Palia, D. (1995), 'Benefits of control, managerial ownership, and the stock returns of acquiring firms', *RAND Journal of Economics*, **26**, 782–94.
Jensen, M.C. (1986), 'Agency costs of free cash flow, corporate finance and takeovers', *American Economic Review*, **76**, 323–9.
Jensen, M.C. (1989), 'The eclipse of the public corporation', *Harvard Business Review*, **67**, 61–74.
Jensen, M.C. (1991), 'Corporate control and the politics of finance', *Journal of Applied Corporate Finance*, **4**, 13–33.
Jensen, M.C. (1993), 'The modern industrial revolution: exit and the failure of internal control systems', *Journal of Finance*, **48**, 831–80.
Jensen, M.C. and Meckling, W. (1976), 'Theory of the firm: managerial behavior, agency costs and ownership structure', *Journal of Financial Economics*, **3**, 305–60.
Jensen, M.C. and Ruback, R.S. (1983), 'The market for corporate control; the scientific evidence', *Journal of Financial Economics*, **11**, 5–50.

Kaestner, R. and Liu, F.Y. (1996), 'Going private restructuring: the role of insider trading', *Journal of Business Finance and Accounting*, **23**, 779–806.
Kaplan, S.N. (1989a), 'The effects of management buyouts on operating performance and value', *Journal of Financial Economics*, **24**, 217–54.
Kaplan, S.N. (1989b), 'Management buyouts: evidence on taxes as a source of value', *Journal of Finance*, **44**, 611–32.
Kaplan, S.N. and Stein, J. (1993), 'The evolution of buy-out pricing and financial structure in the 1980s', *Quarterly Journal of Economics*, **108**, 313–59.
Kaplan, S.N. and Strömberg, P.J. (2001), 'Venture capitalists as principals: contracting, screening and monitoring', *American Economic Review*, **91**, 426–30.
Kieschnick, R.L. (1998), 'Free cash flow and stockholder gains in going private transactions revisited', *Journal of Business Finance and Accounting*, **25**, 187–202.
Kothari, S.P. and Warner, J.B. (1997), 'Measuring long-horizon security performance', *Journal of Financial Economics*, **43**, 301–39.
Kuhn Capital (2003), *Going-Private Equity*, Kuhn Capital Publication.
Lee, D.S. (1992), 'Management buyout proposals and inside information', *Journal of Finance*, **47**, 1061–79.
Lee, C.I., Rosenstein, S., Rangan, N. and Davidson III, W.N. (1992), 'Board composition and shareholder wealth: the case of management buyouts', *Financial Management*, **21**, 58–72.
Lehn, K. and Poulsen, A. (1989), 'Free cash flow and stockholder gains in going private transactions', *Journal of Finance*, **44**, 771–88.
Lowenstein, L. (1985), 'Management buyouts', *Columbia Law Review*, **85**, 730–84.
Marais, L., Schipper, K. and Smith, A. (1989), 'Wealth effects of going private for senior securities', *Journal of Financial Economics*, **23**, 155–91.
Martynova, M. and Renneboog, L. (2005), 'Takeover waves: triggers, performance and motives', Working Paper, European Corporate Governance Institute and Tilburg University.
Martynova, M. and Renneboog, L. (2006), 'Mergers and acquisitions in Europe', Working Paper, European Corporate Governance Institute and Tilburg University.
Miller, G.P. (2000), 'Takeovers: English and American', *European Financial Management*, **6**, 533–41.
Mitchell, M. and Mulherin, H. (1996), 'The impact of industry shocks on takeover and restructuring activity', *Journal of Financial Economics*, **41**, 193–229.
Morck, R., Shleifer, A. and Vishny, R.W. (1988), 'Management ownership and market valuation; an empirical analysis', *Journal of Financial Economics*, **20**, 293–315.
Murphy, K.J. (1985), 'Corporate performance and managerial remuneration: an empirical analysis', *Journal of Accounting and Economics*, **7**, 11–42.
Opler, T. and Titman, S. (1993), 'The determinants of leveraged buyout activity: free cash flow versus financial distress costs', *Journal of Finance*, **48**, 1985–99.
Paul, A. (1994), *United Kingdom. The Mergers and Acquisitions 1994 Yearbook*.
Perry, S. and Williams, T. (1994), 'Earnings management preceding management buyout offers', *Journal of Accounting and Economics*, **18**, 152–79.
Renneboog, L. and Simons, T. (2005), 'Public to private transactions: LBOs, MBOs, MBIs and IBOs', Working Paper, European Corporate Governance Institute and Tilburg University.
Renneboog, L. and Szilagyi, P. (2006), 'How do mergers and acquisitions affect bondholders in Europe? Evidence on the impact and spillover of governance and legal standards', Working Paper, European Corporate Governance Institute.

Schadler, F.P. and Karns, J.E. (1990), 'The unethical exploitation of shareholders in management buyout transactions', *Journal of Business Ethics*, **9**, 595–602.
Shleifer, A. and Summers, C.H. (1988), 'Breach of trust in hostile takeovers', in A.J. Auerbach (ed.), *Corporate Takeovers: Causes and consequences*, Chicago, IL: University of Chicago Press, ch. 2.
Shleifer, A. and Vishny, R.W. (1991), 'The takeover wave of the 1980s', *Journal of Applied Corporate Finance*, **4**, 49–56.
Singh, H. (1990), 'Management buyouts: distinguishing characteristics and operating changes prior to public offering', *Strategic Management Journal*, **11**, 111–29.
Slovin, M.B., Sushka, M.E. and Bendeck, Y.M. (1991), 'The intra-industry effects of going-private proposals', *Journal of Finance*, **46**, 1537–50.
Smith, A. (1776), *The Wealth of Nations*, 1976 edn, Glasgow: Penguin Classics.
Smith, A. (1990), 'Corporate ownership structure and performance: the case of management buy-outs', *Journal of Financial Economics*, **27**, 143–64.
Strong, N. (1992), 'Modelling abnormal returns: a review article', *Journal of Business Finance and Accounting*, **19**, 533–53.
Stulz, R. (1988), 'Managerial control of voting rights, financing policies, and the market for corporate control', *Journal of Financial Economics*, **20**, 25–54.
Toms, S. and Wright, M. (2005), 'Divergence and convergence within Anglo-American corporate governance systems: evidence from the US and UK 1950–2000', *Business History*, **47**, 267–95.
Torabzadeh, K.M. and Bertin, W.J. (1987), 'Leveraged buyouts and shareholder wealth', *Journal of Financial Research*, **10**, 313–19.
Travlos, N.G. and Cornett, M.M. (1993), 'Going private buyouts and determinants of shareholders' returns', *Journal of Accounting, Auditing & Finance*, **8**, 1–25.
Van de Gucht, L.M. and Moore, W.T. (1998), 'Predicting the duration and reversal probability of leveraged buyouts', *Journal of Empirical Finance*, **5**, 299–315.
Warga, A. and Welch, I. (1993), 'Bondholder losses in leveraged buyouts', *The Review of Financial Studies*, **6**, 959–82.
Weir, C., Laing, D. and Wright, M. (2005a), 'Incentive effects, monitoring mechanisms and the threat from the market for corporate control: an analysis of the factors affecting public to private transactions in the UK', *Journal of Business Finance and Accounting*, **32**, 909–44.
Weir, C., Laing, D. and Wright, M. (2005b), 'Undervaluation, private information, agency costs and the decision to go private', *Applied Financial Economics*, **15**, 947–61.
Weston, J.F., Chung, K.S. and Siu, J.A. (1998), *Takeovers, Restructuring and Corporate Governance*, 2nd edn, New York: Prentice-Hall.
White, H. (1980), 'A heteroskedasticity-consistent covariance matrix estimator and a direct test for heteroskedasticity', *Econometrica*, **48**, 817–38.
Wright, M., Thompson, S., Chiplin, B. and Robbie, K. (1991), *Buy-Ins and Buy-Outs: New strategies in corporate management*, London: Graham & Trotman.
Wright, M., Chiplin, B., Robbie, K. and Albrighton, M. (2000a), 'The development of an organizational innovation: management buy-outs in the UK', *Business History*, **42**, 137–84.
Wright, M., Hoskisson, R., Busenitz, L. and Dial, J. (2000b), 'Entrepreneurial growth through privatization: the upside of management buyouts', *Academy of Management Review*, **25**, 591–601.
Wright, M., Renneboog, L., Simons, T. and Scholes, L. (2006), 'Leveraged buy-outs in the UK and Europe: retrospect and prospect', *Journal of Applied Corporate Finance*, **18**, 38–55.

4. Irrevocable commitments, going private and private equity

Mike Wright, Charlie Weir and Andrew Burrows

1. INTRODUCTION

There is growing recognition that hostile, and competing, public bids represent only a small part of the takeover process (Schwert, 1996, 2000; Moeller et al., 2004). Rather, many takeovers are either friendly (Weir and Laing, 2003) or involve private actions and bargaining processes before the bid becomes public (Hansen, 2001; Boone and Mulherin, 2002, 2003).

The goal of this chapter is to add to this debate by addressing an important but neglected aspect of the takeover process, namely irrevocable commitments. These are undertakings given by existing shareholders to agree to sell their shares to the bidder before the bid is announced and so represent a measure of private activity (Berwin, 2003). They are an established feature of takeover transactions and are explicitly recognized in UK corporate law and takeover codes. They are part of the public bid process because they have to be made public when the bid is announced but obtaining them also involves private actions by the bidder prior to the bid announcement. Significant irrevocable commitments are also likely to deter alternative bidders. Gaining irrevocable commitments, therefore, involves actions by a bidder to ensure that they maximize the probability of success. In this chapter, we discuss irrevocable commitments in relation to public to private transactions (PTPs) and examine the factors that determine the level of irrevocable commitments obtained by the bidder from existing shareholders.

PTPs represent a novel form of takeover in which a listed corporation is taken private as an independent company with a new ownership and new financing structure, traditionally involving significant debt. UK PTPs provide a particularly fertile context in which to study irrevocable commitments for a number of reasons. First, the UK has experienced a significant change in the way in which the market for corporate control operates, with PTPs accounting for 30% of all acquisitions of publicly quoted companies by the early 2000s compared with only 4% during the early 1990s. Second, irrevocable commitments play a central role in the sale process of these PTPs (CMBOR, 2003). For example, during the period 1998–2003 the mean level of irrevocable commitments in UK PTPs accounted for 42.25% of equity. Third, the UK PTP sector is characterized by a very low level of public bidding by competing or hostile bidders. Fourth, private equity firms play an important role in negotiating and financing PTPs (CMBOR, 2003). It is therefore relevant to analyse their involvement in gaining irrevocable commitments.

The chapter extends existing literatures on both the bid process and PTP buy-outs. Previous literature on the bid process has considered a number of aspects. One, toehold bids may be used where the seller controls the sale process but may be problematical (Betton and Eckbo, 2000; Bulow et al., 1999). Two, Cornu and Isakov (2000) show that the medium of payment may be used to deter other buyers from entering the market. Three, information may be disclosed privately to a limited number of potential buyers before a takeover bid becomes public (Boone and Mulherin, 2002, 2003). Four, bidders may privately negotiate lock-up options from target management which may deter other bidders (Burch, 2001). Five, and similar to lock-ups, termination fees may be negotiated. These are payable to the bidder by the target if a merger is not consummated after a merger agreement is signed by the company's board of directors (Officer, 2003). An examination of the determinants of lock-up and termination fee usage by Coates and Subramanian (2000) shows that target termination fees are more likely with larger targets and the use of tender offers.

The literature on PTP buy-outs has tended to compare the characteristics of firms going private with those that remained public. These studies have analysed performance (Lehn and Poulsen, 1989; Kieschnick, 1998; Opler and Titman, 1993), governance characteristics (Baliga et al., 1996; Weir et al., 2005a), the potential tax advantages of going private (Kaplan, 1989; Halpern et al., 1999), the wealth effects gained by shareholders in firms going private (De Angelo et al., 1984; Lee et al., 1992; Easterwood et al., 1994; Renneboog et al., 2007), and the role of pressure from the market for corporate control (Lehn and Poulsen, 1989; Halpern et al., 1999). In addition, Citron et al. (2003) have analysed the recovery rates of creditors when management buy-outs fail. The pre-investment valuation methods used by venture capitalists, which play a significant role in the European buy-out market, have been studied by Manigart et al. (2000). The LBO literature more generally has considered the role of the reputation of LBO associations and private equity firms in influencing the longevity of buy-outs (Kaplan, 1991) and in the performance of IPOs of private-equity-backed buy-outs (Jelic et al., 2005).

The chapter builds on these literatures and makes a number of contributions to our understanding of the bid process. First, in contrast to much of the existing LBO literature which concentrates on the end of the PTP transaction, this chapter examines an aspect of the process up to a bid being announced. Second, and related to the first point, an understanding of the importance of private, pre-announcement activity may offer insights into the apparent increase in the frequency of non-hostile takeover activity, for example, only seven, or 4.5%, of our sample experienced a hostile bid. Third, we analyse the factors that influence the willingness of current shareholders to give irrevocable commitments to accept an offer before the bid is made public. Fourth, we analyse differences between internally driven management buy-outs (MBOs) and externally driven management buy-ins (MBIs), since these differences may influence the ability of the bidder to obtain irrevocable commitments. Fifth, we build on evidence of the important certification effect of private equity firms in IPOs to consider whether commitment to a proposed PTP involving a reputable private equity firm signals to existing shareholders that the firm may benefit from being taken private, particularly if there is unlikely to be an alternative buyer.

The basis for the analysis consists of a unique, hand-collected dataset involving PTP transactions completed in the UK during the period 1998–2003. As Figure 4.1 shows, prior to 1998, PTP activity was extremely low so the period analysed covers the years when PTP activity had increased significantly.

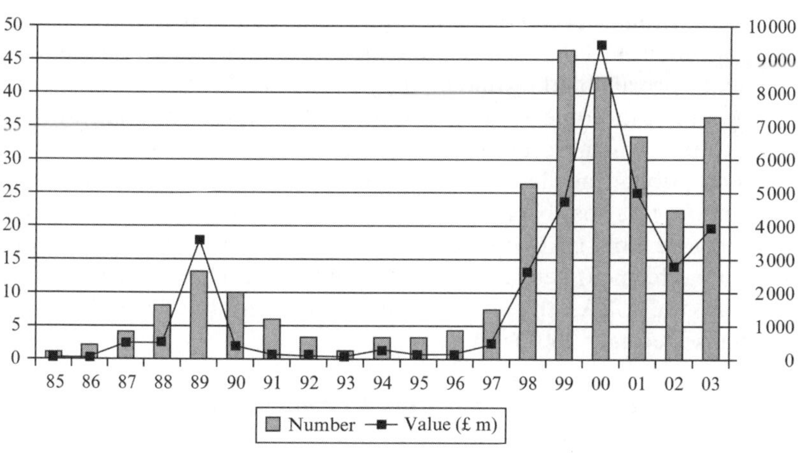

Source: CMBOR.

Figure 4.1 UK public to private buy-outs, 1985–2003

For PTPs in general, we find that the less the takeover speculation, the higher the bid value, and the larger the board shareholdings, the higher the level of irrevocable commitments. We find that those proposing a management buy-out (MBO) are more likely to gain the backing of other shareholders the greater the bid premium and the more likely the private equity backer is to be reputable. Irrevocable commitments are also more likely to be higher if there is less takeover interest from other firms and the larger the value of the bid. In contrast, the MBI results are less encouraging.

The remainder of this chapter is organized as follows. Section 2 reviews the nature of the bid process and irrevocable commitments. Section 3 develops hypotheses relating to the determinants of the level of irrevocable commitments. Section 4 provides an overview of the development of PTPs in the UK. It also describes data sources and examines the sample characteristics, outlines the model specification and defines the variables. The results are presented in Section 5 and the final section presents some conclusions.

2. THE BID PROCESS AND IRREVOCABLE COMMITMENTS

In this section, we provide a discussion of the takeover process and the importance of irrevocable commitments to that process.

2.1 The Sales Process

Boone and Mulherin (2003) identify a five-step sales process consisting of an initiation event, contact with potential buyers, signing confidentiality agreements, private bidding and finally public bidding. They recognize that the initiation can come from either the seller or buyer. This process is similar to that which occurs in the UK. However, as far as we are aware, there is no publicly available information about step four, private bidding. It is therefore not possible to use official documents to assess the extent of activity before a bid is announced. In addition, the private auction process implies an agreement between buyer and seller about the conduct of a bid. Unlike in the USA, this is very uncommon in the UK (Freshfields Bruckhaus Deringer 2002).

2.2 The Sales Process and Irrevocable Commitments

By examining irrevocable commitments it is possible to gain important insights into the bid process because obtaining them involves private actions by the bidder before the bid is announced. Irrevocable commitments are explicitly recognized in UK corporate law and takeover codes. The UK's City Code on Takeovers and Mergers includes both rules concerning the conduct of management buy-outs of listed corporations and restrictions relating to irrevocable commitments in terms of the number of shareholders that can be approached to obtain irrevocable commitments, the prohibition of favourable treatment for those offering irrevocable commitments without Takeover Panel consent, and the disclosure of irrevocable commitments.

The importance of irrevocable commitments to reducing the risk of failure of the buy-out bid is highlighted by both the costs of undertaking such transactions and the regulations governing them in the UK. The costs of undertaking a PTP that fails to be completed can be high and hence gaining irrevocable commitments may be regarded as a means of avoiding these costs. Private equity financiers report that the costs of undertaking a PTP far exceed those involved in other buy-out deals and can amount to 10% of the transaction value (CMBOR, 1999). As PTPs are generally funded by small amounts of private equity and significant amounts of leverage raised specifically to fund the purchase, bid failure may mean that the bidder is left as a minority holder which faces the difficulty of unloading shares to repay debt in what may be an illiquid market. In these circumstances, irrevocable commitments may be especially relevant since they can alleviate some of the uncertainties associated with the bid process.

With respect to takeover regulations, to take a company private in the UK, the bidder must achieve 75% of the equity (Sterling and Wright, 1990). It is unusual for a bidder to declare the bid unconditional when it holds less than the 75% of the ordinary stock it needs to be able re-register the corporation as a private company. However, it is generally necessary to acquire 90% plus of the equity because this enables the bidder to compulsorily purchase the remaining minority shareholdings. If the buy-out bid acquires between 75% and 90% of common stock, the buyer can seek to pass a special resolution to re-register the corporation as a private company. However, minority stockholdings of at least 5% in nominal value of the issued stock or at least 50 members can apply within 28 days to the court to cancel the resolution. If a dissentient minority has 25% plus of the common stock, they can block the resolution to go private. Once a company is re-registered as private, the new owners can take advantage of the private company's exemptions from the financial assistance rules of the Companies Act (Berwin, 2003).

Gaining irrevocable commitments therefore means that the bidder is sending a signal to other non-committed shareholders about the quality of the deal. The announcement of substantial irrevocable commitments may also make other potential bidders less likely to enter the contest with an alternative bid. If they do, a competing bid must be made within 21 days of the posting of the offer documents. It may, however, be difficult for an alternative buyer to complete due diligence within the required time. Private equity firms considering bidding are in particular likely to want to undertake due diligence (Graham, 2001; Berwin, 2003). Existing shareholders may also have the incentive to give irrevocable commitments as they may be able to negotiate conditions that enable them to sell their shares to a new bidder offering a higher price (so-called 'soft' commitments) (Berwin, 2003).

3. FACTORS AFFECTING THE LEVEL OF IRREVOCABLE COMMITMENTS

Having discussed the importance of irrevocable commitments, we consider the following potential influences on the level of irrevocable commitments: the size of the transaction; the bid premium offered; the extent of press speculation about takeovers; the reputation of private equity financiers; the size of shareholding held by board members; and the accounting performance of the firm.

3.1 Bid Value

The problem for acquirers where the target has dispersed stockholders is well recognized (Grossman and Hart, 1980). Given that shareholdings are likely to be more dispersed in larger corporations, it will be more difficult for PTP bidders to gain the support of significant numbers of shareholders. However, the smaller the PTP, the more likely it is that the bidder will be able to gain substantial support for their plans. Hence, we expect that the larger the value of the deal, the more difficult it will be to gain significant irrevocable undertakings. We expect that this relationship will hold for PTPs involving both MBOs and MBIs. Hence:

H1: There is a negative relationship between the value of a PTP and the extent of irrevocable commitments.

3.2 Return on Assets

If a company is performing poorly, with little apparent prospect of recovery, there is less incentive for the shareholders to maintain their stake in the company. Poorly performing firms are likely to offer little in the way of dividends paid or capital gains, which means that existing shareholders are likely to be looking for an exit route. In such cases, institutional investors may be willing to encourage an MBO bid as this may be the only feasible means by which they can effect an exit. In an environment of few hostile bidders competing to take over underperforming assets and replace management, a bid by a corporate acquirer may not emerge. The emergence of MBIs backed by private equity firms provides an alternative where incumbent management may not have performed effectively enough to secure institutional support. Institutional shareholders may be more willing to give irrevocable commitments to MBIs because they expect incoming management to improve performance. It is therefore expected that irrevocable commitments will be higher the poorer the company performance in PTPs involving both MBOs and MBIs. Hence:

H2: There is a negative relationship between pre-PTP performance and the extent of irrevocable commitments.

3.3 Bid Premium

Acquirers typically need to offer a premium on the prevailing share price to persuade existing stockholders to sell. There is extensive evidence that premia are higher in hostile rather than friendly bids (Jarrell et al., 1988). Public to private buy-out transactions also generate significant bid premiums. A series of studies (DeAngelo et al., 1984; Torabzadeh and Bertin, 1987; Kaplan, 1989; Lehn and Poulsen, 1989; Marais et al., 1989b) have each found significant abnormal gains for the target's shareholders around the time of the announcement to go private. The implied bid premium appears even larger than that found in conventional acquisitions as sellers aim to capture some of the expected future gains from the improved incentive and governance mechanisms introduced on buy-out.

In order to persuade existing shareholders to commit to the PTP, bidders may need to offer a premium sufficiently above the current share price that minimizes the likelihood of an alternative bidder emerging and which also reflects at least part of the expected future gains from the PTP. The higher the bid premium, the more likely existing shareholders will support a bid because of the financial windfall. Institutional investors may recognize that managers proposing an MBO may have greater private information about future prospects. For institutional investors to be convinced that incumbents are not exploiting this information to their detriment, they may expect a higher premium to be offered. Management and their private equity firm backers may also recognize that, since it would send a negative signal about their behaviour if they were subsequently to increase their bid, they need to offer a sufficiently attractive bid from the outset. Indeed, following concerns about the offer in the Magnet buy-out in 1989, the Takeover Code in the UK specifically introduced rules concerning the conduct of public to private bids to ensure that a fair price was offered (Wright et al., 1991).[1]

As discussed above, a potential buyer will seek to gain the backing of shareholders by means of irrevocable commitments. It will therefore be important to gain this support as early in the takeover process as possible because a lack of support may result in a bid not being made. This means that an indication of the extent of the firm's current undervaluation will have to be incorporated into the offer price at an early stage of the process. For this reason, the use of abnormal returns around the date of the bid announcement is not appropriate because the time period is too short to take account of the period at which the offer was made. Weir et al. (2005b) show that undervaluation persists over a period of time prior to going private and, using market capitalization data, find significant evidence of undervaluation in firms going private. Given the time involved in completing a PTP transaction, and the need to gain support from existing shareholders early in the process, we argue that the use of market capitalization data offers a useful point of reference against which to measure the extent of the market undervaluation and hence the premium offered. Hence:

H3a: There is a positive relationship between the premium paid in PTP MBOs and the extent of irrevocable commitments.

Management in MBIs are outsiders and may not have access to such information. In addition, MBIs tend to involve more turnaround cases (Robbie and Wright, 1996). However, it is still the case that shareholders have to find an offer financially appealing. Therefore the higher the premium, the greater the irrevocable commitments gained. Hence:

H3b: There is a positive relationship between the premium paid in PTP MBIs and the extent of irrevocable commitments.

3.4 Bid Rumours

The extent to which information is publicly available may guide the private actions of the shareholders. There is evidence that press speculation about possible takeovers does contain valuable information (Pound and Zeckhauser, 1990). Press speculation about a possible acquisition will provide a proxy for potential outside interest in the company (Lehn and Poulsen, 1989).

External shareholders may have a greater incentive to commit to the PTP where they are convinced that the likelihood of a competing bidder appearing is minimal. The less there is press speculation, the less likely it is that other buyers are interested in the company. This will make it easier for those wishing to take the company private to gain support from other shareholders. We therefore expect that less takeover speculation will make it easier to gain backing to take the company private in an MBO. Hence:

H4a: There is a negative relationship between takeover rumours in PTP MBOs and the extent of irrevocable commitments.

The emergence of an MBI bid may suggest to external shareholders that if one outside bidder is available, so are others. Hence, in respect of MBIs we also expect takeover rumours to be negatively associated with irrevocable commitments:

H4b: There is a negative relationship between takeover rumours in PTP MBIs and the extent of irrevocable commitments.

3.5 Private Equity Firms

The growing interest in the role of venture capitalists (VCs) and private equity firms and the stock market has tended to focus on IPOs of VC-backed firms (Brav and Gompers, 1997; Lerner, 1994; Espenlaub et al., 2000). The presence of venture capital and private equity investors has an important influence on the going-public process, particularly if these financiers are more experienced and reputable. Supportive evidence from IPOs of venture-backed firms is provided by Megginson and Weiss (1991) and Gompers (1996), and for IPOs of private-equity-backed LBOs by Jelic et al. (2005). Going private also usually involves the participation of private equity providers, some of which may have strong reputations as specialists in buy-out transactions (Kaplan, 1991; Baker and Smith, 1998).

It is reasonable to argue that the choice of private equity provider may be linked to the provider's reputation (Kester and Luehrman, 1995). One with a successful track record may encourage shareholders to commit to a deal because they will regard this as providing some sort of seal of approval to the plan and that the equity provider will be able to secure sufficient funding for the deal.

Reputable private equity firms may therefore be more able to persuade existing shareholders to commit to a buy-out bid. Their idiosyncratic skills may enable reputable private equity firms to identify and realize gains that others cannot and hence offer a more convincing rationale to existing shareholders. More reputable private equity firms backing management in an MBO may also provide a certification role in that they may be perceived to be associated with offering a fair priced deal to protect their reputation in order to access future deals. Thus the higher the reputation of the private equity firm, the more likely that shareholders will commit to the deal, especially in PTPs involving MBOs. The above arguments also apply to MBIs. Therefore, for MBOs and MBIs, the higher the reputation of the private equity provider, the greater the irrevocable commitments. Hence:

H5: There is a positive relationship between the reputation of the private equity firm supporting a PTP and the extent of irrevocable commitments.

3.6 Board Ownership

Evidence of higher board shareholdings in firms going private was found by Maupin (1987) and Halpern et al. (1999). An MBO's irrevocable commitments will normally include all or most of the current management's shareholdings in addition to any external backing they may receive. Therefore as board ownership increases, irrevocable commitments will also increase. Although there is an inherent conflict of interest between institutional shareholders and managers in an MBO bid, it is likely that significant board ownership will encourage other shareholders to back the bid to go private since a board shareholding that is sufficiently large may make an opposing bid unlikely (Song and Walkling, 1993). Thus, for MBOs, we expect that the higher the board shareholdings, the higher the irrevocable commitments. Hence:

H6a: There is a positive relationship between board shareholdings in PTP MBOs and the extent of irrevocable commitments.

With respect to MBIs, if the outside buyers wanted to complete the process without informing the management of the takeover bid, the buyers would simply gain as much support as possible from other shareholders. Insiders who are not involved in an MBI attempt may be concerned that a successful hostile MBI may lead to their removal. Where boards are dominated by internal management, evidence suggests that management may not be able to influence the outcome once a hostile bid occurs (Sudarsanam, 1995; O'Sullivan and Wong, 1999). This suggests that where institutional shareholders are unhappy with incumbent management's performance, yet incumbent board members have large equity stakes, they may try to increase the probability of an outside bid succeeding by being even more willing to offer irrevocable commitments. PTPs involving hostile MBI bids are, however, rare (CMBOR, 2003).

An alternative explanation is that external buyers may have the incumbent management on their side. This may arise, for example, where the PTP is initiated by a private equity firm that recognizes that there is a need to supplement at least some of the incumbent team with stronger external management; incumbent management may be retained as they have important specific knowledge about the business. In these cases, it may be easier to persuade other shareholders to support the bid before it is made public. This would also suggest a positive relationship between irrevocable commitments and board ownership for MBIs. Hence:

H6b: There is a positive relationship between board shareholdings in PTP MBIs and the extent of irrevocable commitments.

4. UK PUBLIC TO PRIVATES: SECTOR AND SAMPLE ISSUES

4.1 UK Public to Private Characteristics and Issues

In the USA, PTPs first appeared in significant numbers in the 1980s. In the UK, PTPs were in evidence from the mid-1980s but, as Figure 4.1 shows, activity was modest (Wright et al., 2000). The UK experienced a significant increase in the number and value of PTPs during the late 1990s. During the eight-year period 1990–97, only 37 PTPs took place in total (an average of 4.6 per year) whereas during the three-year period 1998–2003, there were 205 PTPs (an average of 34 per year) (CMBOR, 2003). The average value of each deal was £29.8 million for 1990–97 and £136.28 million for 1998–2003, which represents a 4.57-fold increase in deal size. Many firms that go private are relatively small. For example, even in the period 1998–2003, 90% of PTPs had a market capitalisation of less than £300 million (approx. $570 million). The increased importance of PTPs in the overall MBO market is highlighted by the fact that from accounting for 2.8% of the total MBO market value over the period 1990–97, they accounted for 26.2% during the period 1998–2003. We therefore focus on the period in which there was a significant increase in PTP activity.

4.2 Data

Data were obtained for PTPs completed in the UK during the period 1998–2003. The data included performance, ownership, takeover speculation and private equity provider information. This gave us a final sample of 155 PTPs. The names of firms going private were provided by the Centre for Management Buy-out Research (CMBOR), which is based at the University of Nottingham, and which comprises the effective population of buy-outs in the UK. The CMBOR database is compiled from a wide range of sources including twice-yearly surveys of private equity and debt providers to buy-outs,[2] press releases by these financiers, the financial press, stock exchange circulars issued by companies and companies' annual reports. The database has no lower size cut-off. Information about irrevocable commitments was obtained from the offer documents, FT Intelligence and Vickers (2000). CMBOR also provided data on the private equity providers funding and their reputations. Data on the value of the bids were obtained from CMBOR. Information relating to takeover rumours was taken from FT Intelligence. Data on board shareholdings were taken from the PriceWaterhouse Corporate Register. Accounting data were taken from Company Analysis.

The distribution of the sample over each of the years 1998–2003 is shown in Table 4.1 in terms the total value, total number and mean value per deal.

In our sample, the value of PTPs increased from £2,739 million in 1998 to £4,437 million in 2000 and by 2003, it was £1,790 million. In total, the sample's value of bids was £17,863 million. The average value of bids over the period is £115.25 million. The average value increased from £105.34 million in 1998 to £164.43 million in 2000 but has been declining since, to £68.84 million in 2003. This indicates that PTPs are on average getting smaller even though the number has been increasing. A similar pattern applies to MBOs, with the mean value of deals increasing from £105.3 million in 1998 to £164.4 million in 2000 and subsequently falling to £68.84

Table 4.1 Descriptive statistics of deals

Year	Total value of deals £ m			Number of deals			Mean value per deal £ m		
	PTP	MBO	MBI	PTP	MBO	MBI	PTP	MBO	MBI
1998	2739	54	2235	26	13	13	105.34	38.77	171.92
1999	3605	1976	1629	33	25	8	109.79	79.04	203.63
2000	4437	1707	331	27	20	7	164.43	85.35	390.00
2001	4070	3739	331	28	21	7	145.37	178.04	47.34
2002	1222	138	1084	15	8	7	81.46	17.31	154.73
2003	1790	557	1239	26	18	8	68.84	60.62	154.90

Notes: Descriptive statistics on sample value of PTP, MBO and MBI deals, the number of deals by PTP, MBO and MBI and the average deal value for PTPs, MBOs and MBIs. The figures relate to the years 1998–2003. This table presents data on the total transaction value, the number of PTPs and the mean value of PTPs by the year of deal completion. Some numbers do not sum because of rounding.

Source: CMBOR.

Table 4.2 Sample industrial classification distribution of deals

Sector	Number of deals			Percentage of sample	Percentage of firms in sector
	Total PTP	MBO	MBI		
1100 Chemicals	2	0	2	1.3	1.22
1300 Building and Construction	9	9	0	5.8	2.07
2400 Diversified Industrials	4	1	3	2.6	6.25
2500 Electronic and Electrical Engineering	3	2	1	1.9	0.82
2600 Engineering	15	7	8	9.7	2.85
3100 Automobiles	2	2	0	1.3	2.38
3200 Alcoholic Beverages	2	1	2	1.3	3.85
3400 Household Goods	19	17	2	12.3	3.74
3600 Healthcare	6	4	2	3.9	2.33
4300 Food Producers	9	6	3	5.8	2.74
5100 Distribution	10	7	3	6.5	2.16
5200 General Retailers	13	6	7	8.4	2.63
5300 Leisure and Hotels	12	6	6	7.7	2.24
5400 Media	7	6	1	4.5	1.00
5600 Food Retailers	4	4	0	2.6	3.13
5800 Support Services	14	10	4	9.0	1.57
5900 Transport	5	4	1	3.2	1.63
7800 Water	2	1	1	1.3	2.78
8600 Real Estate	11	8	3	7.1	1.81
8700 Other Financial Services	1	0	1	0.6	0.14
9300 Information Technology Hardware	1	1	0	0.6	0.46
9700 Software and Computer Services	4	3	1	2.6	0.41

Notes: Sample industrial classification distribution by the number of deals by PTP, MBO and MBI, the percentage of the sample and the percentage of the total number of firms in the sector over the period 1998–2003.

in 2003. Although there were more MBOs in 2003 compared to 2002, the number is lower than in 1999. The number of MBIs has remained relatively stable over the period but there have been substantial changes to the average value of deals, with the figures ranging from £390 million in 2000 to £47.34 million in 2001.

Table 4.2 shows the distribution of the sample by sector. We find that PTPs occur in a wide range of sectors, with the most common being Household Goods, Engineering, General Retailing and Support Services.

Table 4.3 Irrevocable commitments by quintile

	PTP (%)	MBO (%)	MBI (%)
1	23.40	24.08	19.28
2	37.42	37.04	36.63
3	50.06	50.57	49.46
4	57.84	60.52	55.02
5	>57.84	>60.52	>55.02
Median	44.60	45.86	42.10

Notes: The percentage of PTPs, MBOs and MBIs that had irrevocable commitments in each quintile. Quintile 1 is lowest 20% of irrevocablen commitments and quintile 5 is highest 20% of irrevocable commitments. The median figure for each type of transaction is also given.

Other sectors with relatively large numbers of PTPs are Distribution, Leisure and Hotels and Real Estate. The final column in Table 4.2 shows the number of PTPs as a percentage of the total number of firms in each of the industrial classifications over the period 1998–2003. PTPs are relatively more common in a number of sectors, particularly in Diversified Industrials, Alcoholic Beverages, Household Goods, Food Retailers and Engineering. In contrast, they are less common, relative to the number of firms, in Media, Other Financial Services, Information Technology Hardware and Software, and Computer Services. MBOs are also more frequent in Building and Construction, Household Goods, Media and Support Services. MBIs are relatively more common in sectors such as Engineering, General Retailers and Leisure and Hotels.

Table 4.3 presents the range of irrevocable commitments gained for PTPs, MBOs and MBIs. In relation to PTPs in general, 23.40% of the sample gained up to 20% irrevocables and some 60% achieved at least 50.06% support from shareholders prior to the bid announcement. The most common level of support came in the fourth quintile, with between 50.06% and 57.84% support. MBOs also show significant evidence of pre-bid support, with 40% of MBOs winning more than 50.76% acceptances before the bid announcement. The top quintile achieved over 60% acceptances. MBIs also achieve substantial pre-bid support, with 60% gaining the support of at least 36.62% of the shares before the bid announcement. In general, MBI irrevocable commitments are slightly lower than those for MBOs but the difference is not significant.

The table shows clear evidence of private activity and that the bidders had been successful in gaining significant support for their bids prior to the bids being made public. The median irrevocable commitments figure for PTPs is 44.06%; for MBOs it is 45.83%; and for MBIs it is 42.10%. These figures indicate that the bidders were in an extremely strong position as soon as the announcement of the bid was made public and that potential alternative bidders would be in a difficult position if they put forward an alternative bid. Irrevocable commitments therefore offer an additional insight into the workings of the takeover process.

4.3 Model Specification

The hypotheses developed in Section 3 are tested using OLS. Specifically, we operationalize the following general model:

$$Irrevocables_i = \alpha_0 - \alpha_1 Bidvalue_i + \alpha_2 Premium_i - \alpha_3 Rumours_i + \alpha_4 Reputation_i - \alpha_5 ROA_i + \alpha_6 Boardsh_i + \varepsilon_i$$

The variables used in the analysis are defined as follows:

i. *Dependent variable*
Irrevocables, as the dependent variable, is the percentage of equity committed to the bidder by the existing shareholders before the bid announcement.

ii. *Independent variables*
Ln*BidValue* is the log of the value of the bid (Hypothesis H1). Performance is measured by return on assets, *ROA*, which is defined as earnings before interest and tax deflated by the book value of total assets at the last published accounts (Hypothesis H2). The bid premium, *Premium*, is the value of the bid deflated by the firm's market capitalisation at the date of the last accounts (Hypothesis H3). Speculation about a possible takeover, *Rumours*, is a dummy variable that takes the value of one if the financial press had reported rumours of takeover interest and zero if not (Hypothesis H4). It refers to the reporting of takeover speculation over the period 1–18 months prior to the announcement of the PTP. We use all press speculation, as Lehn and Poulsen (1989), as a measure of pressure from the market for corporate control because this reflects the extent of publicly available information about possible outside interest in the company. The standing of a private equity provider was measured by *Reputation*, a dummy variable which took the value of one if a private equity provider was used in more than two public to private deals in our sample and zero if not (Hypothesis H5). *Boardsh* measures equity ownership of the board deflated by total assets at the last published accounts (Hypothesis H6). We adjust for size because there is evidence that board ownership and company size are negatively related: Mikkelson and Partch (1989) and Song and Walkling (1993).

5. RESULTS

5.1 Descriptive Statistics and Correlations

Table 4.4 provides an overview of the sample's characteristics and correlations. The mean percentage of irrevocable commitments received was 42.25%, although there was a large standard deviation around this level of 20.86%. The median was 44.60%. The public to private firms were on average of modest size, with a mean bid value of £115.25 million but there was a large variation around this position, with a standard deviation of £184.91 million. The mean deflated board shareholding was 1.10 with, again, a large standard deviation of 4.76. On average, 52% of the sample experienced rumours of takeover interest as reported in the financial press. Overall, 32% of the deals used venture capital firms that were involved in more than two of the deals in the sample. The average return on assets was 4.90%.

Table 4.4 also reports the correlation matrix for the independent variables. High correlations indicate the presence of multicollinearity. None of the correlations are excessively high and when the regressions were run, neither the eigen values, which ranged from 0.048 to 0.0925, nor the variance inflation factors, which ranged from 1.064 to 1.406, were near their critical levels for indicating the presence of multicollinearity.

5.2 Multivariate Results

We present results for three sets of dependent variable (Table 4.5). Model 1 refers to all PTPs, model 2 refers to MBOs only and model 3 refers to MBIs. Model 1 shows that as hypothesized, for all PTPs, bid value (Hypothesis H1) and press speculation (Hypothesis H4) are both negative and significant. We also find, again consistent with our hypothesis, that board shareholdings are positive and significant (Hypothesis H6). However, contrary to expectations, neither bid premiums (H3) nor the return on assets (H2) are significant. The model has normally distributed residuals and is significant at the 5% level.

The results for MBOs offer stronger support for our hypotheses. Model 2 shows that, as hypothesised, irrevocable commitments are lower the larger the bid value (Hypothesis H1), indicating that the more diffuse nature of shareholdings in larger firms makes it harder to gain irrevocable commitments. We also find that, consistent with Hypothesis 3a, higher premiums bring about greater irrevocable commitments. Thus existing shareholders are more likely to commit to a buyer, the greater the financial benefit gained from the bid. Consistent with our expectations, we also find that

Table 4.4 Descriptive statistics and correlation matrix

	Mean	SD	*Irrevocables*	*Bidvalue*	*Premium*	*Rumours*	*Reputation*	*Boardsh*
Irrevocables	42.25	20.86						
Bidvalue £m	115.25	184.91	−0.2526					
Premium	1.38	0.61	0.04.9	0.2420				
Rumours	0.52	0.50	−0.2098	0.2437	0.0612			
Reputation	0.32	0.47	0.0158	0.0826	0.0726	0.2248		
Boardsh	1.10	4.76	0.2215	−0.3607	−0.0612	−0.1314	−0.339	
ROA (%)	4.90	17.21	−0.0783	0.3167	−0.0577	0.1340	0.2196	−0.0232

Notes: This table provides means, standard deviations (SD) and correlation matrix for the variables included in the analysis. *Irrevocables* is defined as the percentage of shares committed to the bidders before the public announcement of the bid, *Bidvalue* is the value of the bid in millions of pounds, *Premium* is defined as the value of the accepted bid divided by the market capitalisation at the date of the last accounts, *Rumours* is a dummy variable which takes the value of one if rumours of a takeover had been reported in the financial press over the previous year and zero if not, *Reputation* is a dummy variable which takes the value of one if the private equity provider had been involved in more than two deals in the sample and zero otherwise, *Boardsh* is the percentage of issued capital owned by the board deflated by total assets, and *ROA* is the return on assets defined as earnings before interest and taxes deflated by total assets. SD is the standard deviation.

Table 4.5 OLS regression with the percentage of irrevocable commitments as the dependent variable

	Model 1 PTP sample [n = 155] Model 1	Model 2 MBO sample [n = 105] Model 2	Model 3 MBI sample [n = 50] Model 3
Premium	3.3867	9.8701	−2.5881
	(1.02)	(2.81)***	(1.11)
ROA	−0.0151	−0.0200	0.0494
	(0.12)	(0.13)	(0.34)
Rumours	−5.9871	−9.5508	−4.0660
	(2.11)**	(2.45)**	(0.59)
Reputation	2.5637	7.3628	−6.6058
	(0.73)	(1.77)*	(0.85)
Ln*Bidvalue*	−2.6385	−4.3403	−1.1756
	(2.26)**	(2.77)***	(0.55)
Boardsh	0.6156	0.4205	6.4870
	(3.01)***	(2.58)**	(5.36)***
Constant	49.3410	47.0390	49.9000
	(8.39)***	(6.79)***	(5.14)***
F test	3.28***	4.08***	1.63
R^2	0.12	0.20	0.12
Residual normality chi square	1.95	0.76	0.65

Notes: This table presents OLS regression results where the dependent *Irrevocables* is the percentage of equity committed to the bidder by the existing shareholders before the PTP bid announcement. Ln*Bidvalue* is the natural log of the value of the bid. *ROA* is the return on assets defined as earnings before interest and taxes deflated by total assets. *Premium* is defined as the value of the accepted bid divided by the market capitalisation at the date of the last accounts. *Reputation* is a dummy variable which takes the value of 1 if the private equity provider had been involved in more than two deals in the sample and zero otherwise. *Rumours* is a dummy variable which takes the value of 1 if rumours of a takeover had been reported in the financial press over the previous year and zero if not. *Boardsh* is the percentage of issued capital owned by the board deflated by total assets. *t*-values in parentheses are calculated from heteroscedasticity-corrected standard errors (White, 1980). Significance levels are: *** – significant at the 1% level; ** – significant at the 5% level; * – significant at the 10% level.

irrevocable commitments are higher where takeover speculation is lowest, suggesting that shareholders are more willing to commit to a bidder if there is less likelihood of an alternative buyer (Hypothesis H4a). The private equity provider coefficient is significant and positive, as predicted (Hypothesis H5). This indicates that dealing with a highly reputable private equity provider increases irrevocable commitments. This could work through the signal that it sends to shareholders, that is, that the management is serious in its attempt to go private because it has employed a highly reputable private equity provider. It could also be the result of the ability of the private equity provider to persuade other shareholders to back the bid. Consistent with Hypothesis 6a, we find that irrevocable commitments are higher the greater the board shareholdings. Although negative as predicted, the return on assets was not significant. The equation has normally distributed residuals and is significant at 5%.

In contrast to the MBO sample, the results in Model 3 show that it is much less successful in explaining the extent of irrevocable commitments for MBI transactions. Board shareholdings (Hypothesis 6b) is significant and positive as hypothesized. However, the other variables are insignificant and the F value of Model 3 is also insignificant.

We extended the analysis to take account of the way in which differences in the stock market, as the result of the dot.com boom (and bust), may have affected the willingness of shareholders to give irrevocable commitments. Given the general fall in the stock market, it might be expected that shareholders would be more willing to agree to grant irrevocable commitments as a means of realising some of the lost value suffered by the market downturn. We constructed a dummy variable that took the value of one for the post dot.com boom, 2001–3, and zero for the period of the boom, 1998–2000. The variable was positive but insignificant, showing that irrevocable commitments were not dependent on the change in stock market conditions.

Song and Walkling (1993) reported a non-linear relationship between managerial ownership and size. We followed Song and Walkling and took the square root of board ownership. It was insignificant for PTPs and MBOs, with the MBI equation remaining insignificant. This suggests that non-linearities in the board ownership–size relationship are not present in PTPs. We also extended the analysis of the importance of ownership by assessing the impact of CEO, institutional and blockholding shareholders. In the UK, shareholdings in excess of 3% are reported. We obtained data for total institutional shareholdings in excess of 3% and for total blockholdings in excess of 3%. Institutions were defined as pension funds, insurance companies and investment funds. We expected a positive relationship between irrevocable commitments and institutional shareholdings. Blockholders were defined as private individuals or family members that were not on the board. We expected a positive relationship between irrevocable commitments and blockholder shareholdings. We found that institutional shareholdings were not significant in all three equations. Blockholdings were positive and significant at 5% for all PTPs but insignificant for MBOs and non-MBOs. We also found that CEO ownership was positive and significant at the 1% level for all PTPs and MBOs but was insignificant for non-MBOs. These results show that the support of key ownership groups or individuals is an important element in taking a firm private.

6. CONCLUSIONS

The chapter has contributed to the debate about the sale process by analysing the factors that influence the sale of firms going private. It has shown that bidders involved in PTPs gain substantial backing from shareholders before the bid is made public. It has also provided one of the first analyses of the factors that affect the extent of irrevocable commitments negotiated by potential buyers prior to the public announcement of a bid. We have shown that the model explains MBOs much more effectively than MBIs. It was found that the irrevocable commitments for MBOs could be explained in terms of the value of the bid (Hypothesis H1), the premium offered to other shareholders (Hypothesis H3a), the extent of takeover speculation (Hypothesis H4a), the reputation of the private equity provider used (Hypothesis H5) and board ownership (Hypothesis 6). The Hypothesis H5 result is important because it shows that private equity firms and management involved in public to private MBOs were actively involved in gaining support for the deal by obtaining irrevocable commitments.

The results provide an additional insight into the way in which PTPs take place. Our results suggest that irrevocable commitments are used in an attempt to prevent alternative bidders from entering the bidding process. Consistent with Boone and Mulherin (2002), the results show that, for PTPs in general and MBOs in particular, private activity that takes place before the actual announcement of the bid can have an important impact on the process of going private.

ACKNOWLEDGEMENTS

Financial support from Barclays Private Equity and Deloitte is acknowledged. The helpful comments of John A. Doukas and two anonymous referees are acknowledged with thanks. We would also like to thank David Laing and Louise Scholes for research assistance. We would also like to thank participants at seminars at Cass Business School, Cranfield Business School, King's College London University and at the Department of Trade and Industry. The usual disclaimer applies.

NOTES

1. A number of PTPs failed to complete in the period covered by this study (1998–2003) because the price was reported to be too low (e.g., Litho Supplies) and/or because of failure to convince key block shareholders to sell (e.g., Capitol and Professional Staff).
2. These surveys generally obtain a 100% response rate from all the financiers active in the buy-out market as they receive a free copy of a quarterly review of aggregate market trends based on the data they supply which is recognized as the leading source of information in the market.

REFERENCES

Baker, G. and Smith, G. (1998), *The New Financial Capitalists: KKR and the Creation of Corporate Value*, Cambridge: Cambridge University Press.

Baliga, B., Moyer, R. and Rao, R. (1996), 'CEO duality and firm performance', *Strategic Management Journal*, **17**, 41–53.

Berwin, S.J. (2003), *Public-to-Private: an overview*, London: SJ Berwin.

Betton, S. and Eckbo, B.E. (2000), 'Toeholds, bid jumps and expected payoffs in takeovers', *Review of Financial Studies*, **13**, 841–82.

Boone, A.L. and Mulherin, J.H. (2002), 'Corporate restructuring and corporate auctions', Working Paper, College of William and Mary.

Boone, A.L. and Mulherin, J.H. (2003), 'How are firms sold?' Working Paper, College of William and Mary.

Brav, A. and Gompers, P. (1997), 'Myth or reality? The long-run underperformance of initial public offerings: evidence from venture capital and nonventure capital-backed companies', *Journal of Finance*, **52**, 1791–822.

Bulow, J., Huang, M. and Klemperer, P. (1999), 'Toeholds and takeovers', *Journal of Political Economy*, **107**, 427–54.

Burch, T. (2001), 'Locking out rival bidders: the use of lockup options in corporate mergers', *Journal of Financial Economics*, **60**, 103–41.

Citron, D., Wright, M., Ball, R. and Rippington, F. (2003), 'Secured creditor recovery rates from management buy-outs in distress', *European Financial Management*, **9**, 141–61.

CMBOR (1999), 'Recent developments in the UK public to private buy-out market', *Quarterly Review from the Centre for Management Buy-out Research*, Nottingham University Business School, Winter, pp. 19–40.

CMBOR (2003), *Quarterly Review from the Centre for Management Buy-out Research*, Nottingham University Business School, Spring.

Coates, J. and Subramanian, G. (2000), 'A buy-side model of M&A lockups: theory and evidence', *Stanford Law Review*, **53**, 307–96.

Cornu, P. and Isakov, D. (2000), 'The deterring effect of the medium of payment in takeover contests: theory and evidence from the UK', *European Financial Management*, **6**, 423–40.

DeAngelo, H., DeAngelo, L. and Rice, E. (1984), 'Going private: minority freeze outs and stockholders' wealth', *Journal of Law and Economics*, **27**, 367–402.

Easterwood, J., Singer, R., Seth, A. and Lang, D. (1994), 'Controlling the conflict of interest in management buyouts', *Review of Economics and Statistics*, **76**, 521–2.

Espenlaub, S. Gregory, A. and Tonks, I. (2000), 'Reassessing the long term performance of underperforming UK initial public offerings', *European Financial Management*, **6**, 319–42.
Freshfields Bruckhaus Deringer (2002), *Public Takeovers in the UK*, London: Freshfields Bruckhaus Deringer.
Gompers, P.A. (1996), 'Grandstanding in the venture capital industry', *Journal of Financial Economics*, **42**, 133–56.
Graham, C. (2001), 'The venture capital perspective: why do a public to private?', Presentation at IBC Conference on Public-to-private Takeovers, London, 26 November.
Grossman, S. and Hart, O. (1980), 'Takeover bids, the free rider problem, and the theory of the corporation', *Rand Journal of Economics*, **11**, 42–64.
Halpern, P. Kieschnick, R. and Rotenberg, W. (1999), 'On the heterogeneity of leveraged going private transactions', *Review of Financial Studies*, **12**, 281–309.
Hansen, R. (2001), 'Auctions of companies', *Economic Inquiry*, **39**, 30–43.
Jarrell, G.A., Brickley, J.A. and Netter, J.M. (1988), 'The market for corporate control: the evidence since 1980', *Journal of Economic Perspectives*, **2**, 49–68.
Jelic, R., Saadouni, B. and Wright, M. (2005), 'Performance of private to public MBOs: the role of venture capital', *Journal of Business Finance and Accounting*, **32**, 643–82.
Kaplan, S.N. (1989), 'The effects of management buyouts on operations and value', *Journal of Financial Economics*, **24**, 217–54.
Kaplan, S.N. (1991), 'The staying power of LBOs', *Journal of Financial Economics*, **29**, 287–313.
Kester, C. and Luehrman, T. (1995), 'Rehabilitating the leveraged buyout', *Harvard Business Review*, **73**, 119–30.
Kieschnick, R. (1998), 'Free cash flow and stockholder gains in going private transactions revisited', *Journal of Business Finance and Accounting*, **25**, 187–202.
Lee, C.I., Rosenstein, S., Rangan, N. and Davidson, W. (1992), 'Board composition and shareholder wealth: the case of management buyouts', *Financial Management*, **21**, 58–72.
Lehn, K. and Poulsen, A. (1989), 'Free cash flow and stockholder gains in going private transactions', *Journal of Finance*, **XLIV**, 771–87.
Lerner, J. (1994), 'The syndication of venture capital investments', *Financial Management*, **23**, 16–27.
Manigart, S., De Waele, K., Wright, M., Robbie, K., Desbrieres, P., Sapienza, H. and Beeckman, A. (2000), 'Venture capitalists, investment appraisal and accounting information: a comparative study of the USA, UK, France, Belgium and Holland', *European Financial Management*, **6**, 389–403.
Marais, L., Schipper, K. and Smith, A. (1989), 'Wealth effects of going private for senior securities', *Journal of Financial Economics*, **23**, 155–91.
Maupin, R. (1987), 'Financial and stock market variables as predictors of management buy outs', *Strategic Management Journal*, **8**, 319–27.
Megginson, W. and Weiss, K. (1991), 'Venture capitalist certification in initial public offerings', *Journal of Finance*, **46**, 879–903.
Mikkelson, W. and Partch, M. (1989), 'Managers' voting rights and corporate control', *Journal of Financial Economics*, **25**, 263–90.
Moeller, S.B., Schlingermann, F.P. and Stulz, R.M. (2004), 'Firm size and the gains from acquisitions', *Journal of Financial Economics*, **73**, 201–28.

Officer, M.S. (2003), 'Termination fees in mergers and acquisitions', *Journal of Financial Economics*, **69**, 431–67.
Opler, T. and Titman, S. (1993), 'The determinants of leveraged buyout activity, free cashflow versus financial distress costs', *Journal of Finance*, **48**, 1985–99.
O'Sullivan, N. and Wong, P. (1999), 'Board composition, ownership structure and hostile takeovers: some UK evidence', *Accounting and Business Research*, **29**, 139–55.
Pound, J. and Zeckhauser, R. (1990), 'Clearly heard on the street: the effect of takeover rumors on stock prices', *Journal of Business*, **63**, 291–308.
Renneboog, L., Simons, T. and Wright, M. (2007), 'Leveraged public to private transactions in the UK', *Journal of Corporate Finance*, forthcoming.
Robbie, K. and Wright, M. (1996), *Management Buy-ins: Entrepreneurship, active investors and corporate restructuring*, Manchester: Manchester University Press.
Schwert, G.W. (1996), 'Markup pricing in mergers and acquisitions', *Journal of Financial Economic*, **41**, 153–92.
Schwert, G.W. (2000), 'Hostility in take-overs: in the eyes of the beholders', *Journal of Finance*, **55**, 2599–640.
Song, M. and Walkling, R. (1993), 'The impact of managerial ownership on acquisition attempts', *Journal of Financial and Quantitative Analysis*, **28**, 439–57.
Sterling, M. and Wright, M. (1990), *Management Buy-outs and the Law*, Oxford: Blackwell Scientific.
Sudarasanam, S. (1995), 'The role of defensive strategies and ownership structure of target firms: evidence from UK hostile takeover bids', *European Financial Management*, **1**, 223–40.
Torabzadeh, K.M. and Bertin, W.J. (1987), 'Leveraged buyouts and shareholder returns', *The Journal of Financial Research*, **20**, 313–19.
Vickers, M. (2000), *Public to Private Takeovers: The new paradigms*, London: Ashurst, Morris Crisp.
Weir, C. and Laing, D. (2003), 'Ownership structure, board composition and the market for corporate control in the UK: an empirical analysis', *Applied Economics*, **29**, 579–611.
Weir, C., Laing, D. and Wright, M. (2005a), 'Incentive effects, monitoring mechanisms and the market for corporate control: an analysis of the factors affecting public to private transactions in the UK', *Journal of Business Finance and Accounting*, **32**, 909–44.
Weir, C., Laing, D. and Wright, M. (2005b), 'Undervaluation, private information, agency costs and the decision to go private', *Applied Financial Economics*, **15**, 947–61.
White, H. (1980), 'A heteroskedasticity-consistent co-variance matrix estimator and a direct test for heteroskedasticity', *Econometrica*, **49**, 817–38.
Wright, M., Thompson, S., Chiplin, B. and Robbie, K. (1991), *Buy-ins and Buy-outs: New strategies in corporate management*, London: Graham & Trotman.
Wright, M., Robbie, K., Chiplin, B. and Albrighton, M. (2000), 'The development of an organizational innovation: management buy-outs in the UK 1980–97', *Business History*, **42**, 137–84.

5. Information sharing, price negotiation and management buy-outs of private family-owned firms

M. Louise Scholes, Mike Wright, Paul Westhead, Andrew Burrows and Hans Bruining

1. INTRODUCTION

Corporate governance and the ownership transfer process are attracting academic and practitioner attention. Prior ownership and governance configurations have been linked with the hostile bid takeover process (Song and Walkling, 1993; O'Sullivan and Wong, 1999), as well as in relation to leveraged buy-outs of listed corporations or their divisions (Thompson and Wright, 1995; Halpern et al., 1999; Weir et al., 2005). Currently, there is a dearth of empirical evidence relating to how private firms move across ownership thresholds, defined as the transition from one phase of a firm's life-cycle to another. Theorists suggest that the process of moving across thresholds needs to be explored with regard to contrasting governance structures (Lynall et al., 2003; Filatotchev and Wright, 2005). In this study, we focus on the ownership transition process relating to private family-owned firms that have reported an ownership transition through a management buy-out (MBO) or a management buy-in (MBI). An MBO is the purchase of a business by its management, usually in cooperation with outside financiers such as a venture capital firm. In an MBI, the firm is sold to managers who are external to the business, with this new management team taking a controlling stake. MBO/Is account for about half of all takeovers in the UK, and around a fifth of all MBOs and MBIs in Europe relate to the takeover of private family-owned firms (Centre for Management Buy-out Research (CMBOR), 2005). Several studies have focused on the ownership transition process relating to succession in private family-owned firms (Handler, 1994; Morris et al., 1996, 1997; Birley et al., 1999; Bjuggren and Sund, 2001; Sharma et al., 2003a; Westhead, 2003; Sharma and Irving, 2005). Scholars have, however, neglected the gap in the knowledge base relating to the MBO/I succession option; this study is the first to examine this context.

The purpose of the study is to provide fresh insights surrounding the links between ownership and governance structures of private family-owned firms and two aspects of the MBO/I transition process. Specifically, in this chapter, ownership structure refers to the presence of the founder of the firm and non-family managers who have an ownership stake before the transition, whilst governance structure relates to the presence of non-executive or outside directors (NEDs) before the MBO/I and the influence of the venture capital firm (when present) in succession planning. Two specific aspects (or dependent variables) associated with the MBO or MBI of former private family-owned firms were monitored: whether information was shared equally between vendors (i.e., family firm owners) and purchasers (i.e., MBO/I management teams) and whether agreement was achieved on a mutually beneficial price (i.e., a mutually agreed price as opposed to one or other party imposing a 'take it or leave it' fixed sale price that was to their advantage), as these have been shown to be associated with perceptions relating to whether the MBO/I was successful and the price paid had been fair (Howorth et al., 2004). The post-deal performance of the family firm after the MBO/I may depend on the nature of the business sale negotiation process. If both parties are not satisfied with the deal, the agreed (and in some instances contracted) relationships may not be exhibited in the post-deal period. The performance of the purchased family firm may be retarded if the MBO/I management teams are unable to incentivize the former family owners to transfer tacit knowledge (i.e. knowledge which is only known to the owners and is hard to share with someone else), provide legitimacy or to maintain crucial business relationships with former loyal suppliers and customers (Howorth et al., 2004).

Guided by insights from agency theory, game theory and negotiation theory, a conceptual framework is presented suggesting links between private family-firm ownership and governance structures and the two selected MBO/I process outcomes. Corporate governance theorists utilize the agency perspective to explore control issues in listed firms with diffuse ownership (Hart, 1995; Keasey et al., 2005). An agency perspective has been utilized to explore governance issues in venture-backed private firms (Sahlman, 1990; Lerner, 1995; Kaplan and Strömberg, 2001). The typical family firm has been assumed to be owned and managed by a concentrated group of family members where the firm's objectives are closely linked to family objectives (Zahra et al., 2004). In these circumstances, the traditional agency cost issue may not apply. However, to grow and survive, some private family-owned firms may no longer have aligned ownership and management in the same 'family' hands, and this raises the potential for agency issues between separated family owners and non-family managers. Agency theory has already been utilized to explore the behaviour of family firms that do not have aligned ownership and management. Also, agency theory has been shown to be useful in understanding the relationship between family owners and non-family managers (Chua et al., 2003). Stewardship theory also has some relevance to the study of the family firm succession process where family firm managers may act as stewards. These non-family managers would seek to protect the assets of the family firm rather than to pursue interests which maximize their own personal gain (Donaldson and Davis, 1991).

Recent studies (Schulze et al., 2001, 2002, 2003; Westhead et al., 2001) have highlighted the important influences of firm ownership and governance as well as firm objectives on the strategic behaviour of family firms (Brunninge et al., 2005). However, as noted above, there is scant evidence relating to the purchase of the private family-owned firm by existing (non-family) managers through an MBO, or the external purchase by outside managers through an MBI.

Game theory provides a formal way of analysing competitive (or cooperative) interactions among people who are making decisions; in this case the vendors (i.e., the family firm owners) and purchasers (i.e., the MBO/I teams). Moreover, negotiation theory has been utilized to explore what makes people work together towards a cooperative solution as opposed to trying to maximize individual gains. The probability of a cooperative MBO/I negotiation process can be reduced in the following contexts: family firms have dispersed ownership and governance/management structures; there are high information asymmetries between vendors and purchasers; and the interested parties' objectives are not aligned (Axelrod, 1980; Friedman, 1990; Fudenberg and Tirole, 1991; Cable and Shane, 1997). This raises two key aspects of the family firm MBO/I negotiation process. The first relates to the extent to which information about the firm is shared between the vendors and purchasers. In an ideal situation, all information about the firm would be available to all parties. Both vendors and purchasers require diverse and accurate information surrounding the firm's assets and liabilities in order to set a mutually agreed purchase price for the firm. The second concerns the extent to which the parties cooperate in achieving a mutually agreed price, or whether each party attempts to impose a price that maximizes their own benefit. If information is not available or not disclosed, the vendor, for example, could be at an advantage by knowing what the firm is actually worth. Vendors seeking to maximize the sale price may not disclose all relevant information to the purchasers. The presence of different parties in the ownership and governance of the firm prior to the sale, for example, through the active role of a venture capital firm, can increase the probability that a mutually agreed price is achieved between the vendors and the perspective purchasers.

The study focuses on private family-owned firms that received venture capital and had completed an MBO/I between 1994 and 2003. Information was consistently gathered from the senior executives of 114 private firms in several European countries that had reported an MBO/I deal. The following two broad research questions are explored:

Q1: Are the ownership and governance structures of former private family-owned firms reporting 'information was shared equally' between vendors and purchasers during the MBO/I sale process different from those reporting 'information was not shared equally'?

Q2: Are the ownership and governance structures of former private family-owned firms reporting a 'mutually agreed price' was achieved between vendors and purchasers during the MBO/I sale process different from those reporting 'no mutually agreed price'?

This chapter is structured as follows. Studies focusing on private family-owned firm succession routes are briefly discussed in the following section. The conceptual framework guiding the study is then discussed. In the following section, several hypotheses are derived relating to company ownership structure, governance structure and company objectives. The data collection process and the research methodology are discussed in the next section. Results are then presented. Finally, conclusions and implications are discussed.

2. PRIVATE FAMILY-OWNED FIRM SUCCESSION ROUTES

The survival of family firms is an important entrepreneurial sustainability issue (Westhead, 2003). Further, the failure to carefully consider succession issues may have a detrimental impact on the long-term survival of family firm economic units and the social cohesion of local communities (Wright et al., 1991). Transferring ownership beyond the founder and/or the dominant family group presents major challenges for private family-owned firms where the dominant family group owns the majority of ordinary voting shares in the business (Lansberg, 1999). The majority of family firms fail to plan for generational succession (Cliffe, 1998), and the process is not fully understood (Shepherd and Zacharakis, 2000). Most studies have exclusively focused upon succession within the family (Handler, 1994;

Morris et al., 1996, 1997; Birley et al., 1999; Bjuggren and Sund, 2001; Sharma et al., 2003a; Westhead, 2003; Sharma and Irving, 2005). For the business to prosper, it may be appropriate for the dominant family owning the business to exit (sell) the firm (Willard et al., 1992). International evidence suggests that, in some instances, owners may perceive that there are no suitable family members willing or able to take on the ownership and/or the management of the family firm (Wright et al., 1992; Birley et al., 1999).

Various ownership succession options are available beyond passing the business to the next generation of members drawn from the dominant family or kinship group. The family firm can be sold through a trade sale[1] (Cromie et al., 1995), or through an initial public offering (IPO). Although family firm owners may be willing, in principle, to consider these options (Bleackley et al., 1996), IPOs are rarely feasible (Poutziouris, 2002) and trade sales may be unattractive to vendors if they are associated with a loss of a firm's independent identity. A third option is the transfer of family firm ownership to internal incumbent managers through an MBO, or the transfer to external managers through an MBI (Bachkaniwala et al., 2001). Post-MBO/I there is a greater possibility that the firm's identity and ethos will remain the same, both of which are important for family firm owners (Westhead, 1997). An attractive feature of both MBOs and MBIs is that many incumbent managers may remain in place and family members can continue to be involved (Wright and Coyne, 1985). Family owners may make it a condition of the deal that they retain some involvement in the firm even though they relinquish both ownership and managerial control.[2] European evidence suggests that MBO/Is are viewed, in principle, by owners of family firms as a good way to solve ownership succession problems (Bygrave et al., 1994; Bleackley et al., 1996). In some countries, such as France, government schemes have been designed to ensure MBO/I exit routes (a means for the family to exit the business) are attractive succession options (Wright et al., 1991).

3. CONCEPTUAL FRAMEWORK

3.1 Context

Family firm owners can be viewed as principals whilst non-family managers can be regarded as agents. Agency theorists assume a performance-based system with a focus on financial objectives and self-serving owners who focus upon personal gains which can be achieved by maximizing firm performance. Agency problems may arise where there is separation of ownership and control (Jensen and Meckling, 1976; Fama and Jensen, 1983). It is frequently assumed that private family-owned firms do not suffer from agency problems because, in many cases, ownership and control are aligned in the hands of a dominant kinship group related by blood and marriage who are organization serving (Davis et al., 1997; Arthurs and Busenitz, 2003; Randoy and Goel, 2003). Scholars guided by a stewardship perspective assume that a family firm is a relationship-based system with a focus on non-financial objectives. A strong psychological ownership of the firm and a high occurrence of altruism are assumed (Schulze et al., 2003). The firm's objectives are entangled with family objectives with little outside influence (Zahra et al., 2004). A degree of overlap between the family, ownership and management sub-systems in terms of people and objectives is also assumed (Chrisman et al., 2003a). However, some family firms have diverse ownership and control structures (Litz, 1995; Westhead et al., 2001). If the objectives of owners and management differ there can be agency problems (Schulze et al., 2001; Morck and Yeung, 2003). Owners focusing on financial objectives (Smyrnios and Romano, 1994) may introduce agency control mechanisms such as performance-related pay (Schulze et al., 2003) and NEDs (Westhead et al., 2001) to enhance firm performance.

Family firms associated with 'family agendas' may be owned and managed differently (Dyer, 2003). In line with the stewardship perspective, stereotypical family firms that are closely held, family owned and family managed may focus on non-financial interests.[3] Their prevailing culture may be organization (family) serving. Conversely, in line with the agency perspective, family firms with more diluted ownership and management may focus on financial objectives and exhibit a self-serving culture.

The family firm succession process involves the negotiation of firm ownership transfer from family to a new set of non-family shareholders. Family vendors and non-family purchasers may emphasize individual or joint gains, and these goals may shape the negotiation behaviour (Dabholkar et al., 1994). The prisoner's dilemma in game theory focuses on the conditions under which parties will cooperate or defect in bargaining situations associated with asymmetric information (Axelrod and Dion, 1988). A cooperative strategy involves the seeking of mutual gains at the expense of short-term self-interest. Conversely, defection strategies emphasize the seeking of short-term individual gains at the expense of the other party, as well as long-term mutual benefits. Incentives to cooperation in negotiations between entrepreneurs and venture capitalists, for example, have been associated with goal congruence, relative power relations, trust and communication (Cable and Shane, 1997). The latter variables may also be relevant with regard to the family firm succession context.

In this study, we explore whether the likelihood of the two selected MBO/I succession process outcomes are linked to a private family-owned firm's company ownership structure, company governance structure and company objectives. These three themes are discussed in turn below. In relation to these three themes hypotheses are derived in the following section.

3.2 Company Ownership Structure

To ensure business growth, owners of some family firms may sell ordinary voting shares to 'outsiders' who are not drawn from the dominant group of family shareholders. This dilution of ownership may enable non-family members to impact favourably on company objectives and development (Schulze et al., 2002). Where family objectives are important, the family may retain a majority stake in the business to ensure future family control and the retention of family members in key executive positions. As intimated above, separation of ownership and control of the firm provides the potential for changes to the management structure, and the possibility of agency control mechanisms (Randoy and Goel, 2003). As family firms progress from one generation to the next, the structural form of ownership and management may change (Lansberg, 1999). Where firms are characterized by complexity of ownership, shareholdings will become more diverse, introducing potential agency costs. Individual shareholders with less control may request extra monitoring to ensure that their interests are secured. This could lessen the emphasis on family objectives and there could be a move away from a stewardship towards an agency perspective.

3.3 Governance Structure

The size of the board is generally related to the size and the complexity of the business. Daily (1995) found that chief executive officers (CEOs) of smaller firms with larger equity holdings had smaller boards with less 'outside' representation. Agency issues may arise in family firms associated with large boards of directors and more outside directors, as well as firms with high proportions of non-family managers. Non-family professional managers with broad expertise may be recruited to deal with a principal's governance concerns (Ensley and Pearson, 2005). For example, the recruitment of NEDs may be initiated to professionalize the family firm, to ensure 'family agendas' and to avoid conflict between the non-economic objectives of family owners and the economic objectives of non-family shareholders (Mitchell et al., 2003). Family firm owners may obtain external finance from venture capitalists to ensure business development. Representatives of a venture capital firm will join the family firm board as NEDs to protect the interests of the financier. These latter NEDs may, in addition, provide advice and expertise that can be leveraged by the board to address obstacles to business development (Sahlman, 1990; Pruthi et al., 2003). Such change can bring in diversity that may act as a counterpoint to the dominant perspective of the founders and family owners (Forbes and Milliken, 1999). However, evidence suggests that family firms are less likely to report entry and exit of team members (Ucbasaran et al., 2003). The evidence is also mixed regarding the nature of boards in family firms. Some studies suggest that few family firms use NEDs (Westhead et al., 2001). Moreover, when boards exist they may not be functional in the conventional sense (Huse, 2000). Other evidence suggests that some family firms do have active boards with active non-family members (Corbetta and Salvato, 2004).

3.4 Company Objectives

Family firms may differ with regard to the extent that family objectives are emphasized (Leenders and Waarts, 2003; Steier, 2003). Wealth creation may not be the major objective cited by family firm owners (Chrisman et al., 2003b). Some family firms choose to exchange profit maximization for benefits relating to 'family agendas'. Owners of family firms generally cite the following objectives: transfer ownership to the next generation; maintain financial independence of the family and the business; favour family members in managerial positions; and to ensure the survival of the family business as a going concern (Westhead, 1997).

4. DERIVATION OF HYPOTHESES

4.1 Company Ownership Structure

As noted above, the nature of the ownership structure of the firm raises potential agency problems. A family firm's profile (i.e., ownership structure, governance structure and company objectives) may increase the likelihood of information asymmetry between family firm owners (i.e., vendors) and potential MBO/I teams (i.e., purchasers), creating agency costs. If solely family members own the firm, the information flow about the firm between owners and non-family management during the MBO/I sale process may be asymmetrical. While financial information may be known to incumbent management who may undertake an MBO, external managers undertaking an MBI may be less aware of future market threats and opportunities, the status of major contracts with customers and suppliers, and/or the objectives of family owners (Robbie and Wright, 1995; Howorth et al., 2004).[4]

Family owners may be reluctant to transfer their tacit knowledge to 'outsiders'. Problems may be exacerbated if the original intention of the family firm owners was to pursue intergenerational succession. Chua et al. (2003) suggest that relationships between family owners and non-family management increase in importance with greater business size, and with the criticality of non-family management to the business. Conversely, in some cases, non-family management may be more closely involved in the day-to-day running of the business (Howorth et al., 2004). The latter managers may have the most up-to-date information surrounding the firm's financial and market position. Non-family managers seeking to pay a lower price for the firm may not be willing to share this information with family owners. Information asymmetry, which as agency theory suggests is more likely when there is a conflict of interest due to the separation of ownership and management, may shape the business sale negotiation process. Most notably, the process may not be balanced if management seeks to leverage this additional information to their own advantage.

Both the above conditions suggest that family firm owners and non-family management are likely to defect from cooperative approaches involving information sharing during the business sale negotiation process, and the pursuit of a mutually agreed price for the firm. Family firm owners seeking to align the interests of non-family management with those of the family may disperse some shares to non-family managers. This decision may lead to the eventual takeover of the family business by non-family management shareholders.

Game theory suggests that cooperative solutions may be more likely where there is greater goal congruence (Apfelbaum, 1974), a more even balance of power (Pruitt and Kimmel, 1977), and more communication between the vendors and purchasers (Lindskold et al., 1986). Low levels of non-family management shareholdings may be associated with goal diversity, imbalance of power and weak communication (Schulze et al., 2002, 2003). It is, therefore, reasonable to assume that firms associated with higher levels of non-family management shareholdings would report fewer imbalances during business sale negotiations. Moreover, the subsequent business sale negotiation process may be associated with greater information sharing between family firm owners and non-family management shareholders, and the pursuit of a mutually agreed price may be the goal of both parties. This discussion suggests the following hypotheses:

H1a: Private family-owned firms that cited higher proportions of non-family managers were shareholders prior to the MBO/I were more likely to report that 'information was shared equally' between vendors and purchasers (i.e., low information asymmetries).

H1b: Private family-owned firms that cited higher proportions of non-family managers were shareholders prior to the MBO/I were more likely to report a 'mutually agreed price' was achieved between vendors and purchasers.

Whether the private family-owned firm was founded rather than bought or inherited may be associated with the decision to pursue the MBO/I succession route. The succession process can be problematical if the key owner of the firm refuses to let go, or to delegate responsibilities to successors. Founded firms generally have founders who are still involved in the ownership and the management of their firms. This aligned ownership and management reduces agency costs and may ensure information flows between the owner/manager and the incumbent non-family management team prior to and during the business sale negotiation process. MBO/I negotiations may be cooperative if founders are committed to the long-term future of the firm, and they have good relationships with (non-family) management. Greater sharing of information is expected if owners/managers are seeking some long-term involvement in the firm after the MBO/I, implying greater goal congruence with management (Apfelbaum, 1974). Founders may be more likely to seek this involvement because they may be reluctant to fully let go of the firms they have created and nurtured. Emotional attachment to the family firm (Harveston et al., 1997), lingering doubts as to whether (non-family) management can run the business effectively (Westhead et al., 2001) and concerns about the loyalty and commitment of non-family managers (Chua et al., 2003) in part explain the desire of some founders to maintain some involvement in 'their' business (Dyer, 1992; Lansberg, 1988). Conversely, owners that have inherited or purchased the private firm may be less likely to cite the values and traditions reported by firm founders (Dyer and Handler, 1994). In contrast to founders, these owners may have career interests, psychological needs and life-style needs that are met from outside the firm (Handler, 1992). Owners of purchased firms may thus simply view the firm as a tradable asset that enables them to pursue these interests and needs. This discussion suggests the following hypotheses:

H1c: Founded private family-owned firms, rather than bought or inherited family firms, prior to the MBO/I were more likely to report that 'information was shared equally' between vendors and purchasers (i.e., low information asymmetries).

H1d: Founded private family-owned firms, rather than bought or inherited family firms, prior to the MBO/I were more likely to report a 'mutually agreed price' was achieved between vendors and purchasers.

4.2 Governance Structure

The governance structure of the family firm can consist of executive directors, NEDs (especially non-family NEDs) and managers (i.e., family and non-family). Barach (1984) found that many family firms had small boards and that family directors dominated these boards. Larger boards of directors and more outside (non-family) directors may be associated with growing family firms and/or firms dealing with agency issues. Directors who are members of the dominant family group can exert pressure to ensure that family agendas and the cultural foundations of the business are uppermost in importance. Also, they can favour the recruitment of family members in relation to key executive positions. Owners and directors who focus more on wealth creation and business development may prefer to recruit non-family professional managers.

Goal congruence may lead to more cooperative bargaining solutions (Apfelbaum, 1974; Cable and Shane, 1997). Some NEDs can be used to reduce conflict between the non-economic objectives of the family and the financial objectives of non-family owners. As earlier intimated, relatively few private family-owned firms use NEDs. The presence of NEDs, especially non-family NEDs, on the firm's board, however, may shape information sharing and the business sale negotiation process. NEDs may help to align the interests and aims of owners and managers during the business sale negotiation process. This discussion suggests the following hypotheses:

H2a: Private family-owned firms that cited non-family NEDs were on the board prior to the MBO/I were more likely to report that 'information was shared equally' between vendors and purchasers (i.e., low information asymmetries).

H2b: Private family-owned firms that cited non-family NEDs were on the board prior to the MBO/I were more likely to report a 'mutually agreed price' was achieved between vendors and purchasers.

Family firm owners (i.e., vendors), incumbent non-family management, external management and private equity investors can be involved in the succession planning process. If this planning is carried out in an atmosphere of mutual trust and respect, balanced succession planning may be the cooperative outcome (Steier and Greenwood, 1995). From a game theoretic perspective, more even bargaining power between the parties may contribute to a cooperative solution (Pruitt and Kimmel, 1977). To ensure a mutually beneficial succession route, vendors may hold discussions with non-family managers and private equity firms. The involvement of non-family management in succession planning could ensure even information flows between vendors and non-family managers. However, for many non-family management teams, the MBO/I will be their first experience of the business sale negotiation process. Non-family management may, therefore, be reluctant to challenge a dominant family owner because they do not want to risk losing the deal or their jobs (Wright and Coyne, 1985).

The knowledge and experience of the venture capital firm can be leveraged by an MBO/I team to ensure that the non-family management team is in a stronger position to negotiate with the vendor during the business sale negotiation process, suggesting potential agency issues. The potential for asymmetric information problems between vendors and venture capital firms are, however, acknowledged (Amit et al., 1993). Venture capital firms employ various strategies to obtain information to enable them to make more informed investment and valuation decisions (Admati and Pfleiderer, 1994; Wright and Robbie, 1996; Manigart et al., 2002; Wright et al., 2002). An MBO/I team utilizing the experience of a venture capitalist firm will generally be in a stronger position than non-family management alone to challenge a vendor who has proposed a fixed price that maximizes their own (family) gain. To even up the bargaining power between the vendor and the purchaser, a non-family management team may utilize a venture capital firm to facilitate a mutually agreed price between both parties (Howorth et al., 2004). This discussion suggests the following hypotheses:

H2c: Private family-owned firms that cited venture capital firms were involved in succession planning prior to the MBO/I were more likely to report that 'information was shared equally' between vendors and purchasers (i.e., low information asymmetries).

H2d: Private family-owned firms that cited venture capital firms were involved in succession planning prior to the MBO/I were more likely to report a 'mutually agreed price' was achieved between vendors and purchasers.

4.3 Company Objectives

As earlier intimated, game theory suggests that cooperative bargaining solutions may be reported in contexts where there is goal congruence between the parties involved (Apfelbaum, 1974; Cable and Shane, 1997). The objectives of the family firm owners can range from protecting purely 'family agendas' at one end of the spectrum to pursuing 'non-family agendas' focusing on the financial development of the business at the other end. Some family firm owners choose to exchange profit maximization for benefits relating to the family. Evidence suggests that wealth creation may not be the major objective for many family firm owners (Chrisman et al., 2003b). Family owners may align family and business objectives, reducing agency costs. For example, family firm owners may consider longer-term objectives but they may be reluctant to introduce changes, which reduce the probability of an intergenerational transfer (Schulze et al., 2002). If the objective of family firm owners is to develop the business in the future at the expense of family-oriented objectives they may need to utilize the experience of professional (non-family) managers to achieve this goal. Information sharing between owners and non-family managers may be poor if the firm's objectives are solely family oriented. High information asymmetries may lead to a biased succession planning process and the subsequent business sale negotiation process may favour the dominant family owners.

Objectives cited by family owners may be markedly different from those reported by non-family owners. The desire to retain the family link with the firm may not be strongly cited by some non-family owners. Similarly, non-family managers with no equity stakes in their family firms may report objectives that are not strictly aligned with those cited by family firm owners, indicative of agency issues. Most notably, non-family managers may seek to maximize financial rather than family objectives. The strategic objectives of the family firm may, therefore, shape the succession planning process and the business sale negotiation process. Further, strategic objectives of the firm may differ depending on the ownership and governance structures of the family firm. This discussion suggests the following hypotheses:

H3a: Private family-owned firms that stressed financial strategic objectives prior to the MBO/I were more likely to report that 'information was shared equally' between vendors and purchasers (i.e., low information asymmetries).

H3b: Private family-owned firms that stressed financial strategic objectives prior to the MBO/I were more likely to report a 'mutually agreed price' was achieved between vendors and purchasers.

A central objective of family owners may be to ensure the survival of the business (Westhead, 1997). With respect to the succession planning process, even if the owners take the view that there are no suitable family members to takeover the business (i.e., no suitable family successor), founders and other family owners may still seek to ensure the firm's survival as an independent entity for both social and emotional reasons, rather than succession involving sale of the business to another corporation. In addition, a favourable external perception of the family's standing in the local community may be ensured if the employees are seen to be treated fairly. Conversely, a negative external perception may be reported if the family firm fails, or is taken over by a larger group that has no emotional commitment to the local community. To protect the family's standing in the local community, family owners may actively seek a cooperative solution. If the intergenerational ownership transfer solution within the family cannot be achieved, some family firm owners will seek to ensure there is a more even balance of power between the vendors and the MBO/I team (Pruitt and Kimmel, 1977). To ensure the survival of the independent firm, founders and family firm owners may be more willing to share information with prospective MBO/I purchasers. In addition, vendors may be more willing to agree a mutually beneficial purchase price rather than one that maximizes the sale price in favour of the family vendors alone. Numerous family firm owners have reported philanthropic behaviour. Generosity may also encourage a cooperative solution (Axelrod, 1984). Family firm vendors may signal that they are not hiding information and they are not seeking to maximize the sale price. These signals may be seen as an act of generosity that leads the MBO/I purchasers not to defect by concealing information they possess, or to press for a lower price that maximizes their interests. This discussion suggests the following hypotheses:

H3c: Private family-owned firms that stressed there was no suitable family successor prior to the MBO/I were more likely to report that 'information was shared equally' between vendors and purchasers (i.e., low information asymmetries).

H3d: Private family-owned firms that stressed there was no suitable family successor prior to the MBO/I were more likely to report a 'mutually agreed price' was achieved between vendors and purchasers.

4.4 Data Collection and Research Methodology

The sample was derived from Nottingham University Business Schools Centre for Management Buy-out Research (CMBOR) database that effectively comprises the population of MBOs and MBIs across Europe. A twice-yearly survey of private equity and venture capital firms, intermediaries and banks is conducted to obtain details on all MBOs and MBIs completed. Respondents are incentivized to supply data with a free copy of a quarterly review of the market. Press and annual corporate reports are used to gather additional data and to validate information gathered from surveys. This study focuses on private family-owned firms that received venture capital and had completed an MBO/I between 1994 and 2003.

A growing consensus suggests that a family firm is one that is owned by a dominant kinship group where the owners operate their firm as a family business (Westhead and Cowling, 1998). A broad definition was adopted, with a family firm defined as having more than 50% of the ordinary voting shares owned or controlled by a single family group related by blood or marriage and the firm is perceived to be a family business.

Guided by the literature as well as discussions with practitioners, a questionnaire was designed to explore several issues relating to the private family-owned firm succession process and the selected MBO or MBI ownership succession option. The questionnaire was designed in English. Variations in practice in each country in Europe were considered during the questionnaire design process. The questionnaire was translated into French, German, Italian and Spanish and then back translated into English. To reduce measurement error, face and content validity issues were considered during a pilot study. Twenty private family-owned firms that had been the subject of a venture-backed MBO or MBI were contacted. After the pilot study, one question was slightly modified.

The postal questionnaire survey was administered between June and September 2004. To reduce measurement error (Hair et al., 1995), respondents were selected who had detailed knowledge surrounding the MBO/I events. Senior management in the purchased private family-owned firms was contacted and they were regarded as the key informants (Kumar et al., 1993). Respondents had been involved in the MBO/I business sale negotiation process and they possessed the detailed information requested. The questionnaire was mailed to the CEO of former private family-owned firms that had effected succession through a venture backed MBO or MBI. Two weeks after the first mailing, a reminder was sent. A week later each non-respondent was contacted by telephone by skilled interviewers located in CMBOR. Further reminders were administered from the European Private Equity and Venture Capital Association (EVCA). In total, CEOs in 1,645 firms were sent a questionnaire. As a result of these efforts, information was gathered from 114 MBO/Is, which equates to a 7% response rate. This response rate is in line with surveys of this kind in Europe (Bygrave et al., 1994). Information was gathered from the following respondents: 83.8% were CEOs/presidents, 5.7% were directors including Deputy CEO, and the remaining 10.5% were senior management.

Response bias was considered. Responses to the survey were compared with the population of private formerly family-owned MBO/Is. Table 5.1 shows that the country distribution of survey respondents does not markedly differ from the national population distribution. Also, Table 5.2

Table 5.1 Survey responses by country

Country	Total number of venture capital backed MBO/Is of former private family firms	% venture capital backed MBO/Is of former private family firms	Total number of questionnaires sent out	Total number of questionnaires returned	Total of all returns (%)
Austria	6	0.30	5	0	0.00
Belgium	28	1.40	25	0	0.00
Denmark	15	0.75	15	3	2.63
Eire	5	0.25	5	0	0.00
Finland	20	1.00	19	2	1.75
France	282	14.11	193	9	7.89
Germany	110	5.51	88	7	6.14
Italy	87	4.35	71	8	7.02
Lithuania	1	0.05	0	0	0.00
Netherlands	58	2.90	43	1	0.88
Norway	8	0.40	7	1	0.88
Poland	2	0.10	1	0	0.00
Portugal	5	0.25	2	0	0.00
Romania	2	0.10	2	0	0.00
Slovenia	1	0.05	0	0	0.00
Spain	68	3.40	60	3	2.63
Sweden	30	1.50	28	3	2.63
Switzerland	28	1.40	25	3	2.63
UK	1242	62.16	1056	74	64.91
Total	1998	100	1645	114	100

shows that the industrial distribution of survey respondents was generally in line with the industrial population distribution. However, respondents engaged in construction activities were slightly over-represented, whilst respondents engaged in computing/electronics were slightly under-represented.

Information from the CMBOR database was used to classify the 114 respondents to the survey. With reference to information sharing during the business sale negotiation process, data were gathered from 112 respondents. Forty-seven respondents (42%) reported that the vendor and management shared relevant information equally. In contrast, 65 respondents (58%)

Table 5.2 Survey responses by industrial distribution

Industrial sector	Survey responses (%)	CMBOR database (%)
Biotechnology	0.0	0.1
Computing/electronics	8.8	12.5
Consumer related	22.8	23.1
Construction	9.6	3.1
Energy	0.0	0.4
Industrial products/services	10.6	13.4
Manufacturing	22.8	19.9
Medical/health related	6.2	3.6
Services	10.6	13.4
Transportation	1.8	2.5
Other	7.0	8.1

suggested that information had not been shared equally. Twenty-four respondents (21%) suggested the vendor controlled all of the information, while a further 23 respondents (21%) indicated that the vendor controlled most of the information. Fifteen respondents (13%) suggested that management controlled most of the information, while the remaining three respondents (3%) reported that they controlled all the relevant information.

Information relating to the prices paid for the private family-owned firms was gathered from 113 respondents. In order to distinguish cases where a price that was mutually beneficial to both parties was achieved (mutually agreed price) from those where one or the other party was advantaged, respondents were presented with a number of options relating to the nature of the sale price process. Sixty-one respondents (54%) reported that a mutually agreed price had been achieved, whilst a further 52 respondents (46%) indicated that a mutually agreed price had not been achieved. The latter response relates to a situation where, typically, the vendor had imposed a 'take it or leave it' price. In total, 29 respondents (26%) reported that the vendor proposed a fixed price that maximized their valuation, 12 respondents (11%) reported that the vendor had suggested a fair price that was in the best interests of the company, five respondents (4%) reported that the management proposed a fixed price, three respondents (3%) reported that the vendor required management to match an outside bid, and a further two respondents (2%) indicated that the vendor offered the company to management at a lower price than an external bid. One respondent selected the 'Other' option and indicated that the company had been sold by public sale.

Measurement error is more prevalent when single-item scales are explored and when respondents are provided with several options on a single scale (Hair et al., 1995). This exploratory study focused on two dependent variables and each related to a single-item scale. To reduce the problem of measurement error, each ranked dependent variable was re-coded into a dichotomous dependent variable. Respondents reporting 'information was shared equally' between vendors and purchasers during the business sale negotiation process were allocated a value of '1', whilst those reporting 'information was not shared equally' between vendors and purchasers were allocated a value of '0' (INFOSHARE). Further, respondents stating that a 'mutually agreed price' was achieved by both vendors and purchasers in the business sale process were allocated a value of '1', whilst respondents reporting 'no mutually agreed price' were allocated a value of '0' (PRICE). The likelihood (or the probability) of the INFOSHARE and PRICE events was explored within multivariate logistic regression analysis frameworks. This technique is appropriate to explore 'assumed relationships between dependent and independent variables . . .' (Hair et al., 1995, 131). An independent variable with a positive coefficient in the multivariate logistic regression model suggests that this independent variable increases the probability of the selected event (or dependent variable), whilst a negative coefficient suggests the independent variable decreases the predicted probability of the event. This technique is appropriate to test the presented hypotheses. In the implications section, we acknowledge that structural equation modelling techniques are warranted to explore causality issues, and the impact of interactions between selected independent and control variables. The latter issues were not specified in the presented hypotheses.

Six independent variables were selected. First, each respondent reported the percentage of shares owned by non-family management shareholders before the MBO or MBI (NFM). Second, respondents reporting that the family business had been founded and not purchased were allocated a value of '1', whilst respondents reporting the business had not been founded were allocated a value of '0' (FOUNDED). Third, respondents reporting that a non-family NED had been used before the MBO or MBI were allocated a value of '1', whilst respondents reporting no NEDs had been employed were allocated a value of '0' (NONEX). Fourth, respondents reporting that a venture capitalist firm had been involved in succession planning were allocated a value of '1', whilst respondents reporting that no venture capitalist firm had been involved in succession planning were allocated a value of '0' (VCSP). Fifth, respondents were asked to rank the strategic importance of the market value increment before the MBO or MBI on a five-point Likert scale ranging from (1) low, (3) average and (5) high (MVI). Sixth, respondents were asked to report whether no suitable successor had been identified on a five-point Likert scale ranging from (1) low, (3) average and (5) high (NSS).[5]

One control variable was operationalized in the reported logistic regression models.[6] Manufacturing firms were allocated a value of '1', whilst non-manufacturing firms were allocated a value of '0'.

5. RESULTS

Table 5.3 provides means and standard deviations for the continuous independent variables. Correlation coefficients between the continuous independent variables are also summarized. The variance inflation factor (VIF) scores suggest that the multivariate logistic regression models were not distorted by multicollinearity.

Multivariate logistic regression analysis models are reported in Table 5.4. Model 1 focuses on whether respondents reported 'information was shared equally' between vendors and purchasers during the business sale negotiation process (INFOSHARE). This model has a pseudo R^2 of 0.15 and is significant at the 0.05 level. Two independent variables were significant. In line with expectation (H1c), founded family firms (FOUNDED) were more likely to report that 'information was shared equally between vendors and purchasers'. Also, as expected (H3a), respondents reporting a focus on the strategic importance of the market value increment (MVI) were more likely to report that 'information was shared equally between vendors and purchasers'. Contrary to expectation, hypotheses H1a, H2a, H2c and H3c were not supported.

Model 2 focuses on whether family firm respondents reported that a 'mutually agreed price' had been achieved in the business sale process

Table 5.3 Correlation matrix relating to the continuous independent variables

	Mean	SD	NFM	MVI	NSS	VIF
NFM	5.478	10.884	1.000	−0.095	0.073	1.050
MVI	3.365	1.403	−0.095	1.000	0.359	1.061
NSS	2.747	1.682	0.073	0.359	1.000	1.034

Notes: NFM = percentage of shares owned by non-family management shareholders before the MBO or MBI; MVI = strategic importance of the market value increment before the MBO or MBI on a five-point Likert scale ranging from (1) low, (3) average and (5) high; NSS = whether no suitable successor had been identified on a five-point Likert scale ranging from (1) low, (3) average and (5) high; VIF = variance inflation factor scores.

Table 5.4 Logistic regression models of independent variables associated with information sharing relating to the MBO/I business negotiation process and the reporting of a mutually agreed price

Variables	β	
	Model 1: INFOSHARE	Model 2: PRICE
Independent		
NFM	0.029	0.023
FOUNDED (yes)	1.289**	−0.244
NONEX (yes)	−0.909	0.131
VCSP (yes)	0.656	1.110**
MVI	0.451**	0.527**
NSS	−0.261	0.540***
Control		
MANUF (yes)	−0.214	1.112*
Constant	−0.990	−4.280
Pseudo R^2	0.150	0.204
Nagel Kerke R^2	0.246	0.329
Overall predictive accuracy (%)	77.8	75.3
Model χ^2	14.644	20.613
Model χ^2 significance	0.041	0.004
n	72	73

Notes: INFOSHARE = information was shared equally between vendors (i.e., family firm owners) and purchasers (i.e., MBO/I management teams) during the business sale negotiation process (1 = yes, 0 = no); PRICE = mutually agreed price was reported as having been achieved in the business sale process (1 = yes, 0 = no); NFM = percentage of shares owned by non-family management shareholders before the MBO or MBI; FOUNDED = the family business had been founded and not purchased (1 = yes, 0 = no); NONEX = non-family non-executive directors had been employed before the MBO or MBI (1 = yes, 0 = no); VCSP = venture capitalist involved in succession planning (1 = yes, 0 = no); MVI = strategic importance of the market value increment before the MBO or MBI on a five-point Likert scale ranging from (1) low, (3) average and (5) high; NSS = whether no suitable successor had been identified on a five point likert scale ranging from (1) low, (3) average and (5) high; and MANUF = manufacturing firm (1 = yes, 0 = no).
Significance: * $p<0.1$; ** $p<0.05$; *** $p<0.01$.

(PRICE). Model 2 has a pseudo R^2 of 0.20 and is significant at the 0.01 level. Three independent variables were significant. As expected (H2d), respondents reporting venture capitalist firms had been involved in succession planning (VCSP) were more likely to report that a mutually agreed sale price had been achieved. In line with expectation (H3b), respondents reporting a focus on the strategic importance of the market value increment (MVI) were more likely to report that a mutually agreed sale price had been achieved. Also, as hypothesized (H3d), respondents reporting that their firms' had no suitable successor (NSS) were markedly more like to report that a mutually agreed sale price had been achieved. Contrary to expectation, hypotheses H1b, H1d and H2b were not supported. The control variable was, however, significant. Manufacturing firms (MANUF) were weakly more likely to report that a mutually agreed sale price had been achieved.

6. CONCLUSIONS AND IMPLICATIONS

6.1 Key Findings

Guided by insights from perspectives relating to agency theory, game theory and negotiation theory, this study utilized multivariate logistic analysis to explore whether private family-owned firms citing specific variables relating to their ownership structure, governance structure and company objectives pre-MBO/I were more likely to report two outcomes: whether 'information was shared equally' between vendors (i.e., family firm owners) and purchasers (i.e., MBO/I management teams) during the business sale negotiation process and whether a 'mutually agreed price' had been achieved. Smoother ownership transitions, as reflected in low information asymmetries between vendors and purchasers, were more likely when the family owners were the original business founders. Moreover, if the vendors exhibited a desire to focus on financial strategic objectives relating to increasing the market value increment there was more likely to be information sharing between the vendors and purchasers. We hypothesized that respondents citing non-family management in the ownership of the family firm pre-MBO/I, venture capital firm involvement, the absence of suitable successor and firms citing the employment of non-family NEDs would be more likely to report 'information was shared equally' between vendors and purchasers. However, these relationships were not statistically significant.

Three hypotheses relating to governance structure and company objectives were supported with reference to the mutually agreed price outcome. As expected, respondents reporting venture capital firm involvement in succession planning, those reporting a focus on the strategic importance of the market value increment, and those citing that no suitable successor had been identified were more likely to report that a 'mutually agreed price' had been achieved. We hypothesized that respondents citing non-family management in the ownership of the family firm pre-MBO/I, those using non-family NEDs and founded firms would be more likely to report a 'mutually agreed price' had been achieved. However, these relationships were not statistically significant.

Presented findings shed light on the neglected area of private firms crossing thresholds in the development of their life-cycle (Filatotchev and Wright, 2005). In particular, we extend understanding of the succession process relating to private family-owned firms (Sharma, 2004), and shed light on the feasibility of alternatives to intergenerational succession (Stokes and Blackburn, 2001). We extend the work of Chua et al. (2003) by highlighting the role of non-family management in providing a succession route for private family-owned firms. However, our analysis indicates that non-family management (and indeed NEDs) may be less critical in the negotiation process than the role of the founder. Also, presented evidence extends the insightful views of Sharma et al. (2003b) relating to the importance of identifying a willing and trusted successor (in this study an internal or external management team), rather than focusing solely on retaining the business in the single dominant family related by blood or marriage.

6.2 Implications for Vendors, Management and Practitioners

Empirical evidence presented raises several important implications for vendors of private firms, potential internal and external management team purchasers, and practitioners including venture capital firms. Issues relating to information sharing and the facilitation of a mutually agreed price are discussed, in turn, below.

6.2.1 Information sharing

The finding that the presence of the founder rather than second- or later-generation family owners was more likely to increase the likelihood that information was shared equally between vendors and purchasers suggests that incumbent managers need to make themselves even more aware of the aims of the vendor with regard to the future of the business post MBO/I. Managers need to understand and to differentiate between the aims of founders as opposed to later-generation family owners. Most notably, managers need to consider whether family owners are seeking continued involvement in the business, or seeking to maximize the value from the sale of the family firm. This finding may also have implications concerning the extent to which management possess information relating to the firm that is not available to the vendors, and how to use any information asymmetry in their favour. For example, if management withheld information on future major orders, this could undermine trust with the vendors who may change their attitude to achieving a mutually favourable deal with management.

If incumbent management is in a stronger position, vendors may need to take advice to ensure that a fairer deal can be reached. Vendors may need to identify advisers who have specialist skills in negotiating MBO/Is. Advisers who focus on tax planning and similar services may have insufficient knowledge to leverage the MBO/I process. A consultant experienced in negotiating with venture capital firms could help provide an intermediary role between the parties involved in the private family-owned firm sale negotiation process.

The use of a NED did not increase the likelihood that information was shared equally between vendors and purchasers. This finding raises questions for vendors surrounding the presence and role of independent NEDs in private family-owned firms. More family firm owners need to be encouraged to consider the potential benefits of developing their governance structures and processes. Family firms need to leverage the expertise of independent professionals who can provide supportive advice surrounding alternative ownership transition options that will meet the objectives of the family owners and the business. As intimated above, vendors seeking smooth ownership transitions should leverage the knowledge of consultants with considerable experience in negotiating trade and MBO/I deals prior to formal discussions with internal or external management teams.

As discussed above, family owners seeking to protect family agendas may resist attempts to open up the share capital of the private family-owned firm to non-family managers. The findings that non-family management shareholdings did not significantly increase the likelihood that information was shared equally between vendors and purchasers raises questions surrounding the extent to which incumbent management are brought into the strategic leadership of the family firm prior to succession planning where ownership transition options are discussed. Vendors may seek to develop cooperative relationships with management well in advance of the ownership transfer event. For example, vendors may more proactively engage internal managers in discussions surrounding the ownership transfer options available, which consider the interests of both parties.

6.2.2 Mutually agreed price

Over a fifth of respondents reported no succession planning had been conducted. The finding that respondents citing that no suitable successors had been identified were more likely to report a 'mutually agreed price' had been achieved suggests that vendors may need to consider the succession planning process carefully well in advance of it becoming a necessity. For example, vendors may find it appropriate to build cooperative relationships with management and prepare managers with regard to the possibility of owning, as well and managing, the business. Family firm founders may also need to obtain external advice which can suggest alternative succession options in the absence of family successors. Most notably, more private family-owned firms should be made aware of the MBO/I ownership transition options.

For incumbent management who envisage that an MBO may be possible, our findings suggest that it may be important for managers to build a dialogue with the founder regarding ownership transition options. This dialogue should identify the founder's longer-term expectations surrounding their involvement with the business, and their likely stance with reference to negotiating any future MBO. Also, this dialogue may highlight the need for managers to secure independent advice for themselves to protect their interests and to ensure a smooth ownership transition, which could be in the interests of both vendors and purchasers. Managers should consider leveraging the finance and knowledge of venture capital firms. Evidence presented in Table 5.4 highlights that the likelihood of a 'mutually agreed price' was increased when a venture capital firm was involved in the business sale process. However, venture capital firm involvement was not found to significantly increase the likelihood of information sharing between vendors and purchasers. This evidence suggests that both family firm owners and MBO/I teams need to consider utilizing the expertise of venture capital firms, particularly if a concern is to achieve a win–win price solution for both vendors and purchasers. In addition, we can suggest that more venture capital firms should pro-actively develop adviser or intermediary relationships with more family firm owners that are likely to face succession issues. The lack of significance attached to the role of NEDs may reflect evidence from elsewhere that they are often appointed by owner/managers because of their close association with them rather than for their independent perspective or professional expertise. This raises a wider question regarding the role of and appointment process for NEDs but perhaps adds to suggestions that owner/managers of private firms might benefit from appointing outside directors who are able to contribute independent expertise.

6.3 Limitations and Implications for Further Research

A number of research strands are emerging with reference to the family firm phenomenon (Sharma, 2004; Zahra and Sharma, 2004). Appropriate databases are required to explore issues relating to how private family-owned firms move across ownership thresholds, particularly those relating to MBO/I succession options. Information relating to the business sale negotiation process is difficult to collect (Birley and Westhead, 1993; Howorth et al., 2004). Several data sources need to be utilized to identify private firms that have been sold (Birley and Westhead, 1990a, b). This study has drawn upon a unique and relatively large database relating to the population of MBO/Is across Europe. Family firms that selected an MBO or MBI were detected with reference to a number of data sources. Additional research is warranted surrounding the data sources that can be utilized to detect the population of family firms considering alternative ownership transitions.

The business sale process can involve several actors. Information from even a single actor is difficult to collect. This study focused on the perspective of the management involved in buying out or buying into the private family-owned firm. Attempts were made to reduce measurement error. Selected key informants had been involved in negotiating the MBO/Is and they possessed the detailed information requested. Respondents had been former CEOs/ Presidents and Directors of former private family-owned firms. Fresh insights relating to the process may be provided when several actors involved in the process are consistently contacted over time. Longitudinal studies need to be conducted prior to the MBO/I, during the MBO/I and after the MBO/I. The perspectives of family owners, non-family managers, venture capitalists and independent consultants could be compared to ensure valid and reliable evidence is collected.

Guided by several theoretical perspectives, a number of hypotheses were tested with reference to cross-sectional survey evidence. Logistic regression analysis is an appropriate technique to explore cross-sectional data. Structural equation modelling techniques, are, however, more appropriate if the aim of the study is test hypotheses that suggest directions of causality between independent and dependent variables, as well as interactions between variables. Additional studies should seek to gather responses from large and representative samples of respondents. Information relating to single-item variables was explored in this study. The latter single-item variables could be associated with measurement error. We acknowledge that some of the reported findings may have been more powerful if more robust variables had been analysed.[7] Additional studies are warranted that ask several questions relating to firm profile characteristics (i.e., ownership structure, governance structure and company objectives) and the business sale negotiation process and outcomes (i.e., 'information was shared equally' and a 'mutually agreed price'). Factor analysis should be used to detect valid and reliable constructs, which can be considered as dependent and/or independent variables in future studies.[8] Information should be collected at more than one point in time with reference to the 'process' and not solely the 'outcomes' from the business sale process. Potential differences between MBOs and MBIs, in relation to information sharing and/or negotiation behaviour, should be investigated further using larger data sets. Additional quantitative studies will provide insights. Several complementary theoretical perspectives should be considered to explore the factors (i.e., ownership structure, governance structure and company objectives) associated with the business sale process issues and outcomes. Additional theory testing studies are also warranted.

Theory-building studies also need to be conducted surrounding the private family-owned firm MBO/I succession options. In-depth longitudinal phenomenological studies that monitor family owners, non-family managers, venture capitalists and independent consultants in relation to ownership thresholds, ownership transitions and critical incidents relating to the MBO/I exit route may provide fresh insights. The latter studies may guide subsequent qualitative and quantitative studies. The pre- and post-MBO/I succession effects of family firm ownership structure, governance structure and company objectives need to be explored in a variety of industrial, national and cultural contexts.

This study highlighted that respondents relating to founded family firms rather than purchased family firm were more likely to share information. Additional research relating to the attitudes and cognitive profiles of key founders/managers may provide insights into MBO/I ownership transitions, and the subsequent development of the purchased firm after the deal. More fine-grained research may be needed to explore the nature of founders' attitudes towards their businesses. Founders may vary in their intention to carry over to the next generation; some may plan from the start to sell or harvest the firm, while others may intend from the outset to hand the firm on to the next generation of family members. Future studies should explore whether younger founders of family firms desire a career in entrepreneurship, and whether they leverage their family firm ownership experience to become serial or portfolio entrepreneurs (Westhead et al., 2005a). Additional studies could explore whether individuals with prior business ownership experience relating to the private family-owned firm context identify and exploit business opportunities in specific sectors, whether they transfer the former family firm ethos as well as governance and management structures on the subsequent firms they establish and/or purchase, and whether the experience and knowledge accumulated during the ownership of prior private firms is leveraged to enhance the ability of subsequent firms owned to be associated with superior levels of firm and entrepreneur performance (Westhead et al., 2003, 2005b). Another area worthy of exploration is the impact the pre-MBO ownership structure has on the post-MBO strategy and performance of the firm.

Future research on ownership and governance and the link with information sharing and mutually agreed business sale negotiation could consider differences between the processes of sale to an MBO/I, sale to a corporate acquirer, and succession to family members. Comparative studies may also shed light on differences in negotiations between vendors and management in the absence of private equity investors. Finally, it would be very interesting to look at performance differences post-MBO/I associated with different pre-MBO/I ownership and governance structures.

NOTES

1. This is a common method of exit involving sale to an existing trading corporation. This can either allow owners/management to withdraw from the business, or it may open up the prospect of working in a larger enterprise.
2. Former family owners may retain minority equity stakes and advisory management positions in firms purchased through an MBO or MBI (Howorth et al., 2004). With reference to a MBI exit route, family owners may be reluctant to sell to completely unknown 'outsiders' whom they do not trust to maintain the firm's ethos. Moreover, the performance of the purchased firm may be enhanced due to the employment of some former family firm members. The latter family members, for example, may have a role in reducing information asymmetry problems and transferring tacit knowledge to the new owners of the business.
3. This may include, for example, the provision of employment for family members at levels for which they are not fully qualified or high discretionary expenditures on company cars, second homes, etc.
4. Suppliers, for example, may not provide favourable purchasing arrangements secured by family firm owners to MBO/I business purchasers. Information relating to the latter issue may be difficult to uncover during due diligence.
5. Robustness tests were conducted. Each continuous variable reported in Table 5.4 was log-transformed. For space reasons, the logistic regression models relating to the log-transformed continuous variables are not reported. No difference in results at the 0.1 level of significance was detected.
6. The logistic regression models reported in Table 5.4 relate to respondents who provided complete information for all the selected control variable and independent variables. Due to limited degrees of freedom, it was decided to include only one control variable in the presented logistic regression models. Although not reported, logistic regression models were computed including two control variables. Robustness tests were conducted with the inclusion of alternative control variables. For space reasons, the additional logistic regression models are not reported. A control variable relating to the type of exit route selected was considered. MBO firms were allocated a value of'1', whilst MBI firms were allocated a value of '0'. The results were substantially consistent with the models reported here. The only difference of note was in the information sharing model where venture capital firm involvement and a lack of suitable successor became more important at the expense of founder presence. This is an area for further research. A business age variable was also considered and it was not found to be significantly associated with either dependent variable.
7. Hair et al. (1995, p. 9) have asserted that, 'the "true" effect is partially masked by the measurement error, causing correlations to weaken and the means to be less precise'.
8. Hair et al. (1995, p. 9) suggest that 'Reducing measurement error, while taking effort, time and additional resources, may improve weak or marginal results and strengthen proven results as well'.

REFERENCES

Admati, A. and P. Pfleiderer (1994), 'Robust financial contracting and the role of venture capitalists', *Journal of Finance*, **49** (2), 371–402.

Amit, R., L. Glosten and E. Muller (1993), 'Challenges to theory development in entrepreneurship research', *Journal of Management Studies*, **30** (5), 815–34.

Apfelbaum, E. (1974), 'On conflicts and bargaining', in L. Berkowitz (ed.), *Advances in Experimental Social Psychology*, New York: Academic Press, pp. 103–56.

Arthurs, J.D. and L.W. Busenitz (2003), 'The boundaries and limitations of agency theory and stewardship theory in the venture capitalist/entrepreneur relationship', *Entrepreneurship Theory and Practice*, **28** (2), 145–62.

Axelrod, R. (1980), 'More effective choices in the prisoner's dilemma', *Journal of Conflict Resolution*, **24** (3), 379–403.

Axelrod, R. (1984), *The Evolution of Cooperation*, New York: Basic Books.

Axelrod, R. and D. Dion (1988), 'The further evolution of cooperation', *Science*, **242** (4884), 1385–90.

Bachkaniwala, D., M. Wright and M. Ram (2001), 'Succession in South Asian family businesses in the UK', *International Small Business Journal*, **19** (4), 15–27.

Barach, J.A. (1984), 'Is there a cure for the paralyzed family board?', *Sloan Management Review*, **26** (1), 3–12.

Birley, S. and P. Westhead (1990a), 'Private business sales environments in the United Kingdom', *Journal of Business Venturing*, **5** (2), 349–73.

Birley, S. and P. Westhead (1990b), 'Private advertised business sales in the United Kingdom', *Area*, **22** (4), 368–80.

Birley, S. and P. Westhead (1993), 'The owner-managers' exit route', in H. Klandt (ed.), *Entrepreneurship and Business Development*, Aldershot: Gower, pp. 123–40.

Birley, S., D. Ng and A. Godfrey (1999), 'The family and the business', *Long Range Planning*, **32** (6), 598–608.

Bjuggren, P.-O. and L.-G. Sund (2001), 'Strategic decision-making in intergenerational successions of small- and medium-size family-owned businesses', *Family Business Review*, **14** (1), 11–23.

Bleackley, M., M. Hay, K. Robbie and M. Wright (1996), 'Entrepreneurial attitudes to venture capital investment realization: evidence from the UK and France', *Entrepreneurship and Regional Development*, **8** (1), 37–55.

Brunninge, O., M. Nordqvist and J. Wiklund (2005), 'Corporate governance and strategic change in small firms: untangling and combining the effects of ownership, board structure and top management teams', paper presented at the Conference on Private Firms and Corporate Governance, Max Planck Institute, Jena, Germany, 11 October.

Bygrave, W.D., M.G. Hay and J. Peeters (eds) (1994), *Realizing Investment Value*, London: Pitman Publishing.

Cable, D. and S. Shane (1997), 'A prisoner's dilemma approach to entrepreneur – venture capitalist relationships', *Academy of Management Review*, **22** (1), 142–76.

Centre for Management Buy-out Research (CMBOR) (2005), *Data Extracted from the CMBOR Database in June 2005*, Nottingham: Centre for Management Buy-out Research, Nottingham University Business School.

Chrisman, J.J., J.H. Chua and P. Sharma (2003a), 'Current trends and future directions in family business management studies: toward a theory of the family firm', *Coleman WP Series*, www.usasbe.org.

Chrisman, J.J., J.H. Chua and S. Zahra (2003b), 'Creating wealth in family firms through managing resources: comments and extensions', *Entrepreneurship Theory and Practice*, **27** (4), 359–66.
Chua, J., J. Chrisman and P.P. Sharma (2003), 'Succession and nonsuccession concerns of family firms and agency relationship with nonfamily managers', *Family Business Review*, **16** (2), 89–108.
Cliffe, S. (1998), 'Facing up to succession', *Harvard Business Review*, **76** (3), 16–18.
Corbetta, G. and C. Salvato (2004), 'The board of directors in family firms: one size fits all?', *Family Business Review*, **17** (2), 119–34.
Cromie, S., B. Stephenson and D. Monteith (1995), 'The management of family firms: an empirical investigation', *International Small Business Journal*, **13** (4), 11–33.
Dabholkar, P.A., W.J. Johnston and A.S. Cathey (1994), 'The dynamics of long term business-to-business exchange relationships', *Journal of Academy of Marketing Science*, **22** (2), 130–45.
Daily, C.M. (1995), An empirical examination of the relationship between CEOs and directors', *Journal of Business Strategies*, **12** (1), 50–68.
Davis, J., F.D. Schoorman and L. Donaldson (1997), 'Toward a stewardship theory of management', *Academy of Management Review*, **22** (1), 20–47.
Donaldson, L. and J.H. Davis (1991), 'Stewardship theory or agency theory: CEO governance and shareholder returns', *Australian Journal of Management*, **16** (1), 49–65.
Dyer, W.G. (1992), *The Entrepreneurial Experience*, San Fransisco: Jossey-Bass.
Dyer, W.G., Jr (2003), 'The family: the missing variable in organizational research', *Entrepreneurship Theory and Practice*, **27** (4), 401–16.
Dyer, W.G. and W. Handler (1994), 'Entrepreneurship and family business: exploring the connections', *Entrepreneurship Theory and Practice*, **19** (1), 71–84.
Ensley, M. and A. Pearson (2005), 'An exploratory comparison of the behavioral dynamics of top management teams in family and non-family new ventures: cohesion, conflict potency and consensus', *Entrepreneurship Theory and Practice*, **29** (3), 267–84.
Fama, E. and M. Jensen (1983), 'Separation of ownership and control', *Journal of Law and Economics*, **26** (2), 301–25.
Filatotchev, I. and M. Wright (2005), *The Life-cycle of Corporate Governance*, Cheltenham, UK and Northampton, MA, USA: Edward Elgar.
Forbes, D.P. and F.J. Milliken (1999), 'Cognition and corporate governance: understanding boards of directors as strategic decision-making', *Academy of Management Review*, **24** (3), 489–505.
Friedman, J. (1990), *Game Theory with Applications to Economics*, London: Oxford University Press.
Fudenberg, D. and J. Tirole (1991), *Game Theory*, Cambridge, MA: MIT Press.
Hair, J.F., Jr, R.E. Anderson, R.L. Tatham and W.C. Black (1995), *Multivariate Data Analysis with Readings*, 4th edn, Englewood Cliffs, NJ: Prentice Hall International.
Halpern, P., R. Kieschnick and W. Rotenberg (1999), 'Why firms engaged in levered recapitalisation rather than levered buy-outs', University of Texas at Dallas, Working Paper.
Handler, W. (1992), 'The succession experience of the next generation', *Family Business Review*, **5** (3), 283–307.
Handler, W. (1994), 'Succession in family business: a review of the research', *Family Business Review*, **7** (2), 133–57.

Hart, O. (1995), 'Corporate governance: some theory and implications', *Economic Journal*, **105** (430), 678–89.

Harveston, P.D., P.S. Davis and J.A. Lyden (1997), 'Succession planning in family business: the impact of owner gender', *Family Business Review*, **10** (4), 373–96.

Howorth, C., P. Westhead and M. Wright (2004), 'Information asymmetry in management buyouts of family firms', *Journal of Business Venturing*, **19** (4), 509–34.

Huse, M. (2000), 'Boards of directors in SMEs: a review and research agenda', *Entrepreneurship and Regional Development*, **12** (4), 271–90.

Jensen, M. and W. Meckling (1976), 'Theory of the firm: managerial behavior, agency costs and ownership structure', *Journal of Financial Economics*, **3** (4), 305–60.

Kaplan, S. and P. Strömberg (2001), 'Venture capitalists as principals: contracting, screening and monitoring', *American Economic Review*, **91** (2), 426–30.

Keasey, K., S. Thompson and M. Wright (2005), *Corporate Governance: Accountability, enterprise and international comparisons*, London: Wiley.

Kumar, N., L.W. Stern and J.C. Anderson (1993), 'Conducting interorganizational research using key informants', *Academy of Management Journal*, **36** (6), 1633–51.

Lansberg, I. (1988), 'The succession conspiracy', *Family Business Review*, **1** (2), 119–43.

Lansberg, I. (1999), *Succeeding Generations: Realizing the dream of families in business*, Boston, MA: Harvard Business School Press.

Leenders, M. and E. Waarts (2003), 'Competitiveness and evolution of family businesses: the role of family and business orientation', *European Management Journal*, **21** (6), 686–97.

Lerner, J. (1995), 'Venture capitalists and the oversight of private firms', *Journal of Finance*, **50** (1), 301–18.

Lindskold, S., B. Betz and D.D. Walters (1986), 'Transforming competitive or cooperative climates', *Journal of Conflict Resolution*, **30** (1), 99–114.

Litz, R.A. (1995), 'The family business: towards definitional clarity', *Proceedings of the Academy of Management Best Papers Entrepreneurship*, pp. 100–104.

Lynall, M., B. Golden and A. Hillman (2003), 'Board composition from adolescence to maturity: a multi-theoretic view', *Academy of Management Review*, **28** (3), 416–31.

Manigart, S., K. Waele, M. Wright and K. Robbie (2002), 'Determinants of required return in venture capital investments: a five country study', *Journal of Business Venturing*, **17** (4), 291–312.

Mitchell, R.K., E.A. Morse and P. Sharma (2003), 'The transacting cognitions of nonfamily employees in the family business setting', *Journal of Business Venturing*, **18** (4), 533–51.

Morck, R. and B. Yeung (2003), 'Agency problems in large family business groups', *Entrepreneurship Theory and Practice*, **27** (4), 367–82.

Morris, M.H., R.W. Williams and D. Nell (1996), 'Factors influencing family business succession', *International Journal of Entrepreneurial Behaviour & Research*, **2** (3), 68–81.

Morris, M.H., R.O. Williams, J.A. Allen and R.A. Avila (1997), 'Correlates of success in family business transitions', *Journal of Business Venturing*, **12** (5), 385–401.

O'Sullivan, N. and P. Wong (1999), 'Board composition, ownership structure and hostile takeovers: some UK evidence 1975–1984', *Accounting and Business Research*, **29** (2), 139–55.

Poutziouris, P.Z. (2002), 'The financial affairs of smaller family firms', in D.E. Fletcher (ed.), *Understanding the Small Family Business*, London: Routledge, pp. 111–26.

Pruitt, D.G. and M.J. Kimmel (1977), 'Twenty years of experimental gaming: critique, synthesis and suggestions for the future', *Annual Review of Psychology*, **28**, 363–92.

Pruthi, S., M. Wright and A. Lockett (2003), 'Do foreign and domestic venture capital firms differ in their monitoring of investees?', *Asia Pacific Journal of Management*, **20** (2), 175–204.

Randoy, T. and S. Goel (2003), 'Ownership structure, founder leadership, and performance in Norwegian SMEs: implications for financing entrepreneurial opportunities', *Journal of Business Venturing*, **18** (5), 619–37.

Robbie, K. and M. Wright (1995), 'Managerial and ownership succession and corporate restructuring: the case of management buyins', *Journal of Management Studies*, **32** (4), 527–49.

Sahlman, W.W. (1990), 'The structure and governance of venture-capital organizations', *Journal of Financial Economics*, **27** (2), 473–521.

Schulze, W.S., M.H. Lubatkin and R.N. Dino (2002), 'Altruism, agency and the competitiveness of family firms', *Managerial and Decision Economics*, **23** (4/5), 247–59.

Schulze, W.S., M.H. Lubatkin and R.N. Dino (2003), 'Toward a theory of agency and altruism in family firms', *Journal of Business Venturing*, **18** (4), 473–90.

Schulze, W.S., M.H. Lubatkin, R.N. Dino and A.K. Buchholtz (2001), Agency relationships in family firms: theory and evidence', *Organization Science*, **12** (2), 99–116.

Sharma, P. and P.G. Irving (2005), 'Four bases of family business successor commitment: antecedents and consequences', *Entrepreneurship Theory and Practice*, **29** (1), 13–33.

Sharma, P. (2004), 'An overview of the field of family business studies: current status and directions for the future', *Family Business Review*, **17** (1), 1–36.

Sharma, P., J. Chrisman and J. Chua (2003a), 'Predictors of satisfaction with the succession process in family firms', *Journal of Business Venturing*, **18** (5), 667–87.

Sharma, P., J. Chrisman and J. Chua (2003b), 'Succession planning as planned behavior: some empirical results', *Family Business Review*, **16** (1), 1–15.

Shepherd, D.A. and A. Zacharakis (2000), 'Structuring family business succession – an analysis of the future leader's decision making', *Entrepreneurship Theory and Practice*, **24** (4), 25–39.

Smyrnios, K. and C. Romano (1994), *The Price Waterhouse/Commonwealth Bank Family Business Survey 1994*, Sydney: Department of Accounting, Monash University.

Song, M.H. and R. Walkling (1993), 'The impact of managerial ownership on acquisition attempts and target shareholder wealth', *Journal of Financial and Quantitative Analysis*, **28** (4), 439–57.

Steier, L.P. (2003), 'Variants of agency contracts in family-financed ventures as a continuum of familial altruistic and market rationalities', *Journal of Business Venturing*, **18** (5), 597–618.

Steier, L.P. and R. Greenwood (1995), 'Venture capitalist relationships in the deal structuring and post-investment stages of new firm creation', *Journal of Management Studies*, **32** (3), 337–57.

Stokes, D. and R. Blackburn (2001), *Opening up Business Closures: A study of businesses that close and owners' exit routes*, Kingston: Kingston University, Small Business Research Centre.

Thompson, S. and M. Wright (1995), 'Corporate governance: the role of restructuring transactions', *Economic Journal*, **105** (430), 690–703.

Ucbasaran, D., A. Lockett, M. Wright and P. Westhead (2003), 'Entrepreneurial founder teams: factors associated with member entry and exit', *Entrepreneurship Theory and Practice*, **28** (2), 107–28.

Weir, C., D. Lang and M. Wright (2005), 'Incentive effects, monitoring mechanisms and the threat from the market for corporate control: an analysis of the factors affecting public to private transactions in the UK', *Journal of Business Finance & Accounting*, **32** (5/6), 909–43.

Westhead, P. (1997), 'Ambitions, "external" environment and strategic factor differences between family and non-family companies', *Entrepreneurship and Regional Development*, **9** (2), 127–57.

Westhead, P. (2003), 'Succession decision-making outcomes reported by unquoted family companies', *International Small Business Journal*, **21** (4), 369–99.

Westhead, P. and M. Cowling (1998), 'Family firm research: the need for a methodological rethink', *Entrepreneurship Theory and Practice*, **23** (1), 31–56.

Westhead, P., M. Cowling and C. Howorth (2001), 'The development of family companies: management and ownership issues', *Family Business Review*, **14** (4), 369–85.

Westhead, P., D. Ucbasaran and M. Wright (2003), 'Differences between private firms owned by novice, serial and portfolio entrepreneurs: implications for policy-makers and practitioners', *Regional Studies*, **37** (2), 187–200.

Westhead, P., D. Ucbasaran and M. Wright (2005a), 'Policy toward novice, serial and portfolio entrepreneurs', *Environment and Planning C: Government and Policy*, **22** (6), 779–98.

Westhead, P., D. Ucbasaran, M. Wright and M. Binks (2005a), 'Novice, serial and portfolio entrepreneur behaviour and contributions', *Small Business Economics*, **25**, 109–32.

Willard, G.E., D.A. Krueger and H.R. Feeser (1992), 'In order to grow, must the founder go: a comparison of performance between founder and non-founder managed high growth manufacturing firms', *Journal of Business Venturing*, **7** (3), 181–95.

Wright, M. and J. Coyne (1985), *Management Buy-outs*, Beckenham: Croom Helm.

Wright, M. and K. Robbie (1996), 'Venture capitalists, unquoted equity investment appraisal and the role of accounting information', *Accounting and Business Research*, **26** (2), 153–70.

Wright, M., S. Thompson, B. Chiplin and K.K. Robbie (1991), *Buy-ins and Buy-outs: New strategies in corporate management*, London: Graham Trotman.

Wright, M., S. Thompson and K. Robbie (1992), 'Venture capital and management-led, leveraged buy-outs: a European perspective', *Journal of Business Venturing*, **7** (1), 47–72.

Wright, M., S. Pruthi and A. Lockett (2002), 'Internationalization of Western venture capitalists into emerging markets: risk assessment and information in India', *Small Business Economics*, **19** (1), 13–29.

Zahra, S.A. and P. Sharma (2004), 'Family business research: a strategic reflection', *Family Business Review*, **17** (4), 331–46.
Zahra, S.A., J.C. Hayton and C. Salvato (2004), 'Entrepreneurship in family vs. non-family firms: a resource-based analysis of the effect of organizational culture', *Entrepreneurship Theory and Practice*, **28** (4), 363–81.

PART IV

Entrepreneurship and Value Creation

6. Management control systems and strategy change in buy-outs

Hans Bruining, Marcel Bonnet and Mike Wright

1. INTRODUCTION

Management buy-outs (MBOs) represent an important threshold in the life of a company, creating a juncture at which to reconsider the strategy of a firm and its associated management control system. Jones's (1992) study of 17 MBOs completed in 1984 and 1985 shows that the budget preparation process became more appropriate, including an increase in participation. Owner-managers initiated improvements in the quality of information, intensified formal controls, introduced more disaggregated feedback and used existing management accounting techniques to communicate managerial philosophies. These early MBOs were strongly dominated by restructuring buy-outs that take actions to enhance efficiency and protect the firm against downside risks (Wright et al., 2000).

More recently, MBOs frequently take revitalization and entrepreneurial measures to exploit the upside potential of the firm (Wright et al., 2000). In 1994, Rehab (a pseudonym) was privatized through an MBO, taking over service contracts for disabled persons with local authorities in competition with other companies. After privatization it introduced a wheelchair renting system that lowered costs by 20% and led to 25% savings on the budgets for the municipalities. In addition to being price competitive, the firm improved service levels and developed new orthopaedic products in order to grow organically. The firm created an own dealers network, and acquired a care products firm, so that by 1997 employment had risen from 240 to 1000 full-time employees. Also in 1994, Packaging (another pseudonym), which manufactures synthetic packaging for the consumer market in the food sector, was sold by its heavily constrained state owned Austrian parent in a management buy-out. After initially improving efficiency and exploiting synergies between its business units, the firm developed into a specialist in providing a wide range of specialist packaging services that demand high speed, capacity imagination and innovation. This included development of a high barrier packaging which keeps fruit fresh, allows customers to see the product and has an easy opening facility.

Otley (1999) stresses the importance of studying management control in situations like MBOs where managers become responsible for strategy, management control and operational control. Both firms faced major opportunities and challenges that have implications for the interaction between management control systems and competitive strategy formulation, implementation and modification (Atkinson et al., 1997). The literature on management control systems has tended to focus on isolated elements in organizations such as organizational design, allocation of responsibility and accountability, planning and budgeting, reward and incentive structures, information systems and performance evaluation practices (Speklé, 2001). These cases emphasize the importance of adopting a comprehensive control system framework rather than examining isolated control mechanisms and management accounting techniques (Jones, 1992). Simons's (1995) model of the dynamic relationships between management control systems and strategic change is an attempt to offer a coherent and comprehensive body of management control theory. His framework contains four levers of control that represent important variables from literature with clear linkage to achieve strategy, e.g. beliefs systems, boundaries systems, the traditional diagnostic control systems and interactive control systems. In this chapter, we use Simons's framework to explore the development of management control in these newer forms of buy-out that have significant upside entrepreneurial opportunities. We examine the questions: what changes in the content and process of the firm's strategy take place after the buy-out, and why and how do the directors of the firm change their management control systems to implement these strategies?

The structure is as follows: after defining an MBO, we describe the framework of levers of control. Then we link the MBO to the framework in order to highlight the role of buy-out management along four levers of control in relation with strategy. The research methodology used and data gathered are explained in the following section. Using two case studies, the role of the buy-out managers pre- and post-MBO are analysed with regard to their potential to contribute to each of the four control levers. In a comparative analysis of the cases the differences in the way buy-out managers undertake management control activities are explained. The discussion section considers the case study evidence in the light of the existing literature and develops theoretical insights. The last section summarizes the major conclusions regarding the contribution of this chapter and identifies the implications of the study for researchers and practitioners.

2. MANAGEMENT BUY-OUTS

An MBO involves members of the incumbent management team acquiring a significant equity stake as individuals with institutional support in order to control the company (Robbie and Wright, 1996). The structuring of a buy-out traditionally involves the introduction of significant equity incentives for the entrepreneurs involved, together with substantial external funding and active monitoring by investors (Jensen, 1993; Wright et al., 1994) in order to control agency costs. The emphasis in buy-outs in the US has typically focused on the debt providers who provide substantial amounts of leverage. However, in Europe venture capital firms play a major role in funding buy-outs. In the UK, for example, the vast majority of buy-outs with a transaction value above £5 million involve venture capital finance (CMBOR, 2001). In the Netherlands, the value of private-equity-backed buy-outs amounted to €4339 million in 2001 (CMBOR, 2002) (Table 6.1).

The traditional agency theory perspective has viewed MBOs as involving cost reduction, low growth prospects and few investment demands (Jensen, 1989; Kaplan, 1989; Phan and Hill, 1995). However, many have gone beyond efficiency incentives to become a vehicle for entrepreneurial initiatives and expansion of managerial discretion (Zahra, 1995; Bruining and Wright, 2002).

MBOs backed by venture capital lead to significant changes in a firm's ownership composition, and can contribute to subsequent growth and changes in strategy, organizational structure and entrepreneurial practices (Reid, 1996; EVCA, 2001). Venture-capital-backed buy-outs may especially involve cases that are more than the organizational efficiency tools traditionally discussed in the MBO literature. Wright et al. (2000, 2001) signal a shift from cost reduction and strategic reorientation in mature sectors to creating value in technology sectors through product development and innovation. They label these buy-outs revitalization buy-outs if they complement their efficiency focus with incremental innovations and entrepreneurial

Table 6.1 Number and total value (million euro) of buy-outs in the Netherlands (1991–2001)

Year	1991	1992	1993	1994	1995	1996	1997	1998	1999	2000	2001
NR	44	50	55	41	57	56	61	69	42	75	54
€	594	446	579	1258	856	1030	1082	3457	4463	1785	4339

Source: Centre for Management Buy-out Research (CMBOR).

buy-outs if they combine this with strategic innovations that emerge. Extensive screening by venture capitalists at the time of investment appraisal places considerable emphasis on the entrepreneurial skills of the managers leading a proposed buy-out or buy-in (Robbie and Wright, 1995; Bruining and Wright, 2002). Venture capitalists that have a reputation for providing capital for growth, use long-term incentives to encourage process or incremental innovation by managers and show good understanding of the industry and business in the post-investment period will attract most of these deals. These aspects of MBOs and venture capitalists' behaviour emphasize the potentially important interactions between management control systems and strategy formulation, implementation and modification post-buy-out.

3. CONCEPTUAL FRAMEWORK: FOUR LEVERS OF CONTROL

We agree with Atkinson et al. (1997) that management control systems must provide the stability necessary to meet users' needs efficiently, while simultaneously creating an information environment that permits managers to envision, and respond to, new directions for the firm. As a result, we expect that the control needs of manager-owners in revitalization and entrepreneurial MBOs requiring product development or innovation go beyond the use of the accounting control system to achieve the financial targets agreed between management and investors. Careful analysis and understanding of critical performance variables is important to keep things on track, but to implement changes in strategy after an MBO effectively, top management needs more than what the classical accounting control system provides. To focus on the involvement of the buy-out management in performance measurement and control to promote upside potential of the MBO firm and to protect it against downside risk, the four levers of control in the framework of Simons (1995) are used, as follows.

3.1 Control Levers

At the core of the analysis of the four levers of control is the firm's strategy. This represents how the firm competes and positions itself *vis-à-vis* its competitors in the market. Successful implementation of the firm's strategy depends on understanding the constructs (Simons, 1995, p. 6), which put into perspective that organizations are created for a purpose and that interaction among participants is needed to keep the organization's purpose clear and in harmony with the environment. A different system, or lever, controls each construct.

First, *beliefs systems* are used to inspire and direct the search for new opportunities; provide basic values, purpose and direction for the organization. Second, *boundary systems* are used to set limits on opportunity-seeking behaviour. The first lever reinforces seeking opportunities and the second lever selects acceptable ones in order to delineate an acceptable domain. Simons (1995, p. 38) concludes that beliefs are tools for articulating and communicating missions, credos and goals of the organization, that assist managers to transform these vague beliefs into focused activity. Managers need to understand the beliefs of the organization and to participate in transforming beliefs into action to become enthusiastic participants in the search for opportunity (Westley, 1990).

With respect to the second lever, boundaries can be distinguished into business conduct and strategic boundaries. Of particular importance here are strategic boundaries, where senior managers place boundaries on opportunity-seeking behaviour by specifying the range of business opportunities where they do not want to expend resources.

The last two levers aim to control the implementation and formulation of the business strategy. *Diagnostic control systems* are used to motivate, monitor, and reward achievement of specified goals. *Interactive control systems* are used to stimulate organizational learning and the emergence of new ideas and strategies. The third lever introduces ex post monitoring to pay attention to critical performance variables in order to implement preset goals by taking corrective measures (Ouchi, 1977; Merchant, 1985). Profit plans, budgets and variance analysis are the most pervasive diagnostic control systems in modern business firms.

With the fourth lever, interactive control systems stimulate search and learning and allow new strategies to emerge. Interactive control systems build internal pressure to break out of narrow routines, stimulate opportunity-seeking and encourage the emergence of new strategic initiatives as future states are re-estimated.

Two opposing forces can be depicted in organizations based on these levers: one is aimed at expanding opportunity-seeking and learning and the other at focusing on search and attention (Volberda, 1998). For the former, the firm needs managers that combine the capabilities of stimulating creativity and innovation of its employees (dynamic capabilities that enhance dynamic control by using beliefs and interactive controls). For the latter, there is a need to minimize surprises and take corrective actions (specialized routines that enhance static control using boundaries and diagnostic control). In MBOs, the balance of these two opposing forces may depend on whether the firm is in a mature market, with stable cash flow and few investment opportunities, or whether it has significant entrepreneurial opportunities.

4. LINKING MBOS TO THE FRAMEWORK

In this section we develop the link between MBOs that take entrepreneurial measures and the framework of the four levers of control. We start with the firm's strategy and highlight the respective levers of control. It is well known that managers pre-MBO typically face investment restrictions from headquarters because their firms are peripheral to the product line of the parent company (Wright et al., 2001). These restrictions reduce the scope for responding entrepreneurially to market developments. Pre-MBO, buy-out firms, if they are peripheral to the core business of the parent, may not be allowed to have growth-oriented strategies and organizations. This conflict between subsidiary management and headquarters is often an indication that a buy-out may be appropriate (Bruining, 1992; Wright et al., 2001). A significant share of MBOs divested from parent companies change to more growth-oriented strategies.

In a buy-out, distance between policy and implementation is likely to become significantly shorter, because of the remarriage of ownership and control (Alchian and Demsetz, 1972). Jones (1992) found that chief executive officers/managing directors used existing management accounting techniques to communicate their managerial philosophies concerning the internal functioning of the firm that was reflected in increased importance of participation in budgeting. However, new owner-managers may show higher levels of commitment to the implementation of a growth-oriented strategy than before the MBO (Zahra, 1995; Wright et al., 2001). In turn, this is likely to change the organizational culture to one that is more entrepreneurially driven (Green, 1992). There may, therefore, be a need for management to stimulate entrepreneurial initiatives that fit their vision and the firm's mission. This will make beliefs a more explicit tool for managers to provide inspiration and organizational direction for focused, purposive activity by its employees that is more externally focused.

Top managers experience more immediate freedom and independence, which enables more flexible decision-making, more delegation, quicker action and easier consensus among manager/owners and shareholders (Bruining, 1992). This creates greater scope for autonomy but may also introduce the need for the formulation of specific boundaries for employees post-MBO, such as return on investment, selection of product-markets and business conduct rules. This creates accountability by establishing rules and using sanctions. These boundaries may be communicated by the buy-out management to allow participants to achieve flexibility and creativity in domains with acceptable risks.

Buy-outs typically involve increased levels of external funding. The costs of servicing debt and fixed dividend commitments act as a discipline to allocate resources to operations with the strongest cash flow and eliminate unprofitable operations (Jensen, 1993; Wright et al., 1994). In addition, buy-outs are actively monitored by investors in order to control agency costs. Jones (1992) reports increases in the quality of information used for operational control, an intensification of formal controls, more disaggregated feedback to increase operational efficiency and fulfil profit standards, and a more positive attitude of employees towards accounting control systems to facilitate participation following buy-out. Jones also reports an increase of perceived importance of accounting control systems, indicating a change in the way the established management accounting techniques were applied. Jones concluded that the independence gained by the MBO firm improved the matching between accounting control systems and contextual variables. These findings signal pressures to improve efficiency after MBO and an increased reliance upon accounting control systems. In venture capital investments generally, Mitchell et al. (1997) show enhanced accounting information systems are introduced at the request of financial investors, particularly with respect to monitoring reports and budgetary components.

By definition the incumbent management of an MBO takes a significant equity stake in order to control the company. The incentive compensation for the MBO managers is dependent on achieving targets for profits and turnover. Buy-outs provide not only equity incentives for managers but also control mechanisms introduced by financial investors that were previously lacking, to ensure the implementation of the ambitious growth targets of the new owners. Diagnostic controls play an important role after the buy-out in enabling the financial targets agreed upon between management and investors to be achieved. Using diagnostic control systems as tools of strategy implementation requires a careful analysis and understanding of critical performance variables.

Instead of obeying orders from headquarters that block innovation and investment in order to optimize goals of the diversified parent company, the buy-out managers have discretionary power to decide what is best for the business, how to organize and lead the company, and how the business plan can be carried out most profitably (Wright et al., 2001). In his research of 47 MBOs, Zahra (1995) shows that substantial investment took place in research and development, the creation of new business and product development. Interactive control systems, involving interactions both inside and outside the firm, may stimulate search and learning to allow these innovative strategies to emerge as participants throughout the organization respond to perceived opportunities and threats.

These arguments suggest that post-MBO business strategy needs to be controlled in a more dynamic way. The shift from maintaining the status quo pre-MBO to acting more efficiently and entrepreneurial post-MBO requires more organizational flexibility than before the buy-out. Dependent on the new owners' conception of the environment and perspective of the organization–environment relationship, the firm has to develop flexibility, for example the capability for facilitating emergent, spontaneous strategies, terminating unprofitable existing activities and developing flexible resources for effective response to (un)anticipated changes (Volberda, 1998, p. 43).

In order to address these control lever issues discussed above, the study examines the questions: what changes in the content and process of the firm's strategy take place after the buy-out and why and how does the management change their management control systems to implement these strategies? Section 5 explains the research methodology and data gathering process adopted in the study.

5. METHODOLOGY AND DATA GATHERING

We use case studies to analyse the interaction between strategy and management control in buy-out situations. The cases can be seen as specification case studies (Keating, 1995), to get a better view of the interaction between post-buy-out strategies and management control. The empirical evidence is based on two detailed case studies selected from the Centre for Management Buy-out Research database, effectively the population of buy-outs in Europe. They were selected to show different efforts to increase product innovation post-MBO. In particular, building on Wright et al. (2000, 2001), we selected cases where there was substantial post-buy-out innovation that may be expected to place considerably greater demands on management and accounting control systems than in traditional buy-outs in stable sectors that have been the focus of previous analysis. To provide some comparison between the cases we identified one case as an entrepreneurial buy-out and one revitalization buy-out in Wright et al.'s (2000, 2001) terminology. Rehab can be identified as an entrepreneurial buy-out fostering strategic innovation and entrepreneurial cognition. Strategic innovation emerges because high-powered incentives and discretion are given to owner/managers. Rehab is a privatization buy-out of a government-owned agency supplying paramedical advice, orthopaedic and rehabilitation products to individuals with a physical functional limitation for lodging, working and living. Rehab is the first business to sell their method for reintegrating handicapped persons to employers and their approach to recycling orthopaedic and rehabilitation products. Packaging is a revitalization buy-out involved in process and incremental imitation innovations, which complement an efficiency focus. Packaging is a managers'-investors' buy-out (MAINBO) of a division from a foreign parent company, which manufactures and sells synthetic packaging for the consumer market in the food sector. It has built on the one-stop shop business concept for packaging in the food sector in addition to its efficiency focus.

Separate face-to-face interviews with the CEOs, the COOs and directors of production, all involved in the buy-out, were carried out during 1998 and 1999. These initial interviews lasted at least 2 hours each and were also followed by a discussion involving all interviewees. To provide further triangulation, we also interviewed the executives of the venture capital firms involved in funding and monitoring the two companies for 2 hours each, as well as using company documentation and press reports. The interviews contained semi-structured questions in retrospect about the content and the formulation of the strategy and the applied levers of control pre- and post-MBO (see Appendix 6A). These questions were developed from the existing literature relating to buy-outs and control (Green, 1992; Jones, 1992; Simons, 1995; Wright et al., 2000). The questions referred to two years before and two years after the MBO.

Coupled with within-case analysis, cross-case comparisons were carried out. Using information from these two distinct cases highlights the role of the levers more transparently. Applying the framework in a variety of buy-outs enables us to verify the relationships in the framework in a way that contributes to development of management control theory (Eisenhardt, 1989). Choosing these buy-outs from the period 1992–94 allowed sufficient time for the operational, organizational and strategic consequences of the change in ownership to be implemented.

The operationalization of the variables in the control levers framework was based on the measures used by Simons (1995). Other sources of information used included business plans, annual reports and press articles. In one of the cases a stock exchange prospectus was available. Interviews were conducted with all three managers to triangulate views about changes in strategy content and strategy formulation as well as in management control activities (Eisenhardt, 1989). Full write-ups of the company studies were sent for comments to the respondents. This approach was adopted as a more appropriate instrument for capturing the complexity of the strategy and management control changes taking place following the transfer of ownership (Green, 1992) than would be possible by a survey.

6. CASE STUDY EVIDENCE

The respective sources of the buy-outs vary, but all share pre-MBO a common lack of investments for innovation and renewal purposes. The health care privatization of Rehab transferred its activities from a task for government to a more commercial private sector focus. Packaging was not central strategically to its parent and was divested by a management and investors buy-out. We report in the following the changes in strategy content and strategy process as well as the related changes in the control levers (for a summary see Appendix 6B).

6.1 Strategy

The content of strategy following the buy-out in both cases shows a sharp increase in market and/or product focus. In addition to internal growth, both firms use external vehicles for growth post-MBO, such as (inter)national acquisitions and alliances. These changes were influenced both by management being able to take advantage of opportunities that they had previously perceived but were unable to exploit under the former ownership regimes and by changes in environmental conditions (regulation and competition).

Until 1994 Rehab functioned as a public municipal medical service. Following criticisms of the public service because of its complex and bureaucratic way of organizing, its low-cost consciousness and difficulties in managing numerous contracts with many small suppliers, new legislation made the municipalities responsible for more cost-efficient and customer-oriented supply of paramedical advice, and orthopaedic and rehabilitation products. Therefore, Rehab with 240 employees was privatized and took over service contracts for disabled persons with local authorities on a decentralized level in competition with other companies. Within two years the dealer network was built comprising 85 shops in 60 different locations.

Packaging has been affected by trends such as increasing buyer concentration, short-to-medium-run volumes of specialized packaging and the increasing responsibility of the packaging industry for environmentally friendly production processes and products. An effective strategic response was required by increasing operating scale on an international basis and by being more receptive to customization and the environment. The Austrian parent company of Packaging was not able to support this response with the necessary investments:

> Our former parent Austria Metall was too slow in authorization of investments and lacked the market knowledge where Packaging was active. The European packaging market is growing annually at two percent and on the supply side there is overcapacity. In East Europe our turnover is growing with 30 percent per year. If Packaging wants to grow fast after the MBO, then we have to look around for international acquisitions in the industry that add to our business concept of one-stop shop and to shareholder value. (CEO of Packaging)

Rehab shows a transformation from a monopolistic supplier of wheelchairs to a market-oriented competitor in the fast-growing market for healthcare services and equipment. It acquired a number of similar operations throughout Holland and soon after the MBO it provided a full service package of equipment supply, consulting and advisory services to healthcare organizations, hospitals, nursing homes, corporations and individuals. This strategy required the development of new services such as the recycling of paramedical devices and car rental. The CEO of Rehab reported that he was convinced that the company's positioning of itself as market leader in the field of orthopaedic services, wheelchairs, advice of physicians to municipal councils, increased competition and the quality of products lowered prices and reduced costs to municipalities by approximately 25%. The decrease in costs was due to speeding up the processing time for the rental of these auxiliary medical devices.

Packaging developed from high-volume packaging production to high-value-added, custom-made goods. After the buy-out, the firm preferred to concentrate on the development of its 'one-stop-shop solution' packaging concept by leveraging synergies between the business units (folding cartons, flexible packaging and plastic packaging) in the group through cross-selling services. Two years after the MBO it developed partnerships with large international food firms to increase its production innovation capacity, indicating a shift from mere efficiency to a value-added innovative focus. During 1997 it introduced supply chain management in order to minimize the costs and logistical complexities clients face in maintaining stocks of packaging. To strengthen its international capability, it acquired a French flexible packaging firm in 1998. The CEO of Packaging reported that immediately after the buy-out his firm concentrated on improving short-term financial performance and market orientation. This meant that the firm did not fully address strategic reorientation of the packaging business to incorporate trends in buyer concentration, customizing market needs and responsibility for environmentally friendly production processes and products.

6.2 Beliefs Systems

Pre-MBO we found no beliefs systems in the sense of formal business philosophies relating to how to create value. Post-MBO these beliefs are formalized in a culture that stimulates intrapreneurship, and supports customer focus and quality control orientation. The need for this change in culture was brought about as a result of changes in the competitive environment (deregulation and increased competition in the provision of services for the disabled in Rehab and greater need for competition on the basis of quality differentiation in Packaging) that placed emphasis on utilizing the detailed market knowledge of employees throughout the organizations. In the context of an ownership change that both opened up new opportunities and made the buy-out firms more commercially exposed, there was a need to capture this knowledge in a commercial way.

In the case studies we found a variety of organizational arrangements through which a change in culture was stimulated. Rehab produced a mission statement that sets out the commitment of the firm to enhance the ability of temporarily handicapped persons to help themselves at home and at work. In order to achieve this goal, the company offers services and devices at socially acceptable market prices. Regional meetings between the CEO and the managers from the dealer network were used to discuss how to anticipate opportunities and in what direction. An analysis of strengths and weaknesses of every manager was made in order to determine their training needs and the firm's replacement policy. During the regional 'soapbox' meetings the main core values that promote a business mind were: learning to work efficiently, stimulating a commercial attitude among salespersons and teaching physicians as fee earners to become more cost conscious in the post-MBO situation. The CEO has very clear view on the need for employees to adopt the new beliefs and culture:

> A lot of privatisations fail because the management does not communicate clearly. Our people have to realize from the very start what the ambitions of Rehab are! (Quoted in Shoemakers, 1996)

The CEO characterized the transformation for the company's employees as follows: 'we moved from getting pocket money to earning our own salary in the marketplace', indicating the ending of an era of security for all employees and the beginning of a period of uncertainty. The CEO explained that this shift also involved new rules such as 'work till you are finished', 'be better than your competitor', 'know your costs and your profit'. There was a lot of trust of the venture capitalist and the employees in the top management team, the knowledge and the enthusiastic spirit of the employees and two strong products with a good track record. Most employees invested in sales and account training to adapt to their new job requirements; others left the organization because they could not meet the new performance standards. In the first six months the company made a net profit of DFL 800 000. This helped to stimulate the employees and signalled to them that the transformation was being successful. To motivate the employees financially to make the cultural change, they were invited to take part in the equity of the firm; one-third did so.

The growth of Rehab brought an end to the soapbox meetings with the CEO, with the works council requesting that such meetings be reinstalled. Now formal mechanisms of recruitment, selection and training have gradually taken over from informal ways to communicate the values of Rehab to its employees. For example, for some of its dealer locations Rehab recruited managers from Nissan Motors. It remains to be seen whether this shift will have an adverse effect on beliefs systems.

Both firms used internal business magazines to support the communication of missions and credos, and to inform people in the firm about current business developments. In Packaging, reflecting the less dramatic environmental developments, attempts to change beliefs and culture were less radical than in Rehab. Management was actively involved in communicating that product quality would be achieved by the way customers, suppliers and employees work together in continuous improvement projects. In the first year after the buy-out (1995) the CEO wrote in the annual report:

> the firm has achieved genuine commercial and strategic and financial improvements, confirming that the company is on the right track to use the strength of making use of one another's complementarity.

Two years later he was much clearer about the relationship with the customer in his mission statement:

> We take a long-term perspective because our aim is to forge long-term relationships with our clients. We are constantly planning, investing and looking ahead in order to produce effective solutions that meet the demands of tomorrow's consumers.

This shift in mission indicated the change from a financial short term to a more strategic focus. Self-managing teams consisting of technical and commercial people negotiated the contracts with customers.

6.3 Boundary Systems

The boundaries with regard to product markets and investment were much more clearly specified post-MBO. Before privatization, in Rehab attention was not given to strengths or weaknesses of the firm, nor was any form of entrepreneurship promoted that involved risk-taking. After privatization a lot of time was invested in product innovation and in the exploration of the market, which resulted in the development of guidelines to approach a variety of customers. In this firm, the strategic domain developed after four to five years. This was demonstrated by divesting in 1998 a consulting advisory service acquired in 1995 and at the same time starting activities like recycling of paramedical devices and car rental for the disabled. Rehab also decided to differentiate its core business of advice to disabled persons in their homes by providing advice on the seriousness of employees' disability problems and offering appropriate solutions. In buy-outs where managers perceive new entrepreneurial opportunities, there may be a need to provide scope to exploit those opportunities. The perception of new opportunities and the establishment of clear performance targets influenced the need to set clear boundaries on activities. The potential problem is that unmonitored management may go beyond their idiosyncratic skills and pursue apparent opportunities that do not contribute to the meeting of targets (Castanias and Helfat, 2001). Financial investors may therefore have a role to play but may need to have some understanding of the market in order to be able to contribute to the setting of boundaries that allow the appropriate scope for taking innovative actions. While management in Rehab were most involved in setting these boundaries, the venture capitalist representative on the board also played a key role in focusing management's attention. When asked about the contribution of the venture capitalist on (re)positioning of products, the venture capitalist representative on the supervisory board referred to the discussion with the management team on wholesale activities versus consumer convenient products. During one of the company's annual strategy away-days the decision was made not to try to control the whole medical sector, but to focus on parts.

In Packaging, boundaries were mainly found in guidelines such as return on investment targets and limitation to pre-selected product–market combinations, which were absent pre-MBO. For example, the aim was set to provide a one-stop shop for specialist packaging for Europe's leading consumer brands such as Unilever, CPC and Polaroid. As in Rehab, the venture capitalist representative contributed to the awareness among the Packaging management that some markets were too small to achieve an annual growth rate of 10–15%. The new shareholders were only willing to accept investments in the food and dairy sector which comply with environmental rules that are expected to achieve ROI's above 20%. With 300 million consumers, Eastern Europe is an important target. Two loss-making companies were divested following the MBO because they lacked the potential to contribute profitably to specialist packaging services.

6.4 Diagnostic Control Systems

Before privatization, a framework for diagnostic control in Rehab was missing. Instruments for planning, cost control and performance measurement developed gradually following privatization through a dynamic process rather than there being a simple once-for-all change. Initially, as part of the development of an entrepreneurial culture, control occurred on a more informal basis. After a couple of years the subsidiaries became profit centres and measured the success of managers in the beginning only by turnover targets. In practice this led to a severe 10% loss of personnel caused by heavy pressure by the management to reach turnover goals. Management focused on the sales of wheelchairs because of the higher margins compared to the wheelchairs for hire. This was at the expense of the wheelchair rentals, thus decreasing the chances for employees to satisfy customer needs, and causing higher costs of supplies. The company was forced to differentiate its diagnostic systems in relation to performance evaluation from a single focus on turnover to a more balanced set of criteria. Achievement of the targets set for these criteria determines the flexible component in the reward structure of the managers. This is based on different weights comprising profit margin 30%, accounts receivable, cost targets and stock control targets 20%, and last but not least turnover targets 10%.

According to the director of the business unit of Rehab involved in advisory services, who had undergone a change from physician to business unit manager, not everything went well at the beginning of the transformation. The main problems related to a lack of local approach to customers. Initially Rehab's employees were seen as arrogant and inflexible in their relationship to customers and not particularly good in contract negotiations and setting prices. However, more than 50% of municipalities were now customers of Rehab (35% market share) and employees were learning fast.

After some time these performance management problems were resolved by decentralizing responsibilities for contracts and prices, replacing managers that were not able to make the move to a commercial firm, and implementing account management, thus increasing the ability to serve the clients better. Furthermore, quality controls were implemented to enhance delivery times of rental services and customer satisfaction. Performance measurement information used internally by the investee consisted of turnover analysis, labour cost analysis and net profit. Following venture capital investor involvement, specific information about financial ratios as ROE (employed), ROA and sales/assets invested and cash flow was developed and reported. The monitoring was further developed and financial budgets were fine-tuned because the venture capitalist was focused on governing the business to achieve the exit agreed upon with the management. The frequency of financial reporting was increased from annual, bi-annual and quarterly before buy-out to monthly after involvement of the venture capitalist. Before the buy-out Rehab did not provide reports on cash flow but now these are provided on annual, bi-annual, quarterly and monthly bases. After the buy-out, reports about capital expenditure were developed and also used on annual, bi-annual and quarterly bases; the annual headcount reports were supplemented by bi-annual reports.

Operational, organizational and strategic decision-making information was available but the quality was further developed in order to monitor the results better and take corrective action earlier for the firm and the venture capitalist. For example, when the company acquired another firm which was not well organized and managed with respect to financial controls, the decision was taken on the initiative of the venture capitalist to let the acquired company stand alone for three years, meanwhile improving management control systems before integrating them into the Rehab organization and management information systems.

Following the MBO in Packaging, the managing directors played more 'hands-on' roles than before, focusing on intensifying machine utilization and efficiency, lowering costs and increasing capacity. After two years of restructuring, performance measurement based on critical success factors was extended to factors that support close working relationships between the firm and its industrial customers. This was implemented by appointing account management teams for several clients. For example, the firm uses electronic data interchange to integrate its planning system with the clients' planning systems, enabling more accurate scheduling of production and deliveries. Just in time delivery systems and other logistic support help minimize clients' inventories and ensure receipt of their packaging at short notice. As a result, 100 of the 140 employees participate after the MBO in the budget process in order to control costs, sales and profits. As the director of one of the Packaging subsidiaries reported:

> Before the buy-out our Austrian parent insisted on having budgets. Although they were abstract at the company level, they fitted the performance indicators for managing a large portfolio of companies. After the buy-out we need budgets to manage the company. The budgets are better structured and the subsidiaries use a planning and control cycle for management information of one month, enabling senior management to make quarterly adaptations. I am convinced that our budgets are qualitatively better because the knowledge of the market of our employees has improved strongly.

The venture capitalists represented on the supervisory board show more involvement post-MBO with the company than the representatives of the parent company pre-MBO. Their sounding board function, personality and business experience influence their openness to exchange ideas with the management team on how the operations are progressing in the company's profit centres. Rather than imposing a monitoring system on management, this suggests that diagnostic controls are developed between the two parties. As the venture capitalist representative reported:

> Our role is to confront the management with problems and to invite them to present solutions; we do not choose business measures. For example, one of the subsidiaries had to adapt its cost levels in order to compete more efficiently.

All the profit and loss components and financial ratios reported to the venture capitalist were used before the MBO. After the MBO, the two venture capital investors put more emphasis on cash flow in management reports in order to focus more on operational efficiencies and meeting targets. Instead of quarterly, monthly cash flow reporting now takes place. These actions helped bring the company back into profit (from a loss of DFL 1.7 run in 1994 to a profit in 1995 of DFL 9 million).

6.5 Interactive Control Systems

In Rehab, interaction took place through the strategic appointment to the supervisory board of the chairman of the Dutch Council for the Disabled. Top management now receive up-to-date information from the political decision-making process on the deregulation of certain industries and on legislation with regard to individuals with a physical functional limitation. This enables management to detect and remove major strategic uncertainties for the firm. Another example is the establishment of a consumer council where on a regular basis the supply of products and services is discussed between the responsible managers and their customers. Besides changes in the strategy content, we observed changes in the process of strategy formulation. But these changes may not be instigated by management alone. Post-MBO in Rehab, strategies were formulated by the management team and the supervisory board with representatives of the venture capitalists. Interaction between the management team, the supervisory board and the venture capitalist concerning strategy development involved the supervisory board having a marketing view on the company, while the venture capitalists had a financial view. This interaction aided the learning process. The venture capitalists examined together with the CEO and the COO what businesses to grow internationally and appropriate lease financing packages for activities abroad. The venture capitalist representative noted that:

> For Rehab's success it was absolutely important to obtain national market coverage penetration to generate demand for its products in a fast and massive way.

> Originally we invested DFL 10 mn but this was increased due to heavy investment needs to DFL 22.5 mn.

The venture capitalist representative observed how this interaction also involved other outsiders' participation in the annual strategy away-day of Rehab:

> We had briefings from other medical disciplines to discuss mobility problems [of people] in new and old market segments and the consequences for the firm in terms of whether it should enter new fields or outsource the business because of the danger of becoming too fragmented.

The venture capitalist that funded Packaging was not involved in formulating the original strategy, but explained that he preferred to take a prudent stance in strategy formulation and implementation, and sometimes had to say no to the entrepreneurial plans of the management that had conducted the buy-out.

Packaging faces serious threats because of increasing pressures from the need to produce environmentally friendly products, increasing buyer concentration and bargaining power and the need to provide rapid, short-to-medium-run volumes of specialized packaging. These changes required effective strategic response by being more receptive to requests for customization and by recognizing the need to take account of environmental factors. The one-stop-shop and supply chain concepts are triggers for the company's proactive and innovative approaches to packaging. In response, Packaging has developed interactions with consumers through the introduction of decentralized self-managing teams with seats on consumer panels that have the authority to make decisions concerning production, costs and prices. As the director of one of the Packaging subsidiaries noted:

> Greater uncertainty in the markets has led to stronger involvement of our employees and to a much better and open interaction in the planning process. There is intensive briefing between employees and managers about the critical factors for the firm, for example, the design of our partnerships with customers.

Quality management training programmes are used to ensure that skills keep pace with technological and market developments. The firm is thus able to respond rapidly to the latest consumer trends. These partnerships with large customers are used to establish a position of sustained growth. This interaction of employees with customers has similar features with that adopted in Rehab. However, as noted in the diagnostics section, in Rehab the nature of the interaction was initially inappropriate and inflexible in the absence of sufficient support and monitoring.

6.6 Comparisons between Cases

There are some notable points of comparison in systems between the two MBOs that reflect their different environmental conditions. In Rehab, which faced more radical environmental changes giving rise to greater entrepreneurial opportunities than in Packaging, beliefs were introduced first to provide a basis for change in attitude and behaviour. In addition, interactive control has top priority at the senior management level. Boundaries (strategic and behaviour) and diagnostics were developed later on in an iterative manner. In contrast, in Packaging, diagnostics came first in order for the firm to become cost efficient and cost effective in the face of competition. Subsequently, the ambition of the company had to change because of emerging trends in the packaging sector. As a result, beliefs were developed, boundaries became clearer (pan-European buying; environmental requirements; fast and small production runs) and interactive control at the operations level was organized in self-managing teams. These differences suggest that in more entrepreneurial buy-outs there is a need to focus more on beliefs and interactions systems. On the other hand, focusing only on diagnostic systems may be detrimental if environmental factors require major changes to beliefs and interaction systems.

7. DISCUSSION

In this section we consider the evidence from the case studies in the light of the existing literature and develop theoretical insights. The companies in this study show an increase in the market orientation of their strategies post-MBO. The new owners/managers are adapting their firms strategically through innovation, marketing and organization design to different market niches and contexts. These findings supplement the study of Jones (1992), where for the majority of companies the state of environmental dynamism was unaltered, thus enabling the companies to intensify the use of their existing accounting techniques of formal control such as budgets. In contrast, in the buy-outs examined here, the change in control systems arose firstly because there was a need to adopt new ways of coping with changes in the competitive and regulatory environment, and secondly because management had identified new market opportunities as a result of these changes. The evidence from the two case studies supports the view of Wright et al. (2000) that managerial incentives in buy-out firms can foster revitalization or strategic innovation after a period of neglect. The new owners are released from the investment constraints of the former parent company that blocked innovation and can carry out their own ideas on how to make profits.

Management control goes beyond management accounting systems in buy-outs where entrepreneurial opportunities exist. In addition to the existing formal controls, these companies use other management control techniques to match the changing environmental conditions. With the conceptual framework of the 'levers of control', practices are identified that reflect the choice of which management control activities are selected in cases where the companies want to add value to the business through new products/new market developments that were frustrated by the parent prior to the MBO.

One of the new controls is the increase in use of *beliefs*. The business philosophy regarding how to reach customers is formally communicated by management to employees in a variety of forms in all the companies. Affirmation is explicitly sought about the direction of the firm, its ambition and the essential capabilities and attitudes of its employees that stimulate entrepreneurship. Pre-MBO the respective parent companies did not develop initiatives to use these beliefs systems explicitly.

The Jones study focused on existing accounting control systems as a channel for effecting changes in organizational culture, such as managerial philosophies to promote participation in budgets. Participation was not extended beyond middle managers, which contrasts with the apparently more entrepreneurial oriented leadership style used by top managers in our case studies. We see the reported increase in use of beliefs in our study as a move towards improved matching of an entrepreneurial culture with the organizational context, where financial risks increase after becoming an independent company. Changing organizational cultures is problematical but may be achievable under conditions of major 'shocks' or 'propitious moments' that create organizational breaks (Trice and Beyer, 1993), such as the juncture created by a management buy-out. For cultural change to be effective there is a need not just to change cultural beliefs but also to change people's experiences and what they learn from them so that assumptions and core values are altered (Whipp et al., 1989). In this respect, training can serve as a 'rite of passage' that resocializes current employees while the exit of employees that represent the old culture can have important symbolic and practical consequences for the culture. Innovative cultural leaders who are committed to the new culture and trusted are important in convincing employees to follow the new vision and to overcome resistance. The buy-out was indeed found to involve an organizational break that provided the opportunity to change the culture (Trice and Beyer, 1993) and employees' experiences (Whipp et al., 1989). Consistent with the buy-out literature (Green, 1992; Zahra, 1995; Wright et al., 2000; Bruining and Wright, 2002), the new owner/managers with high levels of commitment were eager to implement growth-oriented strategies to exploit the upside potential of the firm. In so doing, management set about introducing an entrepreneurially driven culture that encourages initiatives by employees to detect profitable opportunities. We suggest from our evidence that in more entrepreneurial buy-outs there is a need for management to be more proactive in taking the initiative to effect changes in culture rather than relying on accounting control systems, and that this action has to be pervade the organization. Our cases suggested, however, that a potential problem in effecting changes in beliefs and culture may arise from implementation failure (Trice and Beyer, 1993). That is, while this process may begin as a more informal one, it may need to evolve over time. Important issues concern whether this evolution to a more formal approach takes place when the new culture is sufficiently embedded or whether a more formal approach undermines the culture.

The introduction of managerial incentives, active involvement by investors and commitment to service external funding is traditionally argued to focus attention on the *boundaries* of buy-outs (Jensen, 1989, 1993). If boundaries are lacking (as in Rehab) before the buy-out, top management gradually set standards for investment volumes, return ratios and for well-defined markets. From the beginning in Packaging, the selection of market niches and minimum return on investments were cited as boundaries. The finding of renewed boundaries is consistent with the delegation of decision-making to lower levels in the organization. Decrease in size and complexity of the organizational structure stimulate decentralization after buy-out (Phan and Hill, 1995), and top managers experience more immediate freedom and independence, which enables more flexible decision-making and delegation. Thus, within the new boundaries the employees and managers are free to generate proposals. This also represents an interesting development on the findings of Jones (1992). The observed increase in emphasis upon planning, reported by Jones, gave rise to an improved match with the organizational context, and implicit in planning would be improved knowledge of the environment. Our data provide explicit details indicating the importance of managerial idiosyncratic actions (Castanias and Helfat, 2001), not just systems and techniques, in effecting changes post-MBO. For example, the management developed guidelines to approach customers and choices for the strategy domain. We suggest that in more entrepreneurial buy-outs this is a dynamic search process of development rather than a once-for-all shift. However, because of the potential downside of managerial discretion, the venture capitalist may play an important role, especially in terms of setting appropriate boundaries on management's entrepreneurial efforts.

Before the MBO the employees of the companies examined here experienced *diagnostic control* systems as distant, not realistic, not tailor made to their own information needs and top-down enforced. This changed post-MBO. Freedom from conformity with the practices of the former parent resulted in management control activities being more closely matched with organizational contexts. The involvement of employees in the formulation of budgets increases, as well as their experience in using budgets, became as an important navigation tool. Planning took place more accurately as employees and managers developed information systems that were more appropriate to their needs. A major difference with regard to the budgeting processes was the shift from top-down to bottom-up budgeting.

This finding is supported by Jones (1992) on buy-outs and also by Mitchell et al. (1997) for venture capital investments generally. Jones provides evidence that following buy-out more relevant control systems are developed that match the environment. Jones found that planning systems became more meaningful, were connected to real strategy and were part of the routines. Changes in attitudes towards management control were associated with and facilitated by managerial philosophies, which extended informal control through participation, as well as formal control through documentation and meetings. Removing barriers between management and workers is seen as necessary to prepare budgets with more commitment and reality. We suggest that diagnostic control systems in more entrepreneurial buy-outs may adapt as in other types of buy-out. However, important issues are raised concerning how this match develops. This adaptation may be part of a dynamic process rather than a simple once-for-all change because the entrepreneurial search for profitable new markets takes place in an environment of great uncertainty. Our evidence leads us to suggest also that there may be a need for the financial investor to develop the existing control system as a means of monitoring managerial behaviour (Reid, 1996). At the request of the venture capitalist, fine-tuning measures may be taken to supplement the monitoring on cash flows and contribution to profit on a product basis. Venture capital investors may play an important role in guiding management to underpin their more entrepreneurial beliefs and interaction systems with appropriate diagnostic control systems that keep the buy-out on track to meet agreed targets for the realization of capital gains. It is also clear that diagnostic control is a process. While the financial investor helps to ensure that appropriate systems are in place, these systems are the basis for a dialogue with management to identify solutions to problems. These circumstances arise as management is likely to have more information than financial investors. This is consistent with arguments that a strict principal–agent approach to monitoring by financial investors has to be tempered by recognition of the need to develop a strong cooperative relationship with management (Sapienza and Korsgaard, 1996; Cable and Shane, 1997).

In the Jones study regular but less formal discussion of operational and policy matters took place only at the management level. The planning system developed to provide additional information concerning the interface between external environments and internal operations. In our study, changes in the strategy formulating process were characterized by interactive controls. However, the frequency with which strategic information about competitors, products, politics and technology was analysed by management varied. *Interactive control* is typically used selectively to sustain revitalization and innovation strategies. Key personnel at different levels of these companies, including non-managerial levels, are involved in discussions with top management about strategic uncertainties relating to the intended strategy based on experience gleaned from their decentralized interaction and negotiation with customers.

We suggest that these organizational arrangements extend insights into the adaptation of planning systems to environmental factors identified by Jones (1992). A notable change in both companies was that, rather than just the incorporation of competitors' actions in planning techniques as identified, interactive control systems developed with both the financial investor and external actors. This interaction was viewed as an important part of a dynamic process of search and learning, to access insights and information that would be valuable in creating a competitive advantage in a changing market environment. The resource-based and capabilities views of the firm suggest that an important way that a firm gains competitive advantage is by management having the skills to develop activities that are difficult to imitate (Barney, 1991; Barney et al., 2001). Information in the public domain is less likely to contribute to developing a competitive advantage than private information. Firms need to have the ability to recognize the value of new information and assimilate it (Cohen and Levinthal, 1990). This ability or absorptive capacity (Zahra and George, 2002) provides firms with the strategic flexibility to adapt and evolve in changing environments. Our study, therefore, suggests that an important aspect of interactive controls is both to access the more detailed private information that is important in enabling management to develop a competitive advantage and to recruit management and employees with the capabilities to obtain and use this information.

8. CONCLUSIONS

Overall, we conclude that post-MBO there is a need to develop coherence between a change in strategy and the application of levers of control. The coherence of management control and management accounting systems, which was lacking pre-buy-out, developed dynamically post-buy-out. We suggest that the development of belief and interaction control systems is of particular importance in more entrepreneurial buy-outs and serves as a valuable complement and extension to but not replacement of the more traditional diagnostic control systems post-MBO.

The analysis has implications for practitioners involved in buy-outs. The study adds to insights regarding the development of management control in different types of buy-out. For practitioners, the findings suggest the need to adopt approaches to control according to whether the MBO is in a traditional sector with limited investment opportunities or whether the firm has significant scope for innovation. It is well established that the change in ownership provides scope for accounting control and planning systems in traditional buy-outs in stable sectors to become more relevant. Our evidence suggests that this also seems to be the case in more entrepreneurial buy-outs in more uncertain environments. However, it was also evident that problems may arise where such systems are too informal and narrowly specified in an entrepreneurial environment. Rather, there appears to be a need to develop appropriate systems through a dynamic, flexible process. What is distinctive about more entrepreneurial buy-outs appears to be the need to develop other dimensions of control that facilitate entrepreneurial and innovative activity. As illustrated by the case of Rehab, for example, this involved the development of focused communication mechanisms that helped to inculcate an entrepreneurial culture that involved employees learning to anticipate opportunities. There also appears to be a need to develop proactive interactive control with both clients and the market in order to reduce strategic uncertainties and to make the firm more market responsive.

Our study also suggests that management in more entrepreneurial MBOs need to find private equity investors with more than just diagnostic financial monitoring skills. This in turn indicates that private equity firms may need to develop their range of human capital to include skills that enable them to contribute to the development of the growth of MBO investees. In addition, this also suggests a need for private equity firms to develop relationships with management rather than relying solely on contractual monitoring arrangements. More generally, our evidence leads us to propose that there is a need to find a fit between the nature of the buy-out and the nature of the private equity investor. While venture capital firms investing in early-stage investments possess these skills, this is less true of private equity firms investing in traditional MBOs in stable sectors with few growth opportunities where the requirement is to improve incentives and financial control systems (Lockett et al., 2002; Wright et al., 2001).

With respect to researchers, our study has a number of implications. First, the study suggests that change in ownership provides a major opportunity to effect changes in beliefs and the interaction between management control systems and competitive strategy formulation, implementation and modification. In extending Jones's (1992) study to buy-outs involving major entrepreneurial opportunities for growth rather than restructuring of mature businesses, we would suggest that our findings extend the contingency perspective on control systems. Control systems in buy-outs lead to a better fit with environmental contingencies but these control systems also appear to be influenced by the nature of the buy-out. These contingent aspects relate not just to the structure of control systems but also to the process of control, notably in terms of the processes involved in communicating beliefs, processes of interaction and the budgetary process. The contingency perspective may also be extended to the application of an agency theory approach to monitoring and control in MBOs that focuses on contractual financial control arrangements. The agency theory perspective may be more appropriate in traditional mature sectors where the need is to enhance cost efficiencies. In more dynamic markets with growth opportunities, a broader approach appears to be required that keys into resource-based and capabilities perspectives. There appears to be a need to develop further research that explicitly links the different control systems to these concepts.

In contrast to more traditional management buy-outs, managers' concerns about risk appear to be less important in our cases than their recognition of new opportunities. Strategic information on opportunities emerges from managers' experience and their rapid interpretation of the changing business environment and less from formal control systems. In this context, financial investors provide support through both traditional controls as well as attaching importance to strategic controls and sharing strategic insight. These investors allow the new owners to exploit their entrepreneurial skills instead of constraining them by high debt repayments and tight contractual arrangements (Wright et al., 2000).

Although we have focused only on the management buy-out context, a second implication concerns the more general questions of how these interactions change during the various 'thresholds' in the life-cycle of firms and what are the barriers to these changes being effective (Daily and Dalton, 1992). These thresholds can be identified in terms of initial start-up, entry of an external financier (especially venture capital firm), the move from private company to listed company in an initial public offering, subsequent takeover (or buy-out of all or part of the company), and possible entry into administrative receivership when there may be a need to reconsider the direction of the firm in order to rescue it. Further research might usefully examine these various threshold junctures in conjunction with strategy change and management control actions.

This point, in turn, raises a final implication for researchers as it suggests a need to undertake more longitudinal studies of the development of the full scope of information and control systems in MBOs. Our analysis provides some indication of the dynamics of the mechanisms for developing beliefs and interactions. It would be interesting to examine how these change further as the pressures and desires emerge to exit the buy-out arrangement, either through sale to another corporation or stock market flotation.

APPENDIX 6A

Questionnaire checklist about strategy and control levers pre- and post-MBO

General
- Background of the interviewee
- Role of the interviewee held within the firm
- Changes in their role post-MBO?
- History of the firm
- General information about core products and organization
- General information about industry, market and technology development
- External shareholders/financiers

Strategy
- Reason for the MBO vision on management
- Underlying strategic goals
- Strategy content
- Strategy process
- Effectiveness strategy
- Adaptations strategy

Beliefs systems
- Presence of shared vision
- Use of missions, vision, credos
- Does it affect your role in any way?
- Involvement of employees/management
- Is there a cultural change programme?
- Relationship-shared vision and new opportunities

Boundary systems
- Boundaries for the firm in seeking chances and opportunities
- The risks avoided?
- Operating rules/behavioural codes managers
- Sanctions for opportunity-seeking behaviour

Diagnostic control systems
- Firm's key performance indicators
- Critical success factors; responsibilities
- Involvement with translation strategy in budgets
- Are any changes made? Reasons?
- Standards, output measures, incentives budgets
- Role of monitoring performance
- Fine-tuning budgets post-MBO
- Monitoring role of external shareholders
- Frequency of budget adaptations
- Attention and attitudes of employees towards budget
- Information needs and current performance measures

Interactive control systems
- Nature of involvement of employees in non-routine decisions
- Experiments, knowledge systems, management development, learning
- Items from operations on strategic agenda of top management
- Frequency of attention to budgets from all management levels
- Frequency of discussion strategic items between management levels
- Changes in assumptions of firm's strategy

APPENDIX 6B SUMMARY

	Case 1: 'Rehab'	Case 2: 'Packaging'
Company strategy	Products for physically handicapped	Packaging
Content	From monopolist to market-oriented advice, products, distribution	From volume to 'one-stop shopping'/tailor-made solutions buyers
Goal	25% market share	Every subsidiary competitive and profitable
Process	Post-buy-out governance with venture capitalist and management team	Delayering firm, self-managing customer-oriented teams
Beliefs	From passive to active solution seeking From no corporate entrepreneurship to intrapreneuring	From passive to active attention to quality and customer orientation through mission

Boundaries	From job descriptions to guidelines to approach a variety of customers by new product development	From no selection to delineating products and markets: only food sector which comply to environmental rules Minimum ROIs
Diagnostic controls	Post buy-out: responsibility accounting with appropriate accounting measures developing over time	From targets figures on division level to contracts per team Budgets and personal setting of tasks Just in time delivery
Interactive controls	Interactive control mainly between top management and venture capitalists Creating learning organization through soapbox, recurrent consultation with employees and customers	Consultation about transfer of new production with reference to new legislation Consultation about partnership with large customers; synergy between subsidiaries

ACKNOWLEDGEMENTS

Thanks to the senior management of the case study companies for their time. We acknowledge with thanks the helpful and constructive comments of two anonymous referees and the editor.

REFERENCES

Alchian, A.A. and Demsetz, H. (1972), 'Production, information costs, and economic organisation', *American Economic Review*, **2**, 777–95.

Atkinson, A.A., Balakrishnan, R., Booth, R.P., Cote, J.M., Groot, T., Malmi, T., Roberts, H., Uliana, E. and Wu, A. (1997), 'New directions in management accounting research', *Journal of Management Accounting Research*, **9**, 79–108.

Barney, J. (1991), 'Firm resources and sustained competitive advantage', *Journal of Management*, **17**, 99–120.

Barney, J., Wright, M. and Ketchen, D. (2001), 'The resource-based view of the firm: ten years after 1991', *Journal of Management*, **27**, 625–41.

Bruining, J. (1992), 'Performance improvement after management buy-out', unpublished PhD, Erasmus University, Rotterdam.

Bruining, J. and Wright, M. (2002), 'Entrepreneurial orientation in management buy-outs and the contribution of venture capital, *Venture Capital* **4**, 147–68.

Cable, D. and Shane, S. (1997), 'A prisoner's dilemma approach to entrepreneur–venture capitalist relationships', *Academy of Management Review*, **22**, 142–76.

Castanias, R. and Helfat, C. (2001), 'The managerial rents model: theory and empirical analysis', *Journal of Management*, **27**, 661–78.

CMBOR (2001 and 2002), *Quarterly Review From The Center for Management Buy-out Research*, Nottingham University Business School.
Cohen, W.M. and Levinthal, D.A. (1990), 'Absorptive capacity: a new perspective on learning and innovation', *Administrative Science Quarterly*, **35**, 128–52.
Daily, C. and Dalton, D. (1992), 'The relationship between governance structure and corporate performance in entrepreneurial firms', *Journal of Business Venturing*, **7**, 375–86.
Eisenhardt, K.M. (1989), 'Building theories from company study research', *Academy of Management Review*, **14**, 532–50.
European Private Equity and Venture Capital Association (EVCA) (2001), 'Survey of the economic and social impact of management buy-outs and buy-ins in Europe', Research Paper, Zaventum, Belgium.
Green, S. (1992), 'The impact of ownership and capital structure on managerial motivation and strategy in management buy-outs: a cultural analysis', *Journal of Management Studies*, **4**, 513–35.
Jensen, M.C. (1989), Eclipse of the public corporation', *Harvard Business Review*, **67**, 61–74.
Jensen, M.C. (1993), 'The modern industrial revolution, exit and the failure of internal control systems', *Journal of Finance*, **48**, 831–80.
Jones, C.S. (1992), 'The attitudes of owner–managers towards accounting control systems following management buy-out, *Accounting, Organizations and Society*, **17**, 151–68.
Kaplan, S.N. (1989), 'The effects of management buyouts on operating performance and value', *Journal of Financial Economics*, **24**, 217–54.
Keating, P.J. (1995), 'A framework for classifying and evaluating the theoretical contributions of case research in management accounting', *Journal of Management Accounting Research*, **7**, 66–86.
Lockett, A., Murray, G. and Wright, M. (2002), 'Do UK venture capitalists still have a bias against investments in new technology firms?', *Research Policy*, **31**, 1009–30.
Merchant, K.A. (1985), *Control in Business Organisations*, Marshfield, MA: Pitman.
Mitchell, F., Reid, G. and Terry, N. (1997), 'Venture capital supply and accounting information system development', *Entrepreneurship Theory and Practice*, **21**, 45–62.
Otley, D. (1999), 'Performance management: a framework for management control systems research', *Journal of Management Accounting, Research*, **10**, 363–82.
Ouchi, W.G. (1977), 'The relationship between organisational structure and organisational control', *Administrative Science Quarterly*, **22**, 95–113.
Phan, P. and Hill, C. (1995), 'Organizational restructuring and economic performance in leveraged buyouts: an ex post study', *Academy of Management Journal*, **38**, 704–39.
Reid, G.C. (1996), 'Fast growing small entrepreneurial firms and their venture capital backers: an applied principal–agent analysis', *Small Business Economics*, **8**, 1–14.
Robbie, K. and Wright, M. (1995), 'Managerial and ownership succession and corporate restructuring: the case of management buy-ins', *Journal of Management Studies*, **32**, 527–50.
Robbie, K. and Wright, M. (1996), *Management Buy-ins: Entrepreneurship, active investors and corporate restructuring*, Manchester: Manchester University Press.
Sapienza, H. and Korsgaard, A. (1996), 'Procedural justice in entrepreneur-investor relations', *Academy of Management Journal*, **39**, 544–74.

Shoemakers, I. (1996), 'Ledereen moet zijn eigen broek ophauden', Interlnfo, October, 22–4.

Simons, R. (1995), *Levers of Control: How managers use innovative control systems to drive strategic renewal*, Cambridge, MA: Harvard Business School.

Speklé, R.F. (2001), 'Explaining management control structure variety: a transaction cost economic perspective', *Accounting, Organizations and Society*, **26**, 419–41.

Trice, H.M. and Beyer, J.M. (1993), *The Cultures of Work Organizations*, Englewood Cliffs, NJ: Prentice-Hall.

Volberda, H.W. (1998), *Building The Flexible Firm*, Oxford: Oxford University Press.

Westley, F.R. (1990), 'Middle managers and strategy: microdynamics of inclusion', *Strategic Management Journal*, 10–32.

Whipp, R., Rosenfeld, R. and Pettigrew, A. (1989), 'Culture and competitiveness: evidence from two mature UK Industries', *Journal of Management Studies*, **26**, 561–85.

Wright, M., Robbie, K., Thompson, S. and Starkey, K. (1994), 'Longevity and the life cycle of MBOs', *Strategic Management Journal*, **15**, 215–27.

Wright, M., Robbie, K., Chiplin, B. and Albrighton, M. (2000), 'The development of an organisational innovation: management buy-outs in the UK', *Business History*, **42**, 137–84.

Wright, M., Hoskisson, R.E., Busenitz, L.W. and Dial, J. (2000), 'Entrepreneurial growth through privatization: the upside of management buyouts', *Academy of Management Review*, **25**, 591–601.

Wright, M., Hoskisson, R.E. and Busenitz, L.W. (2001), 'Firm rebirth: buyouts as facilitators of strategic growth and entrepreneurship', *Academy of Management Executive*, **15**, 111–25.

Zahra, S.A. (1995), 'Corporate entrepreneurship and financial performance: the case of management leveraged buyouts', *Journal of Business Venturing*, **10**, 225–47.

Zahra, S.A. and George, G. (2002), 'Absorptive capacity: a review, reconceptualization, and extension', *Academy of Management Review*, **27**, 185–203.

7. Entrepreneurial orientation in management buy-outs and the contribution of venture capital

Hans Bruining and Mike Wright

INTRODUCTION

Buy-outs have traditionally been viewed as involving firms in mature sectors with few investment demands and low growth prospects (Jensen, 1989). However, the main rationale for buy-outs has shifted from cost reduction and strategic reorientation in mature sectors to creating value in technology sectors through product development and innovation (Wright et al., 2000, 2001). A shift is occurring in the buy-out market from downside protection in deals led by LBO (leveraged buy-out) associations to venture capital firms (VCs) that look for the upside potential of firms. The market is moving to find added value in deals, because auctions increase deal prices and fund providers are looking for higher returns. Research from the US, UK and Continental Europe shows that buy-outs are often followed by increase in (new) product development (Bruining, 1992; Wright et al., 1992; Zahra, 1995). In the US, traditional LBO associations have been joining forces with venture capitalists for this reason.

Many venture capitalists label themselves today as long-term committed and active shareholders that have a 'buy-and-build' strategy. In our view, long-term committed VCs have a focus on value creation in the business and supply additional capital for internal growth and/or acquisitions. Being an active investor implies a need for development of in-house technical expertise about the business and management support, and creates prospects for VCs and buy-out firms to link (Wright et al., 2000). In contrast to studies that highlight the role of the venture capitalist in start-up firms, research about how the role of the venture capitalist fits into this newer growth orientation in management buy-outs is lacking. This chapter aims to fill this gap by analysing the entrepreneur–venture capitalist relationship in two mature buy-out firms in order to obtain insight concerning where and how the venture capitalist's commitment contributes to the entrepreneurial practices in the management buy-out (MBO) firm. The study examines the questions: how do MBOs improve their entrepreneurial orientation (EO) and to what extent does the venture capitalist contribute to the EO of the buy-out firm?

Our theoretical framework uses the EO concept of Lumpkin and Dess (1996, p. 152) which conceptualizes the relationship between entrepreneurial practices and firm performance. The role of the VC is highlighted as a long-term committed and active shareholder and extends conceptualization of how environmental and organizational variables impact the EO–performance relationship in the context of buy-outs.

The structure of this chapter is as follows: after defining an MBO, we link it to the EO framework, and the VC role is highlighted along the EO dimensions. The research methodology used and data gathered are explained in the following section. From two case studies the role of the VCs after the MBO is analysed, as is its potential to contribute to the EO of the firm. In a comparative analysis of the case studies the differences in the way VCs arrange post-investment assistance are explained. The last section draws the major conclusions of this study.

MBOs

An MBO involves members of the incumbent management team acquiring a significant equity stake as individuals with institutional support in order to control the company (Robbie and Wright, 1996).

The structuring of a buy-out involves the introduction of significant equity incentives for the entrepreneurs involved, together with substantial external funding and active monitoring by investors (Jensen, 1993; Wright et al., 1994) in order to control agency costs. The emphasis in buy-outs in the US has typically focused on the debt providers who provide substantial amounts of leverage. However, in Europe venture capital firms play a major role in funding buy-outs. In the UK, for example, the vast majority of buy-outs with a transaction value above £5 million involve venture capital finance (CMBOR, 2001). In the Netherlands, the value of private-equity-backed buy-outs amounted to €3457 million in 1998 and €4463 million in 1999 (CMBOR, 2000) (Table 7.1).

MBOs backed by venture capital lead to significant changes in a firm's ownership composition, and can contribute to subsequent growth and changes in strategy, organizational structure and entrepreneurial practices (Reid, 1996; EVCA, 2001). This is especially the case in those MBOs that are not traditionally perceived as an organizational efficiency tool to streamline processes and decrease unit costs (Wright et al., 2000).

Table 7.1 Number and total value (€ m) of buy-outs in the Netherlands (1989–99)

Year	1989	1990	1991	1992	1993	1994	1995	1996	1997	1998	1999
NR	52	36	44	50	55	41	57	56	61	69	42
€	368	195	594	446	579	1258	856	1030	1082	3457	4463

Source: CMBOR.

Extensive screening by VCs at the time of investment appraisal places considerable emphasis on the entrepreneurial skills of the managers leading a proposed buy-out or buy-in (Robbie and Wright, 1995). VCs that have a reputation to provide capital for growth, use long-term incentives to encourage process or incremental innovation by managers, and show good understanding of the industry and business in the post-investment period will attract most of these deals. The extent to which VCs are able to enhance EO in their investees is the subject of this chapter.

CONCEPTUAL MODEL OF ENTREPRENEURIAL ORIENTATION

To focus on the involvement of the VC in promoting the entrepreneurial upside potential of an MBO firm, the EO model of Lumpkin and Dess (1996, p. 152) is used. The EO dimensions are defined, and how these link to MBOs is shown. The range of areas where the VCs are more likely to intervene in the various elements of the model is identified.

EO Dimensions

EO highlights practices, decision-making styles and methods managers use to let firms act entrepreneurially and offers an opportunity to examine where the VC contributes to enhancing the firm's upside potential. Lumpkin and Dess (1996) argue that an entrepreneurial firm is any firm that engages in an effective combination of five dimensions. First, innovativeness is the tendency of an organization to engage in and to support new ideas, novelty, experimentation and creative processes that result in new products, services or technological processes. This study includes in this definition incremental product/service innovation because this also opens windows of opportunity for the firm. Second, proactiveness involves the process of anticipating and acting on future needs by seeking new opportunities, introducing new products ahead of competition, and strategically eliminating declining operations. Third, competitive aggressiveness is a firm's propensity to outperform industry rivals in the marketplace. Fourth, risk taking is the degree to which managers are willing to make large and risky resource commitments. Fifth, autonomy is the extent to which a team or an individual in the firm is free to bring forward and implement a vision or an idea.

These process dimensions are intermediate factors between external (environmental) and internal (organizational) variables that drive firm performance and lead to 'new entry', the essential act of entrepreneurship. At the firm level, new entry involves actions initiated by the firm to promote upside potential and the strengthening of competitive advantage. As such, the EO concept offers an additional explanation for performance improvement following buy-out that goes beyond agency cost arguments involving efficiency improvement to protect the firm against downside risks (Phan and Hill, 1995). In buy-outs which need at least some innovation, environmental and organizational factors play an important moderating role in enhancing the EO of the firm.

Environmental Factors

Several environmental variables moderate the entrepreneurship–firm performance relationship. The EO–firm performance relationship is positively/negatively moderated by the extent of hostility in the firm's environment. It is well known that managers pre-MBO face investment restrictions from HQ because their firms are peripheral to the product line of the parent company (Wright et al., 2001). This decreases the possibilities of responding entrepreneurially to market development. After the buy-out this situation is reversed. The same can be argued for the other environmental factor – dynamism. This variable expresses the extent to which the needs of customers change and the extent to which technology changes. Pre-MBO, buy-out firms, if they are peripheral to the core business of the parent, are not allowed to have growth-oriented strategies and organizations. This conflict between subsidiary management and HQ is often an indication that a buy-out may be appropriate (Bruining, 1992; Wright et al., 2001).

Other environmental factors in the model are heterogeneity and technological sophistication. The first expresses the diversity in customer needs and expectations, thus offering a firm many or few opportunities for additional innovation and market development. Heterogeneity can enable firms to apply lessons learned in one market to other markets. Technological sophistication is indicative of more demand for new technologies.

Organizational Factors

Knowledge about the interaction between organizational factors and EO dimensions is crucial for understanding the dynamics of the buy-out firm and the possible supportive role of the VC. A significant share of MBOs divested from parent companies face changes to a more growth-oriented strategy and in the process of strategy formulation. Instead of obeying orders from headquarters that block innovation and investment in order to optimize goals of the diversified parent company, the buy-out managers have discretionary power to decide what is best for the business and how the business plan can be carried out most profitably for themselves as a firm (Wright et al., 2001).

The distance between policy and implementation becomes significantly shorter because of the remarriage of ownership and control (Alchian and Demsetz, 1972). It is likely that the new owner-managers show higher levels of commitment to the implementation of a growth-oriented strategy than before the MBO. In turn, this is likely to change the organizational culture to one that is more entrepreneurially driven. Other organizational factors that stimulate efficiency and decentralization after buy-out are the decrease in both size and complexity of the organizational structure (Phan and Hill, 1995). Top managers experience more immediate freedom and independence, which enables more flexible decision-making, more delegation, quicker action and easier consensus among manager/owners and shareholders (Bruining, 1992). This creates greater room at the firm level for the autonomy dimension of EO. Buy-outs typically involve increased levels of external funding. The costs of servicing debt and fixed dividend commitments act as a discipline to allocate resources to operations with the strongest cash flow and eliminate unprofitable operations. Finally, the experience of incumbent senior management is a crucial basis for their ability to act entrepreneurially.

This commitment to EO by the incumbent management is crucial to the development of a joint venture relationship with the VC that will contribute to achieving the growth objectives of the buy-out.

VCs and Entrepreneurial Orientation

In principle, VCs can make a contribution to the entrepreneurial orientation of their investees through the support they provide following investment. Previous literature suggests that VCs investing at early stages emphasize market growth and uniqueness of products rather than demonstrated market acceptance as in later-stage investments (Elango et al., 1995). Amason et al. (1994) show that VC involvement increases as the need arises. This is more likely in riskier, earlier-stage deals. Supportive of this are the findings of Sapienza et al. (1994) that frequency of interaction depends on the degree of the CEO's venture experience, the venture's stage of development and the degree of technical innovation.

Macmillan et al. (1989) find that the highest degree of involvement of the VC concerns acting as a 'sounding board', together with obtaining alternative sources of equity financing, interfacing with the equity group, monitoring financial performance and obtaining alternative sources of debt. Gorman and Sahlman (1989) stress the consultancy nature of the role VCs play in their investment. Littler and Sweeting (1989) observe that VCs provide access to networks among suppliers, customers, competitors and backers. Venture capitalists may provide significantly more value added if they control the board and if they have operating rather than purely financial expertise (Rosenstein et al., 1993). The contribution of non-executive directors may vary quite considerably (Sweeting and Wong, 1997). Sahlman (1990), in comparing LBO associations with venture capitalists, notes that executives in the former assume control of the board of directors and are less likely to assume operational control than venture capitalists investing in new ventures.

Venture capitalists, especially in Europe, may also invest in management buy-outs. Among the few studies to consider the role of VCs in MBOs, Wright et al. (1992) report that 30% of the buy-out managers considered VC involvement very helpful. While some 62.3% of buy-outs introduced new products as a result of the greater freedom of the buy-out, the study does not reveal how the VCs enhanced these entrepreneurial measures. In a study of management buy-ins (MBI),[1] Robbie and Wright (1996) show that the efficacy of direct board representation varies from a proactive stance and protection of their financial position to not being able to justify further investment because of spending a disproportional amount of time and cost to achieve satisfactory restructuring. Hatherly et al. (1994) suggest that relationships between VCs and CEOs of buy-out firms are best characterized as a joint venture. The relationships of trust, openness and mutual support that prevail are arguably important in facilitating VC/CEO interaction on non-routine issues. A recent study by Wright et al. (2001) identifies different types of buy-outs and suggests that different types of financial investor may have different roles to play in monitoring. In the more traditional highly leveraged buy-outs, LBO associations may be more appropriate as they are adept at financial monitoring. In contrast, in buy-outs requiring some limited form of investment and innovation (revitalization buy-outs) or involving major entrepreneurial innovation (entrepreneurial buy-outs) venture capital firms may have a greater role to play as there is a need for technical as well as financial monitoring skills.

This review suggests that while buy-outs have traditionally been seen as requiring less investor involvement than earlier-stage investments, some MBOs may have significant entrepreneurial opportunities that require greater involvement by VCs. In particular, VCs may have an important role to play in developing the EO dimensions of buy-out firms.

The EO model also suggests that VCs' involvement is required in accumulating and applying knowledge of sector-specific environmental factors such as technology, dynamism, hostility and the heterogeneity of markets in order to take appropriate pre- and post-investment decisions. Alliances with venture capital funds may be an important route to gain early access to developments emerging from the fast-moving Internet and communications sectors.

With respect to organizational factors, compared to the relationship with head office before the buy-out, greater interaction is expected to take place between the board of directors, key managers and the VC. Monitoring by VCs, together with substantial management equity stakes, are expected to be primary factors in meeting the costs of servicing external finance and in taking entrepreneurial actions associated with the generation of enhanced cash flow. The VC may play a key role in scrutinizing the expertise of management, with only those able to develop the newly independent firm likely to be acceptable as equity-holding insiders to the VC (Robbie and Wright, 1996).

The next section explains the research methodology and data-gathering process adopted in the study in order to address these issues.

METHODOLOGY AND DATA GATHERING

The empirical evidence is based on two detailed case studies. A two-stage research approach was carried out during 1998. After piloting a questionnaire in three MBOs, supplemented with face-to-face interviews, information was first gathered from CEOs by questionnaires.[2] The questionnaire contained five-point Likert scale questions with regard to external and organizational factors that may affect the relationship between EO and buy-out performance. The questions referred to the period of two years before and two years after the MBO. The MBOs selected had 50–100 employees and the deal prices varied between Dfl 5 and 10 million. The firms were divested by their Dutch parent companies by means of an MBO. Choosing MBO firms from the period 1992–1995 allowed sufficient time for the operational, organizational and strategic consequences of the change in ownership to be implemented. Another criterion for selection was that the firms had to be venture capital backed by leading Dutch VCs, all of whom are experienced in financing buy-outs. These VCs were involved from the very start of the MBO and have representatives who are chairmen of the supervisory board, guaranteeing that they are well informed about the likely development of entrepreneurial practices and their relationship with the CEO.

The operationalization of the variables in the conceptual model was based on measures taken from the widely used studies of Miller (1983) and Covin and Slevin (1986, 1989). After completion of the questionnaire, more detailed face-to-face interviews were conducted with the CEOs. Other sources of information used included magazines, product development brochures, annual reports and, in one case, the flotation prospectus. This approach was adopted as a more appropriate instrument for capturing the complexity of the managerial, entrepreneurial and organizational changes taking place following the transfers of ownership (Green, 1992). Full reports of the case studies were sent for comments to the CEOs.

This exercise laid the basis for the second part of the research. The EO profiles of the CEOs were subsequently sent for comments to the representatives of the respective VCs, who included the chairmen of the supervisory board and the investment manager.[3] Interviews were conducted with both to triangulate views about changes in the EO profile following buy-out (Eisenhardt, 1989). Post-MBO both VC representatives remain in contact with each other and receive the same financial information. In addition to the EO questionnaire, a second set of questions, based on the work of Rosenstein et al. (1993) and Mitchell et al. (1999), was used in face-to-face interviews to focus on the venture capital firms' practices and their specific information requirements in the operational and strategic monitoring of the investee.[4] This enabled identification of the areas where venture capitalists gave assistance to the CEO and his management team to act more entrepreneurially.

MBO firms were selected that showed strong differences with respect to the VC's governance system, exit strategy and the voting position of management based on their equity stakes. In case study 1 the VC used a dual governance system, had a majority equity stake and was aiming at a trade sale exit. In case study 2, the VC used no dual governance, had a minority equity stake and was aiming at exit through a flotation. Using information from these two distinct cases highlights the role of the VC along all EO dimensions more transparently than expected (Eisenhardt, 1989). Coupled with within-case analysis, cross-case comparisons were also carried out.

CASE STUDY RESULTS

This section first presents a synopsis of the main features of each case and, based on information post-MBO, identifies the changes in dimensions of

EO, and the VC's role post-MBO along these changes and dimensions. In the second section, a cross-case comparison is developed to analyse differences and similarities in the contribution of the VCs to the EO of the buy-out firms.

Case Study 1

Synopsis
Company 1 is a pet food manufacturer with Dfl 60 million turnover and 60 employees; it exports 90% of its products to the expanding markets for pet food in Scandinavia, Germany, Belgium, Spain, Portugal and Greece. Company 1 was bought by its management team for Dfl 8.5 million in 1995 from the parent company Cebeco-Handelsraad, a large co-operative firm producing vegetables, flowers, seeds and food. Alpinvest, which was recently acquired by NIB Capital and which has 41% of its total investment portfolio of Dfl 300 million invested in MBOs/MBIs, backed the company. The firm's target rate of return for MBOs is 15%–40% on an annualized basis. The pet food producer belongs to the mid-range size of Alpinvest investments. Alpinvest owns 43% of the shares, another large Dutch VC, NPM Capital also has 43%, while a minority of the shares (14%) is owned by the CEO, the financial controller and the director of production. At the time of the buy-out the financial leverage measured by equity to total assets was 42%. In 2001, seven years after the buy-out, the firm was sold to Provimi, one of Europe's largest pet food producers. Alpinvest and NPM Capital distinguish between an investment manager who does the deal and a supervisory board member taking care of operational post-investment activities. However, the investment managers receive the same financial information about the firm as the member of the supervisory board and stay in contact with the latter. Alpinvest's representative is the chairman of the supervisory board and has a background as a consultant and entrepreneur in the industry. From the very start of the MBO, a modest 6% dividend was paid, indicating a longer-term investment attitude of the VC firm to let Company 1 first repay the debt and allow investments to improve the business, without neglecting the reward for the new shareholders. After paying off the amount of debt and amortization of 'goodwill', the payout of dividends increased. The following sections discuss EO dimensions, environmental and organizational factors, and the contribution of the VC to developing EO as outlined earlier with respect to this case.

EO dimensions
The company's parent, Cebeco, paid little attention to Company 1's new product ideas because pet food was peripheral to its main focus on

vegetables and flowers. After the MBO the management became more proactive in both product development and rationalization. The company started developing new products on its own. The trend towards humanizing animals created ample opportunity for increasing quality and product margins. This increased the firm's proactiveness. The company as a small player had to act smart in its efforts to differentiate and develop new products. The ENMAX exhibition in Chicago became an integral part of the product innovation programme of the firm. Active search for new opportunities required an increase in expenditures for research and development by more than 50%. After the MBO the firm renewed its equipment for the production of varying percentages of fat in order to anticipate healthier animal snacks for the whole animal life-cycle without adding colouring agents. One of its new successful products was the puppy-snack. This is evidence of strengthening innovativeness.

Following the MBO there was an increase in autonomy at the workgroup level. Pre-MBO the CEO as subsidiary director was responsible for the marketing, production and financial decisions at the operational but not the strategic level. This changed after the MBO but he was forced to listen to younger ambitious specialists in the fields of marketing and nutrition of which he lacked understanding.

Management became more willing to take risks. Top management developed a strategic focus on retail and distribution, indicating a preference for projects which could yield relatively higher added value and thus a higher return on investment (ROI) than was the case before the MBO. A high price/quality strategy was adopted that signalled the firm's increased competitive aggressiveness. The role of marketing changed. The marketing department had to obtain orders from superstores and convince them of the healthier status of the company's products, and had to be more active in gathering product ideas from the industry itself. In dealing with the competitors after the MBO the company typically seeks to avoid competitive clashes, targeting peripheral markets, e.g. the Finnish market, where it succeeded in becoming market leader within six months of the MBO.

Environment

In order to differentiate oneself in the pet food industry, technology is a key factor. Products and the related technologies become obsolete rather quickly, because of the need for frequent innovations involving healthy pet food products. Consumer tastes are fairly easy to predict but competitor actions are becoming more unpredictable. Although hostility is not seen as a threat for survival in the short term, the danger of price competition remains in the home market.

Organizational factors

Before the MBO management did not focus on the firm's core competencies and its objectives. After the MBO, the management developed a clear strategy, mission and vision as a niche player in order to grow internally in the expanding markets for pet food. Ideas for new products now originate more from visits to important international industry conferences such as the Chicago pet food exhibition. The retail and distribution function is crucial to creating a strong position by changing the food ingredients needed in a timely manner. The firm now takes a longer-term perspective for planning its future growth. Investment proposals are carried out on the basis of own cash flows, indicating the need for profitable growth and attractive payout figures on which realistic budgets can be made.

More things had to be done after the MBO by the same amount of people, causing a need to delegate by installing self-managing teams. After the MBO, communication developed more intensively between the management team and employees because management was forced to adopt the latest developments from retail and distribution and marketing. Despite his autocratic style of leadership, the CEO changed his attitude towards the retail and distribution and marketing function, whereas before the MBO he considered this primarily as a cost. Several innovation working groups and quality platforms were installed with regular meetings. These groups determined the direction for product development. Ideas for product development are developed during brainstorming sessions between teams of workers and management. In this sense the organization became flatter and adopted a stronger results-oriented attitude towards work. However, the planning of capital expenditures as well as the use of operational budgets are examples of the drive for tight centralized financial control after the MBO and thus the need for more formalization.

After the MBO the company began to imitate new products launched by international leading pet food firms such as Hills in the US. It also started its own new product development. Compared to its competitors, time to market has been reduced since the MBO from nine to approximately six months, because the firm began to target foreign niche markets to minimize the problems of price competition in its home market. By hiring engineers from the Agriculture University of Wageningen the firm was able to anticipate the new technological developments necessary to produce improved animal food for these niche markets. The emphasis on the top quality pet food segment of the market required increasing efforts to qualify for International Standards Organization (ISO) certificates and the more recently acquired Hazard Analysis Critical Control Point. New quality control procedures were introduced. The drive for tight cost control after the MBO resulted in better control of costs and working capital. For

Table 7.2 Economic performance, Company 1 (× Dfl 1000)

Years	Net profit/sales × 100%	Net profit	Sales
1992	1.1	1051	96 587
1993	0.2	178	74 385
1994	0.1	58	60 356
1995	5.5	3351	61 156
1996	5.7	3350	59 046
1997	4.3	2602	61 099
1998	6.3	4090	65 284
1999	9.6	6652	69 016
2000	6.0	4438	73 933

example, accounts receivable decreased by 17% (i.e. Dfl 580.000). These kinds of activities enable the firm to undertake investment in contrast to before the MBO.

While top management considers that it has the same degree of experience compared to pre-MBO, there have been important changes in management development. For example, the supervisory board has been very constructive in developing the focus of the CEO from a predominant emphasis on the bottom line to broader, more professional management. It is notable that not all disciplines are represented on the management board of Company 1. The sales manager and the nutritionist are both not formally part of the management team, but attend on request. The director of finance also became the director of human resources in the post-buy-out period. Most of the employees are not rewarded in relation to performance. However, besides equity stakes, the CEO and his financial controller and deputy directors of production enjoy profit related payments. In 1996 bonuses amounted to approximately Dfl 150 000 each. Top management is clearly better incentivized than before the MBO.

Net profit as a percentage of sales of Company 1 improved dramatically after the buy-out in 1995 (Table 7.2). The divestment of the soya business decreased sales but not the firm's profitability. In 1995, the year after the MBO, a substantially higher level of net profit was reached due to the higher-margin strategy. In 1997 net profit decreased by 20% because of increased input prices which reduced profit margins. In 1998 this situation was reversed.

VC and entrepreneurial orientation

The VC contributed to developing proactiveness by approving and stimulating the implementation of a value-added strategy. With regard to another aspect of proactiveness, the VC also played an important advisory role in discussions about decisions to cut unprofitable activities. He actively suggested that the firm invested in a non-stop production process facility, decreased its workforce (five people) and divested the soya beans unit, thus rationalizing production in order to realize higher margins.

The VC played an important role in promoting innovativeness since, in the period immediately following the MBO, it reviewed the quality of the retail and distribution plans several times a year. Later on, because of the satisfactory results, the involvement of the VC decreased to once a year, and focused on the status of projects. The VC stimulated Dfl 1 million of investment in management information systems. These systems included the introduction of barcodes and software packages as well as systems covering the understanding, control and distribution of information.

The VC played an important informal role in stimulating the development of autonomy since at the VC's instigation, a process was introduced whereby proposals were initiated by the marketing manager and ratified and monitored by management and the VC. The VC approved the direction of the marketing plan, paying particular attention to pricing and sales forecasts, which was important in achieving financial control of the strategy.

A characteristic of this case was the intervention of the VC in the sales strategy following the MBO. This happened during 1997 when Company 1 faced downward pressure on product margins due to higher purchase prices of raw material that could not be passed on to customers. An extremely important consequence was that the investment programme based on internal finance was endangered. The management board and the VC in the supervisory board discussed whether to stop the investment programme and accept the lower margin on sales or to keep the investment programme in operation and focus sales effort at the higher price/quality segment of the market. The VC succeeded in convincing the buy-out team of the usefulness of a higher added value strategy for Company 1 and in maintaining a focus on sales effort aimed at the higher price/quality segment. In this way, the VC also contributed to increasing the willingness of management to take risks. Moreover, with the help of the VC the attention of management shifted from mere price- to more quality-driven competition.

This evidence indicates that the VC stimulated the entrepreneurial practices initiated after the MBO in order to control the projected economic performance of the venture. The intervention by the VC in Company 1's business strategy corrected the actions of the top management team in a timely manner. In this case the management had to learn to carry out a new value-added strategy and re-allocate resources in order to anticipate effectively trends in technology, markets and specific dangers such as increased price competition. Retail and distribution sources from own cash flow, product development and marketing plans, management information system, leadership style of the CEO, delegation and performance-related rewards for the buy-out managers are seen as enablers of developing appropriate levels of EO and involved the VC from the start of the MBO.

Case Study 2

Synopsis

Company 2 is a manufacturer of computer aided design (CAD) and computer aided manufacturing (CAM) systems and creates one-stop solutions for the carpet, printed textiles and woven fabrics industries. It develops, manufactures and markets dedicated software and services for textile design, colour matching, colour separation, fabric simulation, 3D presentation and production of textiles. Turnover is Dfl 13 million, of which 70% is exported. Besides these systems the firm is also a producer of Geographic Information Systems (GIS) for municipalities. The company operates in a relatively young niche market where technology is changing very fast and price competition is very fierce. With headquarters based in the Netherlands, offices in the UK, France and the US with a worldwide agent network, Company 2 positions itself to market and sell its products on a worldwide scale.

The company was backed by Gilde Investment, which is based in Utrecht and is one of the leading investment banks in the Netherlands. From its buy-out fund 74% is invested in MBOs, totalling approximately Dfl 300 million. Company 2 belongs to the middle-range class of Gilde's investments with a target rate of return between 20% and 30%. The total amount of equity invested in Company 2 by Gilde was Dfl 5 million equity, giving it a minority stake of 36%. Top management and 20 employees hold a majority stake of 64%. The financial leverage measured by equity to total assets was 24% at the time of the buy-out. The firm was bought for an undisclosed sum from the receivership of HCS Technology, which went bankrupt in 1992. In this case the investment manager of Gilde is also chairman of the supervisory board and is an experienced financial consultant in the IT sector. In 1998, six years after the buy-out, the intended flotation was realized.

The following sections discuss EO dimensions, environmental and organizational factors, and the contribution of the VC to developing EO as outlined earlier with respect to this case.

EO dimensions

Reducing the time from the initial stage of product development to final production is essential for competitiveness in Company 2's market. Before the buy-out, Company 2 was not capable of seizing these opportunities and offering one-stop solutions. After the MBO, the firm increased its efforts to search for new opportunities, and proactively developed new business opportunities in existing and related markets. At the same time, contracts with suppliers were renegotiated and catering costs were decreased by about 60%. People not able to work in an independent company left. Another example of looking for chances to be ahead of the competition was the acquisition of a French firm specialized in certain weaving techniques, which was used to acquire and develop further new technology and to increase market share in France.

Post-MBO product developments demonstrated the firm's innovative focus on improving communication, networking and multi-media solutions in computer graphics technology and textile technology. The successful launch of new CAD/CAM software Tuft/NT to produce complex carpet designs also demonstrates innovativeness. Further examples of new products are the shrink-wrapped Fashion Flash software, DesignCom software for using design data in other applications and NedGeoDatawarehouse to store geographical and alphanumerical data. Since the MBO the number of software developers has increased from 20 to 30 (25% of the total staff) and substantial investments were made in retail and distribution development (between 7% and 10 % of its annual revenues). After the MBO there was more room for bottom-up communication and quick decision-making, resulting in a richer stream of business proposals with regard to acquisitions and equipment from the business units, thus stimulating autonomy regarding entrepreneurial initiatives. There was a shift towards more flexible use of formal rules and procedures in the firm.

There was a major change in competitive aggressiveness. Company 2 aims to be first with initiatives in the market, with substantial lowering of prices. The marketing stance is encapsulated in the advertising slogan: 'We would have released our windows/NT based software sooner, but we were too busy leaving our competition behind!' Marketing has become important to determine the strategic direction of the firm and generates more products than before the MBO.

Indicative of more risk taking following the MBO was the venture set up in the US. This was a very expensive lesson because this venture failed. After the failure of the start-up, the chief financial officer was given more authority to calculate risks of the firm's strategic decisions. From then on investment opportunities to expand in familiar niches were selected in Europe. After the buy-out Company 2 acquired several companies to expand into the carpet and the printed textile market in the UK, France, Belgium and in its home market.

Environment

Software production technology changes quickly and marketing practices must constantly be adapted to communicate better with industrial customers in order to forecast demand and consumer tastes adequately. Despite the strong price competition for CAD/CAM applications in the carpet industry worldwide and the dynamic environment, the CEO of Company 2 perceives a decrease in threat to survival of the firm, because after the MBO the company invests its own cash flow in its own future, instead of in a financially distressed parent company.

Organizational factors

The financially distressed parent company stifled innovation and investment. After the buy-out the most significant changes occurred in the process and speed of strategy formulation. The longer-term profitability of investments became more important than shorter-term returns. After the MBO the company formulated a mission statement for the development of textile CAD/CAM and GIS. With regard to the former it aims to become the leading supplier of one-stop solutions for all market areas in the textile CAD/CAM market by providing the most comprehensive product line, state-of-the-art PC/Windows/NT-based technology, a high level of support and competitive prices on a worldwide scale. In the field of GIS, the firm strives to be market leader in integrated 'organization-wide' GIS solutions for municipalities in the Netherlands, based on an open-systems concept, universal system integration capabilities, turnkey solutions, a full-service concept and partnerships with users of its systems. The firm became the leader after the MBO in the niche markets involving carpets and printed textiles, strengthening its market focus and enlarging its product range. The emphasis is now on standard quality and low prices in order to increase market share, whereas before the MBO the focus was on low prices. After the MBO in 1992 Company 2 acquired several companies to expand in the US, the UK, France, Belgium and in its home market. The acquisitions were internally financed and concentrated on the standard quality segment.

The company organized itself after the MBO into two independent strategic business units, textile and GIS. Two-way-communication within each strategic business unit has increased and the layers of organization have decreased after the MBO. In contrast to before the MBO, these SBUs meet separately with top management, and if necessary with the VC to evaluate ideas. Instead of painful discussion with the parent company, whose main product line was copiers, the company's culture supports the open expression of novel ideas after the MBO, in contrast to the situation beforehand where the CEO was forced to slow down new business proposals because the directors of the financially troubled parent were not willing to invest in businesses they did not know.

Without the financial limitations imposed by its former parent and with savings on overheads of approximately Dfl 500 000 a year (2% of its sales revenue) and fewer restrictions on financial resources, the firm has experienced more freedom to make investments. After the MBO, personnel are better incentivized. Twenty key managers now have equity stakes. Half the employees (40) of the sales department received a refined performance-related reward system and all employees of Company 2 are given a performance-related bonus in their salary. This relationship was also intensified through arrangements made on an individual basis for those who show ambition to develop certain parts of the market abroad (e.g. Turkey). Other aspects of performance-related pay are aimed at enhancing product development. Employees earn a bonus when they keep product development and maintenance time within certain limits.

The CEO and the CFO have experience with all business functions, but not all disciplines are represented in the management board. The SBU managers of GIS and textile CAD/CAM, responsible for respectively marketing and sales, project engineering, product development and customer support, as well as the HR manager are not formally part of the management board, but attend on request. The characteristic of the top management team remained the same as before the MBO. The CEO was seen in general as a charismatic leader with a strong influence on Company 2 employees.

The years immediately following the buy-out showed the strongest increase in EBIT as a percentage of sales. Despite the failed start-up investment in 1995 in the US it is clear from Table 7.3 that Company 2 showed improved performance post-1992. However, sales growth during 1995–98 was not spectacular.

Table 7.3 Economic performance, Company 2 (€1000)

Year	EBIT as % of sales	PBIT	Sales
1993	11.0	1011	8 711
1994	17.0	1799	10 638
1995	4.8	590	12 264
1996	10.1	1271	12 533
1997	11.6	1569	13 537
1998	13.3	1875	14 048
1999	13.2	2847	21 562
2000	5.9	1536	26 012

Source: Flotation prospectus, 31 March 1998 and annual reports, 1999 and 2000.

In 1998 the company was successfully floated on the NMAX stock exchange. In 2000 the textile and apparel and E-commerce activity are suffering lower demand and tough price competition as a result of market saturation.

VC and entrepreneurial orientation

The VC supported the firm's increased efforts to proactively develop new business opportunities in existing and related markets. In 1995 the VC assisted the CEO to start an IT company in the US and led a consortium of investors to finance that investment. In the stressful period of reorganizing the existing firm due to a sharp fall in profit in 1995 and starting a company abroad, the VC was actively involved in advising management. With respect to greater autonomy, the VC has monthly talks with business unit management, indicating scope for informality. As strategy was not very coherent at the time of the MBO, an INSEAD professor was asked to join the supervisory board at the request of the VC to advise on how to address this problem.

With respect to decision-making information used in Company 2, the VC did not directly intervene in daily operations. Prior to the buy-out, the operating decision-making information used internally and reported to the VC came from marketing and sales. Subsequent to VC involvement, operating decision information was required with regard to finance and personnel. The VC is involved with the operations of the firm through the monitoring of financial information, but its involvement extends further to include the development of strategic decision-making information about acquisitions, product development and marketing actions. The VC's networks are used extensively for advising management. The VC assisted closely in making acquisition decisions, carrying out five acquisitions in Europe. To implement the marketing strategy, the VC was assisted by a Flemish venture capitalist who took an equity stake in the major competitor Sofis, based in Belgium, in order to block competition. Other tasks where the VC showed commitment were counselling for product development and marketing programmes, but also in stressful situations during an IT start-up in the US and early reorganization following the buy-out firm, and last but not least the preparation of flotation. These services enhance most of the EO dimensions of the firm.

With respect to the existing carpet and cartography niche markets, the VC confirmed the CEO's entrepreneurial approach, but assessed the CEO's vision as too narrow in scope to realize diversification opportunities in technology-related markets. The VC tried to create awareness for the relatively small market size and the slow pace of long-term growth, and undertook efforts to renew this strategy. However, the lack of a hierarchical relationship, resulting from the minority shareholding of the VC, limited powerful interaction with top management. The CEO and the VC looked at proposals but did not find anything worthwhile to invest in. According to the VC the CEO was too risk averse in this respect. This was largely due to the fact that in the first two years the VC was the only member on the supervisory board representing a minority shareholding. Therefore the VC could neither provoke action nor promote dynamism to convince others of the right course of action.

COMPARISON OF EO IN COMPANIES 1 AND 2

In both cases evidence was found of actions on the part of the VC to realize long-term benefits. Management and the VC of Company 1 decided to pay a moderate annual dividend of 6% from the start and concentrated on repayment of debt and preparation of the firm for a trade sale. In Company 2, the VC supported the CEO's initiatives for a start-up and required payment of a dividend above a 25% return on equity. After a period of growth, the VC prepared the company for flotation. In both firms the VCs were shareholders for a six- or seven-year period, demonstrating that they were relatively long-term-committed shareholders. Both cases pre-MBO are firms not central strategically to their parents and therefore deprived of investments for innovation and renewal purposes. Using the categorization of Wright et al. (2000), Company 1 can be identified as a revitalization buy-out as it involved process and incremental innovations, while Company 2 is an entrepreneurial buy-out involving strategic innovation.

The extent to which the VCs showed a similar pattern of activities in both companies that enhanced the EO of the firms will now be discussed. Table 7.4 summarizes the different VC governance characteristics and effects found in the case studies.

In both companies major interventions by the VC took place during the buy-out. At Company 1 the intervention by the VC to adhere to the strategy of value adding convinced the CEO and was successful, in contrast to the efforts of the VC in Company 2 to broaden the CEO's view of the market scope of the firm. In Company 1 this probably increased commitment in the inter-organizational relationship between the VC and the CEO (Carnevale and Isen, 1986), producing more innovative solutions. For Company 2 this appeared only valid at the start of the MBO, as shown by the launch of the new IT firm in the US. This failure might have increased the risk aversion of the CEO, because in the years following the MBO, he became reluctant to change the market scope of the firm. Affective commitment in the relationship may have become more problematic from that

Table 7.4 Summary of VC governance differences

Company 1	Company 2
Repay debt first; moderate dividend payment (6%)	Start-up finance; dividend paid if ROE > 25 per cent
Exit: sale to large industrial buyer in 2001	Exit: flotation NMAX in 1998
CEO retired at the time of the sale	CEO sold equity stake at flotation and obtained position on the Supervisory Board; resigned after 2 years
VCs have majority of shares (co-lead)	VC has minority of shares
VC: operational + strategic + financial experience	VC: financial and IT-start up experience
No external specialist advice on strategy and organization, but own advice	External specialist on strategy and organization
Supervisory board member has his own position (independent from VC)	Supervisory board member is investment manager (no independent position from VC)
Dual governance system of VC: board member and investment manager separate persons with close contact	No dual governance system of VC: board member and investment manager in one person
Investment manager: controls contractual data;	One person from the VC controls contractual data and face-to-face interaction for equivocal issues
Board member: face-to-face interaction for equivocal issues	
VC with successful strategy intervention	VC not successful with intervention on market scope
VC significant influence on CEO's leadership style	VC less influence on CEO's leadership style

moment on. Both findings appear to be consistent with the respective influence of VCs on the CEOs' leadership styles. In Company 1 the problematic authoritarian style of the CEO changed in order to integrate the contribution of specialist managers to product and market development. In Company 2 the strong charismatic leadership of the CEO did not generate potential successors from within the firm.

In Company 1 the VC brought in an experienced entrepreneur in the food industry as a business consultant, whereas the VC of Company 2 is a financial specialist in IT business. Both are experienced in developing strategies with the board of directors, but the former possesses more awareness of operational details. The absence of an external specialist at Company 1 in the field of strategy and implementation in contrast to Company 2 supports this observation. Convincing people on the basis of one's own qualities may increase mutually affective commitment in the post-investment relationship between CEO and VC and emotional attachment to the organization in the long run. Post-investment relationship building between the VC and CEO may prosper more from attention to operational rather than financial detail (Rosenstein et al., 1993).

Another finding which has a likely impact on the relationship between the CEO and the VC is the hierarchical position of the parties in relation to each other based on the size of their equity stakes. In the case of Company 2 the VC had a minority shareholding in the firm and had to wait until flotation when the CEO sold his equity before the firm's strategy could be adapted. The VC lacked hierarchical power to control top management. However, concrete proposals to invest in other markets were also absent. In Company 1 the VCs had a majority equity stake and were able to supervise the necessary changes before the exit of the firm. At the time of the trade sale exit of Company 1 the CEO retired.

The VCs differ also in the way they organized post-investment assistance. In both cases, post-investment involvement went beyond financial control. The VC in Company 1 appointed an independent supervisory board member. He had his own personal and legal basis for giving advice in the interest of all the firm's stakeholders. Neither of the VCs can give him orders, although he works closely with them. His fee is paid by Company 1 in contrast to the fee of the VC representative in Company 2, which is paid to Gilde. The latter, therefore, does not have such an independent position for its supervisory board member. The VC representatives in Company 1 – the investment manager and the supervisory board member – get the same contractual data, only the latter specializes in face-to-face communication with the CEO. The investment manager stays in close contact (a half day per quarter) with the CEO and the supervisory board member, but continues to search for new deals. This situation is different for the VC in Company 2 that prefers to have its own people on the supervisory board. Here the representative monitors contractual data and performs a sounding board function in addition to his role in looking for new venture capital investments.

CONCLUSION

This chapter has sought to analyse how buy-outs improve their EO following the change in ownership and how VCs contribute to this process through the development of post-investment relationships. The chapter also sought to validate the EO model in the context of MBOs.

The case studies show that buy-outs do occur where entrepreneurial opportunities exist and provide support for Wright et al. (2000), who argue that buy-outs do not simply involve improving efficiency in companies in mature sectors. With the framework of EO, entrepreneurial decisions and practices are identified that add value to the business through new product/new market development in their companies that were frustrated by the parent prior to MBO. The firms in our study act more entrepreneurially than pre-MBO.

VCs' enhancement of EO in MBOs appears more likely in the following post-investment activities. The first where the VCs intervene is in integrating the contributions of specialists in top management decision-making; influencing the leadership style of the CEO; keeping value added strategy on track; approving bonuses for top management; assisting in new ventures (consortia)/new acquisitions; and broadening market focus. They all frequently face situations where they have to advise on difficult problems or have to select consultants in order to implement appropriate strategies. This is an important field where the VC's knowledge can contribute to the EO of the firm by developing the CEO's vision and keeping the strategy focused. Last but not least, the VC uses its network to reduce the negative impact of competition and to select key figures as CFOs and new CEOs. The second is where VCs put effort into reviewing and monitoring the quality of research and development investment plans, budgets and marketing plans. Sometimes the VC needs to invest in management information systems to modernize management in order to control entrepreneurial decisions better.

An important characteristic of the CEO–VC relationship is the knowledge transfer and learning that takes place, indicating interdependency of the participating parties that enabled the companies to act entrepreneurially. It is crucial, however, for the VC to understand the technology sufficiently in order to be able to assess investment in product development and acquisitions, and subsequently to monitor it effectively. Also the VCs must understand the complexity and the uncertainty entrepreneurs face, and the way they take strategic decisions. The VC must be skilled in developing informal co-operative relationships that stimulate exchange of high quality information, which in turn enables reliable and convincing interventions that enhance EO. In these situations the articles of association and other contracts appear to have little impact on enhancing EO.

As our case studies show, the success of post-investment relationships depends not only on effective informal relationships but also on the position of the VC as a majority shareholder. There is a need for further investigation of the post-investment involvement of the VCs to distinguish those buy-outs that can be better supervised with contractual relationships compared with those where greater emphasis on relationship building between the VC and CEO is likely to be more effective in enhancing EO.

The EO model has been validated in this study in the context of MBOs. The EOs of the firm pre- and post-MBO were compared and similar patterns of increased proactiveness, innovativeness, risk taking and autonomy in two buy-outs which varied in terms of the VCs' governance system, voting power of management and exit strategy were observed. The EO model is therefore appropriate for analysing MBOs with upside potential and the role of VCs in realizing that potential. The multidimensionality of the model offers a variety of possibilities to relate the EO dimensions to external and organizational factors that affect the EO–performance relationship. Organizational factors such as strategy, resources, leadership styles and delegation moderate this relationship because the strength of the relationship between EO and performance varies as a function of these factors. The chapter has extended the EO model of Lumpkin and Dess to include variables that represent the financial and personal motivating mechanisms in MBOs, notably increased management holdings and interactions with the VC. In terms of the framework, these factors stimulate interaction between EO dimensions and external/organizational factors in the specific situation of the MBO and have probably played an important role in improving economic performance.

NOTES

1. MBIs share the change in ownership with MBOs but in contrast to the latter external managers buy the firm. This may be an indication for the management's less deep knowledge of the business.
2. This is available from the first-named author on request.
3. This governance situation is quite similar with the dual form of governance in the UK. One of the differences is that a non-executive on behalf of the Dutch VC is appointed in the supervisory board as member or as chairman, but has no seat on the board of directors. Some VCs appoint their investment managers as supervisory board members; others appoint professionals with entrepreneurial and industry experience. The supervisory board has the legal authority to defend the interest of the company as a whole. It is obligatory for public limited companies and facultative for private limited companies. The supervisory board has to approve the firm's policy, the remuneration of the directors, whereas in the UK the shareholders control the company. New legislation will transfer some of the authorities of the supervisory board to the general meeting of shareholders (e.g. settlement of annual report, appointment of supervisory board members). In the Netherlands some VCs use a dual model for monitoring their investees: an investment manager who does the deal and takes care of the routine financial monitoring afterwards, and a supervisory board member who takes care of the informal communication and coaching part. In our case studies Company 1 makes use of the dual model whereas Company 2 does not.
4. The checklist is available from the first-named author on request.

REFERENCES

Alchian, A.A. and Demsetz, H. (1972), 'Production, information costs, and economic organization', *American Economic Review*, **62**, 777–95.
Amason A.C., Sapienza, H.J. and Manigart, S. (1994), 'The level and nature of venture capitalist involvement in their portfolio companies: a study of three European countries', *Managerial Finance*, **20** (1), 3–17.
Bruining, J. (1992), 'Performance improvement after management buy-out', PhD thesis, Erasmus University, Rotterdam.
Carnevale, P.J.D. and Isen, A.M. (1986), 'The influence of positive affect and visual access on the discovery of integrative solutions in bilateral negotiation', *Organizational Behaviour and Human Decision Process*, **37**, 1–13.
CMBOR (2000 and 2001), *Quarterly Review*, Nottingham, UK: The Centre for Management Buy-out Research, Nottingham University Business School.
Covin, J.G. and Slevin, D.P. (1986), 'The development and testing of an organizational level entrepreneurship scale', in R. Ronstadt, J.A. Hornaday, R. Petersen and K.H. Vesper (eds), *Frontiers of Entrepreneurship Research*, Babson Park, MA: Babson College, pp. 628–39.
Covin, J.G. and Slevin, D.P. (1989), 'Strategic management of small firms in hostile and benign environments', *Strategic Management Journal*, **10**, 75–87.
Eisenhardt, K.M. (1989), 'Building theories from case study research', *Academy of Management Review*, **14** (4), 532–50.
Elango, B., Fried, V.H., Hisrich, R.D. and Polonchek, A. (1995), 'How venture capital firms differ', *Journal of Business Venturing*, **10**, 157–79.
EVCA (2001), *Survey of the Economic and Social Impact of Management Buy-Outs and Buy-Ins in Europe*, Zaventum, Belgium: European Private Equity and Venture Capital Association.
Gorman, M. and Sahlman, W. (1989), 'What do venture capitalists do?', *Journal of Business Venturing*, **4**, 231–48.
Green, S. (1992), 'The impact of ownership and capital structure on managerial motivation and strategy in management buy-outs: a cultural analysis', *Journal of Management Studies*, **4**, 513–35.
Hatherly, D., Innes, J., Macandrew, J. and Mitchell, F. (1994), 'An exploration of the MBO–financial relationship', *Corporate Governance*, **2** (1), 20–29.
Jensen, M.C. (1989), 'Eclipse of the modern corporation', *Harvard Business Review*, **67** (5), 61–74.
Jensen, M.C. (1993), 'The modern industrial revolution, exit and the failure of internal control systems', *Journal of Finance*, **48** (3), 831–80.
Littler, D.A. and Sweeting, R.C. (1989), *Management Accounting: The challenge of technology innovation-management accounting in technological business*, London: Chartered Institute of Management Accountants.
Lumpkin, G.T. and Dess, G.G. (1996), 'Clarifying the entrepreneurial orientation construct and linking it to performance', *Academy of Management Review*, **21** (1), 135–72.
Macmillan, I.C., Kulow, D.M. and Khoylian, R. (1989), 'Venture capitalists' involvement in their investments: extent and performance', *Journal of Business Venturing*, **4**, 27–47.
Miller, D. (1983), 'Entrepreneurship correlates in three types of firms', *Management Science*, **29**, 770–91.

Mitchell, F., Reid, G. and Terry, N. (1999), 'Accounting information system development and the supply of venture capital', in M. Wright and K. Robbie (eds), *Management Buy-Outs and Venture Capital*, Cheltenham, UK/Northampton, MA, USA: Edward Elgar, pp. 263–79.

Phan, P. and Hill, C. (1995), 'Organizational restructuring and economic performance in leveraged buyouts: an ex post study', *Academy of Management Journal*, **38** (3), 704–39.

Reid, G.C. (1996), 'Fast growing small entrepreneurial firms and their venture capital backers: an applied principal–agent analysis', *Small Business Economics*, **8**, 1–14.

Robbie, K and Wright, M. (1995), 'Managerial and ownership succession and corporate restructuring: the case of management buy-ins', *Journal of Management Studies*, **32**, 527–50.

Robbie, K and Wright, M. (1996), *Management Buy-Ins: Entrepreneurship, active investors and corporate restructuring*, Manchester: Manchester University Press.

Rosenstein J., Bruno, A.V., Bygrave, W.D. and Taylor, N.T. (1993), 'The CEO, venture capitalists and the board', *Journal of Business Venturing*, **8**, 99–113.

Sahlman, A. (1990), 'The structure and governance of venture capital organizations', *Journal of Financial Economics*, **27**, 473–521.

Sapienza, H.J. and Gupta, A.K. (1994), 'Impact of agency risks and task uncertainty on venture capitalist–CEO interaction', *Academy of Management Journal*, **37** (6), 1618–32.

Sapienza, H., Amason, A. and Manigart, S. (1994), 'The level and nature of venture capitalist involvement in their portfolio companies: a study of three European Countries', *Managerial Finance*, **20** (1), 3–17.

Sweeting, R.C. and Wong, C.F. (1997), 'A UK "hands-off" venture capital firm and the handling of post-investment investor–investee relationships', *Journal of Management Studies*, **34** (1), 125–52.

Wright, M., Thompson, S. and Robbie, K. (1992), 'Venture capital and management led leveraged buy-outs: the European perspective', *Journal of Business Venturing*, **7**, 47–71.

Wright, M., Robbie, K., Thompson, S. and Starkey, K. (1994), 'Longevity and the life-cycle of MBOs', *Strategic Management Journal*, **15** (3), 215–27.

Wright, M., Hoskisson, R.E., Busenitz, L.W. and Dial, J. (2000), 'Entrepreneurial growth through privatization: the upside of management buyouts', *The Academy of Management Review*, **25** (3), 591–601.

Wright, M., Hoskisson, R.E. and Busenitz, L.W. (2001), 'Firm rebirth: buyouts as facilitators of strategic growth and entrepreneurship', *The Academy of Management Executive*, **15**, 111–25.

Zahra, S.A. (1995), 'Corporate entrepreneurship and financial performance: the case of management leveraged buyouts', *Journal of Business Venturing*, **10**, 225–47.

8. Management buyouts and restructuring Japanese corporations

Mike Wright, Motoya Kitamura and Robert E. Hoskisson

INTRODUCTION

Japan's long period of economic growth came to an end in the early 1990s. The poor economic growth, as well as greater global competition and excessive enterprise debt, put pressure on large corporations to restructure. However, non-performing loans among banks and financial institutions restricted the traditional flow of capital to Japanese firms. In the US and Europe buyouts have become well established as a vehicle to facilitate corporate restructuring. Now buyouts are emerging in Japan, providing a means for Japanese corporations to restructure in order to face up to the challenges of difficult economic conditions and increasing competitive pressures.

One example occurred in October 1998 when, in response to external pressures to restructure, the senior management of Sumitomo Corporation, one of the leading companies in the Sumitomo keiretsu, developed a reform package to improve performance. Part of this strategy involved exiting from non-core businesses. One business viewed as non-core with low growth prospects, and therefore a candidate for disposal, was Sumisho Alis. Takenori Fukui, Sumisho Alis's president, proposed a buyout. He used his retirement funds to purchase equity in the business and therefore has a greater incentive to perform than he had as a salaried manager. However, Mr Fukui stresses the positive side of the change. His company is now free to explore new business opportunities that were impossible when it was part of the Sumitomo keiretsu.

Although rare at the time, buyouts like that of Sumisho Alis are becoming more common in Japan. As noted in Table 8.1, the year 1998 marked the de facto birth of the buyout market in Japan with nine transactions including several landmark cases–the first buyouts from receivership and the first leveraged buyout where the buyout company's cash flow projection was taken as collateral. In 2001 the number of deals reached a record 22

Table 8.1 Trends in buyouts in Japan

Year	Number	Value (¥ billion)
1998	9	5.1
1999	19	31.8
2000	11	40.4
2001	22	116.5

Source: Mitsubishi Research Institute/CMBOR/ChuoAoyama Audit Corp.

and the total value jumped almost three times over the previous year, from ¥40 billion to ¥116 billion. In this chapter we examine the role of buyouts as an important tool in corporate restructuring in Japan, particularly through spinning off underperforming affiliate firms as larger diversified business groups refocus.

This chapter presents the first systematic analysis of the Japanese buyout market and is aimed at providing managers with insights into its importance. We outline a general conceptual framework for understanding the types of buyouts and provide definitions of management buyouts. We then consider the dominant factors that led Japanese management to undertake corporate restructuring. In turn we explain how our framework should be adjusted and analyse the role of the different types of buyout in Japan relative to the factors that are facilitating the development of that market. In a final section, we discuss the implications of our findings for corporate managers in Japan, for managers of subsidiaries considering a buyout, for venture capital firms, for the government seeking to promote buyouts as a restructuring tool, and for foreign entrants to the Japanese buyout market. To inform these issues and the implications of our analysis, we draw on our three comprehensive annual surveys of the Japanese buyout market completed in the period 2000–2002 (Box 8.1).

BOX 8.1 THE SURVEY

In each year, a three-staged approach was used to collect data on buyouts in Japan. First, a questionnaire was sent to all the main buyout financing firms and banks as well as the buyout companies we were able to identify through press announcements as well as other companies that were potentially interested in funding buyouts. The questionnaire to buyout financing firms requested details of the transactions they had completed. The buyout firms filled in the questionnaires that gave information on reasons for sales, etc. In 2002, the questionnaire was sent to 20 financiers, all of whom provided a full response. Second, we conducted face-to-face interviews to collect case study material. Cases were selected that represented examples of emerging trends. Interviews were conducted with the senior executive involved in the buyout. Based on a questionnaire successfully used in the UK buyout market, the survey aimed to identify the extent to which buyouts were successfully functioning as vehicles for restructuring Japanese corporations, by providing enhanced monitoring and upside incentives to management. Finally, we drew on secondary data, such as press announcements related to the development of the buyout market.

MANAGEMENT BUYOUTS

Buyouts are intended to change the incentive and governance structure of the company. In a buyout, senior management typically obtains a significant share of the equity, with institutional investors providing the balance. The subscribers of this private equity, whether a leveraged buyout association or a private equity firm, provide close monitoring of the newly independent buyout firm through requirements for detailed information, board representation, etc.[1] Taking on significant debt to fund the purchase of the company introduces a major commitment to service this financing due to the threat of bankruptcy should interest payments not be met. As such, debt providers also set and monitor a range of covenants as a condition of extending loan finance.[2] In some cases, where incumbent management does not possess the requisite skills, external management may be brought in as significant equity holders, creating a management buy-in.[3] Through these arrangements, both private equity and debt providers have the incentives and the means to monitor management, and management has the equity incentive to perform.

The buyout concept has wide applicability for the restructuring of enterprises. In western economies, previous research has identified three main types of buyout: efficiency buyouts, revitalization buyouts and entrepreneurial buyouts.[4] In what follows, we summarize the framework, define these buyout types and then explain how they may be adapted to the Japanese context.

In traditional 'efficiency buyouts', the target business unit is viewed as underperforming due to the absence of adequate incentive and control mechanisms. This may be due to management having invested in too much product diversification or over-investment in vertical integration. Such problems often give rise to a situation where divisional management has insufficient incentives and where corporate level control is weak because head office managers may have insufficient strategic monitoring expertise and where outside investors are unwilling or unable to exert control. In these cases, the incentive and control mechanisms introduced through a buyout can produce efficiency improvements in underperforming divisions. Such buyouts often include higher levels of debt in the capital structure and therefore restrict managerial discretion, forcing the firm to pay out free cash flow that would otherwise be invested in sub-optimal projects.

Buyouts can also have an impact in terms of enhancing the growth prospects of former divisions to create what we term 'revitalization buyouts'. Large organizations often lack reliable performance measures and resort to bureaucratic measures to ensure performance. In such organizations, divisions with profitable and innovative investment opportunities may be disadvantaged if their division is not regarded as strategically central to the parent. When proposals for new investment are presented, corporate management is likely to reject them, preferring to divert resources to more core activities. There is also evidence from buyouts in the UK that standardized corporate decision-making processes may be inappropriate for the market sector in which a particular division operates, which may further disadvantage the division in gaining investment funds.[5] Managers may become frustrated with such bureaucratic structures and the stifling effect on investment and development, and seek the opportunity for a buyout. In these cases, a buyout may enable divisional management to obtain finance for investment that enables them to catch up with their competitors, revitalizing the business.

The buyout concept is also increasingly being applied to situations involving significant innovation, such as technology and software sectors.[6] Standardized corporate decision-making processes may find it especially difficult to accommodate newly emerging market sectors with little if any trading history or hard information on market size and prospects. Here the combination of management with an entrepreneurial mindset, private equity providers with financial and technical monitoring skills and lower leverage provide opportunity for 'entrepreneurial buyouts' that allow entrepreneurial initiative to be realized and performance to be improved.[7]

RESTRUCTURING AND BUYOUT OPPORTUNITIES IN JAPAN

Buyouts are emerging in Japan and present a means by which Japanese corporations can effect much-needed restructuring. Anglo-American companies have generally become familiar with corporate restructuring. A feature of this restructuring has often been to divest distant subsidiaries or divisions. Anglo-American firms operating in Japan may, therefore, seek to dispose of these activities where they are under pressure to restructure in their domestic markets. These activities may then be potential buyout candidates. Notable examples of this kind of buyout in Japan include Proudfoot Japan from its UK parent Proudfoot in 2000, and Tower Records in Japan from its US parent MTS Corporation in 2002.

However, a dominant feature of the Japanese corporate landscape is the keiretsu structure in which almost all firms have close links with a main bank and extensive ties with their suppliers and distributors.[8] The nature of these ties differs depending on whether the firm is part of a horizontal keiretsu, a vertical keiretsu, or an independent firm.[9] The main bank supplies debt and equity finance for other keiretsu members.[10] Horizontal keiretsu, or financial or bank-centred keiretsu, are groups of firms that span many industries, including manufacturing, financial and service. The horizontal keiretsu are centred around a commercial bank. There are currently four major keiretsu groups: Mitsui–Sumitomo, Mitsubishi, Mizuho and UFJ.[11] Under each keiretsu umbrella are large numbers of affiliate firms, which themselves may be diversified. Vertical keiretsus have a dominant firm that is analogous to a corporate parent and have clear parent–affiliate firm ties. For example, Nissan Motors and Toyota Motors have extensive parts supplier networks and many suppliers are partially owned subsidiaries of these corporations.[12] Horizontal keiretsus may include vertical keiretsus. For, example, Sumitomo Alis is part of a vertical keiretsu within the horizontal keiretsu Mitsui–Sumitomo. Many large independent firms, such as Sony and Matsushita, are also highly diversified. Both keiretsu groups and other large diversified firms have governance and incentive problems because of the important role of inside managers. A criticism of insider systems such as those in Japan is that they fail to ensure exit from non-viable projects in a timely fashion.[13]

Pressure from global competition and an increasing presence of global shareholders have produced consolidation both within and between keiretsus as companies seek to develop their own corporate shareholder relationships. These developments have led to inter-keiretsu alliances such as between Mitsui Chemicals and Sumitomo Chemical, and between Kawasaki Heavy Industries and Mitsui Engineering and Shipbuilding. They have also involved alliances with foreign firms, as for example the announcement in 2000 by DaimlerChrysler that it would acquire a 3.4 per cent stake in Mitsubishi Motors to gain majority control. These consolidations also reduce the mutual reliance of the companies within each group. For example, in October 1999 Nissan Motors announced that it would cut business relationships with keiretsu subcontractors by selling its ownership in them. This resulted in subcontractors no longer being part of the firm's balance sheet, and also changed the basis of the trading relationship so that Nissan was freer to select other suppliers and the former affiliates could seek other customers.[14] Keiretsu-affiliated firms and associated banks have also begun to realize that they can no longer afford to retain inefficient subsidiaries supported by bank loans on favourable terms.

This change in the attitude of corporate managers is reflected in a 1998 report by the Ministry of International Trade and Industry that found that 24 per cent of large firms stated that in the future they would withdraw from a business when it failed to meet targets, compared with 12.6 per cent saying they would previously have done so. This intention was realized in the first half of 2002, as evidenced by M&A activities resulting from corporate group restructuring. Such activity increased 40 per cent over the same period in 2001 to 375 transactions. This includes the restructuring of corporations through the divestment of unprofitable units.[15] For example, major domestic electrical appliance firms such as Hitachi and Toshiba, large steel companies such as Nippon Steel and NKK, and large trading companies such as Nissho Iwai and Sumitomo have spun out subsidiaries since 1999.

The example of Sumitomo Corporation illustrates the execution of a restructuring strategy. In response to external pressures to restructure, the senior management of Sumitomo Corporation developed a reform package for the period up to March 2001 in order to improve its performance. A major feature of the restructuring of conglomerates in the US and Europe over the past two decades has been the refocusing on core businesses. This thinking now appears to be permeating the strategies of Japanese corporations. The strategy adopted by Sumitomo was to grow core businesses, improve the quality of assets and cost competitiveness, consolidate profitable smaller companies in similar sectors and exit from non-core businesses.[16] Three quantitative targets were set: to improve the consolidated risk adjusted return ratio to a minimum 8 per cent by fiscal 2000 (15 per cent over the longer term); to reduce consolidated risk adjusted assets by ¥200 billion by the end of fiscal 2000; and to recover consolidated shareholders' equity to a minimum ¥700 billion (¥600 billion on a non-consolidated basis) by the end of fiscal 2001. Companies to be divested or closed were identified as having low growth potential and with free cash flow/risk asset ratio below 8 per cent. Some 120 companies have been identified as targets for divestment or closure. So far, 40 companies have been divested, closed or combined with another subsidiary. One of the activities divested as a buyout was Sumisho Alis quoted at the beginning of this chapter.

Table 8.2 Nissan Motor's subsidiaries divested through management buyout

Subsidiary	Business	Month/year	Buyout fund acquired	Transaction price (¥ billion)
Vantec	Distribution	Jan 2001	3i	15
Niles Parts	Manufacturer of car parts	Apr 2001	Ripplewood Holdings	10
Zero	Transportation of cars	Apr 2001	AIG Japan, Tokio MarineCapital	5
Altia	Manufacturer of car accessories	Oct 2001	Fuji Capital Management	5
Iid	Research	Oct 2001	NIF Ventures, Fuji Capital Management	N/A
Kiriu	Manufacturer of car parts	Dec 2001	Unison Capital	13.3

A second example is provided by Nissan Motors, which has gone through a major restructuring process since Renault acquired 36.8 per cent of its equity and appointed a new CEO, Carlos Ghosn, in 1999. Nissan is a major keiretsu member of the old Fuyo group (now part of Mizuho). Fuyo group's main bank, Fuji Bank, consolidated with two other banks last year, which makes the Fuyo group a looser keiretsu. Corporate governance by the main banks was too weak in terms of their balance sheets and their know-how to be effective in exerting pressure that would revitalize performance. The appointment of a new CEO has seen the pursuit of aggressive restructuring strategies that previously were only talked about. Rapid restructuring of the car industry at a global level has necessitated greater flexibility. These developments have led Nissan to concentrate managerial resources on the core business of cars. Nissan, through its 'Nissan Revival Plan', sold its non-core assets worth more than ¥400 billion from 1999 to 2002. Out of ¥400 billion, ¥200 billion was stock, ¥100 billion property, and ¥100 billion non-core subsidiaries. Included in this restructuring effort were six buyout transactions in 2001 listed in Table 8.2. In addition to these cases, Sumisho Alis was bought out from the Sumitomo Corporation, Digit was bought out from Mitsui and Nissho Iwai Alconix was bought out from Nissho Iwai, a major trading firm of the old Fuyo Group.

BUYOUTS IN JAPAN

The general change in the mindset of corporate managers regarding the nature of the boundaries of their organizations has enabled buyouts to become accepted as an important aspect of restructuring. Our identification of what is effectively a comprehensive list of management buyouts in Japan shows that more than 85 per cent of these transactions have involved divestments from Japanese corporations. Portfolio restructuring was generally specified as the reason for the buyout. Specifically, the most important reasons why parent company management wanted to sell the company as a buyout in 2001 were that the company was peripheral in terms of product markets (11 companies, 79 per cent of those answering this question), because the company was too small (three companies, 21 per cent) and two companies reporting that an underperforming parent was being restructured. In this section, we show how these rationales for divestment have led to the adaptation in Japan of the three types of buyout identified earlier.

Efficiency Buyouts

In Japan, the high indebtedness of companies may seem to make efficiency buyouts infeasible for groups as a whole because of the difficulty in taking on and servicing further borrowings to fund the purchase.[17] However, the debt covenants in the Japanese banking system have been quite 'soft' and have resulted in the bank consolidation mentioned earlier.[18] By 'soft' we refer to banks being willing to help out when a member firm was in financial distress: norms put an obligation on the bank not to allow group member companies to fail.[19] As such, where affiliates or subsidiaries have not had a separate financing structure from the group, it may be feasible to effect divestment as a buyout through highly leveraged arrangements where the covenants are more restrictive and monitoring is more intense. In contrast to a main bank in a Japanese firm, LBO associations and private equity firms are argued to perform a more active monitoring role in their buyout investments.[20] They also typically own larger equity stakes in the buyout firm than is the case for the main banks in the keiretsu system or among independent Japanese firms. Although main banks can only own up to 5 per cent of the equity in any firm, they usually only intervene as a last resort.

The example of ICS from WDI illustrates an efficiency buyout in Japan (see Box 8.2). The financial structure involved a high degree of leverage with close financial monitoring being introduced. Shortly after the buyout, senior workers were interviewed and branch offices inspected with a view to identifying areas for restructuring. Specific performance targets (EBITDA etc.) and financial covenants were agreed upon and a performance-orientated compensation system was introduced. The senior management team was reformed with the introduction of six executive directors and a reduction in the management team from nine to six. The organization structure was also slimmed down. Since the buyout the number of employees has decreased from 100 to 84, and sales have dropped from ¥5.8 billion to ¥4.5 billion in 2001. The profits are unknown but there are indications that ICS has been underperforming as it has had three different CEOs since the buyout, manifesting the abrasion between the buyout firm (JAFCO) and the management, which is very unusual in Japan. Although it is too early to determine the fate of ICS, it has been adversely affected by the events of September 11 which discouraged Japanese citizens from flying to the US. ICS, supporting study-abroad programmes, suffered from cancellations of 60 per cent of its clients who had intended to enrol in US schools.

BOX 8.2 ICS AN EFFICIENCY BUYOUT FROM WDI

ICS was founded in 1971 and specialized in supporting study-abroad programmes, including publishing a monthly journal. With its business declining, it was acquired in 1989 by WDI, which manages restaurants including Hard Rock Café Japan. As WDI had strong links with foreign countries, it thought it could add value to ICS. ICS was subsequently divested in 1998 because, although value had increased since the acquisition, it was a non-core subsidiary in a sector quite distinct from restaurant management. Because about 50 out of 100 employees at ICS held shares in ICS, it was agreed that a management and employee buyout would be a better way to spin it off from WDI than an IPO or third-party sale. Fuji Bank agreed to provide senior debt with Tokyo Marine and Fire Insurance, based on a seven-year cash flow prediction. The collateral was the predicted cash flow and ICS's entire assets. This was the first time cash flow was used as security in a Japanese buyout and the first time mezzanine debt was arranged. The total amount of debt was ¥2.7 billion, accounting for 71 per cent of the ¥3.8 billion total transaction value. Private equity finance was provided by JAFCO. JAFCO introduced periodical financial monitoring by an accounting firm and examination of management data and internal documents.

BOX 8.3 VANTEC: A REVITALIZATION BUYOUT FROM NISSAN OF THE FUYO KEIRETSU

In January 2001, 3i, the UK venture capital company, funded the management-led buyout of the logistics subsidiary of Nissan Motors for slightly more than ¥15 billion, making it one of the largest deals of this type in Japan to date. Some 55 per cent of Vantec's sales are with Nissan Motors and its subsidiaries. The Nissan Motors group holds about 74 per cent of Vantec. 3i and Vantec management contributed about ¥7–8 billion in funds, while Industrial Bank of Japan led a group of banks providing a syndicated loan to cover the rest of the funds. Vantec plans to increase its revenue – which was ¥63.5 billion in the year ended March 2000 – to at least ¥82 billion in two years. 3i will leverage its own relationships with US and European firms and data networks to help increase the corporate value of Vantec, with the intention of subsequently taking the firm public or selling it to another company.

Revitalization Buyouts

Pressures to restructure corporate groups are leading to the divestment not only of inefficient affiliates but also to the disposal of unrelated businesses that may have good performance prospects. Because banks pursue a conservative approach to managerial decision-making and because other keiretsu member firms who have cross-ownership may not want significant change, risk aversion and inertia may result.[21] For instance, the structure of Japanese keiretsus may mean that one firm's plans to expand are frustrated by being in direct competition with other parts of the keiretsu, which would undermine collective norms. Buyouts may present significant opportunities for parts of keiretsus because they eliminate the excessive conservative governance embodied in collaboration and the main bank system. In these situations, the buyout can provide enhanced incentives, better assessment of managerial talent and increased freedom of decision-making, as well as better monitoring and access to finance.[22] These factors enable revitalizing changes to occur in activities that were not regarded as core to the parent.

The Vantec buyout from Nissan is an illustration of a revitalization buyout that has interesting implications for future restructuring of large Japanese corporations (see Box 8.3). As a logistics subsidiary of Nissan, Vantec had substantial trading links with the parent group. After Renault became Nissan's largest shareholder and decided to narrow its core business, Vantec was recategorized as non-core. Vantec, which had been constrained when it was part of Nissan, now had opportunities to expand outside the group by developing its import and export activities and attracting new customers. For Vantec the buyout produced greater freedom to explore other businesses and other clients, which already made up 45 per cent of revenues at the time of the buyout. For Nissan, Vantec's divestment and buyout means freedom to choose other logistics companies. Links with Nissan have been changed from a guaranteed long-term relationship to more of a contractual one that is flexible.

Entrepreneurial Buyouts

Relational capital markets as found in Japan enable stable and close long-term relationships with financiers and other firms and are advantageous in mature industries and in financing innovations involving lower risk. However, these arrangements are less appropriate for financing more explorative innovation entailing higher unpredictability. Similarly, internal labour markets, while promoting firm-specific knowledge, tend to engender inward-looking solutions, which is problematic for innovations that require radical change in relation to existing technology. Hence, Japanese firms have been highly effective in producing process innovation rather than product innovation, and in adapting and improving on existing technology rather than creating new technology.[23]

This suggests that Japanese managers who perceive radical entrepreneurial opportunities are likely to be frustrated within large firms with networked relationships. With the emergence of the buyout concept in Japan, managers have another avenue to realize entrepreneurial opportunities. The management buyout of Digit (see Box 8.4) represents an entrepreneurial buyout. With a previous background in the computer and publishing business, Digit started a magazine *Home PC* and an internet entertainment project 'i Cupid'. These early successes encouraged CEO Katsumi Ureshino's entrepreneurial spirit, as he sought more rapid expansion, but Digit needed more investment for such development. Meanwhile, Mitsui was not as enthusiastic because it had already extended a loan to Digit which it had no intention of increasing. Moreover, Mitsui did not see itself being further committed to the publishing business, which it perceived as a non-core activity. Given this context, in October 1999, CEO Mr Ureshino and the board director at that time proposed a buyout. Digit developed rapidly after the buyout because Mr Ureshino was now able to pursue his ideas for new internet tools that he had been unable to do under the Mitsui Media Business division. Mr Ureshino obtained additional investment of ¥500 million from other corporations by the end of 1999. With increased capital at its disposal, Digit was able to develop the 'i Cupid' product into 'CG–i Cupid', featuring major entertainers introduced through computer graphics. This project developed into collaboration with NTT Docomo, which would provide the major entertainers in 'CG–i Cupid' in its mobile phones. Digit also founded a joint venture company 'i Money', specializing in providing online financial services information.

BOX 8.4 DIGIT: AN ENTREPRENEURIAL BUYOUT FROM THE MITSUI KEIRETSU

Founded by Mitsui and Dai Nippon Printing in December 1996, the Tokyo-based firm Digit was under Mitsui's Media Business division. In order to enable adaptation to the rapidly changing internet market, the division enjoyed a certain degree of flexibility in its ability to collaborate with outsiders. As of February 2001 the division held 71 subsidiaries, of which approximately 20 were subject to consolidated accounting. Digit was established within this framework as part of Mitsui's growing interest in the BtoC internet market. Digit runs an internet portal targeted at individual PC users. Another mainline operation is an entertainment business in which the company publishes images of singing idols and movie stars both on the internet as well as in magazines. The company was bought out in late 1999. Negotiations with Mitsui lasted approximately three months and centred on the acquisition price which was established at ¥20 million. Venture capital firms and banks were not involved in the funding of the deal. Before the buyout, Mitsui held 91 per cent, Dai Nippon Printing 5 per cent, and Mr Ureshino 4 per cent of the equity. Digit's biggest challenge was that it had to restructure the bank debt, as it had been almost guaranteed due to its affiliation with its parent Mitsui group. Digit generates 70 per cent of its total revenue from collecting advertising fees from corporate sponsors. After its IPO, Digit merged with Brain.com in 2001 and now has 250 employees.

INSTITUTIONAL CHANGES FACILITATING BUYOUTS

As noted above, buyouts are now being successfully adapted to the Japanese context. However, other changes have taken place in the institutional environment of Japan that also facilitate buyout opportunities. These include factors encouraging managers to become entrepreneurial, a supportive legal and taxation framework including government support measures, sources of funds and the feasibility of realizing gains for investors.[24]

Changes in Managerial Attitudes towards Entrepreneurship

According to an annual survey by International Management Development (IMD), Japan ranked 47th among 47 nations on 'creation of firms' and 'entrepreneurship', and 45th on 'shareholder value' in 1999.[25] The prevalence of internal labour markets in Japanese firms creates difficulties in providing strong incentives for risk-taking, due to the internal norms of equity and fairness. Traditional labour practices also emphasize seniority and tenure. Hence, managers are unlikely to be induced to pursue explorative and revolutionary innovations. Firm-specific knowledge and social capital are reinforced by internal labour markets which are supportive of exploitative and incremental innovations. The lack of external labour markets traditionally makes the costs of exit from current employment exceedingly high, particularly where there may be scope for redeployment of managers elsewhere in the group. However, as the spread of corporate restructuring in Japan heralds a change of expectations about lifetime careers with the same corporation, managers may become more positive towards entrepreneurship. The unemployment rate in Japan rose to a record high of 5.6 per cent in December 2001.

Although the impact of these changes on managerial attitudes to entrepreneurial endeavours may occur slowly, evidence from our surveys of buyouts shows that an important reason why managers were willing to buy the companies at which they were formerly employed was that they had been stifled by a lack of market-based incentives and by their former employers in their attempts to develop the business. The most frequent reason cited for a management buyout was their desire to control their own business (59 per cent of respondents). Better financial rewards were cited by 47 per cent of the respondents, a major increase from the 11 per cent recorded for pre-2000 deals.

New Accounting Standards

New accounting standards introduced in 2001 are helping to facilitate restructuring and the emergence of buyouts. Such changes are necessary in the context of Japan's ranking close to the bottom in a study of 47 countries in terms of shareholder value, rights and responsibilities of shareholders and financial institutions' transparency. Consolidated accounting standards will force companies to emphasize groupwide performance and require corporate assets to be estimated at market value instead of book value. In response, banks and companies are already disposing of latent losses on cross-held shares, causing considerable change to the traditional keiretsu system. Companies will also be obliged to report interim consolidated earnings but many corporations are introducing these changes ahead of the requirement.

Government Support

As part of the government's programme to revive the economy, measures have been introduced to support corporate restructuring. A report published in 1999 by a study group established by MITI, consisting of 18 venture capitalists, bankers, academics, consultants and analysts, recommended active steps to facilitate and support buyouts as a form of restructuring.[26]

These recommendations were incorporated alongside measures to promote restructuring M&A into the Law on Special Measures for Industrial Revitalization in 1999. The measures for buyouts include simplified procedures for spinning off divisions to form subsidiaries and the extension of stock option programmes to subsidiary employees. The Industrial Structure Improvement Fund, consisting of public money, is also allowed to provide equity and/or guarantee loans for buyout projects if they qualify as divestments as defined by the government. To qualify, the main conditions to be met are that the vendor must prove that the divestment will enhance the productivity of the parent, will certainly take place, will not interfere with harmonious growth of the domestic economy, and will not unreasonably interfere with employees' status. The K.Maikai's management and employee buyout (MEBO) divestiture from Norton KK, in which both management and employees became equityholders, was the first buyout to benefit from these new policies. K.Maikai was the Drilling Products Division of Norton, which in turn is a fully owned subsidiary of the French group Saint-Gobain. Out of the ¥195 million of senior debt provided in the transaction, the Industrial Structure Improvement Fund guaranteed ¥175 million to facilitate implementation of the buyout. In 2002 the Ministry of Economy, Trade and Industry (METI), the reorganized executive branch of

MITI, formed another study group on buyouts and is gathering policy recommendations to remove further legal obstacles to restructuring and buyout activities.

Private Equity Providers

In western markets, the presence of private equity firms and leveraged buyout associations helps facilitate management buyouts in two ways: it makes finance available to effect buyout purchases; second, the skills of private equity firms enables them to monitor and support newly independent management through the taking of non-executive director seats on boards, the specification of requirements for detailed financial reporting, etc. New financial institutions, such as venture capital firms, providing finance and monitoring for innovative sectors, are viewed as having an increasingly important role to play in Japan.[27] Our survey shows that so far in Japan, some 69 per cent (45) of buyouts include private equity while 31 per cent (20) do not.

There has been marked entry by European and US private equity funds and M&A funds (see Table 8.3).[28] Some foreign funds have allied with Japanese counterparts: Apax and Patricof, 3i, Rothschild, Ripplewood Holdings, Goldman Sachs and Lehman Brothers, while some foreign financiers such as Ripplewood Holdings, Carlyle Group, GE Capital, Cerberus Group and EM Warburg Pincus have established independent

Table 8.3 Major private equity/M&A funds in Japan in early 2002

Investors	Size (¥ Billion)
Ripplewood Holdings, Marriott	400
GE Capital	200
Cerberus Group	200
Ripplewood Holdings	120
Ripplewood Holdings, Mitsubishi Corporation	110
GE Capital, Sumitomo Corporation, etc.	100
Carlyle Group	75
Unison Capital	40
Advantage Partners	30
Jafco	28
3i	20
Apax Globis	20
Schroder Ventures	17

Source: Press reports.

funds of their own (see Table 8.4). Some firms such as Cerberus, Lone Star, Goldman Sachs and GE Capital entered the market by buying distressed assets, notably property. Major trading houses such as Mitsubishi, Mitsui and Marubeni head the list of Japanese investors. Seeing M&A advisory work as a new line of business, they are aiming to invest in restructuring M&A projects, including buyouts.

3iBJ, established in April 1990 as a joint venture between then Industrial Bank of Japan (IBJ) (60 per cent ownership) and 3i (40 per cent ownership) and comprising one UK executive and two from IBJ, played a pioneering role in arranging two MBOs in 1996 and 1998. In 1999, however, 3i group had parted with IBJ and had become 3i Asia Pacific Japan. Venture capital firms, such as JAFCO (the Japanese Associated Finance Company – a consortium of banking, industrial and securities firms and Japan's first venture capital fund), the biggest venture capital firm in Japan, and MKS Partners, formerly known as Schroder Ventures, along with other competitors, are seeking buyout opportunities through their long-established networks with small and medium-sized companies. Executives in the London branch of JAFCO had experience in doing buyouts in Europe and this expertise is being used to develop buyouts in Japan. JAFCO recruited specialists in May 1998 to handle such Japanese buyouts. In December 1998, JAFCO led the management buyout of ICS, a consulting firm for people intending to study abroad, with Fuji Bank (now Mizuho Bank) providing debt. Our survey indicates that, while most Japanese venture capital firms are affiliates of large financial institutions, independent local venture capital firms, such as Globis Capital (as Apax Globis Partners, a joint venture between Apax and Particof), Advantage Partners and Unison Capital, have successfully established their own funds from institutional investors from Japan, the US and Europe. Apax Globis Partners and Advantage Partners have already arranged and invested in several buyout cases. These independent players have collected funds and identified target cases utilizing their personal networks and are expected to develop as major players in the Japanese buyout market.

Venture capital investment in Japan has not been characterized as 'high risk, high return', where the venture capital firm invests at an early stage and then tries to increase the investee company's value with hands-on commitment to the management. In contrast, Japanese venture capitalists' investment emphasizes later-stage investments for firms that have already proven to be successful and are ready for an IPO. According to a survey by the Japanese government, in 1996 more than 37.6 per cent of the venture firms that received equity investment from venture capitalists in Japan were more than 20 years old, whereas only 26 per cent were under five years old. This is in sharp contrast to US venture capital, where in

1996 Venture One's survey showed that 64 per cent were less than five years old.

Venture capital firms in Japan have traditionally relied heavily on advice from the main banks regarding investees as these banks enjoy better access to small firms. The strong connection between the main banks and venture capital firms is evidenced by the fact that about 80 per cent of the venture capital firms are subsidiaries of major financial institutions. Venture capital firms often provide funds through loans to more traditional manufacturing and service sector firms, rather than to high-technology ventures, so that their skills are more likely to involve financial monitoring rather than specialist skills for evaluating high-technology investments.[29] This suggests that the main banks' passive mode of corporate governance may extend to monitoring by Japanese venture capital firms.[30] While this appears to have been the case in the early stages of buyout market development, our surveys show that financiers are now imposing more formal monitoring conditions on buyouts than in earlier transactions, suggesting increasing sophistication in the market (see Table 8.4).[31] The most frequent mechanism in 2001 was monthly financial reports, present in 87.5 per cent of cases compared with 39.5 per cent before 2000. Asset disposal was influenced by financiers in 68.8 per cent of cases while this was only present in 15.8 per cent of cases before 2000. This increased involvement by financiers in buyouts reflects

Table 8.4 Conditions of investment required by financiers regarding MBO investees

Conditions of investment required by financiers of MBO investees	2001 (no.)	2001 (%)	1998–2000 (no.)	1998–2000 (%)
Nomination of chairman by financier	10	62.5	9	23.7
Nomination of other directors by financier	9	56.3	6	15.8
Provision of monthly financial reports to financier	14	87.5	15	39.5
Changes to accounting methods	7	43.8	5	13.2
Change of auditor	7	43.8	4	10.5
Changes in products	4	25.0	4	10.5
Asset disposal	11	68.8	6	15.8
Asset purchase	9	56.3	5	13.2
Investments	10	62.5	7	18.4
Base for %	16		38	

Source: Mitsubishi Research Institute/CMBOR/ChuoAoyama Audit Corp.

the rapid development of the market. Our interviews with financiers indicate that from their initial transactions they have learned the importance of monitoring and also equipped themselves to press for greater monitoring involvement during deal negotiations.

Realization of Gains

Management buyouts are typically not an open-ended new ownership form.[32] In order to satisfy their funds providers, private equity firms need to realize their gains within a particular time period. Management may seek to exit the business as a buyout form either because they too want to realize gains or because they perceive that they can better pursue their career development through a new ownership form. For the business itself to survive, it may need to change its form in order to access further finance or economies of scale and scope. For these reasons, the state of development of stock and takeover markets are likely important facilitators of buyouts in Japan.

In Japan, two particular issues may influence realization of gains. First, while in western markets 'exit' within a given time period through IPO or sale is accepted as a way to enable private equity providers to realize their gains, the notion of 'exit' in Japan has long meant a finale, an almost ceremonial event for venture firm entrepreneurs after their long period of involvement in the firm. This suggests a different and longer-term perspective on the realization of gains in Japan than in other buyout markets. Second, a major barrier affecting the growth of the Japanese buyout market has been the difficulties in seeking to exit. In 1999, however, the US National Association of Securities Dealers (Nasdaq) and Softbank launched a new initiative to attract foreign investments to growing Japanese firms, as well as Japanese investors putting more money into other Nasdaq markets. This development provoked the Tokyo Stock Exchange to introduce a new market at the end of 1999 called 'Mothers (Market of the High Growth and Emerging Stocks)' which has attracted investment from venture capital funds. These new markets create more opportunities for buyout exit.

The emergence of Nasdaq Japan and Mothers has revitalized the IPO market in Japan. As Table 8.5 shows, the number of IPOs has substantially increased since 1998. However, in mid-2002 Nasdaq announced that it was considering closing its Japanese operations due to lack of investors and IPOs, competition from other exchanges and regulatory constraints and resistance from smaller local brokers that had made it difficult to introduce a new trading system.[33]

Although the number of IPOs has increased, the only recent buyout exit through an IPO was that of Digit in September 2000 on Nasdaq Japan. The

Table 8.5 IPO market in Japan: number of companies listed each year

Market	1998	1999	2000	2001
Jasdaq*	62	73	97	98
Mothers	–	2	27	7
Nasdaq Japan	–	–	40	43
Total	62	75	164	148

Note: * Japanese Association of Securities Dealers Automated Quotation.

Source: Tokyo Stock Exchange and Osaka Stock Exchange.

firm expected pre-tax profits of ¥140 million in the year ending December 31, 2000 compared with a loss of ¥27 million the previous year. In September 2000, the company obtained a listing on Nasdaq Japan at a market capitalization of ¥2.19 billion (131 times the MBO value). The proceeds from the IPO will be used mostly to repay loans. The rest will be set aside as operating funds. The main objective is to grow the value of the company. Digit was the first known buyout to exit in Japan since Wilson Learning Worldwide was listed in 1995 on the OTC market. Other buyout cases all took the form of sales to a third party including Pasona Tech, Nihon Athletics Systems and KISCO Exit Solutions. Therefore, more development of the market for exits needs to take place in order for buyouts to become more firmly established.

DISCUSSION

This chapter has presented the first exploration of the consistent implementation of buyouts in Japan. Our analysis has shown that, although the market is still very undeveloped, there are clear signs that buyouts are emerging as a significant factor in the restructuring of corporations in Japan. The implications of these developments are discussed below regarding policy, corporate governance and managerial concerns.

Implications for Management of Large Corporations

In the context of low economic growth and a need to restructure, there is increasing recognition that buyouts might be an effective tool in undertaking necessary corporate reforms to focus on core businesses. The need to restructure keiretsu groups to increase their competitiveness has meant that keiretsu-affiliated companies are increasing their mobility and flexibility by divesting unprofitable and non-core units. It is here that significant potential for buyouts is likely to emerge, at least in the long run. Most deals have been divestments by Japanese corporations. Although a few buyouts have been associated with restructuring of the four major keiretsu groups, most have not been. The main buyouts from a major keiretsu group so far include Alis from Sumitomo, Digit from Mitsui, six subsidiaries from Nissan Motors, and Nissho Iwai Alconix from Nissho Iwai. Restructuring of keiretsu groups is probably happening only slowly because of the continuing linkages and complementarity of their activities.[34] The more likely short-term candidates for buyouts seem to be peripheral operations that are easier to disentangle from keiretsu monitoring and cross-ownership arrangements and are thus able to stand more easily as independent entities. For example, the buyout of Vantec from Nissan illustrates the opportunities for divestments to buyouts that involve significant trading relationships with former parents. In some contrast to the development of the buyout market in the West, where transactions focused on underperforming divisions that provided opportunities to make efficiency gains, buyouts in Japan are seen to be of particular relevance in the spinning-off of underperforming divisions where management's opportunities for growth are frustrated by bureaucratic internal control systems, creating opportunities for revitalization and entrepreneurial buyouts. Although independence from the parent company or keiretsu group may facilitate revitalization and entrepreneurship, such independence may be difficult to achieve for more interdependent subsidiaries. Accordingly, where a buyout could help to revitalize a part of the firm with continued interdependence, some form of buyout hybrid, where the parent firm maintains an ownership interest, may be necessary. These kinds of buyout are long established in developed markets such as the UK. They may be especially attractive to corporate management as the retention of an equity stake enables continued influence. Additionally, future gains may be difficult to value when the activity being bought out has not been operating as a separate profit centre and its development prospects are uncertain. Thus, continued partial ownership by the parent may be necessary until the valuation of gains can be determined in order to avoid the problem that the firm subsequently appears to have been sold too cheaply.

Implications for Managers of Subsidiaries

Both corporate management and the management buying out need to recognize the increased risk of failure that is involved and the changing nature of the relationship between parent and former subsidiary. Managers buying out clearly need to consider the risk of failure from their own financial point of view. Divesting parent corporations may need to ensure that management buying out are not taking an unfair advantage. They may also need to take measures to give the buyout a fair chance of surviving as an independent entity because of the reputation implications for any future buyouts it may wish to initiate.

These issues are illustrated in the case of Sumisho Alis with which we began this chapter. A potentially important issue concerns the loss of the association with the former groups. The company is more open to failure as it may no longer enjoy protection from Sumitomo's main bank as lender of last resort and customers may feel less confident as they are no longer dealing with a member of the Sumitomo group. This in turn may lead to a loss of customers who feel that the business is less financially sound. Contractual arrangements may be needed to deal with the issue of possible future competition between the two parties. Sumisho Alis had to agree to cease using the 'Sumisho' brand name. Sumitomo Corporation agreed not to sell products (17 products were specified in the contract) that competed with Alis's products to Alis's affiliated retail shops and not to interfere with Alis's sales and contracts with its affiliated retail shops. Interestingly, the fear that some of the affiliated retail stores would terminate their contracts with Alis because of the disappearance of the Sumitomo brand name was misplaced as only 14 retail stores out of about 200 did so.

Interestingly, a positive sign in Alis was that some employees from Sumitomo left the company to work for the buyout. The harmonious and relationship-orientated business culture in Japan traditionally guaranteed lifetime employment and gave little incentive to aggressive entrepreneurship. However, our survey indicated a high degree of buyout initiative being taken by management. The spread of corporate restructuring, heralding a change to expectations about lifetime careers, may contribute to a more positive attitude to entrepreneurship, but such changes may be slow because of the need for complementary changes in institutional arrangements. Hence, while there is a potential loss of status related to leaving a group affiliated through a buyout, the undermining of traditional notions such as lifetime employment may make this less of a barrier to buyouts.

Implications for Venture Capital Firms

It will be interesting to see how the market for venture capital evolves in Japan. There has been an entry of both existing and new private equity providers into the buyout segment of the market, indicating less emphasis on riskier early-stage investments. Developments in the buyout market are also linked to greater attention to the need for timely realization of investment gains. It was clear from the survey that venture capitalists initially had relatively little involvement in the hands-on monitoring of investee companies but this seems to be changing in more recent transactions. In part, this may have been due to inexperienced venture capital executives, but it may also reflect cultural factors relating to the reluctance of Japanese monitors to intervene. In this sense, buyouts so far in Japan seem to be different from their counterparts in the US and Europe, but this may change. As suggested above, to move into conducting buyouts of more interdependent businesses in a keiretsu group may require even further innovation from venture capital partners. Perhaps this could be done by venture capital units formed by keiretsu groups.

Implications for Government Policy

The governmental support scheme to aid qualifying buyout projects may have had an important effect. Some observers believe the government has sent a message to the market that Japan has developed an awareness that buyouts are an effective tool in the corporate restructuring process. An important issue may be to ensure that the process for qualification does not become too bureaucratic and slow.[35] There is also a need to promote the concept of entrepreneurship and risk-taking in Japan to help encourage managers to pursue a buyout of the businesses with which they are affiliated. As noted above, Japan ranks as one of the lowest major industrial countries in terms of entrepreneurial culture.

There remains a need for policymakers and practitioners to overcome a number of obstacles to completing deals. Respondents to our survey cited the most common problem as the valuation of the company (55 per cent of the total sample). This proved to be a problem in all the 10 buyouts that emerged from the failed Okura group as well as in five other cases. Negotiating the transaction was equally felt as problematic (55 per cent), while 25 per cent of the sample felt that negotiating with the financiers was a problem area.

However, one of the major legal barriers to the implementation of buyouts in Japan, the requirement for newly established special purpose companies to be examined by an inspector, has now been overcome. The need for inspection as part of the buyout process in Japan introduced cost, delay and uncertainty. Because of the buyout of ICS, the government approved a simplification of the procedure for creating a special-purpose company to facilitate the acquisition of a target buyout company. Thus, rather than unnecessary inspection, all that is needed is a statement of proof that the company is established for a bona fide purpose (such as buyout) by a lawyer or accountant. The inspection system is still in place and the exemption is only possible when the buyout deal is authorized under the government buyout law. The government's study group on buyouts is examining the possibility of abolishing the inspection regime for buyouts altogether.

More generally, realization of the full potential of buyouts in Japan may require the development of complementary institutions supporting change rather than piecemeal adjustment of the system. The Japanese corporate governance system has traditionally been characterized by the complementarity between its bank-centred, relationship-orientated financial system and internal labour market practice of lifetime employment. The decade-long slowdown of the Japanese economy has forced many Japanese firms to revise employment practices and place more emphasis on qualifications and competence than on age and tenure. However, these developments appear to be limited. As such, the long-term development of human capital inside the firm and a managerial ethic based on benevolent responsibility have not changed substantially.[36] Continuing major cultural gaps between Japanese and Anglo-American contexts remain and seem unlikely to change except on an incremental basis.

Implications for Foreign Investors

For non-Japanese investors entering this market, our findings have a number of implications about the type of approach that may be required. An important aspect of market entry is identifying satisfactory deals. Also, our survey results identified that the negotiation and valuation of deals posed problems which may be different in Japan from the domestic markets of new entrants.[37] In the Japanese environment it is crucial for a foreign entrant to access networks for the identification and completion of potential buyouts of Japanese parent corporations.[38]

The buyout concept has been directly imported into Japan without a lot of forethought, given the different culture. Experienced foreign investors may have a competitive advantage over local investors with respect to the hands-on monitoring required to turnaround buyouts experiencing difficulties. Moreover, given the existing monitoring situation in Japan, efforts may be required to convince managers to accept such monitoring. This suggests that if buyout investors are to exert influence on their investees it will need to be through greater emphasis on the informal and non-rule-based approaches that are an important part of Japanese corporate governance.[39] Our most recent survey evidence suggests that more formal governance mechanisms are emerging but convergence with the Anglo-American model seems unlikely.[40]

Finally, differences in approach to the life-cycle of an investment between Japan and Anglo-American buyout markets are evident and may have implications for limited life funds that need to realize their investment within a particular time period. The development of stock markets may help to facilitate exits but our study indicates that there may need to be a shift in mindset among investees concerning the notion of a life-cycle of investment.[41] Perhaps partial funding by venture capital units of the main banks in Japan would be an answer. They are more likely to understand how Japanese business groups are interconnected.

These points suggest that, as in other buyout markets, foreign entrants may seek to adopt a market segmentation strategy based on the strengths they have developed elsewhere.[42] Divestments of Japanese subsidiaries by US parent corporations may provide a means of establishing an initial market presence where contacts already exist with the parent company. As with the example of Tower Records from its US parent MTS Corporation in 2002, such divestment buyouts are already occurring. Whether a distinctive Japanese-style buyout may emerge would seem to depend on the speed of restructuring of core activities of keiretsu groups. However, different approaches to monitoring and the life-cycle of investments would appear to be necessary for foreign investors. Perhaps partnering with venture capital units of main banks in Japan, as suggested above, may be one answer.

CONCLUSION

This chapter has presented the first examination of management and leveraged buyouts as a tool for restructuring Japanese corporations. Using a framework of buyout types developed in western markets, we have shown that these are likely to be adapted in Japan because of the nature of Japanese corporations and the changing institutional environment. In contrast to the widespread efficiency buyouts in many western markets, we expect that buyouts in Japan are more likely to involve revitalization and entrepreneurial buyout types. Although the buyout market is developing significantly, realization of the full potential may require the development of complementary institutions to support the restructuring needed rather than piecemeal adjustment of aspects of the institutional system. Alternatively, adjustments to the approach to buyouts may require strategic adjustments in regard to funding and buyout type such new hybrid buyout types which are evolving to become more consistent with relationship-orientated economies.

ACKNOWLEDGEMENTS

Financial support from Deloitte & Touche, Barclays Private Equity and Mitsubishi Research Institute is gratefully acknowledged. Comments on a previous draft from three reviewers and the journal editor are also acknowledged.

NOTES

1. For leveraged buyouts in the US see: M. Jensen, 'The modern industrial revolution: exit and the failure of internal control systems', *Journal of Finance*, **48**, 831–80 (1993). For management buyouts and buy-ins in the UK and Europe, where venture capital/private equity firms play a more important role in the buyout market, see: M. Wright and J. Coyne, *Management Buyouts*, Beckenham: Croom Helm (1985).
2. D. Citron, K. Robbie and M. Wright, 'Loan covenants and relationship banking in MBOs', *Accounting and Business Research*, **27** (4), 277–96 (1997).
3. K. Robbie and M. Wright, *Management Buy-ins: Entrepreneurship, active investors and corporate governance*, Manchester: Manchester University Press (1996).
4. See M. Wright, R.E. Hoskisson, L. Busenitz and J. Dial, 'Entrepreneurial growth through privatization: the upside of management buyouts', *Academy of Management Review*, **25** (3), 591–601 (2000).
5. C.S. Jones, 'The attitudes of owner–managers towards accounting control systems following management buyout', *Accounting, Organizations and Society*, **17**, 151–68 (1992).
6. In the US the blurring between LBO associations and venture capital firms has been noted with respect to technology investments with computer sector buyouts such a Big Online and Zilog being completed. Similarly, in the UK, technology sector buyouts have also become more in evidence including the buyouts of Sanderson and Q Group, both in computer software (see CMBOR, *Management Buyouts Quarterly Review*, Spring 2000).
7. Wright et al., 'Entrepreneurial growth'.
8. P. Sheard, 'The main bank system and corporate monitoring and control in Japan', *Journal of Economic Organization and Behavior*, **11**, 399–422 (1989).
9. N. Namiki, 'Parent–subsidiary relationships in Japan: some observations from financial statement data', *S.A.M Advanced Management Journal*, **64**, 15–19 (1999); R. Belderos and L. Sleuwaegen, 'Japanese firms and the decision to invest abroad: business groups and regional core networks', *Review of Economics and Statistics*, **78**, 214–20 (1996); M. Bolton, R. Malmrose and W. Ouchi, 'The organization of innovation in the United States and Japan: neoclassical and relational contracting', *Journal of Management Studies*, **31**, 653–79 (1994); C Ahmadjian, 'Keiretsu, governance and learning: case studies in change from the Japanese automotive industry', *Organization Science*, **12**, 683–701 (2001); K. Dewenter, W. Novaes and R.H. Pettway, 'Visibility versus complexity in business groups: evidence from Japanese keiretsu', *Journal of Business*, **74**, 79–100 (2001).
10. The keiretsu is a somewhat looser version of the old zaibatsu, a pre-Second World War group of conglomerates that once dominated Japan's economy. Zaibatsu consisted of about 10 conglomerates, with Mitsui, Mitsubishi, Sumitomo and Yasuda at the core. Zaibatsu conglomerates were dissolved during the post-war occupation.
11. Following extensive mergers and consolidations in all cases, Dai-Ichi Kangyo and Fuyo (Fuji) consolidated to create Mizuho; Sanwa became UFJ; Mitsui and Sumitomo combined to form Mitsui–Sumitomo; and Mitsubishi remained as such.
12. Namiki, 'Parent–subsidiary relationships'.
13. C. Mayer, 'Stock markets financial institutions and corporate performance', in

N. Dinsdale and M. Prevezer (eds), *Capital Markets and Corporate Governance*, Oxford: Clarendon Press (1994).
14. http://www.nissan-global.com/EN/HOME and interview with CEO of Vantec who was formerly a board member at Nissan.
15. Although the agenda has focused on restructuring large companies, surveys strongly suggest that a lack of successor is high on the list of problems for small and medium-sized companies. MITI's survey shows that 32 per cent of privately owned companies regard succession as a problem and 65 per cent of all small–medium companies have not yet identified their successor. Buyouts could serve as a solution to the succession problem in Japan as is the case in Europe, but so far this has occurred in only one case in Japan.
16. Sumitomo Corporation defines its core business by stating on the first line of its website 'We have been selecting our core businesses with high profitability and growth potential since 1998 . . . '. http://www.sumitomocorp.co.jp/english/ir—e/annual/ar 2000/img/ar 6-11.pdf.
17. E. Berglöf and E. Perotti, 'The governance structure of the Japanese financial keiretsu', *Journal of Financial Economics*, **36**, 259–84 (1994).
18. J. McGuire and S. Dow, 'The Japanese keiretsu system: an empirical analysis', *Journal of Business Research*, **55** (1), 33–40 (2002). W. Wan and R. Hoskisson, 'A social exchange approach to explain Japan's banking crisis', paper presented at Academy of Management Conference, Denver, August 2002.
19. Sheard, 'Main bank system' provides quotes to support this view from a former executive of the Sumitomo Bank. The close social ties that characterize keiretsu relationships suggest that pushing for drastic restructuring or even bankruptcy risked damaging the level of solidarity and trust in a main bank among keiretsu member firms. Dewenter et al., 'Visibility versus complexity', also comment that the keiretsu groups provide substantial support to group members in times of financial distress that amounts to an implicit group guaranty.
20. Jensen, 'Modern industrial revolution'.
21. H. Kim and R.E. Hoskisson, 'Japanese governance systems: a critical review', in Benjamim Prasad (ed.), *Advances in International Comparative Management*, Greenwich, CT: JAI (1996).
22. S. Kaplan, *Top Executive Rewards and Firm Performance: A comparison of Japan and the US*, Graduate School of Business, University of Chicago (1993). Kaplan shows, for example, that CEOs in Japan held on average 0.24 per cent of shares in their corporations compared with 0.67 per cent for the US.
23. E. Mansfield, 'Industrial R&D in Japan and the United States: a comparative study', *American Economic Review*, **78** (2), 223–8 (1988).
24. For discussion of the general factors necessary for the development of a buyout market, see M. Wright, S. Thompson and K. Robbie, 'Management-led leveraged buyouts: a European perspective', *Journal of Business Venturing*, **7** (1), 47–71 (1992).
25. The Japanese bankruptcy laws do not appear to be particularly adverse towards entrepreneurship. Bankruptcy is decided by the courts. There are limits to the amounts of a claimee's assets that creditors can recover as such assets could include those that are indispensable for the claimee's living. If the claimee clears the debts then he is free to start another business but could be blacklisted by the banks, although this does not necessarily mean that all banks will not lend to the person concerned.
26. The report recognized that M&A had an important role to play in effecting corporate restructuring and that buyouts were a 'friendly' form of M&A in the sense that they lower the risk of drastic job cuts and the sudden changes in business terms associated with hostile takeovers. Buyouts were thus seen to be in line with the Japanese corporate mentality.
27. Y. Yafeh, 'Corporate governance in Japan: past performance and future prospects', *Oxford Review of Economic Policy*, **16** (2), 74–84 (2000).
28. Venture capital firms/funds tends to be focused on early-stage investments while private equity firms/funds tend to focus on later-stage investments such as management buyouts and development capital. In Europe both venture capital and private equity firms co-exist as members of national venture capital associations.

29. B. Black and R. Gilson, 'Venture capital and the structure of capital markets: banks versus stock markets', *Journal of Financial Economics*, **47**, 243–277 (1998).
30. There is some evidence that Japanese venture capital firms have traditionally been less involved in monitoring investees than their US counterparts. See D. Hurry, A. Miller and E. Bowman, 'Calls on high-technology: Japanese exploration of venture capital investments in the United States', *Strategic Management Journal*, **13** (2), 85–102 (1992).
31. M. Wright, S. Thompson and K. Robbie, 'Buy-ins, buy-outs, active investors and corporate governance', *Corporate Governance: An International Review*, **4** (4), 222–34 (1996). In the UK, monthly financial reports are required in over 80 per cent of cases while board representation is required in about half of cases.
32. M. Wright, K. Robbie, S. Thompson and K. Starkey, 'Longevity and the life-cycle of management buyouts', *Strategic Management Journal*, **15** (3), 215–28 (1994).
33. D. Ibison, 'Nasdaq Japan faces up to an uncertain future', *Financial Times*, August 15, 2002.
34. Y. Yafeh, Corporate governance in Japan: past performance and future prospects', *Oxford Review of Economic Policy*, **16** (2), 74–84 (2000).
35. A comparable scheme in France, introduced in France under La Loi De Delors in 1984, had to be modified shortly afterwards because the administrative procedure was too slow. C Heuze, 'Buyouts in France', *Acquisitions Monthly–MBO Supplement*, October (1991).
36. A. Holzhausen, 'Japanese employment practices in transition: promotion policy and compensation systems in the 1990s', *Social Science Japan Journal*, **3**, 221–35 (2000); R. Dore, 'Will global capitalism be Anglo-Saxon capitalism?', *Asian Business and Management*, **1**, 9–18 (2002).
37. Different approaches to the valuation of venture capital investments have been identified across countries. See e.g. S. Manigart, K. de Waele, M. Wright, K. Robbie, P. Desbrières, H. Sapienza and A. Beekman, 'The value of private equity investments by venture capital firms: a comparative study of the US, UK, France, Belgium and Holland', *European Financial Management*, **6** (3), 389–404 (2000).
38. S. Makino and P. Beamish, 'Matching strategy with the choice of joint venture ownership structure', *Academy of Management Executive*, **12** (4), 17–27 (1999).
39. Informal relationships do form an important aspect of monitoring buyouts in the West but there appears to be a greater contractual underpinning of relationships. See D. Hatherly, J. Innes, J. MacAndrew and F. Mitchell, 'An exploration of the MBO–financier relationship', *Corporate Governance: An International Review*, **2** (1), 20–29 (1994). This is similar to arguments in regard to supplier–carmaker relationships that trust (versus formal contracts) is more important in Japan than in the US or other western countries. See J.H. Dyer and W. Chu, 'The determinants of trust in supplier–automaker relationships in the US, Japan, and Korea', *Journal of International Business Studies*, **31**, 259–85 (2000).
40. A. Boltho and J. Corbett, 'The Assessment: Japan's stagnation – can policy revive the economy?', *Oxford Review of Economic Policy*, **16** (2), 1–16 (2000).
41. M. Wright, K. Robbie, S. Thompson and K. Starkey, 'Longevity and the life-cycle of management buy-outs', *Strategic Management Journal*, **15** (3), 215–28 (1994).
42. G. Baker and G. Smith (1998), *The New Financial Capitalists: Kohlberg, Kravis and Roberts and the Creation of Corporate Values*, Cambridge: Cambridge University Press.

PART V

Impact of Buy-outs

9. Assessing the impact of management buyouts on economic efficiency: plant-level evidence from the United Kingdom

Richard Harris, Donald S. Siegel and Mike Wright

1. INTRODUCTION

During the 1990s, there was a resurgence in management buyouts (MBOs) in the United Kingdom, with the value of assets transferred rising from £3 billion in 1990 to £17 billion in 1999. In an MBO, senior managers purchase a controlling interest in a firm's common stock, typically using funds borrowed against the firm's physical assets or cash flows as collateral to finance the acquisition. Divisional buyouts and buyouts of privately held firms are also quite common.

A critical policy issue concerning MBOs is whether they enhance economic efficiency. The standard empirical approaches to addressing this question are to analyse the impact of buyouts on stock prices or accounting profits (see Kaplan, 1989 and Jensen, 1993). These methods are problematic for several reasons. First, many economists are increasingly skeptical about the *efficient markets* hypothesis (Shleifer, 2001), which asserts that changes in share prices following announcements of buyouts reflect changes in future real performance or economic efficiency. Second, accounting profits are not necessarily perfectly correlated with real performance. Policy decisions regarding the optimal level of buyout activity hinge mainly on its impact on economic efficiency (i.e., the *social* returns to buyouts), not on their effects on share prices or profitability (i.e., the *private* returns to buyouts). Finally, most buyouts involve privately held companies or divisions of larger, publicly held firms, which precludes an analysis of stock prices or accounting profits. Thus, analyses of buyouts based on publicly available datasets (e.g., COMPUSTAT or DATASTREAM) could generate misleading estimates of the social returns to buyout activity.

To overcome these limitations, Lichtenberg and Siegel (1990) (henceforth, LS) asserted that it is more desirable to assess the *total factor productivity* (TFP) of *plants* before and after MBOs. Based on an analysis of the US Census Bureau's Longitudinal Research Database (LRD), which contained data on more than 19 000 mostly large US manufacturing plants for the years 1972–1988, the authors found that MBO plants had higher TFP than representative establishments in the same industry before they changed owners. However, they also reported that MBO plants experienced significant improvements in TFP after the MBO. More importantly, the authors also found that this enhancement in economic performance could not be attributed to reductions in R&D, wages, capital investment, or layoffs of blue-collar personnel.

The purpose of this chapter is to extend this type of productivity analysis in three important ways. First, we analyze a considerably larger sample of MBOs. Second, we employ more sophisticated econometric techniques and include more control variables than in the previous study. Finally, we have many more recent data, as our buyouts occurred during the years 1994–1998.

2. REVIEW AND CRITIQUE OF EVIDENCE ON UK MANAGEMENT BUYOUTS

Statistics on various *types* of UK MBOs are presented in Table 9.1, based on the number and market value of transactions, respectively. These figures indicate that most MBOs occur below the firm level, with the typical deal representing the divestment of a subsidiary of a large firm or a transaction that affects only a few plants. Table 9.1 also reveals that most buyouts involve privately held companies. Full-firm MBOs of publicly traded companies constitute only a very small percentage of aggregate buyout activity.[1]

These stylized facts underscore the difficulties of gathering pre- and post-buyout performance data. Two concerns are that there are few publicly available data on divisions and individual plants. Note also that the entities involved in these transactions are privately held after the MBO occurs, even in the case of a full-firm MBO involving a publicly traded company. Interestingly, it is actually easier to collect information on the characteristics of privately held firms in the United Kingdom than in the United States, due to the existence of the FAME and ONESOURCE UK Private + databases. The two files contain similar firm-level data from corporate financial statements, as do COMPUTSTAT and its British equivalent, known as DATASTREAM.

Amess (2003) presents UK evidence on the effects of full-firm MBOs on TFP, based on ONESOURCE company-level data. We assert that it is

Table 9.1 Characteristics of UK management buyouts (percentages by number and value of deals)

Year	Full-firm MBOs of publicly traded companies		Full-firm MBOs of privately held companies		Divisional MBOs		Other	
	Number	Value	Number	Value	Number	Value	Number	Value
1982	2.0	46.9	8.5	6.3	58.7	27.7	30.8	19.1
1983	0.8	0.4	10.8	8.5	63.8	74.7	14.6	16.4
1984	0.4	0.2	13.1	9.5	59.8	71.8	16.7	19.5
1985	2.7	6.6	23.2	10.1	59.0	77.8	15.1	5.5
1986	7.6	18.1	20.7	10.8	59.0	59.5	12.7	11.6
1987	10.8	17.1	27.1	8.8	45.0	62.6	17.1	11.5
1988	6.6	21.3	32.3	13.1	46.8	60.0	14.3	5.6
1989	7.0	58.1	33.4	6.8	50.7	32.8	8.9	2.3
1990	3.5	12.2	30.1	16.5	47.3	58.2	17.1	13.1
1991	2.0	3.1	26.7	16.5	47.8	62.4	24.6	18.0
1992	3.3	1.9	27.6	17.7	46.8	64.7	22.3	15.7
1993	2.6	1.0	26.8	12.0	47.0	70.5	23.6	16.5
1994	1.6	6.2	34.4	22.1	45.4	51.5	18.6	20.2
1995	1.7	1.4	39.2	29.7	42.2	52.2	16.9	16.7
1996	1.2	0.9	36.9	17.2	40.8	49.5	21.1	32.4
1997	1.9	4.8	40.6	22.0	38.0	59.8	19.5	13.4
1998	4.8	18.5	41.0	18.3	38.5	47.1	15.7	16.1

Source: CMBOR (2002).

inappropriate to estimate TFP using such data, for two reasons. First, the construction of TFP measures requires reliable and comprehensive information on capital and intermediate materials. These variables are typically not reported in financial statements and thus are not contained in COMPUSTAT, DATASTREAM, or ONE-SOURCE files. Second, the accuracy of TFP measures also depends on the accuracy of input and output price deflators, because inputs and output should be computed in constant dollars. The problem is that many large firms have plants in diverse industries, where there may be substantial variation in price changes. However, in files such as COMPUSTAT, these organizations must be classified, at the corporate level, into a single four-digit SIC industry. As shown in Lichtenberg and Siegel (1991), the use of a single set of output and input deflators can introduce substantial measurement error into the calculation of TFP measures. And finally, as mentioned previously, much MBO activity occurs below the firm level. Thus, it is best to use plant-level data to examine the impact of MBOs on economic performance.

3. ECONOMETRIC MODEL

The first and only plant-level study of the relationship between MBOs and TFP was LS (1990). These authors employed a two-stage approach to assess the impact of MBOs on TFP. In the first stage, they computed residuals from within-industry (four-digit SIC) OLS (ordinary least squares) regressions of Cobb–Douglas production functions of the following form (with error terms suppressed):

$$\ln Y_i = \sum_{k=1}^{k} \beta_k \ln X_{ki}, \tag{9.1}$$

where Y is output, X is a vector of k inputs, and i refers to a plant. The second-stage equation was

$$RELPRO_{i,t+m} = f(MBO_{it}), \tag{9.2}$$

where *RELPROD* is the productivity residual of plant i in year $t+m$, and where *MBO* is a dummy variable that equals 1 if the plant was involved in an MBO in year t, and 0 otherwise.

In contrast, our approach is based on GMM (general method of moments) estimation of within-industry (two-digit SIC), one-stage augmented Cobb–Douglas production functions. A one-stage estimation procedure provides more efficient econometric estimates of the conventional arguments of the production function and other determinants of productivity (e.g., a set of MBO dummy variables) than those generated using the two-stage approach. We estimate variants of the following equation:

$$\begin{aligned}\ln(OUTPUT_{it}) = {} & \beta_0 + \beta_1 \ln(CAPITAL_{it}) \\ & + \beta_2 \ln(LABOR_{it}) + \beta_3 \ln(MATERIALS_{it}) \\ & + \beta_4 PREMBO_{it} + \beta_5 POSTMBO_{it} + \beta_6 \ln(AGE_{it}) \\ & + \beta_7 AA_{it} + \beta_8 t + \beta_9 US_{it} + \beta_{10} EU_{it} + \beta_{11} OFO_{it} \\ & + \sum_{j=1}^{18} \theta_j SIC_{ij} + \sum_{k=1}^{11} \gamma_k REG_{ik} + a_{it},\end{aligned} \tag{9.3}$$

where *OUTPUT* is real gross output; *CAPITAL* refers to plant and machinery capital stock;[2] *LABOR* is total employment;[3] *MATERIALS* is real intermediate inputs; *PREMBO* is a dummy that equals 1 if the plant was involved in a MBO during 1994–1998, *POSTMBO* is a dummy that equals

1 in each year after a buyout occurs; *AGE* is the number of years the plant has been in operation;[4] *AA* is a dummy that equals 1 if the plant is located in an Assisted Area of Great Britain; t is a time trend; *US*, *EU* and *OFO* are dummies that equal 1 if the plant is owned by a US, EU, or other foreign parent company; the first sigma sign contains 18 industries (SIC codes); *SIC* is a dummy for the two-digit SIC industry of the plant (1980 SIC); the second sigma sign contains 11 regions; *REG* is a dummy that is equal to 1 if the plant is located in a specific standard UK region; and a_{it} is an error term.

This error term is assumed to consist of three components:

$$a_{it} = \eta_i + \vartheta_t + e_{it}, \qquad (9.4)$$

with η_i affecting all observations for cross-section unit i, ϑ_t affecting all units for time period t, and e_{it} affecting only unit i during period t. We assume that e_{it} is serially correlated so that

$$e_u = \rho e_{u-1} + u_{it}, \qquad (9.5)$$

where u_{it} is uncorrelated with any other part of the model, and $|\rho| < 1$. As shown in Blundell and Bond (1999), if we invoke these assumptions, equation (9.3) can be transformed into a dynamic form involving first-order lags of the variables and a well-behaved error term.

The inclusion of age, foreign ownership, assisted area, and regional dummies as control variables is critical, given recent empirical evidence, based on the Annual Respondents Database (ARD), indicating that these factors explain significant variation in TFP across plants (see Griffith, 1999, and Harris, 2002). Because our final sample consists of 35 752 plants, we have sufficient degrees of freedom to include two-digit SIC industry dummies and to interact the industry dummies with capital, labor, materials, and the MBO dummies. Thus, we estimate separate pre- and post-buyout production functions for each industry.

Equation (9.3), or its dynamic counterpart, can be estimated using the Arellano–Bond (1998) GMM systems method in PcGive (dynamic panel data analysis), because this is sufficiently flexible to allow for the endogeneity of inputs (through the use of appropriate instruments) and a first-order autoregressive error term. We use the GMM systems approach to estimate the model in levels and first differences. Blundell and Bond (1999) argue that including both lagged levels and lagged first-differenced instruments leads to significant reductions in finite sample bias as a result of exploiting the additional moment conditions inherent in adopting their system approach. All data also need to be weighted to ensure that the samples are representative of the population of UK manufacturing plants.[5]

4. DATA AND EMPIRICAL RESULTS

To assess the impact of MBOs on the productivity of UK manufacturing plants, we merged two files. The first is the ARD, constructed by the UK Office for National Statistics, consisting of individual establishment records from the Annual Census of Production.[6] The ARD file contains detailed data on output, materials, energy, employment, and numerous plant and firm characteristics. This information can be used to construct measures of TFP, based on estimation of plant-level production functions.

Griffith (1999) and Harris (2002) provide overviews of the ARD database. Each year, information is collected from approximately 14 000–19 000 establishments (known as *reporting units*), based on a sampling methodology that is biased toward larger establishments. However, the ARD file contains a higher proportion of smaller plants than the version of the LRD examined by LS. More importantly, the ARD is an unbalanced panel, in contrast to the extract of the LRD used by LS, which consisted mainly of continuous plants. The unbalanced nature of the ARD is useful, for there is considerable entry and exit over a long sample period such as ours (1982–1998). Indeed, our final sample consists of 35 752 establishments.

The second file contains comprehensive data on the characteristics of UK buyouts from the Centre for Management Buy-out Research (CMBOR) at the University of Nottingham, consisting of the population of UK MBOs since the early 1980s. The primary source of information is a biannual survey of all private equity and debt providers in the buyout market.[7] Other data sources include press releases, company reports and stock exchange circulars. This approach enables extensive cross-checking of data to ensure reliability. CMBOR (2002) reports that there were 1564 buyouts in the United Kingdom during 1994–1998, approximately half involving manufacturing firms.

ONS linked the ARD and CMBOR files, by matching names, addresses and postal codes from the CMBOR file to comparable information in the ARD from the ONS interdepartmental business register (IDBR), which was introduced in 1994.[8] It appears that we matched at least one plant for almost the complete universe of MBOs in manufacturing, for we were able to locate 979 of 1564 buyouts (62.6%) in the ARD (using the IDBR). This high rate of matching implies that many firms classified in services at the corporate level have manufacturing establishments.

The end result is that we have a much larger and more representative sample than LS, who identified 48 MBOs and 399 plants. The corresponding numbers for our final sample are 979 MBOs and 4877 plants that experienced an MBO during the years 1994–1998. Another improvement is that we have a more unbalanced panel of establishments. Table 9.2 presents

Table 9.2 Comparison of mean values of output, capital, labor, and other variables used in the production function analysis (for MBO and non-MBO UK manufacturing plants, 1994–1998)

Variable	MBO plants	Non-MBO plants	*t*-tests for differences in means
Real gross output (£m, 1990 prices)	3.3	4.2	6.29**
Real value of plant and machinery capital stock (£m, 1980 prices)	0.7	1.1	5.95**
Plant employment	59	54	1.75
Percentage foreign-owned	6.9	11.9	13.44**
Percentage located in Assisted Areas	40.3	39.5	−1.15
Number of plants	4877	30 875	

Note: ** Significant at 5% level.

Source: Authors' calculations based on the linked ARD–CMBOR data set.

mean values of variables used in the plant-level production function analysis. It appears that MBO plants produce less output and consume less capital than non-MBO plants.

Table 9.3 reports parameter estimates of equation (9.3). Given that the model contains 148 parameters, we report only those coefficients that are statistically significant. Two sets of results are presented: short-run and long-run estimates, where the long-run estimates were derived from the short-run dynamic results. The short-run regressions include lagged values of *OUTPUT*, *LABOR*, *MATERIALS* and *CAPITAL* as regressors. The diagnostic tests reveal that the model appears to be well specified; that is, we appear to have a first-order autoregressive error term and an appropriate set of instruments. Recall that our model assumes that there should be negative first-order serial correlation of differenced residuals, but an absence of second-order serial correlation. Note that the Sargan (χ^2) test of overidentifying restrictions does not allow us to reject the null hypothesis that the instrument set is valid. The parameter estimates suggest that there are constant returns to scale in UK manufacturing, as the estimated elasticities of output with respect to capital, labor and materials sum to 1.03. Consistent with Harris (2002), we find that foreign-owned plants tend to be more productive than domestic plants, whereas older plants and those in Assisted Areas tend to be less productive.

Table 9.3 General Method of Moments estimates of plant-level augmented production functions for 35,752 UK manufacturing establishments for the years 1988–1998 [equation (9.3)]

Coefficient on	Short run		Long run	
	$\hat{\beta}$	*t*-value	$\hat{\beta}$	*t*-value
In *(LABOR)*	0.2380	13.50	0.2574	13.74
In *(MATERIALS)*	0.6569	22.60	0.6629	25.89
In *(CAPITAL)*	0.1321	5.20	0.1336	5.79
AGE	−0.0631	−4.62	−0.0808	−4.69
AA (Assisted Area)	−0.0165	−4.09	−0.0212	−4.09
US-owned plant	0.0689	10.00	0.0882	10.27
Other foreign owner	0.0615	6.43	0.0788	6.50
PREMBO	−0.0157	−2.70	−0.0202	−2.70
POSTMBO	0.7049	4.94	0.9032	4.96
PREMBO × *SIC24* (nonmetallic minerals)	0.4641	2.55	0.5946	2.55
POSTMBO × *SIC24* (nonmetallic minerals)	−0.9969	−4.45	−1.2773	−4.45
PREMBO × *SIC25* (chemicals)	0.2874	7.70	0.3683	7.65
POSTMBO × *SIC25* (chemicals)	−0.3915	−3.64	−0.5017	−3.64
PREMBO × *SIC33* (office machinery)	−0.1081	−2.14	−0.1385	−2.14
POSTMBO × *SIC34* (electrical eng.)	−0.0598	−2.78	−0.0767	−2.78
POSTMBO × *SIC42* (drink and tobacco)	−0.2333	−5.09	−0.2990	−5.11
PREMBO × In *(LABOR)* × *SIC24*	−0.1410	−3.25	−0.1806	−3.25
POSTMBO × In *(LABOR)* × *SIC24*	−0.2721	−2.09	−0.3486	−2.09
PREMBO × In *(MATERIALS)* × *SIC24*	0.2664	3.22	0.3413	3.22
POSTMBO × In *(MATERIALS)* × *SIC24*	0.9069	5.28	1.1619	5.27
POSTMBO × In *(CAPITAL)* × *SIC24*	−0.9202	−6.91	−1.1790	−6.88
POSTMBO × In *(LABOR)* × *SIC25*	0.0510	2.57	0.0653	2.57
PREMBO × In *(MATERIALS)* × *SIC25*	−0.1957	−4.16	−0.2507	−4.14
PREMBO × In *(CAPITAL)* × *SIC25*	0.1597	3.75	0.2046	3.73
POSTMBO × In *(LABOR)* × *SIC31*	0.0332	2.99	0.0653	2.99
POSTMBO × In *(MATERIALS)* × *SIC31*	−0.1317	−3.53	−0.1687	−3.53
POSTMBO × In *(CAPITAL)* × *SIC31*	0.0528	2.41	0.0677	2.41
PREMBO × In *(LABOR)* × *SIC34*	0.0155	3.60	0.0199	3.59
PREMBO × In *(LABOR)* × *SIC35*	−0.0281	−2.73	−0.0360	−2.75
POSTMBO × In *(LABOR)* × *SIC35*	0.0500	2.93	0.0640	2.94
PREMBO × In *(MATERIALS)* × *SIC35*	0.1183	3.74	0.1515	3.77
POSTMBO × In *(MATERIALS)* × *SIC35*	−0.1786	−3.72	−0.2289	−3.73
PREMBO × In *(CAPITAL)* × *SIC35*	−0.0490	−2.49	−0.0628	−2.50
POSTMBO × In *(CAPITAL)* × *SIC35*	0.0944	2.51	0.1210	2.51
PREMBO × In *(MATERIALS)* × *SIC41*	0.0674	2.53	0.0863	2.54
PREMBO × In *(LABOR)* × *SIC42*	0.0282	3.65	0.0361	3.68
PREMBO × In *(CAPITAL)* × *SIC42*	−0.0404	−4.30	−0.0518	−4.33
POSTMBO × In *(CAPITAL)* × *SIC42*	0.0569	2.68	0.0729	2.68

Table 9.3 (continued)

Coefficient on	Short run		Long run	
	$\hat{\beta}$	*t*-value	$\hat{\beta}$	*t*-value
PREMBO × In *(LABOR)* × *SIC43*	0.0208	3.96	0.0266	3.98
POSTMBO × In *(LABOR)* × *SIC43*	−0.0301	−2.46	−0.0386	−2.47
PREMBO × In *(MATERIALS)* × *SIC43*	−0.0702	−5.18	−0.0900	−5.17
POSTMBO × In *(MATERIALS)* × *SIC43*	0.1651	3.82	0.2115	3.83
PREMBO × In *(MATERIALS)* × *SIC45*	0.0573	2.23	0.0734	2.23
POSTMBO × In *(LABOR)* × *SIC46*	0.0361	2.12	0.0462	2.12
POSTMBO × In *(MATERIALS)* × *SIC46*	−0.1073	−2.63	−0.1374	−2.63
POSTMBO × In *(CAPITAL)* × $SIC46_i$	0.0479	2.38	0.0614	2.38
PREMBO × In *(MATERIALS)* × *SIC47*	0.0199	1.89	0.0255	1.90
POSTMBO × In *(MATERIALS)* × *SIC48*	0.0734	1.85	0.0941	1.85
PREMBO × In *(CAPITAL)* × *SIC49*	−0.0375	−2.06	−0.0480	−2.06
POSTMBO × In *(MATERIALS)* × *SIC49*	−0.0700	−3.05	−0.0896	−3.03
POSTMBO × In *(CAPITAL)* × *SIC49*	0.0721	4.14	0.0924	4.12
t	0.0050	2.47	0.0065	2.47
Nonmetallic minerals *(SIC24)*	0.0397	3.62	0.0508	3.63
Office machinery *(SIC33)*	0.2548	13.30	0.3264	13.42
Textiles *(SIC43)*	−0.0817	−9.14	−0.1047	−9.36
Paper, publishing *(SIC47)*	0.0505	6.69	0.0648	6.64
East Anglia	0.0202	2.70	0.0258	2.70
East Midlands	−0.0170	−2.83	−0.0218	−2.83
Yorks–Humberside	−0.0146	−3.26	−0.0187	−3.27
North–West	−0.0124	−2.36	−0.0159	−2.36
North	−0.0120	−2.19	−0.0154	−2.19
Wales	−0.0130	−2.18	−0.0167	−2.18
Northern Ireland	−0.0266	−3.39	−0.0340	−3.40
Diagnostic tests*				
Sargan ~ χ^2	1.666	[0.65]		
ml ~ *N(0,* 1)	−24.180	[0.00]		
m2 ~ *N(0,* 1)	1.900	[0.06]		
Zero-slopes ~ χ^2 (×10^5)	26.220	[0.00]		
No. of plants	35 752			
No. of observations	195 676			

Notes: Dependent variable: real gross output. The short-run regressions include lagged values *of OUTPUT, LABOR, MATERIALS* and *CAPITAL* as regressors, with coefficients and í-values (in parentheses) of 0.220 (24.60), −0.037 (−10.04), −0.140 (−10.90) and −0.028 (−4.07), respectively. The model was estimated in PcGive10; all *t*-values are based on robust standard errors; m1 and m2 are tests for first- and second-order serial correlation; the GMM estimator has instruments back to $t-12$ for the model in first differences and $\Delta t-11$ for the model in levels.

* *p*-values in brackets.

We now turn our attention to the coefficients on the pre-and postbuyout dummies. In contrast to LS, we find that, on average, plants involved in MBOs were *less* productive (–1.6% and –2.0% less efficient in the short and long run, respectively) than other plants in the same industry before experiencing a buyout. However, consistent with LS, it appears that MBO plants experience a substantial increase in TFP after an MBO (+ 70.5% and + 90.3% more efficient in the short and long run, respectively). These productivity gains are higher than those reported in the United States. More importantly, these findings appear to be pervasive across sectors, as the average manufacturing plant experienced a substantial increase in TFP in 14 out of 18 industries.

In an effort to 'explain' these efficiency gains, we present mean values of the ratio of post- to pre-MBO levels of output, TFP, labor productivity, employment, capital/labor ratio and materials/labor ratio in Table 9.4. Representative MBO plants generate considerably less output in the post-buyout period, yet downsize their workforce even more dramatically. This results in a significant increase in labor productivity and TFP. These findings, in conjunction with evidence on changes in capital/labor and materials/labor ratios, imply that the improvement in efficiency may be due to measures undertaken by new owners or managers to reduce the labor intensity of production, via outsourcing of intermediate goods and materials.

5. CONCLUSIONS AND SUGGESTIONS FOR ADDITIONAL RESEARCH

Based on comprehensive plant-level data, our results suggest that MBOs may be a useful mechanism for reducing agency costs and enhancing economic efficiency. More generally, the findings are consistent with recent theoretical and empirical evidence (Jovanovic and Rousseau, 2002), suggesting that takeovers shift a firm's resources to more efficient uses and to better managers.

An extension of our analysis would be to examine the productivity impact of different types of MBOs. For instance, private firms could have lower agency costs than publicly traded firms, because they are usually owned and managed by a small, concentrated group of shareholders (e.g., a founder and his family). Thus, we could examine whether differences exist between the TFP effects of public-to-private and private-to-private MBOs. It would also be interesting to assess whether differences exist between the efficiency effects of domestic and foreign MBOs. Finally, there is the phenomenon of the *reverse* buyout (Degeorge and Zeckhauser, 1993), which

*Table 9.4 Mean values of ratio of post-MBO to pre-MBO levels of real output, labor productivity, employment, capital/labor ratio and materials/labor ratio**

Industry (SIC)	Output	Total factor productivity	Labor productivity	Plant employment	Capital/labor ratio	Materials/labor ratio
Total manufacturing	50.5	108.6	112.0	39.0	84.9	137.9
Metal manufacturing (22)	49.1	103.3	124.6	47.8	40.0	113.4
Nonmetallic minerals (24)	14.7	167.0	33.4	15.4	60.5	106.8
Chemicals (25)	36.4	93.1	74.4	32.7	68.1	113.2
Metal goods n.e.c. (31)	54.8	102.4	135.2	46.1	84.5	116.4
Mechanical engineering (32)	88.5	101.6	148.7	68.9	75.2	143.8
Office machinery (33)	147.5	107.8	277.9	71.2	50.5	199.0
Electrical and electronics (34)	53.2	100.2	144.6	42.1	66.3	134.3
Motor vehicles (35)	57.0	100.4	101.1	52.2	135.1	120.4
Other transport equipment (36)	29.9	99.2	117.6	26.8	122.4	132.0
Instrumental engineering (37)	61.3	100.9	117.1	51.8	207.8	111.9
Food (41)	76.8	103.5	122.7	69.2	68.9	104.3
Drink and tobacco (42)	48.5	96.9	80.7	48.9	71.9	107.8
Textiles (43)	112.5	99.9	127.3	80.6	95.8	150.2
Footwear and clothing (45)	89.1	100.0	112.4	70.1	73.6	128.7
Timber and wood (46)	60.8	101.8	137.3	52.0	87.8	111.1
Paper and publishing (47)	59.7	107.9	147.4	46.4	76.1	139.3
Rubber and plastics (48)	69.0	102.5	149.3	60.6	84.5	126.5
Other manufacturing (49)	82.6	100.6	107.2	62.9	230.3	122.6

Note: * All figures are weighted percentages. Only plants that experienced an MBO are included in this analysis (4877 plants).

occurs when an MBO goes public again. It might be useful to analyze TFP before and after reverse MBOs.

ACKNOWLEDGMENTS

We thank Daron Acemoglu, Boyan Jovanovic, Catherine Morrison Paul, two anonymous referees, and participants at the June 2002 North American Productivity Workshop at Union College for comments and suggestions.

NOTES

1. As noted in Lichtenberg and Siegel (1990), this is also the case in the United States.
2. See Harris and Drinkwater (2000) for a discussion of how capital stock measures are constructed using the ARD.
3. Unfortunately, data on hours worked are not available.
4. Plant age is only available from 1970. Thus, plants in existence before 1970 are coded as if they started operations in 1970.
5. Data were weighted prior to use in PcGive10, and thus any automatically generated constant terms were suppressed.
6. The US counterpart of the ARD, the LRD, has been analyzed fairly extensively in recent years. Reviews of LRD-based studies are presented in Caves (1998) and Bartelsman and Doms (2000).
7. This survey yields virtually a 100% response rate, due to CMBOR's reputation for preserving confidentiality and its pledge to provide respondents with a detailed report of trends regarding MBOs.
8. This explains why we only observe buyouts that occurred during 1994–1998. Prior to the introduction of the IDBR in 1994, ONS had a different system for tracking establishments and their corporate parents over time, called the CSO register. Unfortunately, the CSO register was not available after 1994, so we could not identify buyouts that occurred before 1994.

REFERENCES

Amess, Kevin (2003), 'The effects of management buyouts on firm-level technical efficiency: evidence from a panel of U.K. machinery and equipment manufacturers', *Journal of Industrial Economics*, **51** (March), 35–44.

Arellano, Manuel and Stephen R. Bond (1998), 'Dynamic panel data estimation using DPD98 for GAUSS', CEMFI mimeograph, ftp://ftp.ceinfi.es.pdf/papers/ma/dpd98.pdf.

Bartelsman, Eric J. and Mark Doms (2000), 'Understanding productivity: lessons from longitudinal microdata', *Journal of Economic Literature*, **38** (September), 569–94.

Blundell, Richard and Stephen Bond (1999), 'GMM estimation with persistent panel data: an application to production functions', IFS Working Paper no. W99/4.

Caves, Richard E. (1998), 'Industrial organization and new findings on the turnover and mobility of firms', *Journal of Economic Literature*, **36** (December), 1947–82.
CMBOR (2002), 'Trends in UK buyouts', *Management Buy-outs – Quarterly Review from CMBOR* (Spring), 1–14.
Degeorge, François and Richard Zeckhauser (1993), 'The reverse LBO decision and firm performance: theory and evidence', *Journal of Finance*, **48** (September), 1323–48.
Griffith, Rachel (1999), 'Using the ARD establishment level data to look at foreign ownership and productivity in the United Kingdom', *Economic Journal*, **109** (June), F416–F442.
Harris, Richard I.D. (2002), 'Foreign ownership and productivity in the United Kingdom: some issues when using the ARD establishment level data', *Scottish Journal of Political Economy*, **49** (August), 318–35.
Harris, Richard I.D. and Steven Drinkwater (2000), 'U.K. plant and machinery capital stocks and plant closures', *Oxford Bulletin of Economics and Statistics*, **62** (May), 239–61.
Jensen, Michael C. (1993), 'The modern industrial revolution: exit and the failure of internal control systems', *Journal of Finance*, **48** (July), 831–80.
Jovanovic, Boyan and Peter Rousseau (2002), 'Mergers as reallocation', National Bureau of Economic Résearch Working Paper no. 9279.
Kaplan, Steven (1989), 'The effects of management buyouts on operating performance and value', *Journal of Financial Economics*, **24** (October), 217–54.
Lichtenberg, Frank R. and Donald Siegel (1990), 'The effect of leveraged buyouts on productivity and related aspects of firm behavior', *Journal of Financial Economics*, **27** (September), 165–94.
Lichtenberg, Frank R. and Donald Siegel (1991), 'The impact of R&D investment on productivity – new evidence using linked R&D–LRD data', *Economic Inquiry*, **29** (April), 203–28.
Shleifer, Andrei (2001), *Inefficient Markets*, New York: Oxford University Press.

10. Post-privatization effects of management and employee buy-outs

Mike Wright, Trevor Buck and Igor Filatotchev

1. INTRODUCTION

About a decade ago, there was considerable debate about the role of managerial and employee ownership in the privatization of state-owned enterprises in both developed and transition economies (e.g. Ben-Ner, 1993; Smith, 1994). Privatization is now a worldwide phenomenon, with numerous studies available concerning its impact on enterprise strategy and performance. Megginson and Netter (2001) and Djankov and Murrell (2002) provide reviews of the impact of privatization worldwide. Both reviews conclude that privatized firms generally become more efficient and more profitable following the change in ownership. However, their reviews do not explicitly address the impact of privatization through management and employee buy-outs. Although this form of privatization has not tended to involve the largest enterprises in developed market economies, this has been the case in many transition economies. Moreover, numerically, management and employee buy-outs have been used extensively around the world to privatize medium-sized enterprises (Wright et al., 1993b; and below). There is, therefore, a need to synthesize the effects of the management and employee buy-out mode of privatization on enterprises.

This chapter is structured as follows. The first section presents definitions and trends in privatization buy-outs. The second section discusses conceptual issues concerning the expected effects of privatization buy-outs in terms of both performance and longevity or survival. The third section reviews empirical evidence in terms of the impact of buy-outs on productivity and profits performance, attitudinal influences on performance, strategic choices and alternative measures of performance including employment changes, restructuring outcomes, buy-out longevity and the realization of capital gains. The discussion distinguishes the effects of buy-outs in developed and transition economies. The review presented is, therefore, complementary to those of Megginson and Netter (2001) and Djankov and Murrell (2002) by focusing on management and employee ownership after privatization and a wider range of variables. In the final section, some conclusions and policy implications are drawn.

2. DEFINITIONS AND TRENDS

The key general features of buy-outs are: the transfer of ownership of an enterprise to a new legal entity in which managers and employees are significant if not majority shareholders; the recognition of new property rights of managers and employee shareholders through direct share ownership; the importance of monitoring by financing institutions through both mechanisms which result from commitments to service external borrowings and other finance taken out to effect the acquisition, and other processes such as board representation.

Buy-outs can involve a variety of organization forms with various groups of equity holders. The main distinguishing criteria are whether ownership is by management alone (a management buy-out, MBO), evenly spread across all employees (an employee buy-out, EBO), by inside managers and employees (a management-employee buy-out, MEBO), by managers entering the ownership of the firm from outside (a management buy-in, MBI), or by a combination of both outsiders and insiders (a buy-in/buy-out, a joint buy-out, or a voucher buy-out).

In privatization buy-outs, the government may dispose of all or part of the equity of an entity, in the latter case retaining an equity stake which may serve to reduce the need for external finance and/or to exert continuing influence over the firm. Privatization buy-outs may involve the sale of whole enterprises, the divestment of divisions and the break-up of an entire enterprise into many parts. In OECD countries, privatization buy-outs typically involve the sale of assets or shares. In some transition economies, assets may be leased to management, with or without the option to buy, or may be virtually 'given away' through voucher mechanisms. In a voucher buy-out a proportion of the shares in an enterprise are made available to employees either in return for vouchers that have been issued to all adults or at a preferential rate for cash, or both. Where the sale of assets is involved, a financing institution is highly likely to provide both funding and monitoring. Employee share ownership may be effected either through direct share purchase or indirectly through an employee share ownership plan (ESOP). In the case of voucher buy-outs, the introduction of new financing and monitoring by outside institutional shareholders is unlikely.

The UK has seen the largest number of public sector privatizations through management and employee buy-outs among developed countries (Table 10.1). These deals have been identified in the UK since the early 1980s, a total of 273 having been completed. Few of these buy-outs are straight EBOs, MEBOs being more common. These buy-outs covered a wide range of sectors, most notably in respect of the break-up of state- and local-government-owned local bus service providers and the state-owned rail organization. Other significant numbers of privatization buy-outs involved divestment from state-owned steel and car producers as well as local government services and other state government agencies. Large numbers have also been completed in Germany, though these principally relate to the Treuhandanstalt privatizations of the early 1990s. In France, privatization buy-outs in the mid- to late 1980s mainly concerned the divestment of parts of large manufacturing conglomerates, either just before or just after the stock market flotation of the parent company. Although the scope for extensive privatization buy-outs across countries in continental Europe has been much discussed, it is evident that elsewhere

Table 10.1 Number of privatization buy-outs/buy-ins by country: developed economies

Country name	To end 1992	1993	1994	1995	1996	1997	1998	1999	2000
Austria	13	3	6	3	2	0	0	0	0
Denmark	0	0	0	0	0	0	0	0	0
Eire	0	0	2	1	0	0	0	0	0
Finland	4	3	3	2	0	0	3	0	1
France	27	2	2	1	1	3	5	2	0
Germany*	59	43	26	4	0	2	1	0	1
Italy	4	1	2	2	1	2	0	1	1
Netherlands	2	0	2	0	1	0	0	0	0
Norway	1	0	0	0	0	0	0	0	0
Portugal	1	1	0	2	1	0	0	0	0
Spain	1	0	1	0	1	0	0	1	0
Sweden	16	2	1	0	1	1	0	0	1
Switzerland	0	1	1	0	0	0	0	0	0
Total continental Europe	128	56	46	15	8	8	9	4	4
UK	161	13	25	15	33	19	4	1	0
Total	289	69	71	30	41	27	13	5	4

Note: * Includes Treuhandanstalt privatizations.

Source: CMBOR/Barclays Private Equity/Deloitte & Touche.

such transactions have been generally spasmodic except in Austria (Wieser et al., 1997) and Sweden up to the early 1990s.

The importance of MEBOs in privatization in transition economies varies considerably (EBRD, 1997). Direct sales of enterprises as MEBOs were the primary method of large enterprise privatization in nine out of 22 countries in transition and the secondary method in four others. Hence the rankings in Table 10.2 primarily reflect the value of enterprises privatized. Most of these countries were outside the former Soviet Union (FSU), except Tajikistan, Ukraine and Uzbekistan. In Hungary, for example, approximately a third of enterprises disposed of under the self-privatization programme were sold as buy-outs using ESOPs (Karsai and Wright, 1994). In Georgia, Russia and Moldova, management and employee ownership was mainly achieved through 'give-away' buy-outs through privatization voucher programmes that favoured insiders (Estrin and Wright, 1999). In addition, buy-outs have also been widely used for the privatization of large numbers of small and medium sized enterprises (Table 10.2 notes). In emerging markets, privatization management and employee buy-outs have also been notable in Zambia, with small numbers in evidence in sub-Saharan African countries and Malaysia (Wright et al., 2000a).

3. CONCEPTUAL ISSUES

Theories of self-management traditionally provided the basis for the analysis of the effects of enterprise ownership by employees (Stephen, 1984). In practice different employee ownership constitutions (e.g. labour-managed firms, worker-managed firms) complicated the approach, and ownership by senior managers, as a subset of employees in general, presented a further problem. In these circumstances, agency theory has gained wide acceptance as a convenient theoretical lens through which to analyse insider ownership and control (Shleifer and Vishny, 1997).

A major conceptual justification for privatization concerns the governance shortcomings of the state as an enterprise principal (Megginson and Netter, 2001). In state firms, a lack of share ownership by managerial and employee agents means that the incentive to raise firms value is weak or missing. Oversight by a ministerial principal may be better suited to revealing gross misconduct but may be ineffective in promoting and monitoring the attainment of performance targets.

MEBOs in developed economies involve the purchase of a business to improve the prospects for addressing agency cost problems through various mechanisms. The introduction of significant, if not controlling, insider equity ownership is expected to increase incentives for employee agents to

Table 10.2 Methods of privatization of larger enterprises in transition economies to 1997

Country	Sale to outsiders	Voucher-equal access	Voucher-insider concessions	MEBO
Albania	1			
Bulgaria	1	2		
Croatia				1
Czech Republic	2	1		
FYR Macedonia				1
Hungary	1			2[a]
Poland	3	2		1
Romania	2			1
Slovak Republic		2		1
Slovenia	2			1
Estonia[b]	1			2
Latvia[c]	2	1		
Lithuania[d]		1		2
Armenia		1	2	
Georgia			1	2
Kazakhstan	2	1		
Kyrgyzstan		1		
Moldova	2		1	
Russia	2		1	3
Tajikistan				1
Ukraine		2		1
Uzbekistan				1

Notes: 1= primary method; 2= secondary method; 3= tertiary method.

[a] See Karsai and Wright (1994).

[b] OECD estimates to 1995 show among large enterprises 357 trade sales and 120 majority management–employee buy-outs, reflecting the relative importance of privatization methods for the value of enterprises. The relative importance of different methods in terms of the volume of transactions is shown in MEBOs' preference for smaller privatizations which led to 450 employee-owned small enterprises Jan. 1991 to May 1992. Nov. 1992 to Dec. 1995 200–300 insider-owned large enterprises mainly by management. Approximately 36% of privatized enterprises majority owned by insiders, half mainly owned by management and half by a broader group of employees (Mygind, 1997, Table 2 .3 and p. 57).

[c] OECD estimates to 1995 indicate 200 majority management–employee buy-outs, 45 trade sales and 39 minority mass privatizations. Small privatizations in 1992–93 with preferences for employee ownership created 200 MEBOs. 200 insider-owned decentralized privatizations 1992–94. Large privatizations 1994–95 majority outsider with minority stakes through vouchers (Mygind, 1997).

[d] OECD estimates to 1995 show 1500 minority MEBOs, 2920 majority mass voucher privatizations and 63 trade sales.

Source: EBRD Transition Report 1997, p. 90, Table 5.7.

perform. Importantly, insider share ownership is on an individual basis providing the scope to overcome the problems of collective employee ownership (Estrin, 1983; Ellerman, 1993). Closer monitoring, including board representation, by a small group of outside institutional shareholders with commercial objectives can alleviate the problems of government interference. The use of external finance, which carries with it a commitment to servicing that finance, also provides a hard budget constraint that was typically much softer under public sector ownership. The incentive and control effects of insider holdings in buy-out structures may be enhanced where shareholdings are themselves dependent upon the medium-term performance of the firm. The nature of the incentive, control and financing mechanisms involved in privatization buy-outs can be adapted to provide the appropriate balance of managerial and employee discretion that minimizes opportunism and enables entrepreneurial opportunities to be exploited. Both of these issues may have been problematical under public sector ownership (Wright et al., 2000b). However, in former state-owned enterprises, especially in transition economies, managers may not possess the requisite human capital skills to be able to respond effectively to changes in incentives. In these circumstances, an MBI may be appropriate to introduce entrepreneurial managers from outside (Barberis et al., 1996).

The extension of shareholdings to the wider body of employees, either through direct purchase or through an ESOP, to some extent converts employees from agents into principals. The result is closer alignment of employees' goals with those of equity-holding management and any outside investors, leading to improved incentives to enhance productivity and performance. By becoming shareholders, employees may be encouraged to monitor themselves, reinforcing the vertical supervisory structure. This may be especially important where tasks are non-routine, requiring judgement, particularly entrepreneurial judgement, on the part of employees. The extent to which employee ownership in a buy-out generates these gains may, however, be dependent on employees' participation in decision-making and perceptions of whether they 'feel like owners' (Pendleton et al., 1998).

Besides these positive benefits, however, insider ownership (without external monitoring) can in theory also lead to negative, entrenchment behaviour by employee agents, as they forgo increases in firm value to protect their own job security and job-based sources of utility (Shleifer and Vishny, 1997). This possibility is exacerbated in transition economies, where capital markets are under-developed, and 'give-away' privatizations render unnecessary any investments from insiders' own funds, where executives in any financing institutions may not have the requisite monitoring skills, and credit may not be 'hard' where bankruptcy legislation is weak and/or where the extension of inter-firm credit is prevalent.

In MEBOs that arise from 'give-away' voucher privatization programmes, incentive and control mechanisms may be problematical. The general absence of the need to take on external finance to fund the purchase weakens or removes the governance effect from the pressure to service credit. In the absence of outside pressure, the extent to which restructuring will take place depends on the motives for insiders to hold shares. Management and employees may acquire shares for insurance (i.e. entrenchment) as well as for equity investment purposes. In the former case restructuring is expected to be low as insiders seek to protect their positions. A culture of social ownership of assets may have an important influence on the choice of some of insider ownership as the preferred privatization mode and reinforce this kind of entrenchment attitude. If insiders acquire shares for asset purposes, they may decide to sell shares to outsiders once private information about company prospects has been reflected in share prices. Management may prefer outside control where they are oriented towards restructuring since outsiders can provide the necessary injection of funds. Acquisition of shares by outsiders may lead to a change in control and the ability to effect restructuring. Moreover, outsiders may be the only feasible source of finance for investment. Employees may be tempted to sell shares where they need to realize capital gains to purchase consumer goods and where their dispersed shareholdings convey little influence on the control of an enterprise (Earle and Estrin, 1996).

Agency theory, therefore, identifies the capacity of manager and employee ownership to generate negative entrenchment effects, as well as positive effects flowing from improved incentives, with 'give-away' privatizations tilting the balance towards a net negative outcome. In addition it must be recognized that any positive feelings of 'belongingness' felt by employee owners towards their firm can be negated by ownership without a significant share of control in the form of concrete participation in important enterprise decisions. As with the potential agency trade-off between improved incentives and insider entrenchment, it is to be empirically determined whether employee participation and belongingness, on the one hand, or disillusion and cynicism with token participation, on the other, are dominant in the west and in transition economies. The balance of these forces of course influences productivity.

3.1 Longevity and Survival

In general, the longevity and survival of a buy-out structure as a long-run indicator of firm performance is influenced by the objectives of the managerial and employee shareholders, the objectives of any funding institution and the exigencies of the market that affect the firm itself (Wright et al., 1994a). Financing institutions may need to obtain an exit from the buy-out within a particular time period, especially if they are closed-end funds. Life-cycle theories suggest that the most important characteristics likely to influence the longevity of a buy-out are rapidly changing markets, a fast-growing company, the concentration of markets making economies of scale and scope necessary for survival, and relatively high levels of merger activity. Privatization buy-outs whose expansion or development have been frustrated by the constraints of state ownership may pass through an initial growth spurt when they are first privatized, only to come up against new constraints that force them to exit in order to continue to develop or even survive. Privatization policies to restructure industries and markets through the break-up of large state monopolies may be subsequently followed by intensive merger activity as part of the search for a new stable industry structure. In transition economies, the need for finance, especially where privatization has involved a 'give-away' buy-out, may have major implications for longevity and survival. Enterprises may need to seek strategic partners and to make themselves attractive to potential partners. Where this is not possible, enterprises may be expected to languish for some time, especially if the enforcement of bankruptcy legislation is weak. Comparing developed and transition economies, developed labour and capital markets in the former may generally provide greater scope for exit by factors of production than in the latter.

ESOPs and other newer forms of employee ownership may appear in principle to offer greater potential for the longevity of MEBOs (Jones and Mygind, 2000). In contrast to cooperatives, there is usually the presence of a commercially oriented managerial cadre and expectations of democratic control, with its downside problems (as well as potential benefits), are typically weaker. In contrast to more narrowly defined MBOs, the presence of a significant, concentrated body of shareholders in the ESOP may reduce the possibility that the firm will be sold over the heads of the employees. However, other factors may create pressures for further ownership change. In leveraged ESOPs, as the head loan is repaid, share values multiply, providing a strong incentive for employees to sell. As dividends are rarely paid, exiting may be more attractive as it provides the only direct financial reward from ownership. The presence of internal share markets can enable employees to sell without the firm itself changing its overall ownership structure. However, it may be the case that share ownership becomes more concentrated over time. Efforts to restrict share sales by imposing lengthy retention periods or limited internal trading may be undesirable since they can tie up the capital of low-income earners and reduce the opportunity to realize gains from investment.

Hence, employee ownership in buy-outs may be a transitional stage in the development of an enterprise. Although this may be undesirable where the objective has been to promote the social aspects of share ownership, wider employee share ownership of a privately held business may be appropriate only for a particular period of time. Changing market conditions and the objectives of the equity holders may mean that, in order to continue to be economically successful, the ownership structure needs to change.

In transition economies, the stability and longevity of insider ownership in voucher buy-outs may depend heavily upon the objectives of employees and managers. If employees value current employment in the firm above future (uncertain) employment in the private sector, they may be reluctant to sell to outsiders who are likely to enforce restructuring (Filatotchev et al., 1999a). If managers prefer insider control, they will buy shares from employees. This approach to entrenching their position may especially arise if they are 'Red Directors' appointed during the Soviet era and are less optimistic about their employment prospects on the external managerial labour market. Managers may be able to influence the nature of share sales by requiring employees to either sell their shares through manager-controlled companies or to offer shares to other managers and employees. These arguments would suggest a persistence of insider control but with a reduction in employee shareholdings and a corresponding increase in managerial shareholdings. Where managers prefer outside control they may still buy shares from employees, reselling them to outsiders at higher prices.

3.2 Methodologies

An empirical review of MEBOs and their impact in the west and in transition economies must confront a host of methodological problems that obstruct comparisons and conclusions.

It must be recognized that assessing the impact of MEBOs, whether purchased or given away, is considerably more problematical than the case of privatization through stock market flotations. The amount of public information available on buy-outs is generally limited by their status as private companies. Ironically, information on the main independent governance variables, i.e. employee ownership and control, is often more freely available in transition economies than in the west as a result of extensive surveys. The measurement of firm performance presents severe difficulties, however. Generally there is a choice between accounting-based variables like profit and productivity that are severely compromised by mis-reporting and inflation-adjustment problems, and 'softer' measures of firm performance (e.g. employment levels, human resource investments etc.), strategies and insiders' attitudes. In the UK, performance data are publicly available for all but the smallest of private companies. Although the relevant financial reporting legislation has been enacted in many transition economies, there are problems in its enforcement especially in private firms where attempts may be made to hide profits from the state and from organized crime (EBRD, 1998). Analysis may be made difficult because of the problems of inflation and devaluation over time and by the fictitious reporting of asset values in an environment where assets may be transferred out of companies by dominant owners (Estrin and Wright, 1999).

As a result, studies often rely on survey questionnaires or case studies rather than archival accounting and financial data, and, of course, performance information collected through surveys may also be subject to measurement error. These problems are exacerbated by the differences between reporting regimes both between developed and transition economies and within each of these blocs. In the case of surveys, a further fundamental problem often prevents assessment of the representativeness of samples: the general absence of information on the population of employee-owned firms.

Once insider governance, strategies, attitudes and performance have been measured, causal ambiguity represents a further major problem. Selection bias may distort results, e.g. preceding performance may influence governance, and resolution of this problem usually requires measures of preceding levels of variables that are often unavailable. Non-governance influences on strategies and performance must also be controlled for. Where feasible, these methodological problems and the way in which they are addressed will be discussed below.

4. EVIDENCE

This section reviews the evidence from developed and transition economies regarding the impact of privatization buy-outs. The analysis begins with a review of evidence on the estimated *productivity and profits* impact of managerial and employee ownership on firm performance in transition economies within the FSU and in CEE. Given the rather ambiguous outcomes from these studies, reported below, the analysis then proceeds with reviews of evidence relating to the *attitudinal* influences on performance, *strategic* influences behind productivity performance, and *alternative*, deeper measures of performance besides profit and productivity.

In each case, comparisons are made with research results in western countries. In this latter respect, fresh evidence is provided from the authors' research on the longevity and survival of MEBOs in the UK and Western Europe and on the gains on realization of investments.

4.1 Productivity and Profits Performance

In this section, we review evidence from developed economies, then individual transition economies and finally from Djankov and Murrell's (2002) meta-study.

Developed economies

D'Souza et al. (2001) find that in their sample of 118 enterprises worldwide privatized through initial public offering (IPO) profitability decreases as employee ownership increases whereas higher amounts of foreign ownership lead to larger gains in post-privatization efficiency. Evidence relating to efficiency gains in privatization buy-outs in the UK, however, is limited to a number of cases studies which may not be representative of the population. In a series of papers, Parker and colleagues (Parker and Hartley, 1991a, b; Martin and Parker, 1995) examine the effects of various forms of organizational status change involving state-owned enterprises in the UK, including IPOs of the major utilities, corporatization of the Post Office, and the MEBO of National Freight (NFC). They find evidence that, in general, labour productivity growth in NFC post-privatization was substantial and above that for most other firms they examined, supporting their argument that performance will increase as firms move closer towards being owner-managed in a competitive environment.

A study of the 22 privatization buy-outs in Austria up to 1995 that were domestically based and which had more than ten employees showed that of the 14 providing data, ten reported an increase in labour productivity in relation to just before the buy-out (Wieser et al., 1997). This growth appears to be related more to reductions in employment than to increases in turnover. In Austria, privatization buy-outs have tended to occur in lower-performing enterprises where few if any other buyers were available.

Transition economies

In contrast with these positive performance outcomes in developed economies, empirical performance studies on employee ownership in transition economies provide, on balance, a rather mixed view. First, we consider single-country studies. We restrict our focus to those studies that provide data on insider ownership compared to other forms.

Productivity performance data suggest that no one ownership form is consistently associated with higher productivity in transition economies. However, nine of the 18 studies listed in Table 10.3 report a significant positive association of insider ownership with some conventional measure of performance, with six inconclusive. A negative association was found in only three studies.

Table 10.3 Summary of effects of buy-outs on productivity and performance

Study	Country	Findings
Panel A: Insider ownership has significant positive association with performance		
Mygind (1997)	Estonia	Productivity higher in EO, MO and minority IO (no figs)
	Latvia	Productivity higher in IO than SOE (no figs)
	Lithuania	Productivity higher in EO, MO, minority IO (no figs)
Jones and Mygind (2000)	Estonia	EO weak significant positive association with total factor productivity in 1994 only; MO not significant, FO significant positive association with 1994 & 1995; domestic individuals (1994) & no majority (1994/5) also significant positive effect
	Latvia	MO weakly significant positive association with total factor productivity in 1994 only, FO not significant, domestic (individual) ownership and cases of no majority significant positive effect
Smith et al. (1997)	Slovenia	EO positive almost significant association with total factor productivity; 1% increase in ownership → increase in added value of 1.4% in EO, 3.9% in FO
Munteanu (1997)	Romania	MEBO weighted average profit rate increases from 6.1% to 6.8% in one year (authors' calculation)
Earle and Telgedy (2001)	Romania	Labour productivity growth increases: FO −0.16 to 0.30, MEBO 0.05 to 0.07; labour productivity: FO 0.27 to 0.42; MEBO 0.11 to 0.16 (depending on specification)
Lajtai (1997)	Hungary	Sales/employee ratios in MEBOs increase 50% and profit/employee ratio increases 25% in first year post privatization
Rapacki (1995)	Poland	Net margins: MEBO (3.7%), capital privatizations (2.9%); SOEs (2.5%); profit/costs: MEBOs (7.4%); capital privatizations (7.2%); SOE (5.1%)
Vaughan-Whitehead (1997)	Ukraine	Sales/employee ratio: EO 20→23%; SOE 11 → 13%; leasehold 21 → 18%; other joint stock 4% → 5% (93–94)
Estrin and Rosevear (1999a, 1999b)	Ukraine	MO, WO not significantly related to profitability; sales adjust better in IO

Table 10.3 (continued)

Study	Country	Findings
Panel B: Insider ownership has indeterminate association with performance		
Jones and Mygind (2000)	Lithuania	Ownership no significant association with total factor productivity
Jones et al. (1997)	Bulgaria	Using stochastic production frontiers, private ownership significant positive association with efficiency, but worker or employee controlled, codetermination, and cooperative ownership not significant
Anderson et al. (2000)	Mongolia	IO no significant association with value added/employee, sales/employee
Earle (1998)	Russia	After controlling for selection bias in initial OLS regressions, only OO significantly associated with productivity improvements
Djankov (1999a)	Georgia, Moldova	MEBOs higher productivity than voucher BOs, which did not restructure more than SOEs
Djankov (1999b)	Russia, Ukraine, Georgia, Moldova, Kyrgyz, Kazakh	No significant link between labour productivity growth (sales/employee) ownership type; MO, EO beneficial to increasing labour productivity at low levels of ownership and also high levels for MO; FO always positive association with labour productivity growth at any ownership level
Panel C: Insider ownership has significant negative association with performance		
Rock and Klinedinst (1997)	Bulgaria	Labour productivity falls in EO and SOE
Frydman et al. (1999)	Czech, Hungary, Poland	Labour productivity increases in OO 9%; IO falls 8% (90–94)
Jones (1998)	Russia	Firms remaining with EO reduce labour productivity 17% compared to SOE; SOE becoming MO reduce labour productivity 73% p.a.; EO becoming MO reduces labour productivity 31%

Notes: OO – outsider ownership; EO – employee ownership; MO – manager ownership; MEBO – management–employee buy-out ownership; IO – insider ownership; FO – foreign ownership; WO – worker ownership; SOE – state-owned enterprise.

Arguably, such a mixed result should be unsurprising in the context of a wide range of contingencies faced by firms, including firm size, industrial classification, national institutions, privatization policies, etc. In addition, attention must be paid to quality considerations in the studies surveyed. For example, in the 'positive' studies in the upper part of Table 10.3, only Mygind (1997) and Jones and Mygind (2000) use large stratified samples of firms. Earle and Telgedy (2001) use robust specifications that are generally matched by two of the 'negative' studies at the foot of Table 10.3, by Frydman et al. (1999) and Jones (1998).

These latter studies at least begin to address the problem of selection bias, i.e. managers and other employees may use their inside information to 'cherry-pick' the best enterprises. In addition, insiders may be able to take advantage of their insider information to understate the true value of the enterprise by under-reporting pre-privatization revenues. In these circumstances, it is not clear whether subsequent increases in productivity and performance are due to the effects of management incentives or to the distortion of initial information. Frydman et al. (1999) test for this selection bias problem, as well as several others, by contrasting the pre-privatization performance of managerially controlled firms in the Czech Republic, Hungary and Poland with that of firms controlled by other types of owners and find no ownership related bias in the selection of firms for privatization. They find that, in contrast to outsider-controlled firms, insider-controlled firms post-privatization do not show increases in revenues and productivity.

Jones (1998) points out that with considerable changes in ownership structures following privatization (see below), there is also a need for studies of productivity to include specifications relating to ownership and control transitions. Using specifications that emulate Frydman et al. (1999), Jones finds for Russian data that the privatization effect on productivity is much weaker. When ownership transitions are incorporated, firms that remained employee owned experienced falls in labour productivity of 17% per annum compared to state firms. Where managers remained as dominant owners, productivity was insignificant but costs fell substantially relative to state firms. However, formerly state-owned firms that became owned by managers during the period to 1996 performed less well, especially where managers had high levels of influence, suggesting entrenchment behaviour (Filatotchev et al., 1999a). Former employee-owned firms that became bank owned showed the greatest increases in productivity.

It can be seen, therefore, that, while the numerical weight of studies surveyed report a significant positive association between insider ownership and performance conventionally measured, two of the 'negative' studies did use more robust techniques.

Besides these individual studies, in their 'survey-of-surveys' (meta-study) covering 37 different reports, Djankov and Murrell (2002) considered all forms of industrial firms and not just privatized ones, both in the FSU and elsewhere in CEE, and they include studies that do not distinguish insider from other forms of private ownership. With a wide range of performance variables (see below) analysed in relation to ownership patterns across a number of countries, time periods and sample structures, meta-analysis presents aggregation problems. Djankov and Murrell (2002) initially provide comparisons of coefficient means for state and privatized firms. They then go on to analyse ownership variations beyond the state/private dichotomy. From 24 studies in 20 countries, they categorize 11 different ownership dummy variables. GLS regressions are then used to provide composite estimates of the association between ownership dummies and performance. However, performance in individual studies was variously measured with reference to labour productivity, total factor productivity, profitability, total sales, etc.

Their overall finding for the FSU was that, using the (negative) performance association with state ownership as a benchmark, manager and employee ownership appear to have opposite and countervailing associations with productivity performance, with managers having, on balance, a positive, and employees a negative, association. In firms that did not distinguish managerial from employee ownership, the net outcome was positive for all insiders, as for managers. For CEE, however, the association of manager and employee ownership with performance was insignificantly different from state ownership.

However, a major concern of Djankov and Murrell (2002) in their meta-study was to evaluate the studies in terms of adjustment for interaction between ownership and performance. This interaction could include selection bias, e.g. a tendency for the state to privatize firms depending on their performance, technology or size, etc., or any propensity for managers to cede ownership and control to outsiders in weakly performing firms. In other words, performance can influence ownership, either lagged or with simultaneous, reciprocal causation (Finkel, 1995). While the use of prior ownership distributions can be used to take advantage of the time precedence criterion, the use of different time lags and 2SLS techniques reduces, but does not eliminate, the problem. Sequential surveys facilitate analysis in terms of change variables, but in this case there is an important need for quality-adjusted price indices in a period of rapid technological change, when, for example, exporting activity leads to improved product quality controls (Grigorian, 2000).

This mass of evidence on the association between insider ownership and conventional performance measures is difficult to synthesize. The finding of a positive association is common in developed western countries, and the numerical weight of studies in transition economies supports this result, but there are serious doubts about possible selection bias in many of these studies. A meta-study finds a positive association for managerial ownership in the FSU (where 'give-away' buy-outs dominated), but not for workers. Neither produced an association significantly different from that for state ownership in CEE, where purchased buy-outs were more usual.

Given this inconclusive outcome, it may be argued that meta-analysis and reviews of studies relying on conventional measures of performance can be usefully complemented by surveys that target other variables. Although Djankov and Murrell (2002) criticize the use of 'softer' internal variables on which there is (p. 9) 'no consensus' in the literature, it seems worthwhile to initiate a supplementary line of investigation that focuses on the strategic decisions that mediate enterprise governance and performance. This seems particularly appropriate when there is also no unanimity on conventional performance measures. Therefore, after a review of *strategic choices* and their association with governance variables, we consider an even *wider range of performance measures*, in order to build up a wide body of evidence drawn from different perspectives.

First, however, it is necessary to investigate the *attitudes* to *employee ownership* that presumably lay behind productivity variation.

4.2 Attitudes to Ownership

Managers' and other employees' actual participation in decisions, and perceptions of where control resides, may be important influences on observed and future productivity levels.

Developed economies

Bradley and Nejad (1989), in their study of the MEBO of the former state-owned National Freight Corporation, found significant differences in perceptions of the impact of ownership on cooperation and identification between employee shareholders and non-shareholders. Evidence from a sample of 234 employees in four UK bus companies privatized using ESOPs shows, using multivariate analysis, that feelings of ownership among employees were positively associated with commitment to the firm, satisfaction and perceived changes in attitudes and behaviour (Pendleton et al., 1998). Employees with a greater feeling of ownership were also less likely to consider quitting the firm. However, work-group relationships were also found to be as powerful a determinant of commitment as ownership. This suggests that changes in ownership may need to be accompanied by changes in the behaviour of other employees if higher levels of commitment and satisfaction are to be secured from individual employees. Opportunities for participation in decision-making were more important in generating feelings of ownership than employee ownership *per se*. The study also suggested that variations in feelings of ownership were associated with the number of shares held by individuals. Employees who have higher relative levels of share ownership and perceptions of participation were significantly more likely to feel more like owners and in turn to have relatively high levels of commitment and satisfaction with the organization.

Transition economies

Russian evidence suggests that although employees may have significant equity stakes, their involvement in boards of directors and other control mechanisms is generally very low (Filatotchev et al., 1996b). Indeed, a substantial majority of workers in privatized Russian firms believed senior managers were the dominant owners of the enterprise, even where workers owned significant shares (Lissovolik, 1997). Earle et al. (1996) show that management and executive boards, followed by managerial shareholders, have the greatest influence on decisions regarding sales, production, employment, social benefits, investment, etc. However, employee ownership was found to be consistently greater than for other actors except management, with workers being moderately influential over the allocation of profits, especially in employee-owned firms.

In the early stages of the transition process, employee board representation appears to have declined between the year prior to privatization and one year afterwards. In contrast, employee participation in decision-making increased a little after privatization in terms of formal and informal consultations, particularly in terms of formal consultation with workers' assemblies on strategic issues. Later evidence indicates that during 1995–97 there was a slight fall in the number of companies in Russia with employees sitting on the board (Filatotchev et al., 1999d). Where they do have board representation, employees on average hold 2.7 seats compared to management's 3.3.

The low level of influence of employee shareholders is also evident from Hungarian enterprises privatized through MEBOs (Karsai and Wright, 1994), with senior managers typically playing a major role as leaders of the ESOP. Employees in these enterprises did not see themselves as owners but rather focused attention on receiving higher wages and keeping their jobs. Similarly, Neumann's (1994) case study of the Kanizsa Brewery buy-out in Hungary illustrates the reluctance of employees to challenge dominant managers even at the shareholders' general meeting. Lajtai (1997) notes management's awareness of the need for frequent communication with employees in his study of six Hungarian buy-outs but finds that the quality of communication is not good, being primarily oral, and performance information being limited. Latjai suggests that managers are reluctant to see employee owners directly involved in strategic decision-making as their background would probably prevent them from participating effectively, although they have no plans to educate employee shareholders. To avoid conflicts of interest where an employee is both president of the ESOP in a firm and an influential member of the board of directors, some firms were reported to be inviting outside professionals on to the board as representatives of the ESOP.

Rock and Klinedinst (1997) report from their survey of 4000 manufacturing employees in Bulgaria in 1992 that only about a quarter were willing to invest in their enterprise at that point, although they comment that this period was very much the low point in the transition process. Nonetheless, there was some agreement by the employees that if they were to purchase shares they would work harder, ensure output quality, etc. They suggest that from their case study evidence, worker participation in decision-making continues to vary widely but has not generally increased during transition. However, in cases where workers have gained majority control of enterprises, participation in decisions has increased dramatically.

As with conventional productivity studies, therefore, the evidence from surveys of MEBO employees' attitudes is also very mixed for developed and transition economies. Besides employees' attitudes, however, firm strategies (e.g. human resource strategies, downsizing, exporting strategies) can mediate governance and performance. This governance–strategy–performance approach seems useful as a complement to direct governance–performance surveys. Reciprocal causation may still be a problem, but in this case any feedback effects of performance on governance structures must first be mediated through strategies. Separate governance–strategy and strategy–performance investigations may be argued to give less ambiguous results.

4.3 Human Resource Strategies

Developed economies

Analysis of buy-outs indicates that, controlling for other factors, the participation of employees in firms' decisions in privatization MEBOs is associated with a different approach to employee relations reported after the buy-out (Bacon et al., 2001). Using a representative sample of 140 UK buy-outs completed between 1994 and 1997, they find that MEBOs, which are generally privatizations, were more likely than other forms of buy-out, including MBIs and MBOs, to report: the existence of an human resource management (HRM) strategy; trade unions recognized for collective bargaining currently and prior to the buy-out; the protection of employment levels; a greater number of methods used by management to communicate with employees; harmonized terms and conditions; annual appraisals alongside merit pay and employee share ownership; and employee involvement in quality circles and teams. In contrast, more narrow MBOs were more likely to report a change in approach to managing employees, annual appraisals for employees and profit-related pay. The introduction of outside managers, as in buy-ins and hybrid management buy-outs/buy-ins, was more associated with lower levels of union recognition, annual appraisals for employees and profit-related pay. In the buy-outs where employees are not involved in ownership, it appears that the main HR lever is to connect pay with the profitability of the buy-out.

Transition economies

Earle et al. (1996) find in Russia that wages were lowest in worker-owned enterprises. A survey of Russian enterprises by the International Labour Organization (ILO), conducted in 2000 and analysed by the present authors, shows that there is no significant association between employee ownership and wages for managers, skilled and unskilled workers. Bonuses for managers and skilled workers were, however, found to be significantly higher when employee ownership was high, and similarly for two categories of workers' benefits. Similar results were found in a survey of Ukrainian enterprises in 2000 by Bucket al. (2001), who report that employees and managers did sacrifice short-term profitability to promote employee benefits, higher wages, training, etc. as immediate sources of employee utility. Higher wages were also associated with higher levels of insider ownership. Buck et al. (2001) also showed that higher spending on social benefits for employees (either on the old Soviet model of welfare provision or on patterns proposed by new, high-commitment HRM) was associated with improved firm performance. Cost-cutting HRM strategies were found to have a consistently negative influence on performance in the context of the FSU.

This study provides a contrast with earlier evidence from ILO surveys in the mid-1990s that show relatively low wages in employee-owned firms compared with other forms of ownership, although employee-owned firms did tend to pay substantial productivity bonuses, social benefits and profit sharing (Vaughan-Whitehead, 1997).

Mygind (1997) finds from a large sample in Estonia that employee and management ownership were associated with downward flexibility of wages. In contrast, in Lithuania, wage levels were generally higher in employee- and manager-owned firms. Evidence suggests that in Polish management–employee buy-outs wages initially rose faster than in other firms, especially in larger firms, but were subsequently controlled (Nuti,

1997; Jarosz, 1994; Filatotchev et al., 1996b). Similarly, in Hungary, Latjai (1997) finds in his study of six buy-outs that wages increased in the year of privatization but had subsequently been controlled.

To summarize this section, there is no evidence that buy-outs in western and transition economies have consistently favoured higher wages for their insider owners, but some indications that progressive HRM strategies have been encouraged. Of course, employment levels are important features of HRM, but these phenomena are considered later under alternative measures of firm performance, below.

The heterogeneity of traditional performance studies surveyed by Djankov and Murrell (2002) and their reliance on accounting data without rigorous adjustments for inflation, financial reporting, etc. suggests that a wider spectrum of alternative measures of performance should at least be considered to widen the evidence base; it is to these that we now turn.

4.4 Employment Performance

Employment levels are a rather ambiguous aspect of enterprise performance, depending on the firm's circumstances. Thus, high employment accompanying high production may indicate success while high employment at other times may constitute blatant overmanning, which has been a main prediction of agency theory.

Developed economies

In Bacon et al.'s (2001) recent study of all UK buy-outs, a majority (60%) of the buy-outs, that were completed at a time of economic buoyancy, indicated an *increase* in the total number of employees compared to before the buy-out. Over a fifth (22%) reported a decrease in employment. Most buy-outs indicated no significant changes in the number of temporary employees, although more reported an increase in the use of temporary labour than a decrease. For example, 24% indicated an increase in the employment of part-time employees (8% reported a decrease), 13% an increase in employees on fixed-term contracts (7% a decrease), 14% an increase in contractors (7% a decrease) and 20% an increase in temporary agency employees (10% a decrease). Comparing the types of buy-out, the most notable change was the increased use of part-time employees reported by those where outsiders were involved, 67% of investor-led buy-outs (IBOs) and 43% of MBIs. In contrast, only about a fifth of MBOs and MEBOs where privatizations were concentrated saw an increase in the number of part-time employees.

Following a shake-out of employment at the time of ownership transfer in Austrian privatization buy-outs, the vast majority of enterprises had increased employment at the time of the survey (Wieser et al., 1997). In comparison, studies of privatizations in developed market economies involving stock market flotations generally find that employment falls post-privatization but is invariably accompanied by large compensating performance improvements (Megginson and Netter, 2001), although D'Souza et al. (2001) find that their sample of 118 enterprises worldwide privatized through IPO achieved performance improvements without reducing average total employment.

In general, therefore, employment levels have been relatively buoyant in western buy-outs, after initial falls post-privatization.

Transition economies

The balance of findings for transition economies in Table 10.4, however, with nine out of 19 studies showing *more* employment reductions in MEBOs, provides a contrast with the west.

Brown and Earle (2002) show that after privatization, job destruction in Russian firms appears to have been focused on firms with the lowest productivity and to have led these firms to create jobs less actively post-reform. However, they do not distinguish insider and outsider ownership in privatized firms. Table 10.4 summarizes studies relating to employment changes following privatization. A number of studies show marked falls in employment but consider only buy-outs or do not distinguish between managerial and employee insider ownership. Table 10.4 shows that generally in the initial period following privatization (usually one to two years) management and employee ownership has been followed by a reduction in employment. There are mixed results regarding whether this is less than under other non-insider ownership forms but on balance insider ownership appears to lead to less reduction in employment than ownership by outsiders, but greater decreases than in SOEs.

In Russian privatization buy-outs, non-managerial employees do not seem to have been responsible for either blocking or promoting restructuring (Earle et al., 1996). Evidence from a sample of 314 Russian enterprises privatized during the voucher programme and surveyed in 1996 suggests that changes in employment are strongly positively correlated with changes in sales rather than the form of buy-out, that is voucher buy-out versus purchase buy-out (Filatotchev et al., 1999b). However, Aukutsionek and Kapelushnikov (1996) find in their survey of privatized Russian enterprises that about 60% suffered from labour hoarding as enterprise directors saw they had a social responsibility to employees; this share was only slightly below that for state-owned enterprises.

Using data from 541 Ukrainian enterprises surveyed in 1994–95 by the ILO, Vaughan-Whitehead (1997) finds that the highest fall in employment

Table 10.4 Employment changes after privatization buy-out in transition economies

Study	Country	Sample	Employment effect
Panel A: Buy-outs associated with significant positive employment effect			
Frydman et al. (1999)	Czech Republic, Hungary, Poland	209 privatized and SOEs	IO firms lay off fewer workers than OO firms
Anderson et al. (2000)	Mongolia	211 privatized firms	IO reduced employment by less than OO firms
Mygind (1997)	Lithuania	484 large manufacturing, construction and trade firms	Employment fell less in EO and more in OO
Jones (1998)	Russia	111 privatized and SOE firms	Employment grew faster in majority EO firms; where majority EO remained dominant, employment grew faster than SOE
ILO (1994)*	Ukraine	311 all types of ownership	Employment falls in all categories, but EO less than others: EO – 4%, SOE – 8%, leasehold – 11%, other joint-stock companies (JSC) – 12% (93–94)
Panel B: Buy-outs associated with indeterminate or no employment effect			
Earle et al. (1996)	Russia	439 all types of ownership	No effect of EO or MO on change in employment 1992–94
Filatotchev et al. (1996a)	Russia	171 privatized firms	After 1 year, 6.5% increased employment, 38% reduced employment by > 10%; 27% reduced employment by up to 10%
Filatotchev et al. (1999b)	Russia	314 privatized firms	Change in employment associated with change in sales not form of buy-out (voucher vs MEBO)
Estrin and Rosevear (1999b)	Ukraine	150 random sample	Ownership type no effect on employment adjustment after controlling for age of capacity, exporting, energy/cost, barter, employment size
Buck et al. (1999)	Russia, Ukraine, Belarus	97 privatized firms	Greater MO significantly reduces employment but not greater EO or OO after controlling for industry decline, country, employment size and sales/employee

Table 10.4 (continued)

Study	Country	Sample	Employment effect
Panel C: Buy-outs associated with significant negative employment effect			
Mygind (1997)	Latvia	5585 across all ownership forms	Employment fell more in IO firms than in SOEs
Karsai and Wright (1994)	Hungary	17 MEBOs	Declined 10–31% in seven cases; only one case increased employment
Lajtai (1997)	Hungary	6 MEBOs	20% average decline in buy-out year; 5% p.a. decline thereafter
Borbély (1994)	Hungary	1 MEBO	Decline
Jarosz (1994)	Poland	110 lease MEBOs	21% halved employment; 40% reduced employment 31–50%, 9% increased employment
Munteanu (1997)	Romania	447 MEBOs	Total employment of sample fell 9.4% in first year post-privatization
Mygind (1997)	Estonia	666 stratified random sample plus SOEs and foreign-owned firms	MO firms increased employment 9–13%; EO stable; Foreign-owned increased 40%; others declined
Vaughan-Whitehead (1997)	Ukraine	541 all types of ownership	Employment falls in all categories, EO greater fall than SOE or other JSC: EO – 10%, SOE – 9%, leasehold – 13%, other JSC – 8% (94–95)
Buck et al. (2001)	Ukraine	1232 all types of ownership	Employment falls in all categories, EO greater fall than SOE or other JSC: EO – 5%, SOE – 2%, leasehold – 7%, other JSC – 4% (99–00)

Notes: IO – insider owned; EO – employee owned; MO – manager owned; OO – outsider owned; * JSC – joint-stock company.

Source: Quoted in Vaughan-Whitehead (1997).

was experienced by employee-owned firms and leasehold enterprises. This decline was greater than that found in the ILO's survey of Ukrainian firms in 1993–94, when employee-owned enterprises had one of the lowest falls in employment. Vaughan-Whitehead finds that employee-owned firms tend to delay lay-offs more than other ownership forms, preferring to seek alternative forms of restructuring. Results from a sample of privatized enterprises in Russia, Ukraine and Belarus surveyed in 1998 also indicates that, contrary to expectations, employee ownership is not significantly related to employment (Buck et al., 1999). Managerial equity ownership, but not non-managerial employee ownership, was significantly negatively related to employment reduction, providing some indication of entrenchment behaviour. Outside institutional shareholders in these three FSU countries were found to have an insignificant impact on changes in employment levels (Filatotchev et al., 2000). Munteanu (1997) also reports on the basis of large-scale data from the State Ownership Fund in Romania that MEBOs in all sectors experienced reductions in the total number of employees, though it should be noted that in Romania conditions attached to obtaining favourable financing placed restrictions on the reduction of employee numbers.

Hungarian buy-out evidence regarding employment changes is mixed and may be the result of small-scale case studies that may not be representative. One study using 17 privatization buy-out cases suggests that managers recognized the need to gain acceptance for restructuring from employees and thus, despite the lack of involvement of employees in formal decision-making, were cautious in reducing employment except where the financial performance of the company had deteriorated substantially (Filatotchev et al., 1996b). Employment rose in only one case while in the seven cases where employment fell, the reduction varied from 10 to 31%. Lajtai's (1997) study of six Hungarian cases privatized as MEBOs finds an average reduction in the workforce of 20% on privatization and 5% per year thereafter. Borbély (1994) cites the case of Metrimpex to illustrate the impact of the pressure to service debt and deteriorating market conditions. Significant reductions in employment in lease buy-outs, exceeding that for the economy as a whole and falling faster than before privatization, is reported in Poland (Filatotchev et al., 1996b). In the Baltic states, Mygind (1997) reports lower reductions in employment in employee-owned firms in Estonia and Latvia but a greater reduction in insider-owned firms in Latvia.

4.5 Restructuring

Besides reductions in employment, restructuring activities and outcomes encompass changes in products, production and service processes, asset portfolio restructuring, and changes in the relative emphasis of domestic and export markets. These aspects are examined below.

Developed economies

Research on restructuring in privatization buy-outs in the UK is primarily case study based, such as NFC (Bradley and Nejad, 1989), RFS Industries from British Rail and Unipart from Austin Rover (Wright et al., 1993a). The MEBO of Unipart from its highly cash-constrained automobile producer Austin Rover was followed by substantial growth over the next decade arising from increased investment in a new part delivery system, diversification away from but also new long-term contracts with the former parent, the adoption of Japanese production methods and the development of a worldwide customer base (Wright et al., 2001). The introduction of a share option scheme linked to employees' individual performance contributed to substantial cost savings. In contrast, although RFS Industries displayed initial improvements, it subsequently experienced major problems (see below).

A study of restructuring in the 22 Austrian privatization buy-outs with more than ten employees found that the most important and widespread changes were more flexible decision-making processes and higher employees' motivation resulting from higher independence following buy-out (Wieser et al., 1997). A reduction in the influence of political factors and trade unions was also widespread. While there was little change in products, reflecting the pre-privatization emphasis on product quality, there was more of an emphasis on cost efficiency and a more market-oriented approach. Employees were reported to be a key factor in effecting corporate changes. The cultural changes in privatization buy-outs appear to be more extensive than in enterprises privatized through stock market flotation. Hence, it is not surprising that the vast majority of enterprises reported financial problems.

The effects of privatization buy-outs in Austria stand in some contrast to UK experience, where changes in cost efficiencies and restructuring were more important and changes to more flexible decision-making processes of lesser importance.

Transition economies

Filatotchev et al. (2000) in a study of manufacturing firms in Russia, Ukraine and Belarus address selection bias by taking the ownership structure that preceded strategic change. The usual controls for size and industrial classification have been employed to reduce the risk of absent variables giving spurious estimates of associations between variables. They find that managerial ownership was associated with a reluctance to take necessary (employment and capital) downsizing actions.

Employee-dominated firms were significantly less likely to involve managerial turnover than outsider-dominated firms but significantly more likely to do so than manager-dominated firms (Filatotchev et al., 1999b). Using qualitative restructuring indices, Estrin and Rosevear (1999b) find that, consistent with Russian studies, ownership type in Ukraine is not related to performance, measured in terms of management and labour restructuring and financial restructuring following privatization, although product and input restructuring was found to be stronger in insider-owned than outsider-owned firms.

Filatotchev et al. (2001b) extend Earle et al.'s (1996) finding that employee-owned and outsider-owned firms in Russia export significantly more than firms with other forms of ownership. They focus on exporting as a percentage of total sales as a key strategic outcome, since this exposes firms to the need for improved quality control. Presenting four different models for the identification of causation (including lagged preceding exporting levels as an indicator of previous exporting experience), they show that, while ownership structure had an insignificant direct association with performance, governance did affect mediating strategies, and different strategies were in turn related to performance. For example, managerial ownership was positively related to a product strategy that focused on domestic rather than export markets, and to a strategy of product diversification through firm acquisition. In turn, these strategies were negatively associated with export performance. In each of these studies, between-country variations were insignificant. If confirmed elsewhere, these findings of managerial ownership apparently holding back necessary downsizing strategies and export-oriented strategies may have serious implications for conventional measures of performance.

Interestingly, the influence of outsiders through board representation may have as important an impact as equity ownership on some aspects of restructuring in the FSU. Despite majority managerial control, outside board representation in FSU enterprises tends to be positively associated with presence of a foreign partner and export-oriented product development (Filatotchev et al., 2001b). Increases in outside control are negatively associated with external acquisitions and positively associated with managerial turnover.

Substantial levels of employee ownership in enterprises may not afford a significant degree of decision control in the face of acute business crisis or the effect of their control may be neutral in retrenchment terms. The unresponsiveness of restructuring to employee ownership may have been because of employees' apathy and social immobility (Bim, 1996), the give-away nature of the share distribution process (i.e. low stakeholder legitimacy), restrictions on share sales that gave employees little incentive to act as shareholders or because of the generally low level of employee representation on boards or strategic decision-making bodies.

Comparative evidence of the effects of buy-out mode on restructuring by Djankov (1999a) relating to Georgia and Moldova shows that enterprise restructuring was faster in companies purchased by insiders, principally managers, at realistic valuations, than in cases where enterprises were given away through voucher schemes that also favoured insiders. Djankov finds that productivity, asset sales and renovations were significantly greater in the 'purchased buy-out' cases, while voucher buy-out cases did not restructure to any greater degree than SOEs. These findings suggest that insiders' incentives to restructure decrease when they perceive ownership as a windfall gain.

Further insights into the impact of privatization type are provided by Barberis et al.'s (1996) study of Russian shops. In their sample of 353 shops providing ownership structures, they find that after adjusting for selection bias through 2SLS, in the 52% of the sample that were MEBOs, there was no evidence that equity incentives had promoted greater restructuring in terms of renovations, longer store hours and lay-offs. In contrast, shops that had been subject to MBIs or other forms of outside ownership did experience significant restructuring. Barberis et al. argue that these findings suggest that human capital skills may matter more than incentives. However, using data from the Czech Republic, Hungary and Poland, Frydman et al. (2006) find no evidence to support this argument but instead suggest that certain ownership types provide the incentives that allow entrepreneurship to manifest itself in performance.

Again, as with strategic choices and conventional performance measures, MEBOs produce a wide mix of evidence, though it seems clear that the worst fears of agency theory in relation to employee entrenchment behaviour have not been widely supported by survey evidence.

4.6 Performance in Terms of Longevity, Survival and Exit Gains

Time is an important variable missing from most of the extensive literature on MEBOs in transition economies. This contrasts with research in the west, which sees enterprise evolution as an important long-run aspect of MEBO performance that extends beyond short-term strategy and performance studies. This is surprising both because of the dynamic nature of transition economies and since a frequently cited objective of MEBOs has been to promote rapid, irreversible privatization, giving enterprises valuable time to prepare for possible flotation and certainly to implement internal restructuring that renders the firm more appealing to outside investors offering more commitment to the firm than mere 'asset-strippers'. In addition, MEBO failure represents the ultimate measure of weak performance.

Developed economies

The existing privatization literature has paid little attention to the extent to which privatization buy-outs are a transitory phenomenon or not. Evidence on longevity is important for a number of reasons. First, it offers insights regarding the duration of policies to promote wider ownership. Second, it provides a further measure of the success of privatization in terms of indirect evidence on longevity of the productivity effects of the governance and incentive structures that are introduced. Third, the extent and timing of failure provide insights regarding issues concerning the use of management buy-outs to privatize poorly performing activities that could not otherwise be transferred to the private sector.

Based on the whole population of privatization buy-outs in the UK, Wright et al. (1994a) show that privatization buy-outs were significantly more likely to change their ownership form and to do so more quickly than non-privatization buy-outs. The analysis of buy-out longevity, i.e. the examination of the number of years for which buy-out structures remain in place, is made difficult since it may take many years for all buy-outs to change their ownership structure. Two main approaches can be adopted. First, comparisons can be made between the percentage of different cohorts of privatization and non-privatization buy-outs that have ceased to have a buy-out ownership structure at the end of a particular period. Second, the population of privatization and non-privatization buy-outs can be compared to identify the percentages of each type that have ceased to be buy-outs after one year, two years, etc.

The study, however, includes data only up to the end of 1992, which was only part-way through the UK government's privatization programme. Updating these data through to 1997, when a change of government virtually brought a halt to privatization, shows that the trend in exits was maintained throughout the programme. Table 10.5 presents comparative evidence of privatization and non-privatization buy-outs analysed by year of buy-out. In general, there is a much higher non-failure exit rate (which includes IPO, sale to third parties and secondary management buy-outs) of privatization than non-privatization buy-outs. The large variations in between-year exit rates for privatization buy-outs reflect the peaks in the sale of particular state-owned activities. This especially relates to buy-outs in the transport sector (bus services and rail) which have been particularly prone to being sold to third parties as the industry restructured following the break-up of large state-owned enterprises that occurred at the time of privatization.

Table 10.5 UK buy-out/buy-in and exit status (%) by vintage year

Deal year	Non-privatization buy-outs			Privatization buy-outs		
	Deals completed in year (no.)	Non-failure exit (%)	Failures (%)	Deals completed in year (no.)	Non-failure exit (%)	Failures (%)
1982	239	36.3	9.2	8	50.0	0.0
1983	242	32.2	9.5	9	66.6	11.1
1984	247	39.7	9.7	4	50.0	0.0
1985	286	33.1	10.5	7	71.5	28.6
1986	353	34.8	10.2	16	75.1	6.3
1987	403	33.2	17.4	33	69.7	9.1
1988	476	59.4	21.8	22	54.5	4.5
1989	512	27.6	20.3	17	45.7	11.8
1990	581	19.9	19.6	23	43.4	8.7
1991	569	43.6	15.6	11	72.7	0.0
1992	584	23.5	8.4	11	81.8	0.0
1993	479	21.1	11.1	13	69.2	0.0
1994	534	23.1	9.9	25	44.0	4.0
1995	583	21.3	11.0	15	33.3	0.0
1996	609	171.0	8.0	33	48.5	0.0
1997	681	12.7	8.4	19	31.6	5.3
1998	681	10.1	5.7	4	25.0	0.0
1999	643	4.7	3.0	1	0.0	0.0

Notes: This table compares the percentage of public sector privatization buy-outs/buy-ins completed in each year (Deal year) and the percentage of non-public sector privatization buy-outs/buy-ins completed in each year (Deal year) that had changed their ownership status through stock market flotation (IPO), sale to a third party (trade sale), secondary management buy-out/buy-in (i.e. non-failure exit of some or all of initial owners and entry of new financial and insider owners while the firm remains an independent entity) or receivership/bankruptcy (i.e. failure) up to June 2001.

Source: CMBOR/Barclays Private Equity/Deloitte & Touche.

The failure rate of UK privatization buy-outs has generally been below that for non-privatization buy-outs (Table 10.5), partly reflecting efforts to ensure the viability of enterprises at the time of privatization. UK evidence has suggested that where privatization buy-outs fail this has been due to diversification that has happened too rapidly outside the areas of firms' core skills and/or erosion of the market as a result of new entries (Wright et al., 1993a). In the case of buy-outs of local authority services, problems have been due to loss of core contracts and problems with commercially inexperienced managers (Robbie and Wright, 1996).

Table 10.6 Cumulative exit status of UK public sector and non-public privatization buy-out/buy-ins, 1981–1998

Age of deal (years)	Non-privatization buy-outs			Privatization buy-outs		
	Total deals[a] (no.)	Non-failure exit (%)	Failures (%)	Total deals[a] (no.)	Non-failure exit (%)	Failures (%)
1	8144	1.5	0.9	273	5.5	0.4
2	8144	4.6	3.4	273	17.5	2.2
3	7977	9.0	5.7	272	29.1	2.2
4	7293	12.6	7.8	268	36.2	2.6
5	6640	16.4	9.1	245	40.0	3.7
6	6003	19.1	10.5	209	47.3	4.8
7	5454	20.7	11.4	195	52.9	6.7
8	4922	22.7	12.2	169	58.2	7.1
9	4445	24.5	13.1	162	58.7	7.4
10	3869	25.8	14.0	150	58.0	8.0

Notes: [a] Total number of deals after each elapsed year since buy-out; number declines as progressively fewer companies have been privatized for each length of time up to June 2001 cut-off. This table shows the percentage of public sector and non-public privatization buy-outs/buy-ins that had changed their ownership status (exit) in each year after buy-out/buy-in through non-failure exit [stock market flotation (IPO), sale to a third party (trade sale) or secondary management buy-out/buy-in (i.e. exit of some or all of initial owners and entry of new financial and insider owners while the firm remains an independent entity)] or failure (receivership/bankruptcy) up to June 2001. Percentages are based on the total number of deals for each number of years elapsed since buy-out.

Source: CMBOR /Barclays Private Equity /Deloitte & Touche.

The generally shorter longevity of privatization buy-outs in the UK is evident from Table 10.6. Based on the population of over 8000 buy-outs and buy-ins completed in the UK from 1981 to 1998, it is clear that 31% of privatizations change their ownership structure within three years, compared to half this level for non-privatizations. By year six after buyout, over half of privatization buyouts have exited compared to only 30% of non-privatization cases. After this period of time, the exit rate then slows.

The longevity of privatization buy-outs appears to be industry and context specific. The exit rate from Austrian privatization buy-outs appears to have been much lower than is the case in the UK (Wieser et al., 1997). The longer average longevity reflects a different business mentality that is reluctant to sell businesses and less developed stock and takeover markets. However, as the business sectors occupied by Austrian privatization buy-outs have generally tended to be specialized, there may also be less scope to sell or float the businesses. Outside Austria in Continental Europe, the exit rate from privatization buy-outs also appears to be below that for the UK, though the Centre for Management Buy-out Research identified only 17 such buy-outs among the countries listed in Table 10.1.

A further measure of the effectiveness of buy-outs is the extent of gains to equity holders when the investment is realized either through a stock market flotation or sale to a third party. These gains may be the result of the efforts of managerial and employee shareholders to create wealth. Importantly, there has been criticism that the gains to insiders have instead largely been due to initial underpricing at time of disposal by government. The underpricing of privatizations has been a general problem relating to both stock market flotations and buy-outs (Hodges and Wright, 1995) in both western and transition economies. The underpricing argument may have particular weight in buy-outs where insiders have access to private information and the sale occurs very shortly after privatization (Wright et al., 1993a). However, from a policy perspective it needs to be borne in mind that there is a trade-off between government objectives to maximize the budgetary revenues resulting from and the need to provide management and employees with sufficient incentives to undertake speedy privatizations. Valuation is always a subjective issue but may be more straightforward in developed as opposed to transition market contexts (Valentiny et al., 1992).

Megginson and Netter (2001) show that there is convincing evidence that initial returns on privatization IPOs are significantly greater than the initial returns earned on private sector IPOs. Examination of the gains on buy-outs poses greater problems than is the case for IPOs. Because of the private nature of information, the initial sale price may not be made public, the nature of the initial ownership structure is not in the public domain, it is not possible to track share prices and an eventual exit price may only be public if the buy-out achieves an IPO. Existing evidence is therefore patchy and has been based on a small number of cases that represent only a small subset of privatization buy-outs in the UK and may thus give a misleading picture.

Thompson et al. (1992) examine the excess returns over and above those available from the market earned between buy-outs and IPO for a sample of 31 UK deals that included privatization buy-outs. Although they find that the coefficient on the dummy variable for privatized firms was large, it was generally insignificant because of high standard errors. Pendleton et al. (1998) note that the share prices in two of the bus companies in their sample companies rose from £0.05 to £4.58 and £3.80, respectively, within little more than five years following privatization as the companies were subsequently sold to third parties. The National Audit Office in the UK showed massive gains to insiders within very short time periods in respect of rail privatizations (NAO, 1998). For example, in the Porterbrook buy-out from British Rail, management increased their equity stake from £0.3 million to £83.7 million in eight months, while management in the Eversholt buy-out achieved an increase from £0.4 million to £57.2 million in one year.

In an attempt to obtain a more general picture, the present authors obtained information concerning privatization buy-outs from CMBOR investment returns and from press coverage. Due to data restrictions, observations were available only for 31 privatization buy-outs (Table 10.6). Bearing in mind its potential limitations, this evidence does indicate, however, that, although the returns in the Porterbrook and Eversholt cases are at the top end of the distribution, the mean return is, nevertheless, substantial (Table 10.7).

A more general investigation by the Public Accounts Committee in the UK provided evidence of excessive gains to insiders in privatization buy-outs that were subsequently sold (CPA, 1998). These gains occurred despite the development of mechanisms over the long period of the UK privatization programme to curtail underpricing problems, such as auctions, claw backs, retained equity stakes and price-escalation (earn-out) clauses. This problem suggests both difficulties in valuing assets where former parts of state

Table 10.7 Gains in UK privatization buy-outs

	Proportionate change in value of management and employee equity from buy-out to exit		Monthly IRR of change in value of management and employee equity from buy-out to exit (%)	
	Non-IPO exits	All	Non-IPO exits	All
Mean	81.5	109.6	20	19
Std deviation	87.7	157.3	0.3	0.2
Median	39.1	56.1	14	15
Minimum	1.6	1.6	2	2
Maximum	336.1	812.6	130	130
N	24	31	24	31

Note: This table presents the gains obtained by management and employees on their equity stakes between the time of privatization and when the buy-out exited, i.e. when the original ownership form was changed through either sale to a third party or flotation on a stock market (IPO). The first two columns relate to the proportionate change in the value of equity during this period. The third and fourth columns calculate the monthly internal rates of return represented by this change in value.

Source: CMBOR. Based on 31 enterprises for which value of initial and exiting managerial and employee equity was available for buy-outs completed up to end 1997.

enterprises have not previously traded as independent entities as well as the effects of the form of privatization on the dynamics of industry structure.

Transition economies

MEBOs in developed economies have been associated with lower failure rates, relatively rapid conversion through flotation and trade sale, and serious doubts concerning undervaluation, which may be interpreted as MEBOs being too successful. However, the analysis of MEBO survival, longevity and exit gains in transition economies is severely restricted by the inability of researchers to monitor cohorts of firms over time, and there are clear opportunities for further research here. The continued expansion of managerial ownership stakes could produce quite a different scenario to that experienced in the west.

One option is to attempt to identify a consensus in the trends from a number of surveys by different authors over time. Estrin and Wright (1999) adopt this approach for Russia. Synthesizing the results from nine separate studies covering the period 1994–97, they find that insider ownership of privatized firms fell over time from a peak in 1994 of 69% to a low in 1997 of 52%. Among insiders there is a decline in employee ownership and an increase in managerial ownership (Estrin and Wright, 1999). The problems here relate to differences in sample coverage of different forms of privatization and the difficulties involved in obtaining representative samples in transition economies.

An alternative approach is to examine changes over time in the same sample of privatized firms, either by identifying the changes retrospectively or by resurveying firms. A synthesis of the available studies is presented in Table 10.8, where Panel A shows changes in the mean stakes held by insiders in the sample over the survey period and Panel B shows changes in the share of firms owned by insiders over the sample period. Bearing in mind that the periods covered by the surveys are typically about three years, the studies in Panel A generally show an overall decline in insider ownership but with management's stake increasing while employees' stakes fall. In contrast, the study by Djankov (1999b) of six newly independent states generally shows an overall increase in insider ownership, with management's mean stakes increasing sharply while employee stakes fall. In those studies relying on resurveys, there may be a selection bias where enterprises not responding to subsequent surveys may be those where the share distribution has changed most, such as through a sale of the business. Similarly, studies taking a sample of enterprises in a later year and looking backwards at changes in ownership over time may also involve selection biases relating to (a) the inclusion only of surviving independent firms and (b) the inclusion of firms that were not privatized at the start of the period. For

Table 10.8 Changes in insider ownership

Country/study	Period	Sample	Mean percentage of equity ownership in sample		
Panel A			IO†	MO†	EO†
Russia					
Buck et al. (1999)[1]	Priv–94*	139	66.1→66.1	19.3→21.7	46.8→44.4
Blasi et al. (1997)[2]	94–96	142–357	65→55→58	25→16→18	40→39→40
Filatotchev et al. (1999a)[3]	94–96	84	64.3→61.5	17.6→18.8	46.6→43.7
Filatotchev et al. (1999b)[4]	95–97	91	55.8→54.6	11.1→15.9	44.6→38.7
Aukutsionek et al. (1998)[5]	95–97	46	57.2→53	9.3→12.8	47.9→40.2
Djankov (1999a)[6]	95–97	682	51.4→59.6	25.4→36.3	26.0→23.3
Filatotchev et al. (2001a)[6]	97–99	150	52.1→46.2	15.1→14.7	37.0→31.5
Jones (1998)[7]	Priv–96*	111	62.2→59.4	7.6→12.9	54.6→46.5
Ukraine					
Djankov (1999b)[6]	95–97	49	37.8→61.5	14.6→46.2	23.6→15.3
Buck et al. (1999)[1]	Priv–95*	93	81.0→80.0	14.1→15.0	66.9→65.8
Filatotchev et al. (1999b)[4]	95–97	35	75.2→69.9	11.3→12.2	63.9→57.7
Belarus					
Filatotchev et al. (1999b)[4]	95–97	39	64.8→68.8	9.9→11.9	54.9→56.9
Georgia					
Djankov (1999b)[6]	95–97	129	50.9→64.0	41.5→53.6	9.4→10.4
Kazakhstan					
Djankov (1999b)[6]	95–97	62	33.8→37.6	23.1 →29.4	10.7→8.2
Kyrgyzstan					
Djankov (1999)[6]	95–97	79	66.4→70.8	28.1→34.4	38.3→36.4
Moldova					
Djankov (1999b)[6]	95–97	137	28.8→38.0	7.2→18.3	21.6→19.7
Poland					
Jarosz (1994)[8]					
Filatotchev et al. (1996b)	91–93	110	85.2→78.9	9.8→12.0	75.4→66.9

Table 10.8 (continued)

Country/study	Period	Sample	Percentage of firms majority/dominant owned by each group		
Panel B			IO†	MO†	EO†
Slovenia					
Smith et al. (1997)[9]	89–92	22 735	–	–	2.7→10.9
Romania					
Earle and Telgedy (2001)[10]	92–98	2354	–	–	0.2→23.6
Russia					
Aukutsionek et al. (1998)[5]	95–97	46	59.1→57.1	8.0→11.2	51.1→45.9
Jones (1998)[7]	Priv–96*	111	40.5→52.2	0.9→6.3	39.6→45.9
Estonia					
Jones and Mygind (2000)[11]	93–96	666	22→22	10→16	12→6
Latvia					
Jones and Mygind (2000)[11]	94–95	5585	11→12	2→7	9→5
Lithuania					
Jones and Mygind (2000)[11]	94–95	484	51→48	26→26	25→22

Notes: → = direction of change from beginning of period to end for each ownership type.

1 One survey, retrospective information.
2 Three surveys, partially overlapping.
3 Resurvey of same sample.
4 Two surveys, retrospective information.
5 Resurvey.
6 One survey, retrospective information.
7 Survey and archival data, retrospective Jones notes that the position of employees diminished markedly in 13 of the 44 firms where they had been the largest group on privatization.
8 Two surveys.
9 Slovenian population with enterprises with missing data removed. Data relate to cases with 'some employee ownership' (Smith et al., 1997, table 1).
10 MEBO participants; Earle and Telgedy (2001) note that MEBOs tended to result in overwhelming employee ownership.
* Priv = from date of privatization.
† IO – insider ownership; MO – manager ownership; EO – employee ownership.

example, the falls from the large mean stakes held by the state reported in Djankov's study suggest that some firms may not have been fully privatized at the beginning of the period.

In Panel B, the Slovenian and Romanian samples relate to whole populations of firms, the increase in employee ownership over time reflecting the development of privatization programmes which masks any post-privatization ownership changes. In contrast, the falls in the percentage of privatized firms that are majority owned by employees and the rise in the percentage that are majority owned by management in Estonia, Latvia and Lithuania reflect post-privatization changes. Jones (1998), and Aukutsionek et al. (1998), who also use changes in panels of privatized firms, find mixed evidence of changes in the importance of insiders as dominant shareholders, with managers appearing to be more likely to take a dominant role than employees. Jones (1998) notes that the method of buy-out privatization is important, with voucher privatizations in Russia displaying greater changes in ownership than is the case for leasehold buy-outs. In comparison with these findings from buy-outs in transition economies, large corporations privatized through IPOs are also found to experience sharp reductions in their number of shareholders following privatization, while the reverse is true for smaller IPO privatizations (Megginson and Netter, 2001).

While buy-outs in the west have generally converted to outside ownership upon IPO, this has not proved common in transition economies. While gradual increases in outside ownership have been prevalent, a unique feature of buy-outs in transition economies has been the gradual build-up of managerial stakes after privatization.

In this context, Russian evidence suggests that managerial purchases of shares from employees are already extensive, and this appears to be aimed at entrenching management's position rather than overcoming employee resistance by concentrating holdings to enable management to restructure (Filatotchev et al., 1999a). Direct evidence of the impact of changes in insider ownership post-privatization is provided for Russia by Jones (1998), who shows that, where managers took over from employee owners, sales and productivity fell and costs increased but not as much as where managers took over from state owners. The greatest gains in productivity occurred where employee-owned firms became bank-owned. Djankov's (1999b) study of six newly independent states in FSU suggests that increasing ownership by managers post-privatization was beneficial to labour productivity and asset sale restructuring. There is a need for further research on the direct impact of changes in employee and managerial ownership post-privatization in other country contexts. It remains to be seen in transition economies whether low failure rates and rapid exit to flotation and trade sale will follow the pattern of developed economies. If so, this may be the greatest achievement of the privatization movement.

5. CONCLUSIONS

This review has extended earlier reviews in terms of both theoretical perspectives and the scope of empirical evidence. The importance of adopting a multiple theoretical lens that goes beyond agency theory to encompass strategy and HRM perspectives has been emphasized. This chapter has also shown the importance of examining dimensions of the effects of privatization other than productivity, notably employment changes, HR, and the longevity of post-privatization ownership forms.

While a meta-study by Djankov and Murrell (2002) concluded that (p. 6) 'privatization to workers has no effect in Eastern Europe and is detrimental in the CIS',[1] it has been argued here that comparisons with buy-outs in the west, a consideration of employee attitudes, firms' internal strategies and wider performance measures qualify this conclusion to some extent.

The main conclusions from the available evidence presented in this survey of the wider impact of privatization MEBOs are as follows. Although in both developed and transition economies, employees may have significant equity stakes, most buy-outs are MEBOs dominated by management in which employees have little participation in decision-making and limited perceptions of ownership. Higher levels of employee share ownership, as in privatization MEBOs in developed economies and voucher buy-outs with large employee stakes in transition economies, are more likely to be associated with a greater degree of employee-oriented HRM strategies including bonus systems. The positive role of employee participation may be enhanced through building institutional arrangements inside privatization buy-outs to facilitate this involvement, which may be either voluntary or mandatory (Fitzroy et al., 1998).

Privatization buy-outs in developed economies are typically followed by reductions in employment in the post-privatization period, with subsequent recovery. In transition economies, employee ownership is so far associated with reductions in employment levels. Although the evidence is mixed, the extent of lay-offs outside Russia and Ukraine appears to be less in insider-owned privatized firms than in outsider-owned firms. It is not clear, however, whether this difference between FSU and CEE countries reflects differences in the treatment of 'surplus' employees. Employees may still be technically employed but on extended leave with little prospect of return.

The performance of privatization buy-outs may be affected by access to finance. State-owned enterprises starved of cash for investment may need substantial funds to bring their production facilities to a standard that makes them competitive. Buy-outs in transition economies may face restricted access to investment funds: voucher ('give-away') buy-outs typically involve no new funds coming into the enterprise, while purchase buy-outs may be burdened by substantial debt repayment costs, even with loans on favourable terms (which themselves may carry restrictions on restructuring). Enterprises that are privatized through sale to outsiders may be less constrained by a lack of finance for investment.

One of our most important conclusions in developed and transition economies is that the impact of privatization on productivity may depend on the form of institutional context and policy, with employee ownership sometimes being more effective than other forms. Restructuring may be greater where insiders have purchased shares rather than having acquired them for free through voucher programmes. However, the longevity of privatization buy-outs in developed economies appears to be heavily dependent on the dynamics of the industrial sector, rather than the mode of buy-out. In transition economies, employee ownership seems to be generally reducing as managers and/or outsiders purchase employee shares. This raises policy concerns about share transferability. At one level, there is a need to ensure transparent and fair valuation and transfer of shares so that the process does not favour only managers. At another level there is a need to consider the relative importance of objectives to promote and maintain insider ownership *per se* and to promote efficiency.

For policymakers, it needs to be borne in mind, however, that the effects of MEBOs need to be seen within the context of the objectives of privatization and the institutional context of particular countries. Privatization programmes typically need to reconcile competing economic, political, social and financial objectives (Wright et al., 1994b). To the extent that other objectives are more important, the impact of buy-outs on efficiency is reduced. In retrospect, the main positive outcome of privatization buy-outs in transition economies is that they facilitated transition and the disengagement of the state from industry at a crucial time when reforms had to be enacted quickly.

Finally, there would seem to be an urgent need for longitudinal case studies addressing the evolution of individual MEBOs over time, in order to test the generalizability of western studies.

ACKNOWLEDGEMENTS

Thanks to Andrew Pendleton, two anonymous reviewers and the journal editor for comments on earlier drafts.

NOTE

1. CIS – Commonwealth of Independent States – 11 member states (Armenia, Azerbaijan, Belarus, Georgia, Kazakhstan, Kyrgyzstan, Moldova, Russia, Tajikistan, Ukraine and Uzbekistan), plus one associate member (Turkmenistan).

REFERENCES

Anderson, J., Lee, Y. and Murrell, P. (2000), 'Competition and privatization amidst weak institutions: evidence from Mongolia', *Economic Inquiry*, **38** (4), 527–49.

Aukutsionek, S. and Kapelushnikov, R. (1996), 'Labor hoarding in Russian industry', *Russian Economic Barometer*, **2**, 3–11.

Aukutsionek, S., Filatotchev, I., Kapelushnikov, R. and Zhukov, V. (1998), 'Dominant shareholders, restructuring and performance of privatized companies in Russia: an analysis and some policy implications', *Communist Economies & Economic Transformation*, **10** (4), 495–518.

Bacon, N., Wright, M. and Demina, N. (2001), 'Management buyouts and employee relations: exploring the impact of buyout type', Business Strategy and Financier Involvement, paper presented at BUIRA Conference, Manchester Metropolitan University, 5–7 July.

Barberis, N., Boycko, M., Shleifer, A. and Tsukanova, N. (1996), 'How does privatization work? Evidence from the Russian shops', *Journal of Political Economy*, **104**, 764–90.

Ben-Ner, A. (1993), 'Organizational reform in Central and Eastern Europe: a comparative perspective', *Annals of Public and Cooperative Economics*, **64** (3), 329–65.

Bim, A.S. (1996), 'Ownership and control of Russian enterprises and strategies of shareholders', *Communist Economies and Economic Transformation*, **8** (4), 471–500.

Blasi, J., Kroumova, M. and Kruse, D. (1997), *Kremlin Capitalism: The privatization of the Russian economy*, Ithaca, NY: ILR Press/Cornell.

Borbely, S. (1994), 'ESOPs, employment and critical issues for trade unions in Hungary', in S. Rainer (ed.), *Bottom-up Privatization, Finance and the Role of Employers' and Workers' Organizations in the Czech Republic, Hungary, Poland and Slovakia*, Geneva: ILO.

Bradley, K. and Nejad, A. (1989), *Managing Owners: The National Freight Consortium in perspective*, Cambridge: Cambridge University Press.

Brown, J.D. and Earle, J.S. (2000), 'Competition enhancing policies and infrastructure: evidence from Russia', CEPR Discussion Paper 3022.

Brown, J.D. and Earle, J.S. (2002), 'Gross job flows in Russian industry before and after reforms: has destruction become more creative?', *Journal of Comparative Economics*, **30** (1), 96–133.

Buck, T., Filatotchev, I., Wright, M. and Zhukov, V. (1999), 'Corporate governance and employee ownership in an economic crisis: entrepreneurial strategies in the former USSR', *Journal of Comparative Economics*, **27** (3), 459–74.

Buck, T., Wright, M. Filatotchev, I. and Demina, N. (2001), 'Employee welfare, firm governance and performance in Ukraine', paper presented at ILO conference on privatization and employee ownership, Kiev, May.

Committee of Public Accounts (CPA) (1998), *Getting Value for Money in Privatizations*, HC 992 (1997/98), London: HMSO.
Djankov, S. (1999a), 'The restructuring of insider-dominated firms: a comparative analysis', *Economics of Transition*, **7** (2), 467–80.
Djankov, S. (1999b), 'Ownership structures and enterprise restructuring in six newly independent states', *Comparative Economic Studies*, **41** (1), 75–95.
Djankov, S. and Murrell, P. (2002), 'Enterprise restructuring in transition: a quantitative survey', *Journal of Economic Literature*, **40** (3), 739–92.
D'Souza, J., Megginson, W. and Nash, R. (2001), 'Determinants of performance improvements in privatized firms: the role of restructuring and corporate governance', University of Oklahoma, mimeo.
Earle, J.S. (1998), 'Post-privatization ownership and productivity in Russian industrial enterprises', SITE Working Paper 127, University of Stockholm, Sweden.
Earle, J.S. and Estrin, S. (1996), 'Employee ownership in transition', in R. Frydman, C. W Gray and A. Rapaczynski (eds), *Corporate Governance in Russia: Vol. 2, Insiders and the State*, London: World Bank/CEU Press, pp. 1–61.
Earle, J.S., Estrin, S. and Leshchenko, L. (1996), 'Ownership structures, patterns of control and enterprise behavior in Russia', in S. Commander, Q. Fan and M. Schae¡er (eds), *Enterprise Restructuring and Economic Policy in Russia*, Washington, DC: Economic Development Institute, EDI Development Studies, The World Bank, pp. 205–52.
Earle, J.S. and Telgedy, A. (2001), 'Privatization and productivity in Romanian industry: evidence from a comprehensive enterprise panel', Institute for the Study of Labor Discussion Paper No. 326, Central European University, Budapest.
EBRD (1997), *Transition Report 1997*, London: European Bank for Reconstruction and Development.
EBRD (1998), *Transition Report 1998*, London: European Bank for Reconstruction and Development.
Ellerman, D. (1993), *Management and Employee Buy-outs as a Technique of Privatization*, Ljubljana: CEEPN.
Estrin, S. (1983), *Self-Management: Economic theory and Yugoslav Practice*, London: Cambridge University Press.
Estrin, S. (1996), 'Privatization in Central and Eastern Europe', LBS and CEP–LSE, London.
Estrin, S. and Rosevear, A. (1999a), 'Enterprise performance and ownership: the case of Ukraine', *European Economic Review*, **43** (4), 1125–36.
Estrin, S. and Rosevear, A. (1999b), 'Enterprise performance and corporate governance in Ukraine', *Journal of Comparative Economics*, **27** (3), 442–58.
Estrin, S. and Wright, M. (1999), 'Corporate governance in the former Soviet Union: an overview', *Journal of Comparative Economics*, **27** (3), 398–421.
Filatotchev, I., Buck, T., Hoskisson, R. and Wright, M. (1996a), 'Corporate restructuring in Russian privatizations: implications for U.S. investors', *California Management Review*, **38** (2), 87–105.
Filatotchev, I., Buck, I., Grosfeld, I., Karsai, J. and Wright, M. (1996b), 'Buy-outs in Hungary, Poland and Russia: governance and finance issues', *Economics of Transition*, **4** (1), 67–88.
Filatotchev, I., Wright, M. and Bleaney, M. (1999a), 'Privatization, insider control and managerial entrenchment in Russia', *Economics of Transition*, **7** (2), 481–504.

Filatotchev, I., Bleaney, M. and Wright, M. (1999b), 'Insider controlled firms in Russia', *Economics of Planning*, **32** (2), 129–51.

Filatotchev, I., Bleaney, M., Buck, T. and Dyomina, N. (1999c), 'Exporting and restructuring in privatized firms in Russia, Ukraine and Belarus', *World Economy*, **22** (7), 1013–37.

Filatotchev, I., Bleaney, M., Buck, T. and Zhukov, V. (1999d), 'Corporate entrepreneurs and privatized firms in Russia, Ukraine and Belarus', *Journal of Business Venturing*, **14** (5/6), 475–92.

Filatotchev, I., Bleaney, M. and Zhukov, V. (2000), 'Downsizing in privatized firms in Russia, Ukraine and Belarus: theory and empirical evidence', *Academy of Management Journal*, **43** (3), 286–304.

Filatotchev, I., Aukutsionek, S., Kapelushnikov, R. and Dyomina, N. (2001a), 'The effects of ownership concentration on investment and performance in privatized firms in Russia', *Managerial and Decision Economics*, **22**, 299–313.

Filatotchev, I., Dyomina, N., Wright, M. and Buck, T. (2001b), 'Effects of post-privatization governance and strategies on export intensity in the former Soviet Union', *Journal of International Business Studies*, **32** (4), 853–71.

Finkel, S.E. (1995), *Causal Analysis with Panel Data*, Thousand Oaks, CA: Sage.

Fitzroy, F., Jones, D., Klinedinst, M., Lajtai, G., Mygind, N., Nuti, D.M., Rock, C., Uvalic, M. and Vaughan-Whitehead, D. (1998), *Employee Ownership in Privatization*, Geneva: ILO.

Frydman, R., Gray, C., Hessel, M. and Rapaczynski, A. (1999), 'When does privatization work? The impact of private ownership on corporate performance in transition economies', *Quarterly Journal of Economics*, **114** (4), November, 1153–91.

Frydman, R., Hessel, M. and Rapaczynski, A. (2006), 'Why ownership matters. Entrepreneurship and the restructuring of enterprises in Central Europe', in M. Fox and M. Heller (eds), *Corporate Governance Lessons From Transition Economy Reforms*, Princeton, NJ: Princeton University Press, Chapter 5.

Grigorian, D. (2000), 'Ownership and performance of Lithuanian enterprises', Policy Research Working Paper #2343, World Bank, Washington, DC.

Hodges, R. and Wright, M. (1995), 'Audit and accountability in the privatization process: the role of the National Audit Office', *Financial Accountability and Management*, **11** (2), 153–70.

Jarosz, M. (1994), (ed.), *Spolki Pracownicze*, Instytut Studiow Politycznych Polskiej Akademii Nauk, Warsaw.

Jones, D.C. (1998), 'The economic effects of privatization: evidence from a Russian panel', *Comparative Economic Studies*, **40** (2), 75–102.

Jones, D.C., Klinedinst, M. and Rock, C. (1997), 'Productive efficiency during transition: evidence from Bulgarian panel data', *Journal of Comparative Economics*, **26** (3), 446–64.

Jones, D.C. and Mygind, N. (1999), 'The nature and determinants of ownership changes after privatization: evidence from Estonia', *Journal of Comparative Economics*, **27** (3), 422–41.

Jones, D.C. and Mygind, N. (2000), 'The effects of Privatization on productive efficiency: evidence from the Baltic Republics', *Annals of Public and Cooperative Economics*, **71** (3), 415–39.

Karsai, J. and Wright, M. (1994), 'Accountability, governance and finance in Hungarian buy-outs', *Europe–Asia Studies*, **46** (6), 997–1016.

Lajtai, G. (1997), 'Successful waves of employee ownership in Hungary', in M.

Uvalic and D. Vaughan-Whitehead (eds), *Privatization Surprises in Transition Economies*, Cheltenham, UK and Northampton, MA, USA: Edward Elgar.
Lissovolik, B. (1997), 'Rapid spread of employee ownership in privatized Russia', in M. Uvalic and D. Vaughan-Whitehead (eds), *Privatization Surprises in Transition Economies*, Cheltenham, UK and Northampton, MA, USA: Edward Elgar.
Martin, S. and Parker, D. (1995), 'Privatization and economic performance throughout the UK business cycle', *Managerial and Decision Economics*, **16**, 225–37.
Megginson, W. and Netter, J. (2001), 'From state to market: a survey of empirical studies on privatization', *Journal of Economic Literature*, **39** (2), 321–89.
Munteanu, C. (1997), 'Employee share ownership in Romania: the main path to privatization', in M. Uvalic and D. Vaughan-Whitehead (eds), *Privatization Surprises in Transition Economies*, Cheltenham, UK and Northampton, MA, USA: Edward Elgar.
Mygind, N. (1997), 'Employee ownership in the Baltic countries', in M. Uvalic and D. Vaughan-Whitehead (eds), *Privatization Surprises in Transition Economies*, Cheltenham, UK and Northampton, MA, USA: Edward Elgar.
National Audit Office (NAO) (1998), *Privatization of the Rolling Stock Leasing Companies*, HC 576 (1997/98), London: HMSO.
Neumann, L. (1994), 'The Kanizsa brewery case: the history of an ESOP privatization in Hungary', in R. Schliwa (ed.), *Bottom-up Privatization, Finance and the Role of Employers' and Workers' Organizations in the Czech Republic, Hungary, Poland and Slovakia*, Geneva: ILO.
Nuti, D.M. (1997), 'Employee ownership in Polish privatizations', in M. Uvalic and D. Vaughan-Whitehead (eds), *Privatization Surprises in Transition Economies*, Cheltenham, UK and Northampton, MA, USA: Edward Elgar.
Parker, D. and Hartley, K. (1991a), 'Do changes in organizational status affect financial performance?', *Strategic Management Journal*, **12** (8), 631–41.
Parker, D. and Hartley, K. (1991b), 'Organizational status and performance: the effect on employment', *Applied Economics*, **23** (2), 403–16.
Pendleton, A., Wilson, N. and Wright, M. (1998), 'The perception and effects of share ownership: empirical evidence from employee buy-outs', *British Journal of Industrial Relations*, **36** (1), 99–124.
Rapacki, R. (1995), 'Privatization in Poland: performance, problems and prospects – a survey article', *Comparative Economic Studies*, **37** (1), 57–75.
Robbie, K. and Wright, M. (1996), 'Local authorities, compulsory competitive tendering and buy-outs', *Local Government Studies*, **22** (1), 127–46.
Rock, C. and Klinedinst, M. (1997), 'Employee ownership and participation in Bulgaria, 1989 to mid-1996', in M. Uvalic and D. Vaughan-Whitehead (eds), *Privatization Surprises in Transition Economies*, Cheltenham, UK and Northampton, MA, USA: Edward Elgar.
Smith, S. (1994), 'On the law and economics of employee ownership in privatization in developing and transition economies', *Annals of Public and Cooperative Economics*, **65** (3), 437–68.
Smith, S., Cin, B.-C. and Vodopivec, M. (1997), 'Privatization incidence, ownership forms and firm performance: evidence from Slovenia', *Journal of Comparative Economics*, **25**, 158–79.
Shleifer, A. and Vishny, R. (1997), 'A survey of corporate governance', *Journal of Finance*, **52** (2), 737–83.
Stephen, F.H. (1984), *The Economic Analysis of Producers' Cooperatives*, New York: St. Martin's Press.

Thompson, S., Wright, M. and Robbie, K. (1992), 'Management equity ownership, debt and performance: some evidence from UK management buyouts', *Scottish Journal of Political Economy*, **39** (4), 413–30.

Valentiny, P., Buck, T and Wright, M. (1992), 'The pricing and valuation of public assets: experiences in the UK and Hungary', *Annals of Public and Cooperative Economics*, **63** (4), 601–20.

Vaughan-Whitehead, D. (1997), 'Employee ownership alongside hyper-stagflation in Ukraine: enterprise survey results for 1993–95', in M. Uvalic and D. Vaughan-Whitehead (eds), *Privatization Surprises in Transition Economies*, Cheltenham, UK and Northampton, MA, USA: Edward Elgar.

Wieser, O., Wright, M. and Robbie, K. (1997), 'Management and employee buy-outs from the Austrian public sector', *Annals of Public and Cooperative Economics*, **68** (4), 689–712.

Wright, M., Chiplin, B., Thompson, S. and Robbie, K. (1990), 'Management buy-outs, trade unions and employee ownership', *Industrial Relations Journal*, **21** (2), 137–46.

Wright, M., Thompson, S. and Robbie, K. (1993a), 'Finance and control in privatization by management buy-out', *Financial Accountability and Management*, **9** (2), 75–100.

Wright, M., Filatotchev, I., Buck, T. Robbie, K. and Ellerman, D. (1993b), *Management and Employee Buy-outs in Central and Eastern Europe*, EBRD/CEEPN Technical Note, London.

Robbie, K., Wright, M., Filatotchev, I. and Buck, T. (1994a), 'Accountability and efficiency in buy-outs in Central and Eastern Europe', *Financial Accountability and Management*, **10** (3), 195–214.

Wright, M., Robbie, K., Thompson, S. and Starkey, K. (1994b), 'Longevity and the life-cycle of management buy-outs', *Strategic Management Journal*, **15** (3), 215–28.

Wright, M., Pendleton, A. and Robbie, K. (2000a), 'Employee ownership of enterprises in Africa and Asia', *International Journal of Human Resource Management*, **11** (1), 90–111.

Wright, M., Hoskisson, R.E., Busenitz, L.W. and Dial, J. (2000b), 'Entrepreneurial growth through privatization: the upside of management buy-outs', *Academy of Management Review*, **25** (3), 591–601.

Wright, M., Hoskisson, R.E. and Busenitz, L.W. (2001), 'Firm rebirth: buyouts as facilitators of strategic growth and entrepreneurship', *Academy of Management Executive*, **15** (1), 111–25.

11. The impact of business ownership change on employee relations: buy-outs in the UK and the Netherlands

Hans Bruining, Paul Boselie, Mike Wright and Nicolas Bacon

INTRODUCTION

Management buy-outs of companies or parts of organizations have become an important development in corporate governance over the past 20 years as a mechanism for rescuing troubled businesses. In the UK buy-outs have increased their importance as part of the broader changes occurring in business structure from an average of 306 per year in the 1980s to an average of 610 buy-outs completed annually in the 1990s (CMBOR, 2002). In the Netherlands, buy-outs rose from an average of 29 per year in the 1980s to an average of 54 per year in the 1990s (CMBOR/Initiative Europe, 1991; CMBOR, 2003). Expressing the value of buy-out markets in the two countries as a percentage of GDP provides a means of comparing their level of development. On this basis, the value of UK buy-outs rose from approximately 0.5 per cent of GDP in 1990 to 2 per cent in 1999. The comparable figures for the Netherlands were 0.05 per cent in 1990 and 0.7 per cent in 1999. The UK had the highest number of buy-outs in Europe in 1999, while the Netherlands was ranked third.

The main aim of a buy-out is to improve organizational performance through ownership change creating new opportunities for strategic reorientation and restructuring of the firm (Thompson and Wright, 1995). This fundamental change in the structure of ownership may affect the way employee relations develop within an organization (Pendleton et al., 1998). Little is known about the impact of buy-outs upon employee relations. This chapter aims to address this gap. We focus on two key questions. First, what are the effects of a buy-out on employee relations in an organization? Second, does the national institutional context affect the impact of buy-outs on employee relations? The chapter considers employee relations issues in the contrasting institutional environments of the UK and the Netherlands. Theoretical insights from the field of human resource management and buy-outs are incorporated to study the effect of ownership change on employee relations in 190 firms.

The structure of the chapter is as follows. First, in the second section of the chapter, we define buy-outs and suggest that buy-outs provide an opportunity for managers to reassess and change employee relations using two different perspectives that may explain these changes: a cost reduction and an investment perspective. In the third section we review the empirical literature relating to the impact of buy-outs on employee relations and contrast findings in UK and Dutch studies. The following section outlines the different institutional contexts in these two countries and presents an institutional perspective that may explain the findings. The methodology presented in the next section is followed by a comparative analysis of the empirical data of 190 buy-outs in the UK and the Netherlands in the sixth section. In the final section we discuss the findings and the limitations of the study, and draw some conclusions.

BUY-OUTS AND EMPLOYEE RELATIONS

A management buy-out (MBO) involves members of the incumbent management team, backed by financial institutions, acquiring a significant equity stake as individuals in order to control the company (Robbie and Wright, 1996). The former parent or private company owners are replaced by a 'fresh' coalition of new investors and owners/managers from inside and/or outside the company. They aim to improve organizational performance through restructuring, cost reduction, strategic reorientation, product development and innovation, or by using a combination of these measures. Sources of buy-outs vary, although most buy-outs result from the rationalization of public firms and ownership succession in private firms. Other buy-outs emerge from privatization and receivership. Embedded in these different buy-out types there is considerable opportunity for change, which we will explain below.

Prior UK research indicates that certain features of employee relations change while others remain constant after a buy-out. Two surveys conducted in the 1980s emphasized continuity, suggesting that management buy-outs resulted in changes, although relatively few in employee relations. Wright et al. (1984) reported that just a few buy-outs involved a subsequent move towards de-recognizing trade unions because managers perceived unions 'as an essential means of communicating with the workforce'.

A greater change was detected with respect to increases in the employment of part-time workers (Wright et al., 1990) and job losses following buy-outs (Wright and Coyne, 1985), although the economic context caused variation in the number of buy-out companies reporting a fall in employment (Wright et al., 1990). In a study of 48 large US MBOs completed between 1980 and 1986, Kaplan (1989) reports a median change in employment following the buy-out for these companies of 0.90 per cent, indicating a slight decrease in employment level. However, employment increased in 50 per cent of the MBO companies, but the growth in employment was 12 per cent less compared to other companies in the same industry. Controlling for post-buy-out divestitures, more than 60 per cent of these companies show a median increase in employment of 4.9 per cent, which is still 6 per cent lower than the industry-adjusted change. The results of this study do not support the view that buy-out gains come from laying off a large number of employees.

Another key feature of buy-outs is that they encourage wider employee share ownership, especially as part of privatization (Bradley and Nejad, 1989; Pendleton et al., 1998; Robbie and Wright, 1996). Employee buy-outs directly increase employee share ownership, although the overall number of employee buy-outs is small (Wright et al., 1989).

Similar reports of wider share ownership following buy-outs emerge from the study of twelve cases by Van Neerven et al. (1996) in the Netherlands. In these cases, buy-out companies spread equity ownership through a variety of mechanisms: direct share ownership as part of the buy-out, granting options on shares or distributing shares under profit-sharing schemes. Several buy-outs also reduced labour costs, with managers adjusting the wages of employees to industry norms and pursuing increased labour flexibility by adjusting the numbers employed to meet changes in demand. In a further attempt to enhance employee commitment, the managers in many of these cases reported an increased use of employee involvement policies and enhanced training to develop employee awareness of customer and business requirements.

These tentative findings from a small number of previous studies suggest we need to know more about how a change in business ownership influences the type of HR system in an organization post-buy-out. Changes in HRM practices following buy-outs may be an important method of aligning the management of employees with the strategic choices of the new owners.

BUY-OUTS: OPPORTUNITIES FOR CHANGE

Buy-outs have traditionally been viewed as involving firms in mature sectors with few investment demands and low growth prospects (Jensen, 1989). Cost reduction and strategic refocusing are used to mitigate the downside problems of mature firms and to create value following the transfer of ownership. However, buy-outs may also involve the creation of value in less mature sectors through attempts to release the upside potential of firms, allowing product development and incremental innovation to take place that was frustrated under the former ownership regime (Wright et al., 2000; Wright et al., 2001). Research from the USA, UK and Continental Europe shows that buy-outs are often followed by an increase in (new) product development (Bruining, 1992; EVCA, 2001; Wright et al., 1992; Zahra, 1995).

The mitigation of downside problems and the release of upside potential are two different strategies that management may pursue. Agency theory offers a useful perspective for understanding how HRM may develop, although the two scenarios lead to different expectations.

In the traditional buy-out literature (Jensen, 1993; Wright et al., 2001) it tends to be argued that cost reduction predominates as managers introduce efficiencies and reduce costs post-buy-out. The agency theory perspective underpinning this claim proposes that managers are motivated to seek 'efficiencies' because tighter financial monitoring and control limits their discretion and makes them more accountable to investors after the buy-out (Jensen, 1986; Long and Ravenscraft, 1993; Phillips, 1995). In addition, discretionary expenditure by managers is limited following a buy-out as cash flow is used to service interest payments on high leverage (Jensen, 1986). Remuneration arrangements in buy-outs also narrow the corporate governance gap between investors and management, with managers incentivized to maximize investor returns. Buy-outs may therefore reduce employment, display subsequent below-industry employment growth (Kaplan, 1989) and decrease expenditure on indirect management activities such as the personnel function (Wright and Coyne, 1985). In particular, there may be an emphasis on those HR practices that are likely to enhance short-term productivity and financial performance and a decrease in those HR practices that might affect performance in the long run but whose effects are more uncertain (e.g. training and development, employee involvement). Thus we might expect lower investments in human capital in mature industries with little possibilities for growth. Hence, we suggest the following propositions:

Proposition 1a: If the downside protection view of buy-outs predominates, we expect a low level of high-commitment HR policies and practices after buy-out.

Proposition 1b: If the downside protection view of buy-outs predominates, we expect a decrease in investment in high-commitment HR policies and practices after buy-out.

Agency theory may also be applied to situations involving innovation. Innovative activity typically involves high risk, unpredictability and long time horizons (Holmstrom, 1989). In large, integrated diverse organizations, obtaining reliable information on innovative activity may be prohibitively costly. Bureaucratic measures may be adopted to try to ensure acceptable levels of performance but these measures may restrict experimentation and constrain innovative activity (Francis and Smith, 1995). Managers in the pre-buy-out situation may thus face investment restrictions from headquarters, particularly where their firms are peripheral to the main product line of the parent company (Wright et al., 2001). These restrictions reduce the freedom to respond to market developments and give rise to opportunities for a buy-out (Bruining, 1992; Wright et al., 2001). Limitations on discretion and incentive alignment may be substitutes (Holmstrom and Milgrom, 1990). The loss of efficiency from restricting managerial discretion through tighter control in large integrated diverse organizations may be outweighed by the benefits of providing the right incentives post-buy-out. It is likely to be difficult pre-buy-out to provide the necessary equity incentives for divisional management that directly relate to performance because of the need to maintain similar remuneration structures across the group and because equity typically relates to the group as a whole, not to individual divisions. After the buy-out this situation might be reversed. Instead of obeying orders from headquarters that block innovation and investment in order to optimize the goals of the diversified parent company, the buy-out creates discretionary power for the new management team to decide what is best for the business, how to organize and lead the company, and how to set up a business plan that is most profitable for themselves and the firm (Wright et al., 2001). Together with a more moderately leveraged financing structure, in these circumstances we expect changes in firm behaviour as the new owners have greater decision-making autonomy. Consistent with this argument, studies have shown the greater importance of increases in managerial equity ownership, as opposed to greater leverage, in enhancing the performance of firms that have been bought out (Phan and Hill, 1995; Thompson et al., 1992).

The shift from maintaining the status quo pre-buy-out to acting more efficiently and entrepreneurially post-buy-out may require the development of HRM to achieve the required levels of organizational flexibility. Management may need to develop employees' awareness and competency in relation to customer and business requirements and to increase their commitment. This may necessitate making employees more market oriented through HR practices involving greater training and employee involvement in decision-making in order to take advantage of the skills and information possessed by employees. There may also be a need to incentivize employees through share ownership to encourage this shift in behaviour. Hence:

> *Proposition 2a: If the release of upside potential view of buy-outs predominates, we expect a high level of investment in high-commitment HR policies and practices.*

> *Proposition 2b: If the release of upside potential view of buy-outs predominates, we expect an increase in investment in high-commitment HR policies and practices.*

The high-commitment HR policies we might expect and measure in this research arise from prior research on high-involvement work practices (HIWPs) and high-performance work practices (HPWPs). This is a specific area of research within the HRM and performance debate that focuses on the HR practices that increase employee commitment (e.g. Appelbaum et al., 2000). For example, Arthur (1994) defines high-commitment HR systems in terms of decentralization, employee participation, general training, skill development, social events, due processes, employee benefits, and high wages. Kalleberg and Moody (1994) argue that high-performance work systems reflect decentralization, job training, compensation (performance-related pay) and firm internal labour markets. Ichniowski et al. (1997) define high-involvement practices in terms of incentive pay, selective recruitment and selection, teamwork, employment security, flexible job assignments, skills training, communication and good labour relations. Bae and Lawler's (2000) high-involvement HR strategies consist of extensive training, empowerment, highly selective training, performance-based pay and broad job design. Therefore we can conclude that decentralization, employee participation, employee development of skills and knowledge, selective recruitment and selection, performance-related pay (in particular, group-based pay), communication and information-sharing and internal promotion opportunities are the building blocks of high-commitment HR policies and practices (see also Batt, 2002; Guthrie, 2001; Ramsay et al., 2000).

In the following section we highlight the different institutional contexts for HRM in the UK and the Netherlands where we conducted our research that may further help to explain differences in post-buy-out HRM in the two countries.

INSTITUTIONAL CONTEXTS FOR BUY-OUTS IN THE UK AND THE NETHERLANDS

Institutional rules on employment, pay and participation set standards with which management needs to comply, thus reducing the range of discretionary HRM policies available to management (Oliver,1997). Regulatory pressures differ between Anglo-Saxon- and Germanic-type environments (Boselie et al., 2001; Gospel and Pendleton, 2003; La Porta et al., 1997), suggesting HRM will not necessarily take the same path in the Anglo-Saxon context of the UK versus the Germanic or Rhineland context of the Netherlands.

Paauwe and Boselie (2003) apply institutional theory (e.g. DiMaggio and Powell, 1983) to explain differences in HR decision-making processes depending on differences in organizational contexts. In general, institutional theory shows how the behaviour of organizations is a response not solely to market pressures but also to formal and informal institutional pressures, regulatory pressures, general social expectations and the actions of leading organizations (Greenwood and Hinings, 1996).

Gospel and Pendleton (2003) make a distinction between the USA and the UK on the one hand and Germany and Japan on the other, based on the idea of fundamental differences in capitalism. The authors argue that the Anglo-American model appears to enhance managerial choice in contrast to the German model and the Japanese model, which can both be characterized by significant regulation or coordination at the macro-level. The Dutch model is much closer to the coordinated market economy of Germany than to the liberal market economies of the UK and the USA, again suggesting significant differences between the UK and the Netherlands. The varieties of capitalism approach focuses on the role of institutions in capital and labour markets and, of particular relevance here, the levels of commitment of shareholders and employees to the firm (Hall and Gingerich, 2001). Hence, in the Netherlands, a more stakeholder-oriented approach traditionally emphasizes the high commitment of employees, while in the UK a more shareholder-oriented approach emphasizes low employee commitment. Industrial relations in the Netherlands are characterized by a high degree of institutionalization in terms of (a) significant trade union influence, for example through collective bargaining agreements (CBAs), (b) strong labour legislation, for example covering employment security, safety, illness, and contingent work, and (c) the legal status of Works Councils in organizations with more than 50 employees.

The United Kingdom is less institutionalized than the Dutch system of industrial relations (Visser and Hemerijck, 1997), with contracting collective bargaining, declining trade union influence, an emphasis on flexible labour markets and works council legislation covering only European Works Councils (Edwards et al., 1998).

Visser (2003) provides more detailed information on two specific indicators that can be used to measure institutionalization: the degree of unionization and the coverage of collective bargaining agreements (CBAs). The degree of unionization is slightly lower in the Netherlands (about 25 per cent in 1997) than in the United Kingdom (about 30 per cent in 1997), but there is a major difference with respect to the CBA coverage in the Netherlands (over 80 per cent of all employees in 1998) compared to the UK (about 30 per cent of all employees in 1998). The latter results reflect the powerful position of Dutch trade unions in the collective bargaining process in spite of the relatively low degree of unionization. Hence:

Proposition 3a: Buy-outs in the Netherlands are significantly more likely than buy-outs in the UK to invest in high-commitment HR policies and practices.

According to DiMaggio and Powell (1983), organizations in a population facing the same set of environmental conditions will come to resemble each other. DiMaggio and Powell (1983) emphasize the concept of institutional isomorphism for understanding similarities between organizations. Three institutional mechanisms drive institutional isomorphism: coercive mechanisms, normative mechanisms and mimetic mechanisms.

Institutional theory suggests that coercive differences at the national level, which arise from influences such as labour legislation and trade unions, are reflected in the degree of institutional isomorphism at the organization level. Extensive legislation and directives at the national level lead to high degrees of HR homogeneity at the firm level. The United Kingdom is less institutionalized in terms of coercive mechanisms than the Netherlands (Edwards et al., 1998; Visser and Hemerijck, 1997; Visser, 1998).

Boselie et al. (2003) found that labour regulations encourage homogeneity in the HR of Dutch organizations as corporatism has withstood the pressures of international competition (Visser, 1998). Based on the likely impact of institutional environments, we expect differences between the highly institutionalized Dutch system and the less institutionalized UK system of industrial relations with respect to the management of employee relations following buy-outs. New institutionalism suggests that the management of employee relationships (e.g. HR practices and policies) is more homogeneous among firms in the Netherlands than among firms in the UK.

Proposition 3b: Employee relations, in particular HR practices and policies, are more homogeneous in buy-outs in the Netherlands than in buy-outs in the UK.

Further, notwithstanding the agency theory perspective, high degrees of institutionalization are expected to lead to restrictions with respect to the discretion to change HR practices and policies. Firms in the Netherlands are more likely to be 'trapped' in a highly institutionalized web of regulations than firms in the UK and therefore are less likely to change their HRM after fundamental organizational changes, such as a transfer of ownership.

Proposition 3c: The changes in HR policies and practices after a buy-out are expected to be bigger in the less institutionalized context of the UK than in the highly institutionalized context of the Netherlands.

These arguments can also be extended to the role of trade unions, both in terms of their recognition for collective bargaining purposes and also in respect of management's attitudes towards union membership. As noted above, Dutch legislation has institutionalized collective bargaining agreements. In contrast, in the UK, collective bargaining is contracting. Thus, at an individual firm level, it is expected that there will be greater recognition of unions for collective bargaining both before and after buy-out. Similarly, there may be institutionalized differences in the attraction of management towards union membership. Hence:

Proposition 3d: The recognition of trade unions for collective bargaining purposes before, immediately after and subsequent to buy-out is expected to be greater in the highly institutionalized context of the Netherlands than in the less institutionalized context of the UK.

Proposition 3e: Management's attitude towards union membership is expected to be more positive in the highly institutionalized context of the Netherlands than in the less institutionalized context of the UK.

DATA COLLECTION AND SAMPLE

A questionnaire with a common core of questions was developed on the basis of prior literature and discussions with practitioners. The survey instrument was piloted among academics, financiers, advisers and buy-out management. The questionnaires, in English and Dutch respectively, were mailed to the general director/owner of the firm, since these directors were assumed to have direct responsibility for their personnel and thus reliable knowledge of employee relations in their firms. The survey was conducted in 1999–2001.

All UK buy-outs completed in the period 1994–1997 and all Dutch buy-outs completed between 1992 and 1998 were surveyed. The overall usable response rate was 18.1 per cent. After reminders and telephone calls we received usable responses from 145 buy-outs in the UK (18.1 per cent) and 45 buy-outs in the Netherlands (18.2 per cent). All the buy-outs in the sample had a transaction value above €7.5m and were supplied by the Centre for Management Buy-out Research at Nottingham University (CMBOR). CMBOR has collected data on buy-outs since the late 1970s and currently has records of over 16 000 buy-outs in the UK and Continental Europe, effectively the population of buy-outs. The minimum size cut-off was taken on the basis that enterprises above this size are likely to employ a significant number of employees and thereby have more formal human resource management procedures to deal with the complex task of management (Sisson and Marginson, 1995). Comparisons of the distribution of the responses with the CMBOR database for each country showed that the sample was generally representative for the population of buy-outs in terms of size, source of transaction and industry. With respect to industry categories and transaction values, chi-squared tests for differences between the sample and population were insignificant in the UK. In the Dutch sample the category of business services is slightly over-represented compared to the population. A chi-squared test suggested no significant difference between the sample and population shares.

In our survey we asked respondents to indicate the presence or absence of a range of high-commitment management practices in the buy-out with questions sourced from several previous studies (Cully et al., 1999; Guest and Hoque, 1994; Wood and Albanese, 1995). High-commitment practices or high-performance work practices are those practices that are presumed to lead to high employee commitment (employee 'devotion'), increased employee flexibility, decreased employee turnover and high productivity standards (e.g. Appelbaum et al., 2000; Batt, 2002; Guthrie, 2001; Ramsay et al., 2000).

We also asked whether a wide range of personnel practices had changed compared to before the buy-out. We used a 5-point Likert-type scale ranging from 'decreased a lot' to 'increased a lot' with respect to total number of employees, HR management issues, for example the amount of training employees receive, and payment and rewards. Employment was measured in terms of whether the total number of employees had 'increased', 'decreased' or 'remained the same' after the MBO. We asked respondents whether real earnings 'increased', 'decreased' or 'stayed the same' as a result of the buy-out for the directors of the MBO, middle managers, line managers and non-managerial employees. Industrial relations are measured by comparing the recognition of trade unions for collective bargaining, the willingness of directors/owners to negotiate with union representatives and management attitude towards union membership among employees (see Tables 11.3 and 11.4). *T*-tests were carried out in order to determine whether or not significant country differences exist.

RESULTS

First, we present the descriptive findings of the comparison between the UK and Dutch buy-outs with respect to the presence of high-commitment management practices. Second, we report changes in employee relations, in particular total employment, HR practices and payment. Third, we focus on changes in industrial relations in the UK and the Netherlands. Fourth, we provide more detailed insights into the changes following buy-outs in two cases from the contrasting institutional contexts of the UK and the Netherlands.

HRM in UK and Dutch buy-outs

Of 20 high-commitment practices measured, ten are reported to be used by over half of the buy-outs in both the UK and the Netherlands (Table 11.1). For example, with respect to employee involvement methods, a majority of the employees in buy-outs in both countries receive information on company performance and nearly half of them are involved in setting performance targets. If we compare the reported high-commitment policies of both samples, a substantial proportion of the employees in both UK and Dutch buy-outs work in formally designated teams and are trained to do jobs other than their own. Other high-commitment management practices applicable in almost half of buy-outs in both countries are the way team members decide how work is done and the use of internal promotion. These findings provide support for Proposition 2a rather than Proposition 1a.

However, there are also some differences in the reported HR policies between the countries. Dutch buy-outs were more likely than UK buy-outs to report the use of thirteen of these practices, while UK buy-outs reported greater use of seven policies. Dutch buy-outs were statistically more likely to report the use of performance appraisal, profit-related pay, newsletters/staff bulletins, team briefings, problem-solving groups, a guaranteed job security or no redundancy policy, a majority of employees having a minimum five days' training per year and employees deciding how their work is done. Buy-outs in the UK reported a statistically significant greater use of merit pay and suggestion schemes. Overall, Dutch buy-outs were

Table 11.1 HR policies reported in buy-outs in the UK and the Netherlands (% reporting)

HR policy	UK	NL	z-test of proportions
Pay systems			
Own shares under share ownership/share option schemes	28	33	1.09
Receive merit payments	72	53	2.38**
Performance appraisal	77	90	1.91†
Profit-related pay	60	80	2.45**
Employee involvement methods			
Daily 'walk around' workplace by senior manager	88	87	0.18
Suggestion schemes	44	27	2.03**
Newsletters/staff bulletins	61	76	1.84
Attitude survey	27	31	0.52
Regular social functions	58	47	1.30
Team briefing	64	84	2.53**
Employees involved in setting performance targets	40	49	1.07
Information given to employees on company performance	76	67	1.20
Problem-solving groups (quality circles)	32	75	5.10***
Other high commitment management practices			
Most employees work in formally designated teams	49	40	1.06
Guaranteed job security or no-redundancies policy	2	16	3.66***
Most employees have minimum five days' training per year	4	24	4.15***
Most employees trained to do jobs other than their own	43	35	0.95
Employees decide how work is done	42	56	1.65†
Temporary staff used only to protect job security of core employees	26	29	0.40
Internal promotion preferred	47	58	1.29

Notes: †$p<0.10$; * $p<0.05$; ** $p<0.01$; *** $p<0.001$.

therefore more likely to report high-commitment management policies. These findings provide support for Proposition 3a.

Change in Employee Relations

Overall, the results in Table 11.2 suggest that employee relations improve as a direct result of the buy-out. Managers reported increases in the total

Table 11.2 Changes in employee relations

Which issues have changed as a direct result of the buy-out:	Mean UK (SD)	Mean NL (SD)	T-test for equality of means (NL = 1, UK = 0)	Levene's F-test for equality of variances
Employment (3-point scale)				
Total number of employees	2.39 (0.82)	2.47 (0.79)	0.54	0.75
HR management issues (5-point scale)				
Importance of HRM issues	3.81 (0.96)	3.47 (0.67)	−2.20*	16.87***
Resources devoted to managing employees	3.63 (1.02)	3.42 (0.54)	−1.33	33.01***
The amount of training employees receive	3.83 (0.98)	3.20 (0.55)	−4.12***	35.23***
The flexibility shown by employees	3.92 (0.94)	3.50 (0.63)	−2.80**	19.92***
Workers' responsibility for their jobs	4.05 (0.90)	3.73 (0.72)	−2.15*	8.39**
The total number of employees working in teams	3.78 (0.95)	3.40 (0.58)	−2.56*	44.61***
Avoiding lay-offs	3.12(0.78)	3.11 (0.71)	−0.03	0.02
The use of internal promotion	3.48 (0.88)	3.27 (0.62)	−1.51	11.31**
Use of temporary workers only to cover shortages	3.25 (0.83)	2.86 (0.93)	−2.61**	1.21
The level of trust between managers and workers	3.94 (0.98)	3.62 (0.78)	−1.97	6.71*
The similarity of terms and conditions between managers and non-managers	3.39 (0.87)	3.22 (0.47)	−1.23	16.55***
Payment & rewards (1) (5-point scale)				
The number of staff whose performance is appraised on an annual or bi-annual basis	3.65 (0.87)	3.47 (0.69)	−1.26	9.31**
The number of staff receiving merit pay	3.69 (0.91)	3.27 (0.73)	−2.81**	18.41***
The percentage of non-managerial employees owning shares in the company	3.27 (0.81)	3.33 (0.92)	0.36	0.80
Degree of employee involvement	4.07 (0.91)	3.80 (0.69)	−1.82	12.36***

Table 11.2 (continued)

Which issues have changed as a direct result of the buy-out:	Mean UK (SD)	Mean NL (SD)	T-test for equality of means (NL = 1, UK = 0)	Levene's F-test for equality of variances
Payment & rewards (2) (3-point scale)				
Earnings of directors	2.48 (0.69)	2.29 (0.66)	$-1.66^{\dagger}$	0.75
Earnings of middle managers	2.70 (0.47)	2.68 (0.47)	−0.24	0.10
Earnings of line managers	2.57 (0.51)	2.41 (0.55)	$-1.69^{\dagger}$	0.62
Earnings of non-managerial employees	2.54 (0.54)	2.51 (0.55)	−0.30	0.04

Notes: $^{\dagger}p<0.10$; * $p<0.05$; ** $p<0.01$; *** $p<0.001$.
Scales were as follows:
Employment (3-point scale): 1 = gone down, 2 = about the same, 3 = gone up.
HR management issues (5-point scale): 1 = decreased a lot; 2 = decreased; 3 = stayed the same; 4 = increased; 5 = increased a lot.
Payment &. rewards (1) (5-point scale): 1 = decreased a lot, 2 = decreased, 3 = stayed the same, 4 = increased, 5 = increased a lot.
Payment &. rewards (2) (3-point scale): 1 = gone down, 2 = about the same, 3 = gone up.

number of employees, the importance of HRM issues, resources devoted to managing employees, the amount of training employees receive, the flexibility shown by employees, workers' responsibility for their jobs and the level of trust between managers and workers. Other issues did not change dramatically but stayed about the same, including: avoiding lay-offs, the use of internal promotion, the use of temporary workers, the similarity of terms and conditions between managers and non-managers, and the percentage of non-managerial employees owning shares in the company. The results suggest that buy-outs create leeway for the new owners to change employee relations, in particular with respect to growth in terms of number of employees, employee participation, employees' trust and earnings. These findings provide support for Proposition 2b rather than Proposition 1b.

Change in employee relations in Dutch and UK buy-outs

To examine whether HR practices and policies are more homogeneous in the highly institutionalized context of the Netherlands compared to the UK we test for the equality of variances for each HR item. We find that UK buy-outs are significantly different from the Dutch buy-outs on practically all the HR issues (Table 11.2, last column). The UK buy-outs show substantially larger variances than the Dutch cases, indicating larger variation in the pattern of change in employee relations in the UK compared to the more homogeneous scores of the Dutch firms. Proposition 3b is thus supported.

The next step in our analysis focuses on significant differences in the impact of a buy-out on employee relations in the UK and the Netherlands. We find significant differences in the changes in employee relations in buy-outs in the UK and the Netherlands (see *t*-tests in Table 11.2). Using t-tests we compared the mean scores of issues between the institutionalized Netherlands and the less institutionalized UK. Although both groups of buy-outs show improvements, statistically fewer improvements in HRM were reported in the Netherlands compared to the UK on six items: 'importance of HRM issues'; 'the amount of training employees receive'; 'the flexibility shown by employees'; 'workers' responsibility for their jobs'; 'the total number of employees working in teams'; 'use of temporary workers only to cover shortages'; and 'the number of staff receiving merit pay'. Proposition 3c is thus supported.

These findings imply that the UK has risen towards, although still does not match, Dutch standards of HRM. The majority of these 'best practices' appear to be institutionalized in the Netherlands prior to the buy-out through labour legislation (e.g. collective health care insurance and pension schemes) or collective bargaining agreements (e.g. wages, employee benefits, training and development). The amount of training employees have to receive is often part of a collective bargaining agreement in the Netherlands represented by a minimum percentage of total wages. Flexibility in terms of contingent work is strictly tied to labour legislation in the Dutch Flexwet, a law on employment security of contingent workers in the Netherlands. As a result of the opposition of Dutch trade unions to individual performance-related payment systems, merit pay for staff is not as widely used as in the UK. Thus, there seems to be logic for the difference between the UK and the Netherlands with respect to the impact of a buy-out on employee relations. What buy-outs in both countries seem to share equally are increases in the total number of employees, their unchanged behaviour with respect to avoiding lay-offs, and the slight increase in the percentage of non-managerial employees owning shares in the firm.

With respect to payment and rewards, Table 11.2 shows that both groups report an increase in earnings for all worker categories (3-point scale) as compared to before the buy-out. However, the Dutch buy-out directors score more moderately than the UK buy-out directors. Increases in pay for UK buy-out directors are significantly higher than their Dutch colleagues (at a 90 per cent confidence interval), while there were no differences in changes in the pay of non-managerial employees between both samples.

Industrial Relations in UK and Dutch Buy-outs

Buy-outs in the UK and the Netherlands operated in different industrial relations contexts. The recognition of trade unions for collective bargaining before the buy-out, immediately after the buy-out and subsequently is significantly higher in the Netherlands than in the UK (Table 11.3). Subsequent to the buy-out, 60 per cent of the Dutch buy-outs at the time of the survey recognized trade unions for collective bargaining, in contrast to 34 per cent of the UK buy-outs. Apparently UK and Dutch buy-out managers do not have a common framework for collective bargaining.

Table 11.3 Recognition of trade unions for collective bargaining

	Total sample	UK	NL	T-test for equality of means (NL = 1; UK = 0)
Before buy-out	41%	34%	62%	3.39**
Immediately after	35%	29%	56%	3.34**
Currently	41%	34%	60%	3.11*

Note: * $p<0.05$; ** $p<0.01$.

Table 11.4 General attitudes of managers towards trade union membership among employees at the establishment

	Total sample	UK	NL	T-test for equality of means (NL = 1; UK = 0)
In favour of membership	9%	10%	6%	−0.61
Neutral to membership	60%	50%	88%	4.89***
Not in favour of membership	29%	40%	6%	−3.90***

Note: *** $p < 0.001$.

The differences in union recognition reflected the general attitude of managers towards trade union membership among employees at the establishment (see Table 11.4). In the Dutch buy-outs, a majority (88 per cent) of directors expressed a neutral attitude towards trade union membership among their employees. This is indicative of the impact of regulations encouraging a strong sharing of values among Dutch managers towards the effects of trade unions on employee relations. Only 50 per cent of the UK buy-outs were neutral towards trade union membership, and in 40 per cent of the UK buy-outs managers were not in favour of membership at all. The negative attitudes of managers to trade union membership in the UK buy-outs differ fundamentally from their Dutch counterparts.

The majority of Dutch buy-outs in this sample have a works council: twenty-nine firms or 64 per cent of the Dutch buy-outs had one installed before the buy-out and thirty firms had one afterwards. In contrast, none of the UK firms reported a works council. Thus, the results with respect to trade union recognition for collective bargaining, general attitude of managers towards trade union membership, and works councils installed demonstrate significant differences between the UK and the Dutch institutional environment and provide support for Propositions 3d and 3e. These empirical findings indicate institutional industrial relations mechanisms continued in buy-outs in the Netherlands, and UK buy-outs faced fewer institutional constraints.

Case Study Evidence

Drawing on two case studies of buy-outs in the UK and the Netherlands, we shall now illustrate in more detail the effects of the institutional differences between the two countries. Data were gathered from interviews with the parties involved in the buy-outs as well as from secondary published information.

Unipart: a UK buy-out

The automotive parts producer and distributor Unipart was formerly part of the then state-owned Rover Group. In 1987, Unipart was privatized in a management–employee buy-out. Seventy managers obtained 10 per cent of the equity and the general body of employees held 12 per cent. Seventy per cent of employees took up the initial offer to buy shares. Private equity firms held 56.3 per cent of the equity, with the balance being retained by the Rover Group. The private equity firms selected took a long-term perspective on their investment.

Prior to the buy-out, HRM in Unipart was influenced by the problems of the troubled parent. Industrial relations had been poor in the group for many years and the need to deal with trading difficulties had led to a focus on rationalization of the workforce and restrictions on investment. In 1985, the period leading up to privatization, employment in Unipart was reduced by 15 per cent.

The management of Unipart explicitly took the approach after the buy-out not to focus on short-term shareholder value (Jackson, 1997). Rather than management taking a large majority of the equity and increasing profits over a two- to three-year period through further rationalization before floating the company, the decision was taken to spread ownership and invest heavily in a new delivery system and to develop long-term trading relationships. This strategy involved a more flexible and developmental approach to HRM.

Following the buy-out, foremen and supervisor positions were replaced by team leaders as the company adopted Japanese approaches to operations. Instead of being based around function, machines were grouped into cells in which small, flexible teams of employees would carry out a variety of tasks. The factory's team of workers have devised new, faster ways of setting up machines to give more flexibility in the production process. The company also developed 'contribution circles' initiated by management and employees that worked on a large number of projects with resultant significant reductions in costs. Seven layers of management between the factory's general manager and the shop floor were cut to three. In early 1992, the company ended trade union recognition on the grounds that the unions were undermining the company's strategy to develop multi-skilling, team briefings, quality circles and direct communication between management and employees.

An important change in employees' remuneration was also introduced. All 4500 employees are assessed on their individual performance annually, with those with higher ratings being eligible for a higher proportion of share options. An employee's performance is assessed as satisfactory, good or excellent. Those assessed as satisfactory are eligible for one share option for each ordinary share purchased, up to two share options for each ordinary share purchased in respect of those assessed as excellent. The company also changed the structure of remuneration so that all workers were paid salaries rather than hourly wages. Recognizing the importance of maintaining the incentive of employee ownership, a share buy-back scheme was introduced in 1988 with the aim of creating a pool of shares that could be distributed to new employees.

In 1993, the company created Unipart University with the aim of enhancing the skills of employees based on the Japanese model of managers sharing knowledge with employees but at the same time managers also learning from employees. The CEO of Unipart clearly expressed a key aspect of HRM following the buy-out: 'We realized that if we were to compete and survive internationally, we had to make a commitment to making our people more skilled . . . The constant search for improvement is now a way of life in Unipart.' By 1994, 90 per cent of employees had undertaken courses at the university. The university plays a key role in retraining workers displaced by cost cutting. This has meant that employees can be retained rather than being made redundant. In the decade following the buy-out there were no forced redundancies, with there being a guarantee of employment continuation for those whose jobs disappear through restructuring.

Boekhoven-Bosch: a Dutch buy-out

The printing company Boekhoven-Bosch was formerly owned by the publishing company Elsevier. In 1987, Boekhoven-Bosch was divested in a management buy-out to its managers backed by two private equity firms. The general manager and the Employee Consortium each owned 5 per cent of the equity, private equity firms owned 58.4 per cent and 31.6 per cent of the shares remained initially with the parent. The private equity funders are known as long-term investors. At the time of the buy-out the workforce comprised 450 employees.

Prior to the buy-out, HRM in Elsevier was prescribed by a headquarters-based department, responsible for coordinating the personnel arrangements, such as labour conditions across all subsidiaries of Elsevier. The HRM department in Boekhoven-Bosch changed after the MBO from a regulating and bureaucratic body to a department with a more central role in the implementation of the HRM policy of the firm (Van Neerven et al., 1996).

In February 1987, and following the withdrawal from purchase negotiations of the US-based printer Donnelley & Sons, the works council invited the CEO Mr Van Ek to relaunch his buy-out plans for the firm. According to the Law on Works Councils, the works council of Boekhoven-Bosch set up a committee to examine the desirability and feasibility of the proposed MBO. The trade union 'Druk en Papier', a union for the printing industry belonging to the largest Dutch trade union FNV, organized meetings with the works council that focused on issues relating to numbers employed, guarantee of job content and job level, and continuation of the collective bargaining agreement of the printing industry. The works council proposed that the employees should participate in the buy-out as compensation for the loss of the former corporate benefits such as free subscription to two daily newspapers, discounts on books published by Elsevier and three-yearly tax-free gifts of 100 Dutch Guilders (around 45 euro or £30). A foundation named 'Employees' Interests Boekhoven-Bosch' was established to implement the workers' participation plan by using part of the individual saving from the salaries for the acquisition of shares by the employees. After six weeks the council supported the buy-out and advised management to proceed. The trade unions were particularly in favour of the MBO because of the experience and recognized skill of the director of the firm who was to lead the buy-out.

In 1988 and 1989 the management invested in robots and computers to take advantage of the trend towards desktop publishing and electronic printing, and to increase the volume of production to reduce costs. Subsequently, management stimulated strong cooperation between the HRM and the quality department in order to integrate the new job requirements and work attitudes of the operating employees with the new quality requirements for meeting printing orders. Post-MBO, employees became process operators, with more autonomy and responsibility for taking the initiative to control operational processes, contact customers, and ensure the quality of products without waiting for orders from their bosses. Accordingly, responsibilities were decentralized. To improve internal communication, team meetings were introduced in each section. Anything that related to the job was open for discussion in both formal and informal meetings (Van Neerven et al., 1996).

In 1990 Boekhoven-Bosch introduced job profiles that described the characteristics and responsibilities of hundreds of jobs, as well as informative and appraisal interviews, linked to a system of career guidance. An annual system of job performance evaluation was started. The resulting individual career development, job rotation and management development were largely neglected prior to the buy-out. This post-MBO change in HRM led to an increase in training for both employees and middle management in order to develop a multi-skilled and flexible workforce. More hours' training were devoted to communicating and work briefing skills. During this period of transition, people from the HRM department and the works council joined forces to control the loss of days caused by sickness. No employees were laid off, but staff vacancies were not filled. With respect to the changes, the CEO of Boekhoven-Bosch clearly expressed the constructive attitude of the firm's works council: 'The works council is a responsible body with an advisory influence on HRM that without doubt has increased post-MBO. I take them seriously but I also demand that they focus on the key issue of the firm's business.' In place of the previous Elsevier terms, a number of new employment terms were introduced, including: profit sharing, the opportunity to purchase share certificates through a seven-year share saving scheme, a five times per year bonus payment of 100 Dutch Guilders to each employee and a free daily newspaper per employee.

Comparing the two case studies we can see that in the Dutch case the works council plays an active role in the re-launch of the MBO plans of the CEO, and, in accordance with the Law on Works Councils (articles 24, 25 and 27), a constructive role in the subsequent stages of gathering information (e.g. employment and business plan), of advising (e.g. reorganization and change in management) and approving HR issues (e.g. pay, pension, profit sharing and job classification) during the buy-out. Representatives of the trade unions were invited as counselling specialists to inform and advise the members of the works council. These institutions both restrain management choice and enable efficient investments in skills and the further development of employee commitment. In contrast, managers in the UK buy-out had greater leeway and chose to implement new HRM practices to develop employee commitment with little recourse to the trade unions. Despite these differences in communication between management and employees in the two MBOs, the cases also have much in common. For example, both pursued upside strategies, with changes in strategy and organization involving increased training in quality and customer service for employees, and resulting changes in job content and other HR policies. These case studies support the findings of the survey data that buy-outs do not generally improve performance through an attack on the terms and conditions of employees.

CONCLUSIONS

The findings reveal buy-outs have a positive effect on employee relations in both the UK and the Netherlands. The high level of investment in high-commitment HR policies and practices and the increase in these investments following a buy-out suggest that buy-outs release their upside potential rather than protect the downside of their operations. Differences in institutional setting between the UK and the Netherlands appear to moderate the effect of buy-outs on employee relations. For example, Dutch managers in contrast to UK managers recognize trade unions for collective bargaining purposes and have neutral attitudes towards union membership, leading to more investment in high-commitment HR practices and policies but also to more homogeneous employee relations in the buy-out firms than in the UK. However, the effect of buy-outs on employee relations is smaller in the highly regulated Dutch context than in the less regulated UK context for six out of eleven HR management issues. The stronger scores on changes in employee relations in UK buy-outs imply that the UK buy-outs raised their standard of HR practice closer to, although still slightly below, the Dutch level. The effect of buy-outs is also positive on the real earnings of directors, middle managers, line managers and non-managerial employees. Although the change does not quite reach statistical significance, the UK buy-out directors and line managers report more frequent increases in earnings than the Dutch.

These findings raise three main questions. First, why do buy-outs affect employee relations positively? Second, why do UK buy-outs have a greater influence on employee relations than Dutch buy-outs? Third, why do employees on the whole appear to benefit from buy-outs?

Referring to our first question, the change of ownership involved in buy-outs may have several positive effects. First, new ownership releases the bought-out company from former company policies and creates the opportunity to reappraise policies. The leeway after the buy-out can be used to expand the number of employees and to invest in employee development. Second, the incentives for investment may have changed. Compared to the business divisions of larger organizations, buy-outs may be more able to invest for the longer term rather than provide cash for the business group. The pay-off from long-term investments may be higher as it may be captured by the buy-out rather than returned to head office. In short, it may be easier to re-invest profits in buy-outs to develop the business. This may involve human capital investments. Third, buy-outs may embark upon a new business strategy that requires a change of HR policies. For example, a new focus on quality service in a niche market may require significant investments in staff training and development. Fourth, the uncertainty created by the change in ownership may necessitate positive HR investments to build employee trust and commitment to the new owners. The application of HR policies and practices, for example, training and development, payment, increasing workers' responsibility, might be a powerful tool for management to gain trust and commitment. The implementation of new HR practices may also be intended as a signal from managers to employees of the sustainability of the organization. Fifth, the introduction of new managers may simply inject new thinking about the value of investing in HRM. All of these appear feasible explanations and future research could explore which is the main mechanism for upgrading HRM in buy-outs. The evidence of both case studies supports these positive effects of change of ownership on HR investment.

The impact of institutional context provides insights into the second question of why UK buy-outs have a more positive influence on employee relations than Dutch buy-outs. As firms are captive in an institutional environment (Tolbert and Zucker, 1983), they gain a 'common understanding of what is appropriate and fundamentally meaningful behaviour' (Zucker, 1983). The recognition of trade unions for collective bargaining, the attitude of managers towards trade union membership and the works council system all prevent Dutch buy-outs from embarking upon radical changes in employment practices post-buy-out. Our empirical findings on industrial relations confirmed that buy-out firms in the Netherlands face a more institutionalized environment than buy-out firms in the UK. In the Netherlands collective bargaining agreements (CBAs) have been institutionalized by legislation with a widely accepted role for trade unions since 1927. Another typical example of the institutionalized Dutch setting is the obligation for organizations with more than fifty employees to install a works council (Works Councils Law, Article 2). These institutional mechanisms, embedded in the industrial relations system, appear to be responsible for fundamental differences between the UK and the Netherlands in the magnitude of change in employee relations after the buy-out. The differences are represented by a high versus low degree of institutionalization in industrial relations, and moderate the relationship between buy-outs and employee relations. As a result, the positive effect of the buy-out on the employment relationship is smaller in the Dutch context than in the UK context. Six out of eleven HR management issues increased more in the UK cases than in the Dutch cases. This suggests that Dutch buy-outs have either less leeway to change the existing HR practice because of legal restrictions or the specific HR practice is already fixed through collective bargaining agreements. Dutch buy-out managers are also pressured into conformity by regulatory structures based on legislation and public expectations (Oliver, 1991). These pressures are less in the UK, where buy-out directors appear to have greater freedom to reassess employee relations. Their actions do not appear to be driven or evaluated by the same institutional normative influences (Davis and Greve, 1997) as in the Netherlands. Therefore they can decide on policies informally and in a non-committed way, in contrast to Dutch buy-out managers who must comply with the minimum standard for employee relations pre-buy-out, which are on a higher level than for their UK counterparts. This explains the relatively stronger effect of buy-outs on the employee relationship in the UK that contributes to narrowing the gap in the level of HR practices between the two countries.

The third question raised by our findings is: why do real earnings increase for all employee categories after buy-out? We believe that earnings are seen as an important means of motivating people for the risk of running a company themselves. The financiers of buy-outs incentivize managers by rewards triggered only when certain turnover and/or profit targets of the buy-out are met. Buy-out managers are also likely to incentivize all their staff to meet these targets and thereby share some of the gains of improved performance. It is also interesting to note that UK buy-out managers more frequently report an increase in pay for directors and line managers than their Dutch counterparts. Although we can only speculate on the causes we can think of two explanations. First, this may reflect market norms and expectations from financiers about appropriate and acceptable trade-offs between risks and pay after a buy-out. The risk may be similar in the two countries but UK entrepreneurs may simply expect larger rewards. Second, the industrial relations structure in the Netherlands may redistribute a share of profits from senior managers to all staff in buy-outs, whereas in the UK managers may take a larger share of rewards. Buy-outs in the Netherlands may follow the Dutch system of ‘concertation with consensus’ and ‘jobs before income’ (Visser, 1998, p. 284), restricting pay rises for managers.

Finally, what lessons can be learned from these findings for future research on the effects of buy-outs on employee relations?

First, we need to study the motives of buy-out teams for developing new HR policies after the buy-out more thoroughly. Longitudinal research in this area on HR investment before, immediately after, and one to two years after the buy-out could explore whether the HR investment is temporary and merely a management tool for signalling the new owners’ best intentions or represents a new and relatively enduring management philosophy of investing in employees.

Second, it may be fruitful to distinguish between different types of buy-outs. In certain buy-outs employees also take an equity share alongside management and we would expect this to deter a cost-cutting approach towards employment. In other buy-outs, external managers ‘buy in’, introducing new ideas and approaches. ‘Buy-ins’ are certainly likely to lead to a change of HRM policies, although we do not know currently whether the effect is to enhance or downgrade HRM overall. It would also be useful to identify the factors that encourage new managers to upgrade HRM.

Third, for a better understanding of the increased leeway after the buy-out we need to examine the role of investors such as venture capitalists and banks. In particular, it would be useful to explore financier involvement and the effect of the financial incentives and targets set for buy-outs. For example, it may be possible to distinguish between different types of financiers of buy-outs. Some financiers may manage only by setting challenging performance targets and seek a quick return from their investment. As a consequence buy-out managers may still face financial restrictions and be deterred from long-term investments in human assets. In contrast, other financiers may take an active involvement in building the business over a longer term and thereby encourage employee development.

Fourth, it would be helpful to explore changes in the business strategies of buy-outs and the implications for HRM. Whereas buy-outs engaged in a 'buy and build' strategy may develop markets and staff, other buy-outs may retrench into cost competition and squeeze labour costs, and yet others may do both.

Finally, the significant differences in employee relations between the UK and Dutch buy-outs teach us to be very cautious with international comparable research in this area. Labour market institutions shape employee relations in organizations as well as the impact of buy-outs. Future work assessing the impact on HRM of changes in corporate governance must account for the effects of national institutional contexts.

REFERENCES

Appelbaum, E., Bailey, T., Berg, P. and Kalleberg, A.L. (2000), *Manufacturing Advantage: Why high-performance work systems pay off*, Ithaca, NY and London: Economic Policy Institute & ILR Press.

Arthur, J.B. (1994), 'Effects of human resource systems on manufacturing performance and turnover', *Academy of Management Journal*, **3** (37), 670–87.

Bae, J. and Lawler, J.J. (2000), 'Organisational performance and HRM in Korea: impact on firm performance in an emerging economy', *Academy of Management Journal*, **43**, 502–17.

Batt, R. (2002), 'Managing customer services: human resource practices, quit rates, and sales growth', *Academy of Management Journal*, **3** (45), 587–97.

Boselie, P., Paauwe, J. and Jansen, P.G.W. (2001), 'Human resource management and performance: lessons from the Netherlands', *International Journal of Human Resource Management*, **7** (12), 1107–25.

Boselie, P., Paauwe, J. and Richardson, R. (2003), 'Human resource management, institutionalization and organisational performance: a comparison of hospitals, hotels and local government', *International Journal of Human Resource Management*, **8** (14), 1407–29.

Bradley, K. and Nejad, A. (1989), *Managing Owners: The National Freight Consortium in perspective*, Cambridge: Cambridge University Press.

Bruining, J. (1992), 'Performance improvement after management buy-out', unpublished PhD, Erasmus University, Rotterdam.

CMBOR (2002), 'Recent trends in UK buy-outs and buy-ins', in M. Wright and A. Burrows (eds), *Management Buy-outs*, Nottingham: Centre for Management Buy-out Research, pp. 9–36.

CMBOR (2003), 'Market overview' and 'The Netherlands', in M. Wright A. Burrows and A. Scholes (eds), *European Management Buy-outs*, Nottingham: Centre for Management Buy-out Research.

CMBOR/Initiative Europe (1991), *Europe Buy-out Review 1990*, London: Initiative Europe.

Cully, M., Woodland, S., O'Reilly, A. and Dix, G. (1999), *Britain at Work*, London: Routledge.

Davis, G.F. and Greve, H. (1997), 'Corporate elite networks and governance changes in the 1980's', *American Journal of Sociology*, **1** (103), 1–37.

DiMaggio, P.J. and Powell, W.W. (1983), 'The iron cage revisited: institutional isomorphism and collective rationality in organisational fields', *American Sociological Review*, **48,** 147–60.

Edwards, P., Hall, M., Hyman, R., Marginson, P., Sisson, K., Waddington, J. and Winchester, D. (1998), 'Great Britain: from partial collectivism to neo-liberalism to where?', in A. Ferner and R. Hyman (eds), *Changing Industrial Relations in Europe*, Oxford: Blackwell, pp. 1–54.

European Private Equity and Venture Capital Association (EVCA) (2001), *Survey of the Economic and Social Impact of Management Buy-outs and Buy-ins in Europe*, Research paper Zaventum, Belgium.

Francis, J. and Smith, A. (1995), 'Agency costs and innovation: some empirical Evidence', *Journal of Accounting and Economics*, **19**, 383–409.

Gospel, H. and Pendleton, A. (2003), 'Finance, corporate governance and the management of labour: a conceptual and comparative analysis', *British Journal of Industrial Relations*, **3** (41), 557–82.

Greenwood, R. and Hinings, C.R. (1996), 'Understanding radical organisational change: bringing together the old and the new institutionalism', *Academy of Management Review*, **4** (21), 1022–55.

Guest, D. and Hoque, K. (1994), 'The good, the bad and the ugly: employment relations in new non-union workplaces', *Human Resource Management Journal*, **5**, 1–14.

Guthrie, J.P. (2001), 'High-involvement work practices, turnover, and productivity: evidence from New Zealand', *Academy of Management Journal*, **44**, 180–90.

Hall, P. and Gingerich, D. (2001), 'Varieties of capitalism and institutional complementarities in the macroeconomy: an empirical analysis', paper presented at the American Political Science Association Conference, San Francisco.

Holmstrom, B. (1989), 'Agency costs and innovation', *Journal of Economic Behavior and Organisation*, **12**, 305–27.

Holmstrom, B. and Milgrom, P. (1990), 'Regulating trade among agents', *Journal of Institutional and Theoretical Economics*, **146**, 85–105.

Ichniowski, C., Shaw, K. and Prennushi, G. (1997), 'The effects of human resource management practices on productivity: a study of steel finishing lines', *American Economic Review*, **87,** 291–313.

Jackson, T. (1997), 'The lean paternalist', *Financial Times*, 14 February.

Jensen, M.C. (1986), 'Agency costs of free cash flow, corporate finance and takeovers', *American Economic Review*, **76**, 323–9.

Jensen, M.C. (1989), 'Eclipse of the public corporation', *Harvard Business Review*, **67**, 61–74.

Jensen, M.C. (1993), 'The modern industrial revolution, exit and the failure of internal control systems', *Journal of Finance*, **48**, 831–80.

Kalleberg, A.L. and Moody, J.W. (1994), 'Human resource management and organisational performance', *American Behavioral Scientist*, **37**, 948–62.

Kaplan, S. (1989), 'The effects of management buyouts on operating performance and value', *Journal of Financial Economics*, **24**, 217–54.

La Porta, R., Lopez-De-Silanes, F., Shleifer, A. and Vishny, R. (1997), 'Legal determinants of external finance', *Journal of Finance*, **3** (52), 1131–50.

Long, W.F. and Ravenscraft, D.J. (1993), 'LBOs, debt and R&D intensity', *Strategic Management Journal (Summer Special Issue)*, **14**, 119–35.

Oliver, C. (1991), 'Strategic responses to institutional processes', *Academy of Management Review*, **1** (16), 145–79.

Oliver, C. (1997), 'Sustainable competitive advantage: combining institutional and resource-based views', *Strategic Management Journal*, **18** (9), 697–713.

Paauwe, J. and Boselie, P. (2003), 'Challenging "strategic HRM" and the relevance of the institutional setting', *Human Resource Management Journal*, **3** (13), 56–70.

Pendleton, A., Wilson, N. and Wright, M. (1998), 'The perceptions and effects of share ownership: empirical evidence from employee buy-outs', *British Journal of Industrial Relations*, **1** (36), 99–124.

Phan, P. and Hill, C. (1995), 'Organisational restructuring and economic performance in leveraged buyouts: an ex-post study', *Academy of Management Journal*, **38**, 704–39.

Phillips, G. (1995), 'Increased debt and industry product markets: an empirical analysis', *Journal of Financial Economics*, **37**, 189–238.

Ramsay, H., Scholarios, D. and Harley, B. (2000), 'Employees and high-performance work systems: testing inside the black box', *British Journal of Industrial Relations*, **4** (38), 501.

Robbie, K. and Wright, M. (1996),'Local authorities, compulsory competitive tendering and buy-outs', *Local Government Studies*, **1** (22), 127–46.

Sisson, K. and Marginson, P. (1995), 'Management: systems, structures and strategy', in P. Edwards (ed.), *Industrial Relations: Theory and Practice in Britain*, Oxford: Blackwell, pp. 89–122.

Thompson, S. and Wright, M. (1995), 'Corporate governance: the role of restructuring transactions', *Economic Journal*, **105** (430), 690–703.

Thompson, R.S., Wright, M. and Robbie, K. (1992) 'Management equity ownership, debt and performance: some evidence from UK management buyouts', *Scottish Journal of Political Economy*, **39** (4), 413–30.

Tolbert, P.S. and Zucker, L.G. (1983), 'Institutional sources of change in the formal structure of organisations: the diffusion of civil service reform', *Administrative Science Quarterly*, **28**, 22–39.

Van Neerven, T., Bruining, J. and Paauwe, J. (1996), 'Managing without traditional owners', in P.C. Flood, M.J. Gannon and J. Paauwe (eds), *Managing without Traditional Methods*, Wokingham: Addison-Wesley, pp. 105–46.

Visser, J. (1998), 'The Netherlands: the return of responsive corporatism', in A. Ferner and R. Hyman (eds), *Changing Industrial Relations in Europe*, Oxford: Blackwell, pp. 283–314.

Visser, J. (2003), 'Arbeidsverhoudingen na de kanteling', in A.G. Nagelkerke and W.F. de Nijs (eds), *Sturen in het laagland: Over continuïteit en verandering van de Nederlandse arbeidsverhoudingen*, Delft: Eburon.

Visser, J. and Hemerijck, A. (1997), *A Dutch Miracle: Job growth, welfare reform and corporatism in the Netherlands*, Amsterdam: Amsterdam University Press.

Wood, S. and Albanese, M.T. (1995), 'Can we speak of a high commitment management on the shop floor?', *Journal of Management Studies*, **32,** 215–47.
Wright, M. and Coyne, J. (1985), *Management Buy-outs*, London: Croom Helm.
Wright, M., Coyne, J. and Lockley, H. (1984), 'Management buy-outs and trade unions: dispelling the myths', *Industrial Relations Journal*, **2** (15), 45–52.
Wright, M., Thompson, S. and Robbie, K. (1989), 'Privatization via management and employee buy-outs', *Annals of Public and Cooperative Economics*, **4** (60), 399–430.
Wright, M., Chiplin, B., Thompson, S. and Robbie, K. (1990), 'Management buy-outs, trade unions and employee ownership', *Industrial Relations Journal*, **2** (21), 136–46.
Wright, M., Thompson, S. and Robbie, K. (1992), 'Venture capital and management-led leveraged buy-outs: the European perspective', *Journal of Business Venturing*, **7**, 47–71.
Wright, M., Hoskisson, R.E., Busenitz, L.W. and Dial, J. (2000), 'Entrepreneurial growth through privatization: the upside of management buy-outs', *Academy of Management Review*, **3** (25), 591–601.
Wright, M., Hoskisson, R.E. and Busenitz, L.W. (2001), 'Firm rebirth: buy-outs as facilitators of strategic growth and entrepreneurship', *Academy of Management Executive*, **1** (15), 111–25.
Zahra, S.A. (1995), 'Corporate entrepreneurship and financial performance: the case of management leveraged buy-outs', *Journal of Business Venturing*, **10**, 225–47.
Zucker, L.G. (1983), 'Organisations as institutions', in S.B. Bacharach (ed.), *Research in the Sociology of Organisations*, Greenwich, CT: JAI Press, pp. 1–47.

12. The wage and employment effects of leveraged buyouts in the UK

Kevin Amess and Mike Wright

1. INTRODUCTION

The leveraged buyout (LBO) has become an important corporate restructuring mechanism internationally (Wright et al., 2005). LBOs have become especially prevalent in the UK. Between 1994 and 2003 the value of such transactions averaged £13.5 billion per annum. As a percentage of the total value of the UK market for corporate control in this period, LBOs averaged about 31% (CMBOR, 2005). The main features of an LBO are: (1) the transfer of assets to a new company, (2) the equity ownership of managers' increases, (3) the company takes on a large amount of debt secured against the firm's assets and/or against future cash flows and (4) active involvement in monitoring the firm by private equity investors. High managerial equity stakes and fixed interest obligations of debt provide incentives that attenuate the agency problems associated with public listed corporations (Jensen, 1986; Thompson and Wright, 1995).

Share price studies (Kaplan, 1989a; Lehn and Poulsen, 1989; Marais et al., 1989), studies using accounting data (Kaplan, 1989a; Smith, 1990; Smart and Waldfogel, 1994) and those using factor productivity data (Lichtenberg and Siegel, 1990) have been supportive of US LBOs producing performance gains.[1] More recent UK evidence (e.g. Amess, 2002, 2003; Harris et al., 2005) has also suggested that LBOs raise real economic performance.

Whilst there is little debate regarding performance findings, there is debate concerning the source of such gains. The mainly US literature on the source of LBO gains has focused on improved operating performance and productive efficiency (Amess, 2003; Harris et al., 2005), corporate entrepreneurship and new product development (Wright et al., 1992; Zahra, 1995), wealth transfers from pre-buyout bondholders (Marais et al., 1989) and equity holders (Easterwood et al., 1994), transfers from taxpayers (Kaplan, 1989b), reductions in R&D expenditure (Lichtenberg and Siegel, 1990; Long and Ravenscraft, 1993), capital expenditure (Kaplan, 1989a; Smith, 1990), and advertising expenditure (Smith, 1990).

The concern of this chapter is the impact of LBOs on employment and wages in the post-LBO firm. These may represent an area of major transfers of wealth from pre-buyout stakeholders to the new owners (Shleifer and Summers, 1988; Fox and Marcus, 1992; Thompson and Wright, 1995) or may be temporary effects as a firm is restructured to be placed on a more secure financial footing. Whilst the employment and wage effects of conventional mergers have received much recent attention (e.g. Conyon et al., 2002a, b), this is not the case for LBOs. Notable exceptions are earlier studies by Lichtenberg and Siegel (1990) and Wright et al. (1992). Lichtenberg and Siegel (1990) find, using US data, that non-production workers experience a decline in annual compensation of 13.7%, which may be explained by a decline in non-production worker employment. Wright et al. (1992) find, from a survey of 182 UK LBOs, that while there is an initial decline in employment (6.3%), this is followed by a subsequent increase in employment (1.9%). Kaplan (1989) and Smith (1990) report small increases in firm employment following an LBO but after adjusting for industry effects find that employment declines.

This chapter seeks to make the following contributions. First, we add to previous corporate restructuring studies which have estimated wage and employment effects separately (e.g. Conyon et al., 2001, 2002a). Such an approach does not fully capture the interdependence of wages and employment. This is the first study to examine the wage and employment effects of corporate restructuring in a simultaneous equations framework. Second, previous LBO studies treat the LBO decision as exogenous. Our analysis considers the impact of treating the LBO decision as endogenous (thus correcting for biases from such endogeneity). Third, with a few exceptions, previous studies have tended to treat LBOs as homogeneous. In this study, we distinguish between those LBOs that involve incumbent management becoming significant owners (i.e., management buyouts, MBOs)[2] and those cases involving acquisition by external management and investors (i.e., management buy-ins, MBIs).[3] This distinction between insider- and outsider-driven deals, which may involve different motivations and differences in the credibility of threat of closure or dismissal, is expected to lead to differential effects on employment and wages. Finally, previous studies have tended to use relatively small samples drawn from particular subsets of the buyout population. We examine these issues using a unique hand-collected data set involving a sample of 1350 LBOs that are representative of the entire population of UK buyouts.

This chapter is organized in the following way. Section 2 outlines the theoretical background with respect to the anticipated effects of LBOs on employment and wages. The data sources and sample characteristics are in

Section 3. The results are presented in Section 4 and conclusions are drawn in Section 5.

2. LBOS: WAGE AND EMPLOYMENT EFFECTS

The corporate governance literature recognizes that managers of public corporations with diffuse shareholders have different objective functions from the company's owners, creating agency costs (Jensen and Meckling, 1976; Fama and Jensen, 1983; Shleifer and Vishny, 1988; Jensen, 1986; Hart, 1995; and Thompson and Wright, 1995). Jensen (1989) argues that the LBO structure provides a superior form of governance that attenuates these agency problems. The alignment of managers' interests with those of the owners occurs for the following reasons. First, increased leverage increases firms' fixed interest obligations, providing managers with incentives to generate cash to service the debt (Thompson et al., 1992) and to reduce sub-optimal investments and redirect this cash towards servicing the debt (Fox and Marcus, 1992). Thus, debt bonding is an important disciplinary device that reduces managers' discretionary behaviour (Thompson and Wright, 1989). Second, managers of LBOs typically have higher equity stakes in the firm compared to those in public corporations, which leads to improved performance (Thompson et al., 1992). Finally, private equity investors typically have board representation, often nominate the chair of the board, and have greater access to information regarding firm performance than that do shareholders of public corporations.[4] This places them in a strong position to monitor strategic decisions and the performance of the firm.

These theoretical arguments lead to the prediction that LBOs have superior performance compared to non-LBO firms with alternative governance structures. As noted in the introduction, empirical studies using a variety of performance indicators have confirmed this supposition. However, concern remains about the source of LBO success (Fox and Marcus, 1992; Thompson and Wright, 1995).

LBOs provide an opportunity to renegotiate implicit and explicit contracts with employees. Wage payments may be renegotiated, particularly those exceeding the marginal product of labour. There will also be a reduction in employment if pre-buyout management pursued sub-optimal discretionary goals because the LBO provides an opportunity for a correction in levels of employment. Like takeovers, LBOs provide opportunities to reduce sub-optimally high levels of employment and wages. The LBO, however, provides stronger disciplinary and incentive mechanisms for managers to make employment changes (Jensen, 1989).

An alternative argument is that LBOs increase employment because they pursue growth strategies (Zahra, 1995; Wright et al., 2000, 2001) that were not otherwise possible. This is because managers are released from bureaucratic decision-making processes, particularly those involved in the buyout of part of a larger organization (Wright and Thompson, 1987). Being part of a large, complex organization may restrict management's ability to undertake entrepreneurial growth actions, particularly where their firms are peripheral to the main activities of the parent and where bureaucratic company-wide incentive and control measures restrict innovation activity (Holmstrom, 1989). These restrictions reduce the freedom to respond to market developments and give rise to opportunities for a buyout. LBOs provide managers with the discretion to decide what is best for the business, how to organize the company, and what business plans to pursue in order to maximize profits (Wright et al., 2001). Given that LBOs typically increase management's equity stake, such decisions will be motivated by managers seeking to maximize their own wealth and income.

Jensen (1989) argues that LBOs achieve performance gains by substituting compensation for monitoring by bureaucratic staff. Lichtenberg and Siegel (1990) suggest that Jensen's argument could be extended to all employees. Thus, wages are used to attenuate shirking and overcome moral hazard problems. This efficiency wage argument predicts that wages are paid in excess of equilibrium market-clearing levels but at a rate that maximizes firm-level labour productivity (Stiglitz, 1987). Lichtenberg and Siegel (1990) offer two predictions: (1) a reduction in the ratio of non-production to production workers (or the ratio of their respective wage bills) and (2) an increase in the wage bill of production workers. They find evidence consistent with both predictions. First, the ratio of non-production workers to production workers employment (wage bill) declines by 6.5% (15.3%) from the year prior to the LBO to two years after the transaction. Second, over the same period, both hourly and annual pay rates increase for production workers by 2.3% and 3.6%, respectively.

These arguments relating to LBOs versus non-LBOs may be refined by recognizing that LBOs can be divided into two broad categories: management buyouts (MBOs) and management buy-ins (MBIs). Whilst there is now a well-developed literature concerning LBOs, few studies examine the relative impact of insider-led (i.e., MBOs) versus outsider-led LBOs (i.e., MBIs). The different role of insiders and outsiders in these deals suggests important different effects on employment and wages.

Incumbent managers in an MBO with insider knowledge may be able to exploit it to introduce new products and enter new markets which were previously restricted, as noted earlier. These actions may result in employment growth. The possession of such knowledge should also aid due diligence by private equity firms funding the MBO. Alternatively, MBOs may be carried out as defensive transactions in the face of an actual or implied threat of closure or dismissal of management, and may be more likely than MBIs to include wider employee share ownership (Bradley and Nejad, 1989; Bacon et al., 2004). Managers carrying out MBOs are also more likely to be motivated to do so because they wish to run the business for reasons of seeking autonomy (Robbie and Wright, 1996). As such, management action post-MBO in these cases may be focused on employment preservation, at least in part to elicit employee commitment to the recovery and success of the firm. This argument may be more important in periods of economic slowdown than during buoyant economic conditions (Wright et al., 1990).

The need to service external funding may mean that employment considerations are offset by a requirement to shift to a greater emphasis on performance-related remuneration for employees and less emphasis on basic wage levels. Where a group of senior incumbent executives become major equity holders instead of just salaried employees, they may have a greater incentive to break implicit agreements.

In contrast to MBOs, outside management and their private equity backers in an MBI may only acquire such knowledge after the LBO (Robbie and Wright, 1996). As outsiders, their ability to conduct thorough due diligence to reveal problems is likely to be severely curtailed, and public information is typically restricted in private firms and divisions of publicly held groups which account for the vast majority of MBIs. In an MBI, private equity bidders may be provided with a detailed information memorandum but access to incumbent management may be quite limited.

The requirement for new management in an MBI indicates a degree of underperformance by the previous management (otherwise, they would have been able to undertake an MBO) that requires the firm to be turned around (Robbie and Wright, 1996). Further, in contrast to managers in MBOs, managers undertaking an MBI are more likely to be motivated by the exploitation of an opportunity and by financial gain and growth (Robbie and Wright, 1996). Although incoming managers may perceive significant opportunities, asymmetric information is likely to render MBIs riskier than MBOs, as reflected in the greater use of performance-contingent equity ownership in the former (Wright et al., 1996). Wealth-maximizing private equity firms supporting MBIs may seek to take decisive action to turn around the firm. The lack of previous connection with the investee firm by both incoming management and the financier may diminish, if not remove, feelings of commitment towards incumbent management and employees. The control mechanisms put in place by private equity firms are also likely to provide for swift action to make changes if problems not identified by prior due diligence emerge following the MBI (Bacon et al., 2004).

Lichtenberg and Siegel (1990) report that all LBO firms have 4.5%, 3.1% and 4.1% higher productivity in each of the first three years post-buyout, respectively. Their findings with respect to the subset of MBOs over the same period suggest greater productivity improvements of 9.4%, 11.4% and 9.9%. These findings are consistent with incumbent managers in MBOs being able to exploit their inside knowledge of the firm. In contrast, Long and Ravenscraft (1993) find no difference between the effect of MBOs and MBIs on research and development. Additionally, Kaplan (1991) finds no difference between the longevity of MBOs and MBIs.

Lichtenberg and Siegel (1990) examine productivity differences between MBOs and LBOs *per se* but do not explore differences with respect to employment practices. Our chapter examines the wage and employment effects of both MBOs and MBIs, and determines and quantifies any differences between the two types of LBO. We predict that MBIs have greater employment and wage effects than MBOs, which may be easier to effect because the new management have no links to the old regime. In contrast, MBOs do not lead to a change in incumbent management and they might consider they have a fiduciary duty to fulfil obligations made prior to the MBO, notwithstanding the financial incentives for making changes.

3. DATA AND SAMPLE CHARACTERISTICS

3.1 Sources and Characteristics

The sample is constructed from two sources: the Centre for Management Buy-out Research (CMBOR) and FAME. CMBOR provided the names of firms that have adopted the LBO governance structure and the period for which the LBO governance structure was in place. The CMBOR database effectively represents the population of UK management buyouts. Its data are primarily obtained from twice-yearly surveys of corporate advisers and venture capital providers active in LBOs. These surveys achieve an almost 100% response rate as respondents appreciate that individual deal data are kept confidential and that participants receive a free detailed quarterly review of market trends. Firms' audited accounts that provide the data used in the empirical analysis are obtained from FAME.

For an LBO firm to be included in the sample it must fulfil the following criteria: each firm must have a unique Companies House registration number, its accounting data must be in the FAME database, and it must have at least two contiguous years of accounting data. Firms on each database are matched using firms' registration numbers. Using the two data sources, 1350 firms were identified as fulfilling the above criteria.

We sought a stratified random control sample of three firms for each LBO firm from FAME. The control sample was randomly selected from the same industry as the LBO firms using the 4-digit SIC code. In some cases it was not possible to obtain three control firms for each LBO firm; nevertheless, each LBO firm has at least one match. The control sample contains 4029 firms. Firms were precluded from the control sample based on the following three criteria. First, firms that were larger or smaller (based on total assets) than the LBO sample were precluded. Second, firms whose total assets increased by at least 100% in a one-year period were also precluded. Following Conyon et al. (2004), we used this 'rule of thumb' in an attempt to avoid mergers and acquisitions entering the control sample. Finally, each firm had to have a minimum run of at least two years of contiguous data for wages and employment.

Table 12.1 shows that the majority of LBOs and MBOs were sourced either from UK divestment or private ownership. Table 12.2 shows the distribution of buyout observations over the sample period. Annual data over the period 1999–2004 are used in this study. Where a complete year of data is unavailable, financial data are transformed on a *pro rata* basis. This transformation is important as ownership change sometimes results in the accounts being reported for only part of a financial year, which is due to the incorporation of a new firm or for accounting reasons. The data are in the form of an unbalanced panel and the balance of the panel is reported in Table 12.3.

Table 12.1 The source of LBO firms in the sample

Vendor source of buyout	Total number of LBOs	Number of MBOs	Number of MBIs
Foreign divestment	140	119	21
UK divestment	503	395	108
Going private	35	29	6
Private	445	304	141
Privatization	47	42	5
Public buy-in	17	2	15
Receivership, independent company	6	1	5
Receivership, foreign group	6	3	3
Receivership, parent group	53	44	9
Secondary buyout	62	48	14
Unknown	36	27	9
Total	1350	1014	336

Source: CMBOR/Barclays Private Equity/Deloitte.

Table 12.2 Distribution of buyout observations by year of deal

Year of buyout	Total number of LBOs	Number of MBOs	Number of MBIs
1999	660	493	167
2000	698	526	172
2001	678	509	169
2002	604	461	143
2003	279	217	62

Source: CMBOR/Barclays Private Equity/Deloitte.

Table 12.3 Balance of panel

Number of time periods	Number of firms
2	789
3	1124
4	1756
5	841

Sample characteristics are reported in Table 12.4. The financial data are deflated using the producer price index for manufacturing firms and the consumer price index for service sector firms (year 2000 = 100). Manufacturing (service) sector firms are defined as those with a 1-digit SIC 2003 code less than or equal to (greater than) 5. We report summary statistics for all LBO firms (*lbo*=1) and the control sample (*lbo* = 0). We also report summary statistics for the subsets of MBO (*mbo* = 1) and MBI (*mbi*=1) firms. The size of LBOs is effectively limited by the size of private equity and venture capital funds and the ability of bought-out firms to service the leverage taken on to fund the transaction (Jensen, 1989). Thus, notwithstanding the stratification criterion that precludes control firms from being larger than the largest LBO firm, the random control sample is on average larger than the LBO firms. Note also that these variables indicate a size difference between MBI and MBO firms. MBIs are typically larger than MBOs because they are primarily instigated by the private equity firms. In contrast, MBOs might not have private equity support and are typically instigated by incumbent managers.

With respect to the overall comparison between all LBOs and the non-LBO control sample, wages per employee are higher for non-LBO firms than for LBO firms. Within the LBO sample, wages per employee are lower for MBIs than for MBOs. LBOs also have inferior labour productivity (profit per employee) than non-LBO firms. It is noticeable that MBOs are

Table 12.4 Sample characteristics: mean (standard deviation)

Variable	*All firms*	*lbo*=1	*lbo*=0	*mbo*=1	*mbi*=1
Turnover	49 807.36	36 945.87	52 638.63	28 847.73	62 001.26
	(189 886.58)	(111 063.32)	(203 066.08)	(84 927.80)	(165 480.93)
Profit	3 783.98	2 387.69	4 091.36	1 869.64	3 990.51
	(22 412.51)	(8 265.16)	(24 440.74)	(7 407.80)	(10 325.67)
Wages	9 246.11	7 095.63	9 719.51	5 702.27	11 406.63
	(33 791.83)	(20 305.31)	(36 073.48)	(14 718.48)	(31 531.51)
Fixed assets	23 305.74	12 268.73	25 735.38	8 070.38	25 258.32
	(140 503.99)	(48 373.66)	(153 426.78)	(42 170.67)	(62 121.52)
Employees	427.08	370.09	439.63	284.64	634.47
	(1 689.50)	(1 194.26)	(1 779.90)	(852.49)	(1 871.35)
Profit/ Employees	22.09	15.22	23.60	15.21	15.25
	(155.89)	(74.67)	(168.56)	(81.38)	(48.35)
Wages/ Employees	28.30	26.23	28.75	27.00	23.85
	(26.37)	(16.39)	(28.07)	(17.77)	(10.78)
Employment/ Fixed assets	0.23	0.16	0.24	0.18	0.13
	(1.71)	(0.35)	(1.88)	(0.37)	(0.28)
Number of observations	16 179	2 919	13 260	2 206	713

Notes:
(1) Financial figures expressed in real terms (2000 = 100).
(2) Financial figures are in £000s.

the group with the lowest labour productivity. Table 12.4 also shows that LBO firms have a lower ratio of employees to fixed assets. This probably reflects the debt used to facilitate the LBO deal being secured against the firm's fixed assets. Thus, LBOs are more likely to occur with more capital-intensive firms.

3.2 Characteristics of LBOs, MBOs and MBIs

Further analysis of the sample characteristics is conducted to examine whether there are firm-level characteristics that distinguish: (i) firms with the LBO governance structure from non-LBO firms that have alternative governance structures and (ii) MBOs and MBIs.

LBOs and non-LBOs

Comparison of the characteristics of LBOs and non-LBOs allows examination of the likelihood of a firm having the LBO governance structure. Following Lehn and Poulsen (1989) a logistic regression is employed with the dependent variable taking the value of one if a firm has an LBO governance structure in place and zero otherwise.

If performance gains accruing to the LBO are simply a consequence of transfers between employees and their new owners or are a consequence of a better utilisation of labour resources, this suggests that such characteristics be incorporated in the logistic regression. We incorporate both wage and employment characteristics in the regression. Both variables are measured relative to the 4-digit SIC averages to determine if non-LBOs have lower average wages per employee and lower average employment than their competitors.

Additional control variables in the logistic regression are the ratio of employees to fixed assets and turnover. These variables are included relative to the 4-digit SIC industry average. We anticipate that LBOs will be less labour intensive because the debt used to facilitate the transaction is likely to be secured against physical assets. We use turnover as a proxy for firm size and anticipate that relatively larger firms are less likely to be subject to an LBO because the financial constraints of private equity firms places a limit on the size of the LBO transactions they fund. Even if they did have the financial resources to fund a large LBO deal, the private equity firms are likely to adopt a portfolio strategy rather than put all their 'eggs in one basket'.

Table 12.5 reports results for a logistic estimation. As predicted in the above arguments, there is statistically significant evidence that LBO firms are smaller (measured by turnover) compared to industry average. There is also evidence that LBO firms are more likely to have higher levels of employment. The remaining variables in the logit analysis are not significant at the 10% level.

MBOs, MBIs and non-LBOs

Further analysis of the sample is conducted using multinomial logistic estimation to examine the separate characteristics of MBOs and MBIs within the LBO sample (Table 12.6). There is statistically significant evidence that MBOs are likely to be smaller than non-buyout firms; however, there is little support for MBIs being smaller. This is consistent with MBIs being driven by private equity firms.

We find that MBOs are more likely to have higher wage rates than non-LBOs; however, there is no such finding for MBIs. This is consistent with incumbent managers being less likely to break implicit contracts after an MBO than a new management team in the case of an MBI (Bacon et al., 2004). Additionally, MBIs are more likely to have superior performance than non-LBOs and MBOs, which are not likely to have significantly different performance to non-LBOs. The employment to capital ratio

Table 12.5 Logistic estimates of LBO characteristics

	Dependent variable = lbo	
	Coefficient	Marginal effects
ln turnover	−0.17 (2.78)***	−0.3
ln (wages/employees)	0.13 (1.51)	0.02
ln (profit/employees)	0.01 (0.42)	1.77e-3
ln (employees/fixed assets)	0.04 (1.43)	5.95e-3
ln employees	0.30 (5.01)***	0.04
Constant	−1.53 (38.25)***	
Wald	46.99 [0.00]	
Observations	16 179	

Notes:
(1) Independent variables are calculated relative to the 4-digit SIC average.
(2) robust *t*-statistics in parentheses.
(3) * significant at 10%, ** significant at 5%, *** significant at 1%.
(4) *Wald* is a test statistic (probability level) of a test of the joint significance of the regressors.
(5) marginal effects are calculated at the average values of the independent variables.

appears to be a distinguishing feature of MBOs. There is evidence that both MBOs and MBIs are more likely to have higher levels of employment.

4. THE MODELLING PROCEDURE

In Section 2 we argued that LBOs will have an impact on wage rates and employment. In order to determine and quantify the effect of LBOs on employment and wages we estimate both employment and wage equations. An employment equation for firm i ($i = 1, 2, \ldots, N$) in period t ($t = 1, 2, \ldots, T$) is:

$$w_{it} = \beta_1 \acute{\omega}_{it} + \beta_2 k_{it} + \beta_3 \pi_{it} + \beta_3\, Time + f_i + \varepsilon_{it}, \qquad (12.1)$$

where (expressed in natural logarithms) w is the real wage rate, $\acute{\omega}$ is the average wage in each 4-digit SIC code, k is firm size (proxied by fixed assets), π are profits, *Time* is a time trend, f_i are firm-specific fixed effects,

Table 12.6 Multinomial logistic estimates of MBO and MBI characteristics

	MBO		MBI	
	Coefficient	Marginal effect	Coefficient	Marginal effect
ln turnover	−0.19	−0.02	−0.13	−4.13e-3
	(4.56)***	(−4.43)***	(1.86)*	(−1.49)
ln (wages/employees)	0.17	0.02	0.02	−3.16e-4
	(2.63)***	(2.63)***	(0.15)	(−0.07)
ln (profit/employees)	−0.01	−2.22e-3	0.10	0.003968
	(0.64)	(−0.85)	(2.43)**	(2.50)***
ln (employees/fixed assets)	0.07	8.12e-3	−0.04	−0.002066
	(3.57)***	(3.69)***	(1.30)	(−1.61)
ln employees	0.28	0.03	0.38	0.013559
	(6.62)***	(6.25)***	(5.40)***	(4.93)***
Constant	−1.81		−2.98	
	(76.77)***		(72.91)***	
IIA	2.02 [0.92]		4.67 [0.59]	
Wald	181.64 [0.00]			
Observations	16179			

Notes:
(1) Independent variables are calculated relative to the 4-digit SIC average.
(2) Robust t statistics in parentheses.
(3) * significant at 10%, ** significant at 5%, *** significant at 1%.
(4) *IIA* is the Small–Hsiao test statistic (probability level) of the Independence of Irrelevant Alternatives.
(5) *Wald* is a Wald test statistic (probability level) of the joint significance of the regressors.
(6) Marginal effects are calculated at the average values of the independent variables.

and ε is a stochastic error term. Average industry wage is included to capture industry benchmarking effects in wage setting. Size is included to capture firms negotiating power when setting wages. We include profits in order to capture any rent-sharing effects (Conyon et al., 2004).

First-differencing equation (12.1) removes the firm-specific fixed effects and creates a constant term from the time trend. Incorporating an LBO dummy variable produces the following equation:

$$\Delta w_{it} = \beta_0 + \beta_1 \Delta \acute{\omega}_{it} + \beta_2 \Delta k_{it} + \beta_3 \Delta \pi_{it} + \beta_4 \, lbo + \Delta \varepsilon_{it}, \qquad (12.2)$$

where Δ is the first-difference operator, *lbo* is a binary variable taking the value one when the LBO governance structure is in place and zero otherwise, and the βs are parameters to be estimated.

In order to examine the impact of LBOs on employment we use a derived demand equation of the following form:

$$n_{it} = \gamma_1 \, w_{it} + \gamma_2 \, s_{it} + \gamma_2 \, Time + f_i + v_{it}, \tag{12.3}$$

where (expressed in natural logarithms) n is the number of employees, w is the cost of labour relative to the cost of capital, s is output (proxied by turnover), *Time* is a time trend, *fi* are firm-specific fixed effects and v is a stochastic error term. Following standard practice in the labour economics literature, the cost of capital is normalized to one and so w is simply the real wage rate (Conyon et al., 2001). If the difference between firms' cost of capital is constant over time this will be captured by the firm-specific fixed effects.

Equation (12.3), in the same way as equation (12.1), is transformed by taking first-differences and an LBO dummy variable is incorporated to yield:

$$\Delta \, n_{it} = \gamma_0 + \gamma_1 \, \Delta \, w_{it} + \gamma_2 \, \Delta \, s_{it} + \gamma_3 \, lbo + \Delta \, v_{it} \tag{12.4}$$

where previously defined variables are the same as above and the γs are parameters to be estimated. Note that when we seek to determine and quantify the separate effects of MBOs and MBIs on both wages and employment we use two binary variables in place of the LBO binary variable in equations (12.2) and (12.4).

5. RESULTS

Previous studies that determine and quantify the effect of conventional acquisitions on wages and employment estimate the wage and employment equations separately (e.g., Conyon et al., 2001, 2004). Arguably, wages and employment are set simultaneously, therefore, we estimate equations (12.2) and (12.4) simultaneously. Parameter estimates for equations (12.2) and (12.4) are obtained using iterative three-stage least squares. This is an iterative generalized least squares estimator.

The results of simultaneous estimation of equations (12.2) and (12.4) are in column (1) of Table 12.7. Estimation of equations (12.2) and (12.4) with the LBO dummy replaced with MBO and MBI dummies is reported in column (2). For both sets of simultaneous equations Wald tests of the joint significance of the regressors indicate that they are significant at the 1% probability level in all equations. Durbin–Wu–Hausman tests of the endogeneity of wages indicate that the null hypothesis of estimating a reduced form employment equation is rejected at the 1% level and that wages are

Table 12.7 Simultaneous equations estimation

	(1)		(2)	
	Wage	*Employment*	*Wage*	*Employment*
ln (average 4-digit SIC wage)	0.01		0.01	
	(2.56)**		(2.56)**	
ln fixed assets	−0.02		−0.02	
	(−8.94)***		(−8.93)***	
ln (profit/employees)	0.04		0.04	
	(21.26)***		(21.26)***	
lbo	−0.01	−0.03		
	(1.88)*	(2.50)**		
ln (wages/employees)		−2.34		−2.34
		(16.27)***		(16.27)***
ln turnover		0.64		0.64
		(45.43)***		(45.38)***
mbo			−0.01	−0.03
			(1.13)	(1.88)*
mbi			−0.02	−0.05
			(2.01)**	(1.97)**
Constant	0.06	0.13	0.06	0.13
	(25.85)***	(13.69)***	(25.86)***	(13.69)***
Durbin–Wu–Hausman	1017.13 [0.00]		995.83 [0.00]	
Buyout			4.95 [0.08]	6.80 [0.03]
Equal			1.42 [0.23]	0.60 [0.44]
Joint significance	751.23 [0.00]	4 497.08 [0.00]	752.70 [0.00]	4 492.61 [0.00]
Observations	11 104	11 104	11 104	11 104

Notes:
(1) Absolute value of *t*-statistics in parentheses.
(2) * significant at 10%, ** significant at 5%, *** significant at 1%.
(3) *Durbin–Wu–Hausman* is the test statistic (probability level) of wage endogeneity.
(4) *Buyout* is a Wald test statistic (probability level) of the joint significance of the *mbo* and *mbi* dummies.
(5) *Equal* is a Wald test statistic (probability level) that coefficients for the *mbo* and *mbi* dummies are equal.
(6) *Joint significance* is a Wald test statistic (probability level) of the joint significance of the regressors.

endogenous. Thus, simultaneous estimation of the wage and employment equations is preferred for both sets of models reported in Table 12.7.

We first interpret the results in system (1). The *lbo* binary variable is of key interest to this study, so we shall discuss this first. The *lbo* dummy in the wage equation indicates that wage growth is 0.01 of a percentage point lower in LBO firms than non-LBO firms. The *lbo* dummy variable in the employment equation indicates that employment growth is 0.03 of a percentage point lower than that for non-LBO firms.

In system (2) in Table 12.7, *mbo* and *mbi* dummies are included in place of the *lbo* dummy. In both the wage and employment equations the coefficient estimates for the *mbi* dummy variables are significant at the 5% level. They indicate that wage and employment growth is 0.02 and 0.05 of a percentage point lower, respectively, compared to non-LBO firms. Wald tests indicate that the *mbo* and *mbi* binary variables are jointly significant at the 8% and 3% levels in the wage and employment equations. Nevertheless, *t*-statistics suggest MBOs do not have a different rate of wage growth from non-LBOs, but there is some evidence (at the 10% level) that MBO firms have employment growth that is 0.05 of a percentage point lower than for non-LBO firms.

Coefficient estimates for the control variables in the wage equations indicate that average remuneration for 4-digit SIC codes has a positive impact on wage growth within firms, consistent with firms setting wages to an industry benchmark. The size of firms has a negative association with wage growth, possibly indicating that larger firms have a stronger bargaining position when it comes to setting pay.[5] Finally, the positive association of the growth in profits per employee on wage growth is evidence of firms' rent-sharing behaviour.

The control variables in the employment equations in Table 12.7 indicate that higher wage growth has a negative impact on employment growth. There is also evidence that growth in firm-level output is associated with employment growth.

Results from models where the restructuring dummies (i.e. *lbo*, *mbo* and *mbi*) are treated as endogenous are reported in Table 12.8. To test whether the appropriate specification involves treating the restructuring dummies as endogenous we conduct a Hausman specification test. The null hypothesis is that iterative 3SLS estimation produces consistent estimates of the restructuring dummies when they are treated as exogenous. For both sets of simultaneous equations reported in Table 12.8 the null hypothesis is rejected at the 1% level. Thus results reported in Table 12.8 are preferred to those reported in Table 12.7.

The system of simultaneous equations (1) in Table 12.8 indicates that the coefficient on the *lbo* dummy is significant at the 1% level. The coefficient

Table 12.8 Simultaneous equations estimates (endogenous restructuring decision)

	(1)		(2)	
	Wages	*Employment*	*Wages*	*Employment*
ln (average 4-digit SIC wage)	0.02		0.02	
	(2.05)**		(2.17)**	
ln fixed assets	−0.01		−0.01	
	(3.03)***		(2.86)***	
ln (profit/employees)	0.04		0.04	
	(13.82)***		(13.47)***	
lbo	−0.53	0.07		
	(6.21)***	(0.41)		
ln (wages/employees)		−2.44		−2.43
		(15.86)***		(14.23)***
ln turnover		0.75		0.75
		(42.17)***		(36.70)***
mbo			−0.31	0.51
			(3.18)***	(2.76)***
mbi			−0.97	−0.81
			(4.30)***	(1.82)*
Constant	0.16	0.11	0.15	0.09
	(10.00)***	(3.29)***	(8.96)***	(2.43)**
Hausman	64.01 [0.00]		114.16 [0.00]	
Buyout			31.05 [0.00]	10.69 [0.00]
Equal			6.80 [0.01]	7.40 [0.01]
Joint significance	268.20 [0.00]	2110.85 [0.00]	247.05 [0.00]	1716.60 [0.00]
Observations	11 104	11 104	11 104	11 104

Notes:
(1) Absolute value of t statistics in parentheses.
(2) * significant at 10%, ** significant at 5%, *** significant at 1%.
(3) *Hausman* is a Hausman specification test statistic (probability level) of the appropriateness of treating the *lbo*, *mbo*, *mbi* dummies as endogenous versus treating them as exogenous.
(4) *Buyout* is a Wald test statistic (probability level) of the joint significance of the *mbo* and *mbi* dummies.
(5) *Equal* is a Wald test statistic (probability level) that coefficients for the *mbo* and *mbi* dummies are equal.
(6) *Joint significance* is a Wald test statistic (probability level) of the joint significance of the regressors.

estimate indicates that LBOs have 0.53 of a percentage point lower wage growth than non-LBOs. In contrast, there is no evidence that LBOs have any significant impact on employment growth. The estimated effect of LBOs on wage growth is greater when the *lbo* dummy variable is treated as endogenous compared to when it is treated as exogenous. Additionally, the coefficient on the *lbo* dummy is not significant in the employment equation when it is treated as endogenous in contrast to when it is considered to be exogenous in the results reported in Table 12.7.

Results exploring the separate effects of MBOs and MBIs are reported in the simultaneous system (2) in Table 12.8. Specification tests indicate this is the preferred model. Coefficient estimates on both *mbo* dummies are significant at the 1% level. They indicate that wage growth is 0.31 of a percentage point lower and that employment growth is 0.51 of a percentage point higher in MBO firms than non-LBO firms. The coefficient estimates on the *mbi* dummies suggest that wage and employment growth are 0.97 and 0.81 of a percentage point lower, respectively, for MBI firms than non-LBOs. The latter result is only significant at the 10% level, however. The effect of treating the *mbi* dummy variable as endogenous appears to magnify estimated wage and employment effects while the effect on MBOs is to change the sign on the estimated coefficient in the employment equation. Wald tests also indicate that the *mbo* and *mbi* dummies are jointly significant in both the employment and wage equation and that their respective effects on wage and employment growth are not equal.

From the data, we calculate average wage growth for non-LBO firms to be 0.93 of a percentage point. Thus the estimated coefficients for the *mbo* and *mbi* dummies indicate that wage growth is 0.62 of a percentage point for MBO firms and −0.04 of a percentage point for MBI firms. These growth rates are relatively small compared to the reported performance improvements associated with adoption of the LBO form. This suggests that performance improvements associated with LBOs are not simply due to a transfer of wealth from employees to the new owners.

Using the coefficient estimates, average pay per employee grows by £83.70 and £231.35 less per annum for MBO and MBI firms, respectively, than that for non-LBO firms. Additionally, the average wage bill for MBO and MBI firms grows by £23 824 and £146 784.63 less per annum, respectively, than that for non-LBO firms. Thus, whilst the wage and employment growth rates are relatively small compared to the reported productivity increases in the LBO literature, the average wage bill of MBI firms in particular grows at a substantially lower rate than that for non-LBO firms yielding significant cash savings.

Average employment growth for non-LBO firms is 0.26 of a percentage point. Estimated coefficients therefore indicate that employment growth for

MBO and MBI firms is 0.77 and −0.55 of a percentage point, respectively. Furthermore, average employment growth is 1.45 and −5.14 employees per annum for MBO and MBI firms, respectively, compared to non-LBO firms. Indeed, employment increases by 2.19 persons per annum in MBO firms but declines by 3.49 persons per annum in MBI firms.

Notwithstanding the economic impact of MBOs and MBIs calculated above, the estimated growth rates are lower than those reported in Lichtenberg and Siegel (1990), who find for the US that the average annual growth rate of pay is 3.6% higher for production workers in LBO plants and the employment growth rate of production workers is 2% lower in LBO plants.[6] In comparison with recent evidence on UK mergers, however, our results are cast in a different light. Conyon et al. (2002a) report that the wage growth effects of mergers are generally statistically insignificant. However, our estimated employment growth rates are similar to those reported in Conyon et al. (2002b), who find that employment growth is 0.19 and 0.08 of a percentage point lower for related and unrelated mergers, respectively.

With respect to the control variables, those in the wage equations relating to average industry remuneration and profit per employee have a positive effect on wage growth. This suggests there is industry benchmarking when pay rises are set and that employees pay growth benefits from rent-sharing, i.e. employees' wages grow when profits grow. In contrast, the size of the firm has a negative impact on wage growth. This is consistent with larger firms being in a stronger bargaining position when it comes to negotiating pay rises. The employment equation estimates indicate that wage rates have a negative effect on employment growth. Thus, as the price of labour increases, the demand for labour falls. The employment equations also indicate that positive output growth has a positive effect on employment growth.

6. CONCLUSIONS

This chapter investigates both differences between LBOs and non-LBOs and, within the LBO sample, differences between MBOs (insider-led LBOs) and MBIs (outsider-led LBOs) towards employment and wage setting. We find that all LBOs together do not have a significant effect on employment growth but they do have significantly lower wage growth than non-LBOs. Both MBOs and MBIs are found to have a negative impact on wage growth over the period of the study. The employment equation, however, indicates that MBOs have higher employment growth and MBIs have lower employment growth than cohorts in the same industry.

Our findings for wages suggest a need to adjust remuneration to a level commensurate with a more sustainable business; this is especially consistent with MBIs involving businesses that are more likely to be struggling prior to the buyout. The higher employment growth in MBOs in the period covered by this study is consistent with them exploiting higher growth opportunities as a consequence of managers being freed from the bureaucratic control of the pre-buyout organizational structure (Jensen, 1989; Wright et al., 2000; Bacon et al., 2004), and less to defensive motives related to the threat of closure. There is no evidence consistent with the argument that LBOs substitute pay for monitoring, as suggested by Jensen (1989) and Lichtenberg and Siegel (1990).

For both MBOs and MBIs, our findings are consistent with managerial equity ownership and debt bonding providing financial incentives to reduce sub-optimally high levels of wage growth. Such financial incentives appear to have different effects on MBIs and MBOs in relation to employment growth. Thus, our findings also suggest that future research should consider MBOs and MBIs as distinct forms of corporate restructuring and not as one type of LBO.

Finally, it should be noted that the figures are annual average growth rates over the period of the study. We would caution that it is not possible from the results reported here to tell whether this is a constant pattern across each year. Prior research, predominantly in the US, has suggested that there is an initial decline in employment and wages as businesses are restructured on a sounder footing, after which there is a recovery. Further research is required to examine this issue.

ACKNOWLEDGEMENTS

Financial support from Barclays Private Equity and Deloitte is acknowledged with thanks. The comments of an anonymous reviewer are also gratefully acknowledged.

NOTES

1. Thompson and Wright (1995) provide a review of this evidence.
2. This group of insider-driven deals also includes management–employee buy-outs (MEBOs).
3. This group of outsider driven deals also includes investor-led buy-outs (IBOs), which are transactions where the private equity firm acquires the company.
4. This arises as financiers are able to negotiate contractual conditions in the shareholders' agreement providing for such disclosure.
5. It has become a stylized fact of empirical wage equations that there is a positive association between the levels of firm size and wages. However, the direction of the relationship

between wage growth and the growth in firm size is less clear. For instance, Barron et al. (1987) find a negative relationship between the wage growth of new employees and firm size, though we find a negative relationship between wage growth and growth in firm size; estimating models in levels and including a time trend yields the following coefficient estimate (t-statistic) for firm size: 0.09 (1.73). We therefore find a positive relationship between wages and firm size, but only in a levels equation.

6. Note that Lichtenberg and Siegel (1990) have more detailed employment and pay data in that they are able to distinguish between production and non-production workers, making direct comparisons with our study problematic.

REFERENCES

Amess, K. (2002), 'Management buyouts and firm-level productivity: evidence from a panel of UK manufacturing firms', *Scottish Journal of Political Economy*, **49** (3), 304–17.

Amess, K. (2003), 'The effect of management buyouts on firm-level technical efficiency: evidence from a panel of UK machinery and equipment manufacturers', *Journal of Industrial Economics*, **51** (1), 35–44.

Bacon, N., Wright, M. and Demina, N. (2004), 'Management buyouts and human resource management', *British Journal of Industrial Relations*, **42** (2), 325–47.

Barron, J.M., Black, D.A. and Loewenstein, M.A. (1987), 'Employer size: the implications for search, training, capital investment, starting wages and wage growth', *Journal of Labor Economics*, **5** (1), 76–89.

Bradley, K. and Najed, A. (1989), *Managing Owners: The National Freight Consortium in perspective*, Cambridge: Cambridge University Press.

CMBOR (2005), 'Management Buy-out Trends', *Management Buy-outs: Quarterly Review from CMBOR*, Nottingham: CMBOR.

Conyon, M., Girma, S., Thompson, S. and Wright, P. (2001), 'Do hostile mergers destroy jobs?', *Journal of Economic Behavior and Organization*, **45** (4), 427–40.

Conyon, M., Girma, S., Thompson, S. and Wright, P. (2002a), 'The productivity and wage effects of foreign acquisition', *Journal of Industrial Economics*, **50** (1), 85–102.

Conyon, M., Girma, S., Thompson, S. and Wright, P. (2002b), 'The impact of mergers and acquisitions on company employment in the United Kingdom', *European Economic Review*, **46** (1), 31–49.

Conyon, M., Girma, S., Thompson, S. and Wright, P. (2004), 'Do wages rise or fall following merger?', *Oxford Bulletin of Economics and Statistics*, **66** (5), 847–62.

Easterwood, J.C., Singer, R.F., Seth, A. and Lang, D.F. (1994), 'Controlling the conflict of interest in management buyouts', *Review of Economics and Statistics*, **76** (3), 512–22.

Fama, E.F. and Jensen, M.C. (1983), 'Agency problems and residual claims', *Journal of Law and Economics*, **26** (2), 327–49.

Fox, I. and Marcus, A. (1992), 'The causes and consequences of leveraged management buyouts', *Academy of Management Review*, **17** (1), 62–85.

Harris, R., Siegel, D.S. and Wright, M. (2005), 'Assessing the impact of management buyouts on economic efficiency: plant-level evidence from the United Kingdom', *Review of Economics and Statistics*, **87** (1), 148–53.

Hart, O. (1995), 'Corporate governance: some theory and implications', *Economic Journal*, **105** (430), 678–89.

Holmstrom, B. (1989), 'Agency costs and innovation', *Journal of Economic Behavior and Organization*, **12** (3), 305–27.
Jensen, M.C. (1986), 'Agency costs of free cash flow, corporate finance and takeovers', *American Economic Review Papers and Proceedings*, **76** (2), 323–9.
Jensen, M.C. (1989), 'Eclipse of the public corporation', *Harvard Business Review*, **67** (5), 61–75.
Jensen, M.C. and Meckling, W.H. (1976), 'Theory of the firm: managerial behaviour, agency costs and ownership structure', *Journal of Financial Economics*, **3** (4), 305–60.
Kaplan, S. (1989a), 'The effects of management buyouts on operating performance and value', *Journal of Financial Economics*, **24** (2), 217–54.
Kaplan, S. (1989b), 'Management buyouts: evidence on taxes as a source of value', *Journal of Finance*, **44** (3), 611–32.
Kaplan, S. (1991), 'The staying power of leveraged buyouts', *Journal of Financial Economics*', **29** (2), 287–313.
Lehn, K. and Poulsen, A. (1989), 'Free cash flow and stockholder gains in going private transactions', *Journal of Finance*, (3), 771–87.
Lichtenberg, F.R. and Siegel, D. (1990), 'The effects of leveraged buyouts on productivity and related aspects of firm behavior', *Journal of Financial Economics*, **27** (1), 165–94.
Long, W. and Ravenscraft, D. (1993), 'LBOs, debt and R&D intensity', *Strategic Management Journal*, **14** (S), 119–35.
Marais, L., Schipper, K. and Smith, A. (1989), 'Wealth effects of going private for senior securities', *Journal of Financial Economics*, **23** (1), 155–91.
Robbie, K. and Wright, M. (1996), *Management Buy-Ins*, Manchester: Manchester University Press.
Shleifer, A. and Summers, L.H. (1988), 'Breach of trust in hostile takeovers', in A. Auerbach (ed.), *Corporate Takeovers: Causes and consequences*, Chicago, IL: University of Chicago Press.
Shleifer, A. and Vishny, R.W. (1988), 'Value maximisation and the acquisition process', *Journal of Economic Perspectives*, **2** (1), 7–20.
Smart, S.B. and Waldfogel, J. (1994), 'Measuring the effect of restructuring on corporate performance: the case of management buyouts', *The Review of Economics and Statistics*, **76** (3) 503–11.
Smith, A.J. (1990), 'Corporate ownership structure and performance: the case of management buyouts', *Journal of Financial Economics*, **27** (1), 143–64.
Stiglitz, J.E. (1987), 'The causes and consequences of the dependence of quality on price', *Journal of Economic Literature*, **25** (1), 1–48.
Thompson, R.S. and Wright, M. (1989), 'Bonding, agency costs, and management buyouts: a note', *Bulletin of Economic Research*, **41** (1), 69–75.
Thompson, S. and Wright, M. (1995), 'Corporate governance: the role of restructuring transactions', *Economic Journal*, **105** (430), 690–703.
Thompson, S., Wright, M. and Robbie, K. (1992), 'Management equity ownership, debt, and performance: some evidence from UK management buyouts', *Scottish Journal of Political Economy*, **39** (4), 413–30.
Wright, M. and Thompson, S. (1987), 'Divestment and the control of divisionalised firms', *Accounting and Business Research*, **17** (67), 259–68.
Wright, M., Chiplin, B., Thompson, S. and Robbie, K. (1990), 'Management buyouts, trade unions and employee ownership', *Industrial Relations Journal*, **21** (2), 136–46.

Wright, M., Thompson, S. and Robbie, K. (1992), 'Management-led leveraged buy-outs: a European perspective', *Journal of Business Venturing*, **7** (1), 45–71.

Wright, M., Thompson, S. and Robbie, K. (1996), 'Buy-ins, buy-outs, active investors and corporate governance', *Corporate Governance: An International Review*, **4** (4), 222–34.

Wright, M., Hoskisson, R.E., Busenitz, L.W. and Dial, J. (2000), 'Entrepreneurial growth through privatization: the upside of management buy-outs', *Academy of Management Review*, **25** (3), 591–601.

Wright, M., Hoskisson, R.E. and Busenitz, L.W. (2001), 'Firm rebirth: buyouts as facilitators of strategic growth and entrepreneurship', *Academy of Management Executive*, **15** (1), 111–25.

Wright, M., Kitamura, M. and Burrows, A. (2005), 'Management buy-outs: from Europe to Japan', *Journal of Restructuring Finance*, **2** (1), 39–54.

Zahra, S.A. (1995), 'Corporate entrepreneurship and financial performance: the case of management leveraged buy-outs', *Journal of Business Venturing*, **10** (3), 225–47.

PART VI

Investment Realization: Success and Failure

13. The impact of corporate governance mechanisms on value increase in leveraged buyouts

Erkki Nikoskelainen and Mike Wright

1. INTRODUCTION

Leveraged buyouts have received a substantial amount of attention within the financial research literature (see Jensen, 1993; Thompson and Wright, 1995 for reviews). While there is extensive evidence of gains in productivity and operating performance, there is a notable lack of research concerning the value increase of buyout targets and returns realized from buyouts at the investment level. Resulting mainly from accessibility of reliable and usually confidential transaction data, studies on buyout returns have focused either on limited samples relating to IPOs among the largest transactions rather than across the range of realization options for the buyout market as a whole (see, e.g., Kaplan, 1989) or on fund-level measures (see, e.g., Kaplan and Schoar, 2005; Ljungqvist and Richardson, 2003; Cumming and Walz, 2004). This emphasis parallels research on realizations in the venture capital market which has also tended to consider IPOs (Barry et al., 1990; Das et al., 2003), although an exception is Cumming and MacIntosh (2003). Much existing research has also focused on US studies, primarily covering the first wave of buyouts in the 1980s, yet there may be important legal differences between private equity markets that influence the nature of exit from investments (Cumming et al., 2006). Buyout markets have developed more recently outside the US, notably in the UK and Europe, where contextual conditions have meant that buyout deals have covered a wide size spectrum and that realizations have relied less on IPOs (CMBOR, 2005). Moreover, while there is some recognition that buyouts are heterogeneous with respect to whether they are driven by insiders or outsiders (Lichtenberg and Siegel, 1990; Robbie and Wright, 1995), and with respect to whether they involve the purchase of full firms or divisions (Muscarella and Vetsuypens, 1990), the implications of these differences have not been incorporated into previous studies of value creation and returns. Studies analyzing the factors that impact realized buyout returns at the target company level using a comprehensive sample of different types of buyouts across the full size range and incorporating strategic sales to a third party, secondary buyouts and failures in addition to IPOs can add to the existing literature on leverage buyouts.

According to Jensen's (1986, 1989) free cash flow theory, leveraged buyouts result in corporate governance mechanisms that reduce agency costs and increase firm value through improved operating efficiency. Central elements of this governance structure are debt, ownership of equity and the presence of active investors. Agency costs of free cash flow arise if generated free cash flow is not invested in profitable development and maintenance of the business or distributed to shareholders. Debt can reduce these costs and serve as a substitute for dividends because it creates an obligation to service periodic interest costs. The inability to service these payments and repay the principal will ultimately cause the company to be liquidated. As leverage in buyouts tends to be high, a significant proportion of free cash flow is likely to be committed to servicing the debt. The threat of bankruptcy created by the failure to pay interest motivates organizations to become more efficient. Intensive use of debt to finance a buyout reduces the share of equity in the financing structure, allowing private equity investors and managers to control the majority of stock which they would otherwise be unable or unwilling to undertake. Concentrated ownership provides private equity investors with the ability to monitor and control the strategy of the buyout target firm through an active presence on the board of directors. The need for monitoring management is partially offset by the effective self-monitoring resulting from managerial equity ownership.

Mixed support for Jensen's free cash flow theory has been documented. Lehn and Poulsen (1989), Kaplan (1989), Smith (1990), Muscarella and Vetsuypens (1990), Cotter and Peck (2001) and Bruton et al. (2002) find that increased leverage and realignment of incentives have positive effects on the operating performance of leveraged buyout companies. Additionally, Bull (1989), Hall (1990), Lichtenberg and Siegel (1990), Opler (1992), Long and Ravenscraft (1993), Ofek (1994), Desbrières and Schatt (2002) and Harris et al. (2005) provide evidence of cost cutting and improved margins and efficiency after buyout. Easterwood et al. (1989), Singh (1990), Smith (1990), Long and Ravenscraft (1993) and Holthausen and Larcker (1996) show reductions in capital requirements after a buyout. Halpern et al. (1999), Opler and Titman (1993) for the US and Weir et al. (2005) and Renneboog et al. (2007) for the UK, however, do not find support for the free cash flow argument as a driver of public to private buyouts.

Operating performance, as well as efficient use of available funding and resources, are fundamental elements of firm value. However, changes in various measures of operating efficiency serve only as proxies, not direct measures of value. Furthermore, changes in operating characteristics can be short-term in nature and may have a negative effect on the future prospects of a company.

Private equity companies (or any other party investing equity, such as management) want to maximize the value of their investments (see, e.g., Jensen, 1989). The returns generated by a buyout fund and avoidance of the liquidation of any investments are crucial for fund income and reputation (Barry et al., 1990; Cumming and MacIntosh, 2003; Das et al., 2003). The returns earned by a fund are the main factors in ensuring that future funds can be raised. Returns can ultimately be measured only when the investment is realized through an exit by IPO, sale to a third party or other means. The value increase (or decrease) and any conclusions about the factors affecting this change must be based on measures comparing the value difference (return) between the time of entry (leverage buyout) and the time of exit (investment realization). This allows for measuring both the success of buyouts and the relative importance of factors affecting the degree of success. While there is evidence relating to the longevity of buyouts (Kaplan, 1991; Wright et al., 1995), evidence relating to the performance of exited buyouts is limited to consideration of those that have exited by IPO in terms of accounting and stock market returns (Holthausen and Larcker, 1996; Jelic et al., 2005).

Wright et al. (1995) indicate that size of buyout is positively related to a short holding period and a high exit probability. Kaplan (1991) finds similar evidence, but his study focused only on larger buyouts. This suggests that the size of the buyout may be influential in determining returns. Private equity funds invest in a number of buyouts and each of these investments contributes to the overall return of the fund. Financial sponsors may wish to invest in sizeable investments that can be expected to provide high absolute returns that will increase the return of fund. Additionally, private equity investors wish to be able to focus their efforts on the boards of those companies that can provide high income, instead of on small companies that require significant efforts in the board of directors and which contribute only marginally to overall fund return even if the percentage return on each individual investment is high. Further, smaller companies may be more difficult to exit due to lack of interest from large industrial buyers and because they do not meet the scale required for a public listing.

In this chapter, we present evidence concerning investor returns from exited buyouts and their determinants. Empirical evidence is presented that value increase and return characteristics are related to corporate governance mechanisms associated with a leveraged buyout. We use a unique hand-collected dataset to examine the internal rate of return (IRR) on enterprise value and invested equity in 321 exited buyouts in the UK in the period 1995 to 2004. These include 52 IPOs, 92 trade sales, 57 secondary buyouts and 121 receiverships (bankruptcies).

This study makes three contributions. First, this chapter adds to limited previous research on investor returns in buyouts. Kaplan's (1989) study that reports investor returns in buyouts is extended by providing measures of actual (realized) internal rate of return of enterprise value (EV) and of invested equity. We find that the mean index-adjusted EV IRR is 22.2% and the average equity IRR is 70.5% for the whole sample. IPO (median EV IRR 44%, equity IRR 99%) exits outperform trade sale (median EV IRR 7%, equity IRR 43%) and secondary buyout (median EV IRR 3%, equity IRR 21%) exits. Second, this chapter extends the studies of Kaplan (1991), Wright et al. (1994), Wright et al. (1995) and Wright et al. (1996) on the staying power and survival of buyouts by providing empirical evidence concerning the relation between the governance structure of a buyout and likelihood of a positive return at investment realization. Prior studies (see, e.g., Wright et al., 1996) have aimed at understanding the reasons for receivership exits (failure) without measuring the relative performance and returns between other exit types. We find that governance mechanisms resulting from a leveraged buyout are not the main drivers of value increase. However, returns are driven by size of buyout and acquisitions done before exit. Third, this chapter adds to studies on buyout success by providing evidence that returns characteristics are different between buyouts and buyins. Buyout returns are driven by acquisitions during the holding time. Our results indicate that buyout equity returns are negatively impacted by divestments while the opposite is true for buyins. This implies that private equity companies that initiate institutional buyins are able to drive their returns through streamlining of target company operations.

The remainder of this chapter is organized as follows. The next section describes the data, sample selection process and tested variables, and also discusses methodological issues. Thereafter the empirical results are reported and potential biases of the sample are discussed. The final section concludes the study.

2. DATA

The sample utilized in this study consists of 321 exited buyouts in the UK between 1995 and 2004. These include 52 IPOs, 91 trade sales to strategic or industrial buyers, 57 secondary buyouts involving sale to another private equity investor who acquires the company through a leveraged buyout transaction and 121 receivership exits where the buyouts have filed for either bankruptcy or bankruptcy protection. The initial sample is constructed by using the Centre for Management Buyout Research (CMBOR) database that provides comprehensive statistics of the population of UK buyout transactions and their private equity and debt financiers. The CMBOR database is compiled from a wide range of sources including twice-yearly surveys of private equity and debt providers to buyouts,[1] press releases by these financiers, the financial press, stock exchange circulars issued by companies and companies' annual reports. The database has no lower size cut-off.

The database consists of 1485 exited leveraged buyouts in the UK since year 1994. Data retrieved include entry time enterprise value (value of buyout), amount of debt and equity invested in the buyout, revenue and operating profit of the target prior to the buyout, management ownership of invested equity, number of participants in the equity syndicate, the number of acquisitions and divestments made by the buyout during the holding period, the cumulative amount of capital the investor (institution) has committed to investments at the time a specific LBO is announced and the cumulative number of investments the investor has completed at that time. Detailed initial transaction structure (buyout financing) data are available for 635 of these transactions (48 IPOs, 332 trade sales, 134 secondary buyouts and 121 receiverships). For IPOs, all other information required for calculating test variables is retrieved from the prospectuses these companies have filed prior to their listing. For four companies, the prospectus was not available and required information was retrieved from the latest annual report prior to the exit date. In addition, sufficient transaction structure details were found from prospectuses and press releases for four additional transactions not included in the CMBOR detailed transaction structure data. This brought the size of IPO exit group to 52 transactions (40 full listings, eight AIM[2] listings or OTC transactions, two listings on the US market and two reverse-in transactions). Prospectuses (and annual reports for four companies) provide annual data reported less than six months before the exit. Therefore, the accuracy of these data in reflecting the financial and operating status of sample companies at the time of exit can be regarded as high.

In the UK private companies are obliged to report their financial accounts to Companies House. The filed accounts are public information and therefore available. For the 332 trade sale and 134 secondary buyout exits, the data required for the calculation of operating and equity value variables are retrieved from the Amadeus database, which provides financial information on European private companies. Criteria for adding a company to the sample is that the Amadeus database must contain annual financial data for the period prior to exit, and the time gap between the latest reporting period end and the exit date cannot exceed 11 months. This ensures that this financial information provides sufficient accuracy about the operating performance and financial condition of the company at the time of exit. In addition, revenue, operating profit (EBIT) data must be available as well as data for net debt calculation. The Amadeus database does not provide information on buyouts in receivership exits, because these companies no longer exist.

2.1 Internal Rate of Return

We measure the return on enterprise value and on equity investment by an index-adjusted internal rate of return (IRR) discount rate that equates the present value of a series of cash flows (positive and negative) to zero. IRR is the most commonly used measure of the return on private equity investments (see, e.g., Kaplan and Schoar, 2005; Ljungqvist and Richardson, 2003). Enterprise value is used because leveraged buyouts can make use of multiple types of capital to finance the buyout transaction. In general, finance can include senior and junior debt like credit facilities, bank debt, mezzanine or high yield. Financial sponsors investing equity may also invest other instruments in the form of strip-financing (Jensen, 1986). Hence, in these cases financial sponsors focus on the return earned on all types of capital they have invested. Furthermore, the distinction between return on enterprise value (EV) and equity return allows for a comparison between value increase and equity return. The literature on buyouts often refers to value creation without addressing how it relates to equity value. Private equity investors participating in buyout transactions are interested in earning a return on their investment. This does not necessarily mean an increase in EV if they only invest equity, but rather operating improvements and repayment of debt (and possibly other financing) combined with a favorable exit. Therefore, an exited buyout may provide a significant return on the invested equity without increasing EV. For the sample used in this study, the correlation between index-adjusted EV IRR and index-adjusted equity (Eq) IRR is 0.62. The correlation is significant (at 1% level) and shows how much variation there is between these two return measures.

Adjusting the exit time value for index movement during the holding period (index increase or decrease between entry and exit dates) allows value creation to be analyzed by isolating market movement effects from the value change. This is important, as favorable market conditions (index movement upward) can generate increased value from the investment without any changes in the fundamentals of target companies. Additionally, this will adjust for pure warehousing of companies, that is, when opportunistic buyout investments are made by assuming returns are based solely on improving market conditions. Index adjustment does not completely eliminate the market effect, because it is not possible to reliably eliminate favorable exit market conditions (high mergers and acquisitions activity) resulting from improving equity markets. The index used for adjusting the values is the FTSE 100 index of the London Stock Exchange (monthly data). This general index, which comprises the 100 most highly capitalized blue chip companies, reflects the general economic climate both from valuation and from mergers and acquisitions perspectives. In favorable economic conditions there are more favorable exit opportunities because both IPO and M&A markets are active. Moreover, during high-volume M&A markets more assets are put on sale, which also results in a higher deal flow to private equity investors. Using the FTSE 100 index instead of other UK indexes ensures that index adjustments made reflect the general market development in the UK. On the other hand, other UK indices that might better reflect the size composition of our sample that consists mainly of smaller companies are highly correlated with the FTSE 100 index, which represents approximately 80% of the capitalization of UK markets. Other suitable indices, such as the FTSE All Share Index, incorporate the companies in the FTSE 100 index. In summary, as we want the index adjustment to eliminate any purely market-related impacts on the returns, the FTSE 100 will ensure a reasonably accurate adjustment for LBO returns in our sample over different time frames for cases when the index has either increased or decreased during the holding time of the LBO.

Equity values at the time of entry and exit must be defined for the calculation of IRR. Equity value at entry is the total equity invested at the time of buyout. This includes all types of equity, including ordinary and preferred shares.[3] For IPOs, equity value at exit is defined as the market value of the company at the beginning of the first day of trading. For trade sale and secondary buyout exits, equity value at exit is calculated by subtracting net debt (interest-bearing debt minus cash and equivalents) from the exit transaction value (enterprise value). Using the book value of debt may bias the equity value calculation, but given the difficulty in valuing non-market traded debt, which is typically the case in UK buyouts,[4] the book value of debt is used.

Receivership exits are assumed to have zero value at exit. The main assumption is that equity investors receive nothing at bankruptcy. Additionally, we assume that enterprise value is zero at exit, because otherwise receiverships would provide high returns whenever there was a low equity ratio in the initial capital structure. For the whole sample we assume that no dividends are paid to equity holders during the holding time. Enterprise value at exit is adjusted for additional financings (refinancing, including all capital types) in 36 cases. Equity value at exit (for the whole sample) is adjusted for additional equity investments during the holding period in 12 cases for which the CMBOR database provides this information.[5] Both entry and exit time equity values are calculated for 100% of shares. The percentage of shares acquired at entry and sold at exit is obtained from the SDC Platinum transactions database. For most of the sample buyouts, both entry (five companies less than 100%) and exit transactions (one company less than 100%) included all shares of the company (100%). This procedure is not done for receivership exits, since for these companies value at exit is assumed to be zero.

2.2. Variables for Corporate Governance Mechanisms

The structure of buyout transactions provides two important variables for measuring the effects of governance mechanisms. Gearing (leverage) shows how much debt is invested in the entity in proportion to equity. It is an important variable to test because the less equity is invested the more debt is required to finance the entire transaction (not taking into consideration other forms of financing). Secondly, the less equity is invested, the greater equity ownership the management usually receives because management is provided with an affordable option to have stronger incentives. Following Kaplan (1989), Thompson and Wright (1991) and Wright et al. (1995), the management ownership variable is the management's share of equity.

The debt ratio (percentage of debt in the initial transaction structure) is not tested separately because it is partially complementary to leverage and the disciplinary effect of debt is measured by debt coverage. Debt coverage is defined as the amount of debt (including all forms of interest-bearing debt such as high yield, senior debt and loan notes) in the initial capital structure of the buyout divided by operating profit prior to buyout. This measure shows how many years worth of current operating profit would be required for repayment of all outstanding debt. Debt coverage used here serves as a proxy for the controlling effect of debt. Cash flow (EBITDA) would be a better measure for debt coverage, but given that EBITDA prior to entry was available only for 30 sample companies (from Amadeus), we decided to use EBIT instead. Seven sample companies had a negative debt coverage ratio and six companies had a ratio of over 100. Therefore, the debt coverage variable is truncated at the 99th and 1st percentiles. Buyouts with negative debt coverage are given the 99th percentile debt coverage value. Availability of debt, debt terms and costs change over time (Figure 13.1). Transaction structure related variables have the weakness of being exposed to economic cycles and availability of funding. In our sample, the year 2002 has the highest average debt coverage and 2001 the lowest. The sample average gearing level is highest for LBOs announced in

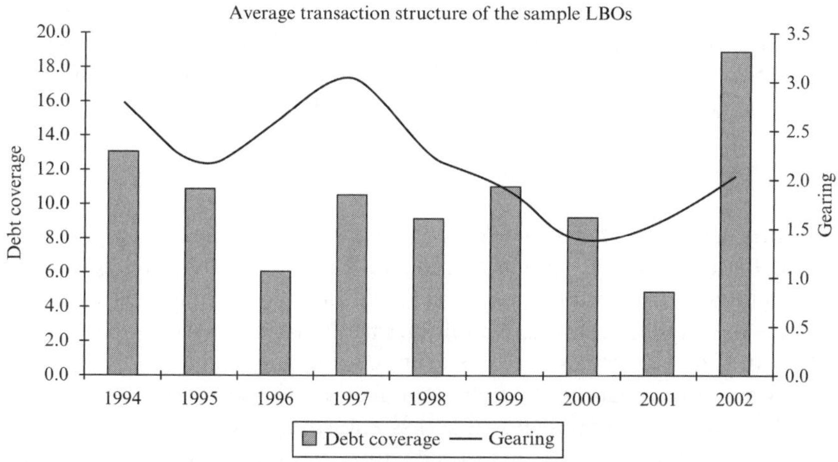

Note: Graph presents the samples' average gearing, amount of debt in initial entry transaction structure divided by amount of equity in initial entry transaction structure and average debt coverage, the amount of debt in the initial entry transaction structure divided by operating profit (EBIT) for the previous fiscal year.

Figure 13.1 Sample average transaction structure and debt coverage

1997 and lowest in 2000. Our sample capital structure and debt coverage largely follow the averages for the whole industry. Various sources report similar patterns where the proportion of invested equity (in proportion to debt) in LBOs increases from the early 1990s to 2000 and started to decrease again after 2000 (CMBOR, 2005).

Often there is more than one private equity investor involved in a buyout transaction. These investors form an equity syndicate whose members agree among themselves the terms under which they, within the syndicate, invest equity. Buyout investors usually have an institutional requirement for a seat on the board of the buyout company or the right to nominate the chairman of the board (Thompson and Wright, 1991; Wright et al., 1995). All participants in the equity syndicate become shareholders in the company. Following Wright et al. (1995), the size of the equity syndicate is measured by the number of participating institutions. Our data do not include the ownership (investment) distribution of the participating institutions and therefore a more accurate measure of each participant's influence cannot be constructed. The number of institutions does however serve as a proxy for the size and attractiveness of the investment. According to Wright et al. (1995), monitoring is more difficult in large boards and therefore buyouts with large syndicates exit sooner. Board members who are nominated by private equity investors act as non-executive directors. As the sample companies were private we have not been able to gather data on the board compositions after the buyout transaction. Hence, we are not able to test board variables, although we acknowledge their importance in corporate governance studies (e.g. Cotter and Peck, 2001; Peck, 2004).

2.3 Control Variables

A number of factors need to be controlled for when the success of LBOs is tested. Descriptive statistics presented in Table 13.1 show a size-related pattern between the four exit types. IPO exits are largest in average size and provide the highest returns. Simultaneously, other governance variables reflect the size characteristics of exit types. Management equity is largest in small companies leading to high managerial ownership in receivership exits. Likewise, high management stakes and small size are associated with a small number of participants in the equity syndicate for this group. The obvious effect of size is the result of the fundamental characteristics of leveraged buyouts.

Financial sponsors frequently seek to invest in buyouts where they can obtain majority ownership. This allows them to control the target's strategy and to take advantage of opportunities that may emerge. Individual managers investing equity seek to maximize their ownership with the capital they can invest. This capital is constrained by the individual's personal wealth and risk profile. Therefore, with a given level of capital invested, management equity ownership in a buyout depends greatly on the target's size. Hence, in small buyouts management may be able to afford to acquire a majority of the equity whereas in large buyouts management usually owns only a small fraction of the equity (CMBOR, 2005).

Size of buyout impacts the availability of different capital types. Providers of debt require collateral for borrowed funds and the amount they are willing to provide depends not only on the assets of the target but also on its operating history and the risks associated with cash flows. Sources of debt finance and capital structure vary with firm size and age (see, e.g., Berger and Udell, 1998). Large companies with steady cash flows and long operating history can choose between different types of debt, pay lower interest and can therefore have higher leverage. The capital structures of large buyout targets can be optimized with, for example, senior debt, high yield and mezzanine financing (CMBOR, 2005). We control for size using the logarithm of the entry time enterprise value of the buyout target.

In this study, we control for the actions of the buyout companies with two dummy variables: acquisitions and divestments. Given that acquisitions and divestments by buyout firms can have significant effects on both operating performance measures, it is important to control for whether

Table 13.1 Descriptive statistics

Variable	Whole sample		Exit type							
			Stock exchange		Trade sale		Secondary buyout		Receivership	
	Average	Media	Average	Media	Average	Media	Average	Media	Average	Media
Return										
Index-adj. IRR (EV)[a]	22.2%	−5.3%	136.9%	44.2%	23.0%	7.3%	10.4%	2.9%	−21.5%	−14.1%
Index-adj. IRR (EQ)[b]	70.5%	−17.8%	423.5%	99.0%	128.6%	43.3%	20.3%	21.0%	NM	NM
Governance variables										
Gearing	3.4×	1.4×	2.8×	1.3×	4.8×	1.5×	5.3×	1.5×	1.6×	1.4×
Debt coverage[c]	NM	4.2×	NM	4.1×	NM	5.4×	NM	4.3×	NM	3.6×
Institutions	2	1	2	1	2	1	2	2	1	1
Mngt equity	37.6%	35.0%	30.9%	24.6%	31.4%	30.0%	32.6%	22.7%	47.1%	49.9%
Control variables										
Size (GBP millions)[d]	55.0	14.7	141.0	23.7	56.7	25.0	52.1	26.5	18.4	6.3
Divestments[e]	39		6		11		16		6	
Acquisitions[f]	62		21		13		23		5	
Type: buyouts[g]	178		28		58		35		57	
Type: buyins[g]	143		24		33		22		64	
Source: whole company[g]	165		23		45		28		69	
Source: divestment[g]	156		29		46		29		52	
Investor investments cumulative value	330	59	316	49	385	64	255	52	NM	NM
Investor investments cumulative amount	2034	1215	1875	1506	2295	1498	1761	859	NM	NM

Table 13.1 (continued)

Variable	Whole sample		Exit type							
			Stock exchange		Trade sale		Secondary buyout		Receivership	
	Average	Media	Average	Media	Average	Media	Average	Media	Average	Media
Other										
Holding time	3.5	3.3	2.6	2.3	3.1	2.8	4.3	4.1	3.9	3.6
Observations	321	321	52	52	91	91	57	57	121	121

Notes: This table presents descriptive statistics for the sample of 321 exited buyouts grouped by type of exit. The variables are: Index-adj. IRR (EV), internal rate of return (IRR) for the holding time using enterprise value (transaction value) at time of buyout (entry) and enterprise value (transaction value) at exit adjusted for FTSE 100 index change between entry transaction and exit transaction dates; Index-adj. IRR (EQ), IRR for the holding time using total equity invested at entry and equity value at exit adjusted for FTSE 100 index change between entry transaction and exit transaction dates; Gearing, amount of debt in initial entry transaction structure divided by amount of equity in initial entry transaction structure; Debt coverage, the amount of debt in the initial entry transaction structure divided by operating profit (EBIT) for the previous fiscal year; Institutions, number of institutional (private equity) investors participating in the equity syndicate; Mngt equity, percentage of common equity held by management after entry transaction; Size, enterprise value of buyout in GBP million; Divestments, number of companies that have made divestments during holding time; Acquisitions, number of companies that have made acquisitions during holding time; Buyout/buyin, the type of buyout as either buyout or buyin; Divest/Whole, the source of buyout defined as either whole company or divestment; Investor inv. cum. value, the cumulative value of the committed capital of the investing institution at the time of buyout; inv. inv. cum. amount, the cumulative number of investments the investor has done at the time of buyout.

[a] Adjusted for refinancing (all capital types) in 36 cases.
[b] Adjusted for additional equity investments (refinancing) in 12 cases.
[c] Buyouts with negative or exceptionally high debt coverage (marginally above zero EBIT) are given 99th percentile value (59.3).
[d] Enterprise (transaction) value at entry. Used as natural logarithm in statistical tests.
[e] Number of companies that have done divestments during holding time. Used as dummy in statistical tests.
[f] Number of companies that have done acquisitions during holding time. Used as dummy in statistical tests.
[g] Denotes number of observations in the sample.

changes in operating performance are of an organic or transactional nature. Controlling for divestments is also important because highly leveraged firms experiencing financial distress may try to improve their operating prospects by selling business lines or assets. Empirical evidence surrounding buyout company divestments is mixed. According to Easterwood (1998), divestments can have significant effects on the value of a divesting buyout company whereas both Smith (1990) and Liebeskind et al. (1992) show that improvements recorded in the performance of buyout firms are more the result of improved management rather than the realignment and streamlining of core businesses through divestments of non-core assets. The CMBOR database provides information for divestments and acquisitions. However, for most of these deals, the transaction value is not available and therefore these are measured as dummies.[6] This does not provide information about their relative effects in terms of size, but allows for a satisfactory amount of control for our analysis. Controlling for divestments and acquisitions measures whether there have been efforts to streamline the buyout targets' businesses or to grow through acquisitions. Because the size of these transactions is not measured, using a count variable could bias results if sample companies have made a large number of small transactions. The acquisitions variable is given a value of one if a company has made acquisitions during the holding period; otherwise it is given a value of zero. The divestment variable is given a value of minus one if a company has divested one or more parts of its business; otherwise it is given a value of zero.

The type of buyout can impact buyout performance. Buyouts by definition are transactions initiated and led by the incumbent management team of the target whereas buyins are leveraged buyout transactions initiated and led by private equity investors together with a partially or completely new management team (CMBOR, 2005). As such there are likely to be informational asymmetry differences between the two types of buyout. Buyins are particularly likely to experience such problems as they involve outsiders, with potential consequences for performance (Robbie and Wright, 1995). In this study, type of buyout is a dummy that is given a value of one if the buyout type is buyin and zero otherwise.

Source of buyout has attracted research attention (Hite and Vetsuypens, 1989; Muscarella and Vetsuypens, 1990; Singh, 1990). Divisional buyouts involve a lack of an observable pre-divestment market value and management may possess private information about their unit that parent management may not. As a result, divisional management may be better able to negotiate a favorable price than are managers taking whole public firms private (Hite and Vetsuypens, 1989). Both Muscarella and Vetsuypens (1990) and Singh (1990) find that divisional buyouts going public generate larger operational performance improvements than whole-firm reverse buyouts, while Muscarella and Vetsuypens (1990) find that divisional reverse buyouts generate greater returns on equity than whole-firm reverse buyouts. Bae and Hoje (2002) find that operating performance characteristics are different between whole-company and divisional (part of company carved out) leveraged buyouts. In our study, source of buyout is a dummy with a value of one if the buyout was a division of a larger company (or otherwise a part of a larger corporation) and zero if the buyout comprised a whole company.

Numerous studies have examined the link between private equity investment performance and private equity investor experience (e.g., Barry et al., 1990; Lerner, 1994; Gompers, 1996; Jelic et al., 2005). Additionally, Cotter and Peck (2001) show that buyout specialists impact structuring of LBO transactions and that when buyout specialists control the majority of the post-LBO equity, the LBO transaction is likely to be financed with less short-term and/or senior debt and less likely to experience financial distress. Building on Jelic et al. (2005) in the specific context of experienced private equity investors funding buyouts in the UK, we control for the degree of experience (specialization) with two variables: the cumulative amount of capital the investor (institution) has committed to investments up to the time the specific LBO in our sample is announced and the cumulative number of investments the investor has completed at that time. These variables are preferred to a simple private equity firm age variable or a (relative) size of private equity firm measure (e.g., Barry et al., 1990; Lerner, 1994) as experience is built up more directly through deal doing. In addition, in the context of UK buyouts, these variables are preferred to a categorization based on exclusive focus on buyouts or not (Kaplan, 1991) as they convey more information about the experience of the private equity firm prior to each deal and there are few pure buyout specialists in the UK market. Similarly, this measure is preferred to a measure of the number of IPOs prior to the focal deal as there are few realizations by this mode per firm in the UK during the period of our study (CMBOR, 2005).

The final sample represents the whole population of UK buyouts in terms of size and exits. We do not limit the sample in any way, other than sufficient data must be available for a buyout to be included in the sample. Some private-equity-related studies suffer from sample selection bias and have created methodologies to overcome these problems. For example, Cochrane (2005) adjusts return variables of venture investments as some of his sample firms may not have received the additional funding needed for the company to reach a trade sale or IPO exit.

In order to model the determinants of rates of return we need to address the potential selection problem relating to non-exited investments

(Cochrane, 2005). Hence, we employ the Heckman two-stage selection model (Greene, 2000, pp. 926–37) which provides a test for sample selectivity (or non-random) bias. From the CMBOR database, we identify the population of 1723 non-exited buyouts completed during the same period as our sample of 321 exited buyouts. In step 1, we estimate the reduced form selection model for the combined population of exited and non-exited buyouts (2044 deals) using a probit and obtain maximum likelihood estimates for whether a buyout has exited or not. In this selection equation, we include variables relating to whether the investment was a buyout or buyin, whether the investment involved a whole-company investment or a divestment, the size of the deal and log of the year in which the investment took place. Buyouts arising on divestment and larger buyouts may be more likely to exit (Wright et al., 1994). Buyouts and buyins have different exit rates (Wright et al., 1995). Older firms may also be more likely to exit and at an increasing rate (CMBOR, 2005; Wright et al., 1995). In step 2, we apply OLS to the determinants of rates of return, conditional on an exit having taken place.

2.4 Descriptive Statistics

Table 13.1 reports selected descriptive statistics for the sample. The average index-adjusted EV IRR is 22.2% and the average equity IRR is 70.5% for the whole sample. The differences in mean-adjusted equity IRRs are significant between all of the groups when tested against each other. The *t*-test statistics are significant at the 1% level between IPOs versus trade sales and IPOs versus secondary buyouts and at the 5% level between trade sales versus secondary buyouts. In both EV and equity IRR terms, IPO exits have outperformed trade sale and secondary buyout exits. The average holding time for the sample is 3.5 years and IPO exits have the shortest average holding time (2.6 years). There is a significant negative correlation between the holding period and IRR variables (at the 1% level). This relationship is also apparent in Figure 13.2A. We assume that this reflects the nature of buyout investments as it indicates that the owners (private equity investors) are taking advantage of favorable exit opportunities even if the holding period is short and planned operating improvements have not been fully executed. Furthermore, prior studies show that larger buyouts tend to exit sooner (Wright et al., 1995). Figure 13.2B illustrates the return distribution of the sample excluding receivership exits, because of the return assumption applied to this exit type. The sample returns are non-normal as are the distributions of the returns between exit types. This can impact the reliability of our results, as our sample distribution violates the assumption of normally distributed returns. The average values for transaction structures show that trade sale exits had the

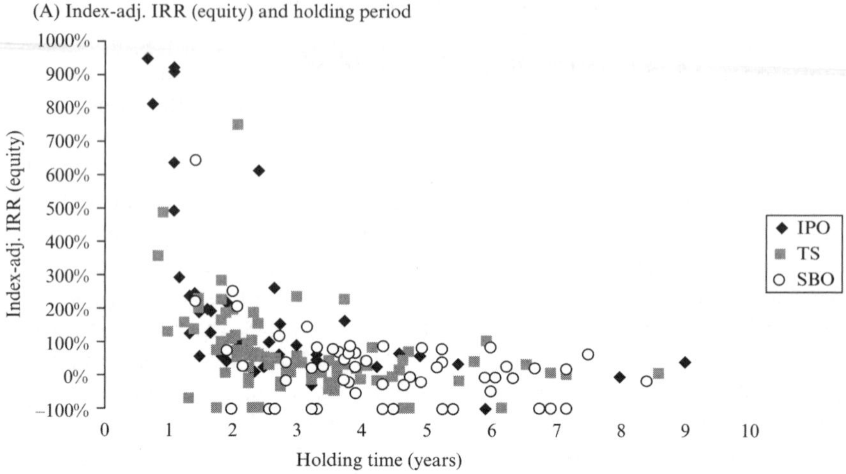

Note: IPO exits and 3 trade sale exits are cut of from the graphs as these have above 1000 % index adj. IRB (Equity).

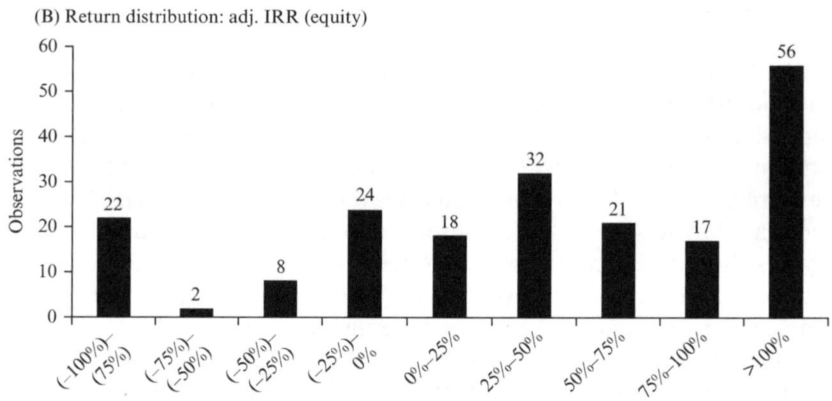

Note: Excludes receivership exits (121) observations.
Graphs illustrate the return characteristics of the sample, presented by the adjusted equity IRR, IRR for the holding time using total equity invested at entry and equity value at exit adjusted for FTSE 100 index change between entry transaction and exit transaction dates. (A) presents the relation between holding time and LBO return for each exit type. (B) shows the return distribution of the sample. Both graphs exclude receivership exits, because of the return assumptions applied to this exit type.

Figure 13.2 Return characteristics and distribution

highest leverage and receiverships the lowest. Management ownership and the number of institutions participating in the equity syndicate do not vary significantly between the three positive exit types, but in receivership exits management's equity stake is noticeably higher.

3. EMPIRICAL RESULTS

Table 13.2 presents regression statistics with both index-adjusted IRR for enterprise and equity value for our sample. Col. (0) for each dependent variable reports the results of the Heckman procedure using the full sample of 2044 exited and non-exited buyouts. The Mills Lambda is significant for the enterprise value (EV) equation but not for the equity value (EQ) equation, suggesting that selection bias may be a problem only for the former. However, the Heckman procedure results are closely consistent with those for the OLS regressions presented in cols (1) and (2) for each dependent variable.

For the index-adjusted IRR of enterprise value (EV) there are significant differences if the investor experience variables are included. Without them debt coverage, management equity, size and acquisitions are significant for both methods. Type of buyout is significant only in the OLS equation without the investor experience variable. Once investor experience variables are included, only gearing and management equity are significant. With index-adjusted IRR of equity value (EQ) as the dependent variable, the size of the buyout and whether acquisitions were made post-buyout are significant in both the Heckman and the OLS regressions. When the investor experience variables are introduced, the amount invested by the investor is significant and negatively associated with EQ but size of the buyout and whether acquisitions were made, as well as the buyout/buyin variable, cease to be significant. However, management equity becomes significant in this latter case. One of the explanations for these results may be related to the size variables. We only have data for the investor variables for 195 of the 321 cases, and these are likely to involve active investors who seek to make these data available as part of their PR. Hence, there may be hidden reasons why investor variables lead to sample selection bias.

To overcome the problem of absence of an exit value for the receivership cases, we undertook logistic regression analysis where both return variables are given a value of one if the index-adjusted realized return was positive and zero otherwise. The assumption of a zero return for receivership exits is alleviated because we argue that the return to private equity firms on receivership exits does not exceed zero, but no assumption of the actual exit time value is required. This allows for analysis of the factors affecting the probability of a positive return. Additionally, this will automatically

Table 13.2 Regression analysis of the whole sample

Dependent variable	Adj. IRR (EV)			Adj. IRR (EQ)		
	(0)	(1)	(2)	(0)	(3)	(4)
Gearing	−0.003	−0.003	−0.006	0.018	0.017	0.001
	(0.03)	(−1.01)	(1.74) *	(0.10) *	(−1.53)	−0.08
Debt coverage	0.003	0.003	0.001	0.000	0.000	−0.012
	(0.01) *	(1.69) *	(0.41)	(0.00)	(0.02)	(1.50)
Institutions	−0.004	−0.013	−0.005	−0.010	−0.037	−0.058
	(0.02)	(0.59)	(0.16)	(0.81)	(0.47)	(0.56)
Mngt equity	0.212	0.232	0.537	0.322	0.362	1.118
	(0.12) *	(1.88) *	(2.87) ***	(0.42)	(0.83)	(1.72) *
Size	0.105	0.070	−0.013	0.403	0.328	0.082
	(0.03) ***	(3.53) ***	(0.39)	(0.09) ***	(4.71) ***	(0.70)
Divestments	−0.018	−0.034	−0.013	0.302	0.270	0.524
	(0.08)	(0.42)	(0.13)	(0.28)	(0.96)	(1.55)
Acquisitions	0.162	0.185	0.104	0.564	0.613	0.237
	(0.07) **	(2.65) ***	(1.25)	(0.24) **	(2.48) **	(0.82)
Buyout/buyin	0.026	−0.106	−0.003	−0.097	−0.373	−0.032
	(0.08)	(2.21) **	(0.04)	(0.27)	(2.21) **	(0.12)
Divest./whole company	0.037	0.015	0.064	−0.007	−0.052	−0.089
	(0.05)	(0.31)	(0.95)	(0.17)	(0.31)	(0.38)
Investor inv. cum. value			0.039			0.357
			(0.50)			(1.30)
Investor inv. amount			−0.123			−0.559
			(1.55)			(2.03) **
Buyout/buyin	0.442			0.442		
	(0.07) ***			(0.72) ***		
Divest./whole company	0.060			0.060		
	(0.07)			(0.07)		

Size	0.144			0.144		
	(0.02) ***			(0.22) ***		
Year	−2.834			−2.834		
	(0.05) ***			(0.05) ***		
Constant	−0.964	−0.189	0.189	−2.366	−0.749	0.526
	(0.37) ***	(1.79) *	(1.07)	(1.24) *	(2.02) **	(0.86)
Observations	2044	321	195	2044	321	195
R^2		0.09	0.11		0.12	0.08
Mills Lambda	0.408			0.852		
	(0.186) **			(0.63)		
Wald chi^2	32.53			43.53		
Prob > chi^2	0.002		0.000			

Notes: Standard errors in parentheses.
(0) Refers to two-step Heckman test. Uncensored observations = 321.
This table presents Heckman regressions for the combined sample of 321 exited buyouts and 1723 non–exited buyouts (col. 0), together with OLS regressions for the exited buyouts (cols 1 and 2) for each dependent variable. In col. (0) variables in italics (buyout/buyin; divest/whole company; size; year) represent the selection equation in the Heckman procedure. The variables are: Index-adj. IRR (EV), internal rate of return (IRR) for the holding time using enterprise value (transaction value) at time of buyout (entry) and enterprise value (transaction value) at exit adjusted for FTSE 100 index change between entry transaction and exit transaction dates; Index-adj. IRR (EQ), IRR for the holding time using total equity invested at entry and equity value at exit adjusted for FTSE 100 index change between entry transaction and exit transaction dates; Gearing, amount of debt in initial entry transaction structure divided by amount of equity in initial entry transaction structure; Debt coverage, the amount of debt in the initial entry transaction structure divided by operating profit (EBIT) for the previous fiscal year; Institutions, number of institutional (private equity) investors participating in the equity syndicate; Mngt equity, percentage of common equity held by management after entry transaction; Size, natural logarithm of entry time enterprise value; Divestments, dummy variable that equals minus one if the company has made divestments during the holding time and zero otherwise; Acquisitions, dummy variable that equals one if the company has made acquisitions during the holding time and zero otherwise; Buyout/buyin, a dummy that is given a value of one if the type of buyout is buyin and zero otherwise; Divest/whole, a dummy that is given a value of one if the source of buyout is a divestment (not whole company) and zero otherwise; Year, the log of a time trend; Investor inv. cum. value, natural logarithm of the cumulative value of the committed capital of the investing institution at the time of buyout; Inv. inv. amount, natural logarithm of the cumulative number of investments the investor has done at the time of buyout.
* Statistically significant at 10% confidence level.
** Statistically significant at 5% confidence level.
*** Statistically significant at 1% confidence level.

truncate return variables to a comparable level. The return earned on a buyout investment at exit depends to a large extent on exit type. Exit decision and exit type depend, among other factors, on the need for investment realization and capital market situations. Therefore, to test the likelihood of success, defined as a positive IRR, buyouts within different exit groups must be comparable.

Table 13.3 presents the results of the logistic regression analysis. For both probabilities, positive IRR of enterprise value and equity return, size and acquisitions are significant. Furthermore, the type of buyout variable is significant when investor experience variables are not present. Moreover, with leverage, the number of institutions (syndication) and management equity variables show signs of statistical significance between 5 and 10%.

As there is some evidence that the type of buyout/buyin variable is significant as reported in Tables 13.2 and 13.3, the sample is divided by type

Table 13.3 Logit analysis of the whole sample

Dependent variable	Probability for positive adj.IRR (EV)		Probability for positive adj. IRR (EQ)	
	(5)	(6)	(7)	(8)
Gearing	−0.013	−0.034	0.001	−0.03
	−0.82	(1.90)*	(0.06)	(1.56)
Debt coverage	0.009	0.004	0.003	−0.011
	−1.11	−0.36	(0.35)	(0.91)
Institutions	−0.1	−0.121	−0.205	−0.322
	−0.84	−0.81	(1.66)*	(2.03)**
Mngt equity	−0.02	1.735	−0.222	0.233
	−0.03	(1.69)*	(0.31)	(0.23)
Size	0.588	0.154	0.773	0.534
	(4.96)***	−0.84	(5.97)***	(2.66)***
Divestments	−0.357	−0.276	0.074	0.736
	−0.81	−0.51	(0.16)	(1.39)
Acquisitions	1.289	0.818	1.465	1.167
	(3.26)***	(1.70)*	(3.48)***	(2.21)**
Buyout/buyin	−0.575	0.243	−0.798	−0.438
	(2.16)**	−0.63	(2.88)***	(1.10)
Divest./whole company	0.115	0.251	−0.212	−0.397
	−0.45	−0.74	(0.79)	(1.12)
Investor inv. cum. value		0.13		0.226
		−0.29		(0.48)
Investor inv. amount		−0.586		−0.736
		−1.37		(1.61)

Table 13.3 (continued)

Dependent variable	Probability for positive adj.IRR (EV)		Probability for positive adj. IRR (EQ)	
	(5)	(6)	(7)	(8)
Constant	−1.845	0.464	−1.748	1.038
	(3.12)***	−0.5	(2.85)***	(1.07)
Observations	321	195	321	195
LR chi^2 (4)	63.810	18.730	86.010	26.590
Prob > chi^2	0.000	0.066	0.000	0.005
Pseudo R^2	0.145	0.077	0.195	0.113

Notes: Absolute value of z-statistics in parentheses.
This table presents logistic regressions for the sample of 321 exited buyouts. The variables are: Index adj. IRR (EV), internal rate of return (IRR) for the holding time using enterprise value (transaction value) at time of buyout (entry) and enterprise value (transaction value) at exit adjusted for FTSE 100 index change between entry transaction and exit transaction dates; Index-adj. IRR (EQ), IRR for the holding time using total equity invested at entry and equity value at exit adjusted for FTSE 100 index change between entry transaction and exit transaction dates; Gearing, amount of debt in initial entry transaction structure divided by amount of equity in initial entry transaction structure; Debt coverage, the amount of debt in the initial entry transaction structure divided by operating profit (EBIT) for the previous fiscal year; Institutions, number of institutional (private equity) investors participating in the equity syndicate; Mngt equity, percentage of common equity held by management after entry transaction; Size, natural logarithm of entry time enterprise value; Divestments, dummy variable that equals minus one if the company has made divestments during the holding time and zero otherwise; Acquisitions, dummy variable that equals one if the company has made acquisitions during the holding time and zero otherwise; Buyout/buyin, a dummy that is given a value of one if the type of buyout is buyin and zero otherwise; Divest/whole, a dummy that is given a value of one if the source of buyout is a divestment (not whole company) and zero otherwise; Investor inv. cum. value, natural logarithm of the cumulative value of the committed capital of the investing institution at the time of buyout; Investor inv. amount., natural logarithm of the cumulative number of investments the investor has done at the time of buyout.

* Statistically significant at 10% confidence level.
** Statistically significant at 5% confidence level.
*** Statistically significant at 1% confidence level.

of buyout. There are 178 management buyouts in the sample and 143 buyins, where either part or whole of the incumbent management team is replaced with new individuals. As reported in Tables 13.4 and 13.5, there are differences between the two types. For buyouts, size and acquisitions are important drivers of returns. Larger buyouts that have done acquisitions have higher returns and higher likelihood of positive IRRs. There is also evidence that buyins have been more successful in making divestments that have increased returns. On the other hand, for buyouts divestments have led to both lower returns and lower probability of positive return.

Table 13.4 Regression comparison between buyouts and buyins

Dependent variable	Adj. IRR (EV)	Adj. IRR (EQ)	Adj. IRR (EV)	Adj. IRR (EQ)
Group	Buyout		Buyin	
	(9)	(10)	(11)	(12)
Gearing	0.002	0.027	−0.01	0.008
	−0.44	(1.81)*	(2.22)**	−0.46
Debt coverage	0.002	−0.009	0.002	0.006
	−0.68	−1.19	−0.96	−0.79
Institutions	0.006	−0.015	−0.027	−0.054
	−0.17	−0.14	(0.93)	(0.47)
Mngt equity	0.443	0.724	−0.130	−0.140
	(2.67)***	– 1.31	(0.70)	(0.19)
Size	0.086	0.404	0.040	0.266
	(2.86)***	(4.02)***	(1.50)	(2.53)**
Divestments	0.082	0.679	−0.177	−0.193
	−0.7	(1.76)*	(1.67)*	(0.46)
Acquisitions	0.281	0.821	0.066	0.345
	(2.71)***	(2.37)**	(0.73)	(0.97)
Divest./whole company	0.031	0.024	−0.003	−0.127
	−0.46	−0.11	(0.05)	(0.48)
Constant	−0.368	−1.104	−0.023	−0.754
	(2.55)**	(2.30)**	(0.16)	(1.35)
Observations	178	178	143	143
R^2	0.11	0.15	0.12	0.11

Notes: Standard errors in parentheses.
This table presents regressions for the sample of 321 exited buyouts divided into two groups by type of buyout. The variables are: Index-adj. IRR (EV), internal rate of return (IRR) for the holding time using enterprise value (transaction value) at time of buyout (entry) and enterprise value (transaction value) at exit adjusted for FTSE 100 index change between entry transaction and exit transaction dates; Index-adj. IRR (EQ), IRR for the holding time using total equity invested at entry and equity value at exit adjusted for FTSE 100 index change between entry transaction and exit transaction dates; Gearing, amount of debt in initial entry transaction structure divided by amount of equity in initial entry transaction structure; Debt coverage, the amount of debt in the initial entry transaction structure divided by operating profit (EBIT) for the previous fiscal year; Institutions, number of institutional (private equity) investors participating in the equity syndicate; Mngt equity, percentage of common equity held by management after entry transaction; Size, natural logarithm of entry time enterprise value; Divestments, dummy variable that equals minus one if the company has made divestments during the holding time and zero otherwise; Acquisitions, dummy variable that equals one if the company has made acquisitions during the holding time and zero otherwise; Divest/whole, a dummy that is given a value of one if the source of buyout is a divestment (not whole company) and zero otherwise.
* Statistically significant at 10% confidence level.
** Statistically significant at 5% confidence level.
*** Statistically significant at 1% confidence level.

Table 13.5 Logit comparison between buyouts and buyins

Dependent variable	Probability for positive adj. IRR (EV)	Probability for positive adj. IRR (EQ)	Probability for positive adj. IRR (EV)	Probability for positive adj. IRR (Eq)
Group	Buyout		Buyin	
	(13)	(14)	(15)	(16)
Gearing	0.031	0.021	−0.105	−0.017
	−1.28	−0.88	(2.30)**	(0.68)
Debt coverage	0.001	−0.009	0.009	0.011
	−0.06	−0.7	(0.71)	(0.86)
Institutions	−0.013	−0.105	−0.137	−0.295
	−0.08	−0.6	(0.73)	(1.54)
Mngt equity	0.917	0.013	−2.057	−0.608
	−1.08	−0.01	(1.51)	(0.47)
Size	0.55	0.8	0.535	0.779
	(3.33)***	(4.44)***	(2.80)***	(3.69)***
Divestments	0.358	1.152	−1.504	−1.130
	−0.58	(1.73)*	(1.94)*	(1.58)
Acquisitions	1.928	1.867	0.617	0.994
	(3.17)***	(2.95)***	(1.04)	(1.64)
Divest/whole company	−0.169	−0.406	0.559	0.041
	−0.5	−1.16	(1.29)	(0.10)
Constant	−2.193	−1.889	−1.499	−2.469
	(2.83)***	(2.37)**	(1.55)	(2.49)**
Observations	178	178	143	143
LR chi^2 (4)	32.03	44.75	51.94	49.02
Prob > chi^2	0.001	0.000	0.000	0.000
Pseudo R^2	0.130	0.181	0.270	0.253

Notes: Absolute value of z-statistics in parentheses.
This table presents logistic regressions for the sample of 321 exited buyouts divided into two groups by type of buyout. The variables are: Index-adj. IRR (EV), internal rate of return (IRR) for the holding time using enterprise value (transaction value) at time of buyout (entry) and enterprise value (transaction value) at exit adjusted for FTSE 100 index change between entry transaction and exit transaction dates; Index-adj. IRR (Eq), IRR for the holding time using total equity invested at entry and equity value at exit adjusted for FTSE 100 index change between entry transaction and exit transaction dates; Gearing, amount of debt in initial entry transaction structure divided by amount of equity in initial entry transaction structure; Debt coverage, the amount of debt in the initial entry transaction structure divided by operating profit (EBIT) for the previous fiscal year; Institutions, number of institutional (private equity) investors participating in the equity syndicate; Mngt equity, percentage of common equity held by management after entry transaction; Size, natural logarithm of entry time enterprise value; Divestments, dummy variable that equals minus one if the company has made divestments during the holding time and zero otherwise; Acquisitions, dummy variable that equals one if the company has made acquisitions during the holding time and zero otherwise; Divest/whole, a dummy that is given a value of one if the source of buyout is a divestment (not whole company) and zero otherwise.

* Statistically significant at 10% confidence level.
** Statistically significant at 5% confidence level.
*** Statistically significant at 1% confidence level.

3.1 Robustness Tests

This study makes the assumption that receivership exits have zero value at exit, as discussed in Section 2.1. This assumption may bias the presented results because in reality receivership exits usually have an exit time value above zero. Citron et al. (2003) find that secured debt providers typically receive an average of 62% of their loan back in cases of receivership and a significant proportion are sold as going concerns. Therefore we test our sample by excluding receivership exits and analyze only other exit types (successful buyouts). Appendices 13.A and 13.B report the results for 200 successful buyouts using the same models as in the tables reported earlier. The observation that receivership exit buyouts are small and management has on average a higher equity proportion in these buyouts explains the results reported for this restricted sample. For IRR regressions, management equity is significant across the board. Moreover, investor experience measured as number of investments is significant with a negative sign for IRR equity. This indicates that private equity investors who invest in a large number of small LBOs (likely with small committed capital) often invest in buyouts that go bankrupt. Additionally, the results indicate that overleveraging of the target companies leads to lower returns.

Additional robustness tests exclude small buyouts. Reflecting the overall population, the sample for this study is somewhat weighted towards small buyouts. Therefore, we perform additional tests with a restricted sample that excludes buyout with enterprise value less than GBP 10 million. We addressed size-related issues in Section 2.3 where we discussed how and why buyout investors prefer to focus on larger transactions. We present results for a size-restricted sample in Appendices 13C and 13D. Similar to the results for the sample excluding receivership exits, management ownership stake is an important driver of returns for larger buyouts. Moreover, this group has the financial muscle to drive value uplift with strategic acquisitions. Furthermore, investors with a large cumulative amount of capital have the experience to drive value up more than private equity companies with a large number of smaller investments.

We undertook further tests of the size effect. First, we divided our sample into three groups by size to reflect practitioners' notions of large, medium and small deal segments of the market (CMBOR, 2005): buyouts over GBP 100 million (35 observations), buyouts between GBP 100 and 10 million (163 observations) and buyouts less than GBP 10 million (123 observations). Following Link et al. (2002, 2005) we first showed with Chow tests that the variances between the three groups are significantly different from each other. We also tried to find structural breakpoints in the data with a cusum test as in Lichtenberg and Siegel (1991) but were unable to find a statistically robust way to divide our sample into size groups. Although not reported in detail here, these results show number of participants in the equity syndicate is positively related to return except in very large buyouts that suffer from syndicates that are too large. Moreover, leverage and debt coverage are positively related to value increase. However, for large buyouts, equity return is negatively related to leverage, the opposite to the expectation that leverage would result in proportionally higher equity returns when enterprise value increases. The proportion of management ownership and the probability of exit through receivership decrease the larger the buyout, and managers either cannot afford or are not allowed to acquire majority stakes in large targets. Large buyouts provide higher absolute returns and receive more attention from outside equity investors who may also invest additional funds in large buyouts if needed. Larger buyouts have higher gearing resulting from alternative capital sources and steady cash flows.

4. CONCLUSIONS

Using a unique, hand-collected dataset, this study examines the IRR of enterprise value and invested equity in 321 exited buyouts in the UK between years 1995 and 2004. These include 52 IPOs, 92 trade sales, 57 secondary buyouts and 121 receiverships. We find that the mean index-adjusted EV IRR is 22.2% and the average equity IRR is 70.5% for the whole sample. IPO exits outperform trade sale and secondary buyout exits. Our evidence relating to return on enterprise value (EV) and equity (EQ) indicates that buyouts do generate value creation as well as equity value. We find some evidence that managerial equity stake in particular is more strongly associated with the EV based measure than for the EQ-based measure.

Our findings do not provide evidence that for all LBOs, the governance mechanisms introduced on buyout are the main drivers of LBO returns. However, our tests on restricted samples suggest that for larger buyouts and among successful buyouts, management's equity stake is a significant factor in determining LBO returns.

The main findings of this study are that size is positively related to value increase, acquisitions during the holding period are one of the main drivers of LBO returns and that there is a difference between the return characteristics of buyouts and buyins.

With respect to size, larger buyouts perform better and provide higher investor returns. One of the main reasons for this is likely to be the higher bankruptcy risk of small LBOs. Small companies are more vulnerable to industry cycles and short-term business disturbance whereas larger corporations likely have better buffers for tougher business environments.

Moreover, large enterprises can have more than one business line that can stabilize enterprises performance through cycles. Furthermore, the investing institutions are likely to provide more assistance and guidance to large companies where they have significant equity investments at risk. This support can also include necessary additional equity injections to keep the company fully operating and to avoid covenant breaches that can result in liquidation decisions from the lenders.

Acquisitions contribute to buyout value increase and especially to the enterprise value uplift. The consistent significance of acquisitions shows that buy-and-build strategies are common among LBO companies. However, acquisitions do not always contribute to equity returns. This finding implies that acquisitions are used mainly as a mechanism to increase scale to ensure lower risks associated with the investments. Moreover, acquisitions can also be a sign of industry consolidation that lower competition and allows to building economies of scale.

With regard to differences between the return characteristics of buyout and buyins, we find that buyout returns are driven by acquisitions during the holding period. There is no evidence that buyin return values would be impacted by acquisitions. Moreover, our results indicate that buyout equity returns are negatively impacted by divestments while the opposite is true for buyins. This finding implies that private equity companies that initiate institutional buyins are able to drive their returns through streamlining of target company operations.

Overall, the reported empirical findings and the resulting conclusions add to work that does not explicitly support Jensen's (1986, 1989) theory that the governance mechanisms of buyouts solve agency problems associated with free cash flow and increase equity value. Rather, our evidence contributes to the heterogeneity view of buyouts, particularly with respect to the size of the transaction and whether it is driven by insider or outsider management. The importance of managerial equity ownership and acquisition activity but not divestment actions is consistent with the importance of incentivized and entrepreneurial management seeking to realize growth opportunities rather than focus on downsizing (Wright et al., 2000).

APPENDIX 13A REGRESSION ANALYSIS OF NON-RECEIVERSHIP EXITS

Table 13A.1 presents regressions for the sample of 200 exited non-receivership buyouts. The variables are: Index-adj. IRR (EV), internal rate of return (IRR) for the holding time using enterprise value (transaction value) at time of buyout (entry) and enterprise value (transaction value) at exit adjusted for FTSE 100 index change between entry transaction and exit transaction dates; Index-adj. IRR (EQ), IRR for the holding time using total equity invested at entry and equity value at exit adjusted for FTSE 100 index change between entry transaction and exit transaction dates; Gearing, amount of debt in initial entry transaction structure divided by amount of equity in initial entry transaction structure; Debt coverage, the amount of

Table 13A.1 Regressions for the sample of 200 exited non-receivership buyouts

Dependent variable	Adj. IRR (EV)		Adj. IRR (Eq)	
Group	Non-receiving exits			
	(17)	(18)	(19)	(20)
Gearing	−0.006	−0.006	0.006	0.001
	(1.82)*	(1.74)*	(0.51)*	(0.08)
Debt coverage	0.003	0.001	−0.004	−0.012
	−1.39	−0.41	(0.56)	(1.50)
Institutions	−0.01	−0.005	−0.071	−0.058
	−0.34	−0.16	(0.69)	(0.56)
Mngt equity	0.514	0.537	1.318	1.118
	(2.90)***	(2.87)***	(2.14)**	(1.72)*
Size	−0.019	−0.013	0.078	0.082
	−0.66	−0.39	(0.76)	(0.70)
Divestments	−0.006	−0.013	0.473	0.524
	−0.06	−0.13	(1.40)	(1.55)
Acquisitions	0.112	0.104	0.298	0.237
	−1.33	−1.25	(1.02)	(0.82)
Buyout/buyin	0.029	−0.003	0.169	−0.032
	−0.4	−0.04	(0.67)	(0.12)
Divest./whole company	0.077	0.064	−0.029	−0.089
	−1.15	−0.95	(0.12)	(0.38)
Investor inv. cum. value		0.039		0.357
		−0.5		(1.30)
Investor inv. amount		−0.123		−0.559
		−1.55		(2.03)**
Constant	0.073	0.189	0.290	0.526
	−0.49	−1.07	(0.56)	(0.86)
Observations	200	195	200	195
R^2	0.09	0.11	0.12	0.08

Notes: Standard errors in parentheses.
* Statistically significant at 10% confidence level.
** Statistically significant at 5% confidence level.
*** Statistically significant at 1% confidence level.

debt in the initial entry transaction structure divided by operating profit (EBIT) for the previous fiscal year; Institutions, number of institutional (private equity) investors participating in the equity syndicate; Mngt equity, percentage of common equity held by management after entry transaction; Size, natural logarithm of entry time enterprise value; Divestments, dummy variable that equals minus one if the company has made divestments during the holding time and zero otherwise; Acquisitions, dummy variable that equals one if the company has made acquisitions during the holding time and zero otherwise; Buyout/buyin, a dummy that is given a value of one if the type of buyout is buyin and zero otherwise; Divest/whole, a dummy that is given a value of one if the source of buyout is a divestment (not whole company) and zero otherwise; Investor inv. cum. value, natural logarithm of the cumulative value of the committed capital of the investing institution at the time of buyout; Investor inv. amount, natural logarithm of the cumulative number of investments the investor has done at the time of buyout.

APPENDIX 13B LOGIT ANALYSIS OF NON-RECEIVERSHIP EXITS

Table 13B.1 presents logistic regressions for the sample of 200 exited non-receivership buyouts. The variables are: Index-adj. IRR (EV), internal rate of return (IRR) for the holding time using enterprise value (transaction value) at time of buyout (entry) and enterprise value (transaction value) at exit adjusted for FTSE 100 index change between entry transaction and exit transaction dates; Index-adj. IRR (EQ), IRR for the holding time using total equity invested at entry and equity value at exit adjusted for FTSE 100 index change between entry transaction and exit transaction dates; Gearing, amount of debt in initial entry transaction structure divided by amount of equity in initial entry transaction structure; Debt coverage, the amount of debt in the initial entry transaction structure divided by operating profit (EBIT) for the previous fiscal year; Institutions, number of institutional (private equity) investors participating in the equity syndicate; Mngt equity, percentage of common equity held by management after entry transaction; Size, natural logarithm of entry time enterprise value; Divestments, dummy variable that equals minus one if the company has made divestments during the holding time and zero otherwise; Acquisitions, dummy variable that equals one if the company has made acquisitions during the holding time and zero otherwise; Buyout/buyin, a dummy that is given a value of one if the type of buyout is buyin and zero otherwise; Divest/whole, a dummy that is given a value of one if the source of buyout is a divestment (not

Table 13B.1 Logit regressions for the sample of 200 exited non-receivership buyouts

Dependent variable	Probability for positive Adj. IRR (EV)		Probability for positive Adj. IRR (EQ)	
Group	Non-receiving exits			
	(21)	(22)	(23)	(24)
Gearing	−0.032	−0.034	0.018	0.030
	(1.94)*	(1.90)*	(1.09)*	(1.56)
Debt coverage	0.009	0.004	−0.004	−0.011
	−0.75	(0.36)	(0.32)	(0.91)
Institution	−0.146	−0.121	−0.340	−0.322
	−0.01	(0.81)	(2.25)**	(2.03)
Mngt equity	1.337	1.735	0.710	0.233
	−1.47	(1.69)*	(0.76)	(0.23)
Size	0.165	0.154	0.472	0.534
	−1.08	(0.84)	(2.83)***	(2.66)***
Divestments	−0.138	−0.276	0.529	0.736
	−0.27	(0.51)	(1.05)	(1.39)
Acquisitions	0.814	0.818	1.098	1.167
	(1.71)*	(1.70)*	(2.13)**	(2.21)**
Buyout/buyin	0.29	0.243	−0.108	−0.438
	−0.8	(0.63)	(0.29)	(1.10)
Divest./whole company	0.267	0.251	−0.341	−0.397
	−0.8	(0.74)	(0.98)	(1.12)
Investor inv. cum. value		0.130		0.226
		(0.29)		(0.48)
Investor inv. amount		−0.586		−0.736
		(1.37)		(1.61)
Constant	−0.23	0.464	0.081	1.038
	−0.31	(0.50)	(0.10)	(1.07)
Observations	200	195	200	195
LR chi2 (4)	13 142	18 730	17 700	26 590
Prob > chi^2	0.142	0.066	0.038	0.003
Pseudo R^2	0.054	0.077	0.074	0.114

Notes: Absolute value of z-statistics in parentheses.
* Statistically significant at 10% confidence level.
** Statistically significant at 5% confidence level.
*** Statistically significant at 1% confidence level.

whole company) and zero otherwise; Investor inv. cum. value, natural logarithm of the cumulative value of the committed capital of the investing institution at the time of buyout; Investor inv. amount, natural logarithm of the cumulative number of investments the investor has done at the time of buyout.

APPENDIX 13C REGRESSION ANALYSIS OF SAMPLE UNDER GBP 10 MILLION BUYOUTS

Table 13C.1 presents regressions for the sample of 204 buyouts with enterprise value under GPB 10 million. The variables are: Index-adj. IRR (EV), internal rate of return (IRR) for the holding time using enterprise value (transaction value) at time of buyout (entry) and enterprise value (transaction value) at exit adjusted for FTSE 100 index change between entry transaction and exit transaction dates; Index-adj. IRR (EQ), IRR for the holding time using total equity invested at entry and equity value at exit adjusted for FTSE 100 index change between entry transaction and exit transaction dates; Gearing, amount of debt in initial entry transaction structure divided by amount of equity in initial entry transaction structure; Debt coverage, the amount of debt in the initial entry transaction structure divided by operating profit (EBIT) for the previous fiscal year; Institutions, number of institutional (private equity) investors participating in the equity syndicate; Mngt equity, percentage of common equity held by management after entry transaction; Size, natural logarithm of entry time enterprise value; Divestments, dummy variable that equals minus one if the company has made divestments during the holding time and zero otherwise; Acquisitions, dummy variable that equals one if the company has made acquisitions during the holding time and zero otherwise; Buyout/buyin, a dummy that is given a value of one if the type of buyout is buyin and zero otherwise; Divest/whole, a dummy that is given a value of one if the source of buyout is a divestment (not whole company) and zero otherwise; Investor inv. cum. value, natural logarithm of the cumulative value of the committed capital of the investing institution at the time of buyout; Investor inv. amount., natural logarithm of the cumulative number of investments the investor has done at the time of buyout.

Table 13C.1 *Regressions for the sample of 204 buyouts with enterprise value under GBP 10 million*

Dependent variable	Adj. IRR (EV)		Adj. IRR (EQ)	
Group	LBOs with enterprise value over GBP10 million			
	(25)	(26)	(27)	(28)
Gearing	−0.002	−0.006	0.018	−0.003
	−0.73	(1.74)*	(1.46)	(0.20)
Debt coverage	0.001	0.001	−0.008	−0.011
	−0.6	−0.29	(1.00)	(1.35)
Institutions	−0.016	−0.014	−0.042	−0.036
	−0.63	−0.44	(0.45)	(0.33)
Mngt equity	0.538	0.68	1.890	2.303
	(3.03)***	(3.13)***	(2.90)***	(3.05)***
Size	0.057	0.002	0.326	0.066
	(1.77)*	−0.06	(2.74)***	(0.48)
Divestments	−0.033	0.001	0.326	0.475
	−0.35	−0.01	(0.95)	(1.32)
Acquisitions	0.118	0.054	0.351	0.046
	−1.42	−0.6	(1.15)	(0.15)
Buyout/buyin	−0.046	0.007	−0.190	0.109
	−0.69	−0.08	(0.79)	(0.38)
Divest./whole company	0.024	0.068	−0.050	−0.001
	−0.39	−0.92	(0.22)	(0.01)
Investor inv. cum. value		0.059		0.555
		−0.69		(1.87)*
Investor inv. amount		−0.127		−0.640
		−1.51		(2.20)**
Constant	−0.228	0.069	−1.066	−0.248
	−1.49	−0.31	(1.90)*	(0.32)
Observations	204	162	204	162
R^2	0.07	0.11	0.09	0.13

Notes: Standard errors in parentheses.
* Statistically significant at 10% confidence level.
** Statistically significant at 5% confidence level.
*** Statistically significant at 1% confidence level.

APPENDIX 13D LOGIT ANALYSIS OF SAMPLE EXCLUDING UNDER GBP 10 MILLION BUYOUTS

Table 13D.1 presents regressions for the sample of 204 buyouts with enterprise value exceeding GPB 10 million. The variables are: Index-adj. IRR (EV), internal rate of return (IRR) for the holding time using enterprise value (transaction value) at time of buyout (entry) and enterprise value (transaction value) at exit adjusted for FTSE 100 index change between entry transaction and exit transaction dates; Index-adj. IRR (EQ), IRR for the holding time using total equity invested at entry and equity value at exit adjusted for FTSE 100 index change between entry transaction and exit transaction dates; Gearing, amount of debt in initial entry transaction structure divided by amount of equity in initial entry transaction structure; Debt coverage, the amount of debt in the initial entry transaction structure divided by operating profit (EBIT) for the previous fiscal year; Institutions, number of institutional (private equity) investors participating in the equity syndicate; Mngt equity, percentage of common equity held by management after entry transaction; Size, natural logarithm of entry time enterprise value; Divestments, dummy variable that equals minus one if the company has made divestments during the holding time and zero otherwise; Acquisitions, dummy variable that equals one if the company has made acquisitions during the holding time and zero otherwise; Buyout/buyin, a dummy that is given a value of one if the type of buyout is buyin and zero otherwise; Divest/whole, a dummy that is given a value of one if the source of buyout is a divestment (not whole company) and zero otherwise; Investor inv. cum. value, natural logarithm of the cumulative value of the committed capital of the investing institution at the time of buyout; Investor inv. amount, natural logarithm of the cumulative number of investments the investor has done at the time of buyout.

ACKNOWLEDGEMENTS

Financial support from Foundation for Economic Education and Suomen Arvopaperimarkkinoiden Edistämissäätiö is gratefully acknowledged; thanks also to Barclays Private Equity, Deloitte, Don Siegel, Douglas Cumming, Michael Jensen, Anders Löflund, Benjamin Maury and an anonymous reviewer.

Table 13D.1 Regressions for the sample of 204 buyouts with enterprise value over GBP 10 million

Dependent variable	Probability for positive Adj. IRR (EV)		Probability for positive Adj. IRR (EQ)	
Group	LBOs with enterprise value over GBP 10 million			
	(29)	(30)	(31)	(32)
Gearing	−0.011	−0.041	−0.001	−0.036
	−0.65	(2.15)**	(0.08)	(1.77)*
Debt coverage	0.009	0.007	−0.002	−0.010
	−0.88	−0.56	(0.22)	(0.81)
Institutions	−0.122	−0.158	−0.229	−0.370
	−0.95	−1	(1.73)*	(2.14)**
Mngt equity	1.734	2.621	1.221	1.758
	(1.90)*	(2.13)**	(1.29)	(1.32)
Size	0.523	0.26	0.744	0.603
	(2.99)***	−1.17	(3.93)***	(1.34)**
Divestments	−0.26	−0.104	0.552	1.064
	−0.54	−0.81	(1.10)	(1.88)*
Acquisitions	1.063	0.674	1.257	0.905
	(2.37)**	−1.33	(2.59)***	(1.60)
Buyout/buyin	−0.142	0.265	−0.474	−0.210
	−0.44	−0.63	(1.42)	(0.47)
Divest./whole company	0.078	0.185	−0.223	−0.363
	−0.26	−0.49	(0.71)	(0.89)
Investor inv. cum. value		0.454		0.396
		−0.97		(0.76)
Investor inv. amount		−0.787		−0.874
		(1.72)*		
Constant	−2.204	0.636	−1.977	(1.74)*
	(2.74)***	−0.54	(2.37)***	(0.20)
Observations	204	162	204	162
LR chi^2 (4)	20 020	18 300	27 370	25 550
Prob > chi^2	0.018	0.075	0.001	0.007
Pseudo R^2	0.072	0.090	0.099	0.136

Notes: Absolute value of *z* statistics in parentheses.

* Statistically significant at 10% confidence level.

** Statistically significant at 5% confidence level.

*** Statistically significant at 1% confidence level.

NOTES

1. These surveys generally obtain a 100% response rate from all the financiers active in the buyout market as they receive a free copy of a quarterly review of aggregate market trends based on the data they supply. The review is recognized as the leading source of information in the market.
2. AIM is the Alternative Investment Market, a secondary tier stock market with less stringent entry requirements than the main market.
3. Note that in buyouts, preferred instruments may include preferred ordinary shares as well as preference shares.
4. Unlike the US, publicly quoted debt is restricted to a very few very large buyouts in the UK (CMBOR, 2005).
5. This figure is low compared to venture capital investments, where multi-round finance is a more common feature.
6. This is a well-known problem with divestment data (see e.g. Haynes et al., 2000).

REFERENCES

Bae, S.C. and Hoje, J. (2002), 'Consolidating corporate control: divisional versus whole-company leveraged buyouts', *Journal of Financial Research*, **25**, 247–63.

Barry, C.B., Muscarella, C.J., Peavy III, J.W. and Vetsuypens, M.R. (1990), 'The role of venture capital in the creation of public companies: evidence from the going public process', *Journal of Financial Economics*, **27**, 447–71.

Berger, A.N. and Udell, G.F. (1998), 'The economics of small business finance: the roles of private equity and debt markets in the financial growth cycle', *Journal of Banking and Finance*, **22**, 613–73.

Bruton, G.D. and Keels, J.K. and Scifres, E.L. (2002), 'Corporate restructuring and performance: an agency perspective on the complete buyout cycle', *Journal of Business Research*, **55**, 709–24.

Bull, I. (1989), 'Financial performance of leveraged buyouts: an empirical analysis', *Journal of Business Venturing*, **4**, 263–80.

Citron, D., Wright, M., Ball, R. and Rippington, F. (2003), 'Secured creditor recovery rates from management buyouts in distress', *European Financial Management*, **9**, 140–61.

CMBOR (2005), *Management Buyouts: Quarterly Review from CMBOR*, Centre for Management Buy-out Research, Autumn, Nottingham.

Cochrane, J.H. (2005), 'The risk and return of venture capital', *Journal of Financial Economics*, **75**, 9–11.

Cotter, J.F. and Peck, S.W. (2001), 'The structure of debt and active equity investors: the case of the buyout specialist', *Journal of Financial Economics*, **59**, 101–47.

Cumming, D. and MacIntosh, J.G. (2003), 'A cross-country comparison of full and partial exits', *Journal of Banking and Finance*, **27**, 511–48.

Cumming, D. and Walz, U. (2004), 'Private equity returns and disclosure around the world', mimeo, available at SSRN: http://ssrn.com/abstract=514105.

Cumming, D., Fleming, G. and Schwienbacher, A. (2006), 'Legality and venture capital exits', *Journal of Corporate Finance*, **12**, 214–45.

Das, S., Jagannathan, M. and Sarin, A. (2003), 'Private equity returns: an empirical examination of the exit of venture-backed companies', *Journal of Investment Management*, **1**, 1–16.

Desbrières, P. and Schatt, A. (2002), 'The impacts of LBOs on the performance of acquired firms: the French case', *Journal of Business Finance and Accounting*, **29**, 695–729.

Easterwood, J.C. (1998), 'Divestments and financial distress in leveraged buyouts', *Journal of Banking and Finance*, **22**, 129–59.

Easterwood, J.C., Seth, A. and Singer, R.F. (1989), 'The impact of leveraged buyouts on strategic direction', *California Management Review*, **32**, 30–44.

Gompers, P. (1996), 'Grandstanding in the venture capital industry', *Journal of Financial Economics*, **42**, 133–56.

Greene, W.H. (2000), *Econometric Analysis*, 4th edn. Englewood Cliffs, NJ: Prentice-Hall.

Hall, B.H. (1990), 'The impact of corporate restructuring on industrial research and development', *Brookings Papers on Economic Activity*, Special Issue Microeconomics, pp. 85–125.

Halpern, P., Kieschnick, R. and Rotenberg, W. (1999), 'On the heterogeneity of leveraged going private transactions', *Review of Financial Studies*, **12**, 281–309.

Harris, R., Siegel, D. and Wright, M. (2005), 'Assessing the impact of management buyouts on economic efficiency: plant-level evidence from the United Kingdom', *Review of Economics and Statistics*, **87**, 148–53.

Haynes, M., Thompson, S. and Wright, M. (2000), 'The determinants of corporate divestment in the UK', *International Journal of Industrial Organization*, **18**, 1201–22.

Hite, G. and Vetsuypens, M. (1989), 'Management buyouts of divisions and shareholder wealth', *Journal of Finance*, **44**, 953–70.

Holthausen, R.W. and Larcker, D.F. (1996), 'The financial performance of reverse leveraged buyouts', *Journal of Financial Economics*, **42**, 293–332.

Jelic, R., Saadouni, B. and Wright, M. (2005), 'Performance of private to public MBOs: the role of venture capital', *Journal of Business Finance and Accounting*, **32**, 643–82.

Jensen, M.C. (1986), 'Agency costs of free cash flow, corporate finance, and takeovers', *American Economic Review*, **76**, 323–30.

Jensen, M.C. (1989), 'Eclipse of the public corporation', *Harvard Business Review*, **67**, 61–75.

Jensen, M.C. (1993), 'The modern industrial revolution: exit, and the failure of internal control systems', *Journal of Finance*, **48**, 831–80.

Kaplan, S. (1989), 'The effects of management buyouts on operating performance and value', *Journal of Financial Economics*, **24**, 217–54.

Kaplan, S. (1991), 'The staying power of leveraged buyouts', *Journal of Financial Economics*, **29**, 287–314.

Kaplan, S. and Schoar, A. (2005), 'Private equity performance: returns, persistence and capital', *Journal of Finance*, **60**, 1791–823.

Lehn, K. and Poulsen, A. (1989), 'Free cash flow and stockholder grains in going private transactions', *Journal of Finance*, **44**, 771–88.

Lerner, J. (1994), 'Venture capitalists and the decision to go public', *Journal of Financial Economics*, **35**, 293–316.

Lichtenberg, F.R. and Siegel, D. (1990), 'The effects of leveraged buyouts on productivity and related aspects of firm behavior', *Journal of Financial Economics*, **27**, 165–94.

Lichtenberg, F.R. and Siegel, D. (1991), 'The impact of R&D investment on productivity – new evidence', *Economic Inquiry*, **29**, 203–29.

Liebeskind, J., Wiersema, M. and Hansen, G. (1992), 'LBO's, corporate restructuring, and the incentive-intensity hypothesis', *Financial Management*, **21**, 73–88.
Link, A.N., Paton, D. and Siegel, D. (2002), 'An analysis of policy initiatives to promote strategic research partnerships', *Research Policy*, **31**, 1459–66.
Link, A., Paton, D. and Siegel, D. (2005), 'An econometric analysis of trends in research joint venture activity', *Managerial and Decision Economics*, **26**, 149–58.
Ljungqvist, A. and Richardson, M. (2003), 'The cash flow, return and risk characteristics of private equity', Working Paper, vol. 9454. National Bureau of Economic Research.
Long, W.F. and Ravenscraft, D.J. (1993), 'LBOs, debt and R&D intensity', *Strategic Management Journal*, **14**, 119–35.
Muscarella, C.J. and Vetsuypens, M.R. (1990), 'Efficiency and organizational structure: a study of reverse LBOs', *Journal of Finance*, **45**, 1389–414.
Ofek, E. (1994), 'Efficiency gains in unsuccessful management buyouts', *Journal of Finance*, **49**, 637–55.
Opler, T.C. (1992), 'Operating performance in leveraged buyouts: evidence from 1985–1989', *Financial Management*, **21**, 27–35.
Opler, T. and Titman, S. (1993), 'The determinants of leveraged buyout activity: free cash flow vs financial distress costs', *Journal of Finance*, **48**, 1985–99.
Peck, S.W. (2004), 'The carrot versus the stick: the role of incentive compensation and debt obligations in the success of LBOs', *American Business Review*, **22**, 1–12.
Renneboog, L., Simons, T. and Wright, M. (2007), 'Why do firms go private in the UK?', *Journal of Corporate Finance*, **13**, 591–628, doi:10.1016/j.jcorpfin.2007.04.005.
Robbie, K. and Wright, M. (1995), 'Managerial and ownership succession and corporate restructuring: the case of management buy-ins', *Journal of Management Studies*, **32**, 525–50.
Singh, H. (1990), 'Management buyouts: distinguishing characteristics and operating changes prior to public offering', *Strategic Management Journal*, **11**, 111–29.
Smith, A.J. (1990), 'Corporate ownership structure and performance: the case of management buyouts', *Journal of Financial Economics*, **27**, 143–64.
Thompson, R.S. and Wright, M. (1991), 'UK management buy-outs: debt, equity and agency cost implications', *Managerial and Decision Economics*, **12**, 15–29.
Thompson, S. and Wright, M. (1995), 'Corporate governance: the role of restructuring transactions', *Economic Journal*, **105**, 690–703.
Weir, C., Laing, D. and Wright, M. (2005), 'Incentive effects, monitoring mechanisms and the market for corporate control: an analysis of the factors affecting public to private transactions in the UK', *Journal of Business Finance and Accounting*, **32**, 909–44.
Wright, M., Robbie, K., Thompson, S. and Starkey, K. (1994), 'Longevity and the life-cycle of management buy-outs', *Strategic Management Journal*, **15** (3), 215–27.
Wright, M., Thompson, S., Robbie, K. and Wong, P. (1995), 'Management buy-outs in the short and long term', *Journal of Business Finance and Accounting*, **22**, 461–83.
Wright, M., Wilson, N., Robbie, K. and Ennew, C. (1996), 'An analysis of management buy-out failure', *Managerial and Decision Economics*, **17**, 57–71.
Wright, M., Hoskisson, R.E., Busenitz, L.W. and Dial, J. (2000), 'Entrepreneurial growth through privatization: the upside of management buyouts', *Academy of Management Review*, **25**, 591–601.

14. Performance of private to public MBOs: the role of venture capital

Ranko Jelic, Brahim Saadouni and Mike Wright

1. INTRODUCTION

Through the 1980s and 1990s there was an improvement in the ability of small to medium-size companies to obtain funds via initial public offerings (IPOs) in the US.[1] The driving force behind this trend was the interplay of an expansion of the venture capital (VC) industry, advances in technologies, and various buy-out transactions using IPOs as an exit route. A similar trend was evident in Europe from the mid-1990s, with leading US venture capitalists entering the European market for the first time.

The UK venture capital market is the leading European market with size equal to the rest of the European market put together (EVCA, 2001). The size and importance of the UK's venture capital market can be explained by an active stock exchange (Black and Gilson, 1998; and Jeng and Wells, 2000). Although the US and the UK are both categorized under the same Anglo-American system, there are notable differences between the countries that may give rise to differences in findings concerning IPOs.[2] For example, Espenlaub et al. (2001) explain significant differences between lock-in agreements in the US and UK by the institutional and legal differences, while Espenlaub et al. (1999) find that UK VCs do not have the same certification effect as in the US. Ritter (2003) reports that a bookbuilding procedure for pricing and allocation of IPOs is more prevalent in the US than in Europe. There are also notable differences in the venture capital and leveraged/management buy-out (L/MBO) markets. The US venture capital market is very much dominated by venture capital firms that are independent limited partnerships and focus on young and high-risk entrepreneurial ventures (Barry et al., 1990). The L/MBO specialists, which are also limited partnerships, are quite distinct and usually invest in mature companies with predictable cash flows. They also have access to equity as well as large amounts of debt.

In marked contrast to the traditional US position, the majority of UK MBOs are financed by VCs (CMBOR, 2002). Also in contrast to the

US, the MBO end of the market in the UK, which accounts for the majority of the value of investments by the venture capital (i.e. private equity) industry, is dominated by captive firms, i.e. those that are subsidiaries of banks, insurance companies and pension funds.[3] These may have different time horizons for investing compared to limited partnerships (Wright and Robbie, 1996). Finally, IPOs are a more important part of the VC exit market in the US compared to the UK (Jeng and Wells, 2000).

In the US there has been some separate examination of venture-backed IPOs (e.g. Megginson and Weiss, 1991; Lerner, 1994; and Brav and Gompers, 1997) and reverse L/MBOs (e.g. Muscarella and Vetsuypens, 1990; DeGeorge and Zeckhauser, 1993; and Holthausen and Larcker, 1996). US studies of reverse L/MBOs have tended to ignore the role of the private equity provider, not least because of the emphasis on debt providers in the US market, although Jalilvand et al. (1996) consider the role of investment banker reputation.

A number of UK studies have identified significant effects on long-term underperformance in IPOs relating to the industrial sector (Levis, 1993; and Espenlaub et al., 1999), the initial returns (Levis, 1993), the proportion of shares sold by the VC and the reputation of the VC (Espenlaub et al., 1999).[4] Espenlaub et al. (1999) fail to find support for the conflicts of interest argument between independent VCs, and VCs affiliated to sponsors and underwriters of IPOs. Barnes (2003) analysed 85 UK, VC-backed IPOs during 1992–99. The results suggest that firms backed by younger VC firms are younger at IPO than those backed by more reputable VCs. Only weak evidence was found to suggest greater underpricing for IPOs backed by younger VCs and that young VCs hold smaller equity stakes. Overall, the author concludes that there is insufficient evidence to support the grandstanding hypothesis for the UK venture capital industry. A common feature of these studies, however, is that they have examined both early-stage and MBO-stage investments combined. MBO firms, however, are quite distinct and are not representative of a typical firm going public, and it is important to study them separately. For example, MBOs undergoing IPOs are less likely to suffer from an information asymmetry problem since they have a relatively longer operating history. In some cases, they may previously have been listed (Jain and Kini, 1995) and, in the UK, will have been obliged to publish their trading accounts even as a private firm. This has potential implications for the certification role of VCs, according to which VC-backed IPOs should, on average, have lower underpricing. Hence, the bundling together of VC-backed MBO IPOs with other VC-backed IPOs may affect interpretation of results reported in previous UK IPO literature.

Similarly, in the literature on corporate restructuring most studies focus on the effects of spin-off and carve-out announcements on parent companies' performance rather than on the financial performance of newly created companies.[5] An analysis of this sub-set of IPOs generally can, therefore, shed more light on the question whether long-run underperformance is common to all IPOs or not, hence contributing to the long-standing debate about underperformance (see Ritter, 1991; Ibbotson and Ritter, 1995; Brav and Gompers, 1997; Fama and French, 2001; and Gompers and Lerner, 2001).

Examination of the role of VCs in MBOs remains an important yet relatively neglected issue. The US L/MBO market traditionally stresses the pressure of debt in effecting gains (Jensen, 1993). This debt is associated with enhanced control and downside protection rather than with upside growth. Studies of US L/MBOs that undergo an IPO have tended to focus on the reverse L/MBO firm rather than on the association of private equity firms and L/MBO (Muscarella and Vetsuypens, 1990; and DeGeorge and Zeckhauser, 1993). For L/MBOs undergoing an IPO, growth prospects may be increasingly important. There is some anecdotal evidence in Europe that institutional investors are reluctant to invest in modest-sized L/MBOs with modest growth prospects (CMBOR, 2002). This may especially be the case in the 1990s compared to the 1980s.[6] VCs can provide an important resource in enabling the MBO to add value and achieve growth, rather than just obtaining value through cost cutting associated with the pressure of debt. Hence, looking at VC-backed versus non-VC-backed IPOs of MBOs is important in a European context.

The objective of this chapter is to examine the short- and the long-term financial performance of UK MBOs that exited through IPOs, and to shed more light on the importance of VCs for the performance of these companies. We also examine the impact of VCs' reputation on the short- and long-term financial performance of listed MBOs. We hypothesize three possible reasons why VCs may affect the performance of these MBOs. First, given the above-mentioned differences between MBO IPOs and other IPOs, as well as institutional differences between US and UK markets, we hypothesize a less important certification role of VCs. Second, if VCs remain as major shareholders in buy-outs after IPO, better long-run performance is expected due to the VCs' monitoring role (Kaplan, 1989; and Holthausen and Larcker, 1996). Third, venture capitalists involved in MBOs face a two-level principal–agent relationship. Besides that which exists between themselves and the managers of the companies in which they invest, there is also a principal–agent relationship between themselves and their providers of capital (Sahlman, 1990). This further implies that VCs' reputation as well as various financing and institutional arrangements between VCs and their providers of capital may result in different roles that VCs play in MBO IPO transactions. To the best of our knowledge this is the first study to examine the role of VCs in the transition from private to public ownership of UK MBOs. Finally, we contribute to the UK IPO and venture capital literature by estimating determinants of initial and long-term returns, after controlling for sample selectivity bias.

2. FINANCIAL PERFORMANCE OF MBOS AND THE ROLE OF VENTURE CAPITAL

Short and Long-term Performance of Private to Public MBOs

The extensive literature on the short- and long-run performance of IPOs reveals positive short-term and negative long-term excess returns internationally (see Loughran and Rydquist, 1994). Theoretical explanations for the observed initial premiums tend to concentrate on the information asymmetry between the various parties involved with IPOs, regulatory issues, ownership issues and market-related issues (see Ibbotson and Ritter, 1995). Information asymmetry theories seem to be best suited to private to public MBO transactions. For example, Leland and Pyle (1977) suggest that fully informed managers sell to imperfectly informed investors (only) when shares in their companies are overvalued. Hence, MBO IPOs are expected to be overvalued and should have positive initial returns:

H1: Private to public MBOs will have positive initial returns.

Theoretical explanations for the negative long-term returns concentrate on irrational strategies by buyers and information asymmetry that exists between insiders and investors (see Ibbotson and Ritter, 1995). For example, Ritter (1991) presents the 'windows of opportunities' hypothesis according to which large cycles in volume and initial returns indicate companies' attempts to 'time' their IPOs.[7] The release of more timely information about the company would lead to a drop in market price and underperformance of IPOs and seasoned issues. This hypothesis is consistent with Myers and Majluf (1984), who suggest that managers may not be willing to sell shares if this would lead to abnormal returns to new investors.

Most previous research on long-term buy-out performance has focused on the first two to three years after buy-out (see Palepu, 1990; Jensen, 1993; and Thompson and Wright, 1995, for reviews) and has mainly concerned the measurement of changes in operating performance before and after the transaction. For example, a series of studies of 1980s and 1990s US L/MBOs reports significant mean improvements in profitability, cash flow and productivity during the period between one year prior to the transaction and two or three years subsequent to it (Kaplan, 1989; Lichtenberg and Siegel, 1990; Singh, 1990; Smith, 1990; and Opler, 1992). In a study of 251 UK buy-outs and 446 non-buy-outs which were tracked for up to six years after the buy-out, Wright et al. (1996) find that buy-outs significantly outperform non-buy-outs in terms of return on assets and return on equity in years 3 to 5 post-buy-out.

There is, however, a paucity of large sample research on the long-term financial performance of going-public buy-outs measured in terms of share price performance. Most evidence on financial performance is related to the performance of reverse L/MBOs.[8] For example, Muscarella and Vetsuypens (1990) find that 72 US reverse L/MBOs during 1983–87 improved operating profitability between the buy-out and IPO and also displayed significant increases in returns on equity in terms of comparisons between share price at time of buy-out and IPO offering price. DeGeorge and Zeckhauser (1993) show that a sample of 62 US L/MBOs outperformed comparable non-buy-out firms in terms of operating profitability pre-flotation but not in the first year post-IPO. Despite this change in relative performance, reverse L/MBOs do not underperform the share price of non-L/MBOs over a two-year period post-IPO, indicating that the market anticipates such a change.

Holthausen and Larcker (1996) examine the accounting and market performance of reverse L/MBOs. Using all 90 reverse US L/MBOs that went public between 1983 and 1988 and which raised at least $10 million, they find that accounting performance relative to industry declines after IPO but that it remains above that of other companies in the buy-out companies' industries for a period of about four years. This change is unrelated to changes in leverage and positively related to changes in insider equity ownership of IPOs. Holthausen and Larcker find little evidence of significant abnormal positive share price performance after the reverse L/MBO. In terms of buy and hold market adjusted measures for 12, 24, 36 and 48-month periods post-IPO, only the 24-month mean return was found to be significant at conventional levels.

Negative long-term performance of private to public MBOs would be consistent with theories and results reported in the IPO literature, but would contradict results for MBOs' operating performance (Kaplan, 1989; and Wright et al., 1996). Hence:

H2: Private to public MBOs neither over- nor underperform in the long run.

VCs' Certification Role

Barry et al. (1990) and Megginson and Weiss (1991) show that VC-backed US companies tend to be younger than their non-VC-backed counterparts. The evidence on association of venture capital backing and underpricing is mixed. Megginson and Weiss (1991) report that VC-backed IPOs are less underpriced than non-venture-backed US IPOs. This has been explained by the certification role of VCs. Other studies report absence of the association (Barry et al., 1990; and Ljungqvist, 1999). More recent studies, however, report positive association of underpricing and venture capital backing (Hamao et al., 2000; and Francis et al., 2001). Espenlaub et al. (1999) report that backing by UK venture capitalists with links to issuing houses reduces initial returns but only if those affiliates are not employed as the actual IPO sponsors. MBOs are more established businesses than is the case for early-stage VC-backed investments and are facing less information asymmetry than other IPOs, Given the MBOs' dominance of the UK venture capital market,[9] the certification hypothesis, therefore, may be less important and venture backing might not be associated with underpricing. Hence:

H3: Venture capital backing is not associated with degree of underpricing.

In venture capital investments, block ownership of equity can be considered as an alternative to takeovers as a governance mechanism for disciplining managers (Wright and Robbie, 1998). Venture capitalists in private companies are typically more actively involved than non-management shareholders in quoted corporations, including institutional shareholders. Although there is some debate about when and how venture capital firms add value (see Sapienza, 1992), monitoring and guidance by reputable venture capitalists are the most often mentioned in the literature. The position of venture capitalists on the board should enable more timely identification of when corrective action needs to be taken and when management should be changed than would be possible by an outsider searching for a takeover target (Romano, 1996). This closer involvement of VCs may be expected to contribute to greater performance in VC-backed buy-outs than in non-VC-backed buy-outs.[10]

Empirical evidence on the long-term performance of venture-backed IPOs is not conclusive. For example, Jain and Kini (1995) find that US venture-backed IPOs have superior post-issue operating performance compared to non-venture-backed IPO firms over a three-year post-issue period. The extent of superior performance is positively associated with the quality of venture capitalists' monitoring. Brav and Gompers (1997) find that venture-backed US IPOs subsequently outperform non-venture-backed IPOs on the basis of equal weighted returns but that the difference is significantly reduced on the basis of value weighted returns. Venture-backed companies do not significantly underperform when compared with various benchmarks and the Fama–French three-factor asset-pricing model. The smallest non-venture-backed firms seem to be the worst performers. Underperformance, however, does not seem to be an IPO phenomenon, since matched non-IPOs perform as poorly as IPOs.

Espenlaub et al. (1999) find that UK IPOs underwritten by issuing houses that are parents or affiliates of the venture capital backers perform better in the long run compared to other IPOs. Rindermann (2003) compares VC- and non-VC-backed IPOs at the German Neuer Markt, French Nouveau Marché, and the British techMark during 1996–99. The results suggest that VC firms did not generally outperform those firms without VC backing. There was only weak evidence suggesting that international venture capital firms appear to have positive effects on both the operating and market performance. The author interprets these results as evidence of the 'heterogeneity' of venture capital and of the lack of 'maturity' and 'critical size' of the European venture capital industry.

Lin and Smith (1998) report a decline in VC board seats after the IPO exits from 13.6% to 4.9%. This further may imply that one should expect the deterioration in performance after the insider's exit. Kraus and Burghof (2003) provided some evidence for the above hypothesis by analysing German IPOs. They report that prior to exit (proxied by expiration dates of lock-ups), VC-backed IPOs outperform non-VC-backed IPOs, but underperform around and after the exit (expiration of lock-ups). Jenkinson and Ljungqvist (2001), however, suggest that negative long-term returns associated with insiders' exit after the IPO should be anticipated by rational investors.

Hence, we test the following hypothesis:

H4: Buy-outs backed by VCs will perform better than non-venture-backed buy-outs, prior to insiders' exit.

VCs' Reputation

A VC's reputation may affect both the timing of an IPO and its performance. Barry et al. (1990) find that venture capitalists have several mechanisms to ensure firms go public at times perceived to be optimal, including board seats and informal advice. Sometimes venture capitalists may offer bad advice in terms of premature IPO timing. This may be the case when venture capitalists want to gain profile and report prior performance in the raising of new funds. Gompers (1996) develops a VC reputation hypothesis (so-called grandstanding hypothesis) suggesting that reputation concerns affect venture capitalists' exit decisions. He demonstrated that IPOs backed by young venture capital firms are younger than those of established venture capital firms. Where VCs are subsidiaries of larger financial organizations, as is typically the case for the more established firms funding MBOs in the UK (Wright and Robbie, 1996), the pressures to grandstand in order to raise further funds may be reduced since these firms do not face the same kind of constraints as limited life independent VC funds (Robbie et al. 1997). Jensen (1989) argues that buy-out investors are expected to take a long-term perspective.

In contrast, Kaplan (1991) finds in the US that buy-outs sponsored by more well-known LBO partnerships[11] are more likely to go public within a particular time period than those sponsored by less well-known LBO financiers, although the differences are not significant. This suggests that reputable VCs and private equity firms financing buy-outs may, because of their greater experience and involvement, be both more adept at picking good deals and more effective at implementing the changes necessary to turn around and grow them. There is extensive evidence that restructuring of buy-outs within a two- to three-year period is key to generating gains (see Thompson and Wright, 1995, for a review). There is also UK evidence that MBOs with board representation from VCs, indicating close involvement, have a lower survivability in the MBO form than those where this is absent (Wright et al., 1995). These VCs are, thus, more likely to bring companies to market sooner. Hence, in contrast to the grandstanding hypothesis, we suggest that:

H5: Buy-outs backed by more reputable VCs will go public sooner than buy-outs backed by less reputable VCs.

A second issue concerns the link between reputation and short- and long-term performance. There is no consensus in the literature on the relationship between sponsors' (underwriters, institutional shareholders, venture capitalists) reputation and the long-term performance of IPOs. Most authors, however, suggest a positive relationship.[12] This is consistent with anecdotal evidence that banks and other financial institutions use data on the long-term performance of their clients in advertising.[13] Empirical evidence also seems to suggest a less severe underperformance of IPOs sponsored by more prestigious underwriters (Michaely and Wayne, 1994; and Carter et al., 1997). However, Franzke (2001) reports that reputable VCs underprice more in the sample of Germany's Neuer Markt IPOs during 1997–2000. Only one study has analysed the certification and reputation roles of sponsors in private to public MBO transactions. Jalilvand et al. (1996) report that investment bankers played only a marginal role in the valuation of US reverse L/MBOs.

Gompers (1996) showed that IPOs backed by less experienced VCs were more underpriced than those of established venture capital firms. On the other hand, more reputable VCs, repeatedly involved in IPOs, do not want to be associated with failures since they want to maintain their reputation. Therefore, they are less likely to overprice stock (or hype the stock) and are more involved in monitoring. This may also imply a better long-run performance of IPOs backed by well-established VCs.

Espenlaub et al. (1999) report that the long-run returns are positively related to the reputation of the venture capital backers, which they attribute to the screening activities of reputable venture capitalists. Barnes (2003) reports only weak evidence to suggest greater underpricing for IPOs backed by younger (more reputable) VCs.

Reputable VCs funding buy-outs may be less restricted by finite time horizons. Some of the major buy-out financiers in the UK are subsidiaries of banking groups.[14] When an MBO investment undergoes an IPO, it may be under less pressure to engage in underpricing and may have the incentive to consider the longer-term performance of the MBO, since they are not so constrained by their funding arrangements to report premature gains and there may be an interest from the parent bank in maintaining the MBO firm as a long-term client. Hence:

H6: Buy-outs backed by less reputable VCs will be more underpriced than those backed by more reputable VCs.

H7: Buy-outs backed by less reputable VCs will have worse long-term financial performance than buy-outs backed by more reputable VCs.

3. DATA AND METHODOLOGY

Data

The sample of private to public buy-outs was collected by the authors as part of the Centre for Management Buy-out Research (CMBOR) database. In contrast to other sources of information on buy-outs, the CMBOR database uniquely comprises a comprehensive coverage of the population dating from the 1960s of all buy-out type transactions in the UK and all size categories. This latter coverage is especially important since buy-outs coming to market may have been relatively small at the time of the buy-out but have subsequently grown to a size where a stock market listing is feasible. Data sources for buy-outs which adopt a relatively large minimum size cut-off may, therefore, present a biased perspective on buy-outs coming to market.

The data are compiled from a variety of sources. These sources include a twice-yearly survey of all financiers and advisers involved in buy-outs with a near complete response rate, text line searches, Stock Exchange circulars, EXTEL, financial press, etc. This data collection exercise enables us to obtain information on the initial transaction value and its financing structure, including the presence or not of an external equity provider (e.g. venture capital firm). We monitor the progress of buy-outs following completion, stock market listings being identified from the same sources as above, plus perusal of prospectuses issued by the companies coming to market.

This process enabled us to collect data on the 167 of the 255 buy-outs which had exited through IPOs in the period 1964–1997 for which data were available. Data for offer prices were collected directly from IPO prospectuses. Data for share prices, FTSE All Share Index and market values were extracted from the Datastream database. Our sample represents about 65% of all buy-outs that exited through IPOs during the period 1964–1997 (Table 14.1). The

Table 14.1 UK management buy-outs (MBOs)

Year	*N*	Total value (£ m)	Av. size (£ m)	Total VC-backed	Total IPO exits	IPO exits for which data available
1964	n.a.	n.a.	n.a.	n.a.	n.a.	1
1984	251	419.3	1.7	n.a.	12	1
1985	293	1227.5	4.2	n.a.	28	1
1986	368	1478.3	4.0	n.a.	36	8
1987	435	3441.8	7.9	n.a.	34	9
1988	498	5015.4	10.1	304	36	14
1989	529	7505.9	14.2	333	14	7
1990	604	3094.7	5.1	296	8	3
1991	580	2914.1	5.0	261	4	3
1992	595	3303.7	5.6	274	11	4
1993	492	2777.9	5.6	193	36	20
1994	559	3738.7	6.7	305	48	29
1995	598	5622.7	9.4	351	29	19
1996	642	7856.3	12.2	383	41	30
1997	700	10311.6	14.7	415	28	18
Total	7144	58707.9		3115	255	167

Note: Data compiled by authors.

Table 14.2 Sample descriptive statistics

Variable	Mean	Median	Min.	Max.	St Dev.
MBO value	53.05	11.64	0.33	2157	197.17
Age	59	40	1	925	92
Time from MBO to exit	47.58	40	2	240	31.77
Management stake pre-exit	53.12	51.9	0	100	30.19
Management stake post-exit	31.00	28.8	0	85	20.61
Institutional stake pre-exit	41.26	38.5	0	100	29.37
Institutional stake post-exit	22.24	22.2	0	70.05	16.73
Private stake pre-exit	5.93	0	0	78.1	14.14
Private stake post-exit	2.86	0	0	43.2	7.88
Public stake post-exit	43.82	43.53	9.1	99	16.03
Market value at exit	76.11	43.16	3.04	919.5	117.95

Notes: MBO value is a value of MBO transaction in million pounds (£); Age is number of months between incorporation and prospectus dates; Market value at exit is market capitalization in million pounds (£) at the end of listing year; Time from MBO to exit is number of months from MBO transaction to listing; Management, Institutional, Public and Private stakes as percentage in total number of shares. Data extracted from various CMBOR/Barclays Private Equity/Deloitte & Touche publications and Datastream.

majority of buy-outs in the sample initially resulted from domestic and foreign divestments (48.7% and 17.1%, respectively). A substantial minority of buy-outs are from privately held family firms (19.6%). The majority of buy-outs which resulted from divestments were, in fact, from listed companies and hence by undergoing an IPO became reverse MBOs.

Descriptive statistics for the main variables are reported in Table 14.2. The mean size of the initial buy-out transactions in the sample is £53.05 million. On average, it takes about 4 years for companies to go from private (MBO) to public status.[15] The average market capitalization, at the end of the listing year, is £76.11 million, with minimum and maximum values of £3.04 million and £919.50 million, respectively. On average, management's stake in the companies drops from 53% before listing to 31% after listing.

Methodology

We measure both the raw and market-adjusted initial returns using the conventional method where the initial return on the first day of trading is calculated as follows:

$$\mathrm{IR}_{i,t} = (P_{i,1} - P_{i,0})/P_{i,0} \tag{14.1}$$

$$\text{MAIR}_{i,t} = (P_{i,1} - P_{i,0})/P_{i,0} - (I_{i,1} - I_{i,0})/I_{i,0}, \tag{14.2}$$

where $\text{IR}_{i,t}$ is the raw initial return of company *i*; $\text{MAIR}_{i,t}$ is the market-adjusted return of company *i*; $P_{i,1}$ is the closing price of company *i* at the end of the first trading date; $P_{i,0}$ is the offer price of company *i* (time index 0 refers to the last day of the subscription period); $I_{i,1}$ is the FTSE All Share Index at the end of the first trading day and $I_{i,0}$ is the FTSE All Share Index company *i*'s IPO prospectus date.

The FTSE All Share Index comprises about 700 companies and accounts for about 99% of UK stock market capitalization. UK reverse MBOs seem to be very diverse companies ranging from very small firms (e.g Capita Group, with MBO value of £0.33 million) to very large companies (e.g. Somerfield, with MBO value of £2157 million). Consequently, the standard deviations for MBO size and market value at exit are 197% and 118%, respectively. An alternative to the FTSE All Share Index, such as the Hoare Govett Smaller Companies Index (HGSC), would be a better benchmark for measuring the performance of smaller companies but not for the larger companies included in our sample. Our sample, therefore, is not typical of the HGSC.

Although the choice of the FTSE All Share Index may not be entirely satisfactory, it does reflect the differences in size in our sample companies, and is consistent with the use of at least one widely inclusive benchmark in previous long-term performance studies (e.g. Ritter, 1991 and Rajan and Servaes, 1997 use NYSE/AMEX; Levis, 1993 and Espenlaub et al., 1999 both use the FTSE All Share Index). By choosing the FTSE All Share Index as one of our benchmarks, we are also able to compare the results of our study with the results reported in previous related literature (Levis, 1993 and Espenlaub et al., 1999).

The market-adjusted (abnormal) returns are calculated for each event month *t* as:

$$ar_{i,t} = r_{i,t} - r_{m,t}, \tag{14.3}$$

where r_{it} is the return of company *i* in event month *t*; $r_{m,t}$ is the return on the FTSE All Share Index in event month *t* and $ar_{i,t}$ is the abnormal return for company *i* in event month *t*. Each month consists of 21 trading days.[16] The average market-adjusted return for a sample of *n* companies in event month *t* is defined as:

$$\text{AR}_t = \frac{1}{n}\sum_{i=1}^{n} ar_{it}. \tag{14.4}$$

The cumulative abnormal return over *T* months starting from month t_0 is the summation of the average abnormal returns:

$$\mathrm{CAR}_{t0,T} = \sum_{t=t0}^{T} \mathrm{AR}_t. \tag{14.5}$$

To test the null hypothesis that abnormal and cumulative abnormal returns are equal to zero, we employ the *t*-statistic following Ritter (1991). The *t*-statistic for AR_t is computed for each month as:

$$t_{\mathrm{AR}} = \mathrm{AR}_t \sqrt{(n_t)}/\mathrm{SD}_t, \tag{14.6}$$

where AR_t is the average abnormal return for month t, n_t is the number of observations in month t, and SD_t is the cross-sectional standard deviation of the adjusted returns for month t.

The *t*-statistic for the cumulative average abnormal return in month t is computed as:

$$t_{\mathrm{CAR}} = \mathrm{CAR}_t \sqrt{(n_t)}/\mathrm{CSD}_t, \tag{14.7}$$

where CAR_t is the average cumulative abnormal return for month t, n_t is the number of firms trading in each month, and CSD_t is computed as:

$$\mathrm{CSD}_t = \sqrt{[t\mathrm{var} + 2(t-1)\mathrm{cov}]}, \tag{14.8}$$

where t is the event month, var is the average (over 36 months) cross-sectional variance, and cov is the first-order autocovariance of the AR_t series.

The buy-and-hold abnormal returns (BHARs) are calculated as the difference of corresponding compounded daily companies' and FTSE All Share Index's returns:

$$\mathrm{BHAR} = R_{it} = \prod_{t=1}^{T} (1 + r_{it}) - \prod_{t=1}^{T})1 + r_{mt}), \tag{14.9}$$

where $R_{i,t}$ is the abnormal return of company i in event month t calculated on a compounded basis, r_{it} is the return for company i in event month t, and r_{mt} is the return of FTSE All Share Index in event month t.

To test the null hypothesis that the mean buy-and-hold abnormal returns are equal to zero, we first use a conventional *t*-statistic:

$$t_R = [\eta(R_t)]/[\delta(R_t)/\sqrt{n}], \tag{14.10}$$

where $\eta(R_t)$ is the sample mean and $\delta(R_t)$ is the cross-sectional sample standard deviation of buy-and-hold returns for the sample of n firms.

Tests for robustness of results

Survivor, rebalancing and skewness biases The results of some recent studies concerning IPOs' long-term returns are not conclusive and highlight the importance of the choice of methodologies. For example, Fama (1998) suggests that cumulative abnormal returns (CARs) may be less biased than buy-and-hold returns as a measure of long-term performance since the latter, calculated on a compounded basis, may exaggerate a single year's poor performance. Lyon et al. (1999) and Kothari and Warner (1997) provide a thorough assessment of various metrics for the measurement of long-term returns. They document three main potential biases in the calculation of long-term returns: (a) survivor bias, which may occur if failing firms are excluded from the sample, (b) rebalancing bias, related to the calculation of cumulative returns and (c) skewness bias due to the fact that long-term returns are typically skewed. In order to minimize these potential misspecifications, we evaluated long-term buy-and-hold market-adjusted compounded returns and cumulative abnormal returns. We also included all failing firms in the calculation of long-term returns. Finally, to account for skewness bias, a non-parametric test[17] and a skewness-adjusted t-statistic with bootstrapped p-values are used to test the null hypothesis that mean buy-and-hold returns are equal to zero:[18]

$$t_{sa} = \sqrt{n}(S + 1/3\,\hat{Y}S^2 + 1/6n\,\hat{Y}), \tag{14.11}$$

where

$$S = \eta(R_t)/\delta(R_t), \tag{14.12}$$

and

$$\hat{Y} = \left\{ \sum [R_{it} - \eta(R_t)]^3 \right\} / [\eta\delta(R_t)^3]. \tag{14.13}$$

The distribution of t-values was simulated by drawing 10 000 resamples of size $n/4$ (167/4, in this case), with replacement, from each return series. The critical t-values for a level of significance (α) were calculated by sorting all 10 000 simulated t-values and by searching for the cut-off points (e.g. top and bottom 42 companies for $\alpha = 5\%$) at which the null hypothesis can be rejected. The critical values are, therefore, obtained by solving:

$$Pr[t_{sa^b} \leq x_1^*] = Pr[t_{sa^b} \geq x_u^*] = \alpha/2, \tag{14.14}$$

where $x_1 = 0.5\%$ and $x_u = 2.5\%$.

Brav and Gompers (1997) report that value weighting significantly reduces performance differences between VC-backed and non-VC-backed US IPOs. We, therefore, measure and compare short- and long-term performance using both equally and value-weighted returns.[19]

Benchmark-related biases, and clustering Dimson and Marsh (1991), Levis (1993), Khurshad etal. (1999) and Espenlaub et al. (2000) emphasize the importance of an appropriate benchmark in the calculation of long-term returns in the UK context. Espenlaub et al. (2000), for example, use four different benchmarks to measure the long-term performance of 588 UK IPOs during the period from 1985 to 1992. They concluded that the CAPM would seem mis-specified due to the importance of size effects and the fact that IPOs are typically small stocks. The results based on Fama and French (1996) style benchmarks may be contaminated due to the nature of the UK book to market value (BV/ MV) data available from Datastream. The authors, therefore, seem to favour two size control models: size control portfolio, and a value-weighted multi-index model using the Hoare–Govett Index as the measure of smaller company performance. The benchmark based on the Hoare–Govett Index, however, suffers from a significant upward bias.

Given the diversity of companies in our sample, and the importance of size control benchmarks, we constructed an additional benchmark from matching firms from the same industries and with similar (end of year) market values to our sample firms. Firstly, we split sample firms into three groups according to prospectus dates. For example, sample firms with prospectus dates between 1985 and 1989 were matched, in terms of industry and market value, with matching firms from 1985. Similarly, sample firms from 1990–94 are compared with matching firms from 1990, and 1995–2000 sample firms are matched with matching firms from 1995. This was necessary so that we do not include any recent IPOs in our matching sample.[20] Secondly, matching firms with closest market values and same industry codes are chosen, and matching firms are used only once. A similar industry code, instead of an exact one, would be used only when there was no firm with a similar market value within the same industry group, or there were not enough firms in the matching group to be able to find an exact industry code.[21] Finally, the returns of the matching firms were calculated in the same fashion and to begin and end on the same day as those of our sample firms.

Ritter (1984) demonstrated waves in IPO activity. The waves may also be reflected in the distribution of VC-backed MBOs during the period of our study.[22] Clustering of IPOs may have an important effect on subsequent performance and statistical tests (Ibbotson, 1975). In order to adjust for the potential problem of clustering we classified MBOs into (calendar time) portfolios depending on the calendar month and year of listing and re-calculated initial returns for the portfolios and repeated the *t*-test.

Sample selectivity bias Our sample descriptive statistics show that VC-backed MBOs tend to be bigger and exit earlier than their non-VC-backed counterparts. The above-mentioned differences suggest that the provision and receipt of VC funding may not be a VC's and/or manager's random choice. This introduces a selectivity bias which needs to be accounted for. In order to address the selectivity bias we employ a version of Heckman's two-step estimation procedure similar to one employed by Lee and Wahal (2004).[23] The procedure involves estimating initially a probit regression with a VC dummy (1 if VC backed; 0 otherwise) as a dependent variable (equation (14.15)). Then, we use the parameters from the probit regression to estimate the probability that a company will receive VC backing. The estimated probabilities (LAMBDA_i) are then added as a regressor to our second stage models for initial and long-term returns. Finally, the second-stage models are estimated by OLS, employing the White (1980) robust standard error procedure and allowing for the sample selectivity equations (14.16) and (14.17).[24]

$$\text{VC}_i = a_0 + \beta_1 \ln(\text{MBOV}_i) + \beta_2 \ln(\text{MBOTOEXIT}_i) + \varepsilon_i, \quad (14.15)$$

$$\begin{aligned} \text{IR}_i = \alpha_0 &+ \beta_1 \text{TOP 3VC}_i + \beta_2 \text{LAMBDA}_i + \beta_3 \text{LNMV}_i \\ &+ \beta_4 \text{GEARING}_i + \beta_5 \text{INDUSTRY}_i + \beta_6 \text{BV/MV}_i \\ &+ \beta_7 \text{SOLD}_i + \beta_8 \text{UNDWT}_i + \beta_9 \text{RISK}_i \\ &+ \beta_{10} \text{REVERSE}_i + \varepsilon_i, \end{aligned} \quad (14.16)$$

$$\begin{aligned} \text{BHAR}_{12,24,36i} = \alpha_0 &+ \beta_1 \text{TOP 3VC}_i + \beta_2 \text{LAMBDA}_i + \beta_3 \text{LNMV}_i \\ &+ \beta_4 \text{GEARING}_i + \beta_5 \text{INDUSTRY}_i \\ &+ \beta_6 \text{BV/MV}_i + \beta_7 \text{SOLD}_i + \beta_8 \text{IR} \\ &+ \beta_9 \text{UNDWT}_i + \varepsilon_i. \end{aligned} \quad (14.17)$$

In regressions (14.16) and (14.17) we test for the importance of VCs' reputation (TOP3VC) for the short- (IR) and long-term performance (BHAR) and control for significant variables identified in previous IPO studies, such as: industry (INDUSTRY), size (LNMV), proportion of shares sold (SOLD), ex ante risk (RISK), underwriters' reputation (UNDWT),[25] and cases of reverse MBOs (REVERSE). In addition, we control for level of gearing (GEARING) and book to market value (BV/MV) since they have been identified as statistically significant in previous literature on properties of expected returns in the UK context (Strong and Xu, 1997).

4. RESULTS

Our sample includes 132 venture-backed buy-outs and 35 non-venture-backed buy-outs. In all but one case, venture capital firms involved in public to private transactions remained involved in the subsequent private to public transactions. Ten venture capitalists were involved in backing around 62% of all venture capital-backed buy-outs during the period.[26] Our criterion for most reputable venture capital firms was the number of completed MBO transactions. We selected the three most reputable venture capital firms that backed at least 3% of all buy-outs and our sample buy-outs.[27] Our top three venture capital firms (3i, NatWest Equity Partners and Barclays Private Equity) together backed around 48% of all buy-outs, and were involved in 62% of our sample buy-outs (Table 14.3). These VCs were considered to be the most prestigious. It is worth noting, however, that our measure of VC reputation implies that the prestige level corresponds to the number of completed transactions and implies that a reputation established before 1980 does not count. However, given the very small number of venture capital-backed MBOs during the 1970s relative to the number of MBOs during the mid-1980s and 1990s, and the presence of very few venture capital firms in this period, we do not consider this to be a major limitation. In order to test for sensitivity of our results with respect to alternative definitions of reputation, and given the dominance of 3i in the UK

Table 14.3 Top ten venture capitalists by number of UK MBOs, 1980–97

Rank	Name	Total/sample buy-outs (%)
1	3i	39.0/43.9
2	NatWest Equity Partners	5.9/10.6
3	Barclays Private Equity	3.3/7.6
	Total/sample	**48.2/62.1**
4	Lloyds Development Capital	2.2/1.5
5	Cinven	1.9/7.6
6	Charterhouse Development Capital	1.9/6.1
7	HSBC Private Equity	1.8/6.8
8	Domestic Trade Interest	1.6/0.7
9	Murray Johnstone Private Equity	1.5/1.5
10	Schroder Venture	1.3/8.3
	Total/sample	**60.4/94.6**

Notes: Data compiled by authors. There were 4080 buy-outs backed by 686 different venture capital firms during the period. Each of top three venture capital firms backed at least 3% of all buy-outs during the period. Together, they were involved in backing of more than 48% and 62% of all and our sample buy-outs, respectively.

Table 14.4 Industry distribution: VC-backed MBOs versus Non-VC-backed MBOs

Industry	VC-backed MBOs (%)	Non-VC-backed MBOs (%)
Distribution	10.6	3.3
Retail	7.0	10.0
Electronic and electrical equipment	14.1	6.7
IT, soft/hardware and services	9.4	6.7
Financial services	2.4	0
Business support	5.9	10.0
Brewers, pubs and restaurants	2.4	0
Chemicals and oil services	4.7	0
Paper and packing	3.5	3.3
Leisure facilities and hotels	7.0	3.3
House building and building materials	2.4	3.3
Construction	1.2	10.0
Transport (shipping, rail, road)	7.1	13.3
Engineering	4.7	10.0
Clothing and footwear	3.5	0
Printing and publishing	3.5	10.0
Others	7.1	6.7
Total	**100%**	**100%**

Notes: Percentage of the sample MBOs by various industries. Industries listed are only those that account for at least 2% of either VC-backed or non-VC-backed MBOs.

VC market, we have compared the results for 3i-backed firms with those for other VCs.

Venture capitalists tend to focus their investment activities on MBOs from certain industries (Table 14.4). For example, distribution, electronic and electrical equipment, and information technology and computer-related activities account for 34.1% of the VC-backed MBOs, but only 16.7% of non-VC-backed MBOs. We, however, could not reject the hypothesis of equality of distributions across industries for VC-backed and non-VC-backed private to public MBOs.[28]

There are statistically significant differences in size, timing of exit and changes in ownership structure in buy-outs after exit according to whether the buy-out was initially venture-backed or not (Table 14.5). Venture-backed buy-outs tend to be larger, exit earlier and tend to have lower management stakes before and after exit. The sample MBOs, on average, retain 56% of shares after the IPO.[29] VC-backed MBOs tend to retain less shares than their non-VC counterparts (54% versus. 62%). Buy-outs backed by the

Table 14.5 Sample descriptive statistics by venture capitalists

Variable	VC	Non-VC	T/MW *P*-value	Top 3 VC	Other VC	T/MW *P*-value
MBO value	62.58	3.23	**(0.00)** **[0.00]**	30.49	78.82	(0.12) [0.13]
Age	51	119	**(0.06)** **[0.29]**	43	52	(0.21) [0.14]
Time to exit	45.64	56.92	(0.12) **[0.05]**	38.28	45.74	**(0.00)** **[0.00]**
Mgt pre-exit	43.57	76.57	**(0.00)** **[0.00]**	53.19	42.46	**(0.08)** **[0.06]**
Mgt post-exit	26.29	46.32	**(0.00)** **[0.00]**	32.29	23.92	**(0.05)** **[0.02]**
Inst. pre-exit	51.26	17.66	**(0.00)** **[0.00]**	44.64	53.31	(0.32) [0.36]
Inst. post-exit	25.93	10.79	**(0.00)** **[0.00]**	23.78	27.31	(0.28) [0.24]
Private pre-exit	5.12	7.09	(0.59) [0.90]	1.82	5.09	**(0.05)** **[0.34]**
Private post-exit	2.34	4.03	(0.36) [0.60]	1.72	1.48	(0.46) [0.62]
Public post-exit	45.69	37.58	**(0.01)** **[0.00]**	43.37	47.12	(0.34) [0.67]
MV at exit	87.22	35.11	**(0.00)** **[0.00]**	88.27	92.87	(0.78) [0.13]

Notes: Average (mean) MBO value is the value of MBO transaction in million pounds (£); Age is number of months between incorporation and prospectus dates; Market value at exit is market capitalization in million pounds (£) at the end of listing year; Time from MBO to exit is number of months from MBO transaction to listing; Management, Institutional, Public and Private stakes as percentage in total number of shares. Data extracted from various CMBOR/Barclays Private Equity/Deloitte & Touche publications and Datastream. *P*-values (•) and [•] indicate the level of significance for 2-tail T and [Mann–Whitney] (MW) test for difference in means and medians for relevant variables.

most reputable VCs tend to be smaller, exit earlier and tend to have higher management stakes before and after exit. VC-backed firms tend to be younger than non-VC-backed firms, and more reputable VCs tend to back younger firms than their less reputable counterparts.[30] This is an interesting result which clearly contradicts the 'grandstanding' hypothesis supported by US data (Gompers, 1996).

Average initial returns are positive and highly statistically significant measured on an equally, value-weighted, and clustering-adjusted basis. The results of both parametric and non-parametric tests reveal no significant

Table 14.6 Average (mean and median) raw (IR) and market-adjusted initial returns (MAIR) by venture capitalists' backing and reputation

		IR (%)			MAIR (%)		
	N (IR/ MAIR)	Mean	Median	St. dev.	Mean	Median	St. dev.
Sample							
Equally weighted	167	8.46***	6.33***	14.67	9.40***	6.99***	16.11
Value-weighted	*155*	*6.00****	*2.26****	*26.94*	5.65***	*2.73****	*17.17*
Clustering-adjusted	167	7.23***	6.91***	6.55	7.99***	6.97***	8.88
VC-backed	132/111	7.79***	6.17***	13.12	8.96***	7.01***	15.03
	117/107	*7.00***	*1.30****	*30.90*	*6.50****	*1.60****	*19.70*
Non-VC-backed	35/33	11.24***	6.63***	20.17	11.03***	6.93***	20.32
	38/36	*2.93****	*1.60****	*4.04*	*3.04****	*1.50****	*3.92*
Differences		−3.45	−0.46		−2.07	0.08	
		4.07	*−0.30*		*3.46**	*0.10*	
Top 3 VC	40/32	9.87***	5.36***	15.48	11.27***	5.30***	22.09
	35/32	*12.90*	*1.00****	*54.90*	*9.10*	*1.10****	*33.30*
Other VC	92/79	6.83***	5.09***	11.86	7.97***	5.74***	10.89
	82/75	*4.50****	*1.50****	*8.96*	*5.43****	*1.70****	*9.22*
Differences		3.04	0.27		3.30	−0.44	
		8.40	*−0.50*		*3.67*	*−0.60*	

Notes: Average returns are calculated on an equally and value-weighted basis. Value-weighted returns are in *italics*. Clustering-adjusted returns calculated as average returns for calendar time portfolios. The levels of significance for the two-tail *T* and Wilcoxon tests of mean/median = 0 vs mean/median ≠ 0, reported as: *** significant at 1% level or better, ** significant at 5% level or better, * significant at 10% level or better. The levels of significance for the differences in mean (*T*-test) and median (Mann–Whitney test) raw (IR) and market-adjusted initial returns (MAIR) for venture backed MBOs vs raw and market-adjusted initial returns for non-venture-backed MBOs, reported as: *** significant at 1% level or better, ** significant at 5% level or better, * significant at 10% level or better.

differences between the average equally weighted initial returns of MBOs backed by venture capital firms and MBOs not backed by venture capital firms (Table 14.6). However, the results for value-weighted MAIR indicate higher underpricing for MBOs backed by venture capital at the 10% significance level. Although more reputable VCs, on average, underprice more, the results suggest no statistically significant differences, at

Table 14.7 Average abnormal (AR) and cumulative abnormal returns (CAR)

M	*N*	Negative AR_t	Positive AR_t	AR_t (%)	*t*-stat.	Negative CAR_t	Positive CAR_t	CAR_t (%)	*t*-stat.
6	164	82	82	1.10	1.45	84	80	1.03	0.34
12	164	84	80	−0.26	−0.37	74	90	0.06	−0.01
18	164	86	78	−0.12	−0.15	100	64	−2.09	−0.40
24	150	78	72	−0.15	−0.16	74	76	0.33	−0.05
30	130	65	65	−1.15	−1.26	71	59	−2.26	−0.30
36	123	78	44	−1.43	−1.48	76	47	−2.40	−0.28

Notes: ARs and CARs calculated as in equations (14.4) and (14.5), respectively. Average returns are calculated on an equally weighted basis without initial premiums; the *T*-statistic for AR_t is computed for each month (*M*) as $AR_t\,(n_t)/SD_t$, where AR_t is the average adjusted return for month *t*, n_t is the number of observations in month *t*, and SD_t is the cross-sectional standard deviation of the adjusted returns for month *t;* the *t*-statistic for the cumulative average adjusted return in month *t* is computed as $CAR_t\,(n_t)/CSD_t$, where n_t is the number of firms trading in each month, and CSD_t is computed as $CSD_t = [t\text{ var} + 2(t-1)\text{cov}]^{1/2}$, where *t* is the event month, var is the average (over 36 months) cross-sectional variance, and cov is the first-order autocovariance of the AR_t series (see Ritter, 1991).

conventional levels, between the underpricing of reputable and less reputable VCs.[31]

Table 14.7 reports the average market-adjusted returns and cumulative abnormal returns (CARs) for 36 months after the MBOs listings. The CARs are positive, but not statistically significant, up to 12 months after IPO. From month 30 through to month 36 CARs are negative, but not statistically significant.

Overall, the sample displays no evidence of statistically significant underperformance (Table 14.8). For example, only negative and statistically significant returns are equal-weighted mean, and value-weighted median returns in months 12 and 36, respectively. In other months, returns are predominantly negative but not statistically significant.[32] The results remain robust after we account for skewness bias, by calculating a skewness-adjusted *t*-statistic with bootstrapped *p*-values. Although buy-and-hold returns exhibit positive skewness, we find only a minimal effect of bootstrapped critical values on our results. The only notable difference arises for the 12-month returns. Using the bootstrapped critical values increases significance from 8% to 1%.

The results based on matching sample and clustering adjusted returns (Table 14.8) are consistent with previously reported results, and indicate a lack of significant underperformance. Our sample companies outperformed the matching sample companies in months 18, 30 and 36. The

Table 14.8 *Average market-adjusted buy-and-hold returns (BHAR), clustering adjusted buy-and-hold returns (BHAR-CA) and wealth relatives (WR)*

M	*N*	Positive BHAR	Negative BHAR	Mean BHAR	Median BHAR	BHAR – Skewness-adjusted *T* – *P*-values		Mean BHAR-CA	Median BHAR-CA	BHR	MBHR	WR
6	164	71	93	−0.22	−0.24	−1.50	[0.13]	0.88	0.27	0.999	1.003	0.996
				0.18	*0.01*							
12	164	79	85	−0.44*	−0.10	−2.40	**[0.01]**	−0.21	−0.23	0.997	0.998	0.999
				−0.19	*−0.07*							
18	164	87	77	0.21	0.06	1.25	[0.23]	0.22	0.20	1.002	1.001	1.002
				0.21	*0.03*							
24	150	72	78	−0.27	−0.23	−0.95	[0.37]	0.72	0.05	0.999	1.005	0.994
				−0.38	*−0.08*							
30	130	63	67	0.08	−0.07	0.44	[0.68]	0.04	−0.10	1.002	0.997	1.004
				−0.01	*−0.05*							
36	123	49	74	−0.29	−0.30	−1.15	[0.30]	−0.18	−0.13	0.997	0.997	1.000
				0.55	*−0.12***							

Notes: Mean and median buy-and-hold market-adjusted percentage returns computed for each month (*M*) as equally, *value-weighted*, and clustering-adjusted (CA) compounded returns using the FTSE All Share Index as a benchmark: average equally weighted buy-and-hold market-adjusted returns calculated as in equation (14.9); weights for *value-weighted returns* computed using the offer size for weights; *P*-values for two tail *T*-test of mean equally, *value-weighted*, and clustering-adjusted (CA) buy-and-hold market-adjusted returns = 0 vs mean equally. *value-weighted*, and clustering-adjusted (CA) buy-and-hold market-adjusted returns ≠ 0, and *p*-values for Wilcoxon-Signed-Rank test for median equally. *value-weighted*, and clustering-adjusted (CA) buy-and-hold market-adjusted returns = 0 vs. median ≠ 0 reported as: *** significant at 1% level or better, ** significant at 5% level or better, * significant at 10% level or better; *P*-values for skewness-adjusted *t*-test for equally weighted mean buy-and-hold market adjusted returns = 0 vs mean equally weighted buy-and-hold market adjusted returns ≠ 0, using a bootstrapping procedure, reported in brackets [•]; sample average buy-and-hold returns (BHAR) and matching firms' portfolio average buy-and-hold returns (MBHR) are computed as equally weighted buy-and-hold raw compounded returns. Wealth relatives (WR) are calculated as BHR/MBHR. The portfolio of matching firms was constructed from firms from the same industries and with similar (end of year) market values to the sample firms.

better performance corresponds with the positive BHAR returns reported for months 18 and 30. The only difference is for the performance in month 36. BHAR, based on the FTSE All Share Index, indicates negative (but not statistically significant) returns whereas corresponding wealth relative indicates absence of any abnormal performance (WR = 1000).

We were not able to identify a break point in the long-term performance of our sample companies by using expiry of lock-up agreements. This may be related to contractual diversity of lock-ups in the UK. For example, consistent with Espenlaub et al. (2001), we find that our sample firms often specify different lock-up expiry dates for the same group of shareholders. In addition, lock-ups are often staggered from 6 to 36 months after the IPOs.[33]

The results of tests of the long-term performance of MBOs segregated by venture capital involvement and their reputation are reported in Table 14.9. The results based on BHAR, the wealth relatives, and clustered adjusted BHAR, indicate a lack of significant underperformance in the long run. VC-backed companies exhibit negative and statistically significant BHAR in month 36, whenever non-backed companies exhibit positive and statistically significant BHAR in month 6. In all other months, returns are predominantly negative but not statistically significant. *P*-values indicating the level of significance for the test of differences in mean (*t*-test) and median (Mann–Whitney test) suggest no statistically significant differences in the performance of MBOs backed by venture capital firms and their non-venture-backed counterparts both on an equally and value-weighted basis. Our results seem to contradict Brav and Gompers's (1997) findings that venture-backed US IPOs subsequently outperform non-venture-backed IPOs, based on equally weighted long-term returns. The results, however, seem to be consistent with Rindermann (2003), who reports that VC-backed hi-tech IPOs in Germany, France and the UK did not outperform their non-VC-backed counterparts.

Venture capital firms' reputation does seem to play a role in the long-term performance of IPOs of UK MBOs (Table 14.9). Companies backed by more reputable VCs perform better in all months. The performance differences are statistically significant (at 10% or better) in months 24 and 36. To check for robustness of our results, we compared the performance of 3i-backed IPOs with the results of IPOs backed by other VCs. The unreported results are consistent with our previous findings: 3i outperformed its counterparts in all months. The performance differences are statistically significant (at 10% or better) in months 6 and 12.

The results of our two-step estimation procedure, with and without allowing for sample selectivity bias, are shown in Table 14.10. The regression for IR, allowing for sample selectivity, explains 23.18% of the variation

Table 14.9 BHAR: venture-capital-backed versus non-venture-capital-backed MBOs

M	VCBHR	NVCBHR	MVCBHR	MNVCBHR	VCWR	NVCWR	BHAR–VC	BHAR–NVC	Difference T *P*-value	Difference MW *P*-value	BHAR–Top 3VC	BHAR–Other VC	Difference T *P*-value	Difference MW *P*-value
6	0.999	1.003	1.001	1.010	0.997	0.993	0.31	1.35**	(0.14)	(0.19)	0.55	0.20	(0.49)	(0.58)
							0.12	*0.38***	*(0.24)*	*(0.13)*	*−0.05*	*0.19*	*0.57*	*0.45*
12	0.999	0.991	0.999	0.910	0.910	0.995	−0.21	−1.30	(0.30)	(0.29)	−0.03	−0.30	(0.43)	(0.36)
							−0.22	*−0.13*	*(0.69)*	*(0.79)*	*−0.00*	*−0.31**	*0.41*	*0.34*
18	1.002	1.003	1.001	0.997	1.001	1.005	0.24	0.10	(0.75)	(0.61)	0.49	0.13	(0.42)	(0.16)
							0.26	*0.06*	*(0.35)*	*(0.69)*	*0.53*	*0.14*	*0.44*	*0.36*
24	0.998	1.007	1.005	1.006	0.993	1.002	−0.41	0.32	(0.34)	(0.89)	0.31	−0.71	(0.10)	(0.18)
							−0.36	*−0.45*	*(0.88)*	*(0.54)*	*−0.59*	*−0.26*	*0.71*	*0.14*
30	1.001	1.008	0.995	1.006	1.006	1.001	0.04	0.23	(0.72)	(0.98)	0.22	−0.03	(0.48)	(0.55)
							−0.01	*−0.00*	*(0.99)*	*(0.83)*	*−0.30*	*0.11*	*0.51*	*0.94*
36	0.999	0.988	0.998	0.990	1.001	0.998	−0.16	−0.83	(0.34)	(0.64)	0.42	−0.38	(0.27)	(0.06)
							*−0.72**	*0.03*	*(0.16)*	*(0.90)*	*0.19*	*−1.05**	*0.08*	*0.10*

Notes: Mean market-adjusted buy-and-hold returns (BHAR) by month (*M*) after listing for venture-capital-backed (VC), non-venture-capital-backed firms (NVC), backed by highly reputable VC (Top 3VC), and less reputable VC (Other VC) reported in percentages. The returns were calculated as equally and *value-weighted returns*. Levels of significance for the two-tail *T* tests of mean = 0 vs mean ≠ 0, reported as: *** significant at 1% level or better, ** significant at 5% level or better, * significant at 10% level or better; *P*-values in parentheses (•) indicate the level of significance for the test of differences ($\eta_1 = \eta_2$ vs. $\eta_1 \neq \eta_2$) in mean (*T*-test) and median (Mann–Whitney test) market-adjusted buy-and-hold returns for sample firms backed by highly reputable venture capitalists and sample firms backed by less reputable venture capitalists. Sample venture-capital-backed average buy-and-hold returns (VCBHR), sample non-venture-backed average buy-and-hold returns (NVCBHR), venture-capital-backed matching firms' average buy-and-hold returns (MVCBHR), and non-venture-capital-backed matching firms' average buy-and-hold returns (MNVCBHR), are computed as equally weighted buy-and-hold raw compounded returns. Venture capital wealth relatives (VCWR) are calculated as VCBHR/MVCBHR. Non-venture-capital wealth relatives (NVCWR) are calculated as NVCBHR/MNVCBHR. The portfolios of matching firms were constructed from firms from the same industries and with similar (end of year) market values to the venture and non-venture sample firms.

Table 14.10 Determinants of long-term returns – with and without allowing for sample selectivity

Step 1: Probit regression		Step 2: OLS – White's regressions									
Dependent variable: VC		Dependent variables:	IR (SS)	IR	$BHAR_{12}$(SS)	$BHAR_{12}$	$BHAR_{24}$(SS)	$BHAR_{24}$	$BHAR_{36}$ (SS)	$BHAR_{36}$
Intercept	−0.008	Intercept	−0.029	0.001	−0.030	−0.15	0.034	0.027	0.037	0.039
MTOEXIT	−0.002	LAMBDA	−0.006		−0.003		0.001		−0.004	
LNMBOV	0.415***	LNMV	0.007	0.006	0.007	−0.002	−0.002	−0.002	−0.001	−0.002
		IR			−0.006	−0.006	−0.011	−0.011	−0.011	−0.011
		INDUSTRY	−0.041	−0.040	−0.003	−0.002	−0.011	−0.012*	−0.010	−0.010
		SOLD	0.001	0.001	0.039	0.038	0.011	0.012	−0.032	−0.032
		BV/MV	0.064	0.065	−0.012	−0.011	−0.011	−0.011	0.004	0.004
		GEARING	−0.003	−0.003	−0.012	−0.014	−0.015	−0.015	0.016	0.016
		UNDWT	−0.038*	−0.039*	0.006	0.006	0.014*	0.014*	−0.007	−0.007
		TOP3VC	0.008	0.008	0.007	0.007	0.009*	0.009*	0.008	0.008
		RISK	1.543	1.545						
		REVERSE	−0.026	−0.027						
		DW–statistic	2.066	2.069	1.868	1.900	1.928	1.931	1.999	2.001
		F-statistic	4.014***	4.483***	1.207	1.323	0.922	1.040	1.325	1.503
Pseudo R^2	0.16	R^2(%)	23.18	23.14	6.75	6.55	5.63	5.61	9.62	9.61
N	160	*N*	144	144	160	160	149	149	122	122

Notes: $BHAR_{12,24,36}$ = first-, second- and third-year market-adjusted buy-and-hold returns, respectively; $BHAR_{12,24,36}$ denoted SS in regressions adjusted for sample selectivity; TOP3VC = dummy variable for top three venture capital firms (1 if backed by top 3 VC; 0 otherwise); IR = row initial returns; SOLD = percentage of equity sold in the IPOs; BV/MV = net tangible assets per share/first trading price; LNMV = natural logarithm of market value (end of listing year); INDUSTRY = industry dummy (1 if from hi-tech; 0 otherwise); RISK = ex ante uncertainty measured by coefficient of variation of returns for the first trading month; MTOEXIT = time from MBOs to listings; REVERSE = reverse MBOs dummy (1 if reverse MBO; 0 otherwise); LNMBOV = natural logarithm of MBO values; GEARING = end of first listing year total debt/total assets ratio; UNDWT = underwriters' reputation dummy (1 if underwritten by highly reputable underwriter; 0 otherwise); LAMBDA = selectivity correction factor estimated from the Probit regression as the inverse Mills ratio; OLS estimations based on White's heteroscedasticity-adjusted standard errors; Levels of significance reported as: *** significant at 1% level or better; ** significant at 5% level or better; * significant at 10% level or better.

in initial returns. The RISK, REVERSE, SOLD, LNMV, UNDWT and TOP3VC variables have the expected signs. The variable UNDWT is the only statistically significant variable (at the 10% level), suggesting that more reputable underwriters have lower underpricing than their less reputable counterparts. The results did not change in the regression without allowing for sample selectivity.

The results for long-term returns provide further support for our findings on the importance of VCs reputation for long-term performance. The TOP3VC variable is positive in all regressions and statistically significant (at the 10% level) in the regressions for 2-year buy-and-hold market-adjusted returns. Interestingly, the only other statistically significant variable, in the regression for 2-year buy-and-hold market-adjusted returns, was UNDWT. VCs' and underwriters' reputations seem to be the most important factors in the long run. Although the *t*-statistic on the inverse Mills ratio variable (LAMBDA) is statistically insignificant in all regressions, some variables tend to be more significant if sample selectivity issues are ignored. For example, the INDUSTRY variable is statistically significant in the regression for 2-year buy-and-hold returns (at the 10% level) only when sample selectivity is not taken into account.

5. CONCLUSION

Using a unique dataset, we examine financial performance and venture capital involvement in 167 MBOs exiting through IPOs on the London Stock Exchange during the period 1964–97. The results suggest positive and highly statistically significant initial premiums (H1), regardless of measurement matrix, but no evidence of a significant underperformance in the long run (H2). The results for long-term performance remain robust after using the matching firms portfolio, as an alternative benchmark, and after computing the clustering and skewness-robust *t*-statistic. The lack of significant underperformance contradicts the findings reported in other UK IPO studies (Levis, 1993; Khurshad, 1999; and Espenlaub et al., 2000) and supports our expectations that the sub-sample of MBO IPOs may perform differently from other IPOs.

Venture capital-backed MBOs tend to be larger and exit earlier than their non-venture capital-backed counterparts. Based on equally weighted average initial returns there are no statistically significant differences between VC-backed and non-VC-backed IPOs (consistent with Espenlaub et al., 1999). However, VC-backed companies seem to be more underpriced than MBOs without venture capital backing (H3) based on average value-weighted returns. This is consistent with more recent international evidence on the VCs involvement in the IPO process (e.g. Hamao et al., 2000; and Francis et al., 2001). We found no evidence that VC-backed MBOs perform better than their non-VC-backed counterparts in the long run (H4). The results remain robust after using the matching firms' portfolio benchmark and after controlling for sample selection bias.

We find that, in contrast to the grandstanding hypothesis, private to public MBOs backed by more reputable VCs in the UK tend to exit earlier (H5). VCs' reputation does not seem to be a statistically significant variable in explaining cross-sectional differences in underpricing (H6). The VCs' reputation, however, seems to play an important role in long-term performance: MBOs backed by more prestigious VCs performed better than those backed by less prestigious VCs, measured by two-year buy-and-hold returns (H7). The results of our two-step estimation procedure on the importance of underwriters' reputation for both short- and long-term performance is intriguing, and calls for further investigation of the associations between UK underwriters and VCs.

The study involved IPOs of MBOs covering the period up to 1997 and thus specifically excluded the effects of the 1999–2000 period which may have distorted returns. During this period and subsequently, the annual number of IPOs of MBOs fell sharply. Correspondingly, the taking private of listed firms, some of which had previously been IPOs of MBOs, increased substantially (CMBOR, 2002). Future research might usefully examine the role-of MBOs in this period.

Evidence from UK IPOs generally shows negative abnormal stock returns at and around lock-up/lock-in expiry commensurate with US evidence, although UK lock-up/lock-in agreements tend to be less standardized (Espenlaub et al., 2001). Further research might, therefore, usefully examine how the nature of VC involvement in MBOs changes after the lock-up period and the consequences for financial performance.

Similarly, it may be the case that, in the longer term, management is able to cash out their gains and leave the firm. Evidence suggests that the extent to which entrepreneurs quit venture-backed investments following exit is extensive (Wright et al., 1997). Further research might be addressed at examining the extent and timing of such exit post-IPO and the impact on long-run IPO performance.

ACKNOWLEDGEMENTS

The authors would like to thank Mike Theobald, Edel Barnes, Douglas Cumming, participants at the 2002 European Financial Management Annual Meeting in London and staff seminars at Lancaster University,

Nottingham University and City University for their helpful comments. They would like especially to thank an anonymous referee for constructive suggestions. The research assistance of Chia Ying Chan and Sushma Iyer is also gratefully acknowledged.

NOTES

1. After 1979, the rate at which new firms are listed on the major US stock exchanges increases sharply. For example, average annual number of new listings changed from about 140 per year to more than 500 per year (Fama and French, 2001).
2. For more on differences between countries in access to finance and legal determinants of finance see La Porta et al. (1997 and 1998).
3. Based on aggregate UK data for private equity as a whole in 1999, the most important sources were: pension funds (31%), banks (25%) and insurance companies (14%); BVK (2000) as reported in Mayer et al. (2002).
4. Studies have examined other variables but results have been less significant: Iqbal (1998) found little evidence of a significant relationship between underwriters' and auditors' reputation and long-term performance of UK IPOs; Espenlaub et al. (2001) find lack of evidence of statistically significant underperformance of IPO stocks around their lock-in expiry dates. Hill and Short (2003) find that firms making a declaration of risk factors cannot be distinguished from firms that do not make a declaration of risk factors. Cai et al. (2003a and 2003b) find that dotcom firms underprice in order to promote demand for subsequent offerings.
5. One of the rare examples is Cusatis et al. (1991). For studies on financial performance of parent companies, see Hulburt et al. (2002).
6. In the 1980s, there was considerable scope to achieve gains from cost cutting, in the 1990s tighter governance in corporations is likely to mean less slack in divisions and auctions for MBOs as a result of the vast amount of funds available for investment. This is likely to mean that MBOs have to generate growth if they are to achieve target rates of return.
7. The periods of high volume and the average initial returns on IPOs are known as 'hot-issue' markets and were first documented by Ibbotson and Jaffe (1975).
8. Reverse L/MBOs are also known as 'secondary IPOs'.
9. MBOs and MBIs constitute at least 70% of total UK private equity investments (BVCA, 1998).
10. But evidence of reduction in VC retained ownership after IPO would contradict this hypothesis (Lin and Smith, 1998).
11. LBO partnerships in the US are responsible for leading the buy-out transaction, typically raising closed end equity funds to be used in conjunction with debt to structure the finance of the buy-out. In Europe, these funds tend to be seen as part of the private equity and venture capital industry.
12. For example, Fields (1995) hypothesizes a positive relationship due to the possible role of banks (and other institutional shareholders) in corporate governance. Chemmanur and Fulghieri (1994) propose that investors assess underwriters' reputation by measuring the quality of firms advised by the underwriters. The underwriters are, therefore, keen to maintain their reputation by being involved in IPOs of high-quality firms.
13. Deutsche Bank advert in the *Financial Times* (24 May 2000, p. 6). *Forbes* and the *Wall Street Journal* provide tables on the correlation between underwriters' reputation and IPO performance.
14. Obvious examples are Nat West Equity Partners, Barclay's Private Equity, Lloyds Development Capital and HSBC Private Equity.
15. It takes, on average 47.5 months for a reverse MBO to switch back from private to public

status. Muscarella and Vetsuypens (1990) report an average of 34 months for US reverse LBOs.

16. For example, the first trading month is from day 2 to day 22, the second month comprises trading days from day 23 to 43, etc.
17. Wilcoxon-Signed-Rank test.
18. Adopted from Lyon et al. (1999).
19. The value weighting was based on size of offers.
20. Nevertheless, in 6 cases matching firms were listed within a 3-year period after the listing of sample firms. There was, however, no statistically significant difference in the results with and without these 6 firms.
21. For example, 2 sample firms from 'construction' were matched with firms from 'house building', 3 sample firms from 'paper and packaging' were matched with firms from 'paper and printing', 2 sample firms from 'chain stores' were matched with firms from 'general retailers', and 5 sample firms from 'road transport' were matched with firms from 'transport'.
22. We ignore geographic concentration of VC-backed IPOs which is shown to be important in the US (see Lerner, 1994) as this applies less to the UK.
23. The Heckman (1979) procedure, also known as the 'Heckit' estimator and/or Endogenous Switching Regression, was developed for the economic modelling of the labour force participation and labour supply decisions. For a description and various applications of the Heckman procedure see Berndt (1991) and Greene (2000). For applications of the Heckman procedure in financial economics see Dunbar (1995) and Madhavan and Cheng (1997).
24. The results are reported with and without allowing for sample selectivity.
25. Underwriters' reputation is measured on the basis of frequency of engagement in underwriting (as a lead underwriter) of sample companies. The highly reputable underwriters are: Barclays de Zoete Wedd Limited, Baring Brothers & Co. Limited, Beeson Gregory Limited, Charterhouse Bank Limited, Henderson Crosthwaite Corporate Finance Limited, Hill Samuel & Co. Limited, J. Henry Schroder Wagg & Co. Limited, Kleinwort Benson Limited, Lazard Brothers and Co. Limited, NatWest Markets and Samuel Montagu.
26. The ten venture capitalists are: 3i, NatWest Equity Partners, Barclays Private Equity, Lloyds Development Capital, Cinven, Charterhouse Development Capital, HSBC Private Equity, Domestic Trade Interest, Murray Johnstone Private Equity and Schroder Venture.
27. There were about 4080 buy-outs backed by 686 different venture capital firms in the 1980–97 period.
28. A χ^2 test could not reject the null hypothesis of equality of distribution across industries for VC-backed and non-VC-backed companies, at the 5% significance level.
29. DeGeorge and Zeckhauser (1993) report that insiders in US LBOs hold, on average, 68% (median 49%) of the shares after the IPO.
30. The difference between average (mean) age for VC-backed and non-VC-backed firms is statistically significant at the 6% level.
31. In cases where more than one VC-backed the IPO, we use the reputation of the leading underwriter in calculation of average returns. Our results do not seem to be sensitive to different criteria for reputation. For example, the unreported results with 3i being the only reputable VC (3i was involved in backing of 44% of our sample companies) confirm our previous findings.
32. Using market capitalization for the end of 1997, only 23% (38) of companies in our sample were ranked among the top 500 UK companies (*Financial Times*, 1999). Since the MBOs in our sample seem to be small to medium, this further implies the absence of severe underperformance in this sector of UK companies. This result contradicts the well-documented severe underperformance of UK small companies during the period 1988–98 (see Dimson and Marsh, 2001).
33. We were able to identify lock-ups in 90 prospectuses. In 40 cases, lock-ups were staggered from 6 to 36 months.

REFERENCES

Barnes, E. (2003), 'Grandstanding in the UK venture capital industry', paper presented at the FMA Conference, Dublin.

Barry, C., C. Muscarella, J. Peavy and M. Vetsuypens (1990), 'The role of venture capital in the creation of public companies: evidence from the going public process', *Journal of Financial Economics*, **27**, pp. 447–71.

Berndt, E.R. (1991), *The Practice of Econometrics: Classic and contemporary*, Reading, MA: Addison Wesley.

Black, B. and R. Gilson (1998), 'Venture capital and the structure of capital markets: banks versus stock markets', *Journal of Financial Economics*, **47** (3), 243–78.

Brav, A. and P.A. Gompers (1997), 'Myth or reality? The long-run underperformance of initial public offerings: evidence from venture and nonventure capital-backed companies', *Journal of Finance*, **52**, 1791–821.

BVCA (1998), Report on Investment Activity.

Cai, X.C., D. Duxbury and K. Keasey (2003a), 'Dotcom IPOs: what factors account for the offer price and level of underpricing?', Working Paper, Leeds University.

Cai, X.C., D. Duxbury and K. Keasey (2003b), 'Manipulation of the IPO market during the dotcom bubble', Working Paper, Leeds University.

Carter, R.B., F.H. Dark and A.K. Singh (1997), 'Underwriter reputation, initial returns, and the long-run performance of IPO stocks', Working Paper, Iowa State University.

Chemmanur, T.J. and P. Fulghieri (1994), 'Investment bank reputation information production and financial intermediation', *Journal of Finance*, **49**, 57–79.

CMBOR (2002), 'Trends in UK Management Buy-outs', *Quarterly Review from CMBOR*, Nottingham: Centre for Management Buy-out Research, Spring.

Cusatis P., J. Miles and J.R. Wooldridge (1991), 'The investment performance of spin-offs', Working Paper 91–1, Smeal College of Business Administration, Pennsylvania State University, as cited in DeGeorge and Zeckhauser, (1993).

DeGeorge, F. and R. Zeckhauser (1993), 'The reverse LBO decision and firm performance: theory and evidence', *Journal of Finance*, **48** (4), 1323–49.

Dimson, E. and P. Marsh (1991), *The Hoare Govett Smaller Companies Index*, Hoare Govett Investment Research Limited.

Dimson, E. and P. Marsh (2001), *Hoare Govett Smaller Companies Report*.

Doukas, J.A. and H. Gonenc (2001), 'Long-term performance of new equity issuers, venture capital and reputation of investment bankers', Working Paper.

Dunbar, C.G. (1995), 'The use of warrants and underwriter compensation in initial public offerings', *Journal of Financial Economics*, **38**, 59–78.

Espenlaub, S., I. Garrett and W.P. Mun (1999), 'Conflicts of interest and the performance of venture-capital-backed IPOs: a preliminary look at the UK', *Venture Capital: An International Journal of Entrepreneurial Finance*, **1**, 325–50.

Espenlaub, S., I. Garrett and W.P. Mun, A. Gregory and I. Tonks (2000), 'Re-assessing the long-term underperformance of UK initial public offerings', *European Financial Management*, **6** (3), 319–42.

Espenlaub, S., I. Garrett and W.P. Mun, M. Goergen and A. Khurshed (2001), 'IPO lock-in agreements in the UK', *Journal of Business Finance & Accounting*, **28** (9/10), 1235–78.

EVCA (1995, 2001), EVCA *Yearbooks*, European Venture Capital Association, Zaventem.

Fama, E. (1998), 'Market efficiency, long-term returns, and behavioural finance', *Journal of Financial Economics*, **49**, 283–306.
Fama, E. and K.R. French (2001), 'Newly listed firms: fundamentals, survival rates, and returns', Working Paper 530, University of Chicago Graduate School of Business.
Fields, L.C. (1995), 'Is institutional investment in initial public offerings related to long-run performance of these firms?', Working Paper, UCLA.
Filatotchev, I. and K. Bishop (2003), 'Board composition, share ownership and "underpricing" of UK IPO firms', Working Paper, Bradford University.
Financial Times (1999), 'Top 500 UK Companies', December.
Financial Times (2000), 'Deutche Bank Advert', 24 May.
Francis, B.B., I. Hasan and C. Hu (2001), 'The underpricing of venture and non-venture capital IPOs: an empirical investigation', *Journal of Financial Services Research*, **19**, 99–113.
Franzke, S.A. (2001), 'Underpricing of venture-backed and non venture-backed IPOs: Germany's Neuer Markt', CFS Working Paper no. 2001/01.
Gompers, P.A. (1996), 'Grandstanding in the venture capital industry', *Journal of Financial Economics*, **42**, 133–56.
Gompers, P.A. and J. Lerner (2001), 'The really long-run performance of initial public offerings: the pre-NASDAQ evidence', Working Paper, Harvard Business School, September.
Greene, W.H. (2000), *Econometric Analysis*, 4th edn, Englewood Cliffs, NJ: Prentice Hall.
Hamao, Y., F. Packer and J. Ritter (2000), 'Institutional affiliation and the role of venture capital: evidence from initial public offerings in Japan', *Pacific Basin Finance Journal*, **8**, 529–58.
Heckman, J. (1979), 'Sample selection bias and a specification error', *Econometrica*, **47**, 153–61.
Hill, P. and H. Short (2003), 'Do risk warnings matter? Implications for the financial reporting of risk based on evidence from four industrial sectors', Working Paper, Leeds University.
Holthausen, D. and D. Larcker (1996), 'The financial performance of reverse leveraged buy-outs', *Journal of Financial Economics*, **42** (3), 293–332.
Hulburt, H.M., J.A. Miles and J.R. Woolridge (2002), 'Value creation from equity carve-outs', *Financial Management*, **1**, 83–100.
Ibbotson, R.G. (1975), 'Price performance of common stock new issues', *Journal of Financial Economics*, **2**, 235–72.
Ibbotson, R.G. and J.F. Jaffe (1975), ' "Hot Issue" Markets', *Journal of Finance*, **30**, 1027–42.
Ibbotson, R.G. and J.R. Ritter (1995), 'Initial public offerings', in R. Jarrow et al. (eds), *Handbook in OR and MS*, Vol. 9, Amsterdam: Elsevier, pp. 993–1016.
Iqbal, A. (1998), 'Initial public offerings performance and financial agents' reputation: the UK evidence', unpublished MA dissertation, Manchester School of Accounting and Finance.
Jain, B. and O. Kini (1995), 'Venture capitalist participation and the post-issue operating performance of IPO firms', *Managerial and Decision Economics*, **16** (6), 593–606.
Jalilvand, A., S.M. Stewart and J.A. Switzer (1996), 'A synthesis on investment banker reputation and pricing of initial public offerings: new evidence on reverse LBOs', *Financial Markets, Institutions and Instruments*, **5** (5), 37–61.

Jeng, L. and P. Wells (2000), 'The determinants of venture capital funding: evidence across countries', *Journal of Corporate Finance*, **6**, 241–89.

Jenkinson, T. and A. Ljungqvist (2001), *Going Public: The theory and evidence on how companies raise equity finance*, 2nd edn, Oxford: Oxford University Press.

Jensen, M.C. (1989), 'Eclipse of the public corporation', *Harvard Business Review*, Sept.–Oct., 61–74.

Jensen, M.C. (1993), 'The modern industrial revolution, exit and the failure of internal control systems', *Journal of Finance*, **48** (3), 831–80.

Kaplan, S. (1989), 'The effects of management buyouts on operating performance and value', *Journal of Financial Economics*, **24**, 217–54.

Kaplan, S. (1991), 'The staying power of leveraged buyouts', *Journal of Financial Economics*, **24**, 217–54.

Khurshad, A., R. Mudambi and M. Goergen (1999), 'On the long run performance of IPOs', Working Paper, Case Western Reserve University.

Kothari, S.P. and J.B. Warner (1997), 'Measuring long-horizon security price performance', *Journal of Financial Economics*, **43**, 301–40.

Kraus, T. and H.P. Burghof (2003), 'Post-IPO performance and the exit of venture capitalists', Working Paper, University of Munich.

La Porta, R., F. López de Silanes, A. Shleifer and R. Vishny (1997), 'legal determinants of external finance', *Journal of Finance*, **52** (3), 1131–50.

La Porta, R., F. López de Silanes, A. Shleifer and R. Vishny (1998), 'Law and finance', *Journal of Political Economy*, **106**, 1113–55.

Lee, P.M. and S. Wahal (2004), 'Grandstanding, certification and underpricing of venture capital backed IPOs', *Journal of Financial Economics*, **73**, pp. 375–407.

Leland, H. and D. Pyle (1977), 'Information asymmetries financial structure and financial intermediation', *Journal of Finance*, **32**, 371–87.

Lerner, J. (1994), 'Venture capitalists and the decision to go public', *Journal of Financial Economics*, **35**, 293–316.

Levis, M. (1993), 'The long-run performance of initial public offerings: the UK experience 1980–1988', *Financial Management*, **22** (1), pp. 28–41.

Lichtenberg, F. and D. Siegel (1990), 'The effects of leveraged buyouts on productivity and related aspects of firm behavior', *Journal of Financial Economics*, **27**, 165–94.

Lin, T.H. and R.L. Smith (1998), 'Insider reputation and selling decisions: the unwinding of venture capital investments during equity IPOs', *Journal of Corporate Finance*, **4**, 241–63.

Ljungqvist, A.P. (1999), 'IPO underpricing, wealth losses and the curious role of venture capitalists in creation of public companies', Working Paper, Oxford University.

Loughran, T. and K. Rydquist (1994), 'Initial public offerings: international insight', *Pacific Basin Journal*, **2**, 165–99.

Lyon, J.D., B.M. Barber and C.-L. Tsai (1999), 'Improved methods for tests of long-run abnormal stock returns', *Journal of Finance*, **54** (1), pp. 165–201.

Madhavan, A. and M. Cheng (1997), 'In search of liquidity: block trades in the upstairs and downstairs markets', *Review of Financial Studies*, **10**, 175–203.

Mayer, C., K. Schoors and Y. Yafeh (2002), 'Sources of funds and investment activities of venture capital funds: evidence from Germany, Israel, Japan and the UK', Working Paper.

Megginson, W. and K. Weiss (1991), 'Venture capitalist certification in initial public offerings', *Journal of Finance*, **46**, 879–903.

Michaely, R. and H.S. Wayne (1994), 'The pricing of initial public offerings: tests of adverse selection and signalling theories', *The Review of Financial Studies*, **7**, 279–319.

Muscarella, C. and M. Vetsuypens (1990), 'Efficiency and organisational structure: a study of reverse LBOs', *Journal of Finance*, **45** (5), 1389–413.

Myers S.C. and N.S. Majluf (1984), 'Corporate financing and investment decisions when firms have information that investors do not have', *Journal of Financial Economics*, **13**, 187–221.

Opler, T. (1992), 'Operating performance in leveraged buy-outs', *Financial Management*, **21**, 27–34.

Palepu, K. (1990), 'Consequences of leverage buy-outs', *Journal of Financial Economics*, **27**, 247–62.

Rajan, R. and H. Servaes (1997), 'Analyst following of initial public offerings', *Journal of Finance*, **52**, 507–29.

Rindermann, G. (2003), *Venture Capitalist Participation and the Performance of IPO Firms: Empirical Evidence from France, Germany and the UK*, Frankfurt: Peter Lang.

Ritter, J. (1984), 'The "hot issue" market of 1980', *Journal of Business*, **57**, 215–240.

Ritter, J. (1991), 'The long run performance of initial public offerings', *Journal of Finance*, **46**, 3–27.

Ritter, J. (2003), 'Differences between European and American IPO markets', *European Financial Management*, **9** (4), 421–34.

Robbie, K., M. Wright and B. Chiplin (1997), 'The monitoring of venture capital firms', *Entrepreneurship Theory and Practice*, **21** (4), 9–28.

Romano, R. (1996), 'Corporate law and corporate governance', *Industrial and Corporate Change*, **5** (2), 277–339.

Sahlman, W.A. (1990), 'The structure and governance of venture-capital organizations', *Journal of Financial Economics*, **27**, 473–521.

Sapienza, H. (1992), 'When do venture capitalists add value?', *Journal of Business Venturing*, **7**, 9–27.

Singh, H. (1990), 'Management buy-outs and shareholder value', *Strategic Management Journal*, **11**, 111–29.

Smith, A. (1990), 'Corporate ownership structure and performance: the case of management buy-outs', *Journal of Financial Economics*, **27**, 143–64.

Strong, N. and X.G. Xu (1997), 'Explaining the cross-section of UK expected stock returns', *British Accounting Review*, **29** (1), 1–24.

Thompson, S. and M. Wright (1995), 'Corporate governance: the role of restructuring transactions', *Economic Journal*, **105**, 690–703.

White, H. (1980), 'A heteroscedasticity-consistent covariance matrix estimator and a direct test for heteroscedasticity', *Econometrica*, **48**, 817–38.

Wright, M. and K. Robbie (1995), 'Managerial ownership and succession and corporate restructuring: The case of management buy-ins', *Journal of Management Studies*, **32** (4), 527–50.

Wright, M. and K. Robbie (1996), 'Venture capital firms and unquoted equity investment appraisal', *Accounting and Business Research*, **26** (2), 153–68.

Wright, M. and K. Robbie (1998), 'Venture capital and private equity: a review and synthesis', *Journal of Business Finance & Accounting*, **25** (5&6), 521–70.

Wright, M. and K. Robbie and C. Ennew (1997), 'Venture capitalists and serial entrepreneurs', *Journal of Business Venturing*, **12** (3), 227–49.

Wright, M., N. Wilson and K. Robbie (1996), 'The longer term effects of management-led buy-outs', *Journal of Entrepreneurial and Small Business Finance*, **5** (3), 213–34.

Wright, M., S. Thompson, K. Robbie and P. Wong (1995), 'Management buy-outs in the short and long term', *Journal of Business Finance & Accounting*, **22** (4), 461–82.

15. Secured creditor recovery rates from management buy-outs in distress

David Citron, Mike Wright, Rod Ball and Fred Rippington

1. INTRODUCTION

Considerable attention has been devoted to the role of debt in management (MBOs) and leveraged buy-outs (LBOs). High leverage has been argued to play an important role in committing management to improve efficiency (Jensen, 1986). MBO loan agreements tend to contain more covenants than general corporate lending agreements with specialist secured creditors also engaging in close monitoring (Citron et al., 1997). Buy-out specialists may increase monitoring that substitutes for tighter debt terms (Cotter and Peck, 2001). High leverage in MBO/LBO transactions has been argued to trigger bankruptcy at a point that preserves greater going-concern value than in firms that are predominantly equity financed (Jensen, 1991). Andrade and Kaplan (1998) show for a sample of 31 highly leveraged transactions (HLTs) that became distressed that the value of the distressed HLTs did not decline and that the costs of financial distress amounted to 10–20% of firm value. This literature suggests that secured creditors will recoup substantial proportions of the funds they extend to finance the initial buy-out. However, as yet there is no evidence either on the extent of credit recovery by secured lenders in MBOs nor on the factors that influence the extent of this recovery.

In order to gain a deeper understanding of the process by which secured creditors recover funds they have extended to MBOs, this chapter utilizes evidence from a unique dataset of 42 failed buy-outs compiled by the authors. Compilation of the dataset involved the monitoring of a cohort of MBOs from deal completion to receivership and detailed archival analysis of the reports of the receivers.

We find that on average, 62% of secured credit is recovered when buy-outs enter the receivership process. This is comparable with the 70% found to be recovered by banks in Franks and Sussman's (2000) study of privately held small and medium sized companies. However, our study finds a lower secured creditor recovery rate for MBOs than those found for non-MBOs in the USA that range from 80.1% to 100% (Weiss, 1990; Franks and Torous, 1994; Tashjian et al., 1996). Using univariate analysis, we find some evidence that secured creditors recover a higher percentage of their lending where there is only one creditor, where asset realization by the receiver is as a going concern, and where the cause of failure is managerial. Recovery rates by secured creditors are lower where the audit report receives a going-concern modification. Recovery rates are not found to vary significantly with duration of the MBO, whether the receivership firm was a Big Six accounting firm, nor according to the size and sector of the MBO nor the state of the economic cycle. Multiple regression and logistic regression analysis showed that the percentage of secured credit recovered is increased where the distressed buy-out is sold as a going concern and where the principal reason for failure concerns managerial factors. The presence of a going-concern qualification in the audit report and the size of the buy-out both serve to reduce the recovery rate by secured creditors. The chapter is organized as follows. The next section briefly outlines the institutional framework in the UK. The third section discusses the expected determinants of the amount of repayment to secured creditors. This is followed by a description of the dataset used. The fourth section presents the results of the study in terms of both univariate statistics and cross-section regression analysis. Finally, some conclusions are drawn.

2. INSTITUTIONAL FRAMEWORK

Administrative receivership, the focus of this study, can be instigated only by a creditor whose security is held as a floating charge (see for example Franks et al., 1996). A floating charge is a form of security over assets which are changing in nature, such as stocks or work in progress. Moreover, administrative receivers owe their prime duty of care to their appointer, the floating charge holder, and few obligations to others.

The administrative receiver has complete control over the firm and can, for example, liquidate the business without the permission of other creditors or the court. In theory, however, fixed charge holders can constitute an important constraint on the activities of the administrative receiver. Fixed charge holders are creditors who hold security over an identifiable corporate asset such as property (real estate) and they have the right to realize their specific security in priority to any other claimants. In practice, creditors usually ensure they hold both floating and fixed charges, the former to give the right of appointment of administrative receiver and the latter to gain priority over certain asset realizations. In UK management buy-outs, banks typically obtain a high level of security by taking a fixed and floating charge over the assets of the company (Sterling and Wright, 1990; Kreuger, 1990; Wright et al., 1990).

3. DETERMINANTS OF RECOVERY RATES

One stream of research into payments by financially distressed firms to their creditors has focused on firms that have not entered formal bankruptcy proceedings. Brown et al. (1994), for example, examine the circumstances under which financially distressed firms pay out the proceeds of asset sales to creditors, and Detragiache (1995) investigates the role of mixed cash and equity payments to creditors in corporate debt workouts.

There has, however, been little previous research into the determinants of recovery rates by creditors from firms that have entered formal bankruptcy proceedings. Prior research into bankruptcy resolution has focused primarily on issues such as the direct costs of the process, the extent of violation of priority rules and the extent of creditor recovery rates under a variety of US bankruptcy resolution procedures, but generally has not investigated the determinants of creditor recovery rates. Regarding specifically secured creditor recovery rates, the focus of this chapter, Weiss (1990) finds that in 33 of his 37 Chapter 7 and Chapter 11 cases the secured creditors recoup 100%. In Franks and Torous's (1994) 37 Chapter 11 cases they receive an average of 80.1%, and Tashjian et al. (1996) find a mean 99.3% repayment rate to secured creditors in 41 prepackaged bankruptcies. Of these studies, Franks and Torous (1994) analyse the determinants of overall recovery rates by all classes of creditors. They find that recovery rates are higher the stronger the performance of the economy but are negatively related to levels of asset sales which presumably take place at prices below their values in best use. Comparisons in recovery rates between jurisdictions are problematical, however, due to differences in institutional arrangements. Chapter 11 procedures in the USA, for example, are more akin to reorganizations whereas UK receiverships are closer to winding ups.

This study therefore extends previous work in the area by focusing on the determinants of secured creditor recovery rates from firms that have entered formal bankruptcy proceedings, and by its use of a new dataset, UK MBOs. The percentage of secured credit recovered is taken to be a function of a vector of MBO firm-specific characteristics related to distress, the effectiveness of monitoring the MBO and the effectiveness of the receivership procedure.

3.1 Distressed MBO Firm Characteristics

In the stylized MBO, the firm is in a mature, niche sector with stable cash flow and low capital investment needs (Jensen, 1991). These characteristics facilitate the taking on of high leverage that, together with significant levels of managerial equity, encourages managers to seek profitable opportunities. In general, therefore, firms may become distressed, that is enter receivership, due to one or more factors related to shortcomings in these operational, financial and managerial aspects (Wright et al., 1996).

The MBO firm's market may not necessarily remain stable post-MBO. A major reason for a parent company to divest a division is market decline. Where the firm fails because of trading problems, recovering significant amounts of secured debt may be more difficult as the indication is that the operational base of the enterprise has been eroded due to market decline.

Trading problems may lead to difficulties in servicing highly leveraged financial structures. However, financial difficulties may also arise due to excessive leverage introduced at the time of the MBO. Bruner and Eades (1992) show in the case of the failed REVCO buy-out that the company's interest and fixed dividend obligations arising from the leverage used to fund the buy-out meant there was a very low probability that the company could survive. Kaplan and Stein (1993) show in their study of larger US buy-outs completed in the late 1980s that the greater amounts of leverage taken on in this period increased the probability of failure. For a sample of 110 failed UK MBOs, Wright et al. (1996) find that the lower the net worth ratio, an inverse proxy for high leverage, the greater the probability of failure.

Even though high leverage leads to financial distress, MBOs may still have viable trading activities (Andrade and Kaplan, 1998). High leverage in MBO/LBO transactions has been argued to trigger bankruptcy at a point that preserves greater going-concern value than in firms that are predominantly equity financed (Jensen, 1991). Hence, the high leverage and loan covenants used in buy-outs may mean that a relatively high underlying value of the enterprise is preserved. In such cases, it may be feasible to recover a high degree of secured debt by selling the business as a going concern either in whole or in part. However, companies that fail with the most acute financial and cash flow problems, perhaps exacerbated by trading problems, may be most difficult to sell on a going-concern basis as it is likely to be difficult to persuade buyers to take on these difficulties.

Management may be incentivized to a greater extent in an MBO than beforehand but their performance may be poor because they do not have the expertise to lead the now independent entity. The MBO financiers' screening process is expected to identify individuals who are unlikely to make the transition from divisional managers to peak tier coordinators.

However, financiers are faced with an asymmetric information problem since they are unable to observe the management performing their new role prior to making an investment. Moreover, financiers may only be able to judge imperfectly the value of managers' private information regarding the firm's future prospects and their ability to act upon it. Managerial problems may thus only become apparent subsequent to MBO. Both the operating activities of the business and financial aspects may have an underlying soundness that can be addressed with the replacement of inadequate management. In the case of MBO failure primarily because of poor management, therefore, it may be expected that secured creditor recovery rates will be relatively high.

Evidence suggests that in general, MBOs do not fail quickly. Wright et al. (1995) find that in a cohort of 158 UK MBOs, less than 1% had failed after three years but that after six years 7% had failed. A shorter period to failure may reflect financial difficulties due to excessive leverage or trading problems due to the loss of major customers. Secured creditors in MBOs tend to receive greater information for monitoring purposes that is used to take corrective actions when covenants are breached (Citron et al., 1997). This monitoring by banks may be closer in the early years of an MBO when there is less track history and risk is high. A longer period to failure is consistent with the relatively slow decline of a market where management are unable to successfully introduce new products. A higher repayment rate might be expected out of longer-lived MBOs as debt outstanding is likely to fall with MBO life. However, in MBOs that enter receivership, debt may not have fallen as much as it would have done in successful MBOs (Wright et al., 1996; Andrade and Kaplan, 1998). In addition, if the trading base has been eroded over time and assets have become old or obsolete due to a lack of cash to replace them, realization values may be low. Hence, it is expected that secured creditor recovery rates will be higher for MBOs that become distressed sooner after buy-out.

Larger and smaller buy-outs are more prone to failure than medium-sized ones (Wright et al., 1996). Informational asymmetries may be greater for smaller transactions whereas larger MBOs typically have complex financial structures and are more prone to excessive leverage (Kaplan and Stein, 1993). It may be possible to generate significant amounts of cash from the disposal of parts of larger MBOs, some of which may be sold as going concerns. However, this may still leave significant problematical activities. It may thus be difficult to find buyers willing to acquire a large troubled business unless they pay a proportionately lower price because of the size and complexity of the restructuring task. Hence, overall larger buy-outs are expected to be negatively associated with higher repayments to secured creditors.

Asset security is an important aspect of lending to MBOs by banks. There is some debate about the impact of the nature of the assets on likely repayment of secured debt. The industrial sector in which a firm is located provides an indicator of the nature of assets. For non-MBOs, LoPucki (1983) shows that manufacturing firms are more likely to reorganize than liquidate and hence lead to greater repayment. However, as the manufacturing firms in her sample tended to be larger than other firms, this finding may also reflect size rather than industry effects. In contrast, and after controlling for size, Campbell (1996) finds also for non-MBOs that construction and manufacturing firms are more likely to liquidate than to reorganize.

Firms in retail and wholesale sectors may be more likely to have assets (stores) that can be sold readily. Such assets are typically used as collateral for higher lending and may be targeted for piecemeal disposal to pay down certain tranches of debt as for example in the cases of the Safeway LBO in the USA (Denis, 1994) and the Gateway LBO in the UK (Wright et al., 1994). Similarly, when such MBOs become distressed, it may be possible to dispose of stores piecemeal to raise cash. However, it is not clear that it will be possible to raise *proportionately* greater amounts of cash from the property of retail/wholesale MBOs in distress than for MBOs in other sectors.

3.2 Monitoring

Two aspects of monitoring that are especially pertinent to recovery rates of secured debt in distressed MBOs concern the audit report opinion and the number of secured creditors.

The presence of an audit report with a going-concern modification may be a signal that the MBO is becoming distressed. Research into listed companies in the UK shows that auditors appear reluctant to modify their audit report for going-concern uncertainties unless the company is already in dire financial straits (Citron and Taffler, 1999). Assuming auditor behaviour is similar in this population of unlisted companies, it is expected that if receivers are not called in until after a modified audit report has been issued, then the secured creditors will obtain relatively low rates of debt recovery.

The effectiveness of the monitoring role of secured creditors may be influenced by the number that are present in a particular deal. Bolton and Scharfstein (1996) show that it is optimal for firms with low credit quality to maximize liquidation values by borrowing from just one secured creditor and by adopting rules that make it easier to complete an asset sale. Liquidation value may be lower with multiple creditors. While difficulties in getting agreement among creditors to sell may increase the sale price to persuade them to sell, this may be more than offset by the unwillingness of potential bidders to sink the costs of becoming informed about the firm's assets. Wilkins and Zimmer (1996) show how an independent third-party adviser to creditors can align the various interests of the various claim-holders.

However, the greater the number of lenders in a loan syndicate, the greater the potential conflicts of interest among claim-holders (Wruck, 1990), the greater the renegotiation costs associated with default (Smith, 1993) and the less likely is private renegotiation of financial distress to be successful (Gilson et al., 1990). Evidence from the syndication of venture capital investments suggests that larger syndicates impose increasingly greater coordination costs (Lockett and Wright, 2001). Where there are syndicates in MBO lending, all primary contacts with the client are generally channelled through the lead (agent) bank so that syndicate members have less influence on monitoring (Citron et al., 1997). As a result, syndicated lending in MBOs leads to significantly longer delays in implementing action than in single creditor lending (Citron et al., 1997). Moreover, such actions are also reported to be significantly less effective in syndicate lending.

It is possible, therefore, that a multiplicity of secured creditors could both lead to delayed corrective action prior to receivership and adversely affect the conduct of the receivership when it occurs. If different creditors have different and possibly conflicting priorities and objectives, the variety of pressures on the receivers and the accompanying coordination problems may result in a lower overall rate of payout to the body of secured creditors.

3.3 Effectiveness of Receivership Procedure

The proportion of debt repayable may be affected by the expertise of the receiver handling the failed MBO. More expert receivers with greater reputations, such as members of Big Six accounting firms, may be expected to be more adept at disposing of failed businesses for higher prices.

Receivers may dispose of failed MBOs in two principal ways. Either the business may be sold as a going concern or liquidated as a set of assets. The highly secured position has led to a suggestion that banks will prefer to liquidate companies prematurely rather than undergo a rescue process. Franks and Sussman (2000) show in their UK study of financially distressed small and medium-sized companies that banks do not automatically liquidate firms upon distress. They find that almost a half of firms placed in bankruptcy are sold as going concerns. US evidence indicates that the prices of asset sales under both reorganization (Chapter 11) and liquidation (Chapter 7) regimes are substantially lower than prices obtained by non-distressed firms as bankruptcy status attracts 'low ball' bids (Pulvino, 1999).

As noted above, the use of higher leverage in buy-outs and closer institutional control may mean that firms signal financial distress earlier than if they were funded substantially by equity (Jensen, 1991). MBO firms that default on loan payments and subsequently enter receivership may retain greater value. As a result, they may have good prospects of being reorganized and sold as going concerns rather than being liquidated. Andrade and Kaplan (1998) show in their sample of HLTs that the majority exit Chapter 11 restructuring as public companies, with only a small number being sold or liquidated.

Shleifer and Vishny (1992) argue that increased liquidity in the market for corporate assets from the 1980s onwards enabled higher leverage to be extended to MBOs since significant amounts of debt could be paid down from the subsequent sale of assets. Franks and Torous (1994), in their study of firms undergoing informal and Chapter 11 bankruptcy resolution, find evidence to support this thesis. This increased liquidity in the market for corporate assets also suggested that it would be more feasible to recoup significant amounts of debt from the sale of MBOs entering bankruptcy. Hence, it is expected that distressed MBOs which are subsequently sold as going concerns will lead to greater percentages of secured debt recovery than cases where sale is piecemeal.

The effectiveness of the receivership process may also be affected by the state of the economic cycle. It may be that those MBOs set up during or close to a period of recession will have more conservative financial structures and be monitored more closely and may, therefore, achieve higher repayments to secured creditors. However, many firms fail as the economy emerges from recession. These companies will have been weakened by the recession years and then find they are insufficiently capitalized to cope with the growth of the immediately post-recession period. Thus the receiverships of these severely weakened firms will be put at a relative disadvantage, as a result of which they may achieve lower repayments than those occurring a number of years after recession. Furthermore, the liquidity of markets for corporate assets may be reduced in conditions of recession, hence potentially reducing the prices at which receivers can sell MBOs in distress (Shleifer and Vishny, 1992; Franks and Torous, 1994).

4. DATA AND METHODOLOGY

The study involved the compilation of a novel dataset of MBOs completed in the period 1992 and 1995 that had subsequently entered receivership.

This period was selected for two main reasons. First, the start date represented a time when the UK economy was still in recession. Second, the end date allowed sufficient time for failures to emerge and for the completion of the receivership process in a significant proportion of cases.

The Centre for Management Buy-out Research (CMBOR) database was used to identify the cohort of buy-outs. The CMBOR database is compiled from a wide range of sources, including twice-yearly surveys of private equity and debt providers to buy-outs,[1] press releases by these financiers, the financial press, stock exchange circulars issued by companies divesting subsidiaries as MBOs and companies annual reports. The database has no lower size cut-off and is unique in effectively representing the universe of buy-outs in the UK. Data on failures of buy-outs and buy-ins are collected by CMBOR from its regular surveys of participants in the buy-out market, Companies House returns and Extel, monitoring of the financial press and the London Gazette.

A total of 2241 buy-outs and buy-ins were completed in the period 1992–95, with a combined transaction value of £15.2 billion. By June 2000, a substantial proportion of these buy-outs and buy-ins had changed their ownership form (Table 15.1), with receivership being the second most common. Some 202 deals had entered receivership, 9% of the total. In value terms, 4.1% of the capital directed at all deals during the period was used for buy-outs with a known value that had subsequently failed by June 2000.

It was possible to obtain Companies House microfiches for 139 of the 202 MBO receivership cases identified on the CMBOR database. Of these, 71 were found to be unsuitable for analysis for a number of reasons such as lack of data on appointment of the receiver or absence of receivers' receipts and payments accounts; receiver appointed very recently; some cases of voluntary liquidations; and problems with establishing correct company identity.

Of the remaining 68 potentially suitable cases, the receivership process was still continuing at the time our analysis was undertaken in 26 firms. It

Table 15.1 Change in status of all buy-outs 1992–95

Year	Total	Float	Trade sale	Second MBO	Receiver
1992	595	27	91	23	47
1993	492	23	71	10	55
1994	557	13	84	25	47
1995	597	19	69	15	53
Total	2241	82	315	73	202
Total (%)		3.66	14.06	3.26	9.01

Source: CMBOR/Barclays Private Equity/Deloitte & Touche.

Table 15.2 Cases analysed by year of MBO and year of receivership

Year	MBO (no.)	Receivership (no.)
1991	1	0
1992	9	1
1993	11	3
1994	16	7
1995	5	7
1996	0	11
1997	0	6
1998	0	6
1999	0	1
Total	42	42

Source: CMBOR/Barclays Private Equity/Deloitte & Touche.

is likely that further amounts will be realized for the secured creditors in these cases. The analysis in this chapter, therefore, relates to the remaining 42 cases (Table 15.2). Of these, in 33 cases (79%) the receivership process was complete, with the company having been struck off. While the remaining nine (21%) of cases were technically continuing, they were treated as completed. These are cases where the receiver has filed the final receipts and payments accounts or strongly indicated that future payments will be insignificant, and one case where the receivers informed us directly that the receivership was effectively complete. The names of the 42 MBOs together with details on the date each MBO was set up, its value at that date, the date it entered receivership and the percentage of secured debt repaid are contained in the Appendix.

Data on the number of secured creditors and the amounts owing to each are obtained from the directors' Statements of Affairs. The mode of sale of the MBO by the receivers, the identity of the receivers, the MBO's industry sector and the cause of failure are obtained from the receivers' report to the creditors. The amount of secured debt repaid by the receivers is determined from their annual receipts and payments accounts. The duration of the MBO from creation until receivership is obtained from the CMBOR database, while the value of the MBO at the date it is set up is taken in 29 cases from the CMBOR database supplemented in nine additional cases by the value of total assets less current liabilities from the first published balance sheet subsequent to the MBO being established.

Accounting data from the MBOs' published financial statements are available for only a subset of our population. Balance sheet and audit report information is available in 23 cases. Where more than one set of

Table 15.3 MBOs in receivership – descriptive statistics (n = 42)

	Mean	Median	Minimum	Maximum	Standard deviation
Average duration of MBO (months)	29.8	29.0	7.0	75.8	16.99
Amount of secured debt due at date of receivership (£ thousands)	980.9	603.5	56.3	7419.6	1374.05
Secured debt repaid (%)	61.7	64.9	5.9	100.0	31.90

accounts is available, the last set prior to the appointment of the receivers is used.

As shown in Table 15.3, the average duration of the 42 MBOs was 30 months. For the 32 cases in our population for which we have data, the mean (median) length of the receivership was 829 days, i.e. 2.3 years (783 days i.e. 2.2 years), ranging from a minimum of nine days to a maximum of 1656 days (4.6 years).

The mean amount of secured debt owing at the date of the receivership was £980 900 (median = £603 500), of which an average of 62% was repaid (all averages cited in this chapter are unweighted, so that no greater weight is given to cases with larger amounts of debt outstanding). Supporting expectations that secured creditors will hold both fixed and flexible charges, of our population of 42 receiverships, in 39 (92.9%) cases the secured creditors held exclusively both fixed and floating charges, while in three cases some creditors held both while others held only fixed charges. This degree of holding fixed and floating charges exceeds the top end of the range of 52.6% to 91.2% across the three banks examined by Franks and Sussman (2000), indicating a higher degree of fixed and floating charge holding by banks in MBOs than in smaller private firms generally.

5. RESULTS

5.1 MBO Firm Characteristics

Cause of receivership

In 37 of the 42 cases the receivers referred to the cause of MBO failure in their report attached to the Statement of Affairs. In Table 15.4, Panel A these causes have been categorized as operational, financial, managerial or other (these being cases where the cause is simply ascribed to losses or inheriting loss-making companies).[2] The mean repayment rate in the 12 cases where cause is managerial or other is 76%, significantly higher (at the 5% level, two-tailed test) than the 54% mean repayment when the cause is operational or financial.

Duration of the MBO

Table 15.4, Panel B shows secured debt repayment analysed by percentage repaid in quartiles, including the number of cases with 100% repaid. It also shows the average duration of the MBOs falling in each repayment category. The table reveals no discernible relationship between percentage repaid and duration of the MBO. While the seven cases in the lowest repayment category (up to 25%) had a relatively short average duration of only 24 months, the average duration of the ten cases achiev-

Table 15.4 Factors affecting creditor recovery: firm characteristics

Factor			No. cases		Secured debt repaid (mean %)	
Panel A: Causes of failure						
Operational			19		54	
Financial			6		55	
Managerial			7		71	
Other ('losses')			5		83	
All			37		61*	
Panel B: Mean duration of MBO (months)[a]						
Secured debt repaid (%)	up to 25%	25.1–50	50.1–75	75.1–99.9	100	Total/avge
Average duration (mths)	24	38	21	38	24	30
No. of cases	7	11	6	8	10	42
Panel C: Industrial sector[a]						
Retail/wholesale			6		44	
Other			36		65	

Notes: This table provides univariate analysis of the variables affecting secured creditor recovery rates for the 42 MBOs in the sample. In Panel A, differences are tested between those MBOs where the cause of failure was managerial/other and those where cause of failure was operational/ financial. In Panel B differences in MBO duration between percentage quartiles of repayment are tested. In Panel C differences in industrial sectors are tested.

[a] Difference between groups not significant.

* Difference between groups significant at 0.05 level.

ing 100% repayment is identical and also below the overall average of 30 months.

The average life of the 24 MBOs in which the repayment exceeded 50% was 27.8 months, while that of the 18 cases with a less than 50% repayment was somewhat longer at 32.6 months. However, this difference is not statistically significant. Looking at the most long-lived MBOs, the five cases which lasted over four years repaid an average of 78% to secured creditors while the other 37 cases repaid only 59%. Again, however, this difference is not statistically significant.

The absence of any significant relationship here may be due to: (a) the countervailing influence of opposing factors such as described at the beginning of this section; (b) the possible overriding influence of case-specific factors. This would point to the importance of carrying out thorough due diligence procedures in each case; (c) the strong influence of a few cases in the analysis given the relatively small number of cases available.

Size

To investigate whether size of MBO is associated with higher payments to secured creditors out of receivership, we look at size as measured by value of the MBO at the date it was established. Data are available on value for 36 of the 42 cases.

While there is a significant positive association between value and the amount of secured debt due at the date of the receivership (correlation coefficient $= 0.46$; $p = 0.005$), there is no relation between value and the proportion of this debt repaid (correlation coefficient $= -0.13$; $p = 0.44$).

Sector

The buy-outs in our sample can be grouped into seven broad industries. Highest repayments to secured creditors range from means of 100% in finance ($n = 1$), 80% in timber/furniture ($n = 5$), 75% in transport ($n = 2$) and 71% in systems ($n = 4$) at the upper end through to 43% in paper/printing/publishing ($n = 7$) and 44% in retail/wholesale ($n = 6$) at the lower end. The 19 manufacturing firms in the sample recouped an average 62% of secured debt.

The mean repayment in the six retail/wholesale cases of 44% compares with 65% for all other 36 companies, although the difference is not significant ($p = 0.16$, two-tailed test) (Table 15.4, Panel C). The lower repayment rate among retail/wholesale companies may be due to lower balance sheet liquidity prevalent in that sector. We explore this proposition by analysing balance sheet ratios taken from the last set of published accounts prior to receivership for the small number of companies for which these are available. The acid test ratio (ratio of debtors + cash/current liabilities) has a mean value of 0.60 (median = 0.67) for the four retail/wholesale companies for which data are available compared with a mean of 0.77 (median = 0.68) for the 19 companies in other sectors, neither of these differences being statistically significant. The mean ratio of debtors to creditors is only 1.01 (median = 0.96) for the four retail/wholesale companies compared with 52.07 (median = 1.70) in the 15 other cases. The difference in medians is marginally significant at $p = 0.07$ using the Kruskal–Wallis test indicative of some lower degree of liquidity among retail/wholesale firms.

5.2 MBO Monitoring

Audit report going concern modification

In only two (9%) of the 23 cases for which audit reports are available did the auditor modify the report on the grounds of going-concern uncertainties (Table 15.5, Panel A). The average repayment rate in these two cases was only 28% compared with 62% in the other 21 cases, a difference significant at the 7% level (one-tailed test). There is thus some evidence that a greater proportion of the value of a business will have been lost if receivers are not called in until a going-concern modified audit report is issued.

Table 15.5 Factors affecting creditor recovery: monitoring

Factor	No. of cases	Secured debt repaid (mean %)	Mean amount of secured debt due at date of receivership (£000)
Panel A: Audit report going-concern modification[a]			
Yes	2	28	
No	21	62	
Panel B: No. of secured creditors			
1	28	67	667.2
2	9	49	762.2
3	4	50	3374.0
4	1	86	2161.1
All	42	62[a]	980.9

Notes: This table provides univariate analysis of the variables affecting secured creditor recovery rates for the 42 MBOs in the sample. In Panel A, differences are tested between those MBOs where there was a going-concern modification to the audit report and where this was not the case. In Panel B, differences are tested between those MBOs having one secured creditor and those having more than one secured creditor.

[a] Differences between groups significant at 0.1 level.

Number of secured creditors

In our sample, 28 cases had one secured creditor while 14 had more than one (Table 15.5, Panel B). The 28 receiverships with a single secured creditor achieved a 66.6% repayment rate on average, while those with more than one secured creditor paid back an average of only 51.9%, a difference weakly significant at the 9% level (one-tailed test).

Interestingly, the only case in the sample with as many as four secured creditors, Coventry Binders, achieved a high 86% repayment. Excluding this case from the analysis produces an even stronger result for the remaining 41 receiverships, with the 66.6% repayment in the 28 single creditor cases now comparing with only 49.3% in the 13 cases with two or three secured creditors (difference statistically significant at the 6% level, one-tailed test).

As can be seen from Table 15.5, there is no difference in repayment rates between cases with two secured creditors as compared to those with three. It would appear, therefore, that the crucial cut-off is having more than one such creditor.[3]

5.3 Effectiveness of Receivership Procedure

Identity of receivership firm

The identity of the receivership firms was also analysed to see if Big Six receivers achieved higher repayment rates (Table 15.6, Panel A). Exactly half of the 42 cases fell into each of the two receiver firm categories. The repayment rates achieved by each group were virtually identical, with the 21 Big Six receivers repaying 63% of secured debt and the 21 non-Big Six firms 61%. This, therefore, is not a determining factor.

Mode of sale

The mode of realization of an MBO's assets is determined by reading the receivers' statements to the creditors. Cases are classified as 'going-concern' sales where this is explicitly stated. The receivers usually try initially to sell the business as a going concern, often to parties with whom the MBO directors have been in contact prior to the receivership. A typical statement is that 'the business was sold as a going concern on (date) for (amount)'. Where an MBO is sold partially as a going concern with the remaining assets sold piecemeal it is classified as a 'mixed' sale, and all other cases are treated as 'piecemeal' realizations.

Eight (19%) of the 42 MBOs are going-concern sales and these achieve a mean 64% repayment to secured creditors (Table 15.6, Panel B). Six cases (14% of the total) are mixed sales with a mean 82% repayment rate, while the remaining 28 cases (67% of the total) repay an average of 57%. Combining the going-concern and mixed cases shows that the mean

Table 15.6 Factors affecting creditor recovery: effectiveness of receivership process

Factor	No. of cases	Secured debt repaid (mean %)
Panel A: Receivership firm		
Big Six	21	63
Non-Big Six	21	31
Panel B: Mode of sale[a]		
Going concern	8	64
Mixed	6	82
Piecemeal	28	57
Panel C: Economic timing		
MBO Pre-94	21	63.5
MBO Post-93	21	59.9
Receivership pre-96	18	65.2
Receivership post-95	24	59.0

Notes: This table provides univariate analysis of the variables affecting secured creditor recovery rates for the 42 MBOs in the sample. In Panel A, differences are tested between those MBOs where the receivership firm was a Big Six accounting firm and those where this was not the case. In Panel B, differences are tested between those MBOs sold as going concern plus those sold through mixed methods and those sold piecemeal.
[a] Difference between groups significant at 0.1 level.

repayment in the 14 cases with a going-concern element in their asset sales was 71% compared with only 57% in the 28 piecemeal realizations, a weakly significant difference at the 9% level (one-tailed test).

Economic cycle

Comparing the repayment rates of the 21 MBOs set up in the recessionary period before 1994 with those for the 21 post-1993 cases, it can be seen that the secured creditors of the earlier MBOs received a 63.5% repayment on average while those of the later cases received a slightly lower 59.9% (Table 15.6, Panel C). However, this difference is not statistically significant.

To test the expectation that receiverships of severely weakened firms may achieve lower repayments than those occurring a number of years after recession, we compare repayment rates for the 18 receiverships dated 1995 or earlier with those for the 24 cases dated 1996 or later. While the 18 earlier receiverships achieved an average payout of 65.2%, the 24 later cases paid back an average of only 59.0%. Once again, however, the difference is not statistically significant.

5.4 Multivariate Analysis

Multivariate analysis is undertaken to examine the relation between each explanatory variable and debt repayment rates while taking account of the effect of the remaining independent variables.

The factors influencing the amounts recovered by secured creditors were analysed in a multivariate framework using multiple and logistic regression. Equations of the following general form were estimated:

$$REC_i = SECCRED_i + SALMOD_i + MBODUR_i + RECTYP_i \\ + FAILCAUS_i + LogSIZE_i + IND_i + ECON_i + QUAL_i$$

For multiple regression the dependent variable (REC)was measured as the proportion of secured debt repaid.[4] With respect to logistic regression, a binary measure was used which took a value of 1 for amounts of recovery at or above the median (64.9%) and 0 otherwise.[5]

The multiple regression and the logistic regression are each run twice, once with the independent variable for the number of secured creditors measured as the actual number of such creditors (SECCREDCONT), and once as a binary variable taking the value 1 where there is more than one secured creditor and the value 0 when there is only one secured creditor (SECCREDBIN).

The remaining independent variables are defined as follows:

SALMOD	= 1 if going-concern or mixed (partly going-concern) sale
	= 0 if wholly piecemeal sale
MBODUR	= life of MBO measured in months
RECTYP	= 1 if receiver is not a Big Six firm
	= 0 if receiver is a Big Six firm
FAILCAUS	= 1 if managerial or other
	= 0 if financial or operational
LogSIZE	= Natural logarithm of value of MBO at date it was established or, if this not available, the balance sheet value of total assets minus current liabilities
IND	= 1 if not retail or wholesale
	= 0 if retail or wholesale
ECON	= 1 if receiver appointed in 1996 or later
	= 0 if receiver appointed before 1996.[6]

Table 15.7 presents the results of the multiple regressions of the above variables on the proportion of secured debt repaid for the 31 cases with full data availability. In the full model, Model 1, two of the independent variables

Table 15.7 Multiple regression of variables associated with proportion of secured debt repaid

Variable	Predicted sign	Model 1 (all variables) coefficient (*p*-value)	Model 2 (reduced) coefficient (*p*-value)	Model 3 (all variables) coefficient (*p*-value)	Model 4 (reduced) coefficient (*p*-value)	Model 5 (all variables) coefficient (*p*-value)	Model 6 (reduced) coefficient (*p*-value)
Number of cases		31	31	20	20	20	20
Intercept	?	0.883	0.857	0.316	0.494	0.185	0.485
		(0.025)	(0.001)	(0.513)	(0.178)	(0.700)	(0.177)
SECCREDCONT	–	0.065	0.062	−0.033	−0.013		
		(0.382)	(0.369)	(0.641)	(0.848)		
SECCREDBIN	–					−0.136	−0.074
						(0.205)	(0.503)
SALMOD	+	0.226	0.215	0.252	0.254	0.238	0.243
		(0.046)	(0.044)	(0.031)	(0.028)	(0.031)	(0.029)
MBODUR	–	−0.002	−0.0003				
		(0.492)	(0.890)				
RECTYP	–	−0.068	−0.059				
		(0.591)	(0.630)				
FAILCAUS	?	0.217	0.241	0.230	0.217	0.230	0.211
		(0.178)	(0.121)	(0.079)	(0.091)	(0.066)	(0.088)
LogSIZE	–	−0.083	−0.076	−0.089	−0.088	−0.082	−0.087
		(0.074)	(0.046)	(0.063)	(0.055)	(0.041)	(0.044)
IND	?	0.014		0.086		0.151	
		(0.942)		(0.651)		(0.428)	
ECON	+	0.121		0.109		0.116	
		(0.320)		(0.319)		(0.286)	
QUAL	+			0.611	0.549	0.657	0.574

			(0.075)	(0.082)	(0.051)	(0.061)
Adjusted R^2	0.151	0.189	0.310	0.361	0.357	0.378
F	1.668	2.167	2.218	3.145	2.509	3.309
F (sig)	(0.163)	(0.082)	(0.108)	(0.041)	(0.077)	(0.035)

Notes: Dependent variable in all models is proportion of secured debt repaid. SECCREDCONT is the number of secured creditors; SECCREDBIN = 1 if more than one secured creditor; =0 otherwise; SALMOD = 1 if going concern or mixed sale; = 0 otherwise; MBODUR = life of MBO in months; RECTYP = 1 if receiver not a Big Six firm; = 0 otherwise; FAILCAUS = 1 if managerial or other; = 0 if financial or operational; LogSIZE = natural log of value of MBO at date it was established or, if this not available, of the balance sheet value of total assets minus current liabilities; IND = 1 if not retail/wholesale; = 0 otherwise; ECON = 1 if receiver appointed 1996 or later; = 0 otherwise; QUAL = 1 if audit report not modified for going-concern uncertainties; = 0 otherwise. The figures in parentheses are the significance levels for the White-adjusted (1980) *t*-statistics.

are significant. As expected, going-concern asset realization (SALMOD)is highly positively associated with higher debt repayment ($p = 0.046$). Also as expected, the larger the MBO (LogSIZE), the lower the repayment rate to secured creditors ($p = 0.074$). The number of secured creditors, measured as a continuous variable, is not significant. However, the overall equation for Model 1 was insignificant at the 10% level. In Model 2, the insignificant variables IND and ECON are removed. The same two variables remain significant with slightly improved significance levels and the overall model is now significant at the 9% level.

In Models 3–6 a new variable, QUAL, representing the presence or absence of a going-concern modification, is introduced as follows:

QUAL = 1 if last audit report prior to failure is not modified for going-concern uncertainties
= 0 if last audit report prior to failure is modified for going-concern uncertainties

Models 3 and 4, like Models 1 and 2, measure the number of secured creditors as a continuous variable while Models 5 and 6 use a binary measure. In addition, in Models 3–6, two of the previously used independent variables are omitted as being significantly correlated with QUAL. These are MBODUR with a correlation of −0.42 ($p = 0.062$ two-tailed) and RECTYP with a correlation of −0.37 (p = 0.110 two-tailed). The number of cases with data availability is reduced to 20.

Models 3–6 have higher adjusted R^2s than Models 1 and 2, ranging from 0.31 to 0.38. Two of the same independent variables – SALMOD and LogSIZE – remain significant, as is the new variable QUAL with the presence of an audit report going-concern modification being associated with a lower repayment rate as expected. Furthermore, an additional variable, FAILCAUS, measuring the cause of failure, is now significant at the 10% level, indicating that a higher repayment rate is associated with cause of failure being managerial or other.

The results of Models 1–6 are tested further using the same independent variables in a logistic regression with the dependent variable = 1 if the percentage of secured debt repaid is above the median of 64.9%[7] and = 0 if below the median. The results, shown in Table 15.8, are very similar to the multiple regression models but with generally stronger significance levels. Models 7–10 are significant overall with high correct classification rates (from 80.7% to 87.1%), and with the same three independent variables – SALMOD (all Models), FAILCAUS (Models 7 and 8) and LogSIZE (Models 7, 8 and 10) – significant with the same signs.

Table 15.8 Logistic regression of variables associated with proportion of secured debt repaid relative to median

Variable	Predicted sign	Model 7 (all variables) coefficient (sig. Wald stat.)	Model 8 (reduced) coefficient (sig. Wald stat.)	Model 8 (all variables) coefficient (sig. Wald stat.)	Model 10 (reduced) coefficient (sig. Wald stat.)
Number of cases		31	31	31	31
Intercept	?	3.488	4.816	2.073	4.434
		(0.356)	(0.081)	(0.588)	(0.069)
SECCREDCONT	–	1.125	1.155		
		(0.183)	(0.159)		
SECCREDBIN	–			−0.425	−0.100
				(0.723)	(0.927)
SALMOD	+	3.641	3.311	2.922	2.467
		(0.035)	(0.034)	(0.032)	(0.036)
MBODUR	–	−0.076	−0.066	−0.033	−0.031
		(0.168)	(0.184)	(0.432)	(0.365)
RECTYP		−1.122	−0.964	−0.930	−0.702
		(0.389)	(0.428)	(0.418)	(0.511)
FAILCAUS	?	2.858	2.485	1.486	1.491
		(0.079)	(0.078)	(0.250)	(0.224)
LogSIZE	–	−1.000	−1.021	−0.641	−0.741
		(0.033)	(0.017)	(0.113)	(0.035)
IND	?	1.326		2.007	
		(0.617)		(0.393)	
ECON	+	0.370		0.061	
		(0.795)		(0.966)	

Table 15.8 (continued)

Variable	Predicted sign	Model 7 (all variables) coefficient (sig. Wald stat.)	Model 8 (reduced) coefficient (sig. Wald stat.)	Model 8 (all variables) coefficient (sig. Wald stat.)	Model 10 (reduced) coefficient (sig. Wald stat.)
Percentage of cases correctly classified		83.87%	83.87%	87.10%	80.65%
Model χ-square		16.442	15.983	14.713	13.812
χ-square sig.		0.037	0.014	0.065	0.032

Notes: Dependent variable = 1 if percentage of secured debt repaid is greater than or equal to the median (64.9%); = 0 otherwise. SECCREDCONT is the number of secured creditors; SECCREDBIN = 1 if more than one secured creditor; = 0 otherwise; SALMOD = 1 if going-concern or mixed sale; = 0 otherwise; MBODUR = life of MBO in months; RECTYP = 1 if receiver not a Big Six firm; = 0 otherwise; FAILCAUS = 1 if managerial or other; = 0 if financial or operational; LogSIZE = natural log of value of MBO at date it was established or, if this not available, of the balance sheet value of total assets minus current liabilities; IND = 1 if not retail/ wholesale; = 0 otherwise; ECON = 1 if receiver appointed 1996 or later; = 0 otherwise; QUAL = 1 if audit report not modified for going concern uncertainties; = 0 otherwise; Wald statistic significance is for two-tailed test.

6. CONCLUSIONS

This chapter has examined the extent and determinants of recovery rates by secured creditors from management buy-outs in distress using a unique data set of 42 management buy-outs that entered receivership.

We find that, on average, 62% of secured credit is recovered when buy-outs enter the receivership process. This is comparable with the 70% found to be recovered by banks in Franks and Sussman's (2000) study of privately held small and medium-sized companies. However, the recovery rate is below that identified in US studies of non-buy-outs (Weiss, 1990; Franks and Torous, 1994; Tashjian et al., 1996). The determinants of secured creditor recovery rates were hypothesized to relate to three areas: the characteristics of the MBO firms, the nature of the MBO monitoring process and the effectiveness of the receivership process. Using various specifications, our multivariate analysis provides evidence of support for elements of each of these three explanations. As regards the characteristics of the MBO firms, we find weak evidence that the percentage of secured credit recovered is increased where the principal reason for failure concerns managerial factors and is reduced the larger the buy-out. With respect to monitoring, the presence of a going-concern qualification in the audit report serves to reduce the recovery rate by secured creditors but the number of secured creditors does not appear to be significantly associated with the recovery rate. The effectiveness of the receivership process is evident in that the percentage of secured credit recovered is increased when the distressed buy-out is sold as a going concern but neither the reputation of the receiver nor the timing of the economic cycle was found to be significantly associated with the recovery rate.

The finding of consistency in the secured credit recovery rate between our study and that of Franks and Sussman (2000) for small to medium-sized non-MBOs suggests that banks may have developed similar monitoring policies across their portfolios (Citron et al., 1997, p. 292). The absence of a significant association between the number of secured creditors and the secured credit recovery rate suggests that coordination of lending syndicates in MBOs is not generally problematical. However, our findings may raise questions about the claimed specialist screening and monitoring by banks engaged in lending to MBOs. The finding of lower recovery rates for larger MBOs is particularly interesting in this context given the general development of larger transactions in the UK MBO market (CMBOR, 2001). While the transactions costs of larger MBOs are often argued by practitioners to be proportionately lower than for smaller MBOs, it is not clear whether the banks are devoting sufficient attention to understanding the value of the asset security, the stability of the cash flows and the complexities involved in the MBOs to whom they lend. This may be particularly problematical in MBOs that were formerly divisions of larger groups, the dominant source of UK MBOs, where detailed pre-MBO information is limited. This suggests that the banks may not be devoting sufficient specialist monitoring attention to MBOs. There is some evidence that the main clearing banks in the UK in particular pass the MBO company to a relationship manager in the branch network (Citron et al., 1997). Further research is required to examine more directly the nature of the link between post-MBO monitoring and subsequent failure.

The apparent difference between the secured creditor recovery rates in the available UK and US studies cannot at this stage be taken as evidence of differences in the effectiveness of bankruptcy regimes in the two countries as the nature of the samples in the two sets of studies was quite distinct. Such comparative analysis was outside the scope of this chapter. Further specifically designed comparative analysis of the effectiveness of different bankruptcy regimes is required.

APPENDIX

Table 15A.1 Summary information on sample of MBOs entering receivership, 1992–99

Company	Date of MBO	MBO value at set up (£ thousands)	Receivership date	% secured debt repaid
Alan Markovits	Mar. 92	750	11.08.95	28
Bickavon	Oct. 93	750	26.06.96	39
Biltons Tableware	Aug. 95	4400	10.07.98	35
Brookfield Farm	Dec. 93	667	28.09.95	36
C.I.S. Windows	Jun. 95	5400	03.05.96	59
Cartons Boulangeries	Apr. 95	5	12.01.96	14
Celtic Meat Company	Oct. 94	150	01.01.96	100
Challis Holdings	Jan. 94	2700	16.01.97	29
Christal Rapid Transport	Sep. 93	1300	01.05.95	100
City Windscreen & Body Glass	Jun. 94	n/a	18.10.96	6
Conrad & Essenhigh	Aug. 92	400	14.12.93	21
Coventry Binders	Nov. 94	2000	20.06.96	86
Devon Conversions	Mar. 94	1400	27.11.96	76
Edwin Trisk	Aug. 93	2000	03.03.99	95
Euro-Asia Trading Company	Mar. 94	16315	22.07.97	36

Company	Date of MBO	MBO value at set up (£ thousands)	Receivership date	% secured debt repaid
Galliard Printers	Mar. 95	194	27.07.98	16
Genesis Fast Food	Oct. 94	10 100	11.07.97	81
GMS Computing	Feb. 93	100	29.07.94	69
HAT Property Services	Feb. 94	3600	02.04.98	100
Herebond	Mar. 94	61	29.07.97	100
HNB Systems	Mar. 94	300	17.09.96	93
Hoyle Butterworth	Mar. 92	100	17.07.98	40
J.L. Joinery (London)	Jun. 93	n/a	26.05.94	100
James Graham & Co. (Timber)	Apr. 92	n/a	13.11.92	68
James Longley Joinery	Mar. 94	489	18.10.96	62
John Barnes	Dec. 93	2500	23.02.98	59
Ken Moore	Dec. 93	33	30.11.95	37
Marr Engineering	Mar. 92	114	30.09.94	80
Media Medica Publications	Apr. 92	650	11.01.94	45
Personality Profiles	Apr. 95	2550	18.03.97	23
Phillips Leeds	May. 94	465	27.02.95	69
Pollards Cornish Ice Cream	Apr. 93	189	29.09.94	76
Premier Footwear	Feb. 94	n/a	03.01.95	100
Pressed Sheet Products (Nottn)	Mar. 92	111	17.01.96	100
Realcraft Finishing Touches	Jan. 93	n/a	01.12.93	100
Redruth Brewery	Jul. 91	700	21.07.94	37
Riverside Foods	May. 94	279	19.12.96	21
Swan Industrial	Jun. 92	7250	07.12.93	8
Travellers Coach Company	Jan. 94	3500	10.11.97	49
Truck & Van	Sep. 93	1500	06.10.95	100
Vic-Tree (B'ham)	Apr. 92	500	16.01.98	95
Woodfield Machinery	Jan. 94	n/a	27.10.94	100

ACKNOWLEDGEMENTS

Financial support from Deloitte & Touche, Barclays Private Equity and Lloyds/TSB is gratefully acknowledged. The chapter has benefited from comments of Eric de Bodt and other participants at the European Financial Management Association (EFMA) 2002 meeting in London. Thanks also to Ameziane Lasfer, Maria Carapeto, Steve Toms and participants at staff seminars at Nottingham University Business School and the Judge Institute, Cambridge, for comments on an earlier version.

NOTES

1. These surveys generally obtain a 100% response rate from all the financiers active in the buy-out market as they receive a free copy of a quarterly review of aggregate market trends based on the data they supply which is recognized as the leading source of information in the market.
2. It is recognized that classifying cause of failure involves an element of subjective judgement. Cause of failure is classified as operational where the problems are primarily external to the company. Cause of failure for Biltons Tableware, for example, is classified as 'operational' as it suffered from the strong pound sterling and economic recession in the Far East, leading to a sharp drop-off in sales. Personality Profiles is classified as 'financial'. The company started life with significant deferred purchase liabilities and unpaid acquisition costs as well as substantial debt. These factors together with sales ledger problems resulted in excessive strain on cash flow. Truck and Van is classified as 'managerial' because when a large loss-making contract was terminated, although required redundancies were identified they were not implemented.
3. Table 15.5 also indicates that a greater number of secured creditors is associated with a larger amount of secured debt outstanding at the date of the receivership. In fact this positive correlation is statistically significant (correlation coefficient $= 0.48$; $p = 0.001$). While the percentage repaid appears to be negatively associated with the amount due, the result is not statistically significant (correlation coefficient $= -0.19$; $p = 0.24$). It therefore seems that it is the number of secured creditors rather than the total amount due that is the stronger driver of repayment rates, but this issue warrants further research.
4. The White (1980) covariance estimator is used to take account of heteroscedasticity.
5. As there was some skewness in the data towards the higher end of the distribution, a second set of logistic regressions was run with the binary measure taking the value 1 where 90% or more of the secured debt was repaid and 0 otherwise was constructed. The overall regressions are as significant as those reported here although the coefficients on individual independent variables are not. These results are therefore not reported in this chapter.
6. 'Regressions were also run with an alternative date cut-off representing whether the MBO was established in 1992/93 or from 1994 onwards. The results are very similar although somewhat less significant than those reported here. It should be noted that there is a positive correlation of 0.518 ($p = 0.003$ two-tailed) between MBODUR and ECON, indicating not surprisingly that the longer-lived MBOs in our sample appointed their receivers at a later date.
7. This is the median for the total sample of 42 cases, not for the 31 cases entered in the logistic regressions.

REFERENCES

Andrade, G. and Kaplan, S., 'How costly is financial (not economic) distress? Evidence from highly leveraged transactions that became distressed', *Journal of Finance*, **LIII** (5), 1998, 1443–93.

Bolton, P. and Scharfstein, D., 'Optimal debt structure and the number of creditors', *Journal of Political Economy*, **104** (1), 1996, 1–25.

Brown, D.T., James, C.M. and Mooradian, R.M., 'Asset sales by financially distressed firms', *Journal of Corporate Finance*, **1**, 1994, 233–57.
Bruner, R. and Eades, K., 'The crash of the REVCO LBO: the hypothesis of inadequate capital', *Financial Management*, **21** (1), 1992, 35–49.
Campbell, S., 'Predicting bankruptcy reorganization for closely held firms', *Accounting Horizons*, **10** (3), 1996, 12–25.
Citron, D. and Taffler, R.J., *Audit Report Disclosures of Going Concern Uncertainties: a Continuing Puzzle*. ACCA Research Report No. 60, London: Certified Accountants Educational Trust. 1999.
Citron, D., Robbie, K. and Wright, M., 'Loan covenants and relationship banking in MBOs', *Accounting and Business Research*, **27** (4), 1997, 277–96.
CMBOR, 'Market developments', *Management Buy-outs: Quarterly Review*, Centre for Management Buy-out Research, Nottingham University, Autumn. 2001.
Cotter, J. and Peck, S., 'The structure of debt and active equity investors: the case of the buyout specialist', *Journal of Financial Economics*, **59**, 2001, 101–47.
Denis, D., 'Organizational form and the consequences of highly leveraged transactions: Kroger's recapitalization and safeway's LBO', *Journal of Financial Economics*, **36**, 1994, 193–224.
Detragiache, E., 'Adverse selection and the costs of financial distress', *Journal of Corporate Finance*, **1**, 1995, 347–65.
Franks, J. and Torous, W.N., 'A comparison of financial recontracting in distressed exchanges and Chapter 11 reorganizations', *Journal of Financial Economics*, **35**, 1994, 349–70.
Franks, J. and Sussman, O., 'Resolving financial distress by way of a contract: an empirical study of small UK companies', mimeo, London Business School. 2000.
Franks, J., Nyborg, K.G. and Torous, W.N., 'A comparison of US, UK, and German insolvency codes', *Financial Management*, **25** (3), 1996, 86–101.
Gilson, S., John, K. and Lang, L., 'Troubled debt restructurings: an empirical study of private reorganizations of firms in default', *Journal of Financial Economics*, **27**, 1990, 315–53.
Jensen, M., 'Agency costs of free cash flow, corporate finance and takeovers', *American Economic Review*, **76** (2), 1986, 323–9.
Jensen, M.C. (1991), 'Corporate control and the politics of finance', *Journal of Applied Corporate Finance*, **4**, 13–33.
Kaplan, S. and Stein, J., 'The evolution of buy-out pricing and financial structure in the 1980s', *Quarterly Journal of Economics*, **CVIII** (2), 1993, 313–59.
Kreuger, J., *Management Buy-outs*, London: Butterworths. 1990.
Lockett, A. and Wright, M., 'Structure, management and information in syndicated venture capital investments', CMBOR Occasional Paper. 2001.
LoPucki, L.M., 'The debtor in full control – systems failure under Chapter 11 of the bankruptcy code?', *American Bankruptcy Law Journal*, **57**, 1983, 99–126.
Pulvino, T., 'Effects of bankruptcy court protection on asset sales', *Journal of Financial Economics*, **52** (2), 1999, 151–86.
Shleifer, A. and Vishny, R., 'Liquidation values and debt capacity', *Journal of Finance*, **47**, 1992, 1343–66.
Smith, C.W., 'A perspective on accounting-based debt covenant violations', *Accounting Review*, April 1993, 289–303.
Sterling, M. and Wright, M., *Management Buyouts and the Law*, Oxford: Blackwell Law. 1990.

Tashjian, E., Lease, R.C. and McConnell, J.J., 'Prepacks: an empirical analysis of prepackaged bankruptcies', *Journal of Financial Economics*, **40**, 1996, 135–62.
Weiss, L.A., 'Bankruptcy resolution: direct costs and violation of priority claims', *Journal of Financial Economics*, **27**, 1990, 285–314.
White, H., 'A heteroskedasticity-consistent covariance matrix estimator and a direct test for heteroskedasticity', *Econometrica*, **48**, 1980, 817–38.
Wilkins, T. and Zimmer, I., 'Economic consequences of debt covenant violation: the case of Inno-Pacific Holdings Limited', *British Accounting Review*, **28**, 1996, 121–37.
Wright, M., Wilson, N., Robbie, K. and Ennew, C., 'Restructuring and failure in buy-outs and buy-ins', *Business Strategy Review*, **5** (2), 1994, 21–40.
Wright, M., Thompson, S., Robbie, K. and Wong, P., 'Management buy-outs in the short and long term', *Journal of Business Finance and Accounting*, **22** (4), 1995, 461–83.
Wright, M., Wilson, N., Robbie, K. and Ennew, C., 'An analysis of management buy-out failure', *Managerial and Decision Economics*, **17** (1), 1996, 57–70.
Wright, M., Normand, J. and Robbie, K., *Touche Ross's Management Buy-outs*, Cambridge: Woodhead-Faulkner. 1990.
Wruck, K., 'Financial distress, reorganization and organizational efficiency', *Journal of Financial Economics*, **27**, 1990, 419–44.

Index